CANADA'S JEWS:
A PEOPLE'S JOURNEY

The history of the Jewish community in Canada says as much about the development of the nation as it does about the Jewish people. Spurred on by upheavals in Eastern Europe in the late-eighteenth and early-nineteenth centuries, many Jews immigrated to the Dominion of Canada, which was then considered little more than a British satellite state. Over the ensuing decades, as the Canadian Jewish identity was forged, Canada underwent the transformative experience of separating from Britain and distinguishing itself from the United States. In this light, the Canadian Jewish identity was formulated within the parameters of the emerging Canadian national personality.

Canada's Jews is an account of this remarkable story as told by one of the leading authors and historians on the Jewish legacy in Canada. Drawing on his previous work on the subject, Gerald Tulchinsky describes the struggle against antisemitism and the search for a livelihood among the Jewish community. He demonstrates that, far from being a fragment of the Old World, Canadian Jewry grew from a tiny group of transplanted Europeans to a fully articulated, diversified, and dynamic national group that defined itself as Canadian while expressing itself in the varied political and social contexts of the Dominion.

Canada's Jews covers the 240-year period from the beginnings of the community in the 1760s to the present day, illuminating the golden chain of Jewish tradition, religion, language, economy, and history as established and renewed in the northern lands. With important points about labour, immigration, and antisemitism, it is a timely book that offers sober observations about the Jewish experience and its relation to Canadian history.

GERALD TULCHINSKY is a professor emeritus in the Department of History at Queen's University.

Canada's Jews

A People's Journey

GERALD TULCHINSKY

UNIVERSITY OF TORONTO PRESS
Toronto Buffalo London

© Gerald Tulchinsky 2008

University of Toronto Press
www.utppublishing.com
Toronto Buffalo London
Printed in Canada

ISBN 978-0-8020-9062-1 (cloth)
ISBN 978-0-8020-9386-8 (paper)

∞

Printed on acid-free paper

Library and Archives Canada Cataloguing in Publication

Tulchinsky, Gerald, 1933–
  Canada's Jews: a people's journey / Gerald Tulchinsky.

  Based on the author's two books, Taking root and Branching out.
  Includes bibliographical references and index.
  ISBN 978-0-8020-9062-1 (bound)   ISBN 978-0-8020-9386-8 (pbk.)

  1. Jews – Canada – History.   2. Canada – Emigration and immigration –
  History.   3. Canada – Ethnic relations.   I. Tulchinsky, Gerald, 1933–
  Taking root.   II. Tulchinsky, Gerald, 1933– Branching out.   III. Title.

  FC106.J5T845 2008   971'.004924   C2007-906318-7

University of Toronto Press acknowledges the financial assistance to its publishing program of the Canada Council for the Arts and the Ontario Arts Council.

University of Toronto Press acknowledges the financial support for its publishing activities of the Government of Canada through the Book Publishing Industry Development Program (BPIDP).

Contents

Acknowledgments vii

Abbreviations xi

Introduction 3

PART ONE: BEGINNINGS, 1768–1890

1 Foundations in the Colonial Era 13

2 Pedlars and Settlers on the Urban Frontiers 37

3 Victorian Montreal and Western Settlement 62

PART TWO: EMERGENCE OF A NATIONAL COMMUNITY, 1890–1919

4 Travails of Urbanization 93

5 'Corner of Pain and Anguish' 126

6 Zionism, Protest, and Reform 165

PART THREE: BETWEEN THE WARS, 1919–1939

7 Jewish Geography of the 1920s and 1930s 199

8 Clothing and Politics   242

9 The Politics of Marginality   283

10 'Not Complex or Sophisticated': Interwar Zionism   328

PART FOUR: THE SECOND WORLD WAR AND BEYOND, 1940–2008

11 Into Battle   371

12 Post-war Readjustments   401

13 Jewish Ethnicity in Multicultural Canada, 1960–1980   427

14 Complexities and Uncertainties   459

Epilogue: *Oyfn Veg* (On the Road)   489

Appendix: *Jewish Population of Major Canadian Cities, 1891–2001*   497

Notes   501

A Select Bibliography of Secondary Sources   599

Index   607

Illustrations follow pages 180 and 380

Acknowledgments

This book is a product of the long journey that started in Brantford, Ontario, where I was born in 1933 and attended school. We were the only Jewish family in our neighbourhood of mostly working-class families only just coming out of the Depression, with many sons, uncles, and fathers, by 1942, in the armed forces, some of them dying in battle or returning home very badly wounded.

Early on, my lion-hearted younger brother, Ted, and I understood the meaning of being outsiders. Taunting, and fist and rock fights, were part of the social landscape at Graham Bell Public School, in the neighbourhood empty lots, and on our daily walk or bike ride to Hebrew school located at our synagogue in another part of town. Nevertheless, we also made some excellent friends among our non-Jewish neighbours and schoolmates.

Judaism was a major part of our lives, in particular, Young Judaea, a national organization that was the youth wing of the centrist Zionist Organization of Canada, with branches all over the country. During our teenage years, Young Judaea kept us socially and intellectually alive with books, films, pamphlets, and letters we received from dear *chaverim* we met at conferences and summer camp. We felt, naïvely, that we were participants – though, in fact, we were just onlookers – in the regeneration of the Jewish people that was taking place in Palestine, soon to be Israel. After finishing high school, with a few dozen other teenagers I attended a one-year stint in Israel at the Machon L'Madrichei Chutz l'Aretz (Institute for Youth Leaders from Abroad), from September 1952 to August 1953. This was the highest point of our lives, and the memory of experiences and people we encountered became so indelibly imprinted on our minds that they return repeatedly to consciousness with enormous clarity and power. For me, it was the interaction with Jewish people from all over the world that I found so moving: the Holocaust survivors, the Sephardim, the pre-war German-speakers, the youth from other countries, and the *chalutzim* from central Europe. The encounter with them and their cultures changed most of us forever.

Returning to Canada and attending the University of Toronto, later McGill, while serving in the University Naval Training Division, then back to University of Toronto for the Ph.D. degree in history – and now happily married – reinforced my childhood formation as a Jewish Canadian, a child of two distinctive and separate cultures which are inextricably intertwined, though not always without tension. The history of the Jewish people – notably in the twentieth century and especially during the Holocaust – was always of enormous interest, and I was often drawn to new books, articles, and reviews about it when I was supposed to be doing such other things as finishing a thesis chapter or preparing for a class, though teaching at Loyola College, the University of Saskatchewan, and, finally, Queen's University was fully absorbing.

So, while writing and teaching courses on Canadian business and urban history, I had, as it were, another life, which over time assumed greater importance to me, the history of the Jewish people in Canada, resulting in *Taking Root: The Origins of the Canadian Jewish Community* (1992) and *Branching Out: The Transformation of the Canadian Jewish Community* (1998) and some shorter pieces along the way. In those books, for which this one is a replacement and an update, I tried to explain the main threads of the social experience the Jewish people had in the British colonies in the northern half of North America (which became Canada in 1867), and to describe what I thought – and still think – is distinctive about these transformations, while comparing them to those of United States Jewry.

To be sure, I stand on the shoulders of forerunners such as Benyamin Gutl Sack, Louis Rosenberg, and David Rome, and am bolstered by the work of my contemporaries, whose scholarly studies have profoundly informed me in ways that even the profuse endnotes herein do not fully acknowledge. They and the new scholars – let's call them '*die yunge*' (the kids) – now entering the field have enabled me to write this present offering as a synthesis of how the Canadian Jewish people got to where they are now, from immigration to integration, in a country in transition from colony to nation.

This book is dedicated to the memory of my mother, Anne Stemeroff z'l, who died in October 2005 at the age of one hundred and one. The

Canadian-born daughter of immigrants from Russia, she was part of the story told here, as well as an inspiration to me and the three succeeding generations of our extended family, whose lives were profoundly touched by her deep wisdom, easy humour, and abiding love. But that is not all, because this book is, in the end, the by-product of all of my other teachers, notably my father, Harry Tulchinsky, who could recite Chayim Nachman Bialik's lengthy Hebrew poem 'Hamatmid' by heart; Rabbi (Rav) Gedaliah Felder, Talmud scholar par excellence; Professor Maurice Careless, distinguished historian of Canada and thesis supervisor; and Ze'ev Mankowitz, deeply thoughtful student of the Holocaust, as well as a host of wonderfully generous colleagues too numerous to mention (but they know who they are), except one, Jack Granatstein, who has encouraged and advised me for years about this and other work. As well, I thank all of my research assistants over many years, most of them Queen's students, who have worked on aspects of this project. And I extend special gratitude to my typist, Vyvien Vella, who insisted on continuing on through her own very difficult year. Linda McKnight of Westwood Creative Artists gave me excellent advice throughout, and Bill Harnum, Len Husband, and Frances Mundy at University of Toronto Press supported this project strongly. Louis Greenspan, Hilary Neary, and two anonymous readers for the Press made helpful comments. I gratefully acknowledge, too, the financial support of the Multiculturalism Branch, the Social Sciences and Humanities Research Council, and Queen's University. I recognize a deep debt also to all the Queen's librarians and public archivists who have given me such valuable help over the years, in particular, Myron Momryk and Lawrence Tapper, formerly at Library and Archives Canada, Janice Rosen at the Canadian Jewish Congress National Archives, Ellen Scheinberg at the Ontario Jewish Archives, and Eiran Harris at Montreal's Jewish Public Library.

I want to give special thanks to Doctors Alan Cruess, Jeffrey Gale, and Wendell Willis for superb eye care and to David Hemings, physician and good friend. Mel Wiebe and Tracy Ware supplied many laughs and good words. And lastly, I thank my family, especially my wife, Ruth, who read every word and gave me tough-minded editorial advice; Steve, Ellen, and Laura and her husband, Rob, who watched and waited; and my grandchildren, Hannah and Jillian, who, I hope, will one day read this book and know why their *Zaidy* and *Bubby* were so busy. This book's imperfections are mine alone.

December 2007

Abbreviations

ACWA	Amalgamated Clothing Workers of America
AJCS	Allied Jewish Community Services
CCF	Co-operative Commonwealth Federation
CGIT	Canadian Girls in Training
CIC	Canada-Israel Committee
CJC	Canadian Jewish Congress
CNCR	Canadian National Committee on Refugees and Victims of Political Persecution
CPC	Communist Party of Canada
CPR	Canadian Pacific Railway
DP	displaced person
FLQ	Front de Libération du Québec
HIAS	Hebrew Immigrant Aid Society (New York)
ICOR	Association for Jewish Colonization in the Soviet Union
IDF	Israel Defense Force
ILGWU	International Ladies' Garment Workers' Union
IRO	Industrial Removal Office (New York)
IUNTW	Industrial Union of Needle Trade Workers
JCA	Jewish Colonization Association
JCC	Jewish Community Council
JEAS	Jewish Emigration Aid Society
JIAS	Jewish Immigrant Aid Society
JNF	Jewish National Fund
NBC	National Budgeting Conference
NRMA	National Resources Mobilization Act
PLO	Palestinian Liberation Organization
POW	prisoner of war

PQ	Parti Québécois
RCAF	Royal Canadian Air Force
RCMP	Royal Canadian Mounted Police
RCN	Royal Canadian Navy
RNWMP	Royal North West Mounted Police (to 1920)
UGWA	United Garment Workers of America
UIA	United Israel Appeal
UJPO	United Jewish People's Order
UJRA	United Jewish Refugee Agency
UJWF	United Jewish Welfare Fund
UNRRA	United Nations Refugee and Rescue Agency
YCL	Young Communist League
YMHA	Young Men's Hebrew Association
YMHBS	Young Men's Hebrew Benevolent Society
YWHA	Young Women's Hebrew Association
WEC	War Efforts Committee
ZOA	Zionist Organization of America
ZOC	Zionist Organization of Canada

CANADA'S JEWS:
A PEOPLE'S JOURNEY

Introduction

> Go catch the echoes of the ticks of time
>
> A.M. Klein, 'Of Remembrance'

Late one afternoon, just before my bar mitzvah in September 1946, I heard loud sobbing coming from downstairs. It was my father; he had just read a letter received that day concerning the fate of his family in Bessarabia (now Moldavia) and Ukraine during the Holocaust. Most had been murdered outright (or done to death in various ways), the letter informed him, and as he read off their names he was overcome. I came downstairs and witnessed his grief for his brothers, sisters, their children, and an extended clan numbering in the hundreds. For him this marked the end of the Second World War, which he had followed with ever mounting concern after 1939. Jews like him, who had lived through the Ukrainian pogroms of 1918 and 1919, had sensed that a cataclysmic disaster was in the making. And he, my mother, and their friends would endlessly discuss the information they gleaned from the radio, newsreels, the Canadian press, and the Yiddish newspapers and magazines mailed to our house.

Most immigrant Jews suspected that the German Nazis and their collaborators were obliterating the Jews of Europe. They also knew that they could do nothing about this mass murder. But they could and did discuss their fears, as their hopes waned of saving even some Jews, possibly their families, from that charnel house. My parents recounted to the family, local friends, and the numerous visitors – usually representatives of the Canadian Jewish Congress and Zionist organizations – their analysis of the news, fragmentary though it was, trying to suck from it such meaning as it had concerning the fate of the Jewish people.

I sensed too, uncomprehendingly, that the world of European Jewry my father talked about was at an end. Not just my uncles, aunts, and cousins – whom I had never met – living in Moldavia and the western Ukraine, but the entire civilization of which they were a part was gone. The thousand-year-old heartland of the Jewish world was being destroyed.

Jews like my grandparents were at one time part of that world. This was a civilization so complex, so nuanced, and so diversified that only with deep study can those who did not experience that world begin to learn of its richness. Between 1901, when my maternal grandparents reached North America, and 1924, when my father landed at Halifax, their old world experienced the most profound changes that modernization, failed revolution, education, enlightenment, Zionism, world war, successful revolution, civil war, and mass murder could bring. And to this country, then the Dominion of Canada, in 1904 enjoying the sunny age of Wilfrid Laurier and in 1924 experiencing the crusading opportunism of Mackenzie King, they brought some of the shards of that world.

Jews and the many other immigrants may not initially have grasped the fact that Canada was in many important ways distinct from the United States. As part of the British Empire, Canadian political institutions had emerged from the venerable tradition of Crown, Parliament, Cabinet, and responsible government. The United States, on the other hand, was born in revolution, and its constitution set out a clear separation of powers among executive, legislative, and judicial branches of government. Canada was a nation of two nations, or 'races,' as André Siegfried – an astute French observer – stated early last century, that had established a delicate equilibrium between French and English 'rights' between the 1840s and the 1860s, when Confederation brought the Province of Canada into union with two Maritime colonies and, less than a decade later, with the rest of British North America (except Newfoundland) as well. If America was different from Europe, then Canada was also different, though to a lesser degree, from the United States.

Although the Canadian Jewish community is one of the oldest ethnic groups in Canada, its numbers are small in comparison to many other Jewish communities in the world, being only fifth in size, while its influence on world Jewish affairs was not, until recently, significant. Now numbering nearly 400,000 people, it is concentrated in major cities and towns, and includes a number of the nation's leading business people, scientists, jurists, intellectuals, artists, and academics. Jews have made notable contributions to virtually every major sector of Canadian life, from agriculture to literature.

To fully recount those achievements would require a multi-volume work. Fortunately, it is not my task to assemble that record, but rather to write a history of the Jewish people's experience in Canada, and an assessment of the community's evolution from its modest beginnings in the eighteenth century until recent days. Like other historians of Jewish life, I am torn between noting the importance of its unique features and stressing the universality of its experiences.[1] The student of modern Jewish history is confronted by the momentous events affecting Jews in the twentieth century: the Holocaust, their worst tragedy; and the rise of the state of Israel, their greatest triumph.

As Robert Harney has pointed out, the multiculturalists' efforts in recent years may well have helped to perpetuate certain myths of immigration history.[2] Moreover, putting immigrants at the centre of Canadian history, and thereby depicting Canada as a country built by successive waves of immigrants, robs the history of its complexity and subtlety. These myths portray the various migrations as due to political or religious persecution, declare that Canada is the sum of all its ethnic groups' cultures and that the immigrants moved up social, economic, and political ladders to success by self-sacrifice and hard work, and claim that immigrants formed cohesive self-supporting communities to assist themselves to move forward and upward through adversity.

Such myths are especially prevalent in some of the popular perceptions of Canadian Jewish history: Jews fled from the persecutions of the Russian-Polish pogroms; they adapted themselves readily to the new environment and became one of Canada's great success stories; they moved quickly up the social and economic ladders and established a well-organized communal life marked by cohesion and self-help, except for certain minor divisions between the earlier and later arrivals. And so on. The trouble with myths is that they usually contain a certain amount of truth, and the difficulty lies in distinguishing between the times and places when they are and are not true. To apply them as universal truths denies the validity of the special and unique.

In the study of Canadian Jewish history, certain questions present themselves, some of them addressing those myths, others raising different issues concerning Jewish immigration, settlement, and adjustment in Canada. As the process began in the old country itself, we must ask why Jews left, and from which elements or classes they were drawn. How were they received in Canada, by Jews and non-Jews, and how did they adjust to their new lives in the urban environment? What types of institutions emerged within the Jewish communities of those cities, and how did these structures change over time as newcomers came to outnumber their forerunners? As these transformations occurred, what kinds of economic, social, and political relationships emerged among different groups or classes within the communities? Through what channels did Jews achieve upward economic mobility? Was it principally by means of schooling, or through business? How effective was the Jewish labour movement (which was focused on the clothing-trade unions) in representing those class differences, and in marshalling the intellectual and political resources of the Jewish working class in a sustained manner to effect change?

What was the source of Jewish workers' social consciousness? Was it Russian socialism, as was the case among many Finns in Canada, or was it some hybrid which also included other admixtures, such as Jewish ethical culture? What explains the early emergence of an unusually strong Zionist movement in Canada? Was it perhaps the existence of a divided Canadian nationalism, or the British imperial relationship, which encouraged the rise of this form of Jewish nationalism? Or was Zionism essentially a combination of philanthropy and cynical self-interest which sent Jews to rebuild Palestine? What distinguishes the history of the Canadian Jewish community from that of American Jewry, with which it has had so much in common? Why has Canadian Jewry been able to organize and sustain strong national organizations and cultural institutions? What explains the promising growth of Jewish agricultural settlements on the Canadian Prairies during the early 1900s, a feature which suggests a commonality with Argentinian Jewish history? An attempt will be made to answer these and other questions in the pages that follow.

This volume covers the 240 years from the beginnings of the Jewish community in the 1760s down to recent times, and of the European upheavals endured by the Jews of Eastern Europe, spurring the massive immigration to the Dominion of Canada. Within a few years, the government would begin to impose new policies restricting Jewish immigration. The 1920s mark, therefore, a watershed in the long formative period of Canadian Jewish history, when the community's social politics witnessed the passage of the old Zionist leadership and the emergence of the short-lived Canadian Jewish Congress, an organization which represented the claims of the immigrants to a share in the formation of the communal agenda for Canadian Jewry. During the ensuing decades when the Canadian Jewish identity was being forged, and its distinctiveness within North America was being defined, the Canadian polity underwent the transforming experiences of separating itself from the mother country and distinguishing itself from the United States. The Canadian Jewish identity was formulated within the parameters of the emerging Canadian national personality, however vague, inchoate, tenuous, and divided that remained.

The community was formed out of the human material that emigrated from Europe to British North America. But while its institutional structure was based on experiences and ideals emanating from the immigrants' old homes, and in response to exigencies and opportunities found in the New World, they did not attempt to re-create the world from which they had come. Therefore, this community was not a fragment of the Old World, a particle flung off and intellectually, or in any other way, congealed. Canadian Jewry grew in every dimension during these twenty-four decades, from a tiny group of transplanted British American Jews professing a Sephardic connection in the 1760s to a fully articulated, diversified, and dynamic national group that defined itself as Canadian while expressing itself in the varied political and social contexts of the Dominion. At the same time, it was a part of a world of political and social change that rendered insignificant the physical distances separating Odessa, Warsaw, and other European sources of inspiration from Montreal, Toronto, Winnipeg – and all the secondary cities and towns where Canadian Jews lived – as letters, books, journals, newspapers, and people crossed and sometimes recrossed the Atlantic. The golden chain of Jewish tradition, religion, language, economy, and history was set down and renewed many times in these northern lands, to take root and branch out in rough symbiosis with a new society that was distinctively North American: overwhelmingly British and French, conservative, traditional, precarious, and defensive.

The Jewish experience takes place, as the philosopher Abraham Heschel reminds us, in space as well as in time. The geographic, political, economic, and social elements form contexts that shaped the evolution of communities in many countries and cultures in which Jews have lived for two thousand years. Countervailing the temporal dimension, moveover, the spatial element permits the continuation of the central elements of Jewish culture over centuries largely influenced by the local context in which Jews live. The constant interplay between culture and context presents the Jewish historian with an erratically moving target, an opportunity and a challenge to understand and describe to his readers the experience of this people both in space – in this case, Canada – and in time, with reference to the eternal coordinates of Judaism.

In the chapters that follow, readers are offered a view of Canadian Jewish history that describes this encounter between continuity and change. Life in the interwar years was undergoing massive social transitions, while immigration was curtailed in a nation recovering from war, a society driven by racial dualism, and an economy largely dependent on raw-material exports in the flux of gyrating world markets. Beginning with foundations in Nova Scotia and Quebec in the mid-eighteenth century, the story surveys the religious, economic, and social evolution through the nineteenth century as the community faced problems created by immigration. Drawing massive resources from abroad, leaders undertook relief and colonization experiments to relieve the strain. Parallel to these works, the immigrants made their own adjustments, seeking economic opportunity while attending to the life of the mind in the cities, neighbourhoods, small towns, and villages of first settlement. Here, too, they again faced antisemitic prejudices but with a distinctive Canadian face. In order to fund communal needs and overseas responsibilities, and address political challenges, the Canadian Jewish Congress was formed in 1919 at the end of a massive campaign by immigrant organizations.

One aspect of that encounter took place in that perennial Canadian hotbed of tension, Montreal. Here the generation-old issue of how Jews fit into the province's confessional school system arose once more and caused bitterness both within the Jewish community and among French-Canadian clerico-nationalists. The question of how Jews, who were defined as Protestants for educational purposes, should define themselves remained moot. But the debate, the resolution, and the aftermath had serious impact for the Jews of Montreal.

By the 1920s 'the great Jewish metier,' to borrow historian Moses Rischin's felicitous phrase, the clothing industry, had come into full flower, notably in Montreal, Toronto, and Winnipeg. Because of competition and pressures to lower costs, this frontier of enterprise was a well-known danger zone for both would-be manufacturers and their workers, some 30 per cent of them Jewish. In the resulting confrontations, the spirit of North American free-enterprise capitalism collided with the collectivist values of East European socialism and brotherhood within the Jewish world.

That socialist outlook, which many Jews shared, was largely coloured by their European backgrounds, where the battles for workers' rights, humanistic values, and democratic government were fought by socialists against the dark forces of reaction and antisemitism. And in the Canada of the 1920s and 1930s, amid recurring unemployment and massive social distress, it seemed that socialism had a future.

Antisemitism was present throughout the interwar period, though its ugliness in Canada was exacerbated by the special situation of Quebec – French, Catholic, and introverted – where fascist-minded ultra-nationalists articulated an especially virulent form of racist Jew-hatred to add to the traditional religious anti-Jewish phobias. Meanwhile, antisemitism flourished amid virulent and violent forms of racism elsewhere in Canada.

Amid all these transformations, which were creating the circumstances for defining a Canadian Jewish identity, Canadian Zionists were involved in the extraterritorial project of rebuilding the Jewish 'national home' in Palestine. But the vast majority of Jews had no intention of personally participating in the Palestine project beyond occasional contributions of money. Instead, Zionism strengthened their identity as Jewish Canadians and provided an important vehicle for political expression and ethnic pride. This became even more clear during the Second World War, when Jews participated honourably in Canada's military endeavour, but only at the same level as all other Canadians, despite widespread understanding that Europe's Jews were the special target of the Nazis. The Canadian environment had helped to transform exile into diaspora for most Jews, who were anxious to become as Canadian as local society would allow.

Zionism historically had deeper roots in Canada than in the United States when measured by per capita financial contributions and volunteering for the Israel Defence Forces during the 1948–9 War of Independence. The rates *of Aliyah*, or migration to Israel, nevertheless were no higher then or later. The post-war era also demonstrated that Canadian Jews as a collective were seeking accommodation and integration into the mainstream, and enjoying economic and social advancement at unprecedented levels. Antisemitism of the most malevolent pre-war forms virtually disappeared, and many of the old barriers against integration gradually fell away. Meanwhile, the community grew through renewed immigration, first of Holocaust survivors, then of Israelis, North Africans, Russians, and, more recently, Argentinians – all of them adding diversity while forming sub-communities within the larger collective. And, at the same time, alongside the Holocaust the existence of Israel became recognized as a vital node of identity, a homeland whose survival, language, and culture became integrated into the Canadian Jewish mentality through schooling and visits.

The post-war migration of Jews, many of them survivors, and the transformations after 1945 saw Canada's Jews moving slowly into the mainstream. In the meantime, overall communal governance and various fundraising structures had changed out of all recognition in response to transforming communal needs.

Canada's Jews, numbering nearly 400,000 persons at the beginning of the twenty-first century, have entered the Canadian mainstream to a degree undreamed of two generations earlier, and constitute a much different community – if they are really still a single body – than they once were. The interface between the eternal values of Judaism and the Canadian context, its broadly conceived social space, when added to the Holocaust and Israel, has produced a much different community than that which existed only a generation before. Strength, confidence, pride, and commitment are now the norm in Canadian Jewry, which is in reality a community of communities, amidst growth and diversity. The look back offered in these pages will perhaps illuminate aspects of our present condition and offer a glimpse into the years ahead.

PART ONE

Beginnings, 1768–1890

1 Foundations in the Colonial Era

When fourteen Jews foregathered to form Canada's first congregation, named Shearith Israel (the remnant of Israel), in Montreal on 30 December 1768, they were continuing a North American Jewish communal tradition that had begun in New Amsterdam 114 years earlier, when a handful of their co-religionists fleeing Portuguese persecution in Brazil had gathered to worship in a small loft on the town's waterfront. To be sure, the members of the small group that assembled in Montreal in 1768 were not the first Jews to reach these shores or to have important contact with Canada. Joseph de la Penha, a Dutch Jewish merchant of Spanish and Portuguese descent, was granted the territory of Labrador by England's King William III in 1697, possibly because one of de la Penha's captains had discovered the area. Aside from an interesting story of a stowaway to New France, Esther Brandeau, in 1738, and a Dutch Jew who converted upon reaching Louisbourg, there is evidence that Jews traded with the French colonies in the Americas, including New France and Acadia, and there may even have been a few Marranos among the French merchants living in Quebec during the last years of the French regime[1] when Abraham Gradis of Bordeaux conducted a huge trade with New France.[2] A small group of Sephardic Jews who had come north with invading British troops in 1759 and 1760 but had soon disappeared.[3] Their Spanish- and Portuguese-sounding names were to be found among Jews in Curaçao, Barbados, and London. Some of them apparently married Christian women. Jacob de Maurera is one example; he had been a sergeant-major in the commissariat branch of the British army and was given a grant of land after reaching Canada about 1760. Changing his name to Jacob Maurer after marrying a local woman in 1768 in Montreal's Christ Church, he integrated into the

French-Canadian community.[4] Other early Sephardim returned to New York or Philadelphia after only brief sojourns.

Even before they settled in Quebec, there was some Jewish mercantile contact with the British colonies in Newfoundland and Nova Scotia, and with the French fortress of Louisbourg on Ile Royale (Cape Breton). In the 1740s the Rodrigues family of the 'nation portugaise' – a contemporary French code word for conversos who had settled in the Bordeaux region – were heavily involved in the Louisbourg trade; a decade later the Gradis shipped goods there. One street in the fortress was known as 'rue des Juifs,'[5] and official records refer to a Jewish conversion. The New York merchant Jacob Franks shipped tea to Newfoundland and Cape Breton in the early 1740s.[6] In 1748 the executive of London's Spanish and Portuguese synagogue, then searching for a refuge for their poor, considered founding a colony in Nova Scotia.[7] Four years later, the project was still alive, as reported in October 1752 in the *Halifax Gazette*: 'The congregation of the [London] Jews in general, that is to say the three synagogues, have chartered three ships of 500 tons each and are going to send 100 poor families over with provisions for a year after their arrival and £10 in goods on three years credit to set them up. They are to sail in three weeks times.'[8] The scheme was mooted for a few years more, though nothing ever came of it.

Considerable numbers of Jewish traders arrived in Halifax shortly after it was founded in 1749 as a British naval and military counterpoise to Louisbourg. A number of Jews moved there from Newport, Rhode Island, in 1751, all of them merchants who dealt in New England colonial goods, manufactured articles from England, and staples from Nova Scotia. One of them even applied for the right to mine coal in Cape Breton.[9] By the 1750s there were many Jews in Halifax among the army and navy purveyors and the merchants who supplied the civilian population, which numbered 4,000.[10] Surviving records indicate that some of these merchants intended to stay. Israel Abrahams's household consisted of three males and seven females, who presumably included his wife and daughters, while the Nathans' family domicile included five males over sixteen.[11] A cemetery was acquired and a fledgling community was established. But it gradually died out in the 1760s as trade with New England dwindled following the American Revolution. The barely used cemetery, located in a prime area, was appropriated for a provincial workhouse.

Outside the capital, a Dutch Jewish trader, Nathan Levy, became a Lutheran in 1752 and settled in Lunenburg, where some of his descendants still reside. Samuel Jacobs (who later settled at St-Denis, Quebec) was present early in 1758 at Fort Cumberland, 'where he apparently engaged in the liquor trade'; he was also a partner in a brewery at Louisbourg between 1759 and 1761.[12] In the early 1750s, Israel Abrahams manufactured potash there and petitioned the Board of Trade to employ him to restrict others in this business. Jacobs and Abrahams were joined by several others, including Naphthali Hart, Jr, who formed a partnership with Abrahams; they became 'large scale merchants and packers of mackerel.' They may have done business with the Newport shipowner Aaron Lopez, whose ships traded with merchants in Newfoundland and the Gaspé. Lopez owned numerous vessels plying the eastern seaboard of North America. His crews engaged in whaling off the Newfoundland coast and traded mustard, rum, cordials, and onions to merchants in Halifax and Quebec City.[13] With other Newport merchants, Lopez had interests in the Gulf of St Lawrence cod fishery, as he 'followed his advantage wherever it beckoned, to nearly every important harbour between Quebec and Florida.' A trader named Nathans ran the Halifax mackerel fishery from nearby Russell's Island (now Horseshoe Island) and, lavished generous hospitality on his friends and associates at his home situated on the Northwest Arm.

At least two Jews were among the Loyalists who sailed from New York to Nova Scotia in 1783, Jacob Louzada from Bound Brook, New Jersey, and Abram Florentine, a Tory businessman from New Jersey and New York; however, no evidence survives of precisely where they settled, or how long they stayed. A few others may have lived in Saint John shortly after it was founded in the 1780s. Isaac DaCosta, an English Jew of Dutch origin and of Spanish-Portuguese lineage, in evidence before the Commission of Enquiry examining Loyalists' losses, testified to having lived in Nova Scotia in 1765–6; his claims included ownership of over 20,000 acres in the province and financing the settlement of six families there. Two Jews, with surnames Abraham and Phepard, acquired land in the 1780s in the border region between Nova Scotia and New Brunswick and assimilated into the local population.

Samuel Hart, formerly a merchant in Philadelphia, moved to Halifax in 1785, perhaps because of his reputed Tory sympathies during the American Revolution. He set up in business as a general merchant and ship chandler, trading with the West Indies and Shelburne County. He was elected from Liverpool to the Nova Scotia legislature in 1791 and took the oath of office 'on the true faith as a Christian,' even though he was still a Jew, though not for long. He was soon baptized an Anglican and became a pewholder in St George's Church. He played a minor though cooperative role in the legislature until 1797, when he was awarded several large land grants by a grateful government. He prospered and within a few years owned more than £4,000 worth of real estate.[14] He maintained a large country estate near Halifax where he entertained lavishly, perhaps too lavishly, because his social ambitions eventually outran his purse. He died in 1810 and was buried in St Paul's churchyard in Halifax. After his demise, a few Jewish merchants continued doing business, but by about 1820 they too had disappeared.

And so, even before Montreal's Jews organized themselves as congregation Shearith Israel on that winter day in 1768, Jews were present in the British Americas that later became part of the Dominion of Canada. In their communities, with ten men present Jews circumcised their sons, married only other Jews, partook of meat and fowl that had been slaughtered according to a rigorous code, and refrained from eating forbidden food. They were required to bury their dead in separate ground, support the sick, aid the poor, and protect the orphaned. They were enjoined by their holy books and hallowed tradition to observe all of these and many other religious and social practices that cumulatively decree and prescribe in minute detail the order of their lives from birth to death, from their waking in the morning until their slumber at night. Thus, wherever Jewish traders might travel, they carried – to a greater or lesser extent, depending on the individual – a need to observe an ancient tradition.

Although most of Canada's first fourteen Jewish settlers who formed Shearith Israel were Ashkenazim (followers of the German order of prayer), they identified themselves as Sephardim (followers of the Spanish and Portuguese order of prayer), not just because of the implicit cachet that the Spanish and Portuguese Jews awarded themselves, but also because the Sephardic tradition was an integral part of the American Jewish culture they shared with congregations throughout the Thirteen Colonies before moving to Quebec.[15] Even though the handful of Sephardim that were in the congregation in 1768 had largely disappeared within a decade, the congregation retained that identity. The congregation's name was taken from that of New York City's major synagogue, and, though dependent on London for religious personnel and guidance, they continued their strong connection to the Jewish communities in New York and Philadelphia,[16] from whom for years they drew financial support. By affiliating itself with Shearith Israel in New York, the Montreal congregation was able to feel it had a 'mother' in the New World and lots of other 'relatives' elsewhere in the Americas.[17] Indeed, some Montreal Jews sought refuge and help from the New York Jewish community, and business and social ties remained strong through the eighteenth century. As British citizens, they enjoyed contacts throughout the British North American colonies.

Given their orientation to trade and commerce, it is not surprising that some Jews were among the suppliers who accompanied or followed the British army that captured Quebec city in 1759 and Montreal in 1760. Alexander Schomberg, post-captain in the Royal Navy, commanded the frigate *Diana*, which in September 1759 participated in that action by covering Wolfe's famous landing above Quebec; he returned the following year to help cement the British victory.[18] Many Jews were operating on the American frontier as fur traders or purveyors to the scattered army garrisons. The forces of General Amherst, commander-in-chief of the British army in North America, included a considerable number of Jewish suppliers, or sutlers, as well as several Jewish officers in the colonial militia regiments that formed part of his army. Following the British conquest, more Jewish merchants moved to Quebec from Halifax, Albany, New York, and Philadelphia, while others came directly from London.

Because they had enjoyed a British identity before arriving in what would later be the Province of Quebec, Jews benefited from all of the rights and the economic advantages of 'old subjects.' British merchants gradually came to dominate the economic life of Quebec by pushing aside the French bourgeois who remained following the Cession of 1763, using their superior political connections and commercial ties to the metropolis of London.[19] Economically aggressive, these newcomers induced a reluctant governor, James Murray, to open the interior fur-trading posts, and they rushed upcountry in the late 1760s to trade their goods with Aboriginal people who, having been held back by war, had several years' worth of rich pelts to barter.

Montreal's promising commercial future rested not just in the fur trade, but also in the lucrative business provisioning the British naval and military forces that were stationed there, at nearby forts like St John on the Richelieu, and in the interior at Niagara and Detroit. When these garrisons expanded during crises like the American Revolution and the War of 1812–14, this business thrived. By the 1780s, commerce also included the supply of goods to new settlers in the western regions of the province, where the Loyalists and later immigrants from the United States seeking refuge and free land under the British flag were beginning to settle. Montreal was rapidly becoming the commercial hub of the north, and here a promising future beckoned.

The experiences of some of the earliest Jewish traders are instructive. In the hope of profiting from the booming fur trade, Lucius Levy Solomons, who came from Albany, moved upcountry from Montreal in 1761. In partnership with his cousin Ezekiel Solomons and several other New York Jews, he reached Michilimackinac with a huge load of trade goods even before the British troops took over from the French. But he lost the entire stake, worth an estimated £18,000, when he was captured by Indians during Pontiac's rebellion of 1763.[20] Solomons and some partners re-entered business a few years later, however, and by 1770 he was again a big player in the fur trade. In the Detroit region, Chapman Abraham, a German-born Jew from Montreal, traded in wine and brandy, and supplied muskets, gunpowder, ball, and shot to the British forces there until he was captured and later released during Pontiac's uprising in 1763.

So many Jews were operating out of Montreal in the 1760s, in the fur trade and in importing, that according to historian Jacob Marcus, they constituted 'at least ten percent of the mercantile community, one of them diversifying even into hogs.'[21]

Not all Jewish settlers lived in Montreal. Samuel Jacobs, an Alsatian Jew who came to Quebec by way of Nova Scotia and resided in St-Denis on the Richelieu, had a store that exchanged a wide variety of foods and goods to local French-Canadian farmers in return for wheat, while British soldiers from the nearby garrison came by for liquor. With branch stores at St Charles and St Ours, Jacobs also diversified with a distillery and a potashery; he remained a major commercial figure in the region until his death in 1786.[22]

One of Jacobs's many business contacts was Aaron Hart, who was the most successful of Canada's first Jewish settlers. His a family became famous and acquired great wealth and influence in Trois-Rivières, where he lived from 1762 until his death in 1800.[23] Like both the Jacobs and the Solomons families, Hart came up to Quebec by way of New York in 1759 as a sutler to the British army. Following the troops northwards, he became a purveyor to the forces stationed at Trois-Rivières, where he ventured into the fur trade and, in partnership with his brother Moses of Montreal, into many real estate transactions: he bought the fief of Bruyères and the seigneuries of Sainte-Marguerite and Bécancour, as well as the marquisate of Le Sable and numerous other properties in and around Trois-Rivières. Having established a strong business presence in the Trifluvien region, Aaron Hart has attracted some attention from historians. The first historical account was unflattering, depicting Hart as a shrewd, oversharp Jew, 'égoiste et mystérieux dans ses desseins,' with an 'ambition dévoratrice.'

Hart also operated a store in Trois-Rivières, where he conducted a diverse wholesale and retail business, and extended commercial and real estate loans throughout a wide area around the town. Prospering by these diverse operations, he bequeathed a huge legacy to his eight surviving children; his four sons inherited the vast bulk of his estate, while his four daughters received £1,000 each. Hart's sons, however, did not fulfil their father's hopes of establishing a dynasty in Trois-Rivières. All of them except Moses eventually left the town, as did most of the daughters. Those who remained gradually blended into the local French-Canadian community and, as Jews, eventually disappeared.

There were other, less famous Jewish families in Sorel, Verchères, St Antoine-de-Padoue, Rivière-du-Loup, Yamachiche, and Berthierville for varying lengths of time, ultimately leaving or, in some cases, like Samuel Jacobs, intermarrying and assimilating. A small community flourished at Quebec for many years, building a synagogue and establishing a cemetery.[24] But the largest Jewish congregation was located at Montreal.

Indeed, the Montreal congregation's first years were difficult because many of its founders were men on the move. Most ventured north looking for quick gains on this commercial frontier and, finding little, drifted off. Some may have despaired at the distance from family and the lack of a Jewish community, or realized the unlikelihood of finding Jewish wives there. Within the decade, therefore, the membership of the congregation had almost completely changed. By 1778 it included thirteen men who had erected a small synagogue on Little St James Street on land owned by David David. Though they apparently used the building for services, the acquisition of its religious accoutrements, notably the sefer torahs (scrolls of the Pentateuch), was not completed until about three years later. They adopted a strict code of synagogue governance, modelled on that in effect in New York, which was based in turn on that governing London's venerable Sephardic synagogue in Bevis Marks. The minutes of the congregation of 1778 record that 'the synagogue as we all comprehend is meant for the use of all Israelites who conform to our Laws and our Regulation and under the management of a Parnass [president], Gabay [functionary], and a Junto [committee] of three of the Elders ...'[25] Levy Solomons was elected parnass and Uriah Judah gabay, while Ezekiel Solomons, Samuel Judah, and Andrew Hays constituted the first junto or governing committee. To ensure participation, a system of stiff fines (£2 10s per refusal) was instituted for those who demurred. Two other honorary positions were that of hatan torah, the man called up to the reading of the last portion of Devarim (Deuteronomy), and hatan Bereshit, the man summoned to the reading of the first portion of Bereshit (Genesis). Both of these observances took place on Simchat Torah, the festival of Rejoicing of the Torah, which ends the festival of Succoth, the feast of Tabernacles. These honours were usually a prelude to synagogue office. The junto was delegated to formulate 'a proper Code of Laws for the better Regulating of this Kahal [congregation].'

That the congregation's minutes were kept in English suggests that most members recognized it as their common language. But the use of Hebrew dates indicates that some members had some Jewish knowledge. Services were conducted according to the Sephardic ritual. Within a year, two Torahs and a shofar, a ram's horn, were acquired from London. There was also a punctilious regard for observance of Jewish laws and traditions. For example, early minutes include a reference to a decision not to bury uncircumcised male babies in the congregational cemetery, to prevent a recurrence of such a burial as that of the child of Ezekiel Solomons, who had married a French-Canadian woman.[26]

To retain tight control, the junto gave themselves and their sons a double vote at congregational meetings. Also, new members could vote only after two years and could assume executive office only after three – provided they paid a stiff entry fee of £10 'to preserve to those Present Subscribers the Founders of this Congregation which have been so far Established at an expense beyond the Bounds of our Circumstances, that we may enjoy certain Privileges beyond any Stranger that may hereafter Settle here.'[27] In order to recruit all the newcomers, however, they stipulated that any Montreal 'Israelite' who did not yet join the congregation within twenty days of coming to town, 'and those out of the Town within Six Months,' would be excluded. The constitution also levied fines for members who caused a disturbance, refused office, failed to perform a mitzvah (duty), or missed a meeting. 'Severe penalties,' moreover, would be imposed 'on those who shall be the Means of giving a bad Name to any of the Congregation, by which a Disgrace may be brought on any of the Israelites,' a provision against slandering fellow members.

Such regulations, if enforced, were bound to cause problems. A dispute erupted within the first year, between Jacob Franks and the parnass, Levy Solomons, who allegedly had 'made use of expressions to the Manifest Injury of the Congregation.' The affair was taken seriously by the junto because 'it appeared to us of the Greatest Consequence to ourselves and the future Welfare of our Religion in this Province.' Found guilty of the infraction, Solomons was immediately replaced as parnass, a stiff rebuke.

While the status of the Jewish religion in Quebec did not yet meet with any public challenge, Jews nevertheless may have felt vulnerable to antisemitism. Of this, as in other British North American colonies, however, there is little evidence. As well, because they were mostly in business, Jews interacted daily with their fellow traders and merchants throughout the province and neighbouring parts of the United States without any commercial restrictions. They bought, leased, and sold property, traded in commodities, imported manufactured goods, participated in joint ventures to own ships, dispatched fur-trading brigades to Michilimackinac and other interior posts. They traded with Indians, contracted to provision and supply British garrisons, signed apprenticeship agreements, joined with other merchants in petitions for liberalization of trade, redress of grievances, and the establishment of a legislative assembly, and supported each other, as well as their non-Jewish colleagues, in meeting their financial obligations in times of economic distress.[28] And that this tiny community of no more than a score of families was able to finance the construction and fitting out of a synagogue indicates both prosperity and confidence in the possibilities of Jewish continuity in Montreal.

The congregation's minutes indicate a continuing serious commitment to Jewish observance. In 1779 an English Jew, Jacob Raphael Cohen, was hired as a combined cantor, teacher, circumcisor, and ritual slaughterer.[29] In 1782 Cohen was succeeded by Hazan de Lara, who remained until 1810. He was assisted by several congregants, who could conduct religious services. But, like his counterparts in the Thirteen Colonies, the colonial Canadian Jew 'lived in a Gentile world without a ghetto and without a rabbinate.' Religious observance diminished when business was conducted on the Jewish Sabbath and holidays, forcing

Jews to neglect major religious obligations and prohibitions. In this free society, then, a decline in formal religiosity was in evidence.

The effects on this community of the American Revolution and the invasion of Quebec by General Montgomery's forces in 1775 have been treated in Jacob Marcus's *Colonial American Jew*, where he points out that only a few of the colony's Jews – like David Salisbury Franks and Levy Solomons – were so sympathetic and helpful to the invaders that they were forced to leave the colony when the Americans retreated south in the spring of 1776.[30] Though actively supporting the establishment of a legislative assembly, along with a majority of their fellow merchants in Quebec, most Jews were not prepared to side openly with the invaders, even though Aaron Hart and Samuel Jacobs – among others – sold goods to them. Like most other Canadians, 'new subjects' or 'old subjects,' Jews preferred to remain neutral.[31]

Although less is known of the lives of Jewish women and children than of men, certain facts are clear. Most of the earliest settlers were unmarried men, and, as there were practically no Jewish women in the colony, they went abroad to marry – like Aaron Hart, who brought his cousin Dorothea back as his bride from London in 1778 – or married non-Jewish women. Fur traders who spent lengthy periods at posts in the interior often took Native 'wives' *selon la coutume du pays*; traders recognized the economic utility of these alliances, as well as the need for emotional and sexual comfort.[32] Jewish contemporary intermarriage rates in Quebec probably mirrored the 28 per cent for American Jewry in the Federal period.[33] The shortage of marriageable Jewish women in eighteenth-century Quebec could account for the fairly high rates of migration in the first wave of Jewish merchants to the larger communities in the United States. Several members were forced to go abroad for wives, but most married women from New York, Newport, or Philadelphia, while others chose local women like the Hart sisters.

Typical of the times, Aaron and Dorothea Hart had a large family – with eight surviving children – and Dorothea's days must have been filled with their care. They were observant Jews – in 1778 Aaron admonished his son Moses to keep the dietary laws and to return to Trois-Rivières for the Passover holiday – and Dorothea would have had a heavy schedule to ensure strict attention to the code. Meat and fowl had to be ritually slaughtered, while dairy and meat foods were to be kept apart and eaten only with separate dishes and cutlery. Even though servants undertook the real work of the kitchen, constant surveillance by the mistress of the house was necessary to ensure correct procedure. Sons were circumcised and given the rudiments of Jewish education by their father, or by itinerant teachers who may also have worked in one of Aaron's businesses. Sons were expected to enter the business, usually after serving an apprenticeship, and daughters to be married off at an early age. Sarah Hart married Samuel David, Charlotte married his brother Moses David, while Catherine married Bernard Judah.[34] Historian Jacob Marcus observed, 'It was not unusual for a woman to step into her husband's shoes after his death.' Phoebe David, a widow and the sole support for five children, carried on her husband's business after he died in 1776.[35] But it is unlikely that many other Jewish women entered business affairs in those early days. Home and childbearing were their destiny. Average family size is unknown, but it likely mirrored that of Jews in American cities. Recent studies of Jewish demographic patterns before 1820 in New York, Newport, Philadelphia, Charleston, and Savannah reveal that the average Jewish family had 5.9 children.

Virtually all of these Jews were middle-class and, as property holders, importers, wholesalers, and retailers, inevitably interacted on all levels with non-Jews. Business dealings meant cooperation in the creation of a favourable environment for commerce; thus many of the earliest settlers supported petitions for the establishment of English commercial law, and other changes to improve the local business climate. As essentially middle-class urbanites, Canadian Jews were in the same economic and political camp as the Anglo-Saxon elites that governed the colony and dominated its commerce.

Between 1760 and the early 1780s, the Canadian Jewish experience began with small but firmly committed steps towards the establishment of a permanent community. In Montreal, a synagogue was built, a cemetery acquired, a code of governance drawn up, a small group of families established, and an identity affirmed. Many of these Jews with American origins were now forced to adjust to a different political and social environment. The Quebec Act of 1774 confirmed the already well-recognized uniqueness of the province by allowing the continuation of the Roman Catholic faith and religious hierarchy, the French laws of real property and inheritance, and the seigneurial landholding system. The Act also implied the official abandonment of attempts to anglicize the French population and the prospect of establishing representative government institutions like a legislative assembly. The governing Executive Council of Quebec was to contain eight French

Canadians among its twenty-two members, thus giving it a 'preponderantly French Canadian ... tone.'[36] Although the British government later made a few concessions to Quebec's English-speaking merchants by allowing the application of English law for the collection of debts and the enforcement of contracts and agreements and suits for damages, these provisions were not enforced, and such matters remained a sore spot for years.

The extent to which Jews were apprehensive about their future in Quebec is not clear. In view of the serious disabilities Jews still suffered in contemporary France, even aside from the reservations they held about the Quebec Act, Jews may well have been concerned about their prospects in a society that was predominantly Catholic and French,[37] although business relations among French Canadians were cordial and Quebec was, after all, a British possession, where their personal liberties were protected. Because they were 'close to that [Protestant] clique and sided with it, literate and with some wealth, the Jews were obviously an important part of the Canadian power structure.' Even so, the possibility existed that the province might again be acquired by France, which still claimed ownership of vast territories in North America. This prospect – however remote – of falling under the dominion of a nation where Jews did not yet enjoy equal status must have caused some Jews anxiety.

The majority of Quebec's Jews strived to blend with the new British community of administrators and businessmen. They spoke English, many had been born in the Thirteen Colonies or in England, and they were virtually all traders whose ultimate political allegiance during the Revolution was to Britain, even though – like most of their business confrères – they were essentially neutral during the early stages of the conflict. Once the Americans abandoned serious attempts to invade Quebec, after the disaster of 1775–6, British residents in the province professed their loyalty to the king, while continuing to petition for the establishment of a legislative assembly that would allow them to participate in the governance of the colony. Many of Quebec's Jews signed the petitions for an assembly and other reforms that were produced by agitators among the 'old subjects' periodically between the Conquest and the Constitutional Act of 1791. Thus, while they identified with the anglophone community, they also supported the institutions of self-government as many had experienced in most American colonies.[38]

The completion of a synagogue constitutes a commitment to define a separate community and to continue their own personal lives as Jews. In contrast to Europe, where the synagogue 'was only one agency of the

Jewish community,' in America it 'became the community.'[39] By building a synagogue and acquiring a cemetery, they bound themselves to submit to a discipline, to pay fines, to obey, and to pursue God's will through observance. By the waters of the St Lawrence, as it were, the 'old subject' Jews awesomely and solemnly reaffirmed the old covenant. They were on the way to formulating a distinctive Jewish identity in a new and somewhat disquieting political and social context – and in a great raw land.

As well as the British-American tension, serious problems arose from the newly emergent French-Canadian nationalism. This challenged the special status and interests enjoyed by the elite British appointed officials in Quebec and the mainly anglophone merchants of Montreal. Thus caught between two conflicting visions of the future of Lower Canada, Jews became involved in a dramatic battle for their civil rights. It began in 1805, when British officials and merchants attempted to create an infrastructure for economic development by introducing a tax on land. The French-Canadian majority of the Legislative Assembly argued that the vast bulk of the population would be adversely affected by such levies. The Assembly raised import duties instead, in an effort to put the financial burden on the English commercial sector. The ensuing Assembly debate was marked by rising acrimony on both sides, and sparked the emergence of the Parti Canadien, which insisted on the principle of the 'supremacy of the legislative branch over the executive authority,'[40] while voicing increasingly assertive expressions of French-Canadian nationalism.

It fell to Ezekiel Hart, the second son of Aaron Hart, to be a casualty in this clash. Ezekiel, like his brothers Moses and Benjamin, took an interest in politics. He ran in a by-election for a seat in the Assembly in April 1807, winning over three other candidates.[41] Hart's second major hurdle was his Jewishness. The electoral officer was a strong supporter of the government, untroubled by scruples of impartiality. Not only did he favour the candidature of Thomas Coffin, but, in the words of the *Quebec Mercury*, he also 'cast ... many aspersions on the situation of Mr. Hart and his brothers' and pointedly 'adverted to the religion of Mr. Hart.' His attack was so hostile that 'no Spanish Monk, in the height of ascetic zeal, could have poured on this subject, more bitter invective or intolerant warmth.' What forces carried Hart to victory are not known, though his brother Benjamin's spirited response to overt antisemitism may have helped. It was a Saturday, the Sabbath, and though Hart demurred at signing various electoral documents, he complied when pressed. He presented himself at Quebec in January 1808, at the opening of the Assembly's next session, ready to be sworn in and take his seat.

In the meantime, his election had already become a minor *cause célèbre* in Lower Canada. His opponents had publicly asserted that Hart could not be sworn in on the grounds that he was a Jew,[42] and the Quebec newspaper *Le Canadien* had carried a letter accusing Hart of 'having employed the most vile and corrupt methods,' while another correspondent held that 'the election of a Jew to represent Trois-Rivières must be regarded as proof of the existence of an influence among the electorate that is stronger than their sense of duty to their country.' The writer continued: 'Everywhere the Jews [are] a people apart from the main body of the nation in which they live ... A Jew never joins any other race.' Warming to his subject, the writer asserted: 'The Jews are united among themselves, however spread out among all countries, forming an entity that has no other centre than itself. If such a confederation, united by a continuous correspondence, does not provoke the jealousy of other people, neither does it merit their encouragement.' No member of this people had a right to represent Trois-Rivières: 'By what right can a Jew who is only worried about himself and his sect expect to look after the interests of the whole nation? And what reason is there to expect that such a man would work in the interests of the common good?' Having elected Hart, the people of Trois-Rivières, the letter stated ominously, should expect 'no indulgence after [making] such an extraordinary choice.' The 1807 election also produced an impromptu, an extemporaneous composition sung to the tune of a popular song which compares Hart's election – unfavourably – to Caligula's appointing his horse as consul of Rome.[43]

When presented with the oath, Hart put his hand on his head as a substitute for the traditional covering, and replaced the word 'Jewish' for 'Christian' at an appropriate point in the recitation. This was not the prescribed oath, however, and various members of the Assembly seized on this to try to prevent Hart from taking his seat,[44] a move that was supported by the provincial attorney-general, a judge who also sat in the Assembly, and by several other English-speaking members. Hart attempted to explain himself, but after some skirmishing, he was ordered to appear at the bar of the House – a serious measure – to debate the legality of his sitting in the Assembly as a Jew who had not taken the proper oath. He appeared and presented his case, but after a spirited debate, the Assembly adopted the resolution that 'Ezekiel Hart, Ecuyer, professant la réligion juive, ne peut siéger ni voter dans cette chambre.' Though Hart protested, 'praying the oath might again be administered to him in due form,' he failed to overturn the measure.

Because the Assembly had been dissolved, he had to wait a year before trying to get re-elected. Admonishing the opposition in the *Mercury*, the government sheet in Quebec, one commentator pointed out, 'The Jews, in the United States, are eligible to any place and hard then would be their lot, if they were denied that privilege in this frigid wilderness.'

Hart tried again. In the next provincial election, in a field of four contestants for two seats, he stood in second place.[45] Re-elected, he appeared at Quebec when the Assembly convened in April 1809 and took the required oath, this time without covering his head or hedging on the oath's Christian character. He was nevertheless ousted, this time simply because he was a Jew. The Jews of Lower Canada, already alarmed by these events, had petitioned the Assembly for redress in March, but their appeal was rejected. During the debate on Hart's eligibility in early May 1808, Jean-Marie Mondelet, member for Montreal East, asked that the Assembly be informed of the manner in which Hart had taken the oath. When told that he had done so 'sur les Saints Évangiles,' Mondelet moved that Mr Hart, being a Jew and unable to bind himself by this oath, could not claim his seat. One member, sensing the opportunity for some drollery in this tedious business, proposed an amendment 'that Mr. Hart should abstain until it was verified that he was a Christian when he was elected.'

The Assembly again resolved: 'Que c'est l'opinion de ce comité que Ezechiel Hart, Ecr., professant la réligion judaique, ne peut prendre place, siéger, ni voter dans cette chambre.'[46] This decision was upheld by the colonial secretary, Lord Castlereagh, on the grounds that a Jew could not sit in the Assembly 'as he could not take the oath upon the Gospels.' Having been expelled a second time, Hart made no further attempts to enter the Assembly. His brother, Moses, ran for one of the Trois-Rivières seats in the next election, but was defeated. The Harts were not resigned to this rejection. Following his second expulsion, Ezekiel tried unsuccessfully to open the issue up for debate.

Several aspects of the affair need to be clarified, argues historian Jean-Pierre Wallot.[47] He places this clash in the context of heated passions over the broad question of eligibility for membership in the House of Assembly. The principal conflict was about the suitability of judges, several of whom had attempted to take their seats following their election. Behind that was 'the political struggle of two ethnic groups, social and religious antisemitism, personal animosities, and weaknesses in the law.' The concern of the Parti Canadien in the Assembly was political, not religious. While keeping Hart out, it was attempting also to expel two French-Canadian judges who were suspected of harbouring sympathies for the ruling English party.

These observations are undoubtedly valid, as is the fact that antisemitism was not restricted to the French Canadians. Governor Craig did not come to the defence of Hart; instead, he exploited the issue to try to teach the Parti Canadien a 'lesson' because of its obstreporousness on several other matters. He dissolved the Assembly after administering a severe tongue-lashing on these issues.[48] Nevertheless, Jews were now officially second-class citizens. They were ineligible for membership in the Assembly and legally unfit to hold any other office, civil, judicial, or military, because they could not be bound by the required oath. Except for the Assembly, however, this ban seems not to have been enforced.

There is no record of any other Jew attempting to gain membership in the legislature of Lower Canada, though several joined the militia, which required a similar oath, and became officers. Others took up minor appointments which likewise demanded swearing-in ceremonies and prescribed oaths. But the contest of 1808 compelled them to take an oath which included the phrase 'on the true faith of a Christian.' This requirement rankled in the Jewish community, especially in the Hart family, still affected by the expulsions of Ezekiel in 1808 and 1809. Ezekiel's son Adolphus Mordecai, and his nephew Aaron Philip, attempted to have the oath reworded, thereby eliminating the disqualification.[49]

Eventually, in March 1831 the legislature passed an act declaring that 'all persons professing the Jewish religion, being natural born British subjects inhabiting and residing in this Province, are entitled and shall be deemed, adjudged and taken to be entitled to the full rights and privileges of other subjects of His Majesty ... to all intents, constructions and purposes whatsoever, and capable of taking, having or enjoying any office or place of trust whatsoever, within this Province.'[50]

Introduced by the popular John Neilson, it had the support of Louis-Joseph Papineau, the leader of the Parti Patriote (as the Parti Canadien had been renamed) in the Assembly, and by Denis-Benjamin Viger, who presented petitions to the Legislative Council.[51] While Papineau's motives might have been essentially political, 'the virulent character of the earlier controversy found no echo in 1832 in the legislative assembly, the council or the press; it was simply treated in a factual manner by both English and French.'[52] Even though the measure passed in the House and became law on 5 June 1832, it was challenged by some members on technical grounds. The challenge was considered by a special committee of the Assembly in 1834, and the law was confirmed.

While the affirmation of Jewish political rights in Lower Canada, and by implication in the rest of British North America, was not achieved until the early 1830s, it must be emphasized that, like their co-religionists in England, Quebec's Jews enjoyed a highly emancipated state. Their status was not defined by special laws; they enjoyed freedom of movement, occupation, and ownership of real estate.

Jews were deeply involved in the major economic transformations of that era. The Hart family's enterprises in Trois-Rivières were thriving. Aaron was growing older, and his son Moses, among all of his eight children, seems to have been the firm's principal businessman. He dealt in urban and rural real estate, while conducting an extensive local trade in virtually all commodities, including furs, and imported manufactured goods, which he sold wholesale and retail over the entire Trifluvien region.

One of the Harts' most important real estate acquisitions was the seigneury of Bécancour, a feudal grant located across the St Lawrence from Trois-Rivières. Purchased in sections between 1791 and 1817, the seigneury gave them ownership of nearly 5,500 arpents, from which they would derive an annual revenue of *cens et rentes* and *lods et ventes* of $4,031.17 by 1858.[53] This, however, was just the beginning. Moses also acquired enormous holdings in the Eastern Townships, and parts or all of the seigneuries of Grondines, Belair, Gaspé, Sainte-Marguerite, Carufel and Godefroy, and Dutort and Courval, besides the marquisate of Le Sable and the Vieuxpont fief. With considerable investments also in Canada's earliest banks and in the development of the St Lawrence River steamboat business, he became an important figure in Lower Canada's economic life.

In Montreal, new economic opportunities opened up with the beginnings of settlement in Upper Canada. David David was perhaps the major Jewish participant in this transforming economy.[54] Starting off as a 'winterer' in the northwest fur trade, he linked up with the North West Company and was admitted in 1817 to Montreal's prestigious Beaver Club. While operating a store in Montreal and dabbling in the wheat trade, he did business with the military. A prosperous man, David supported the formation in 1822 of the Committee of Trade, which was intended to give the business community a stronger voice on trade matters with local and imperial authorities. From 1818 to 1824, he served as a founding director of the Bank of Montreal and acted as one of the promoters of a company to build a canal between Montreal's port and Lachine to improve communications with Upper Canada.

At his death in 1825, David was a rich man. His holdings of Bank of Montreal stock were worth nearly £7,000, and his personal account had a balance of £1,575; his portfolio included over £3,300 in Bank of England annuities and about £24,000 in mortgages, promissory notes, and other assets. He sat on the boards of the Bank of Montreal and the Lachine Canal Company. He also did business with many of the city's biggest import-export houses, and he owned some four thousand acres of rural land in Lower Canada, besides a great deal of urban real estate. Altogether his estate was worth nearly £70,000, about $300,000.

Moses Judah Hayes was another Jew who actively fostered Montreal's economic development. He helped to promote one of the city's early gas companies, and a bank, and in 1832 he bought Montreal's waterworks, which he sold to the municipality in 1845.[55] He then built a four-storey hotel and theatre called Hayes House, an elegant establishment that became a favourite of Montreal's nouveau riche – the merchants, bankers, shipowners, and entrepreneurs and their families who prospered from the city's impressive economic growth as the commercial, financial, and transportation hub of the St Lawrence economy.

Clearly, many of the early Jewish immigrants were deeply involved in the new economic activity dominated by the Scots, English, and Americans in Montreal. David, Hayes, and several members of the Hart family who lived in Montreal and Trois-Rivières did business with French Canadians, as well. Import and export listings record that Benjamin Hart of Montreal exported some of the largest consignments of pot and pearl ash to British ports, while he imported cargoes of metal goods. Levy and Benjamin Solomons ran a prosperous tobacco and snuff importing business, while they also manufactured some of their stock-in-trade. Meanwhile, their relation Henry Solomon, a furrier, required his journeymen to work twelve-hour days, 'sabbath and other holidays of the Jewish religion excepted.'[56]

Business had crossed ethnic, national, and language lines in Lower Canada since the Conquest, even though by the mid-nineteenth century some economic specialization by ethnic groups had begun to emerge in Montreal. 'La bourgeoisie Canadienne-française,' while participating in a small way in financial, commercial, and industrial capital, had its real strength in the real-estate sector, and while French-Canadian businessmen had no monopoly here, 'leur présence est beaucoup plus forte qu'ailleurs .'[57] Jews who bought and sold real estate, therefore, likely would have dealt with French Canadians, and those who sold to country traders, peddled goods in the timber camps, or toured the countryside to purchase commodities undoubtedly encountered French-Canadian businessmen. And so did most of those in Montreal, this city of increasingly mixed cultures and nationalities. In this respect, then, Jews appear to have been no different from most others.

A few Jews could assimilate into one of the two major surrounding cultures, as Samuel Jacobs had done earlier. Levi Koopman, who was born in Amsterdam, came to Montreal in 1826, adopted the name of Louis Marchand, and joined a French-Canadian merchant in business in the Chambly River area; he converted to Roman Catholicism in 1828 and married a local French-Canadian woman.[58]

In Quebec during the early 1840s, Abraham Joseph, an observant Jew and a twenty-something bachelor running his family's business affairs in that city, socialized successfully among the local anglophone business elite.[59] Others adapted in different ways. The norms of propriety observed among Montreal's Jews were shattered with dramatic panache in May of 1840 by Eleazar David. The eldest son of Samuel David and his wife, Sarah Hart, Eleazar was a lawyer who joined the Royal Montreal Cavalry in the 1820s and served during the Rebellion of 1837 as a senior captain in command of a reconnaissance and dispatch-rider unit at the battle of St-Charles-sur-Richelieu. He was 'mentioned in dispatches,' an honour signifying better than average service under fire, and was promoted to major. He commanded a large unit at the decisive battle of St Eustache. Rising up the ranks of the militia after the Rebellion, David saw his promising military, legal, and personal career shattered by his decision to elope with a British army captain's wife, Eliza Harris, with whom he had been conducting a torrid affair. (The elopement was perhaps precipitated by the birth of their child the month before.) They spent the next ten years in exile in the United States, France, Italy, and the West Indies. When they returned to Montreal in 1850, with their five children, David resumed his activity in the militia and in the legal profession, although he was to attract more notoriety some twenty years later.

Yet, for many Jews, an important dimension of their lives was enclosed within the community. Their religion and culture separated them from their fellows by an invisible fence of laws, traditions, language, and history – not to mention, fears and suspicions. In Montreal in the early nineteenth century, a strict degree of Jewish observance was difficult, if not impossible, to achieve. Surviving records of the synagogue and its members indicate how serious those problems were.

The most pressing of these was the synagogue itself. Situated on Little St James Street, not far from Nelson's Column at the top of Place Royale, the small stone structure that had been standing since 1778 was probably still adequate for the community's needs. According to a register of 1832 kept in the Montreal prothonotary's office, there were only fifteen males over the age of twenty-one identifying themselves as Jews. A few more were added during the end of the 1830s, but the total was still very small.[60] Therefore, the problem was not the size of the synagogue, but its location and ownership. It had been built on land donated by David David, on which he held only a life interest. Upon his death in 1824, the property reverted to his heirs, and the congregation was forced to abandon the building. Services were then held in the homes of members, but without a proper religious centre there was no focus for observances and festivities. Though Benjamin Hart attempted, from 1826 on, to galvanize the community to build a new synagogue, the project dragged on for another decade.

Little was accomplished until 1838, when a donation of £575[61] started off a fundraising campaign which extended as far as England – without any success, except for a contribution of £5 from the philanthropist Sir Moses Montefiore. The poor showing, Abraham Hart believed, was 'the complaint ... that you have no Killer [schochet, or ritual slaughterer], and so are not living as Jews.' But enough money came in to begin, and a new structure was planned by a local architect. In March the trustees commissioned the carpentry and masonry. By September 1838 the impressive structure – described as 'a fine specimen of the Egyptian style of architecture' – was ready for use. 'Also in the Egyptian style,' the description continued, 'is a very beautiful mahogany Ark, over which are placed the Ten Commandments, in Hebrew characters, cut in white marble.'

Now the search began in England and the United States for a person who would serve as hazan, mohel, shochet, and teacher. Abraham Hart, who acted as the congregation's agent in London, was pessimistic because 'were he to be met with [it] would not be necessary for him to go to America for a situation [because] his services would be too eagerly sought on this side of the Atlantic.'[62] But soon David Piza, from London, was employed as hazan, mohel, schochet, and teacher.

Other problems ensued, mainly the tensions over the vexing question of which *minhag* (customary) order of service, the Portuguese or the Dutch-German (Sephardic or Ashkenazic) should be followed. The practicalities were significant as Benjamin Hart noted in a letter to fellow congregant Isaac Valentine, in October 1833. 'Provided we have a Portuguese Shool,' he pointed out, 'impressive financial support could be secured from even local Jews and strangers [who] ... have all told me they prefer our [Sephardi] Ceremonies to their own.'[63] But as a safeguard against agitators who might try to change the ceremonies, Hart asked Valentine for the names of those who would vote to retain the established order, so that 'we are perfectly secure from the Dutch, German ...' 'No Dutch will ever have our Shool for their own,' he snorted, '[because] they are themselves ashamed of their ceremonies.' Hart appended several proposed changes to the synagogue's by-laws to strengthen the grip of the old guard and ensure victory for his side. They provided 'that all youths brought up to the Portug. mode of worship, or brought up in this congregation shall at the age of 21 become members – provided they have been seat holders three years.' These provisions also stipulated that, although sermons might be given in English, 'the fixed Prayers shall be read in the Hebrew Language according to the custom of the Spanish and Portuguese Jews and no other.'

But other complications followed, and the joy attending the opening of a new synagogue, and the apparent settlement of the ceremonies issue, did not unite this tiny diverse congregation. Religious leadership and finances remained problematic; even though the community was willing to pay a religious functionary up to five hundred dollars a year, there were no candidates. Sadly, Abraham Hart's dour warnings now proved to be correct. Consequently, several members refused to pay their dues. Isaac Aarons held back on the grounds

> that the regular fixed Prayers have not for eleven months past been read in the said synagogue and that during the said eleven months, no regular performance of divine service according to the portuguese custom (or any other custom of the Jews) have [*sic*] been performed in the ... synagogue ... for the want of a Hazan or reader.[64]

He also pointed out that even the by-laws calling for fixed prayers to be read in Hebrew 'according to the custom of the Spanish & Portuguese Jews and no other' were being violated. Over nearly a year of close observation, he reported indignantly, 'a part of the fixed prayers have been twice or thrice publicly read in the english language in the ... Synagogue.' Clearly, both religious education and religious devotion were at a low ebb.

Worse still was the fact that there was no schochet. Aarons complained:

> A Shochet or Killer of the meat is indispensable in a Congregation of Jews, as it is the first Pillar ... although where a number of Jews are congregated they can dispence [*sic*] with a Hazan or reader and even a Public Synagogue, they can not according to our fundamental rites of religion dispence with the Shochet or Killer.

By the late 1830s, then, there were at least two serious problems: the division over the *minhag* to be observed in the prayers, and the absence of religious leadership and kosher meat. But while there was no one able to conduct services according to the Portuguese *minhag*, there existed a tiny group of members – many of them recent arrivals – prepared to conduct services in the Dutch/German, or Ashkenazic, style. This group was apparently able to provide kosher meat – likely through one of their number who was familiar with the rites of *schechita* (ritual slaughter). By the early 1840s these dissenters had decided to form their own congregation, and in early June of 1845 they began to conduct prayers on their own. In 1846 they secured legal status, through an act of the legislature which authorized 'the diverse persons of the Jewish faith calling themselves German and Polish Jews' to form a separate congregation with the same rights and privileges as the Shearith Israel.[65]

The inevitable split took some time to occur. There had been a slow influx from Germany and Poland to Montreal and, to a lesser extent, elsewhere in the Canadas for a number of years, and though some adhered to the practices of Shearith Israel, others did not. In religious, family, and intellectual life, Lower Canada's Jews were thus able to draw on both the Sephardic and the Ashkenazic heritage and on family connections on both sides of the border. Religious guidance, marriage partners, news, and ideas were sought from these sources, all equally important. Several Montreal Jews were among the earliest subscribers to *The Occident*, a Philadelphia weekly devoted to Jewish news and opinion, when it began to appear in 1843.[66]

Although loyal to their tradition, not every Jew in Lower Canada was religious. Influenced by the writings of eighteenth-century deists – and possibly also by reflection upon the religious intolerance that had kept his brother Ezekiel out of the Legislative Assembly – Moses Hart devoted much thought to religious questions. In a small book entitled *Modern Religion*, which he published in New York in 1816, Hart urged

Jews and deists to adopt what he called a 'universal religious system' in order to 'harmonize the religious contentions of mankind.'[67] While Hart's system proclaimed a belief in a supreme being, or benevolent Creator, he eschewed established religious observances. In their place, he proposed a set of three public festivals and 'duties obligatory,' which included prayers, rites, and blessings on special occasions. Influenced, according to Jacob Marcus, by eighteenth-century ideas of reason and the 'trinity' of God, immortality, and ethics, Hart based his revolutionary new religion on his belief in the general need for a liberal religious faith.[68] But the fact that Jews were among his primary targets for conversion to this 'modern religion' suggests that he was deeply uncomfortable with Judaism. The work was reprinted in the United States, where it had aroused interest among members of Jewish communities contemplating 'Americanizing' their religious practices.

For over fifty years, the Jewish community of Lower Canada had thus undergone enormous pressures. The most important of these was the political reality of the French-English conflict in Lower Canada, and the exposure of Jewish vulnerability in the struggle between French Canada's pursuit of cultural distinctiveness and the Anglo-Saxon forces of economic progress. Jews were squeezed between the upper and nether millstones of nationalism and continentalism, between French resistance to change and British disdain for a way of life and institutions which appeared to hinder economic growth. This was surely the crux of the Hart crisis of 1808 and 1809 – not antisemitism, which was a minor, though ugly, addendum. At least one contemporary, the quixotic American Jew, Mordecai Noah, who attempted in 1825 to set up 'an asylum for Jews' named Ararat on Grand Island in the Niagara River, doubted the sincerity of French-Canadian proponents of liberty.[69]

Had antisemitism been the main issue, then it would have resurfaced when the 1831 bill giving Jews full entitlement was passed in a Legislative Assembly dominated by an assertively nationalistic French-Canadian majority led by Louis-Joseph Papineau. Importantly this 'Jew bill' was a first in the British Empire, preceding by a generation the extension of full civil rights to Jews in Britain. In Europe, full Jewish civil rights were accessible only in France, and even there Napoleon had called a special meeting of Jewish notables in 1809 to discuss Jewish loyalty to the state and establish limits for Jewish uniqueness in a secular society.[70] All the same, the vital comparison is with the United States, where most Jews had enjoyed full civil rights for almost a century, although some states still restricted office-holding to Christians well into the mid-1800s. In the North American context, the political discrimination in Lower Canada was not an anomaly. And antisemitism resurfaced in the aftermath of the failed rebellions of 1837, when some insurgents organized Hunters' Lodges (Frères Chasseurs) which recruited members in both Upper and Lower Canada, but many more in the United States. Before launching an invasion of Lower Canada, according to historian Mason Wade, they announced a program which called for the strangling of all Jews and the confiscation of their property.

For the majority of Jews, the cultural conflict in Lower Canada was a political reality that seriously affected their civil status. Official limitations of political rights not only set up barriers but also established a principle that could have manifested itself in further refinements. Ezekiel Hart was rejected even after swearing an oath of office which included a reference to Christ – thus, even a Jew who publicly abjured his Jewishness (in this one matter, at least) was still unacceptable. The question of what else Jews might be prevented by law from doing, was answered by the legislation affirming their rights. Meanwhile the basic coordinates of their lives went on as before.

Also significant was the emphasis on Sephardic worship at Shearith Israel, Canada's only congregation, and the same kind of insistence on the Ashkenazic in the merging German, English, and Polish congregation. What historian Jonathan Sarna identifies as the 'revolution in American Judaism,' with the emergence of Reform in two congregations in the United States in the 1820s foreshadowing a mighty religious movement, had no counterpart in Canada, where there was little reflection of the Second Great Awakening that so influenced Jews south of the 49th parallel.[71] While similar in so many respects, Canadian and American Jewries were on divergent paths in their religious and political identities: revolution to the south, tradition to the north.

2 Pedlars and Settlers on the Urban Frontiers

As already noted, most Jews made their living from commerce, and the mid-nineteenth-century immigrants were no different. Snapshots of some of these new arrivals demonstrate how they – like their non-Jewish confrères – were involved in the expanding trade of the British colonies, which, in 1867, became the Dominion of Canada.

Mark Samuel, who ran a men's hat shop on Montreal's Notre Dame Street, probably was unaware of the entry on him in the R.G. Dun and Company (the forerunner of Dun and Bradstreet) credit report of 1852.[1] It read, 'said to be a very honest Jew,' signalling to potential creditors the message 'here is one you can trust.'[2] But not all Jewish businessmen in Montreal were accorded such praise. Most were depicted as 'close fisted Jew,' 'trying to get the best of a bargain,' or simply 'Jew, cannot trust.' These descriptions were more derogatory than those usually attached to businessmen of other origins, and no doubt reflected an antisemitism prevalent at the time. Jews had a reputation for shrewdness, toughness, and dishonesty that surpassed the reputed canniness of the Scot or the sharpness of the Yankee trader. Those who reported confidentially to Dun's made certain to find out who was a Jew,[3] tried to scrutinize his dealings more closely than others, and emphasized that in their reports.

One obvious question is: Did antisemitism matter? If it had not existed, would Jews have fared better in the business environment of mid-nineteenth-century Central Canada? As noted earlier, the commercial community that governed the economic life of Montreal had included a small number of Jews since the Conquest – as well as a few Germans and Italians – amid the Anglo-Celtic majority of Scots, Americans, English, and Irish, and the minority of French Canadians. By about

1850, Jews were listed among the local merchants who dominated the increasingly diverse business affairs in the city. Jesse Joseph, for example, president of the Montreal Gas Company and by far the richest Jew in Montreal, was amassing a vast amount of first-class urban real estate.[4]

The Dun register does seem to suggest, however, that the Jewish experience in the business world was distinctive, that Jews constituted a separate business enclave, to a significant degree working apart from the rest in a kind or business ghetto. If so, the question is: was the separation self-imposed or caused by antisemitism? Did antisemitism restrict Jews in business endeavours? Studies of Jewish economic life in the mid-nineteenth-century United States stress that because of anti-semitism and the resistance of Jews to the transparency which credit agencies demanded, they were forced to rely on private credit.[5] Thus, Jews did not fit the norm. But in Canada family connections, inter-city networks, and patterns of ethnic business association were the normal pattern throughout the business world in the mid-nineteenth century.[6] Borrowing from family and friends and forming business partnerships with them were widespread practices, and Canadian Jews generally followed this pattern, as a look at Dun's records – which provide some fascinating information about their capital, connections, and style of business – confirms.

Most Jewish males were in a variety of businesses – jewellery, tobacco, dry goods and textiles, and clothing manufacturing – and all of them benefited from family connections in financing their firms and marketing goods throughout Montreal's expanding hinterlands.

Moses Ollendorf, a forty-four-year-old German Jew, arrived with some capital in 1848 and started by repairing jewellery and engaging in small-scale retailing.[7] After failing in 1852, he recommenced on a modest scale as an importer and wholesaler dealing mainly with Jewish pedlars. By 1862, following a second failure (in which he paid off his creditors), he was reported to be worth some $15,000 and described as 'a shrewd cunning Jew [who] lives in great style.' He assisted a brother, a local soap-maker, and helped his son-in-law, Lewis Anthony, a small-scale clothing manufacturer, establish a business in Toronto. As a member of the English, German, and Polish congregation, Ollendorf contributed handsomely to the campaign to build its first synagogue in the 1850s, and was elected its first president in 1860.[8]

Abraham Hoffnung, also from Germany, arrived in 1855 at the age of twenty-five via St Louis, Missouri, with an inventory of watches worth about $8,000.[9] He was an importer and wholesaler, dealing mainly with London suppliers. He prospered and was estimated to have made a profit of $5,000 to $6,000 within two years, benefiting from the excellent credit he enjoyed in London and, probably, from his marriage to the daughter of John Levy, a well-to-do local tobacco merchant. Hoffnung's business was well regarded, though the Dun reporter complained in October 1858 that he 'belongs to a class regarding whom it is next to impossible to learn anything certain,' a frequent complaint about Jews. By 1860 he was estimated to be worth $10,000, and his annual turnover was judged to be $25,000. In August of 1860, he partnered with a young English Jew, George Wolfe, one of two brothers who had started a small jewellery business since arriving in 1858 with an $8,000 inventory that had been supplied by a sister-in-law.

Gottschalk Ascher was another German who had arrived via Glasgow in 1841, at age fifty. He sold watches and jewellery, importing merchandise from both New York and Glasgow. By 1857 he was thought to be doing well, though the reporter complained about his secrecy. By that time, Ascher had already established a branch store in Toronto run by his sons, Jacob and Albert, who took over the Montreal store. Although this transformation was damaging, he was soon back in business, on a much reduced scale. By that time, his son Albert – who had married into the wealthy Joseph family – was the firm's travelling salesman. The marriage did not help the business, however, and by 1861 it was sputtering.

Michael Dinklespiel, another German, and Michael Bumsel, a Swiss, set up in partnership in 1859. This was a wholesale house, and Bumsel, a former jewellery pedlar, seems to have been its salesman. The leading partner was Dinklespiel, supported by a brother in New York, who became the effective owner of the business by 1861. Despite a good start, the firm closed down in October 1862. Dinklespiel decamped to California, probably as his brother's agent, while Bumsel returned briefly to Europe, possibly to peddle jewellery in the Swiss countryside. Unable to make a go of it there, he then journeyed back to Toronto, where he cut a sad figure.

Henry Davis and Julius Lander, both Germans, began to import jewellery and fancy goods in 1861 through Lander's connections in Germany.[10] They sold mainly at wholesale, to pedlars like Samuel Silverman, whose wife kept a millinery shop in the city, and to Herman Danciger, a German who had migrated to Montreal from New York, where he had run a clothing store for several years. They supplied Simon Hart, who, with his wife and son, Philip, also operated a pawnshop[11] with William

Silverstone, another German. Silverstone left that arrangement in February 1863 and set up his own pawnshop with Louis Albert, a former pedlar.

David Ansell imported various kinds of glassware and toys.[12] An agent for several German firms, he arrived in 1862 from Queensland, Australia, where he had served an apprenticeship in this line. He had excellent connections in Frankfurt, where his father manufactured glassware which he exported to London, Paris, and Hamburg. By 1869 Ansell was reported to be worth from $8,000 to $10,000 and enjoyed a good reputation. 'He evidently knows how to make money,' commented Dun's investigator, after noting that Ansell claimed to have made $10,000 in 1868 alone, 'a result few would expect from the quiet business he does.' Besides turning a handsome agent's profit, Ansell dabbled in real estate, in 1871 building a row of fine stone houses. He employed six travelling salesmen, including one working exclusively in the United States. By 1874 he was reported still to be doing well, though following a 'peculiar style of doing business,' while estimates of his personal wealth ran as high as $50,000. He suffered serious reverses a year later, perhaps because of the depression, and in November 1875 he was forced into bankruptcy with his liabilities totalling $130,000 against assets of $40,000. Although Dun's registers lose sight of him at this point, Ansell went into other business ventures, apparently with great success. He was one of the most important figures in the Jewish community for nearly another forty years, taking an active role in charitable work among immigrants, in colonization projects, and in Quebec political issues that affected Montreal Jewry.[13]

Nearly all of these jewellers were German. Most arrived with capital or inventory, and benefited from business and family connections abroad, which supplied them with vitally important agencies for specific lines of merchandise, credits, and information. Several acted as wholesalers to local pedlars, or upcountry traders, many of whom, apparently, were also Jews. But not all of them prospered; about half enjoyed only transitory business lives.

Montreal's Jewish tobacco traders, by contrast, included practically no Germans. Most ran small-scale enterprises with apparently few family or other credit connections abroad. One exception was headed by Jacob Henry Joseph. The Josephs, who operated on a large scale, originally settled in Berthier in about 1800, then in Quebec City in 1814, and finally in Montreal in 1830.[14] Their business was so large, well-capitalized, and sound that in October 1858 a credit report rated them 'as good as the

Bank. You may trust them [for] all they will buy.' And in February 1859: 'Jews and "Rich as Jews."'[15] The firm occupied huge premises, where the tobacco products were manufactured. By October 1857 the family also held other assets, possibly real estate, worth over $200,000. A year later, Jacob Henry was reported to be building a house for $40,000, and was believed to have a net worth of at least $100,000. He became an officer of the Montreal Board of Trade and the harbour authorities, and supported several charities.[16] In 1866 he took in Alexander Hart as a junior partner, freeing himself to follow other interests in real estate and share holdings in Montreal's booming telegraph, railway, banking, and elevator companies.[17] Jacob Henry Joseph and his brother, Jesse, also a rich and diversified investor, was probably on a par with the super-rich Scottish tycoons who dominated the rising economic empire of the St Lawrence.

Tobacconist Samuel Davis arrived in Montreal from New York with substantial means about 1864. A cigar-maker by trade, he began manufacturing 'medicated' cigars and selling part of his output at two stores he opened in Montreal.[18] If some of his accounts turned sour, he would sell them off at a discount to recoup whatever he could, thus staying as liquid as possible. Though in good standing in Montreal, Davis did not use his credit there, somewhat to the mystification of Dun's reporter, preferring instead to draw on his New York contacts. In August 1868 he brought Lyon Silverman – who invested $4,000 – into the firm as a partner. Eighteen months later, however, despite their preference for 'good accounts,' the firm was forced into bankruptcy as a result of a major creditors' failure. Two years after settling his debts at 40 per cent, Davis was back in business, aided by his New York creditors and a new partner, Jacob L. Moss, a former local pawnbroker, who invested $20,000. By October 1874 their firm was thriving and they employed seventy-five workers, who produced cigars for their retail and wholesale trade in Quebec and Ontario. Less than a year later, they claimed a yearly turnover of $300,000, using substantial lines of credit at both the City Bank and Molson's Bank, thus shifting from sole reliance on New York to the Montreal banks. Samuel Davis's son, Mortimer, infused his enormous energy into the business, which flourished in the 1880s and 1890s, making him Canada's 'tobacco king,' and a multi-millionaire.[19]

By comparison, most of the other Jews in the tobacco business were much smaller fry. Of these, John Levy (whose daughter married the jeweller Abraham Hoffnung) was apparently one of the most successful, at least for a brief period during the 1850s. An immigrant from Manchester, Levy began business in 1843 on a small scale. Ten years later, using credits from New York City firms, he was prospering and, according to the Dun reporter, 'making money ... owns [real estate] and is said to be rich & good.'[20] Thought to be worth from $18,000 to $22,000, he was doing between $60,000 and $65,000 in business annually. A Dun reporter noted that Levy put on 'a princely entertainment' for his daughter's wedding in March 1858. But Levy died the following August, leaving his widow and ten children – and his creditors – with a rat's nest of tangled finances. His wife settled with the creditors, most of them in New York, for fifty cents on the dollar, and continued solely in retail on a much reduced scale. She opened a shop in Quebec City and gave it to one of her sons to manage, but it closed a few years later and Mrs Levy was forced to take in boarders to help meet expenses, while eking out a meagre living in her own small shop in Montreal.

Other transient petty retailers or simple pedlars usually had short-lived careers. Henry Jacobs and Michael Michaels, formerly of Guelph, opened a small retail and wholesale shop in Montreal in 1860.[21] They eked out a living with a modest stock-in-trade and limited credit. Abraham Levey and Humphry Michaels attempted to do the same in their shop, which opened in 1858,[22] but they were soon forced to become pedlars. Rebecca Warner operated a retail store in the 1850s for her husband, an undischarged bankrupt, with the backing, according to Dun's, 'of parties who take a peculiar interest in her.' In November 1858, with heavy debts outstanding, the Warners suddenly skipped town for parts unknown, never to be seen again in Montreal. Then there were Zacharias and Delapratz, German Jewish cigar-makers from Connecticut who blew into Montreal in August 1866, ran up substantial debts, and hightailed it out of town two years later, leaving their creditors high and dry. Samuel Brahadi, an English Jew and a cigar-maker, set up a small shop in 1861 and did a reasonable trade until he was forced to the wall in 1869 as a result of debts accumulated by his brother, Abraham (of whom more later), for whom he stood guarantor. Thus, in the tobacco business, aside from the Joseph and Davis firms, small-scale Jewish retailers and cigar-makers were characterized by financial weakness and transiency.

In all branches of the clothing business, a traditional Jewish area of enterprise, the pattern of their participation was much different. Most Jews operating in this sector manufactured caps and hats and fur goods. Some, like Mark Samuel, the 'very honest Jew' referred to earlier, simply made hats and caps and sold them at retail, in shops which were often managed by family, while his father peddled door to door in town or out in the countryside. Some furriers sold at retail and wholesale in stores in Montreal, like Bernard Levin and Moses Davis, Germans described as 'decent men of their class' who operated a store on Notre Dame Street, where, after 1859, they also sold clothing.[23] Some bought up furs for export. Abraham Brahadi, an Englishman – formerly a professional singer who, Dun's sleuths recorded, had allegedly abandoned his wife and son in London – arrived in Montreal in the late 1840s and gradually developed a business which became so fashionable that it attracted 'the better kind of French Retail Custom' trade.[24]

The most prominent clothier from the mid-1830s until the early 1860s was a native of Manchester, William Benjamin, who, with his brothers Samuel and Henry, owned three distinct but interconnected businesses – clothing, dry goods, and carpets – each operated by one of the brothers.[25] By the end of the 1840s, their aggregate worth was estimated to be about $200,000, and their thriving retail dry goods and clothing stores were rated as the best in town. Consequently, they enjoyed a high rating with creditors in New York and England, especially with a family firm in Manchester. However, by 1860 they were in trouble. Their trade had declined seriously over the previous year or so, according to one report, 'on account of the prejudice felt toward them as Jews,' though another report stated – perhaps more accurately – that 'the retail business in which they are engaged is not successful owing to competition.' In 1861 they liquidated, except for a wholesale dry goods outlet in Quebec, which they left with William, and moved back to Manchester, where Samuel and Henry set up a dry goods export house.

Several Jews pioneered in the manufacture of ready-made apparel as early as the mid-1840s. The Moss brothers, David and Edward – until then importers – were turning out men's work clothes on an enormous scale[26] in a factory next to the Lachine Canal, where they employed eight hundred workers. By 1856 they were exporting $200,000 worth of goods annually to Melbourne, Australia, where their two brothers had wholesale and retail outlets.[27] They were known to be rich, not only from their clothing business, but also because of their sideline of private banking, in which they 'shaved notes,' as the Dun reporter disparagingly described it, by discounting commercial paper.[28] This sideline was so rewarding that, by early 1858, the Mosses started cutting back on manufacturing to concentrate on banking. They retired to England in early 1864, giving the clothing business over to their sons, Samuel and Jacob (Edward's), and Jacob and Hyam (David's). The two pairs of brothers, with occasional guidance from their fathers in London, proceeded to enlarge operations. By January 1873 they had about $250,000 invested in fixed and working capital and had greatly expanded. By 1878 Samuel Moss had become the principal partner in the firm.

Finally, there was Moses Gutman, an American who gave up his trade as an engraver a few years after he emigrated to Canada in 1857 to work for the Mosses as an invoice clerk.[29] Less than a year later, Gutman joined their rivals, the Benjamins, in their Quebec outlet as a bookkeeper. In 1863 he formed a partnership with Mona Lesser, a salesman for a major New York hoop-skirt manufacturer who had moved to Montreal in 1860. Gutman started off with twenty-eight women workers in 1863 to manufacture low-priced lines, while Lesser served as salesman, travelling mainly in the countryside. Gutman soon emerged as the principal partner, and, even though he was an undischarged bankrupt, he commanded substantial credit in New York, where the firm bought almost all of its supplies. Dun's reporters remained cautious about this firm, even though its owners were deemed to be hard-working and steady men who apparently did not seek credit in Montreal. By May 1869, Gutman and Lesser were 'selling goods at cutting prices and pushing trade too hard for their limited means,' a practice which the reporter deemed to be 'a little too sharp.' Gutman left the firm in 1871, while Lesser carried on. By September 1874, however, he was in serious financial trouble. 'This state of things,' it was reported, 'has been occasioned by the many rapid changes of fashion entailing losses to his customers and ultimately on him by which his capital was used up.' After the partnership ended, Gutman opened an outlet in Toronto with two others, Edward Morris and Alexander Saunders, to produce gloves.

In the clothing business, therefore, there were few sparkling performances. The exceptions, the Mosses and the Benjamins, were either well supported by continuous credits from family abroad, or had substantial cash and merchandise in hand. Even in clothing manufacturing, where Jews became so successful, some were just beginning at mid-century. Apparel production in Montreal was booming by the early 1870s.[30] But all the major Montreal manufacturers, aside from Moss's, were owned and operated by anglophones.[31]

Toronto was also enjoying economic change, as its western hinterlands filled up with settlers. Here, Jewish pursuits were focused heavily in jewellery and fancy goods. The brothers F. and E. Gunther started up a small jewellery business in 1856 or 1857, 'without much capital,' according to Dun's reporter.[32] The Aschers of Montreal operated a successful Toronto branch.[33] Michael Bumsel, having failed in Montreal, had retreated to Switzerland, then moved to England, where he failed again before reappearing in Toronto in 1857, attracting the label of 'a hard case'; Bumsel's credit was reported as 'very doubtful at best ... he does not inspire any confidence here.'[34] Soldiering on, Bumsel nevertheless staked out a peddling hinterland between Quebec and London, 'selling jewellery and watch materials to small dealers and retailers.' A few months later, Dun's reporter still described him as a 'hard case' with no property and 'no settled abode,' advising potential creditors to exercise 'the greatest caution' in extending credit to this man of 'irregular habits and general char[acter] ... [with] nothing to bind him here and having no apparent wealth ... a travelling Jew.' Now in bad repute, the feckless Bumsel drifted away, peripatetically peddling out on the Canadian frontier until the end of his days.

M. Feintuch, another jewellery pedlar, showed up in Toronto in the spring 1863. 'A Jew of the regular type,' Dun's man snorted; Feintuch was 'not in good repute and is not sold to here by the trade.'[35] Although he was thought to have 'made some money [by] peddling ... [he] is a risky customer and only pays when he can't help it.' 'He should be avoided,' the entry continued, because he 'could pack up and leave at any moment.' Feintuch, however, was thought to be 'doing well,' despite Dun's disparagement. But he too drifted away, presumably to improve his fortunes elsewhere.

I. Guttstam, a German Jew, reached Toronto in the early 1860s and opened a business dealing in fancy and dry goods. Believed to have 'some money,' Guttstam was not too successful and, according to Dun's reporter, was 'sharp and attempted to smuggle,' presumably a reference to a business manoeuvre which led to a seizure of some of his assets.[36] Guttstam's fortunes apparently improved when he moved to the Bradford area, where he bought a farm, built a new house, and was reputed to have five or six pedlars working for him through the countryside.

Judah George Joseph, the first Jewish settler in Toronto 'prepared to strike roots' in the city, was an optician and stockbroker.[37] When his name first appeared in Dun's records in August 1848, he was noted as 'very respectable, A Jew, s[ai]d to have a gr[ea]t deal of money,' although 'it is not easy to find an est[imat]e of his real w[orth] or position.'[38] He had gone bankrupt in Cincinnati, where he was a lawyer, and 'in various kinds of merc[antile] business,' but in Toronto – where he had been in business since about 1843, according to a Dun's reporter writing in 1854 – Joseph was doing well and enjoyed a good reputation. 'For a Jew his eng[age]m[en]ts are all O.K., I sh[oul]d say Good ... I have a doubt ab[ou]t Jews generally, but consid[er] him an exception.' Until his death in 1857, Joseph's business prospered and his reputation remained intact.

Two other Toronto Jewish families, the Samuels and the Rossin brothers, were also well-to-do. Marcus and Samuel Rossin reached Toronto in 1842, and set up a jewellery and fancy goods business. Wheelers and dealers, the Rossins were 'open to any speculation they think they can make money out of,' the Dun snoop sniffed; they 'will buy anything from Bacon to Silk gloves if they are only sure of a profit.'[39] Anticipating an economic boom in the 1850s as a result of Toronto's extensive new railway linkages to southwestern Ontario, in 1856–7 they built Rossin House, an opulent hotel on King Street – just in time for the commercial depression that struck the city that year. The enterprise was in serious financial difficulties by early 1861. Dun's reporter noted that 'the Rossins had to take or keep [it] to prevent its being closed.' This commitment, along with other speculations in downtown Toronto real estate, put the brothers in financial jeopardy, although they limited their losses by 'getting back into [the] hands of original owners a large amount of RE.' Speculating meanwhile in calf-skins and cigars, the brothers were described as 'sure to make money if they enter trade again as they contemplate doing.' The hotel burned down in November 1862, and within the year the brothers were reported to be manufacturing tobacco products, while contracting for the construction of a railroad in Kansas! Much of their real estate had been seized by various creditors, the rest was heavily mortgaged, and the insurance on the hotel had been paid to other creditors, but the Rossins managed to salvage some of their fortune by selling the property on which the Rossin House had stood. 'If they are successful they will pr[oba]bly be all right,' wrote Dun's reporter, no doubt amazed at their resourcefulness. They were soon to disappear from Toronto forever, Samuel to the United States in 1863 and Marcus, the following year, back to Germany.[40]

Another entrepreneur with connections in the United States was Jacob Englehart; he and a group of other New York Jews associated with Sonneborn Dryfoos and Company, a firm described somewhat mysteriously as 'whisky-rectifiers,' financed the development of the early oil industry in Western Ontario in the 1860s.[41]

Notwithstanding the short-lived prominence of the Rossins, Toronto's premier Jewish family by the mid-1850s – and easily the wealthiest – was that of Lewis Samuel, an Englishman who arrived there in 1855. It was he who took the initiative in mobilizing eighteen Jews to establish Toronto's first Jewish congregation,[42] only a year or so after he had arrived in the city to start a hardware business, after an apprenticeship of seven years in New York, Syracuse, and Montreal.[43]

When they first attracted notice from Dun's reporters, in August 1858, the Samuels – Lewis was joined by his brother, Mark – were 'not cons[idere]d to be of much consequence,' partly because 'there is so little known of them.'[44] Consequently, one reporter complained that 'there is a good deal of contradiction in the reports respecting their standing.' One thing was clear very early: they sold 'at very low rates,' thus undercutting competitors and 'creat[ing], a bad feeling [against] them amongst the trade.' This was possible partly because the brothers kept only a small inventory and 'are exceedingly close, live over their store ... and are very attentive and pushing. They sell at almost anything to get money.' An additional and more important advantage was the fact that they generally paid cash – a practice also employed by their contemporary Timothy Eaton – to buy merchandise at discounts, sometimes even for bargain prices.[45] Thus they could usually undercut their competitors. Another advantage was the connections the Samuels had with suppliers in Quebec, Montreal, and New York 'who purchased bargains in job lots, remnants, etc.' Perhaps most importantly, however, was their access to a ready source of capital from a Liverpool Jewish family, the Hoffnungs, who helped to finance them in their first few years. 'The Hoffnungs opened their hearts to us,' Lewis's son, Sigmund, later recalled; 'over the years they were to lend my Father and Uncle the sum of fifty thousand pounds, without security and at very low interest.' With this kind of backing and the Samuels' 'exceedingly close ... very shrewd ... and persevering character in a g[oo]d many things,' as Dun's reporter put it in September 1860, they had a good start in Toronto's commercial world.

By 1861 their business was doing very well and the firm enjoyed a fine reputation. Dun's reporter described them as '("Jews") of excellent character and business ability.' Their trade was large and profitable, 'making money.' Although their full worth was unknown, they were prompt in meeting their obligations. Mark moved to Liverpool, where he did much of the firm's purchasing, serving in the classic role filled by so many British partners in Canadian firms based on transatlantic partnerships.[46] Dun's reporter was well informed of this feature: 'one of the bro[ther]s now resides in England,' he wrote in November 1863, 'where he picks up job lots,' noting that while they were considered to be good for their 'engagements, ... very little is known of their means.' The Samuels kept their affairs strictly to themselves. But their credit in Toronto was obviously very good nevertheless. In 1869 they were thought to be worth about $75,000 and doing $300,000 a year in business. Therefore, when they bought out the stock of a local metals importer in 1871 for $18,000 – spread out over twenty-four months – the normally cautious Dun investigator did not flinch at this risk-taking of moving heavily into a new line of trade.

In 1871 the Samuels did $350,000 business, but uninsured losses incurred in Chicago – due to the fire that destroyed the city that year – set them back somewhat. Dun's grass often commented favourably on the family's frugal lifestyle, a virtue admired by the Victorians. Despite the onset of a serious depression in 1874, the Samuels were nevertheless able to survive. In December, the Dun report stated that their annual turnover was about $500,000, and their losses so small that they would still make a profit. In fact, the annual statement showed gains of $23,300 and the firm's net assets came to $78,000.[47] The depression and ensuing credit squeeze had apparently not hurt them seriously; in 1875 they were still 'thought to be doing well' and were worth between $75,000 and $100,000.

While they focused on hardware and metals, the Samuels' early business drew them into other fields. Because of a lack of ready cash, 'business often was on a semi-barter basis,' Sigmund Samuel recorded in his memoirs. His father was frequently compelled to accept commodities like hides, tallow, or beeswax in partial payment for goods, and on one occasion exchanged beaver pelts for tin plates. Such were the necessities of trading in the cash-starved frontier economy of Upper Canada in the 1850s and 1860s. Therefore the Samuels moved towards the commodities export trade, which developed into an important part of their business. When Sigmund became a partner in 1869, the firm was exporting wood products.

The Samuels imported pig iron and lead, and many goods and commodities as well. Quantities of copper, tin, zinc, brass, pipes, wire, stove plate, Russian iron, and chemicals arrived by ship and rail. Casks of bristles were brought from Poland to be made into brushes, glass came from Belgium, marble from Italy, and linseed oil, tin foil, and horsehair from other countries. Assisted by the burgeoning railway network spreading from the hub of Toronto, the Samuels sold at both wholesale and retail to customers throughout southwestern Ontario. They did business in Chicago and, after 1881, in Winnipeg during its brief economic boom at the start of the Canadian Pacific Railway's construction.

In nearby Hamilton, virtually all Jewish businessmen were German immigrants and concentrated largely in selling jewellery and fancy goods. The brothers Leander and Leopold Rosenband (the latter in partnership with three Dray brothers) sold fancy goods and cigars.[48] Though they owned no real estate, according to Dun's reporters they did 'a very fair business,' were good businessmen, and enjoyed a sound credit rating, even though Dun complained that 'it is impossible for us to know really what [their] standing [capital] is.' By 1859 the Rosenbands and Drays were apparently doing a large business at a small store in the city, and in peddling and 'getting up raffles' for their merchandise through the surrounding countryside. By October 1859 the partners, 'shrewd keen Jews [with] no visible means,' were doing 'a large trade' and were 'thought to have money.' The partnership was dissolved in 1860, however, the Drays departing the city and Leopold Rosenband continuing on alone. A Dun report of April 1861 rated him as a man of 'very exalted bus[iness] ability good char[acter] + habits. Has always a good bal[ance] to his credit at B[an]k.' With an estimated $12,000 capital, Leopold was able to pick up 'bargains for Cash,' enabling him to sell merchandise at low prices. In Hamilton there was 'nothing against him, except that he is a German Jew, which in some quarters prejudices his credit.' He was certainly a German Jew 'of the better sort,' the report went on, but though 'supp[ose]d good ... no one can tell.' By November 1862, Rosenband had got out of the fancy goods trade and into a tobacco manufacturing concern with Frederick Schwartz, a former brewer who, if also a Jew, was not noted as such that year. Rosenband gave up the Hamilton business scene altogether after the early 1860s, presumably to look for opportunities elsewhere in fancy goods, tobacco, or other ventures.

Two Polish Jews, Prince and Levy, started a jewellery business in Hamilton in the mid-1850s, but by 1857 they were struggling and they failed, leaving furious creditors.[49] Several brothers named Hofeller opened a clothing store in the early 1860s, but they lasted only long enough to attract notice as 'German Jews, not deserving of cr[edit] ... sh[oul]d be avoided.' The same was written of the clothing dealers I. and L. Desbecker, two 'of the numerous German Jews we have here ... no one knows anything about them.' Such was also the case of L. Loeb and Co. – Loeb sold dry goods but 'nothing favourabl[e] [was] known of him' – while L. Levi dealt in fancy goods for a few years in the mid-1860s before drifting off to the United States. Isaac Stine, another German immigrant, set up as a clothier in the early 1860s, was thought possibly to be worth as much as $10,000, but 'possibly he absconds tomorrow ... German Jew, don't trust him.' In March 1862 he was described as 'worthless.'[50] J. Hirschfield sold hoop skirts in the early 1870s, but disappeared.

Off in the hinterland, there were a few Jewish pedlars and storekeepers who operated, mostly transitorily, in towns and villages that served as local market centres. Early nineteenth-century frontier Upper Canada was served by numerous pedlars who helped to provide 'agencies of retail and wholesale commerce.'[51] While Toronto, Hamilton, and many other towns were emerging as significant commercial centres by 1850, there was opportunity in rural areas for these itinerant traders to conduct petty commerce from wagons, horseback, or, at its most primitive level, simple backpack. In Paris, for example, Thomas Coleman, who was described as 'an English Jew,' ran a general store in the 1840s, but by about 1850 he had abandoned business and was living handsomely on the proceeds of his father's estate and some valuable real-estate holdings. A few years later, Coleman departed for St Paul, Minnesota.[52] In nearby Brantford, a rising place in the 1860s, two German Jews named Strauss (possibly father and son) sold clothing; they were thought to have a stock worth $300, to be 'steady and always on hand when any bus[iness] is to be done,' and worthy of 'credit for a sm[all] sum.'[53]

In London, J.W. Ezekiel, a Polish Jew who had lived in London, England, for some years, started a millinery and ready-made clothing business in the early 1850s but came to be known as 'not safe: not a man of principle, a Jew of a 3rd rate stamp ... a rascally Israelite and not to be trusted on any acc[oun]t.' Ezekiel left town in 1856 after closing up business and moved on to Detroit, where he was arrested for debt.[54] B. Morritz operated a clothing store in London from May 1856, did pretty well by all accounts, and was judged to be 'of g[oo]d character and hab[it]s and tho[ugh]t s[a]f[e] for purchases,' but by July 1858 he was out of business and had moved away. Samuel Kohn set up a tobacco shop in the city in 1859 but disappeared within two years.

Jewish traders were also to be found in Brockville, Stratford, Victoriaville, and St Andrews by the 1850s and 1860s, though often for only a year or two before drifting away to look for a better business frontier.[55]

George Benjamin, who had lived in Belleville since 1834 and prospered as owner-editor of the *Belleville Intelligencer* and *Hastings General Advertiser*, served as member of the legislature of the Province of Canada for North Hastings from 1857 to 1863. He was the first Jewish MP in Canada.[56] In nearby Kingston, the brothers Abraham and Samuel Nordheimer gave music lessons and operated a music store between 1840 and 1844.[57] In 1857 German-born Simon Oberndorfer, a cigar-maker by trade, established a successful cigar factory; he became one of the founders of the Jewish community there by the end of the century.[58] There is evidence that numbers of other Jews came, stayed a few years, and drifted away. Men on the move they were, destinations unknown, moving their stock by wagon or buggy, or occasionally even hot-footing it out of town.

Though little is known about the small Jewish enclaves in Ontario, there is some information about a fascinating group located in and around the village of Lancaster, a few miles northeast of Cornwall. This tiny Jewish community was founded by Noah Friedman shortly after he immigrated from Poland in 1857.[59] He was followed by Harris Kellert, his brother-in-law, ten years later. The Jewish population numbered ten persons in Glengarry County in 1861, but many others followed, including Abraham Jacobs and his large family. By 1871 the community numbered thirty-nine, while nearby villages in Stormont County had nineteen Jews and the town of Cornwall had twenty-six. This Glengarry-Stormont-Cornwall group continued for the next twenty years, although its numbers declined slowly. The Jews in Glengarry were essentially pedlars and general store owners, or both. However, many moved to Montreal, drawn by family connections, Jewish facilities, and more opportunities for business – notably in the burgeoning wholesale clothing business. Kellert and Friedman formed a fancy goods wholesale business before becoming clothing manufacturers.[60] The Glengarry experience foreshadowed a pattern: initial settlement, followed by growth over a decade or two, and then decline as the younger generation sought greater opportunities in the cities.

Overall, Jews were, with some notable exceptions, merely petty and transitory retailers or pedlars. Many were driven from their shops by the ill winds of the business cycle, bad luck, mismanagement, incompetence, or under-capitalization. Butchers, bankers, agents, restauranteurs, and auctioneers were also included among the peripatetic penny capitalists who drifted into Canada's cities and towns for a few years and then, blown over by a bad season or two, moved on to try their luck elsewhere – though never far from the scrutiny of R.G. Dun and Company's assiduous sleuths.

Were Jews adversely affected by the antisemitism that was clearly manifest in the business world? Dun's reports indicate that only in very few cases did it matter enough to force a business failure. The evidence indicates that, in the competitive (if not cut-throat) world of business in the mid-nineteenth century, a Jew was as welcome a creditor or client as anyone else – provided, of course, that he allowed transparency and was good for his commitments. Non-Jews did business with Jews despite the existence – possibly even the prevalence – of attitudes that held Jews in contempt, fear, or mistrust. They were, after all, an alien cultural element, most of them relatively new to the scene. At the time 'political and commercial realities ... were multidimensional. Men formed loyalties and took positions on the basis of race ..., religion ..., region ..., national loyalty ..., personal ambition ..., as well as calculated economic interest.'[61] Suspicion was not limited to Jews. Irish and American businessmen in Montreal deeply resented the prominence of the Scottish 'old boy' network in practically all major sectors of the local economy, while French-Canadian businessmen seem to have operated largely in their own sphere. Immigrant Jews – or other outsiders – would not likely be invited into the potentially profitable railway stock flotations and other lucrative ventures that were promoted by Montreal's and Toronto's rich, and politically well-connected, entrepreneurs. Everyone, Jews included, understood that that was the way business was done. Who, except those under duress, would share such deals with perfect strangers – and with Jews, to boot?

It appears, furthermore, that most immigrant Jews preferred doing business with fellow Jews. Time and again, Dun's reporters complained of the difficulty of getting information about Jewish businessmen and said that, when possible, Jews seemed to prefer using their credit with their British and United States connections – often eschewing opportunities for credit in Montreal. To Dun's sharp-eyed spies, it seemed that some Jews were living better than their assumed volume of business would allow, a sign that their real financial standing was unknown. Despite continued snooping, Dun's investigators found it extremely difficult to fully penetrate the veil that hid the business affairs of some Jews, who may have preferred using credit supplied by family or friends than bank loans, believing that relatives and partners were more trustworthy than strangers. The Jews did carry a unique history of persecution, as in

Germany and Poland, where they had long suffered from edicts by the authorities, one of these being the periodic confiscation of accumulated wealth and special 'Jew taxes.'[62] It was perfectly natural therefore that secretiveness should continue to prevail among Jewish immigrants.

For the most part, then, the history of the Jews shaped their business attitudes and behaviour. They were largely marginal to the major economic transformations under way between the mid-1840s and the 1870s. Aside from the Josephs in the Montreal tobacco business and the Moses in the apparel manufacturing trade, they were absent from the dynamic sectors of urban industrialization in Montreal's industrial quarters along the river and the Lachine Canal; nor were they participants in Toronto's and Hamilton's spectacular industrial growth of the 1860s and 1870s. Neither were they much involved in those cities' flourishing banks and insurance companies, and railway and steamboat ventures. As well, with a few exceptions, Jews were absent from businesses importing iron goods, wines, liquors, and textiles, and from those exporting flour, grain, timber, and other commodities. But this was not because of anti-semitism; it was principally due to lack of experience and connections in such enterprises. It is evident, therefore, that at this stage in the development of Canadian capitalism, Jews as a group had no important role. Unlike their co-religionists in Atlanta, Buffalo, and New Orleans – where Jewish businessmen from importers to pedlars developed 'a singularly Jewish trade'[63] in which Jews operated largely within a Jewish business world – their Canadian counterparts do not appear to have been nearly so restrictive. The sale of wholesale and retail clothing provided a major springboard for Jewish entry into the manufacture of men's and boys' apparel, while tobacco merchandising gave them another major manufacturing opportunity in Canada. But the full efflorescence of the Jewish presence in these sectors lay some twenty years in the future.

Elsewhere in British North America, several Jewish merchouts settled in Newfoundland and Labrador outports in the late eighteenth century. A few years later, out in Windsor (not far from Halifax), in the early 1850s, lived B. Louis, who was believed by one investigator for Dun and Company to be of 'Jewish descent,' a feature that possibly explained why there was 'a g[rea]t deal of Wash/[junk]' on his shelves.[64]

Saint John was the base of some Jewish pedlars in the eighteenth century and even of 'an unusually large number of Jewish farmers ... most of [whom] married into the Christian majority.'[65] At Chatham, the booming timber post at the mouth of the Miramichi River, a merchant named Joseph Samuel ran a general store for some thirty years before he retired in 1856.[66] As well as selling imported English goods, Samuel bought up furs, and though regarded as 'a respectable Jew,' he was also thought to be 'cautious like most of his nation.' In 1855 he set up another store in partnership with a nephew, Morden Levy, at Miramichi. Here they engaged in the salmon fishery. Samuel transferred his business interests to his son, Solomon, in 1857 and retired to England. The cousins continued the business, opened a branch at Richibucto, stood well in the community as far as their credit went, and prospered. A contemporary report by an investigator for Dun's observed that Levy 'puts up fish, and does rather extensive bus[iness] at Richibucto and does a quieter bus[iness] at Chatham.' The store at Chatham was sold in March of 1863. Levy died the following year, and though Solomon Samuel carried on for a while, he slips from view in 1865, beset by his growing dispute with the heirs of Levy over the business and other jointly held assets.

Both Prince Edward Island and Newfoundland experienced only sporadic Jewish settlement in the nineteenth century, though Solomon Solomons, Newfoundland's first postmaster, appointed in 1805, may have been a Jew. 'There is more than ample reason to believe that throughout the nineteenth century there was ... a continuous Jewish settlement on [Newfoundland],' in coastal trading and the seal fur business. English Jews named Ezicial settled on the island in the early 1800s, and others like Lacque and Levi were involved in the seal trade in 1834.[67]

The Dominion census of 1871 reported forty-eight Jews living in New Brunswick, mostly residing in Saint John, Canada's third-largest city. A major port and regional banking and commercial city, it was also a promising industrial centre. Most Jews were in some form of business. Solomon Hart, a tobacco merchant who had settled in the city in 1858, was joined in 1862 by Nathan Green, his brother-in-law. Born in Amsterdam, Green apprenticed as a cigar-maker (he claimed to have learned this craft from Moses Gompers, father of Samuel Gompers, the famous American trade union leader), moved to New York in 1850, and finally settled in Saint John. Here he developed a large business in manufacturing and selling tobacco products all over the Maritimes.[68]

The Hart-Green clan of Saint John grew to fifteen by the late 1860s, becoming the nucleus of what was to become the first significant Jewish community of the Maritime region. The Harts and Greens were joined in 1878 by Abraham and Israel Isaacs, who ran a successful cigar factory on Princess Street. Other families followed in the 1880s, and by 1896, when the community numbered some thirty families, a congregation named Ahavath Achim – Brotherly Love – was formed.[69] Close ties were maintained with Boston for both religious officials and supplies of kosher foods. In fact, in the autumn of 1879, Boston's Jewry supplied a cantor, a Torah scroll, and the vital tenth man to make the necessary quorum[70] for the first services. Substantial assistance arrived from Boston and New York to build a synagogue in 1898.

Halifax's Jewish community re-established itself in the last third of the nineteenth century after disappearing in the 1820s. By the 1890s the new community was well in hand, fuelled by a wave of immigrants arriving from Europe, increasing the population from 18 in 1891 to 102 a decade later.[71] The Baron de Hirsch Benevolent Society was formed in 1891, and a synagogue was built on Starr Street four years after,[72] to mark the start of what was to become a thriving community.

Communal beginnings on the west coast were more auspicious than the fragmentary and scattered settlements on the Atlantic. This was in part because a synagogue, with all that its development implied, was built in Victoria in 1863, within five years of the arrival of the city's first Jew. Another major factor was the relative size of the Jewish immigration in 1858. 'As I write these lines there is an extraordinary excitement in California. New gold mines have been discovered in the British possessions north of the Washington Territories on the banks of the Fraser and Thompson rivers,' Daniel Levy gushed in June 1858, in his report from San Francisco for the Paris newspaper *Archives Israélites*.[73] 'There are few Jews among the pioneers who are almost entirely miners with pick and shovels, and a few speculators well provided with capital ... However a few left on the last two steamers.' He recognized that if the Hudson's Bay Company's trading monopoly was extended, keeping out others, 'it will be a real disaster for our co-religionists in commerce here, who would thus see a large part of their trade leave California and would be unable to follow it themselves.' But 'if they are admitted to trade freely there, you will soon hear of new Jewish communities at Victoria ... and other places, which to-day are only small trading posts, but may become within a few years great centres of population and flourishing ports in which the commerce of the world will meet.' No wonder, then, that even before Governor Douglas announced in 1860 that Victoria was a free port, 'the flow of ships brought golden inundation by waves of eager miners' followed by 'entrepreneurs with capital, store and hotel keepers, commission merchants and real estate buyers, who were ready to invest in the business which they envisaged would accrue to Victoria from its service to the gold fields.'[74] Among them were a number of Jews who got passage on the crowded ships that made the four-day trip from San Francisco to Victoria.

Frank Sylvester was among about fifty Jews – most of them moving directly from San Francisco – to reach Victoria in July 1858. He arrived with some cash and high hopes of doing business in the city, which was booming from the traditional trade in furs and fishing, as well as from the lucrative traffic in supplies to the goldfields up the Fraser and Thompson rivers, where burgeoning communities of miners were panning for gold.[75] Sylvester was followed by others, including the five Oppenheimer brothers, who were also attracted to the Fraser River rush. The German-born Oppenheimers – after business ventures in Ohio, Texas, and Louisiana – set up stores at Yale, Fort Hope, Lytton, and Barkerville, in the heart of the goldfields, as well as a store and warehouse in Victoria, which became the base of their operations after gold mining died out in the Cariboo district.[76] Other early Jewish settlers included the brothers Selim and Lumley Franklin, English Jews who arrived via San Francisco in 1858 to become auctioneers and real-estate agents,[77] while numerous others who settled upcountry passed through Victoria.[78] The three Sutro brothers arrived in 1858 to establish a branch of their San Francisco–based tobacco business.[79]

While some migrated from Britain, Australia, or New Zealand, most Jews came from California, where, even though of German or other origins, 'they had already become acculturated to Anglo Saxon society.'[80] Most were pedlars and merchants. The German Jewish traveller I.J. Benjamin noted in 1862, in his *Three Years in America*, that 'about a hundred Jews live here,' continuing:

> Only a few are married. The beginnings of the city of Victoria are really due to the Jews. For, no matter how many persons streamed to the island at the outbreak of the gold fever, they scattered again ... to all corners of the world when their disillusion followed only too quickly ... More and more Jews settled here, and the German element was increasingly represented by them.[81]

By 1863 there were 242 Jews in Victoria, making it the second-largest Jewish community in British North America.[82] Not all of them, however, were permanent residents. Many, like the Oppenheimers, dealt in the interior, while others moved up-island to Nanaimo.[83] But the Jewish population of Victoria fluctuated between 4 and 4.8 per cent of the city's total.

As general merchants, many of the newcomers were acting as agents of family businesses supplying the miners in the interior with most of the non-perishable goods and provisions. Others lived briefly in the interior acting for Victoria-based firms, while others were express agents and pack train drivers to and from the goldfields. Others peddled on their own. By 1863 there was a total of twenty-two Jewish-owned clothing and drygoods stores in Victoria, fourteen grocers and provisors, thirteen tobacconists, and ten others selling various items. This was a major commercial presence in this small town.

The congregation began in 1858 with the formation of a minyan for prayer, and a benevolent society, the Chevra Bikkur Cholim V'Kedusha, for tending the sick and burying the dead.[84] A cemetery was acquired in 1860, and two years later, a constitution.[85] Soon the congregation resolved to build a synagogue.[86] Abraham Hoffman, the congregation's first secretary, invoked the aid of Providence for the young congregation, which

> may one day attain the magnitude of a mighty institution, a shrine for the destitute, a school for our youth and the blessing for those that seek the House of G-d in prayer. [where] we may in the turmoil, troubles and anxieties sometimes cast a lingering look upon the religion that our forefathers upheld so faithfully.[87]

He urged the membership 'to build a synagogue as speedily as possible ... our numbers are certainly large enough and there remains but the will to accomplish our end ... the balance for a commodious place of worship can easily be raised by subscription.' With thirty-five members, construction was begun, and Hoffman reported to Dr N. Adler, the Chief Rabbi of the British Empire, that 'we have resolved with the will of G-d to erect a temple which will be an honour to Him and a credit to us.' Even with sixty-eight members, fifty of them heads of families,[88] financing the new building, he informed the rabbi, they required assistance: I trust that [those] in the Old Country will not refuse to lend their aid which will be the means to accomplish our religious task.' Soon remittances arrived from Baron Rothschild and Sir Moses Montefiore in London.[89]

The synagogue project was also assisted by many of Victoria's non-Jews, who donated substantial sums.[90] The building was completed in early November 1863 and opened amidst celebration and fanfare – including attendance by the local St Andrew's Society, the French Benevolent Society, the Germania Singing Club, Masonic officials, local politicians, and a huge crowd led by the band of HMS *Topaz* from the Royal Navy dockyard at nearby Esquimalt.

However, growth was slow. With the decline of gold-rush fever in Victoria, members began to drift away, not just for economic reasons. Many were young men arriving in 1858 or 1859 as temporary representatives of San Francisco firms, with no intention of staying on; [91] the number of singles declined from a high of thirty-eight in 1858 to twenty-two in 1863, while the number of families grew from thirteen to sixty-five.

A building was one thing; religious observance quite another. M.R. Cohen, the congregation's first 'minister' (a title used by rabbis in England), complained in early November 1863 that 'our synagogue arrangements at present are anything but satisfactory or likely to draw religious light upon us as a Congregation of Israel.'[92] There was no proper schedule for services on the Sabbath or on holidays, 'which keeps the people from attending this Synagogue instead of finding a pleasure in visiting it ... and our rising generation ... must suffer by it, to whom the Synagogue service if properly conducted forms the principal fountain of their religious life.' The children, Reverend Cohen observed, must be taught to 'know the difference between the kernel and the shell and thereby appreciate the time they spent [in synagogue].' 'The present age,' he continued, 'demands of us some improvement in our religious affairs and unless some steps are taken in the matter I fear that all your labour ... in erecting so noble an edifice ... will prove "Labour in Vain."' He called for a public meeting 'of all Israelites of Victoria' to consider this 'and other matters for the welfare of our holy faith.'

The Victoria community's future was in doubt as the economy stalled when gold-rush fever declined after the 1880s, while Vancouver's flourished. They had great difficulty employing a rabbi and supporting a synagogue. Many of the founders were anglicized Jews who mixed easily in the city's social, cultural, and political milieu, as is evident from the public careers of Selim Franklin and Henry Nathan in Victoria, and the Oppenheimers in Vancouver. Franklin was elected to the Vancouver Island legislative assembly in 1860 and, after a challenge similar to Ezekiel Hart's problem in Lower Canada on the grounds that he had not taken the oath 'on the true faith of a Christian,' was allowed to take his seat.[93]

Henry Nathan, who arrived in Victoria in 1862 from England, was elected to the legislature of British Columbia in November 1870 as member for Victoria. Nathan actively promoted British Columbia's entry into Confederation in 1871 and became one of the province's first members – and the Dominion's first Jew – to sit in the House of Commons.[94]

Vancouver's Jewish community began in the early 1880s and grew slowly through the next two decades. In a city that was initially created by the Canadian Pacific Railway as its western terminus and headquarters, the orientation was largely landward. By the early 1880s, David and Isaac Oppenheimer, envisioning the future economic importance of this western terminus,[95] had been buying prime land in the area since 1878 and, with subsequent purchases through their Vancouver Improvement Company, controlled large tracts in the Coal Harbour and English Bay districts. Patricia Roy writes: 'Along with other private landowners, David lobbied the British Columbia government to assist the C.P.R. to extend its line westward from Port Moody and encouraged other private owners to join him in selling 175 acres to the railway.' After opening a wholesale grocery house in 1887, David concentrated on the urban development of the city and got into local politics. Promoting basic urban services and actively encouraging industrial development, he was acclaimed Vancouver's first mayor in December 1887 and helped to organize the Board of Trade. He sought European investment for industrial projects and personally invested in electrical and tramway utilities to serve areas where he owned substantial real estate. While he faced charges of 'boodling,' a contemporary word for corruption, in his own time Oppenheimer continued to enjoy a reputation as the 'best friend Vancouver ever had.'

Slow growth continued, mainly with immigration from Russia and Poland. A tiny Reform congregation was established in 1884 under the guidance of Solomon Philo, a religious leader of German origin.[96] Orthodox services were organized around the same time by Zebulon Franks, an immigrant from Russia. But only in 1910 was the first synagogue built in the city.

In any event, it is evident from these earliest east- and west-coast communities in the nineteenth century that their origins were similar to those of Montreal's communities in the eighteenth century. Most of their initial settlers came from nearby areas of the United States; the majority of Montreal's earliest Jews had moved north from New York, Newport, and

Philadelphia, while Nova Scotia's moved up from New York and Boston, and Victoria's arrived from San Francisco. Those American cities had often been no more than sojourning places for immigrants from Bavaria, Alsace, Posen, Amsterdam, or London who might have lived in several other locations before that. Most of the migrants, then, were young men, often unmarried, who moved to seek opportunity elsewhere, or escape failure. The phenomenon of 'men on the move' affected Jews in the same way as it propelled other people in North America from place to place in search of the fortune that often proved elusive or fleeting.[97]

These Jewish migrations in and out of British North America, usually on to new commercial frontiers, are similar to those of their Christian contemporaries who immigrated from American or British metropolitan centres. Both the Maritimes and Pacific British North America were frontiers on the outer fringes of metropolitan societies. Resources and personnel migrated from the south, though both often originated in Britain or Europe, while the vital structure of government was decidedly British. And the early Jewish presence in Nova Scotia or British Columbia evolved under the British flag, administration, and imperial policies. Thus, both regions were British imperial frontiers. British Columbia was a 'counter frontier ... projected from London and Victoria in response to influences and pressures from other frontiers,' particularly from the United States.[98] Yet, while the governmental context was British, California – mainly San Francisco – was a 'major source of economic influence in British Columbia from Confederation to the 1890s.'[99] Nova Scotia and New Brunswick, on the other hand, were fully integrated into a North Atlantic commercial world centred on Britain.

Just as Lower Canadian Jews sent to New York, Philadelphia, Newport, or London to find wives, borrow funds, or recruit kinfolk to join them in business, or seek religious assistance for their communities, so the Nova Scotia, New Brunswick, and British Columbia Jews often returned to their origins for the same reasons. The key lines of communication, family ties, and economic relations thus ran in two directions – north and south, and east and west across the Atlantic. But until the late 1890s there was no unified Canadian Jewish community; the various centres began largely in isolation from each other, as had those in the United States, where, until the mid-nineteenth century, no organizational structure to provide a semblance of national Jewish cohesion existed.

Another salient feature of British North American Jewry was their mainly English and German origin – with the exception of Montreal, where there were some Polish Jews by the 1850s. And yet the early presence of the German element did not result in the emergence of the Reform movement, as they were less numerous than in the United States. The decidedly British nature of British North America was more important, and religious leadership continued to come from the British metropolis, London.

3 Victorian Montreal and Western Settlement

When Abraham de Sola, the twenty-two-year-old newly appointed spiritual leader of Shearith Israel congregation, reached Montreal from London in January 1847, he had travelled through New York, where he would have observed firsthand the condition of Jewry in the United States. Enervated by growing indifference, drained by high rates of intermarriage, impoverished by ignorance of Jewish religion and culture, reduced by weak leadership, and threatened by confrontation with the rising Reform movement, traditional Judaism in America was challenged by the relative openness of American society and the powerful influences of the Protestant culture.[1] But – once settled in Montreal – de Sola soon would have realized that British North America was a somewhat different society. Its northern cold was a matter for his mordant comment, but the vital fact that half the population of the city, and most of the surrounding countryside, was French and Catholic must have been striking. De Sola's intellectual world was limited largely to Jewish learning and anxiety about the survival of traditional Judaism. The scion of a London rabbinical family, he had received his education from his scholarly father, David Aaron de Sola, a prominent member of London's venerable Bevis Marks synagogue, and from Louis Loewe, an orientalist.[2] Though not an ordained rabbi – he was called chazan (cantor) – Abraham de Sola was Shearith Israel's religious leader, its rabbi in all but name, and he devoted himself to it with missionary zeal. At the same time, he enjoyed the rewards of teaching at McGill College and participated in local numismatic and scientific societies. But he functioned essentially in a Jewish intellectual and social environment that stretched from London to Philadelphia, to persecuted Jews in Persia, to the needs of charities in Palestine, to the threats from reformers in Germany and America, and that included tensions within Montreal Jewry itself.

By the early 1840s, Jews in Lower Canada had obtained full civil and political rights. Their synagogue had been erected on Chenneville Street, and some were prospering economically and socially in anglophone Montreal. As well, they had attained modest recognition in the civic administration, the officer corps of the militia, certain Masonic lodges, and various professions.[3] Small in numbers, closely related, and culturally homogeneous, the Montreal Jewish community had reached a comfortable equilibrium by about 1840.

Though still tiny, the community was growing through immigration. Previously dominated by the older interconnected families like the Harts, Davids, and Josephs, it now included Mosses, Silvermans, and Aschers; while officially Sephardic in its religious rites and English in language and associations, it encompassed increasing numbers of English, German, Alsatian, and Polish Jews used to the Ashkenazic traditions common throughout Central and Eastern Europe. In the 1840s the conjuncture of these elements precipitated changes, and the accompanying tensions would alter the community beyond all recognition over the next forty years, including the formation of a second congregation in 1846, and the establishment of a Hebrew Benevolent Society a year later.

De Sola soon began to invest his learning and energy in Montreal Jewry, while reaching out to the local English-speaking Christian communities. His immediate concern was the revitalization of Shearith Israel's educational, fraternal, and benevolent activities, which had been faltering since the completion of the synagogue in 1838. He started a congregational Sunday school to instruct children in prayer, Hebrew, the Bible, and Jewish history, drawing inspiration from Rebecca Gratz's Sunday school at Philadelphia's Congregation Mikveh Israel in the 1830s.[4] He organized the Hebrew Philanthropic Society to assist Jewish indigents. At the same time, he took on duties as lecturer in Hebrew and oriental languages at McGill College.

While deeply committed to Jewish continuity, de Sola, much like his distinguished British Jewish contemporary Sir Moses Montefiore (to whom de Sola sent reports of his activities), realized that Jews must achieve emancipation in the modern world while preserving their religious distinctiveness. This required, he realized, a delicate balancing act; without it, Jews would be tempted to abandon Judaism altogether. Integration, then, could help insure Jewish survival.[5] In pursuit of this, de Sola sought acceptance by joining many English-language cultural organizations, including the Mercantile Library, Mechanics Institute, Numismatic and Antiquarian Society, and Natural History Society; he also delivered learned papers which won him local renown as a scholar of Judaica. In recognition of these achievements, McGill College awarded him an honorary doctor of laws degree in 1858. In 1872 he opened the United States House of Representatives with prayer, the first Jew and the first British subject to do so. As well, he enjoyed prominence among some of the leading Jewish religious leaders in North America, two of whom, Jacques J. Lyons of New York's Shearith Israel and Isaac Leeser of Philadelphia's Mikveh Israel, collaborated with him in several publishing ventures.

There is little indication of involvement during his thirty-five-year career with the city's French-Canadian intellectuals. While he sought out liberally minded intellectuals in the anglophone community, de Sola seems to have remained aloof from the French-Canadian liberals in the L'Institut Canadien de Montréal, where, in all likelihood, he would have been welcomed as a scholarly, intellectual man.[6] However, de Sola probably had no verbal French and, because of his existing affiliations within the community, understood instinctively that their interests lay with the English. Yet he missed a potentially important opportunity in these formative years to associate with those elements of French-Canadian society who, like Wilfrid Laurier and many others, were attempting in the 1860s and 1870s to create a genuinely liberal Quebec.[7]

His research and writing covered several aspects of Judaic law and history; he wrote articles on the history of the Jews in France, Persia, and England, as well as on various Jewish holidays and festivals for American Jewish publications like Philadelphia's *Occident*, New York's *Jewish Messenger*, and London's *Jewish Chronicle*. In collaboration with Jacques Lyons, in 1854 he published *A Jewish Calendar for Fifty Years, from A.M. 5614 to A.M. 5664*.[8] He also took an interest in natural science, probably influenced by his McGill colleagues William Dawson and William Logan, who were leading geologists at the forefront of the Canadian fascination with science and natural history. His first publication in this field, an 1849 article entitled 'Critical Examination of Genesis 111.16; Having Reference to the Employment of Anaesthetics in Cases of Labour,' was published for the *British American Journal of Medical and Physical Science*, and manifested his concern for reconciling religion and science. This was followed by 'Observations on the Sanatory Institutions of the Hebrews as Bearing upon Modern Sanatory Regulations [*sic*],' in 1852–3, for the *Canada Medical Journal and Monthly Record of Medical and Surgical Science*, which was later published as a book. De Sola thus shared in the modern British spirit of scientific inquiry, along with other Jewish intellectuals who engaged in serious scientific, technological, and advanced medical studies.

Young, well-grounded, and enormously self-confident, de Sola was a one-man whirlwind of activity. As if his philanthropic efforts, running of the Sunday school, and articles for *The Occident* were not enough to keep him fully occupied, he corresponded regularly with one of the major leaders of American Jewry, Isaac Leeser, of Philadelphia,[9] whom he addressed with breezy, though respectful, collegiality, confiding that he had arrived in Montreal with burning evangelical zeal. 'Nothing would give me greater pleasure than to participate in a movement which might (and doubtless would) tend to promote the awfully neglected interests of our much prized faith,' he confided to Leeser in December 1848. 'Anything that would agitate, awake, our community from the tardema [deep sleep] which enwraps and paralyses them, should be encouraged by every lover of God's people.' He was referring, of course, to the whole American Jewish community in the grips of an indifference bred by affluence and smugness. Despite his earnest hard work to foster true Judaism in Montreal – or at least in his own congregation – de Sola felt stymied. Responding in May 1856 to Leeser's request that he encourage increased subscriptions to *The Occident*, de Sola lamented, 'My people are very like their brethren t'other side the line; the Journal, Ledger + Cash Book have great interest as serious reading while for lighter moments the Book of Kings (+ aces) obtain their share of attention.'

Moved by the dire plight of Jews in Middle Eastern countries, in October 1848 de Sola organized the Montreal Committee for the Relief of the Persecuted Persian Jews, to lead a Jewish and Christian protest against the oppression – including many forced conversions to Islam – of Jews in Persia.[10] He was inspired by the visit to Montreal of Rabbi Nissim ben Solomon, a refugee from those horrors, and delivered public lectures on the subject, arousing interest and sympathy for the distressed. 'There was an unusually large audience to hear me,' he reported to Leeser in April 1849, 'since they came numerously to hear about the countrymen of R[abbi] Nissim, notwithstanding that lectures so late in the season are [usually] rather thinly attended.' De Sola supported Leeser's attempts in 1848 to convene delegates from all of America's

Jewish communities to a conference on Jewish concerns. 'God grant that the movement, provided it indeed takes place, may prove an important one and beneficial to this and other generations "yet unborn,"' he prayed.

At McGill, de Sola found a collegial intellectual climate. Here he encountered William Dawson, who, as principal, encouraged the study of Hebrew.[11] Dawson invited de Sola to write a review essay countering some of Ernest Renan's assertions concerning the similarities between Hebrew and the Iroquoian and Algonquin languages. He was promoted to professor – an unpaid position, however – in 1853, awarded the honorary LL. D. in 1858, and delivered the convocation address in the spring of 1864.[12] 'It was gratifying to me,' he informed Leeser, 'the occasion being an unusual one and evincing the liberality of the College authorities, for tho' there are Jewish professors, I believe no one has ever yet been entrusted with giving parting moral advice to graduates.' Indeed, his position at McGill and in Montreal society seems at times to have been as important to him as his work for the Jewish community. When Leeser asked in the spring of 1865 why sales of *The Occident* were not increasing in Montreal, de Sola replied:

> If you have no field here, be comforted with the reflection that neither have I nor anyone else. It is because I have as good a position as a Jew could obtain among Xians [Christians] and that my position at College has greatly improved that I am satisfied with the extent of my Jewish field.

At the Presbyterian College, where he lectured on Hebrew, de Sola was associated with its principal, Daniel MacVicar, and other leaders of that communion. He may well have rubbed shoulders with the noted Montreal Christian free-thought advocate Robert Chambliss Adams, and was undoubtedly aware of his preaching.[13] Such associations are reflected also in the acknowledgment to de Sola by Ellen Ross, in her novel *The Legend of the Holy Stone*, which was published in Montreal in 1878.

De Sola seemed untouched by the currents of religious renewal or regeneration emerging among Jewish religious thinkers during the 1870s and 1880s. Clearly he was too strongly committed to Orthodox Judaism to be swayed. He was influenced, however, by ideas that employed modern scientific knowledge to understand and explain religious beliefs and practices. Like Isaac Leeser, he was influenced by the Jewish enlightenment, which stressed the importance of rationalism and modern secular knowledge among Orthodox Jews for a comprehensive understanding of the place of traditional Judaism in the modern world.[14] While Leeser imagined a unique American role in the achievement of Jewish redemption, de Sola had a similar vision in regarding British North America as holding out great promise for the renewal of faith in a land of British liberty.

Although respectful of some of the new scholarship or ritual, and modern in his use of English in sermons and of new Hebrew-English books in the Sunday school, de Sola nevertheless opposed the Reform movement. 'I too am a reformer as far as endeavours which I believe to be consistent and legal in the manner of synagogue worship are concerned,' he confided to Leeser in 1847.[15] 'I don't think the cause of orthodoxy would suffer much did conservative Synagogues introduce quiet and respectability in their services.' 'Orthodoxy by nature, by age and by character is respectable,' he continued, '[but] absurd and inconsistent novelty in the Synagogue is disreputable in its very essence ...' In 1855 he advised Leeser not to 'attach too much importance to ... the doings of our ultra reformers,' suggesting instead that he expose 'the extreme ugliness of their deformities [to] better serve the cause of historical Judaism than by creating into heroes a few men who have more philosophy than religion.'

De Sola, however, had a grudging respect for some of Reform's leaders, informing Leeser that 'the talent and activity of these ultras cannot but be admired and movement and life are always better than drowsiness and stagnation.' In fact, the real weaknesses of traditional Judaism were more worrisome than the activities of the Reform movement. Still, he described the reformers, as 'flippant [and] shallow German rationalists – who have influence enough to spare.'[16] Some Reform leaders were, in his opinion, less dangerous than others, notably Gustav Poznanski, preacher and reader of Charleston's Beth Elohim (House of the Lord) congregation. 'Can't you get a good man for Charleston,' he wrote to Leeser in June 1866, 'a proper, strong man would now check [the] Reform movement of the old stamp for the next quarter of a century.' So deep was his fear of Reform that he was even prepared to swallow his abhorrence of B'nai B'rith, 'for since this organization, which I view with anything but favour, has assumed its present proportions, I suppose we must look after it, lest our humble modest pious etc. reform brethren use it as a tool – a terrible one too – against orthodoxy.'

Nevertheless, de Sola did reach out to other Jews. He became the leading Canadian officer of the Kesher Shel Barzel (Links of Iron), an American Jewish organization founded in the 1860s to promote fraternal bonds and good works. He visited lodges in Montreal, Toronto, and Hamilton, to address meetings and install officers.[17] But he had to overcome his earlier reservations, which he expressed to Leeser in August 1865: 'I hate the very idea of a Jewish secret society – No Roman Catholic prelate ever hated Masonry [,] Orangeism[,] Ribbonism or any other secret ism more than I abhor such an organization among us – or one at all approaching these Christian religious or political secret societies.' De Sola was opposed to shortening the traditional canons of worship in many synagogues; he fulminated to Leeser:

> The Synagogue in America is fast approaching the state of the Protestant Church there ... The truth is we have too many 'carnal minded Jews' in our midst. Is it the peoples [sic] fault as much as the Doctors [sic] or could the latter play the antics they do? – eating on a Ta'anit tsibur [public fast day] – smoking on a shabbat [Sabbath].

With firm belief in the final religious outcome, he asserted that he had 'too much confidence in the divine strength of our holy faith to suppose that such a set [of reformers] can ... injure it permanently. We may have to witness some "sorry sights" but they will not remain to blast out vision longer than Banquo's ghost.'

Given his origins in London's Spanish and Portuguese community, he supported the Portuguese minhag, which he viewed as both superior to the Ashkenazic and a possible counterpoise to the worrisome advance of Reform. 'When hundreds of German and Polish Congregations are formed under the most unpromising auspices, why in the name of religion should we not multiply – or attempt to multiply – congregations having so superior a ritual as the Portuguese?' he wrote in June 1857.

De Sola's relations with Montreal's rising congregation of Germans, English, and Polish were coloured by his prejudice against Ashkenazi ritual, as well as by his disdain for its 'Pollack' members. His dealings with its religious leaders were not always friendly. 'Entre nous, Mr. Fass is at present too much engaged with manufacturing vinegar, to cultivate pulpit eloquence,' he wrote to Leeser in August 1865.[18] His own congregation's Polish and German members he was prepared to regard as 'brethren.' 'I don't know what I should do without them,' he once told Leeser. 'I sometimes think I am as much a Pollack as any of them.' However, he was not above private expressions of contempt for such people. 'The German [synagogue] ... that formerly existed,' he confided in the mid-1850s, 'is on its last legs. They were but a poor and troublesome set who lately [are] ... neither ornamental nor useful in a Synagogue above all in a Portuguese Synagogue the [minhag] of which they "tont untershtant."'

De Sola contributed news items, sermons, and extracts from his writings over many years to *The Occident*, a weekly edited by Leeser from its founding in 1843 to 1868, and he often purchased books from Leeser at the same time as he sought support for the publication of his own writings. He strongly encouraged Montrealers to subscribe to *The Occident*. 'I am not too proud,' he wrote in February 1848, 'to receive suggestions from you, though I might be from others. I don't mind the stroke of the lion, but I don't like the kick of the ass.'[19] He hoped, by encouraging subscriptions to *The Occident* and distributing prayer books, to advance Jewish learning and observance.

Seeing a need to organize *tsedakah* (charity) in Montreal, de Sola established the Hebrew Philanthropic Society in 1847, especially to aid newly arrived German immigrants.[20] But the crisis passed quickly. As the immigrants departed or settled in, only a few local and transient indigent Jews remained; for these purposes, an occasional passing of the hat seems to have sufficed, and the society disbanded.

By 1863, however, more immigrants had begun arriving, many of them from the United States, while local indigency was also increasing.[21] The pattern of informal collection and handouts was inefficient, and better organization involving both congregations was needed. In July, de Sola convened some thirty men 'to consider the desirability of forming some association to assist our needy or unfortunate co-religionists.'[22] The result, the Young Men's Hebrew Benevolent Society (YMHBS), was limited at first to bachelors, but a few years later the membership also included married men drawn equally from both congregations. The executive was the Relief Committee, which included de Sola and Fass (of the English, German, and Polish congregation). Despite some rivalry between the two synagogues, dispensation of charity was not affected, and in the spirit of sharing, the executive positions were pretty evenly divided between the two congregations.

During its first decade, the relief work of the YMHBS was limited. Although the Jewish population of Canada East (which became the Province of Quebec in 1867) had grown by 1861 to 572 people, mostly in Montreal,[23] over the next ten years numbers actually declined as many residents left the city. But during the 1870s, immigration increased the Montreal Jewish population to about 950 by 1881, and over the next ten years to 2,473 people. Many of the new arrivals came from Central and Eastern Europe in great need of help.

This wave of immigration created stress. In October 1874, members complained that they had to bear heavy financial burdens due to 'many families having arrived here from Germany and other adjoining countries in a state of utter destitution.'[24] Helping forty-two families had cost $542 and depleted the society's resources, forcing it into deficit. But the strain was brief as proceeds from dues, hat-passing, and occasional special appeals, bolstered by theatricals and dances, helped to balance the books. Besides providing necessities such as food, clothing, coal, and medicines, money was also spent on assisting transients to move on.

Reflecting stringent Victorian ideas of charity – and, perhaps, some dilatoriness in the payment of annual dues – one prominent member argued in 1863 that the society 'is not based on the principle of granting permanent relief' and that therefore 'no application [should] receive assistance oftener than once in three months.'[25] He suggested that relief payments be limited to an annual maximum of ten dollars for any single applicant or family group. Recognizing that providing permanent relief would strain their budget, members resolved to provide only 'temporary' relief. Although de Sola opposed such rigidity, recognizing the growing numbers of indigents who needed long-term rehabilitation, he was overruled, 'in view of this Society not having been sufficiently supported by some of our co-religionists.'[26]

Montreal's population, of course, was defined variously by ethnic, linguistic, and religious allegiances, while it was divided economically into several levels, from common labourer to business tycoon, and occupationally into about five major divisions (agricultural, commercial, domestic, industrial, and professional). Disparity in income was apparent in the existence of benevolent societies and, on the other hand, in the evidence of some Jews enjoying an affluent lifestyle. There existed plutocrats, too – like Jesse Joseph. But, occupationally, the Jews of Montreal in the 1850s and 1860s were heavily concentrated in lesser commercial pursuits.[27] In 1861, fully 55 per cent of gainfully employed Jews were in these occupations, almost two and a half times the rate among the city's population as a whole. The 1871 census returns reveal that nearly 63 per cent of working Jews were in commerce, nearly three times the rate of the entire city's population. There were no Jews in agriculture, and only two in domestic service in 1861, four in 1871. The number of Jewish professionals actually declined from fourteen to eleven during these two decades, as did the number and percentage in industrial occupations. Thus, the community was overwhelmingly middle-class and commercial.

This activity did not mean general prosperity. A study of Jewish residential patterns in the 1860s and 1870s revealed that some upper-middle-class Jews could afford to move from downtown Viger Square to the fashionable 'new town' neighbourhood that was opening up south of McGill College. At the same time, however, a new and much poorer Jewish enclave was emerging in the St Lawrence Boulevard area. Here lived most of the people with undocumented lives: pedlars, pawnbrokers, commercial travellers, hatters, tailors, rag-shop owners, silverplaters, and glaziers. Most were Polish-born and were, apparently, recent immigrants. Thus, even before the mass migration of poor Jews from Russia in the 1880s, fairly sharp economic, ethnic, and religious differences existed within the Montreal Jewish community.

Over the next decade, the problem of persistent poverty in the Montreal community intensified. In 1876 attention was drawn to several families who were annually dependent upon the society during 'our long winters' because of their inability to find employment.[28] Members wanted to deny even short-term relief if the indigents refused to move 'to some other place where they might perhaps find friends or relations to assist them or constant work and pay the year round.' This view was supported by some members who even suggested that these families were 'unable to support themselves any longer and should be forced [!] to go away.' The society also wished to limit the intake of the so-called 'too many destitute and helpless Israelites.' In 1875, hearing of a large Jewish migration on its way to Canada, the executive protested in the London newspapers *Jewish World* and *Jewish Chronicle*, in the hopes of preventing Jewish philanthropies, such as London's Ladies Emigration Society, from shunting too many of the European Jews arriving in England to Canada. In October 1875 the *Jewish Chronicle* commented: 'Our transatlantic brethren object – and we confess, very properly so ... to being burdened with the poor and unskillful Jews who are assisted to emigrate from Europe to the United States and Canada.'[29] But such sympathy did not stop these activities. Two years later, the Montrealers complained again that London organizations were sending over too many Jews 'in a state of destitution and generally incapable of self help.' In desperation de Sola was dispatched to London to protest in person to those responsible, the Jewish Emigration Society. While there, he was partly persuaded that 'the statements of the immigrants that they had been sent by the Jewish Emigration Society should not always be accepted.' In any event, following this visit and for the time being, anyway, the export of poor Jews from London ceased.

During the influx of the mid-1870s, there was some duplication of relief efforts. The Ladies' Hebrew Benevolent Society devoted itself to assisting women and children, cooperating with the Young Men's Hebrew Benevolent Society on their clients. However, similar cooperation was not apparent with any of the other newer self-help associations formed by the immigrants themselves. This caused confusion and animosity because of the overlapping appeals for funds. In response to this proliferation of effort, and perhaps also to the success of New York's recently formed United Hebrew Charities, it was suggested in 1874 that a similar body be established in Montreal, the argument being that, 'the interest of charity will be best served by this Society merging itself into a more general organization, embracing all the Jews of Montreal as its members.' Few society members were supportive, however, the majority preferring to retain control and to limit the extent of their obligations. The idea of a mass charity organization was rejected just as immigrants were beginning to outnumber residents. These newcomers were more likely to be receivers than givers of philanthropy, and their concepts of Jewish charity could be more costly.[30]

Meanwhile, tensions within Shearith Israel continued between the followers of the Sephardic order of prayer and the Ashkenazic rite, causing great distress to more religious congregants. Inside the congregation there was also strife between the older community and the newcomers. Of the latter, some had remained in the congregation and were in one way or another 'rather troublesome,' according to the young Clarence de Sola, who was probably reporting his father's impressions of the congregation's annual meeting in his diary in April 1872. In some of his letters to Isaac Leeser, himself of German origin, Abraham de Sola revealed his disrespect for these newcomers who belonged to the other synagogue, which was sometimes referred to as the 'German school' or, derisively, 'dem paleischer Minyan.'[31]

For de Sola, the Victorian era was a period of remarkable integration into the social and economic life of Montreal. Others like Samuel Benjamin, who was elected alderman for Centre Ward in 1849, enjoyed public office,[32] while Dr Aaron Hart David was appointed secretary to the Central Board of Health. Members of the Joseph, Ascher, Davis, and Moss families attained recognition for their business success. The social life of the younger generation included philanthropic endeavours, the bonhomie of sports, as well as the frivolities and flirtations at picnics and parties. Most of the young men belonged to the Young Men's Hebrew

Benevolent Society, and the women, the Ladies' Hebrew Benevolent Society, but they also enjoyed secular pursuits.

De Sola's son Clarence was probably typical of this group. He attended the balls and dances, socializing with members of the Anglo-Saxon elite.[33] His diaries carry no references to antisemitism, in any of his activities. In school, sports, and in genteel social groups, he enjoyed good relationships with all. In school, he was known as 'Historicus' because of his strong interest in history. If his diaries are to be believed, while in his early teens he immersed himself in the classics: Grote's *History of Greece*, Milman's *History of the Jews*, Macaulay's *History of England*, and many others. Although not especially close to the Protestant establishment, he shared many of their attitudes. His closest friends, however, were from the well off families in the Spanish and Portuguese synagogue, including the younger Jacobses, Davises, Aschers, Mosses, Harts, Josephs, Kellerts, and Samuelses.

Clarence de Sola also became involved in Jewish communal welfare during the stressful and transformative 1880s of immigration, new synagogues, and formation of numerous new organizations.[34] In 1882 the arrival of hundreds of refugees from Eastern Europe following the pogroms moved him profoundly. Strongly influenced by British Jewish paradigms, de Sola joined a small group to organize a branch of the London-based Anglo-Jewish Association to press for the protection of Jews overseas.[35] This organization helped to mobilize Montreal's Jews to receive this wave of pogrom refugees during the 1880s. The organization was not only paternalistic and philanthropic, it also – like its English model – reflected ethnic pride, sense of duty, and social conscience. And as the counterpart of ethnic organizations like the St Patrick and St Andrew's societies, perhaps the two most prominent in anglophone Montreal at that time, the Anglo-Jewish Association and the Young Men's Hebrew Benevolent Society were part of the quest for respectability – acceptance, even – in the best social circles.

By 1860, United States and Canadian Jewry were in structure and concerns significantly different. Many of the most pressing issues confronting American Jewry were not prominent on the Canadian Jewish agenda.[36] Reform did not make inroads in Canada until later in the century. When de Sola attempted to join the drive led by Leeser to form a Board of Delegates of Hebrew Congregations in the 1850s, he was unwelcome, an indication that leading American Jews thought Canadian Jewry did not share their concerns. Of course, the distinctions were not just qualitative. In 1850 the American Jewish population numbered some 50,000 souls and fifty congregations, fifteen in New York City alone, whereas in all of British North America there were a mere 451 Jews in 1851.[37] Through the immigration of the 1850s, though Canada's Jewish population more than doubled to 1,186, the number of Jews in the United States increased by about 100,000, to a total of 150,000 by 1860. The number of congregations in Canada had increased from the two in Montreal to a total of five, the additional three being in Toronto, Hamilton, and Victoria, but meanwhile another 135 congregations had emerged in the United States. From 1861 to 1871, Canada's Jewish population increased by a minuscule number to 1,333 persons, while Montreal's actually decreased. These small numbers ruled out religious dissent, except in Montreal – where the second synagogue was every bit as traditional as the first.

The Jews who migrated to Canada in that early Victorian era were probably very similar to those who went to the United States.[38] German Jewish immigrants of the 1850s were mostly 'the poorest and the least educated.' As many as half of them were from impoverished families in Bavaria, while others came from Posen, the eastern-most province of Prussia, and Bohemia and Moravia. The origins of Jews to Canada were similar, but others were British-born, or long-time residents in Britain, a circumstance which affected their political and social outlook.

The crucial difference between the Canadian and American Jewish communities lay in their social and political contexts. In contrast to the United States, where, since 1850, a single – albeit increasingly divided – nation had existed from sea to sea, governed from Washington under a situation 'conceived in liberty,' British North America consisted of separated and widely scattered colonies until Confederation in 1867; indeed, the territorial union was completed only in the 1870s, when the Northwest Territories, Manitoba, British Columbia, and Prince Edward Island were brought into the Dominion. Even then, Canadian national identity relied largely upon British coordinates, while Canadians grappled with the French factor.

In Montreal this fundamental French fact was enhanced by the magnificent new Roman Catholic cathedral arising in the 1850s on Dorchester Street, by the sounds of the French language among about half of the city's population, by the outpouring of journals in the 1840s, by the emergence of powerful personalities like Bishop Ignace Bourget and George-Etienne Cartier, and by the continuing importance of the Sulpician Order in the economic life of the city.[39] The question of Jewish adaptation to the new nation, defined as a 'dominion,' never arose because – unlike the United States, which was based on a statement about philosophically derived first principles – Canada was founded, in the words of the British North America Act, 'under the Crown of the United Kingdom ... with a constitution similar in principle to that of the United Kingdom.'

The rates of departures of Russian Jews fluctuated, in reaction to economic changes and to business cycles in both the country of origin and the countries of destination. Despite push factors, Russian Jewish emigration increased only slowly in the early 1880s, accelerated in the early 1890s, then declined slightly until 1905, when it rose substantially and maintained a high, though uneven, level until 1914.[40] Pogroms and political upheavals – such as the failed revolution of 1905 – were still not the major factors; poverty and dreams of better economic opportunities in America were the principal forces that propelled Jews from the Old World to the New.

The Jews in Eastern Europe during the late nineteenth century were enduring murder in Ukraine and the destruction of property, making it all too clear that equality for Jews was unattainable in the Russian Empire. But the tide of emigration was small until the 1890s, and it was not caused by pogroms alone, which were of minor importance; indeed, emigration rates declined later in the 1880s. Historian Shmuel Ettinger's conclusion that 'this migration was the consequence of demographic, economic and political developments' seems a more accurate summation than his statement that 'this emigration movement was largely a "flight to emancipation."' The average Russian Jew did not aspire to emancipation, even if he could understand what that word meant. He and his brothers and sisters were too poor, too uneducated, and too religious to be influenced by such ideas. Generally speaking, the Haskalah (Enlightenment) never penetrated below the ranks of the Jewish intelligentsia and the middle class, except perhaps in Odessa. Most of the masses were suffering more from poverty than from a lack of political and social emancipation, and even religion was of little solace – as the Talmud says, 'Where this is no bread, there is no Torah.'

Canada took in about 10,000 Jewish immigrants between 1880 and 1900, some in transit to the United States. Their return rate to their countries of origin was extremely low: the net immigration for the period 1908–14 stood at about 93 per cent.[41] Thus, Canada gained about 9,300 of the 10,000 immigrants.[42] With this influx and natural increase,

Canada's Jewish population grew from 2,443 to 16,401 between 1881 and 1901. Decennial censuses distinguished between 'Jews by race' and 'Jews by religion,' the former exceeding the latter by less than one per cent before 1931.[43] The figures of 'Jews by religion' are used here on the assumption that, while not strictly religious, they identified as Jews. Other calculations show that the decennial growth rate of Canada's Jewish population was 164.88 per cent during the 1880s and 157.06 per cent during the 1890s, compared to total population-growth rates of 11.76 and 11.13 per cent. In other words, the Jewish population of Canada grew at about fourteen times the rate of the population as a whole, and enjoyed one of the highest increases of any ethnic community in the country during those decades. And while the Canadian Jewish population grew by about 700 per cent in two decades – some 14,000 people, 9,300 of them immigrants – natural increase minus emigration, mainly to the United States, would account for about half of that growth.

By 1891, Jews living in Canada's major cities included a significant percentage of East European immigrants who had transmigrated from the United States, Britain, or Germany. Many of them had resided in the United States, judging from the birthplaces of their children. Clearly, the complex process of immigration was an important part of what has been described as the mingling of the Canadian and American peoples.[44]

There was a long-standing preference by governments to favour immigration of farmer-settlers to settle the isolated regions.[45] Dominion lands policy became an integral part of Canada's national policy of development. And so, when immigration of Russian Jews began on a small scale in the spring of 1882, questions would naturally be raised concerning their suitability for farming in the vast Northwest Territories.

In January 1882, as reports of persecutions of Jews in Russia began arriving,[46] a Montreal group calling itself the Citizen's Committee Jewish Relief Fund was formed with considerable support in the Christian community, including the *Montreal Gazette*, which urged Dominion officials 'to make proper provision for the hospitable reception of such of them as may land on our shores.' 'The people of their own race and faith, of whom many living amongst us occupy positions of respectability and influence,' the *Gazette* continued, 'will of course do all that is in their power for the succor of their unfortunate brethren, but it is no less incumbent on Christians of all denominations to give a helping hand, which shall atone, to some extent at least, the brutal usage by those who profess to serve the same master.' The Anglican bishop of Montreal,

William Bennett Bond, who headed the Committee, solicited subscriptions and raised over $4,600 by mid-September. By this time, major Jewish charity groups in the city – the Young Men's Hebrew Benevolent Society, the Ladies' Hebrew Benevolent Society, and the Anglo-Jewish Association of Montreal – had joined together to form the Jewish Emigration Aid Society (JEAS) to coordinate refugee assistance, including transportation to other parts of Canada and the United States.[47]

They had not long to wait. On May 15 the first group of 260 Russian refugees – who, according to the *Gazette*, 'were not particularly distinguished for cleanliness' – arrived at Bonaventure Station.[48] Using funds sent from London's Mansion House Committee, a large building on the waterfront was converted to a dormitory, and a relief and medical centre, while some refugees were boarded with local Jewish families. By late June, 180 refugees had been housed and employment had been found for most of them, while many others were helped to move on to the United States, Ontario, and Manitoba. A small group arriving in Winnipeg in late May were greeted by a *Manitoba Free Press* editorial as 'stalwart looking and evidently intelligent' and 'were thought to give promise of making hand-working and valuable settlers of this new country. ' Winnipeg Jews, few though they were, passed the hat to help out the newcomers in the emergency. Similar responses were organized in Toronto, where both Jews and sympathetic Christians contributed to the relief work. Toronto's emergency committee leased an old hotel and even used a synagogue to provide temporary housing.[49] In all three cities, Christians gave strong financial and moral support.

As well as offering a refuge from persecution and poverty, Canada was believed to hold the possibility of widespread Jewish agricultural settlement, a new Eden for a distressed people. The idea of a Jewish colonization society had surfaced in Montreal in 1874, but nothing came of it.[50] Such proposals were gaining considerable support among United States Jewish charity organizations, which were generally opposed to massive immigration of poor Eastern European Jews, who crowded into the cities and placed financial strains on these organizations.

Given the prominence of agricultural settlement schemes, it was very likely that such proposals should be raised in Canada, where the newly acquired Northwest Territories were opened up to settlement through the Dominion Lands Act of 1872, which made possible free homesteads.[51] The Canadian High Commissioner in London, Alexander Galt, an experienced land speculator, who was greatly interested in promoting these schemes, wrote to Baron Rothschild in January 1882, encouraging the migration of 'the agricultural Jews to our North West.'[52] For Galt, who invested in various development projects in western Canada, the prospect of more settlers in the West, and the possibility of enticing London Jewish financial backing for some of these projects, fitted nicely into his new financial interests.[53] With his excellent political and business connections, Galt was in an ideal position to help Jewish settlement projects. He confided to Prime Minister John A. Macdonald that 'a large proportion [of Russian Jews] will still be found with sufficient means to establish themselves in Canada ... I found the American Jews were actively promoting emigration to the United States, and I thought what was good for them, could not be bad for us.'[54]

In fact, however, this proposal was essentially intended to prevent a large-scale influx of 'Old Clo,' a contemptuous reference by Macdonald to the cry of London's Jewish used-clothing pedlars, by which he meant poor Russian Jews. 'Those unhappy Jews take up more time than bargained for,' Galt wrote to Macdonald in early February 1882. 'But it is very necessary, or we might have a lot of them thrown upon our shores unprovided for. By being on the committee I can prevent this.' Galt and Macdonald were not really promoting Jewish settlement on Canada's Prairies, or a few Jewish 'Cheap Jacks' and 'Chapmen,' who would have been useful to the Conservative Party in the West. They wanted what a Jewish colony might provide, which was, as Macdonald put it confidentially to Galt, 'a link, a missing link ... between Canada and Sidonia [Jewish financiers].' In the same letter, he told Galt, 'After years of ill-concealed hostility of the Rothschilds against Canada, you have made a great strike by taking up the old clo' cry, and going in for a Jew immigration into the Northwest ...'[55] Macdonald's real motivation was the hope of attracting some Rothschild money for the Canadian Pacific Railway – then under construction by a company desperately short of funds – or for other development projects. And if acquiescence to some Jewish immigration was the price of an entrée to the Rothschilds and other London Jewish financiers, it was well worth it. Reflecting the politicians' outlook, the governor general's secretary, Colonel I. De Winton, wrote to Macdonald in mid-February, 'if the English Jew will subscribe liberally and settle his Russian brother why shouldn't the Canadian [government] get the benefit of the transaction[?]'[56] Galt had written clearly to Macdonald in late January 1882: 'The Jewish persecution in Russia has induced me to write Rothschild suggesting that I would like to discuss with him the feasibility of removing the agricultural Jews to

Canada – I have only sent my note to-day. It seemed not a bad opportunity of interesting the Hebrews in our NorthWest.'[57]

In contrast to this cynicism and opportunism, at least one official – the Dominion government's Icelandic agent at St Andrew's, Manitoba – appealed to the Marquis of Lorne, the governor general, for a suitable block of land in the Northwest for Jewish settlement, on humanitarian grounds. 'Providing new homes far removed from the cruelties and atrocities so shamefully perpetrated on this people in the name of religion,' he stated, 'would be a lasting credit to this country ...'[58] In May, the lord mayor of London wrote to the president of the Anglo-Jewish Association of Montreal that 'at the suggestion of Sir Alexander Galt, the Mansion House Committee are sending a considerable number of the Russo-Jewish refugees to Canada, the more able bodied to Winnipeg.' He added that 'Sir A. Galt had given my committee so glowing an account of the charity and benevolence of the Canadian Jews that I feel sure that this suggestion will meet with your ready acceptance.'[59]

Encouraged, or maybe intimidated, by such impressive support, early in 1882 several prominent members of Montreal's YMHBS and the JEAS formed a settlement and land company, the International Colonization Association, with a projected capital of one million dollars, to establish communities of Russian and Polish Jews in the Northwest. Given their own financial limitations, they were probably hoping for support from London or other European plutocrats. They proposed to start by moving one hundred families out west the following spring.[60] Backed by other Montrealers and the local press, they sent Lazarus Cohen, a local notable, to Ottawa to confer with the minister of agriculture, who gave assurances of his interest.

Meanwhile, several contingents of Jews, totalling 340 persons, had reached Winnipeg in the spring of 1882, putting a serious strain on the community to house and feed them and to find them employment. One of the newcomers poured out his disappointment in a lengthy letter to *Ha-Melitz*, the Odessa Hebrew daily, which reported regularly on the new agricultural settlements in North America.[61] Informing his readers that he wrote from 'Winnipeg (in the country of Canada, North America) Sunday, week of Parashat hukat ..., 1882 (5652)', he wrote as follows:

> I don't know where to dip my pen as I write these words – shall it be in the inkwell before me or in the abhorrent tears which stream from the cheeks of the people who came here with me. Like an outcast, I sit looking towards the sky, and I hear voices of their weeping, lamenting the days of their

youth which have passed away quickly with poverty and grief in an arid and sunken land. Their words and groans tear my heart and pierce my inner parts to the very depths ...[62]

By September, however, the correspondent was much more optimistic about Winnipeg, then undergoing boom times, and wrote to *Ha-Melitz* readers that 'perhaps I have somewhat exaggerated.'[63] He reported that the immigrants had successfully worked on railway-building and sewer-construction crews, earning between $2.50 and $3.00 per day. Comparing the Winnipeg immigrants with those refugees in New York who still languished in sheltering homes, he continued:

> The farmers, willing to work, endeavour with their own hands to earn their livelihood without relying upon the generosity of strangers ... Here in [their] new Country, even the cultured and well-bred among us have Soon discarded their starched shirts and lacquered shoes, and have set themselves to work.

But while there were employment prospects, he reported on the lack of opportunities for providing children with a Jewish education. 'One is grieved,' he wrote, 'with things educational and spiritual, which are growing Worse daily. Our children wander recklessly about the streets and humiliate us in the eyes of our neighbours.'

After returning to Canada in 1883, Galt continued his efforts on behalf of Jewish colonization, serving as agent for the Mansion House Committee, which collected and distributed money for the welfare of the Jewish refugees of 1882.[64] In early April 1884, he wrote to an official in the Department of the Interior concerning the prospects for settling the forty to fifty Jewish families then standing by in Winnipeg. 'I now have the money to help them from the Mansion House Fund,' he wrote, asking 'as an exceeding important favour' that four homesteads – instead of two, as provided in the Dominion Lands Act of 1872 – be allowed to occupy each 640-acre section in the region.[65] Thus each family would have 160 acres of land. Intensive settlement 'will be of the greatest Service,' he advised. This would allow him to house all four families in one dwelling and supply them in common. Galt insisted on 'good, easy worked land [with] wood, water and proximity to the Railway' and inquired, 'where can you find some ten or twelve sections that combine these qualifications [?]' The matter was urgent, as it was already April 1: 'Time is of so great importance that I have intended to go west the moment I have the answer.'

Galt's plan was approved, and Winnipeg officials of the Dominion Lands Commission decided in May on a site for thirty families in townships 11, 12, and 13, range 2 west of the second meridian. Galt pressed the government 'to reserve the remaining vacant homesteads and pre-emptions in the Townships ... until the result of the present experiment is known,' or about six months.

And so, twenty-eight families formed a colony near Moosomin in 1884 in the District of Assiniboia.[66] The Mansion House Committee provided each family with a loan of up to $600 to buy cattle, implements, and food.[67] In the spring of that year, the settlers arrived. Occupying 8,968 acres – an area which included pre-empted land (additional quarter sections) as well as homesteads of quarter sections – the farmers faced almost insuperable barriers. Support from London was inadequate, and the settlers appealed to the Winnipeg Jewish community, as crops that first year of 1885 were struck down by hail. Morale was dropping precipitously, and when the colony's rabbi was stricken with disaster in 1886, the settlers lost heart. Many began to leave.[68] Their unsuitability for farming was obvious. 'There was not a farmer amongst them nor were they trained mechanics, and they made very poor laborers.'[69] The immigration agent at Brandon reported in 1887 that, though occupying good farmland, they had not done well 'and were never adapted for agricultural pursuits.'[70]

Broken financially and spiritually, the settlers refused to repay the loans they had received from the Mansion House Fund, causing a long legal and political squabble, as well as disputes over the rights of those who had registered their lands. For years, Galt was pestered by the messy financial aftermath of the project. His worry was that a failure to settle the claims 'will close the door upon all further effort on the part of the friends of the Jews in Europe.'[71] Some of the original settlers returned in 1887, bringing others with them in the hope of rejuvenating the project, which they renamed 'New Jerusalem.' A local lands agent reported in 1892 that they had 'built several houses, with the ruins of those houses left by their predecessors.' But they, too, failed after putting in one crop, 'which, unfortunately was so badly frozen that they were discouraged, and this band also deserted ... leaving a few houses and stables ...' after fire ravaged the colony in September of 1889.

Meanwhile, five Jewish families had settled near Wapella, in the District of Assiniboia, in 1886, with the assistance of a London Jewish financier connected with the Canadian Pacific Railway.[72] Led by its founders, John Heppner and Abraham Klenman, the tiny colony grew slowly over the years.[73] Between 1886 and 1907, the Wapella district attracted about fifty Jewish families to local homesteads. Others settled in the towns along the new CPR branch line from Brandon to Estevan, and in 1891 a group of farmers led by Ascher Pierce and his family settled at Oxbow in the Northwest Territories.

Although all these homesteaders shared many challenges, the Jewish farmers suffered additional handicaps.[74] They came with 'virtually no previous farming experience' and had little capital to buy implements, animals, and basic household amenities. Conditions at Wapella during the early years, therefore, were especially harsh and primitive. Homesteading in a wooded area of heavy black soil, where poplar trees provided building materials and fuel, the early colonists, who were drawn mostly from southern Russia and Bessarabia, scratched out a living by hauling wagonloads of wood to nearby towns to sell for a dollar a load, or by working for neighbours. Meanwhile, they cleared their land – a few acres each year – for growing wheat, oats, and barley. The first houses were often just dugouts covered with sod roofs; these were followed by more substantial dwellings built of logs and clay, whitewashed for appearance. Household furniture was scarce. 'Who needed furniture?' Fanny (Pelenovsky) Brotman remembered many years later. 'We were looking for something to eat. You can't eat furniture ... We put hay on the mud floor and we all slept on the floor.' Most of the scant 'furniture' they had was of the crude, homemade variety. Religious services, she recalled, were held regularly on the Sabbath and on the holy days, when Jewish farmers from miles around came to the settlement. 'They would stay over two days on Rosh Hashanah, and they'd come the day before Yom Kippur. We didn't have enough beds, so they slept on the floor. And we would have to cook for everyone.' One of the colonists was specially trained in *shechita*, so it was possible to have local kosher chicken and meat. But they had a hard life and many drifted away.

Ekiel Bronfman was one of the early Wapella settlers. He arrived there with his wife, Mindel, and three children in the summer of 1891 and experienced the harsh conditions of long dry summers and early frosts.[75] These disasters made a lasting impression on four-year-old Harry Bronfman, who later recalled that the family's wheat froze and that his father spent the winter of 1891–2 'going into the bush, cutting logs, loading them onto a sleigh and drawing them twenty miles' to sell for 'money to buy a sack of flour, a few evaporated apples, dried prunes and probably some tea and sugar to bring back to his family.'

No other new settlements materialized during the 1880s, even though Galt publicly professed to take an interest in such projects, which for some years, according to his official biographer, 'kept him in close touch with the Montagus, Rothschilds, and other leaders of the Jewish community in London.'[76] Privately, Galt felt deep disappointment. 'I regret to say my Jewish colony at Moosomin is a failure. The [settlers] have sold their cows – the cattle I gave them – and turned to their natural (!) avocation of peddling,' he wrote in early 1888 to an official in Ottawa. Referring to the failed settlers as 'vagabonds,' he continued, with utter disregard for the facts: 'The only comfort I have is that from the start I protested against the experiment as I never thought they would make farmers.'[77]

A more ambitious western settlement project was begun in 1892 by the Baron de Hirsch Institute – as the YMHBS had been renamed in 1891 – which met with greater success. Baron Maurice de Hirsch gave huge sums of money to various Jewish charities[78] to try to solve by radical means some of the main problems facing the Jews of Eastern Europe. He believed that they must not only be removed from the congestion, poverty, and hatreds of their environment, but must also be rehabilitated in such a way that these conditions could never reoccur. Jews must, he thought, be made more like their neighbours, and settled in large numbers as sons of the soil in new lands like Argentina and Canada. Thus Jewish life must be reconstituted in a revolutionary manner. The baron emphasized that the social and economic structure of Jewish life in Eastern Europe had to be reformed from the bottom up. In this way, his outlook was similar to that of the Jewish radical socialists, who insisted that a national home was not enough, but that the very fabric of Jewish society had to be reconstructed to achieve normalization.

The baron made use of Montreal's Baron de Hirsch Institute to further his plan of settling Jews in the Canadian Northwest.[79] Prospective colonists petitioned the Montreal Committee, in late March 1891, stating that 'they have been residing in this city from one to five years and have been engaged [unsuccessfully] in various occupations.' They asked for 'assistance ... to go to the North West where they would be able to farm.' The Committee wrote to the minister of agriculture and sent a delegation to Ottawa to pursue another Jewish settlement in the West. An appeal was sent to the baron 'acquainting him of our circumstances and the negotiations in progress for colonising our unfortunate coreligionists in the Canadian North West,' and in September 1891 the society established a separate Colonization Committee headed by Montreal merchant David Ansell, who continued contact with the Dominion government. In Ottawa, Lands Branch officials – perhaps mindful of the Moosomin failure – reacted cautiously to these overtures.[80]

In November,[81] trying to prepare the ground for spring activities, Colonization Committee members interviewed the prime minister on the subject of suitable lands, proposing that the abandoned Moosomin colony site, which was still held in trust for the Mansion House Committee by Galt, be turned over to the new project. Meanwhile, the Montreal colonists informed the board that they intended to approach the Jewish Colonization Association (JCA) in Paris to request direct assistance from Baron de Hirsch, and asked the board for 'general support in their undertaking.' Obviously annoyed with such independence, the Committee 'strongly advised them to abandon this ill advised scheme. It was fallacy to imagine that their attendance would have any weight and it was only wasting money to proceed on their journey.'

But the colonists' delegates went to Paris anyway. In February 1892, Dr Sonnenfeldt, director of the JCA, sent out a list of the settlers, asking whether Montreal would establish and supervise the project if the JCA gave it financial backing. The board agreed, provided they retained the right to select the colonists, since 'they certainly could not accept the list as it stood,' and the JCA agreed to the hiring of an expert to supervise and assist the settlers. An experienced and reliable person, a Mr C. McDiarmid – formerly a farmer in Huntingdon County, Quebec – was sent to the Northwest to survey a number of suggested sites.

In March, news came from Paris that a grant of 100,000 francs would be provided by the JCA and the Alliance Israélite Universelle. A committee was appointed to select 'not more than 40 men ... to be ready at a moment's notice to proceed to land, the females and the children to be left behind till the weather was more favourable.' McDiarmid was appointed to supervise the colony and immediately began purchasing supplies. Ascher Pierce[82] advised a location near Oxbow, which was found acceptable. By now it was April, and the food supplies, horses, tools, and implements were being assembled.[83] The remittance of the necessary money from Paris was being arranged and the final selection made of twenty-six families, who were joined by ten more from Winnipeg and three from Regina. McDiarmid was dispatched west again to prepare as much as possible for the colonists. A shochet was employed, and a sefer torah was borrowed from the Shaar Hashomayim synagogue. And all was in readiness for the tedious rail journey to Oxbow. On April 19 the settlers appeared before the board to sign the agreements, which were, their minutes recorded, 'translated into Hebrew and German [Yiddish] so that everyone should thoroughly understand its contents ... They were then addressed collectively and informed of the duties they would be expected to perform and exhorted to be industrious in their new station in life and to live peaceably with their neighbours and respect the rules and laws of the country which they had now adopted as their own.' Pomposity had its place in nineteenth-century philanthropy.

An eleventh-hour delay developed when McDiarmid telegraphed on April 24 that he was investigating another parcel of land 'a few miles beyond [west of] Oxbow.' This gave the board further opportunity to plan the colony, and it determined that the colonists should 'work first as a community and proceed as rapidly as possible with ploughing and seeding' and that no division of property should be made for several weeks after they arrived. Until then, four work parties were to be formed, each under a local farmer selected and supervised by McDiarmid.

McDiarmid then wired that he had selected lands from the new tract in the District of Assiniboia, and that the colonists could now be sent west. When the board determined that the group should leave the following day, several colonists vehemently protested against having to leave on Thursday, meaning that they would have to travel on the Sabbath. However, 'they had since consulted their Rabbi and were informed that in cases of necessity it was perfectly allowable.' On Thursday, then, the men, some with their families, left by CPR from Windsor Station. Some of their friends and the loved ones who would follow came to see them off, as did most of the Baron de Hirsch Institute board members.

The colonists of the new settlement – named Hirsch, aptly enough – required material assistance and technical advice for several years. Their communications to Montreal reflect the weariness of their labour, their poor crop yields in the early years, and their loneliness, without even the railway locomotive's whistle to break the silence of the prairie night. But these records also show that the institute shared in these strains. The Colonization Committee maintained regular correspondence with McDiarmid, who wrote often about the stock in the general store, the cost for necessary supplies, and the needs of colonists themselves.

The institute soon proposed establishing a school in the colony and approved the hiring of a midwife. As early as August, they were worrying about ensuring an adequate supply of coal, and in February about matzos for Passover. (It was eventually decided that the matzos would be baked at Hirsch itself.) Full of optimism, they even speculated on the possibility of expanding. They sent voluminous reports to the baron, often enclosing letters from the farmers themselves to impress him with the need for more funds. In mid-July, two Montrealers visited the colony to supervise the allocation of a quarter section of land to each settler.[84] On their return, they reported at length on the state of the settlement and on some of the burgeoning problems. A second group of colonists was getting organized during the summer of 1892,[85] but the society viewed many of them as 'not proper people to be sent away as they were already earning a living in the City,' reflecting an outlook that colonization was a form of philanthropy.

The Montreal group then sent a delegate from the new settlement to Paris in August, to protest directly to the JCA and the Alliance against the decision to refuse them support. It worked; two months later, an additional twenty-two families were sent out to the colony, only a few days after the JCA telegraphed its intention of sending another $16,500 to 'complete the purchase of cattle, implements and food for the [new] colonists.' By now, some Montrealers believed that the Alliance and the JCA in Paris should take complete charge of the colony.

And problems abounded at Hirsch. McDiarmid was recalled to Montreal in late November 1892 to answer numerous complaints from colonists. Realizing that the colony would require continued assistance at least until the next year's crop could be harvested, the board appealed to the baron, who replied that the JCA would send a further $12,000 to pay outstanding accounts and buy the necessary supplies, 'but that under no circumstances would any further sum be given.' Despite this warning and the profusion of difficulties, the board continued to manage Hirsch. New managers were appointed and sent out west in February, while an employee of the institute was also dispatched to deal with legal and financial matters.

By early May 1893, the institute's executive considered that most of their work would soon end, and that the colony should, within the foreseeable future, be able to manage itself. Each settler now had his own homestead of 160 acres, some draught animals, at least one cow, and a supply of tools, while some of the larger and costlier implements were provided for common use. Most encouraging of all, the first harvest had been substantial. The settlers were developing a community life and would soon enjoy their own school and synagogue. A post office was to be opened, and it was rumoured that the CPR would build a branch line from Oxbow to Hirsch.

But Hirsch colonists needed further assistance, largely because of subsequent crop failures. Also, the JCA found it impossible to supervise the Jewish farmers in Canada from its offices in Paris and refused to provide for a paid official in Canada; and so, reluctantly, the institute's board members felt morally bound to continue as the beneficiary of much of the baron's philanthropy.

In mid-October of 1893, a robbery at the colony's store and a disturbing report that 'the Colonists were trying to sell their cattle and farming implements' made it clear to the board that 'the condition of the Colonists was very distressing' and that because the whole project was in jeopardy they appealed to the baron for help. Meanwhile, in late November, board member Lazarus Cohen left to assess the situation at Hirsch;[86] he fired the manager and put Hirsch in the hands of the most reliable colonists he could find,[87] later reporting that at least $15,000 was required to keep Hirsch going until spring. Another appeal for assistance was sent off to the baron, whose stolid silence to the previous request was unnerving. Meanwhile, further trouble in the colony was reported in February. With still no answer from the baron by March, the board was desperate. Seed had to be bought soon. The colony still had no manager, and the board asked the local Hudson's Bay Company agent to recommend a suitable replacement. Another temporary manager arrived in Hirsch, where he settled outstanding business accounts and attempted to reassure the distraught colonists. On his return in September 1894, he set out a plan of temporary assistance for the colonists.

These measures, however, made little difference. During 1894 and 1895, farms were abandoned, crops were poor, and the settlers were experiencing considerable privation. The novelty of establishing a colony had disappeared, and the ongoing tedium remained. Nonetheless, hope prevailed, and the gradual recruitment of eager new colonists brightened everyone's hopes. When several Jewish families farming near Red Deer pleaded for help, they were removed to Hirsch, where they took up some of the abandoned farms. The colony struggled on through the late 1890s, though it relied on continuing handouts from the JCA.

The Baron de Hirsch Institute provided assistance and guidance to the Jewish colony which had sprung up, spontaneously, near Wapella.[88]

In 1900 the JCA's colonization work was taken out of the institute's hands, and the manager of Hirsch was given direct charge over all JCA settlement work in the Canadian West, leaving as the institute's only responsibility the supervision of the school at Hirsch. The JCA set up its own Canadian committee in 1908, and three of its six members were from the institute. But this was a tenuous connection with colonization, compared to the early years of involvement in some of the most minute details of life at Hirsch – as when the board had decided, early in 1893, that 'no new Passover dishes be purchased but that lye be procured and the Colonists directed to clean their dishes therewith.'[89]

As was the case with other such projects, Jewish colonization in Canada was complicated, hazardous, and expensive. On the Prairies, experiments in settling other ethnic groups – Hungarians, for example – in the 1880s and 1890s had met with mixed results, including significant rates of departure by original members.[90] In fact, 'the record of the first Hungarians in the West closely resembles that of the pioneer Jewish homesteaders.' Overall, statistics of homestead abandonment indicate that failure rates among western Canadian farmers were extremely high.[91] Jews were no more successful than others, and probably less so than Mennonites, Doukhobors, and Mormons, who brought substantial communal unity and farming experience with them and wisely settled in adjacent colonies.[92] From this perspective, Hirsch has to be judged at least a limited success. While the lure of the open plains as a place for the rehabilitation of East European *luftmenschen* continued to interest many, the JCA's Paris officials were less sanguine about Canada than about Argentina, where enormous sums of money were invested in the settlement of tens of thousands of Jews in colonies on the pampas.[93]

Canada's Jewish farm colonies, like those begun in the United States during the 1880s and 1890s, were small and poorly organized. But there were differences between the American and Canadian experiments. The American Jewish colonies were established as agricultural utopias by leaders who were 'sublimely indifferent to the need for careful planning,' and thereby, to some degree, fit into the American tradition of such experiments.[94] In the Canadian colonies, on the other hand, such utopian ideals appear to have been less prominent. The colonies were initiated by people who felt the call to farming to improve their material lives, and who appealed to philanthropies in Montreal and Paris for support. After the JCA became more involved in Canada in the early twentieth century, the differences between the major Canadian and American

Jewish agricultural experiments became much sharper. Whereas, in the United States, by the 1920s virtually all efforts at Jewish colonization were abandoned (except in places like Woodbine, New Jersey, located close to New York), in Canada attempts were made to strengthen the major farm colonies. Thus, while colonization constitutes a brief paragraph in American Jewish history, it is a significant chapter in the history of Jewry in Canada. What is more, the Canadian Jewish farming experience was unique in the British Anglo-Saxon countries. In South Africa, New Zealand, and Australia, no such organized experiments were undertaken, even though those three dominions possessed large tracts of unsettled land. Canada's history of Jewish colonization was similar to Argentina's, where, by the early 1900s, efforts were in full flower.[95]

At the end of the 1890s, however, Jewish colonization attempts in Canada's West were, at best, a qualified success. It was becoming clear that Jewish immigration must be based on the expectation that Jews would migrate to urban centres, and that their prospects for success were therefore limited by the absorptive capacity of the Canadian economy. In a survey of economic conditions in 1907, a year of serious recession, the JCA's agricultural expert, Dr Sonnenfeldt, was not optimistic and recommended that Paris should 'not plan on sending [to Canada], in the coming years, more than 10,000 people a year, until industry develops and provides work for more hands.'[96] Dominion officials had also formed an extremely unfavourable opinion of Jewish farmers. They blamed Jews for their own administrative bungling, 'and the complexities inherent in the legislation regarding colonization companies tended to be forgotten in the shuffling of papers related to the troublesome "Jewish business" as it came to be known.'[97]

That such a substantial part of Canadian Jewish assistance took the form of western colonization efforts underscores the fact that Canada (or Montreal, at least) believed it could not cope with the influx in any other way. Nevertheless, Canada was a refuge – though a poor second to the United States, which took in over 80 per cent of those leaving Russia and similar proportions from Austria-Hungary and Romania. Canada's political economy was at a less advanced stage than that of the United States during these decades. The West still beckoned, as it had in the United States a generation earlier, and the unofficial national agenda was to conquer that territory. And if these attempts to populate the Prairies with Jewish families were unsuccessful, the idea did not die. In 1906 the New York Jewish philanthropist Jacob Schiff offered $500,000 to kick off a project to move some two million impoverished Russian Jews to the Canadian Prairies.[98] The scheme was stillborn, as immigrants wanted to live in cities. The influx resulted in the substantial growth of the Jewish communities in Montreal, Toronto, and Winnipeg, both in numbers and in the very character of their communal life. The Eastern Europeans had arrived, and the semblance of a Canadian Jewish community had come into view.

PART TWO

Emergence of a National Community, 1890–1919

4 Travails of Urbanization

The influx of Eastern European immigrants created such enormous burdens in Montreal and Toronto that community leaders appealed to Western European and British Jewish organizations to stem the flow of immigrants and help support those who had already arrived. But the financial assistance which came from agencies like London's Mansion House Committee and Paris's Jewish Colonization Association was never enough.

The sheer numbers of immigrants were staggering. While Montreal's total metropolitan population grew by some 55 per cent in the 1880s and by 25 per cent in the 1890s, in the same period the city's Jewish population rose from 811 to 2,473 and up to 6,941 – an average of nearly 300 per cent in each decade.[1] The growth was accompanied by demographic change, as reflected in school enrolments, urban patterns, and the location of synagogues. While the immigrants were concentrated in the downtown area, those established had already begun to move uptown, west, and north into the salubrious new suburbs at the foot of Mount Royal. In 1882 the English, German, and Polish congregation, Shaar Hashomayin (Gates of Heaven), transferred from its building on St Constant Street to a classy new synagogue near McGill University. Ten years later, Shearith Israel, located since 1839 on Chenneville Street, also migrated to an impressive edifice uptown. Meanwhile the Reform congregation, Temple Emanuel, which had originated in 1882, also settled into a new structure in the tony west end of town.

As the older community shifted, the newcomers filled – and overfilled – the spaces they had left. A new congregation of Russians, B'nai Jacob (Sons of Jacob), occupied one of the vacated downtown synagogues, while newly arrived Romanians, who had organized themselves as the

Beth David (House of David) in 1886, also acquired an abandoned shul. There was Beth Yehuda (House of Judah), another group of Russians, organized in the 1890s; Chevra Kadisha (Holy Brotherhood), which was formed in 1893 and worshipped in an old factory; and Chevra Thilim (Brotherhood of Psalms), a group of Russians and Lithuanians which started about 1903 in a downtown flat.[2] Meanwhile, a small synagogue was erected in 1900 in the industrial suburb of Lachine. Besides these, there were other groups which met for prayer in rented rooms or apartments.[3]

As well as religious associations there were socialists, anarchists, and free-thinkers.[4] Groups came together for friendship and mutual aid. A typical organization, known as a *landsmanshaft* (hometown association), arose to provide sick benefits, prepaid burials, and temporary help to widows and orphans.[5]

Jewish immigrants also faced need for credit to meet business or family needs. Some of these funds were available in small amounts from the numerous *landsmanschaften*, while a more formal community-wide organization, the Montreal Hebrew Free Loan Association, was created in 1911 – just when the caisses populaires, with similar purposes in French Canada, were being formed – to broaden and regulate this important function.[6]

Some immigrants took to peddling various goods around the city or out in the countryside – the same kind of penny capitalism often pursued by many others a generation earlier. In Montreal the Baron de Hirsch Institute even provided small loans for some of these pedlars in the early 1880s. Their numbers proliferated so much that by 1905 established businesses were loudly complaining.[7] Other forms of petty commerce abounded: retail clothing, confectionery, fish and grocery stores, kosher bakeries and butcher shops. Some were employed as religious slaughterers, teachers, or rabbis. These and other service workers, many of them self-employed, may have constituted as much as 30 per cent of the Jewish gainfully employed, the same level they obtained in Russia in the 1890s.

The production of ready-made clothing was flourishing in Canada in the 1880s and 1890s. Protected by high tariffs and stimulated by rising demand, the industry doubled the value of output in the 1870s and increased it further in the 1880s. By 1900, clothing production was Montreal's second-largest industry[8] and was booming in Toronto and Hamilton as well.

Apparel of all kinds was produced in Montreal, the major centre since the 1850s,[9] and the demand for labour was constant during short production seasons. Jews became clothing workers in factories, where all of the production was carried out on the premises, or in home workshops, where parts of the pre-cut garments were sewn up. By the 1880s manufacturers Harris Vineberg, Mark Workman, Harris Kellert, David Friedman, Solomon Levinson, and Lyon Cohen were breaking new ground in this industry, which had been dominated by large and powerful non-Jewish firms.[10] The example of Jewish advancement within the industry in Britain and the United States was emulated time and again in subsequent years. Besides the Mosses and the Benjamins of an earlier generation, the immigrants were witnesses to outstanding contemporary Jewish success in this business.[11]

Noah Friedman and his son David, for example, started in a small way in 1881, after years of running a store in Lancaster. They were joined two years later by Noah's brother-in-law, Harris Kellert, also newly arrived from Lancaster, to form the Freedman Company, which grew into an immense business selling men's ready-to-wear across the Dominion.[12] Harris Vineberg, once a pedlar in the Ottawa Valley, started manufacturing men's and boys' suits in 1882 as the 'Progress Brand' company. Abraham Jacobs, Solomon Levinson, and Jacob Cohen, after serving business apprenticeships as pedlars and petty retailers around Lancaster, also moved to Montreal during the 1870s and set up successfully as menswear manufacturers. Levinson established a retail clothing business in Montreal in 1874, and began producing clothing using home labourers in the countryside, to supply his store. Having a surplus of goods, he established a wholesale outlet in 1880. In 1894 he was joined by his son, and in 1900 by his brother, to form a firm which became one of the largest in Canada. Many others were drawn to this business because as former traders and retailers, they understood merchandising. Also, with little capital required, cheap sewing machines available, and a large immigrant labour pool, costs were kept low. Many Jewish immigrants, including experienced tailors, were willing to endure the abysmal conditions brought to light during the royal commission investigations into labouring conditions in 1889, 1896, and 1898.

Evidence at the royal commission inquiries into labour conditions in the 1880s and 1890s noted the increasing presence of Jews; in Montreal and Toronto many were operating as contractors in very poor conditions. In 1886, Montreal wholesale clothier James O'Brien testified that he employed several Jewish contractors, some of whom hired up to thirty workers, toiling long hours at home or in filthy garrets, warehouses, or cellars with poor air circulation, dampness, and no sanitary facilities. Some of these contractors attested that many of their employees were members of their own families, including many children.[13] By 1895, out of two dozen major men's clothing contractors, most were Jews with small shops employing up to twenty workers in the heart of the Jewish quarter.

The report of the Commission on the Sweating System in Canada in 1896 produced further evidence that Jews acting as contractors for large clothiers were in some cases exploiting others.[14] Two years later, the report authored by future prime minister William Lyon Mackenzie King on the production of post-office uniforms highlighted this same pattern of small-scale Jewish contractors. So pointed were references to Jewish sweatshops in his report and in a feature article he wrote for the *Montreal Herald* that the *Jewish Times* published a strong editorial attack on these conditions. Meanwhile, evidence presented by Quebec's inspectors of industrial establishments confirmed the existence of a serious problem in this industry.

Throughout the immigrant districts of Toronto and Montreal, King's investigation revealed, there was a widespread system of oppressive, unhealthy conditions. In unsanitary, crowded, poorly ventilated, and dangerous shops, their workers were very poorly paid on a piecework basis, labouring a sixty-hour week. King found that one Toronto contractor worked his operatives thirteen hours a day, seven days a week.[15] Wages varied considerably, depending on the specific job performed and the worker's skill. When production was in full swing, operators, basters, and pressers earned an average of between $9 and $12 per week, although an efficient presser could earn $18 to $20 per week. However, young women in their early teens, who were deemed apprentices, took home a scant $3 to $5. In many shops, these girls were unpaid while they learned the trade, and were often fired when they demanded wages.

Piecework and subdivision of labour resembled an assembly line. In the production of a coat or jacket, for example, fifteen separate processes were involved; these called for the work of a trimmer, pocket-maker, seamer, stitcher, lining-maker, joiner, sleeve-maker, under-baster, finisher, sleeve-lining feller, basting feller, button-seamer, hand presser, edge-presser, and seam-presser. King recognized that 'all this division of labour tends to make men mere cog in wheel – if he had whole section [garment] he could exercize brain – if [only] one cog – can't do anything else, nerve wracking.' He identified a serious problem in the modern industrial process – the separation of the worker from the end product of his or her labour. While King did not comment on the industry's seasonality, which resulted in lengthy, large-scale layoffs, this too was a major problem. Although some manufacturers employed small numbers during the slack seasons, many hundreds were out of work during the slow winter months. These employees thus experienced serious privation, as did those a generation later, when in the winter of 1913, a serious depression hit the city.[16]

All three royal commissions pointed out that only the merchant tailors, milliners, and dressmakers manufactured entirely on their own premises, though even some of them contracted out part of their output. However, the vast majority of those manufacturing large production runs of clothing – mainly cheaper grades of menswear – utilized outworkers hired by contractors. The clothier or manufacturer, who acted as a wholesaler, produced specific garments; he sold either at his own factory, through travelling salesmen, or at retail in his own store. The pieces of these garments were cut at his factory from whole cloth, with tailor's shears, bench-mounted knives, or the new steam-powered machines that could slice through twenty thicknesses at once. He sought out contractors, and, once price and delivery date were decided, the pieces were marked, matched, and bundled. Contractors took them to their workers, who operated either at their homes or in the contractor's own shop.

Because contractors needed little capital, it was easy to enter into this business. Many Jews who had some knowledge of clothing production or marketing even became subcontractors, taking on part of the contractor's work. Manufacturers would therefore put the work out at low prices, counting on the likelihood that some needy contractor would have to accept his terms. He, in turn, would offer his operatives low piece rates determined by competition for work in the trade. Workers could accept or reject, but could rarely improve the terms.

In this Hobbesian, crushing system of undeclared economic war of 'all against all,' the wages for all but the highly skilled were kept low and working conditions were abysmal.[17] Should workers complain, contractors, known as 'sweaters,' could always find other willing hands, in the city itself or in the surrounding countryside. Low wages and poor working conditions were 'all the fault of the "sweaters",' one contemporary observed, 'as they are constantly undercutting the prices in order to get the work and the wholesalers are continually playing one lot against the other.' Married women workers – most of them employed at home, because of social custom and domestic responsibilities – were open to severe exploitation. To the bosses, it did not matter who did the work, as long as it was done properly, on time, and at the lowest possible price.

Reports by provincial factory inspectors on the sweatshops received full exposure in the *Jewish Times*. In February 1898, it noted that

> the space is small, badly aired, and unprovided with special conveniences for women ... The workshops ... are most defective. Located in old buildings, private houses, lanes, and back-yards, sometimes in basements, but oftener in garrets, they lack equally in air, light and cleanliness. Besides the hygienic question, the other abuses are excessive working hours and low wages ... Piece-work is responsible for many evils.[18]

The paper called upon the 'Baron de Hirsch' to start a program of training Jewish immigrants in a variety of trades. 'But a surer remedy,' it continued pointedly,

> lies with the wholesale merchants themselves; for if, instead of becoming philanthropists for one day at the annual meeting of the Benevolent Society [the 'Baron de Hirsch'], they would examine the condition of their work people and determine that the misery which these wretched people undergo should not be laid at their door, a different state of affairs would exist.

A year later, when the inspector issued another report condemning Jewish sweatshops, the *Times* again did not mince words:

> The conditions under which Jews are thus publicly reported as being in the habit of conducting their industries requires plain speaking. They should not be tolerated. Not only in physical matters, but morality, the character and reputation of the Jews of Montreal are at stake. Those who are in touch with the parties indicated should spare no effort in the endeavour to bring about a better state of affairs.

Yet, despite these exposures and exhortations for reform, the evil continued unchecked.

In response to these conditions, in the early 1890s Jewish workers in Montreal and Toronto formed branches of the United Garment Workers of America, marking the entry of Jews into the labour movement.

The unions attempted to exploit the retailers' vulnerability, as work stoppages or strikes at the beginning of a season could ruin a manufacturer. As well, unions provided an additional vehicle for economic and political self-expression among the immigrants, like the new synagogues and *landsmanshaften*. They also highlighted growing divisiveness within the Jewish communities. This was natural enough. Jews had never been homogeneous, and a gulf existed between the established community and the immigrants. By the 1890s, charities were dominated by those who had arrived between the 1840s and the 1870s. The more established members of the Spanish and Portuguese community were not as involved in running these organizations as were members of the English, German, and Polish congregation. However, members of both congregations came together in many contexts, not the least important being the marriage canopy under which, for example, a Vineberg would marry a Hart. They also shared the Montefiore Club, a business and social association of the Jewish well-to-do, who were excluded from the clubs to which Montreal's anglophone elite belonged.

And they had lots to do. With help from its benefactor, the Baron de Hirsch Institute started up relief and education programs. In response to urgent appeals for help, the baron made the Montrealers a $20,000 grant in 1890. A small building was purchased where institute's activities were focused, providing temporary accommodations for immigrants. Some of them were newly arrived families of men who had preceded them. While attempts were made to reunite the families, the wives and children remained in the 'home,' the children attending school in the same building. Frequently a husband had died or disappeared completely, and the widowed or deserted woman was sent back to Europe or to friends elsewhere in Canada or the United States.

The 'Baron de Hirsch,' as the building and the organization were now known, was located near the Champ de Mars, in the heart of a largely Jewish district. Various social and cultural organizations began using the building regularly, and it became a major social hub for the community. But its most valuable use was as a school, established early on and providing free education for the poor and pre-school preparation for the newly arrived.

Although of vital importance, this school, with an initial enrolment of more than two hundred pupils, was short of funds. What remained of the baron's grant was rapidly being used for immigrant relief and colonization. The Paris-based Alliance Israélite Universelle sent regular but meagre assistance; occasionally the baron or the Jewish Colonization Association sent further remittances. However, this was still inadequate, and other sources of revenue were soon explored. With funds for their school in short supply, officers of the Baron de Hirsch soon came to demand a portion of the school taxes paid on property owned by Jews in the city of Montreal. This brought them into direct conflict with the Spanish and Portuguese synagogue, in a contest which highlighted the complex question of the legal position of Jews in Quebec's educational structure, which was established under the British North America Act in 1867, mandating separate confessional school systems for Protestants and Roman Catholics.

The Shearith Israel had long operated a day school for their own children under the direction of their minister, Reverend Meldola de Sola, son of Abraham and brother of Clarence de Sola. To finance it, the members of the congregation in 1886 exercised their right under Quebec law to allocate their school taxes (levied on their real property) to the Roman Catholic board of school commissioners. This body, which had only a very small number of Jewish pupils – Montreal's Jews overwhelmingly attended Protestant schools – agreed to turn back 80 per cent of these monies to the Spanish and Portuguese congregation, retaining 20 per cent for acting as broker. This arrangement compromised the position for the increasing numbers in the Protestant school system. The Protestant board did not get much financial support from the immigrant parents, most of whom were poor and unlikely to own real estate; it was the established Shearith Israel members who possessed property. Out of a total of $2,800 levied in school taxes paid by Jews in the city in 1892, $2,200 came from members of that congregation. In 1889, the Protestant board had attempted to have the provincial legislature pass a bill which would interfere with this arrangement, but the congregation successfully fought it.[19]

The Baron de Hirsch officers believed that, as their enrolment exceeded that of the synagogue school, their institute should receive a portion of this Jewish tax money. But they were rebuffed by the synagogue's officers, and the issue simmered ominously.[20] In May 1892, the Baron de Hirsch appealed directly to the provincial government to intervene,[21] asserting that the reason why the Spanish and Portuguese continued their own school was because they were unable 'to have their minister [Meldola de Sola] appointed under salary as the Hebrew teacher in the Protestant Schools.' The Spanish and Portuguese private deal with the Roman Catholic board was 'against the whole tenor and spirit of the School Acts, which were framed for the education of the masses, and not for the benefit of any particular individual or Congregation.' And while the Spanish and Portuguese school was supposedly open to all Jewish children in the city, regardless of ability to pay, it was in fact inaccessible to most because of its location in the west end. David Ansell argued for the Baron de Hirsch that the solution lay in a proportional distribution of all school taxes derived from Jewish-owned property. He also reminded the government that the 250 Jewish pupils who attended Protestant schools were backed by only $600 in Jewish tax money and warned that the Protestants 'have threatened to close their doors to Jewish children, if the present state of affairs continues.'

While the matter remained unresolved, the provincial government warned Meldola de Sola that since 'we feel that the distribution of the Jewish school taxes are not as equitable and fair as they should be ... it will suffice to call the attention of the interested parties to those facts.'[22] If the question was not fairly settled within a few months, provincial secretary Louis Pelletier continued sternly, 'the Government will decide as to what course ought to be adopted.'

De Sola's evasive answer to this warning and to Ansell's appeals was met with the renewed government threat of an imposed settlement. A few days later, de Sola offered $800 to settle an issue now so notorious that it was being freely discussed in local newspapers.[23] The institute's school committee again refused, demanding at least $1,000. The congregation demurred, trying everything possible to stave off government legislation that would impose a per capita division. When Premier Taillon visited Montreal in December 1892, Meldola de Sola tried to convince him 'that the matter should be looked into anew when he returned to Quebec.'[24] A bill that was introduced in the Legislative Assembly in early February to settle the issue once and for all was stalled, and the whole issue remained in limbo during 1893 and most of 1894. Faced with the resolve of both the government and the Baron de Hirsch, the Spanish and Portuguese congregation finally surrendered in late 1894, reassigning Jewish school taxes to the Protestant board, on the understanding that Meldola de Sola would be appointed as Hebrew teacher to these schools.[25] While the Protestants were placated, the claims of the Baron de Hirsch were still not settled. But the Protestant board recognized the value of the school for their own system and decided to subsidize it with an annual grant of $1,500, placing it on a more assured financial basis.

The dispute was now resolved but, despite the impressive victory, there was a downside. The Protestant board was now more conscious of the injustice of having to educate a rapidly growing number of Jewish children without adequate compensation from school taxes on Jewish-owned property. Even though it now received all Jewish school tax monies, these amounts did not cover its costs. By 1899, when Jewish enrolment stood at 749 – having increased from 269 in 1890 – and when Jews constituted over 8 per cent of the total student body in Protestant schools, the board was deeply worried about the costs of accommodating them.[26] In an ominous public statement issued in mid-February of 1898, one board member indicated their frustration:

> It is all very well for people to talk about children of different creeds sitting together on the same bench, a very nice phrase, and I would like it if all could be educated together, but I suppose the [Jews] on the bench have no legal rights there, and they are pushing off those who have and who pay for the bench.[27]

Two years later, in order to gain public attention, the board changed its regulations, to admit only children of Jews who paid their school taxes to the Protestant board. Henceforth children of Jewish non-taxpayers would be admitted only as a matter of grace.

Outraged and alarmed, the Jewish leaders prepared to fight what would turn out to be a very long, bitter, internally divisive, and, ultimately, losing battle. It would arouse strong feelings in francophone Montreal as well, particularly in the Roman Catholic hierarchy. At least one newspaper, the militantly ultramontane *La Croix de Montréal*, used this issue as a springboard for an antisemitic campaign that lasted through 1894 and 1895.[28]

The work of the Baron de Hirsch school continued despite these clashes over finances. Here emphasis was placed on ensuring that the children quickly learned English, and other subjects too, including Hebrew. Some parents chose special Jewish schools – attached to the new synagogues and the smaller congregations springing up in the Jewish district – or private teachers. The Baron de Hirsch school attempted to inculcate a sense of pride in Canada as well as in Jewish traditions. In 1898 a cadet corps known as the Hirsch Cadets, affiliated with the Jewish Lad's Brigade of England, was formed. They were equipped with uniforms, and, with their wooden rifles shouldered, they were drilled up and down the nearby Champ de Mars.

The rising tide of Jewish immigrants during the late 1890s determined much of the Baron de Hirsch activity. The number of people in the home; the cost of feeding, clothing, and housing them; their transference to other places; the amount, kinds, and costs of medical treatment in both outpatient clinics and hospitals; and even the number of burials in the newly acquired cemetery, all absorbed the resources of the society. By far the largest proportion of the immigrants were from the Russian Empire, although precise figures are not known.[29] Nor do we know the numbers of petitions for assistance in any one year, as the records are sparse. Yet there are constant references in the minute books to immigrants arriving, to their being met at the ships, to lost baggage and searches for lost family members. Many needed at least temporary lodging, besides meals and clothing; some wanted to be sent to New York, Winnipeg, Toronto, Chicago, Cincinnati, Omaha, or – in a few cases – back to Europe.

Towards the end of the decade, Romanian Jews began to outnumber the Russians. In 1900 alone, 2,202 Romanians arrived in Montreal, most of them needing assistance. They posed tremendous problems and raised hackles among government officials, who, worried by this and other backlashes, wired the Montreal office of the JCA: 'This department protests against this class of immigration and will take steps to prevent any further numbers arriving.'[30] Through July and August, nearly 300 arrived each week. The society resettled many and enlisted the aid of ad hoc committees elsewhere, although the majority settled in and around Montreal.

Most of the financial support came from abroad, supplementing the baron's original gift of $20,000 many times by special grants. The Paris-based Alliance Israélite Universelle also supported the school generously, while the Baroness de Hirsch donated $20,000 for a new school building, and left the institute almost $89,000 when she died in 1899. By contrast, funds raised in Montreal were abysmally low. In 1900, when the JCA sent $12,000 to help support some 2,880 immigrants, $1,500 for the home and $10,000 towards the construction of a new building (and the Protestant school board donated $2,000 towards the school), the institute raised a paltry $1,100 from local Jewish supporters (along with a few special donations for matzos and coal),[31] revealing a startling discrepancy between local and outside contributions. On the other hand, the executive and many other members volunteered numerous hours on all the various committees. Without fees, the institute physician worked two days each week, and made house and hospital visits. Both the notary and the solicitor spent much *pro bono* time on complicated and expensive legal work. Board members would often pay for their trips to Quebec City or to Ottawa to discuss relevant issues. Members of the executive met new immigrants, found them lodging and jobs, offered advice, and at times sent them to their destinations elsewhere.

Nonetheless, the off-shore funding relegated the institute into an administrative agency of the baron and the JCA's funds. Directives from Paris accompanied most of these grants, requiring detailed financial reports. Their purposes were changing to suit the designs of the JCA, and Montrealers complied in fear of losing support. Montreal was at the end of a migration chain that began far off in eastern Europe. Jewish committees in Germany and Austria were unable to turn the migrants back; if they and the JCA could not stem the tide, the Montreal organization could surely not control the flow.

While the Baron de Hirsch spoke for the majority of the Montreal Jews and, with colonization and immigrant services, served a national role as well, other organizations followed. In 1893 their middle-class sisters in the East had established the National Council of Women of Canada – which had distinctly Christian overtones – to advance a number of important women's causes, and Jewish women followed suit in 1897. The National Council of Jewish Women was organized in Toronto and later spread to other major cities, focusing on programs to help new immigrants, with visitations and English classes. The council also assisted children with summer camps, recreational activities for girls, and help for problem children.[32]

Public reaction to the increasing number of Jews in Montreal was, with some exceptions, fairly benign. The major newspapers manifested no alarm or animosity, although Jules-Paul Tardivel's Quebec City newspaper, *La Vérité*, began publishing antisemitic articles in the early 1880s, most of them drawn from militant ultramontane publications in France.[33] In 1886, Tardivel made favourable references to Édouard Drumont's diatribe *La France Juive*, and to other French antisemitic publications, and in the early 1890s he began writing such screeds himself. In October of 1890, he urged his readers 'to be on guard against the Jews, to prevent them from establishing themselves here ... The Jews are a curse, a curse from G-d.' *La Vérité* also published pieces by other French-Canadian antisemites, such as Zacharie Lacasse and Raoul Renault, while Tardivel's antisemitism was echoed by Amédée Denault, who, in his newspaper *La Croix de Montréal*, published much of this material between 1893 and 1895, either borrowed from French antisemites or locally produced. Many of these articles were published between November 1894 and March 1895, in the first stage of the infamous Dreyfus case.[34]

The Dreyfus affair, which fostered a crescendo of virulent abuse against Jews in France, found only faint echo, however, in Quebec. The Montreal daily *La Patrie* approved the verdict of treason in the court martial in 1894, and reported some of the antisemitic material from the French press during the related libel trial of Émile Zola in 1898, and a few independent French-Canadian newspapers were pronouncedly anti-Dreyfusard and antisemitic throughout.[35] In a lead editorial during the second Dreyfus trial in 1899, *La Presse* – the French daily with the largest circulation – on the other hand, proclaimed that 'we are neither Dreyfusist, nor anti-Dreyfusist,' and reminded its readers: 'As we in this country follow English law in criminal matters, we do not accept, especially during a trial, that the accused should be considered guilty.'[36] *La Presse* was headed by leading journalist Jules Helbronner, an Alsatian Jew, a staunch liberal, and a champion of workers' rights. Widely known as a Jew, Helbronner – who never denied that fact – nevertheless enjoyed a lengthy career in the French press and wide respect among French-Canadian liberal thinkers.

The most avowedly antisemitic of the major Montreal newspapers was not a French-Canadian publication at all, but the daily serving the city's English-speaking Catholics, the *True Witness and Daily Chronicle*, which carried strongly partisan material during both the Dreyfus and Zola trials. The lead editorial of 11 December 1897, proclaimed:

> [It] should be borne in mind that the highest authorities in the French Army, and all the members of the court martial by which he was tried, have declared their belief that he did commit the crime of selling important military secrets to the German War Office. The Chamber of Deputies has also by a very large majority affirmed its conviction that the charge was fully proved.[37]

This was, on the evidence to date, not an unreasonable position. But the *True Witness* then elaborated on 'the rise of antisemitic feeling on account of the undue prominence attained by Jews in the financial, political and journalistic world.' From this point onwards, the paper was unabashedly anti-Dreyfusard. In reply to a complaint in the *Jewish Times*, the *True Witness* replied that 'nothing could have been further from our minds than to attempt "to poison the minds of our readers" against the Jews ... [However], because a man is a Jew, it does not follow that he is incapable of committing a crime.' In the wake of Zola's libel conviction in February 1898, after he published *J'accuse,* a letter alleging conspiracy in the Dreyfus case, the *True Witness* editorialized that 'no one who has read the letter ... can have the least doubt as to his guilt ... Fancy France's honour being personified by the filthy novelist Zola.' Referring to other recent cases of treason in the French army and navy, the newspaper continued: 'None of these cases excited more than passing interest, but ... had these men been Jews, it would have been otherwise.' To the credit of the editors, they did backtrack considerably after learning that Dreyfus might have been innocent all along. In late September 1898, the newspaper referred to Dreyfus as 'this unfortunate man' and to his public degradation and humiliation before the garrison of Paris followed by his 'banishment to a lone and barren isle.' The *Montreal Star,* on the other hand, strongly proclaimed Dreyfus's innocence throughout the second trial in September of 1899. As for *La Minerve,* it demonstrated a patronizing, amused, and sometimes genuinely curious attitude towards the culture of these new arrivals. If it was occasionally mildly prejudiced, it could not be described as antisemitic in its pages.[38]

Therefore, there is little apparent difference between the attitudes of the mainstream anglophone and francophone Montreal press towards the Jewish community in these years. If a certain ethnic stereotyping was current – sometimes aimed at Italians – in Montreal, at least, it was seldom vicious; nothing like the virulent anti-Asiatic campaigns that were then under way in British Columbia.[39] Some nasty, even rabid, printed antisemitism did exist, as in *La Vérité* and *La Libre Parole* (*Illustrée*), which propagated some poisonous anti-Jewish libels. While overt antisemitism was present in Montreal, it was at this point no stronger amongst francophones than anglophones.

Still, the Dreyfus case had had a marked effect on segments of Montreal Jewry. Lyon Cohen and Samuel Jacobs, a prominent lawyer and influential figure in the Liberal Party, founded a weekly newspaper, the *Jewish Times,* for 'the advocacy as well as the defence of Jewish rights as free citizens of a free country.' In its first issue, in December 1897, the *Times* editorial declared that the conviction of Dreyfus was a 'dark constitutional crime ... an antisemitic plot which showed the weakness of the French judicial system and the inability of the French government to protect its citizens.'[40] The *Jewish Times* continued to publish numerous reports on the case, supporting Dreyfus and opposing the resulting local antisemitism.

Throughout its seventeen-year existence and changing ownership, the *Jewish Times* remained the newspaper of the West End Montreal Anglo-Jewish community. It reached into Ontario, the Maritimes, and, to a lesser extent, the Prairies. Editorials championed the equality of Jews and Christians; indeed, the *Times* employed the ideas of Darwinism, including race science and eugenics, in the fight against antisemitism, which was taking an increasingly racist direction,[41] and stressed Jewish loyalty to Canada and the British Empire.

After the outbreak of the Boer War in 1899, the paper urged Jews to support the empire, while the exploits of local Jewish volunteers such as Captain Hyman Lightstone in the Canadian Contingent, and Dr J. Alton Harris, who joined the British army, received considerable coverage – as did the award of the Victoria Cross to an English Jew.[42] Jewish military achievements past and present were glorified, while Jewish participation in the American naval and military forces during the Spanish-American War was also highlighted. (Revenge, at last, for the Expulsion of 1492 and the Inquisition!) The *Times* reported, for example, that eleven Jewish sailors had been killed when the *Maine* blew up in Havana harbour. In an era that extolled military achievements, the *Times* emphasized that such valiant warrior Jews were a great boost to Jewish pride.

In August of 1900 the paper reported that, on a visit to Winnipeg, Rabbi Aaron Ashinsky of Shaar Hashomayim, Cohen and Jacobs's own synagogue, had delivered a rousing speech extolling British supremacy. Because British institutions were based on justice and equality, he predicted that Anglo-Saxons would eventually rule the world. Jews, the rabbi urged, should pray for the Queen twice a week, because 'it would be through the British that the Jews would ultimately be returned in full possession of their Holy Land.'

The *Jewish Times*, then, was not just to report but also to educate non-Jew and Jew alike in their perceptions of Jewish life in Canada. And the regular column 'As Others See Us' included instruction about the social graces, the lack of which, they warned, excluded Jews from polite society.[43] Jews who sought admission to fancy resort hotels without learning the proper manners were an embarrassment: 'These are the sort of people who have brought discredit on Jews as a whole and, until they learn better manners, we will all have to suffer for their sins.' Other editorials voiced concerns about the development of a specific Jewish quarter: 'those of our community who have the good of our people at heart should do all in their power to prevent the formation of a Ghetto in this city' by inducing Jews to spread out.

This type of emphasis left the *Times* little room for discussion of the complex life of downtown Jewry. Instead, the Baron de Hirsch, the Ladies' Hebrew Benevolent Society, the Young Ladies' Sewing Circle, and other uptown charities received major coverage. Reporting on the concerns of the downtown Jews was almost always condescending and emphasized their poverty. There was little significant attempt to inform, analyse, or comment on the social and economic changes in Quebec, wrought by massive industrialization and urbanization. Nor were the far-reaching effects of French-Canadian nationalism objectively evaluated, although its antisemitic aspects were featured. The importance of these matters was minimized, although, on the other hand, the major French and English newspapers published detailed accounts of many events within the Jewish community of Montreal.

After hesitating initially, the *Jewish Times* openly supported Zionism as a solution to the 'Jewish problem,' and, in particular, the territorial Zionism of Theodor Herzl. A homeland for the Jews, not necessarily in the Land of Israel, must be created, and with the outbreak of new pogroms in Kishinev in 1902, Herzl began favouring a proposal to establish a temporary refuge in British Uganda. *Jewish Times* editorials supported this project and the subsequent formation of the Territorialist Organization, which backed a Jewish homeland anywhere, not necessarily in Palestine, and continued quixotically to support the Uganda project even after it was finally rejected. Zionism, which served both philanthropic and communal purposes, attracted substantial support from the Montreal Jewish elite.

By 1900 Montreal's Jewish community had a more decidedly East European flavour. A distinct class structure existed, tending to sharpen differences; workers, machinists, tradesmen, pedlars, and small storekeepers had different attitudes and needs than the established uptown bourgeoisie. They employed different strategies for pursuing economic security. Toronto and Hamilton were much newer communities. Off in the west, Victoria's had already peaked in size. And although those in London, Saint John, and Halifax were by the 1880s numerous enough to establish minyanim, the synagogues would come later.[44] These centres experienced slower rates of growth than Montreal's 280 per cent increase during the 1890s. Toronto's Jewish population, for example, grew by slightly more than 100 per cent during the same decade, Hamilton's by

50 per cent, and Winnipeg's by about 90 per cent. Ottawa's Jewish population, on the other hand, rose by 800 per cent during the 1890s, both Windsor's and Saint John's by over 900 per cent, and Quebec City's by 600 per cent.[45] More significantly, by 1900, all of these communities had reached sufficient size to establish various institutions. All of them, as well as Halifax, London, and Vancouver, now possessed synagogues – most of them rather modest structures, but nevertheless major bridgeheads to communal strength, and symbols of continuity.

Out in Winnipeg, the tiny Jewish group, numbering only a few families in 1881, had grown to 645 persons by 1891 and to 1,156 a decade later. The Shaarey Zedek (Gates of Righteousness) congregation was formed in 1880, and the Rosh Pina (Head of the Corner) followed in 1890.[46] Many Jews took to peddling, and because they competed with the established merchants, pedlars' licence fees were suddenly raised in March 1891. This imposition was accompanied by a rise of antisemitism in local newspapers. Winnipeg Jews put forward a candidate for alderman 'largely as a defense mechanism to ward off [the] aggression and hostility' that had arisen in the city, 'and to achieve acceptance and equality.'

The Toronto Jewish community, although only half the size of Montreal in 1900, had similar social and economic patterns. Instead of two older synagogues, Toronto possessed only one, Holy Blossom, which had begun in 1856 and had been housed since 1875 in a modest new downtown building, which was replaced in 1898 by a magnificent new uptown edifice. The congregation had now adopted elements of Reform, including services largely in English, mixed seating, organ music, a choir, and more permissive rabbis.[47] Yet more divisive than these practices were social and cultural barriers. Sigmund Samuel, the son of a well-to-do hardware merchant who had been the moving spirit in building the first synagogue, records that, while he received his secular education at Upper Canada College and the Toronto Model School, his formal Jewish education was limited to after-school tutoring for his bar mitzvah. Although he experienced some anti-Jewish discrimination, Samuel became very wealthy and circulated among Toronto's best circles. Other Toronto Jews – the Nordheimers are a case in point – were so assimilated that by this time they were regarded as Gentiles.

Canada's Jewish population rose from 2,443 to 16,401 between 1881 and 1901,[48] bringing great changes. Russian and Polish immigrants carried with them tensions between two post-liberal ideologies that had emerged from the failure of the Haskalah to solve the 'Jewish problem.' They were grappling with socialism, the Jewish Bund, which strove for the realization of Jewish national autonomy within a socialist state, and with Zionism, a nationalistic movement dedicated to a political and cultural revival in the land of Israel. Others were more radical, including followers of anarchist or communist ideals.

With most immigrants concentrated in the metropolitan centres, between 1901 and 1911 Montreal's Jewish population grew by more than 400 per cent, Toronto's by nearly 600 per cent,[49] although the growth rates between 1911 and 1921 were a more modest 60 and 70 per cent respectively. The secondary Jewish centres of Ottawa and Hamilton also grew dramatically by about 400 per cent from 1901 to 1911 and 70 and 50 per cent respectively during the next decade.

The most spectacular growth between 1901 and 1911 occurred in the West, where Winnipeg's Jewish community experienced a staggering 800 per cent increase and Vancouver's nearly 500 per cent. Calgary's Jewish population rose from 1 to 604, while Edmonton's, Regina's, and Saskatoon's rose from zero to 171, 130, and 77 respectively. Fort William increased from 13 to 267, Port Arthur from 3 to 76, and Brandon from 73 to 271.[50] As well, Jews began to settle in many smaller western towns: Selkirk, Portage la Prairie, Dauphin, and Winkler in Manitoba; Melville, Yorkton, Moose Jaw, Canora, Lipton, and Estevan in Saskatchewan; and Lethbridge in Alberta. By about 1921 the numbers in most of these places had stabilized, while many declined sharply during the 1920s.[51]

The same was also occurring in central Canada, especially in southwestern and northern Ontario. London's Jewry grew from 206 to 571 to 703 from 1901 to 1911 to 1921, Kitchener's from 10 to 226 to 298, and St Catharines from 30 to 109 to 225, while figures for St Thomas, Owen Sound, Peterborough, Brantford, Guelph, Chatham, and Sarnia rose markedly. In 'New Ontario,' Sudbury and Sault Ste Marie grew, while Cobalt, Cochrane, Englehart, Timmins, and North Bay developed sizeable Jewish populations. At the same time, Jewish concentrations in the Maritime provinces also increased. Saint John and Halifax more than doubled from 1901 to 1911, while new communities sprang up in Glace Bay, Yarmouth, Moncton, Fredericton, and, over the next decade, in New Waterford.[52]

Thus, Jews were moving in response to economic opportunity. This was reflected in changing regional distribution: by 1911 roughly 21 per cent of the Canadian Jewish population lived west of the Ontario-Manitoba border, an increase of 4 per cent over the previous decade.[53] On the other hand, in 1901 some 5 per cent of the country's Jews lived in the Maritimes; this decreased to a little over 3 per cent in 1911 and to

2.7 per cent in 1921. Ontario's percentage of the Canadian Jewish population rose from 32 in 1901 to 35 in 1911, and increased again to nearly 38 per cent by 1921, while Quebec's percentages dropped steadily from 45 to about 35 between 1901 and 1921.

The Jewish communal experience[54] in such places as Glace Bay, Brantford, and Moose Jaw differed greatly from life in large centres. Jews were too few in number to form a distinctive neighbourhood. They were on a kind of cultural frontier where, living and doing business with non-Jews, they were directly exposed, on the one hand, to Christian influences and, on the other, to the need to assert their Jewish identity on a daily basis. Their major forms of association were fixed: the local synagogue, the B'nai B'rith lodge, and, for the women, Hadassah and the synagogue Ladies' Auxiliary. The youth, after 1917, had their Young Judaea clubs. Most cultural influences came filtered through the organizations within that structure, as well as in the metropolitan Yiddish newspapers and magazines or from an occasional speaker, frequently a Zionist fundraiser. People huddled close to each other for mutual support: here, nothing could be taken for granted.

The first communal obligation was to purchase land for a cemetery. The biggest task, however, was the establishment of a synagogue. Initially gathering for prayers in a home, the community would later meet in a room above a downtown store, then move to a converted house, and, much later, to a commodious, modern structure designed by an architect (whose plans might be amended several times after heated disputation among local 'experts'). These little shuls were adorned only by stars of David in a few windows and an embroidered curtain in front of the Ark containing Torah scrolls. Occasionally, biblical symbols of lions, menorahs, and eagles would be painted, and one wall of Windsor's Tifereth Israel was graced by a passage from *Pirke Avoth* (Sayings of the Fathers): 'Be bold as a leopard, light as an eagle, fleet as a hart, and strong as a lion, to do the will of thy Father who is in heaven.'[55]

In these towns and cities, the synagogue became the centre of Jewish life. Members drew up constitutions for their governance. 'All men of Jewish faith can become a member of this Corperation by making application and paying three dollar fees,' the 1902 constitution of Kingston's Independent Hebrew Congregation solemnly declared, but continued: 'any person marrying contrary to the law of Judaism shall be excluded from the rights and privileges of this Corperation.'[56] Here English, Galician, Lithuanian, Polish, Ukrainian, and Russian Jews – and perhaps, later, a few Germans and a sprinkling of Czechs and Hungarians – came together uneasily, but of necessity, to assemble and pray in awkward unison.

All of the town's Jews, religious and non-religious, yeshiva graduates and those with lesser learning, Zionists and Bundists – even the town communist – gathered on the High Holy Days, and faced east towards Jerusalem to sing the Lord's praises and utter ancient pleas for redemption. With members of diverse backgrounds, these unique communities emerged where their tiny numbers forced Jews into a unity, sometimes discordant, and an unnatural cohesion which enabled the establishment of national organizations like the Federation of Zionist Societies. For many years, the Federation (later the Zionist Organization of Canada), along with the Hadassah and Young Judaea organizations, provided vital linkages to the metropolitan centres and programs for Jewish identification.

Here there was no Jewish working class; the majority engaged in storekeeping, usually in men's or women's clothing, furniture, or shoes. Others might operate a grocery wholesale, a theatre, a flour mill, a candy store, or a dry cleaning shop.[57] Many of these people began as pedlars selling merchandise from small carts or buggies in rural areas, or along the streets in towns and villages, securing the merchandise on credit from a metropolitan wholesaler.[58] In a few years, he might have done well enough to open a small store. Instead of cash, some pedlars took livestock or produce as payment, while still others accepted any scrap metal, hides, or furs that farmers had for barter. Those seeking scrap metals, for example, sometimes offered new kitchen utensils to farmers in exchange for cast-off implements. Such metals would be hauled back to the pedlar's yard, knocked apart with crow bars and sledge hammers, thrown into piles, and sold off to brokers who shipped it by rail or truck to the steel mills in Hamilton, Sydney, and Sault Ste Marie. Others collected rags, cleaned and shredded them, and sold off the product as 'shoddy' to mills. Some dealt in hides and furs, which they assembled, cleaned, sorted, and sold to brokers from the city.[59] These dealers served as commercial intermediaries between the nearby farms and the metropolitan centres. Pedlars and storekeepers offered much the same kind of link between the rural community and the growing populations in their towns, while, as purchasers from Montreal, Toronto, and Winnipeg wholesalers, they also linked the towns to the metropolises.

Although Jews accepted work in a variety of occupations, they gravitated to commercial pursuits. According to a well-informed observer of life and labour in northern railway-construction camps from 1903 to 1914:

Few Jews engage in manual work. There are exceptions, however, and persistent able workers they are even in the most strenuous tasks. But they usually prefer to do their own planning. As tailors, peddlers, jewelers, and small traders of various kinds they follow the steel, locating temporarily in the small towns which spring up in its wake.[60]

The community provided for religious needs, such as kosher meat and fowl, instruction of children, and prayers. Teachers who doubled as ritual slaughterers were employed, among them saintly men who served all their lives accepting minimal wages. Some were ordained rabbis, graduates of great Polish or Lithuanian talmudic academies, cast ashore, as it were, in Halifax or Brantford, brimming with learning and zeal for the Torah, but usually required to spend most of their lives providing rudimentary religious services in these isolated communities. Missionaries they were, to their bewildered people scattered across half a continent.

By 1921, Winnipeg – the emporium of the West – had 14,837 Jews,[61] who constituted a larger percentage of the total civic population than in any other Canadian city. By 1920 the community had established a parochial school system embracing separate institutions for children of religious or left-wing families. Groups for theatrical and choral performances, for reading, discussion, and debate, and for numerous Zionist, mutual aid, and philanthropic purposes sprang to life. A newspaper, *Dos Yiddishe Vort*, was founded in 1911, and a few years later the *Jewish Western Bulletin*, an English-language weekly, began publication.[62] Both circulated throughout the Prairies.

Location, as well, contributed to this dynamism. Winnipeg was situated in a region where many non-anglophone immigrants, designated as 'foreigners,' were a political and social fact. Jews were included among Ukrainians – sometimes known as Galicians or Austrians – Poles, and Germans, in an ethnic agglomeration that constituted nearly half the city's population by 1913. In one North End school in 1911, Jewish pupils constituted the largest single group by nationality, but they were a minority among children of Christian immigrants.[63] In such a variegated population, the Jews, like the members of other ethnic groups, perhaps felt the need to assert their group identity the more strongly.[64]

The area of first settlement was the North End, located north of the CPR yards and its main line east and west. This included Ward 3, where between 1901 and the 1930s upwards of 88 per cent of the Jewish population resided[65] as well as large proportions of other immigrant communities. Early on Jews were concentrated in a fairly narrow belt between Main and the Red River. By 1921 their centre of population was located at Selkirk Avenue. While they constituted a majority in certain parts of these districts, Jews lived close to Ukrainians, Poles, and Germans. The basic demands of life diverted attention away from the renewal of old acrimonies, while the diversity of the city's social setting temporarily overrode those old feelings.

But soon old animosities re-emerged: Ukrainians, to many Jews, were murderous, drunken barbarians, while Jews, to many Ukrainians, were Christ-killers, unmanly weaklings, and ruthless exploiters.[66] Neighbours in these areas, Jews and Ukrainians began to compete with each other in municipal politics as a vehicle for gaining acceptance in the larger society. Efforts to elect aldermen and school trustees who had the support of both communities broke down after 1911, and 'the unfriendliness of the Jewish-Ukrainian political competition ... brought to the surface hatred and fear' in the 1914 municipal elections. While the tensions did not end and 'political rivalry between Jews and Ukrainians ... continued ... in Winnipeg until well into the post–World War period,' left-wing Jews and Ukrainians eagerly supported Communist candidates in the interwar period.

The Jewish influx included a substantial number of Zionists and radicals. Their top priority was the education of their children in their ideology, and thus they rejected the existing schools.[67] In 1906 the Zionists started their own school, attached to the new B'nai Zion synagogue in the North End. Within a year, the school, now called the Winnipeg Hebrew School–Talmud Torah, had an enrolment of 150 pupils. Six years later, it moved to larger quarters and became for some years 'the heart of the Winnipeg Jewish community.'

The radicals' literary and cultural club, the Yiddisher Yugend Farein (Jewish Youth Organization), launched the National Radical School in 1914, following lengthy disputations over the content of the curriculum, the language of instruction (whether Yiddish or Hebrew), and the precise ideological pitch of socialist teachings. Discord on the last question led to a split in 1914, the radicals leaving to form their own school. Called the Arbeiter Ring (Workmen's Circle) School, it started in 1918 with a program that included Yiddish language and literature as well as Jewish and working-class history. Meanwhile the Shaarey Zedek congregation had operated its own religious school since 1915. As well, many a *melamed* (private teacher) also served the area. Thus, Winnipeg may have been one of the best-endowed Jewish communities in North America. These varied schools served not only as conduits of Jewish culture but as 'prime socialization agents' for the adoption of immigrant children into Canadian society.[68]

Small Jewish communities in Calgary, Regina, Edmonton, and Saskatoon also grew with remarkable speed. Jews had figured among fur traders at Rocky Mountain House as early as 1869, storekeepers at Qu'Appelle in 1877, and CPR construction gangs in 1882, and were among the founders of Calgary and Edmonton.[69] In 1906 Calgary Jews purchased land for a cemetery, rented space for religious services, and hired a shochet. In Edmonton a congregation was organized that year, and in 1907 a Hebrew school was opened. The Jewish community of Saskatoon was founded around 1905.[70] Regina's was begun the same year and grew quickly, to 130 people in 1911, 495 in 1916, and 860 in 1921, by which time a synagogue, a rabbi, a cemetery, and a school had been acquired.[71] The groups in Prince Albert, Moose Jaw, and Medicine Hat, flourished too, along with those in a number of other towns and villages that sprang up during the western wheat-boom years between 1900 and 1913.

In the early twentieth century, colonization efforts continued out on the Prairies. Following the establishment of Hirsch in 1892, the colony experienced serious tensions which resulted 'in a frequent movement of settlers out of the colony with new ones recruited in their place.'[72] Nevertheless, the JCA persevered. In 1901 some 365 Romanian Jews were established in the Lipton-Cupar area of the Qu'Appelle Valley, even though government officials were sceptical, given their inexperience in farming.[73] The Paris-based JCA, operating through a committee of the 'Baron de Hirsch' in Montreal, responded to complaints of inefficient management by shifting control of its Canadian operations to an affiliated New York organization, the Jewish Agricultural and Industrial Aid Society. This was also unsatisfactory, and in 1907 the JCA established its own Canadian organization with an office in Montreal.

In total, the JCA discovered that Hirsch had only twenty-four farmers, with 2,529 acres under cultivation, while the Lipton-Cupar settlement had fifty-six farmers who had put only 500 acres under plough. Despite these modest results, the JCA persevered. Some colonies began spontaneously, like Bender Hamlet in 1903, at Narcisse, north of Winnipeg, and Edenbridge, in 1906, near Melfort, Saskatchewan. Another, Sonnenfeld, was established in 1905.[74] Other Jewish homesteaders settled on the Prairies before the First World War, with or without the JCA support. It is not clear, however, if the level of success depended on JCA support.

The lives of the Jewish families in these settlements are examined in the published memoirs of a few early settlers such as *Land of Hope*, by Clara Hoffer, and *Uncle Mike's Edenbridge*, by Michael Usiskin. Something of these challenges can be derived from Clara Hoffer's diary in Yiddish about the experiences she shared with her husband, Israel Hoffer, and his father, Reb Moshe, who had come to Saskatchewan from Galicia in 1906:

> It was true God was everywhere. But to go to the wild sprawling prairie countries where there were no Synagogues, no scroll, and not enough Jewish men for a minyan, was the height of madness ... what was he doing here ... In the Old Country he had been revered as a learned, as a respectable man. Pah on his son's obstinacy.[75]

The displacement was – at least in retrospect – deeply depressing to a man of Reb Moshe's age, fifty-seven. 'This is the place my son wants to call home,' he said bitterly to a visitor, 'this wilderness with no trees and no water except what is in the slough.' In the rough atmosphere of the Canadian frontier, the ignorance of Jewish customs that prevailed among other farmers could lead to some embarrassing, even perilous situations.

After thirty-three years of working on his farm at Edenbridge, Mike Usiskin recalled the appeal directed at London Jews in 1906 by the 'rabbi' of the colony:

> Flee, my friends, from the London fogs and the chaos that eats away at your hearts. Flee from the confusion of busy streets ... flee from the tenements and the bosses that live off your blood, sweat and tears; flee from that two-faced society where politicians don't say what they think, and don't think what they say. Come to Edenbridge. Come where the air is fresh. Everything is so peaceful ... The forest here is so vast that personal expansion has no bounds. You can live here by your own resources ... Come help us tame this wild land ... we need you. Come please come! You will not regret it.[76]

Usiskin succumbed to the call, travelled to Canada, and when he got to Edenbridge encountered Jews who came from all over the world – '[South] Africans, Europeans, Americans, and a new breed called Canadians.'

The settlers' most important preoccupations, judging from these memoirs, were about relationships with Christian neighbours and tensions emerging within the Jewish community itself, while Usiskin's overriding concern was the realization of his youthful ideals of building in rural Saskatchewan a new arcadian Jewish life far from urban travails. The women of these colonies appear to have left almost no memoirs, and we can only imagine their perspectives on lives of domestic toil in harsh surroundings, with husbands ground down by incessant labour and uncertain rewards, while their children were growing up as strangers to them in this new land. Doctors were often far away, most close family and friends were still living in the old country, and the ways of this new country were so unfamiliar. These women look out from old photographs with puzzled sadness or wry hopefulness, and almost palpable weariness.

The accomplishments of colonization were both actual and mythical. The colonies, though small, existed for some seven decades, demonstrating Jewish ability to cope successfully with an agricultural life in which, though many failed or gave up, some survived. The soil did indeed beckon to and nurture a small number who would never trade the broad prairie sky for the narrow horizons of a Canadian city, or the feel of their own wheat between their fingers for the dubious touch of a clothing contractor's garment pieces.

The big cities experienced the problems associated with immigration, including poverty, mental illness, crime, juvenile delinquency, desertion, and child abuse. In Montreal, the Baron de Hirsch and its associated charities were extremely busy after 1900 attempting to meet many pressing responsibilities. There were so many burials of Jewish indigents (including 139 children) in 1908, for example, that available spaces in local Jewish cemeteries were all used up.[77] Because the charity's doctors' caseloads jumped from 787 to 2,162 between 1907 and 1913, the Herzl Health Clinic was established to cope with the sick, many with tuberculosis. For these cases, the Mount Sinai sanatorium was established in the Laurentian highlands near Ste-Agathe, while in response to the need, an orphanage was built in the city's western suburbs. Jewish immigrants also required credit to meet business or family needs. Some help came in small amounts from the numerous *landsmanschaften*; while a more formal community-wide organization, the Montreal Hebrew Free Loan Association, was created in 1911 – just when the caisses populaires, with similar purposes in French Canada, were being formed – to broaden and regulate this important function.[78]

Toronto's principal Jewish neighbourhood was the inner city 'Ward,' or 'St. John's Shtetl.'[79] In this narrow downtown area there lived about half of all the city's Jews, a majority of the Ward's total population. A slum by early-twentieth-century standards, it attracted notoriety for its crowded conditions, filth, squalor, poverty, and inadequate sanitation. But it did serve as a reception area for most of the Jews arriving in the city in the Laurier years, and by 1912, 87 per cent of the pupils in the district's two elementary schools were Jews. Here they created 'a miniature Jewish civilization in the heart of Anglo-Saxon Toronto,' with all of 'the amenities and security of the shtetl' they had left behind. Convenient to the enormous factories erected nearby in 1910 by the T. Eaton Company, the Ward also offered cheap housing, especially in the rear tenements filled with tiny, dark rooms. As Jewish children crowded the classrooms of the Ward's Hester How Public School, as 'foreigners,' school officials worried about how to 'Canadianize' them.[80]

Poverty notwithstanding, the light of Torah shone forth. Synagogues abounded. The magnificent Goel Tzedec (the Lithuanian shul), modelled on London's Roman Catholic cathedral of Westminster, was opened on University Avenue in 1907; the Machzikei Ha Das (the Galicianer shul), a less impressive edifice, was built the year before, on Terauley Street.[81] Numerous others arose: the Shomrei Shabbos (Sabbath Observers) on Chestnut Street, four major congregations on Centre Avenue, and several *shtiblach* (prayer rooms) elsewhere in the Ward. Stores selling Jewish foods, kosher restaurants, delicatessens, candy stores, offices of steamship agents, clothing stores, sweatshops, and Jewish bookstores added to the shtetl-like ambience, whose Jewish population was already declining. The move had begun, and the centre of Toronto Jewish life re-emerged in the next decade in the Spadina area to the west.

A number of mutual benefit societies appeared in Toronto in the early 1900s, helping in their way to lessen the pain 'of alienation, loneliness and rootlessness in a strange new country,' as well as the economic problems of adjustment.[82] Membership consisted mostly of Jews who could not afford synagogue affiliation or were secularists. There were three types of mutual benefit societies: the non-partisan and ethnically mixed, the left-wing, and the *landsmanshaften*, whose members were all from the same hometown. By 1925 there were thirty such organizations in the city: ten *landsmanshaften*, eight ethnically mixed societies, and twelve branches of the left-wing Arbeiter Ring, with memberships ranging from 80 to 500.

The Pride of Israel and the Judaean Benevolent and Friendly Society assisted workers with benefits, including payments during illness (excluding those caused by immoral actions) for the member and his family, doctors' visits, and free burial in the society's own cemetery. Many also provided small loans at low interest rates. The price of this protection cost each member as much as two weeks' wages annually.

Just as important were the social and psychic benefits provided by the *landsmanshaften* through associations with fellow townsfolk who could share a reminiscence about now-rosier old times in, say, Czestochova, Miedzyrecz, Ostrow, or other Polish towns and cities, where bearded rabbis, town fools, pious women, village peasants, and cheder (Jewish school) children crowded the square on market days, collecting in front of memory's camera and calling out in Yiddish: 'Lang leben zolstu' (Long life to you); 'Don't forget us'; 'Come back for a visit, rich Canadian.' The Workmen's Circle lodges provided the cohesion of an ideology that stressed left-wing politics and Jewish cultural autonomy, a comfort both to working men in an exploitative economic climate and to Yiddish speakers who supported the rich efflorescence of that language in the early twentieth century.

To those without such protection, cash, coal, food, bedding, and cooking utensils were dispensed by the Toronto Hebrew Ladies Aid, from 1899 on; specific congregations, along with charities, offered maternity and child care and other social assistance needs.[83] And in 1909 the Jewish dispensary was set up to supply the poor with medicines and medical advice. An orphanage was established in 1910 and an old-age home in 1913.

In Winnipeg, in 1909, the Hebrew Benevolent Society, which since 1884 had provided relief for the needy, jobs for the unemployed, railway tickets for those intending to resettle elsewhere, help for the farm colonies, and assistance for other communal efforts, was reorganized as the United Hebrew Charities.[84] Conflicts over priorities between the poorer and more numerous Jews of the North End and those of the prosperous south side were resolved by an amalgamated organization called the United Relief of Winnipeg in 1914.[85] Two orphanages were established by 1917, and in 1919 the Jewish Old Folks Home of Western Canada was founded.

Orphanages housed not only those children without parents, but also those abandoned, or left with only a single parent – usually a woman – who had too many children to look after adequately. Besides these unfortunates, there were children who were so badly abused or improperly cared for by unfit parents that they had to be taken into communal care.

Criminality was not unknown, including the nefarious 'white slave' traffic. In 1920, Lillian Freiman of Ottawa voiced deep concern in an address to Hadassah members over the fate of orphaned Jewish girls in Eastern Europe who were being lured to South America 'into a future worse than death [by] these human vultures.'[86] While traffic was limited in Canada, the Baron de Hirsch cooperated with international organizations and the National Council of Jewish Women in attempting to arrest its spread. From time to time, Montreal was alleged to be the scene of some of this activity, and Vancouver a way station on the Pacific.[87] In September of 1908, the Toronto newspapers reported the arrest and deportation to the United States of two local Jews, well known to the Chicago police as brothel keepers, who were wanted on charges of white slavery.[88] And the 1915 Toronto Social Survey Commission noted that a few Jewish pimps were doing business in the Ward, probably servicing mainly a Jewish clientele, and there were allegations that most of the city's bootleggers were Jews and Italians.[89] Some prominent Montreal Jews – like Samuel Schwartz and Rabbi Nathan Gordon – aided in various campaigns to suppress corruption and vice, including rampant prostitution, indicating their progressive and reformist impulses rather than any sense of guilt over Jewish participation in such crimes.[90] In sharp contrast to notorious criminality in Buenos Aires, New York, and other American cities, no serious charges were made against the Jewish communities in Canada, although occasional allegations were voiced.[91] Perhaps this reflected the fact that Jewish criminality was never a significant public issue in this 'peaceable kingdom.'

In larger centres, juvenile delinquency attracted the attention of the Baron de Hirsch and affiliated organizations. The orphanages were sometimes used as repositories for unmanageable children. Jewish boys were being arrested for selling newspapers without municipal licences; others were in court on criminal charges. One magistrate publicly noted the fact that large numbers of Jewish youths were being tried on a variety of charges. So many of these boys were convicted and sent to a provincial correctional farm at Shawbridge that the Institute was forced to mount a special rehabilitative program for them. In Toronto, meanwhile, a Jewish branch of the Big Brother movement was organized in 1914 to respond to juvenile delinquency, which was on the rise, one contemporary later reflected, 'in undue proportion to the population' and 'becoming more serious daily.'[92]

The lives of Jewish immigrants were dominated by the search for economic survival in this new land, where, in the early twentieth century, the wheat boom, war, and recovery created enormous growth and rapid modernization. Immigrants pursued different strategies to seek a livelihood; their family biographies tell of the struggle, confusion, and anguish that were common to many. Allan Grossman, born in Toronto's 'Ward' in 1910, was the seventh child of Moses and Yetta Grossman, whose migration from Poland to Canada stretched over two years, from 1907 – when Moses came with his son Levis – until 1909, when Yetta landed with the rest of the family.[93] While waiting for his family, Moses did a succession of labouring jobs, including laying railway ties. In 1912 he became a pedlar and, like so many others, collected rags and bones for recycling by paper and glue manufacturers. Pushing their little carts along city streets crying out, 'Rags, bones and bottles. Any rags today, lady?' these pedlars became a fixture of the urban scene.

Moishe Lazarovitch migrated from Romania to Montreal in 1911 and was followed two years later by his wife and children.[94] A religious Jew who was unable to find work in his occupation of bookkeeping, Lazarovitch spent his days in study and prayer at home and in a local synagogue, seeking redemption in the slums of Montreal, 'a dark, brooding, silent man' with 'a strong sense of the unimportance of this world,' while his family struggled to make ends meet. In 1912, Louis Zuken, a pottery worker from Gorodnize, Ukraine, unemployed after leading an unsuccessful strike, arrived in Winnipeg, where he found work in a meat-packing house; two years later, he brought over his wife and their children to live in the city's North End.[95] In December of 1921, Joshua Gershman left Warsaw to join his father, who farmed near Winnipeg, only to find that his father was dead. He had left the family behind in Poland in 1913, hoping to save enough to send for his wife and children.[96]

Kalman and Yetta Klein reached Montreal in the summer of 1910 with three children, their five other offspring having preceded them to North America.[97] Formerly a pedlar in pottery items, Kalman found work as a presser and laboured over hot irons for the rest of his working life in the sweatshops along St Lawrence Boulevard. Eleven years later, Morris Lewis, a leather worker, left Svisloch in Belorussia for Montreal; in a few months, he brought over his wife and their three children.[98] He got work in the clothing industry and joined the Amalgamated Clothing Workers of America (ACWA or 'The Amalgamated'), striving towards recognition of labour's dignity and the brotherhood of all workers.

The transition from Old to New World exposed – and in many instances created – certain social problems. Among the most serious was the breakup of families. While East European Jews had a very high rate of migration in family units – compared, for example, with pre-1914 Italian immigrants – many Jewish male breadwinners did immigrate ahead of wives and children. Others left their families at ports of debarkation like New York and Montreal while they sought employment elsewhere. In the process, contact was sometimes lost, through accident or neglect, or even by design, as some husbands sought to escape their responsibilities. Such desertion became so grave a problem that American Jewish charities organized the National Desertion Bureau in 1911 to track down husbands 'on the lam,' many of whom had skipped over the Canadian border.[99]

Early in 1913, New York's Industrial Removal Office (IRO) relayed to Winnipeg a message received from their St Petersburg correspondent, who was trying to locate a man who, six years before, had emigrated to Fargo, North Dakota, 'leaving his old parents in Russia. As there are now 2 years that he sends neither letters to his parents, who besides are sick and without means, we request you ... to get information ... regarding the reason for his silence and urge him to care for his old parents.'[100]

Other correspondence between Canada and the IRO illustrates the range of obstacles experienced by immigrants. One man claimed he could not help his brother and sister come to Winnipeg because he had been unemployed for some time. A husband and father who worked on a dairy farm pleaded for help in bringing his family from New York to Winnipeg, where 'he would be in a position to support them on their arrival.' Another asked for help on similar grounds, claiming that while with earnings of nine dollars a week 'he could nicely support his wife ... if they were together ... [he] is unable to contribute anything towards transportation as he has to prepare a house and some furniture for the arrival of his family.' A Montreal junk pedlar, who was a distant relative of two recent arrivals, offered to furnish them with handwagons so that they could start peddling. A Montreal Jewish official offered to bring the sick husband of a distraught woman to the city from New York only if he agreed to have a physical examination 'as you know that unless the man can stand the severe Canadian climate he will only become a burden to this community.' An official writing to the IRO from Toronto in August 1913 stated that the children of a tailor who still resided in Europe 'are not well disposed to their father and do not wish him to come' to Toronto, where they now lived.[101]

The stories of working children are especially heart-rending. A home visitor for the Baron de Hirsch reported in December 1907 on thirty-four hard-luck cases.[102] Ten-year-old Mary Vangorofsky worked as a tailor for $1.50 a week to help her widowed father support two other children. Golde Steinberg, age thirteen, assisted her mother, who worked as a washerwoman to help sustain four other children. Fannie Hofobovitz, age thirteen, earned $2.00 a week working as a tailor, while two sisters aged eighteen and fifteen made another $14.00 to assist a widowed mother and another sister. Fannie Ganofsky and a seventeen-year-old sister together earned $7.00 a week making cigarettes to provide for a widowed father and three other children. Max Kaufman, a teenaged orphan, was paid $3.00 a week as a messenger at a downtown department store. Fannie Taitelbaum, age twelve, toiled in a clothing factory earning $2.50 a week to aid her widowed shoemaker father take care of five other children. Myer Klagman earned $4.00 a week as a clothing-factory worker to finance an unemployed father and four other children. Pasa Bookman, who made paper boxes for $2.00 a week, was the sole breadwinner in her family of four, including an unemployed father. The same was true of Peritz Chedlac, age twelve, who earned $2.00 as a tailor. Most of the child operators, pressers, tailors, and workers were employed in Jewish-owned clothing firms like Hart's, Vinebergs, and Kellerts – most of them apparently did not go to school. It is clear, then, that Jewish immigration in this period was fraught with much chaos, confusion, and crushing poverty.

The immigrants came from a culture in which men and women traditionally, throughout their lives, had sharply defined gender roles in the family as well as in their economic and religious activity. But the New World social context effected some changes. With only fragmentary evidence, generalizations are risky, but, even in Europe, some Jewish women were striving for educational and economic improvement. In pre-revolutionary Russia, a girl from a traditional family, Rae Stillman, insisted on being allowed to learn to read and write Russian 'like the other [Christian] girls and be good at it.'[103] Against her parents' wishes, she learned Russian and found a job in a factory; at age seventeen, she married her boyfriend and left her family for Canada. Fanny Sky recalled that her mother, the daughter of a well-off family, had a good education and wrote letters for people in her town, while Rose Wohlgelertner attended a business academy in her native Lvov. Bella Isaac graduated from the gymnasium in Marburg, Germany, and Elizabeth Kestler from a junior high school in Zilina, Slovakia. There was apparently a significant number of exceptions to the general rule that girls were taught only domestic skills to prepare them for life as 'a good wife, able to raise her children, and also [to] help her husband whenever she could. Nobody had a special occupation. They were just housewives.' Or, as Betty Mazerkoff succinctly remembered: 'Housewives were different, they didn't expect much out of life.' Whether in Eastern Europe or in Canada, such was indeed the pattern for most women: endless drudgery in the home, numerous pregnancies, and subordination to males in the home, synagogue, and society.

But this 'world of our mothers' began to change in Canada. Here, as Paula Draper and Janice Karlinsky point out, 'the relative wealth and high degree of acculturation of Jews from western Europe allowed for rapid adjustment to New World feminine ambitions, just as it reinforced their fear of any threat to their integration into Canadian life.'[104] The first generation of Jewish mid-nineteenth-century women immigrants from Central Europe were influenced by social reform ideas to try to emancipate themselves, and while their eastern European sisters who reached Canada a generation later formed the Hadassah organization in 1917 for the welfare of women and children in Palestine, the Jewish women arriving after 1900 were often workers in factories. Because of their awkwardness with the English language, they 'shied away from joining English-speaking groups like Hadassah.' Their class culture inclined them to socialist organizations, like the Labour Zionists, the Social Democratic Party, and the Bundist Workmen's Circle. Despite barriers put up against them by the Jewish unions and their Jewish co-workers, 'Jewish women played an important part within the Jewish labour movement ... [with] militancy and class consciousness ...'[105] In Winnipeg radically inclined women – some of them well-versed in European secular culture – organized Muter Farein, mothers' clubs to bolster efforts of the Peretz Shule and Arbeiter Ring and *layenkrayzn* (reading circles) to advance their self-education.[106] Conditions in North America were impacting on segments of Jewish society and changing the role of women within the community.

The enlargement of the Canadian Jewish community during the years between 1900 and 1920 brought into play both realities transferred from Eastern Europe and particular social imperatives in the contemporary Dominion of Canada. A culture of ancient lineage that had long been subjected to the social and political forces of the Pale of Settlement came into a nation whose promise was as yet unfulfilled. The adjustment of these immigrants, and the routes by which they sought accommodation to their new environment – their survival strategies – demonstrate the resulting interaction between their imported cultural context and the raw realities of a nation whose economic destiny was still publicly defined in terms of staple production, and whose identity was obscured by unreconciled national dualities. In the clothing industry, traditional Jewish occupations like tailoring provided an entrée and a springboard for Jewish-led trade unions, a kind of immigrant success story in which – to a great extent – Europe imposed itself on Canada. The modest success of Jewish farm settlements demonstrates, conversely, that, in the short run, at least, this fragment of the European context could not easily be transplanted to the new environment.

5 'Corner of Pain and Anguish'

Jewish immigrants would not escape antisemitism, although animosity towards Jews was sometimes indistinguishable from a general disdain for immigrants. Preceding the First World War, Jews were unwelcome settlers, but so were other ethnic groups, on the grounds of their racial 'inferiority,' dress, or habits.[1] The book by Methodist minister and Social Gospeller J.S. Woodsworth, *Strangers within Our Gates*, echoed the racism typical of the time, although he regarded Jews as more adaptable, assimilable, and culturally suitable than most other non-British immigrants. The Winnipeg General Strike of 1919 witnessed more anti-foreign than specifically anti-Jewish sentiment, despite the fact that Jewish support for the strike probably equalled that of the East Europeans, and Abraham Heaps – an English Jew – was among its major leaders.

Jews' entry into the country was comparatively easy before 1914. Riots and bloodshed against Orientals occurred on the West Coast, but nothing comparable happened to Jews.[2] The latter, in fact, may have enjoyed certain advantages. After all, the community had established an evident economic, social, and political presence and had a steadily rising population from only 6,501 in 1891, to 74,564 in 1911. Also, the Canadian response to Jewish sufferings (at various times during the late nineteenth century) had been empathetic and generous. Jewish organizations had, with varying success, interceded with political authorities to facilitate immigration and settlement. By 1917, Canadian Jewry was present politically. Sam Jacobs from Montreal was a member of Parliament, and there were aldermen in Montreal and Toronto. A small number of wealthy Jews with connections lobbied effectively on behalf of their community; most other ethnic communities had no such power. Hence, during this period, antisemitism was part and parcel of the antipathy for foreigners.

Goldwin Smith, a leading intellectual in the late nineteenth century, was Canada's best-known Jew-hater. Although he was otherwise recognized as a liberal spirit, Smith's virulent antisemitism was notorious throughout the English-speaking world. His tirades included claims that the cause of the Boer War was Britain's demand that the franchise be extended to 'the Jews and gamblers of Johannesburg'; that Jews were gaining control over the world's press and influencing public opinion; that 'the Jews have one code of ethics for themselves, another for the Gentile'; that Disraeli was a 'contemptible trickster and adventurer, who could not help himself because he was a Jew. Jews are no good anyhow'; that 'the Jew is a Russophobe'; and so on.[3]

Smith had embraced antisemitic views since the late 1870s, expressing them often in print with force, conviction, and skill. These articles appeared in highly regarded journals, such as the *Nineteenth Century*, the *Contemporary Review*, and the *Independent*, as well as in his own Toronto papers, the *Bystander*, the *Week*, and the *Weekly Sun*. While he had eclectic interests (and several other long-standing hatreds), antisemitism was a major preoccupation.[4] In Smith's mind, the very presence of Jews in society posed serious problems that required urgent resolution. Their removal from Europe, he asserted ominously in 1878, would take away a 'danger from Western civilization.' And he prophesied that unless Jews turned to 'the grand remedy' of assimilation, 'there is further trouble in store ... collisions which no philanthropic lecturing will avert ... [the Jews'] end will come.'

While the origins of Smith's antisemitism are obscure, some of his diatribes reflect attitudes prevalent in early-nineteenth-century England.[5] By the late 1870s, Smith believed that Judaism endangered Western civilization itself. Early in 1878, he described Judaism and the Jews as 'another element originally Eastern [which] has, in the course of these events, made us sensible of its presence in the West.'[6] During the debate over possible British intervention in the Turkish-Bulgarian war, in which Jewish financial interests were allegedly involved, he contended that 'for the first time perhaps Europe has had occasion to note the political position and tendencies of Judaism ... In fact, had England been drawn into this conflict it would have been in some measure a Jewish war, a war waged with British blood to uphold the objects of Jewish sympathy, or to avenge Jewish wrongs.' The nations of Europe 'have acted on the supposition that by extending the principle of religious liberty they could make a Jew a citizen, as by the same policy citizens have been made of ordinary Nonconformists,' but they were in error. Jewish monotheism was 'unreal' because the Jewish God 'is not the Father of all, but the deity of His chosen race.' After 'the nobler part of the Jewish nation, the real heirs of David and the Prophets, heard the Gospel, and became the founders of a human religion: the less nobler part ... rejected Humanity, and ... fell back into a narrower and harder tribalism than before ... bereft of the softening, elevating, and hallowing influences which ... link patriotism with the service of mankind.'

Smith contended that Jews could not be loyal citizens because their allegiance was to their own people, 'the religion being identified with the race, as is the case in the whole group of primeval and tribal religions, of which Judaism is a survival. A Jew is not an Englishman or Frenchman holding particular tenets: He is a Jew, with a special deity for his own race. The rest of mankind are to him not merely people holding a different creed, but aliens in blood.'[7] Reflecting influences from contemporary racial antisemitism, he asserted that 'the secret of Lord Beaconsfield's life lies in his blood.'[8]

Jews were 'Christ-killers' and 'plutopolitans.' They were guilty of 'wealthworship, stock-jobbing, or any acts by which wealth is appropriated without honest labour.' Smith was echoing the latest wave of antisemitism in Central and Western Europe. From Canada, with no public perception of a 'Jewish problem,' he joined the international brotherhood of antisemitic propagandists, while actively soliciting the latest fashionable new anti-Jewish ideas.[9] He absorbed and propagated these notions throughout Britain, the United States, and Canada in potent antisemitic prose, challenging the right of the Jewish people to survive as a distinct cultural group. This was antisemitism of the most fundamental and dangerous kind.

Smith alleged Jewish control over the press, thus explaining why the truth could not reach the public. 'What organs can they not command,' he asked rhetorically in July 1883, when dealing with Jewish claims of persecution in Europe. In July 1897 he wrote in the *Weekly Sun* that 'the Jews control the European press. They are sometimes found behind even Christian religious journals.'[10] His claims were bolstered by information from his London contact, Joseph Laister, which Smith subsequently retailed to his readers. 'Is there such a thing as a paper or periodical which is not controlled by Jews or afraid to print the truth ... about them?' Smith lamented to a friend in May 1906. 'They seem to be behind the press everywhere, or at least be able to muzzle it.'

The Talmud, the great storehouse of Jewish law and commentary, held for Smith, as for many antisemites, an enormous fascination. The

Talmud and 'Talmud Jews' were frequently derided, and he repeated old myths about biblical Judaism, which he regarded as legitimate, and Talmudic Judaism, which he excoriated as evil.[11] In a lengthy article for the *Nineteenth Century* of November 1882, he wrote:

> Talmudism is the matter from which the spirit has soared away, the lees from which the wine has been drawn off ... It is a recoil from the moral liberty of the Gospel in a legalism which buries conscience under a mountain of formality, ceremony and casuistry ... It is a recoil ... to a religious philosophy which ... makes the chief end of man consist in the pursuit of wealth, as the means of worldly enjoyment.

Smith argued that Jews would be acceptable only if they assimilated. Yet, in demanding the eradication of Judaism, he was really calling for an anti-Jewish crusade.

Smith repeated canards current among Russian antisemites that Jews lacked 'civic honesty,' exploited their female servants sexually, corrupted the Russian peasants with drink, abused Christian burgesses, raised prices of food unjustly, mixed vodka with impure substances, traded on the Christian Sabbath and holidays, and put peasants into debt.[12] He referred to 'facts' such as 'the fact that the Oriental character, in its leading features, is inferior to the European ... race.' Jews who wished to remain fully Jewish should emigrate to Palestine; however, 'those who refuse to mingle with humanity must take the consequences of their refusal. They cannot expect to enjoy at once the pride of exclusiveness, and the sympathies of brotherhood.' In a piece for the *Weekly Sun* in July 1897, he wrote: 'The discovery of the Ten Lost Tribes is another religious fancy of which we ought to have heard the last. "I am very much out of funds," was the reply of one who had been asked to subscribe for that object, "and I really cannot afford at present to give any thing to your association for finding the Ten Tribes, but if you have an association for losing the Two Tribes, poor as I am, I will try to contribute."'

To Smith the major threat was Jewish financial power: 'Their usurious oppression of the people' would have to be given up before they could be absorbed into their host societies.[13] Fearing the effects of public sympathy because of the Russian atrocities, he gave the consular reports large play in Britain and Canada, claiming that Jewish losses 'were in most cases exaggerated, and in some to an extravagant extent.' Blaming the victims, he said, the troubles started over 'bitterness produced by the exactions of the Jew, envy of his wealth, jealousy of his ascendancy, combined in the lowest of the mob with the love of plunder.' He repeated these allegations when, in 1907, anti-Jewish pogroms broke out in Romania: 'Any race, let its religion and its historical record be what they might, which did what the Jews have done would have provoked the same antipathies with the same deplorable results.'

Jews had invited antisemitism by persecuting others. 'To pronounce the antipathy to the Jews utterly groundless is in fact to frame an indictment against humanity.' Had not Tacitus and Juvenal written about Jew-hatred in the ancient world, and did not Gibbon find evidence of it in his research? In medieval times, Smith averred, Jews 'provoked the hatred of the people by acting as the regular and recognized instrument of royal extortion';[14] they avoided military service; they bought land and thereby undermined the feudal system; they attacked Christian religious processions; they lent money at high interest; they sympathized with and supported the forces of Islam, notably in medieval Spain; they showed themselves to be intolerant of religious dissenters in their own ranks, like Spinoza and Acosta. Jews such as Disraeli and the merchants of Johannesburg fostered war for their own financial gain. In Russia, Jews were 'eating into the core of her Muscovite nationality,' while in Germany they 'lie in wait for the failing Bauer,' and in the southern United States 'a swarm of Jews' had engaged in 'an unlawful trade with the simple negroes ... [thus] driving out of business many of the old retailers.'

It is impossible to estimate Smith's influence on public opinion or policy. Outside of the Jewish community, there appears to have been little reaction, although in a review of Smith's *Essays on Questions of the Day*, George Monro Grant, principal of Queen's University, wrote that Smith tended to blame the victims for the rise of antisemitism: 'The fault is thrown wholly upon the Jews and not upon those who treat them with brutal violence.'[15] While Smith's views did not have any discernible influence on immigration policy during his life, his disparagements may have contributed to the general tensions over immigrant issues during the 1890s and 1900s. However, his sporadic writings lacked fervour in criticism of existing policies. 'What is the use of excluding the Chinaman when we freely admit the Russian Jew?' he asked despondently in July 1897. Ten years later, he lamented: 'we have been welcoming a crowd of ... Russian and Polish Jews, the least desirable of all possible elements of population.' Nor did Smith, a prolific writer of letters to prime ministers Sir John A. Macdonald and Sir Wilfrid Laurier, even raise this question with them.

Still, Smith's fulminations challenged the right to live as Jews in civil society. He paid for professional assistance on this subject, and continued his writings for over thirty years. He channelled some of the worst forms of European antisemitism to North America and personally endorsed these prejudices.[16] He declaimed his views widely, and his influence on at least one young student at the University of Toronto in the 1890s was profound. Writing in his diary in February of 1946 about the threat of Communism, Prime Minister William Lyon Mackenzie King confided: 'I recall Goldwin Smith feeling so strongly about the Jews ... that they were poison in the veins of a community ... in a large percentage of the race there are tendencies and trends which are dangerous indeed.'[17]

Antisemitism was widespread in the late nineteenth and early twentieth century. Politicians alluded to unscrupulous business practices of Jews, as did the Honourable John Thompson in Antigonish in December 1878, when he said that Nova Scotia 'was getting into the hands of the "Jews and shavers of [Halifax's] Hollis Street."'[18] Phyllis Senese, in her study of the reaction to the Dreyfus case in the western Canadian press, discovered 'that a habitual, unthinking, unarticulated, but very real antisemitism was for many [Western Canadians] a part of their way of thinking.' There were distinctly antisemitic overtones both to a riot in early August 1903 at Inverness, Nova Scotia, and in the smashing up of a Jewish-owned liquor store at Londonderry, in June 1904.

In 1904 the Lord's Day Alliance, an organization devoted 'to establishing what they called the "English Sunday" as an invented Canadian tradition,' viciously attacked Orthodox Jews who had complained about Sunday observance laws.[19] Jews, one of the organization's pamphlets contended, 'had sought out our land FOR THEIR OWN GOOD' and should conform to Canada's 'civil customs.' Jews were among the groups who, in the mind of Reverend S.D. Chown, head of the Canadian Methodist Church in the early 1900s, were parasites in the national bloodstream. Clara Brett Martin, Canada's first woman lawyer, in a letter in March 1915 to the Ontario attorney general, attacked alleged Jewish real-estate malpractises and recommended amendments to the Registry Act 'to prevent this scandalous work of foreigners.' As late as 1920, Dr C.K. Clarke, the Dominion's leading psychiatrist, argued strenuously against allowing the immigration of refugee Jewish children from the Ukrainian famine on the grounds that they 'belong to a *very neurotic race,* and while many of them are of unusual ability, yet a certain proportion prove to be mental defectives.' Leading Toronto Presbyterian Reverend John Chisholm pointed out that 'Jews have much to do with commercialized vice.'[20]

The fact that these sentiments were so often directed against Jews does suggest a well of deep antipathies towards them. In 1913, Halifax was the scene of an interesting controversy over the Jewish method of slaughtering cattle. A police court magistrate had found an individual, who claimed to be a rabbi and had slaughtered a heifer according to the Jewish mode, guilty of cruelty to an animal, implying that Jewish practices were inhumane.[21] An eloquent response to these charges published in the *Halifax Herald*, and in other Canadian newspapers, reflected increasing Jewish sensitivity to such vicious attacks.

In his 1909 novel, *The Foreigner*, the popular Canadian writer Ralph Connor depicted the Jew as the 'middle-man acting dishonestly as interpreters and business agents for less educated immigrants,' and as a powerful metaphor for greed, conniving, immorality, and oppression – the very antithesis of individual freedom, democracy, and Christian decency.[22]

Universities were rife with antisemitism. Assertions of Christian supremacy surfaced during the 1912 controversy at Queen's over the new provincial act which defined the constitution of the university. One member of the board of trustees insisted that a phrase be added affirming that 'the University shall continue distinctively Christian and the trustees shall satisfy themselves of the Christian character of those appointed to the teaching staff.'[23] In spite of some strong Jewish protest, this provision was nevertheless included in the act. Seven years later, a serious antisemitic incident arose as a result of remarks by the new principal of Queen's, Dr R. Bruce Taylor, at a luncheon meeting of the newly formed association of the university's Montreal alumni. Dr Taylor congratulated himself 'that Queen's unlike McGill was not situated in a great centre of population (mostly Jews) and of wealth (mostly held by Jews).' When challenged for an explanation, Dr Taylor warmed to his subject. 'He was rather proud of the fact that there were only five Jews at Queen's,' recalled one member of his audience. 'The presence of many Jews tended to lower the tone of Canadian Universities,' Taylor continued, and he claimed to have been told by Dean Moyse of McGill that he 'deplored the presence of so many Russian Jews in his English classes – These Jews he said, when they came to him, were not even conversant with Shakespeare':

> Speaking frankly, and among ourselves, we should do our best to keep their numbers [the Jews] from increasing in our Universities. No wonder

they did so well in school, they stayed at home and studied when their place was at the front [during the war].

Protesting to the chancellor, one Queen's graduate pointed out that of the four Jews at Queen's in 1914, two had enlisted immediately, and asked whether Jews could continue to attend that university. The chancellor replied lamely that 'Principal Taylor's remarks were, I think, phrased in such a way as to be misunderstood and did not convey his meaning.'

A few years earlier, Lewis Namier's application for a lectureship at the University of Toronto had been turned down despite the opinion of his Oxford tutor, who wrote: 'I started on him with the normal prejudice about Jews, but now I can not speak too highly of him.'[24] Namier was regarded by all as a brilliant prospect, but the Toronto professors who interviewed him felt, as Professor James Mavor put it, 'the major drawback about [Namier] evidently is that he has the misfortune to have the Jewish characteristic of indistinct articulation strongly developed.' A Board member wrote: 'nor do I like the choice of a Polish Jew as an interpreter of history ... who by his broken accent constantly proclaims it.' Still, he thought, Namier was 'a man whose brilliance would bring [the university] much honor.'[25] Yet even a Jew with impeccable articulation, Ontario-born Abraham I. Willinsky, struggled to find an internship at a local hospital when he graduated from the University of Toronto medical school in 1908.[26] At McGill, steps were taken to reduce the number of Jews. While they constituted 25 per cent of arts students, 15 per cent of medical students, and 40 per cent of law students in 1920, university officials imposed stiff quotas that would severely reduce those percentages during the interwar years.

Meanwhile, the Jewish presence in Quebec elicited a French-Canadian response, marked by the desecration of the Jewish cemetery in Trois-Rivières and the re-emergence of the school question in 1901, local Sunday closing legislation in 1904, and the Plamondon libel of 1910. The Jews of Montreal felt besieged on all fronts, and their reactions to these threats impacted significantly on the social politics of the community. Jew and non-Jews met, in the Montreal Board of Trade and, inevitably, in business, schools, university, and the professions. And while Jews were almost exclusively part of the anglophone community, both in business and education in the Protestant system, they had some contact with French Canadians; a few attended the law school at Université Laval à Montréal or the medical school at the Université de Montréal. In a generally tolerant atmosphere, efforts to convert the Jews by both Protestant and Catholic organizations were a constant reminder that their religion was viewed with disdain.

The Presbyterians were particularly zealous in this endeavour. Back in the mid-nineteenth century, they had sent a Jewish convert to preach in Palestine, and in the 1890s they had set up conversion missions in both Toronto and Montreal.[27] The Toronto Presbytery reactivated its missionary efforts in 1907, led by a former rabbinical student, Shabbatai Benjamin Rohold, whose efforts aroused powerful opposition in the local Jewish community. Rohold nevertheless insisted that his 'unconditional, whole-hearted, sincere love without interest' had paid off. In 1910 he reported that large numbers of Toronto's poor Jews had taken advantage of his Christian charity: 8,234 had visited his Terauley Street reading room, 292 had enrolled in English-language classes, 58 in sewing classes, and 3,142 had been treated in the dispensary. Still, although 9,000 Christian tracts had been distributed, only seventeen Jews had converted. Rohold soldiered on, however, until in 1921 he departed Toronto for Palestine, still contending that he had planted the seeds of Christian beliefs among many more Jews who feared to openly profess them.

The situation in Quebec changed drastically towards the end of the nineteenth century. By 1901, Jews had become the largest single ethnic group in the province after French, British, and Native Canadians.[28] Some 6,000 of the Jews were of Russian origin, mostly poor, and heavily concentrated in the central core of downtown Montreal. The Catholic Church, strongly ultramontane in spirit and drawing inspiration from Rome and France, began to perceive the Jews as even more dangerous aliens than before. Accused of being allied with the anti-clericals, socialists, and Freemasons, they were seen as threats to the preservation of a Catholic Quebec, while some young nationalists viewed them, along with the English, as an entirely foreign and dangerously disruptive element. The publication in 1886 of Édouard Drumont's virulently antisemitic book *La France juive* was warmly received by part of the French-Canadian press,[29] and among Quebec church leaders and laymen who, like Drumont, believed that modern civilization, 'which had impoverished and degraded man and robbed life of its poetry and truth,' held out special dangers for the survival of French-Canadian civilization. As the 'spearhead' of modern capitalism, the Jews were perceived by some as exploiters and destroyers of the purity and sacredness of Quebec's rural way of life. Prominent Montreal journalist and labour activist Jules Helbronner (who had little to do with the Jewish community) was nevertheless attacked for his Jewish heritage, which he stoutly defended in numerous libel suits.[30]

Leading intellectual and newspaper editor Henri Bourassa had only contempt for the poor ghetto dwellers, and in his remarks to the Commons on the proposed Lord's Day legislation in 1906, he displayed utter disregard for the bill's effect on observant Jews.[31] He objected to provisions of the bill which would exempt Jews. These were added, he charged, 'in order to pander to the Jewish vote.' Citing the views of Goldwin Smith, he stated that Jews 'are the least remunerative class [of immigrants] that we can get – that class which sucks the most from other people and gives back the least ... they are the most undesirable class that can be brought into the country.' To Bourassa, Jews were 'vampires on the community instead of being contributors to the general welfare of the people' and are 'detrimental to the public welfare.' According to historian Pierre Anctil: 'the founder of *Le Devoir* believed it was necessary to construct a coherent and striking response to this massive and unprecedented presence of immigrants in a society born, in practice and in law, from the encounter of two competing colonial empires on a new continent.'

But aside from an article critical of Clarence de Sola (reported in the *Jewish Times* of September 1910) in which it was suggested that 'Jews had no place in the high offices of a Christian society,' in Bourassa's newspaper, *Le Devoir*, there were no editorial attacks on Jews. There were, however, numerous impartial reports before 1920 on many aspects of Jewish communal activity. Indeed, one lengthy editorial in April of 1914 – possibly written by Bourassa himself – argued constructively that to relieve tensions between the Montreal Jewish community and the Protestant school commission, Jews should be able to set up their own school system: 'Le moyen de profiter du principe général de liberté qui est à la base de notre loi.' His co-editor, Armand Lavergne, an MP and a nationalist, was sympathetic to Jews and during the 1906 debate said: 'we should treat them as Canadians ... I should [not] want another minority to be deprived of what they have a right to do.' One of several articles in *Le Devoir* by columnist Orner Héroux was entitled 'L'exemple des Juifs,' a laudatory account of the Montreal Hebrew Free Loan Association; 'la chose ne vaudrait-elle pas la peine d'être étudiée par les chrétiens?' Héroux asked. A few years later, *Le Devoir* published a translation of a *Keneder Adler* article lauding the newspaper *Le Pays*, which had battled vigorously and for many years against antisemitism in Quebec. In March of 1919, *Le Devoir* reported the proceedings in Montreal of the Canadian Jewish Congress. Thus, throughout its first decade of existence, *Le Devoir* – the premier journal of French Canada's rising spirit of nationalism – was not spreading antisemitism among its readers.

However, after 1900, the number of threats to Jews increased within Quebec. The desecration of the Jewish cemetery in Trois-Rivières by the municipality, which had been judicially sanctioned to expropriate the property – and the removal of bodies and reinterment without religious services – was a reminder of the vulnerability of Jews in an insensitive, if not hostile, environment.[32]

The re-emergence of the school question in Quebec (which since Confederation had confessional schools that mandated separate Protestant and Catholic systems) not only bedevilled Jewish-Protestant relations for the next thirty years, but caused serious divisions among Jews themselves. In 1894 the Protestant school board of Montreal had accepted responsibility for providing elementary schooling for the city's Jewish pupils in return for school taxes on property owned by Jews, and had agreed to pay a salary of $800 annually to a teacher who would provide religious and Hebrew-language instruction to the Jewish pupils. The Protestants had also agreed to support the 'Baron de Hirsch' school in providing early elementary schooling for immigrant Jewish children unable to cope with English instruction. However, by 1900 the Protestants faced serious financial difficulties. The proceeds from Jewish school taxes and fees did not meet all the costs. In the late 1890s, as Jewish immigration increased, the Protestant board considered reactivating the whole issue. In the 1900–1 school year, the number of Jewish pupils reached 1,153. According to the board, they cost $34,351.35 to educate, while revenue from Jewish school taxes and fees was $11,016.24.[33] There was a loss of over $20 on every student. To make their point, the board served notice that Jewish pupils would not be eligible for prizes and scholarships awarded for academic achievement.

In 1901, Jacob Pinsler – a ten-year-old pupil at Dufferin School, in the heart of the Jewish quarter – was accordingly refused a prize for free tuition which he had won with an average of 83 per cent.[34] Pinsler's case became a cause célèbre around which this whole issue was publicly debated. It was clear to all concerned that the quarrel involved the government of Quebec as well. While the Jews had been semi-officially part of the Protestant community, for educational purposes, since 1894, this was not recognized by the government when it divided up the provincial education grant, or by the City of Montreal in its allocation of proceeds from the Neutral Panel, into which school taxes paid by corporations were deposited. Hence, the Protestant schools derived no funding for their Jewish pupils from these substantial sources. By forcing the issue of Jewish rights in the schools, the Protestant board hoped to rectify this pressing financial question. All Jewish children who applied were taken into the Protestant schools and were not penalized for refusing religious instruction. However, they were, in subtle ways, made to feel unwelcome, and Jewish teachers were not employed.

So the Protestant school commissioners were unapologetic. The Jews simply did not fit into either of the established school systems. They had no clear claim upon either the Protestant or the Catholic board to educate their children, unless they were property owners and assigned their school taxes appropriately. (Protestants, on the other hand, were guaranteed education whether their families paid taxes or not.) As the Protestant board declared in 1901:

> A resident of the Jewish religion who, although an owner of real estate, has not adopted as to his school tax, or who does not own real estate, cannot claim as of right to have his children admitted to the public schools ... such admission is given by grace and subject to whatever conditions the commissioners choose to impose, inclusive of non-eligibility for the scholarship in question.[35]

This relegated all Jews in Quebec to second-class citizenship, and the Jewish leadership challenged the Protestant commissioners in the courts. But they lost. In his reluctant judgment against Jacob Pinsler in 1903, Justice Davidson urged the lawmakers to change the existing situation.[36] The judicial decision in the Pinsler case threatened both segments of the community: the downtowners because their children might be denied places in the schools, and the uptowners because of the implication of incomplete civil rights of Jews. Already alarmed by local reaction to the Dreyfus affair and by the desecration of the Trois-Rivières cemetery, both elements were determined to insist on full social equality. The uptown Jews, with their legal advisers, skills in English, and comparative wealth, immediately became the spokesmen of the action. They were supported by vocal demonstrations and protests from downtown, and a formidable (if temporary) force was created.

At a mass meeting on the crisis in February 1903, a committee headed by Maxwell Goldstein, a lawyer prominent in Montreal Jewish affairs, was appointed to discuss the entire school question with the Protestant board. Goldstein was well connected both outside and within the Jewish community. In a series of meetings with the board, he reached an agreement providing that the Jewish population would be included within the Protestant school system,[37] which, while 'distinctly Protestant, and therefore Christian,' would allow a conscience clause protecting the religious convictions of Jewish scholars. Accordingly, in the 1903 provincial act[38] that legalized this agreement, all Jewish proprietors would pay school taxes to the Protestant board, and Jews would be counted as Protestants in the per capita allocation of school taxes from the Neutral Panel and from legislative grants. The act also provided that 'the children of persons professing the Jewish religion shall have the same right to be educated in the public schools of the province as the Protestant children, and shall be treated in the same manner as Protestants for all school purposes.' A conscience clause which provided that 'no pupil of the Jewish religion can, however, be compelled to read or study any religious or devotional books or to take part in any religious exercises or devotions' meant that the school system would retain its exclusively Protestant orientation.

Subsequent attempts by the Montreal Jewish community to gain equality in the school system, through election to the Protestant school board and the hiring of Jewish teachers, fell afoul of the board's insistence – easily defended in law – that their schools remain 'Christian and Protestant.'[39] Eligibility for election to this body seemed logical and desirable, but from the standpoint of the Protestant board, such an election would undermine the character of their school system.

By 1909 the Jewish student component was more than one-third of the total Protestant school enrolment, and immigration numbers were increasing. Even Jewish leaders expressed concern. In an interview published in Britain's *Jewish Chronicle*, and reprinted in Montreal's *Jewish Times*, Maxwell Goldstein explained that among the 'problems' facing Canadian Jewry was the difficulty posed by an influx of 'foreign Jews' who formed ghettos and fostered prejudice among the French Canadians[40] – a curiously one-sided idea coming from a community leader. 'These foreign Jews,' Goldstein continued, 'form their own synagogues ... and have had the temerity to select their own chief rabbi [probably a reference to Rabbi Simon Glazer, known as "the people's rabbi"] whom the uptown Jews refused to recognize.' These immigrants, he warned, had to be persuaded to 'recognize their duties to the community'; the challenge lay in assimilating the newcomers, and Goldstein even supported a temporary restriction in immigration until this had been achieved. Thus the pain and anguish of East European Jewry counted for less, in his view, than the embarrassment he and his fellow West Enders felt when these rather bedraggled immigrants arrived at the Montreal docks and proceeded up St Lawrence Street to take their precarious place in the crowded Jewish quarter. While the West Enders were striving for dignity, propriety, and acceptance, the continuing arrival of large numbers of their co-religionists, unkempt and poor, radicals, nationalists, or Orthodox, speaking a Yiddish whose sharp accents the uptowners were trying hard to erase from their own speech, interfered with reaching that goal.

The *Jewish Times*, mirroring the views of anglophile Jews like Goldstein, editorialized in April 1905 that sectarian education was 'entirely out of harmony with the times and genius of democracy.'[41] But for the Protestants to yield on the religious character of their educational system, in the sectarian atmosphere of Quebec, would drastically weaken the coherence and survival of the whole minority Protestant community. The Protestant board therefore felt justified in resisting these changes. After all, the Jews were newcomers to the scene; if they were unwilling to accept the existing system, perhaps they should set up their own. Certainly the prospect of employing Jewish teachers in the schools of the existing sectarian system was totally unacceptable.

The struggle was bound to become bitter and protracted, with both sides equally determined. Jewish children were virtually the majority in some downtown schools, and no Jewish teachers were hired. This meant a complete absence of moral instruction in school, as Protestant teachers were debarred by the 1903 law from teaching religion to Jewish pupils, who could excuse themselves from these classes under the 'conscience clause.' Equally serious was the limitation on employment opportunities for qualified Jewish teachers. A letter headlined 'No Jewish Teachers Need Apply' to the *Jewish Times* in January 1910 angrily asserted that 'until something is done by ... the set of so-called leaders who claim to represent public Jewish opinion ... to endeavour to rectify the glaring abuse, our self constituted leaders cannot hope to have the confidence of the rank and file of Montreal Jewry.'[42] Even though the Protestant board decided in June 1913 to permit the hiring of Jewish teachers, very few of them were employed, and the issue continued to fester.

For all the commotion over education and civil rights, the most blatant threats to the Jews in Montreal were the attacks on their religion and on their persons. Such assaults served to remind them of the familiar kind of antisemitism in Eastern Europe. Catholic clergymen frequently reviled Jews, as did journalists and intellectuals – one declared at a meeting in Trois-Rivières that the Jews were a tragedy for Canada[43] – and occasional dust-ups occurred in the streets. While Quebec at its worst was never comparable to the pogroms of Eastern Europe, many immigrant Jews were sometimes reminded of their old hometowns in the Jew-baiting on the streets, and the small-scale riots down in the Jewish quarter, when gangs of ruffians came in looking for action – and found it. During one such punch-up in late August of 1909, a running battle between French Canadians and Jews raged up and down St Lawrence Boulevard (the Main) for several hours before police were able to separate the combatants – and arrested only Jews. At times, Jewish pedlars going through the tough Point-St-Charles section were beaten up and robbed by local hooligans.

Borrowing from his experience in Europe, where self-defence groups sometimes succeeded in fighting off pogromchiks, an activist named Rosenberger organized a large 'vigilance committee' to protect Jewish lives, honour, and property. This initiative attracted criticism from the *Jewish Times* and from Lyon Cohen (living safely in upper Westmount), who argued that such tactics would only provoke more incidents, and who preferred instead to rely on the police for protection.[44] But this potential for anti-Jewish violence added a certain degree of anxiety to downtown Jewish life in Montreal.

Ultimately, however, the most sinister threat was the open support by some segments of the Quebec Catholic community to the most obscene medieval myths and superstitions about Jews. A tide of vicious antisemitic propaganda pervaded many of Quebec's nationalist and clerical newspapers. Antisemitic articles had appeared in several minor French-Canadian newspapers since the early 1900s.[45] A major complaint was the increasing Jewish purchases of houses and businesses in the areas where both communities lived side by side: in the Quebec City suburb of St-Roch and in Montreal's St-Laurent and St-Louis quarters, especially on St Lawrence Boulevard and on Ste-Catherine and Ontario streets. After 1910, much of this hate literature circulated in the clubs of the newly organized Association Canadienne de la Jeunesse Catholique, an association of French-Canadian youth dedicated to nationalist and religious action.

Some of this literature was pretty virulent stuff. In the summer of 1909, *La Libre Parole* described Jewish and Syrian pedlars as 'une épidemie ... qui passent par les paroisses ...'[46] In October the same newspaper featured an article with the headline 'La Gangrene Juive,' in which 'Youpins' – a contemptuous reference to Jews – were spreading 'dans notre bonne ville de Québec.' The Quebec suburb of St-Roch was becoming especially 'gangrené,' and within ten years, *La Libre Parole* predicted 'la plus grande partie de St. Roch sera juive.' Readers were implored to boycott these 'youpins' and to buy what they needed instead from their own kind. These writings referred to French-Canadian young women, 'petites Canadiennes,' as being somehow especially susceptible to the blandishments of Jewish pedlars, a suggestion, perhaps, of dangers which could not be discussed openly. 'La Juiverie à Montréal. Elle S'Impose de Jour en Jour,' announced a minor headline in one December 1909 issue of *La Libre Parole* concerning Montreal Jews getting their names on voters lists, while other entries such as 'La Race Juive' and 'La Presse et les Juifs' seem intended to arouse fears of the spread of a 'Jewish peril' and Jewish control of the American press. Soon *La Libre Parole* was including Jews among the other enemies of French Canada, the Freemasons and the Orangemen, but the descriptions of Jews as parasites and filthy vermin, as the forces behind every villainy and scandal, and as 'seducing' girls into buying things they don't need, were apparently intended to invoke powerful emotions. In its 1910 New Year's Day issue, *La Libre Parole*'s editors published a veritable cornucopia of antisemitic writings. One writer demanded that readers 'mettre les Juifs au ban de la société,' then turn the Jews loose, apply the whip ('allons donc! fouetter les Juifs'), and drive them out of Quebec. The same issue contained a lengthy denunciation of 'Jewish trusts,' a report on alleged Jewish brothel-keepers in Toronto, and a joke about Jews.

Jews were among French Canada's most serious enemies, along with freemasonry, alcohol, cigarettes, novels, and magazines – and candy stores.[47] And what was needed were 'des ligues anti semites' to keep out Jews who were 'plus sale que ces parasites,' the leaders of revolutionary movements, strikers, and Freemasons. One of the reasons for supporting the nascent Caisses Populaires movement was the need in Quebec to stop 'la coopération universelle de la juiverie pour étrangler [strangle] le peuple chrétien.'

While not a major newspaper, *La Libre Parole* and another antisemitic journal, *L'Action sociale* (which printed virulent attacks on Jews in 1910), nevertheless can be assumed to have had some effect on readers. Moreover, the existence of such publications was an indication of an antisemitic movement – however limited its support – in Quebec.

On 30 March 1910, Quebec City notary Joseph Édouard Plamondon delivered a lecture at Jeunesse Catholique which contained some of the foulest lies about Judaism, including the old calumny of ritual murder. Plamondon's charges added to the store of antisemitic incidents, causing considerable apprehension.[48] Rabbi Simon Glazer wired the federal minister of justice, asking him to 'direct [the] attorney general of Quebec to stop antisemitic agitation and [calls] for massacre against the Jews of Quebec. Large meetings to plan riots against Jews take place Wednesday night Quebec City.' The Jewish community sued Plamondon for libel.

Plamondon had echoed the writings of Édouard Drumont and other nineteenth-century French antisemites. These were summed up by Samuel Jacobs, KC, one of the community's lawyers, in a letter to an enquiry from the United States:

> [The] defendant ... has circulated statements to the effect that Jews are enemies of the faith, honor, lives and well-being of their Christian fellow-citizens; that Jews are thieves, corrupters of women, assassins of Christian children, instigators of revolutions; and that they have done these things wherever they lived, and will attempt to do the same in the Province of Quebec, as soon as they are sufficiently powerful; also that Jews offer sacrifice to God by shedding blood of non-Jews.[49]

Plamondon added that, being a menace to the country, Jews should not be given the same rights as other citizens;[50] rather, they should be governed under special laws similar to those enacted by medieval popes and potentates in order to establish and give legal sanction to their inferiority. Better still, they should be excluded from the country.

The case came to trial at Quebec City on 19 May 1913, in Superior Court, before Mr Justice Malouin. Representing the plaintiffs, Lazarowitz and Ortenberg of Quebec City, were two of Montreal's brilliant young Jewish lawyers, Sam Jacobs and Louis Fitch. As witnesses on his behalf, Plamondon summoned Abbé Grandbois, professor of theology at Laval, Abbé Damours, editor of *L'Action Sociale*, and Abbé Nadeau, professor of Greek history at the Collège de Levis. The community's witnesses included Dr Herman Abramowitz, rabbi of Montreal's Sha'ar Hashomayim synagogue, Montefiore Joseph, a Quebec City merchant, Canon Scott, rector of Saint Matthew's Church in Quebec City, and Dr Ainslie Young, principal of the high school in Quebec City.

While the plaintiffs alleged that, as a result of Plamondon's charges, they had suffered financial losses and personal physical harassment, the case obviously had far wider implications. The Jewish people were being slandered, and their tradition – including the text of the Talmud, which

Plamondon claimed justified these abominations against non-Jews – was being ridiculed. In Eastern Europe such myths resulted in bloody pogroms.[51] Jews understood the sinister power of such lies as the blood libel and that, while pogroms were unlikely, deep-seated Christian anti-semitism could be reinvigorated by such conditioning, and lead to unpleasant manifestations. Louis Fitch, in summing up for the plaintiff, put it succinctly:

> Fortunately we live in a civilized country here: I do not expect that the adherents of Mr. Plamondon will murder us, or rape our women, or rob us of our property ... But I say the effect is to excite hatred among the people with whom we live, and, though perhaps to a lesser extent, bring disastrous results.[52]

Concentrating his remarks on the blood libel so recently revived during the Beilis case in Kiev, Sam Jacobs put his case this way:

> If the Christian inhabitants of St. Roch's believed these charges to be true, and were convinced that Jews practised a religion which ordered them to commit such offences, is it not reasonable to conclude that they would and ought to take the most stringent means of ridding themselves of such a danger lurking in their midst?

Despite such argumentation, the libel action was lost. It was not enough for Jacobs and Fitch to brilliantly demonstrate that Plamondon and the witnesses who appeared on his behalf were totally ignorant of the Talmud – which they cited as the source of their allegations – nor was it sufficient for Dr Abramowitz, who had studied the Talmud for twenty-five years, to categorically deny the blood libel and other charges, and demonstrate that the evidence of Plamondon's witnesses was completely unfounded. Even calling the two prominent Christians, Canon Scott and Dr Ainslie Young, to testify that Jews were decent, upstanding, and law-abiding citizens did not help. The problem was a technicality: the law of libel did not cover group defamation, and, since Plamondon was not accusing any particular Jew of these abominations, the court found for the defendant. Quebec's Jews were deprived of an important legal victory, however impressive their triumph in disproving all of Plamondon's charges.[53]

The Plamondon libel had a galvanic impact upon the Jews of Quebec. The repetition of the ancient charges brought a collective shudder of disgust and fear to all Jews. Thus, a number of Montreal's Jews decided to appeal, and a fund was collected for this purpose by the Baron de Hirsch legislative committee.

To demonstrate their concern over the fate of Mendel Beilis in Kiev, the Jews of Montreal had held a huge rally at the Gaiety Theatre in October 1913. All of the West End 'prominents' were present, as well as many representatives of the East End. The battery of speakers, Sam Jacobs, Rabbi Abramowitz, Rabbi Nathan Gordon, Peter Bercovitch, and Louis Fitch – along with Montreal's mayor, Louis Arsène Lavallée – denounced the blood accusation as baseless. All of them condemned the tyranny and antisemitism of the Russian authorities, to the applause of 5,000 Jews inside and outside the theatre.[54] In Winnipeg, over 6,000 people, including politicians, gathered to protest, while in Toronto similar events occurred.[55]

Meanwhile the blood libel was still not dead in Quebec. In July 1914, Abbé Antonio Huot, a prominent Catholic priest, would publish an inflammatory pamphlet with allegations that, while the accusation could not be made against Jews in general, 'certain dark and secret (Jewish) sects ... used Christian blood for ritual purposes.'[56] Still, this and many future events, symbolized a degree of community cooperation on perceived threats, and though Anglo-Jews and immigrants assessed these perils differently, they all nevertheless possessed a clear perception of danger. Though there might be disagreement on the degree of danger, some apprehended no better than a qualified answer to the eternal question that stemmed from centuries of insecurity – 'Is it good for the Jews?'

At the same time, however, compared to Eastern Europe, life in Canada was good for most Jews, even for the majority of newly arrived, struggling immigrants. Manifestations of antisemitism were, on the whole, not very dangerous. Jewish men (and a few women) still attended universities, Jewish storekeepers and pedlars plied their trade, Jewish workers laboured alongside non-Jews and walked the same picket lines, and Jewish householders shared neighbourhoods with Christians. And, not infrequently, Jews and their culture elicited favourable comment from the press and others who observed them. At higher levels, government officials publicly manifested sympathy for Jewish suffering. In January 1882 the Canadian high commissioner, Alexander T. Galt, joined British luminaries at a public meeting in London to protest against atrocities in Russia.[57] In January 1906 a public meeting in Ottawa to protest against Russian pogroms was addressed by Prime Minister Sir Wilfrid Laurier, who offered refugees 'a hearty welcome' in Canada. Official condemnations of the Beilis 'blood libel' were expressed in several Canadian cities. Reverend A.N. McEvoy, an Anglican minister, wrote in a letter to the *Toronto Daily Star*: 'I know the purity of their family life, their affection and sense of responsibility for their children. I know ... their quietness, industry, thrift and temperance.'[58] The Dominion of Canada allowed these and other possibilities for the blessings of peace, freedom, and opportunity.

It should also be noted that in North America, the Quebec context was unique, exposing Canadian Jews to a distinctive kind of antisemitism. While a poisonous variety existed in the contemporary United States, it was not as structural as it was in Quebec. Canadian Jewry, nearly one half of whom lived in the province, therefore, developed a special sensitivity and consequently more powerful defence organizations than Jews in the Republic deemed necessary.

Parallel with these political tensions, economic adjustment was proceeding apace. As the Canadian clothing industry expanded during the first two decades of the twentieth century, Jewish participation increased enormously. Capital requirements were relatively low, cheap labour was plentiful, and markets abounded. Clothing manufacturing thus offered an attractive frontier of enterprise, especially for Jewish immigrants, who possessed minimal capital, a capacity for very hard work, and a willingness to take a chance, often as contractors who undertook to sew up garments for manufacturers.

As Jewish contractors proliferated, some of them prospered so much that, as Montreal's *Journal of Commerce* observed in February of 1906,

> [Jewish immigrants] are driven to make their own garments at home and readily adapt themselves to doing repairs for the second hand shops, and gradually become workers for the wholesale houses. Eventually these people buy their own materials and manufacture for the consumer directly. Many have made a name for themselves in Montreal.[59]

As new firms developed and older ones declined, the *Journal* noted that a number of Jews had emerged as important manufacturers. Competition was rife, and expanding markets placed a premium on flexibility, price-cutting, mobility, and exploitation of workers, particularly women, children, and immigrants.

In this industry, it was difficult to organize trade unions. High turnover rates, the ready availability of part-time workers, the relative mobility of factories (the so-called runaway shop, which was moved out of town to escape unions and use cheap labour), and the tradition of craft unionism, which tried to restrict entry to skilled workers, militated against the organization of the unions. Tailors' unions, emerging since the 1820s, proved inadequate for the organization of masses of semi-skilled workers in clothing factories.

The United Garment Workers of America (UGWA) arose in the United States in the 1890s and quickly organized locals in Toronto, Hamilton, and Montreal.[60] In Montreal the union engaged in a fierce but losing strike at Mark Workman's factory in September 1900. The union charged that Workman, who specialized in making uniforms, had laid off nine workers and hired imported Romanian Jews allegedly willing to work for one-third the wages. While Workman denied any illegality, he did not deny the firings. The union demanded an increase in wages, which were as low as $5 per week for workers labouring sixteen-hour days. Workman continued production with barely a pause.

Unable to prevent the use of cheap labour, the UGWA could do little to stop the replacement of salaried tailors by women on piecework, or to keep employers from slashing salaries and forcing workers to forgo their Saturday half-holidays without compensation,[61] which was especially oppressive for Sabbath-observant Jews – although some Jewish employers allowed work on Sunday instead. Jewish workers were sometimes militant in defending their religious holidays. During a needle-industry strike in Hamilton in April 1913, they insisted on recognition of Passover, 'during which time,' a Department of Labour official reported, 'none of the Jewish people, and there are many of them among the strikers, would return to work until this particular holiday was over.'

Serious confrontations were also erupting in the women's wear sector. In March 1904, workers at Star Mantle Manufacturing Company walked out under the leadership of the newly organized International Ladies' Garment Workers' Union (ILGWU), which won major concessions from the firm's owners.[62] Strikes at other women's clothing companies were often accompanied by violence, arson, lockouts, threats, and rapidly rising bitterness on both sides. In February and March 1910, a lengthy and serious confrontation broke out in the dress and cloak factories owned by Abraham Sommer, a prominent activist in the Jewish community.

Piecework, contractors, crowded conditions, dirty garret shops (which caused high rates of tuberculosis),[63] immigrant labour – the hated 'sweating system' – had not improved by the early 1900s, despite the publicity given to it since the late 1880s. Several leaders of the Montreal labour movement pinpointed specific evil conditions. B.A. Larger, president of the Montreal UGWA, argued in 1904 that imported female factory workers, many of them mere children who worked for $2 to $3 per week, were depressing wages generally in the industry. Seasonality was another problem; in the periods between the major production runs of July to September for fall deliveries, and January to March for spring deliveries, there were long layoffs for cutters, and only part-time work for operators. Such conditions made it easy for employers to dictate terms of employment. During a powerful open-shop drive in May of 1904, the *Montreal Star* observed, jobs were so scarce in Montreal that a strike would be ineffective. One firm forced its employees to post a forfeitable $25 deposit each as a personal guarantee that they would not strike, a form of extortion, as some workers pointed out; the employer could foment a strike and pocket the money. Allegedly, some did so.

The UGWA's growing Jewish membership added a socialist tinge.[64] Four major garment strikes were called against a large number of Montreal firms in autumn 1907, to secure union recognition, substitution of wages for piecework, and cleaner factories. The union demanded that young girls begin work at 7:30 a.m. instead of 7:00, so that they could eat breakfast at home, and decried the practice of forced 'deposits' against strikes. In factories producing women's clothing, a group of Jewish pressers and cloakmakers battling for union recognition had to confront intra-ethnic animosity, as employer A.J. Hart – himself a Jew – demanded that 'foreign [Jewish] agitators be deported,' claiming that 'not one of our native born employees were affected.' In March 1908, the workers at Freedman Company – owned by community leader Lyon Cohen – struck for a reduction in their work week from sixty-one hours to forty-eight. Other fierce battles ensued all across Canada. In Winnipeg, a bitter and unsuccessful strike by the UGWA in 1908, which included 'many Jewish tailors' at the ladies' clothing firm of Jacob & Crawley, lasted more than a year.

But while minor gains were occasionally achieved, employers successfully resisted unionization, as well as attempts to prevent them from employing contractors, whose outside shops were so numerous, so difficult to regulate, and so transitory that they were almost impossible for health inspectors to police effectively, or for unions to penetrate.

The tension caused by increasing competition and rising union militancy brought a rash of strikes in Toronto, Montreal, and Hamilton in 1912. In Toronto, a two-month walkout by the mostly Jewish Cloakmakers' Union against the T. Eaton Company in the winter of 1912 ended in failure, despite efforts by luminaries in the Jewish community to broker a settlement.[65] The confrontation began in Montreal in early June when an industry-wide strike erupted against the member firms of the Montreal Clothing Manufacturers' Association, which included all the major men's clothing producers. The dramatis personae in this protracted and bitter struggle included many prominent members of Montreal's Jewish community, indicating their close identity with the needle trades and the deep class divisions that existed among them. Jewish manufacturers included such community worthies as Solomon Levinson, Harris Kellert, Noah Friedman and his son David, Lyon Cohen, Harris Vineberg, Jacob Elkin, and Samuel Hart – most of whom were connected by marriage or by business ties going back to the 1860s and 1870s, when many of them had been storekeepers and pedlars around Lancaster, Ontario. Well-to-do, established, and powerful men, they had made the slow transition from merchants to manufacturers as contractors on the fringes of the industry, and had emerged as successful industrialists who distributed product across the country and employed hundreds in their large shops, which were located in the city's garment district around lower St Lawrence Boulevard. Members of the venerable Spanish and Portuguese synagogue, Shaar Hashomayim, or the Temple Emanuel, they lived in fashionable West End suburbs, supported local Jewish charities, and took a keen interest in Jewish public affairs.

The most prominent and active of these worthies was Lyon Cohen; he was born in 1868 in Poland, grew up in Maberly, Ontario, and joined his father, Lazarus, in a Montreal coal and dredging business. He established a brass foundry and in 1906 bought the Freedman Company, which became one of the city's largest and most successful men's clothing firms. As a vehicle for the vigorous defence of Canadian Jews against antisemitism – and as a public service to the Jewish community – in 1897 Cohen founded the *Jewish Times*. He chaired a committee set up to advance Jewish rights in the Montreal Protestant school system and served as president of the Baron de Hirsch. Well-off, prominent, energetic, and articulate, Lyon Cohen was also charitable, and looked with deep compassion on the sufferings of his people. However, understanding went just so far. For Cohen and his colleagues, their vital economic interests took precedence, even though a large percentage of their workers were Jews. Also at issue was their own amour propre, which they refused to diminish even for the welfare of their fellow Jews – especially those who did not share their values. Thus, they supported the denunciation of 'professional agitators [who] have created all the trouble,' and they refused to 'permit irresponsible demagogues to dictate the terms upon which we will deal with those we employ.'[66] They may also have suspected that these organizations were dominated by radicals who would undermine the social order – and bring shame on the Jewish community.

Who were these 'professional agitators' and 'demagogues'? Opposing the manufacturers in the summer of 1912 was a joint executive board of forty local UGWA members, headed by a union official from Baltimore, and Victor Altman, a representative from one of the three striking Montreal locals. Included in the union's demands were the reduction of the workweek from an average of fifty-five hours for men and fifty-two for women to a nine-hour day, a five-day week, and an overtime rate of time-and-a-half.

Most manufacturers refused to meet with the union representatives.[67] On June 6, one union organizer had triumphantly reported to the press that seventeen firms, mostly small manufacturers, had come to terms with the union. Workers could sense an early victory and ran a successful tag-day throughout the Jewish community to raise money for the strikers' families, indicating substantial public support. But violence erupted, and the promise of an early general settlement was shattered. Picketers were beaten up by toughs who turned out to be either private detectives or Montreal police plainclothesmen hired by the employers. In turn, non-striking workers were attacked by union sympathizers, who inflicted serious injuries. Employers, now determined to starve the union out, closed down their factories on June 18. Workers responded with parades and giant rallies at Coronation Hall and out in Fletchers Fields, where they shouted their determination to continue and were bolstered by speeches from some of the city's leading union leaders. The manufacturers charged that the strike had been called by the parent union in New York to coincide with similar strikes in the United States, to prevent Canadian workers from emigrating there as scab labour. (Seasonal or permanent migration of workers in both directions across the Canadian–American boundary was a well-established phenomenon, and there is evidence of this kind of labour transiency among clothing workers, especially among the highly skilled designers and cutters.) Manufacturers also alleged that the union leaders in New York wanted to narrow the price differentials on manufactured clothing in order to keep Canadian goods out of the United States market.

The real inspiration behind the 1912 strike was Hananiah Meir Caiserman, a twenty-six-year-old accountant who had emigrated from

Romania only two years earlier and worked in a clothing factory. Caiserman was determined to raise the class consciousness of the city's Jewish workers, who were now probably 30 per cent of the work force in the industry.[68] Besides organizing the garment workers into separate locals according to trades (cutters, pressers, cloakmakers), Caiserman also inspired Jewish bakery workers, using rallies, street demonstrations, and fiery oratory to force employers to accept the union label. As well, he organized cultural evenings for these workers and gave courses on political economy.

Assisted by a devoted team between 1911 and 1913, Caiserman built the separate locals into a well-organized, financially sound, loyal, and militant union that was affiliated with the Poale Zion (Labour Zionists), which had spread rapidly among Jewish manual workers, students, and intellectuals in Europe, Palestine, and North America.[69] It provided Caiserman and his associates with the inspiration for militant strikes for the UGWA and, a few years later, for the Amalgamated Clothing Workers of America (ACWA). They were battling not just for improved wages and working conditions, but for social justice and recognition of the dignity of labour. When the June 1912 strike began, Caiserman had behind him all the Montreal Poale Zion clubs, which taxed each of their members a day's wages. The clubs solicited funds from Poale Zion groups in other cities to support the $7,000 strike fund and called a conference of all Montreal labour organizations to build up support for the strike. Morris Winchevsky, the noted and revered left-wing Jewish poet, came from New York to inspire the strikers.

The workers showed spirited defiance. Two hundred women members donned red sashes and took to the streets at five o'clock one morning to sell copies of *Cotton's Weekly*, a local socialist newspaper, containing a long review of the causes of the strike. At the same time, they warned the Montreal police that, if they interfered, the paper's editor would be brought to Montreal to sell them.[70]

Valuable allies were Montreal lawyer Peter Bercovitch, who interceded with the police on behalf of the strikers, and Reuben Brainin, editor of the *Keneder Adler*. Bercovitch had a reputation as a champion of the Jewish poor, underprivileged, and workers. As *Keneder Adler* editor, Reuben Brainin – Montreal's leading Jewish intellectual – attempted on a number of occasions to arbitrate between the disputing parties in the clothing industry. In the meantime, the *Jewish Times* of 19 July 1912 – now edited by a progressive-minded young lawyer, Marcus Sperber – recognized that 'there is a continual hostility between capital and labour ...

[making] strikes ... inevitable' but '... regretted this strike in question because most of the participants in it are Jews.' It called on both sides 'to patch up the differences':

> For shame! You leaders of thousands of men, and you captains of industry should be more considerate, should be more human than to allow the wretchedness and misery consequent upon the strike to continue, because, forsooth, you are proud, and wish the other party to rap at your door.[71]

The manufacturers, unrepentant, resorted to smear campaigns, violence, and 'runaway shops.' In early July, four major firms announced that they would relocate their factories, Brothers and Hart to Sorel, J.E. Elkin to Joliette, Crown Pants to Cornwall, and Union Clothing to St Jean.[72] Finally, after many weeks of bitterness, the manufacturers and union representatives reached a compromise on July 29. But the union achieved only a partial victory: a staged reduction in weekly hours from fifty-five to forty-nine and an increase in piecework rates. The union was forced to drop its demands for wages instead of piecework and for time-and-a-half overtime pay. Worse still was the fact that the manufacturers were able to retain the open shop, the union's biggest target.

Conditions were largely unchanged in the Montreal men's needle industry since the late 1880s and 1890s, when factory inspectors had deplored the pitiable working and living conditions. But industrialization had now facilitated a measure of labour solidarity, even class and ethnic consciousness, among workers who had previously been segregated from each other in small workshops, similar to what urbanization created among South Italians in American cities.[73] In the needle industry, identity from the workplace was becoming as important as religious or regional identity. The Poale Zion and Arbeiter Ring, which were organized in 1905 and 1907 respectively, had social, political, and economic goals, and were part of the immigrants' 'cultural baggage' rather than products of North American acculturation. But some of their Montreal leaders, like Hananiah Meier Caiserman and Hershl Novak of the Poale Zion, became leaders in the clothing unions,[74] because they recognized that solidarity was vital to economic betterment for the workers. The unions – the UGWA in the men's trade and the Cloakmakers (a forerunner of the International Ladies' Garment Workers' Union) in the women's trade – promoted acculturation and consciousness raising, as well as economic goals.

While the needle industry symbolized a certain kind of transformation and unification in Canadian Jewish urban life, it also set the stage for economic warfare of the kind which the strike of 1912 foreshadowed: bitter and bloody, Jewish workers locked in a struggle with Jewish employers, Jewish strikebreakers, and allegedly even Jewish gangsters. These confrontations, which continued for another generation,[75] created deep and long-lasting divisions within communities where the needle industry was significant. Beneath the surface, Jewish communal solidarity was thin and fragile.

And these divisions also reflected cultural gulfs. Battle lines in these disputes coincided closely with those rifts caused by the Jewish school question, and which would emerge sharply during the future debate over the formation of the Canadian Jewish Congress. Thus, while the emergence of two contending forces at the 'Corner of Pain and Anguish' clearly expressed a classic economic conflict, the associated cultural and social dimensions were also of far-reaching importance.

In Toronto a 1912 strike of the Journeymen Tailors' Union, involving 550 workers, lasted a year but was unsuccessful in its struggle for a minimum wage scale for a forty-nine-hour week, better piecework rates, sanitary shops, and equal pay for women.[76] The UGWA struck some fifty-four contractors' shops producing men's clothing, singling out Rasminsky and Stein, one of the city's larger contractors, for unionization; but the firm refused to yield, and the workers returned.

Here, however, Jewish participation in the garment industry was less than in Montreal. Although by early 1913 the overwhelming majority of the city's fifty-four men's clothing contractors' shops were Jewish, few Jews had become full-fledged manufacturers. One recent scholarly study of the Toronto industry reveals that by 1901, while some 15 per cent of clothing firms were owned by Jews, 'Jewish businesses accounted for only two per cent of the total value of garment factories in Toronto.'[77] Though Jewish entrepreneurial participation increased subsequently, historical geographer Daniel Hiebert found that 'by 1915, a few men's wear factories and approximately 50 per cent of all women's wear firms were owned by Jews ... they accounted for less than 15 per cent of the production in the industry.' In Toronto, moreover, factory production of clothing was overwhelmingly dominated by the T. Eaton Co. At this stage, then, there were few counterparts to the prominent Jewish clothiers in Montreal. Numbers may have influenced this; the Jewish population of Toronto in 1921 was 34,770, while Montreal's was 45,802.

Contracting was less lucrative than in Montreal because of slight wage differentials and the greater availability in and around Montreal of part-time workers. Although many Jewish workers were employed by contractors, large numbers of them were also hired by non-Jewish firms, including Eaton's.

Here, too, mainly Jewish tailoring union locals existed from the early 1900s. In fact, Toronto hosted the UGWA in 1906. The union's organizer for Canada, H.D. Rosenbaum, recruited many workers and by early 1913 had forced one of the city's largest manufacturers, Randall and Johnston, to encourage its contractors to accept union members.[78] Conditions in Toronto, however, remained poor. When thirty-three firms granted more than 2,000 workers wage increases of between 10 and 20 per cent, a Department of Labour reporter stated: 'Conditions among Gentile girls said to be very good. Among Jewish girls not so good, owing to the fact that a large number of Jewish girls are employed in outside contract shops, also that there is a sub-contracting system.' In Hamilton the settlement of an industry-wide strike was delayed until after the Passover holiday because of the large number of Jews among the workers.

In the women's clothing sector, where Jewish manufacturers and contractors were also increasingly evident before 1910, Jews likewise assumed greater visibility. The Independent Cloakmakers' Union of Toronto went on strike in April 1910 in an attempt to force union recognition. 'Many of the strikers,' the *Labour Gazette* noted, 'are of the foreign element, Jews and others.'[79] In sympathy with the aims of the ILGWU, many workers strongly supported a Toronto organization drive that began two years later. In June of 1912, the eleventh annual convention of the ILGWU was held in Toronto to bolster the efforts of a full-time organizer, M. Koldofski. A strike against the John Northway and Pullan companies early that year resulted in recognition of the union, as well as major improvements in working conditions.

A strike at the Dominion Cloak Company between April and August of 1914 lasted for twenty weeks, which were filled with widespread violence, especially after the company hired strikebreakers; by the end of the month, nineteen police court cases – mainly assault charges – were pending, fifteen of them against union members, most of whom were Jewish. The firm's plant was sabotaged, and private detectives were hired as more violence and more arrests ensued. By early August, the workers and the union were so exhausted that they were forced to call off their strike and admitted defeat. A month later, eighty of the employees were still without work.

Relative peace, prosperity, and full employment marked the menswear industry after the bitter 1912 strike and on into the early years of the First World War. Rapid mobilization resulted in full order books for manufacturers, who were generally willing to concede higher wages and better conditions to keep production flowing, and the number of strikes in the industry fell rapidly. In 1916, however, inadequate wage settlements and a new drive for union recognition caused a major upheaval. Since the huge split in the ranks of the UGWA at its convention in 1914, a new and more radical industrial union had arisen in the North American industry. Led by Sydney Hillman and Joe Schlossberg, the Amalgamated Clothing Workers of America was formed. This was an industrial union with a combative style, Jewish leadership, and an emphasis on social justice and collective bargaining which appealed strongly to the Jewish clothing workers.[80] Tens of thousands of them joined during its early organizing drives across the United States and Canada. In Montreal and Toronto, support for the Amalgamated spread among the UGWA's Jewish members, who sent a delegate – the revolutionary enthusiast, Elias Rabkin[81] – to the union's first convention in New York. He reported that 'the tailor unions in Canada have been ruined and ... the conditions of labour have, in the course of the past two years, been reduced to the very lowest state, particularly in the clothing centres of Montreal and Toronto.' The Amalgamated New York office sent up an organizer, and Canada's first local of the ACWA, No. 277 (the pantsmakers), was established in Montreal in 1915.

UGWA organizers established several locals to cover all of Montreal's twenty major menswear factories, where 5,000 tailors were employed. Affected by the rise of the Amalgamated Clothing Workers of America, which challenged the UGWA, Caiserman and his group favoured the switchover to the Amalgamated.[82] They formed new locals and concentrated on organizing workers in large plants and forming joint boards to coordinate locals in both Montreal and Toronto. Recognition would then be sought as sole bargaining agent in all factories and contractors' shops – creating the union shop. If the giant firms were organized, it was assumed that all others would fall into line.

In July 1916 the union called its first strike against John W. Peck, a large, well-established Montreal firm. The results were excellent for the union; it won the company's recognition as bargaining agent for the 400 workers, who were granted a substantial increase in wages.[83] Four months later, another strike, involving all five locals, against the huge Fashion Craft, resulted in another impressive victory. The firm agreed to stop contracting out work, to recognize the union, to increase salaries by 10 to 15 per cent, and to keep to the nine-hour day and forty-nine-hour week.

Buoyed by these victories and a successful organizing drive and strike at the Davis Brothers plant in Hamilton in July, the Amalgamated tried to negotiate similar terms with Montreal's Semi-Ready. But by now the manufacturers too were organizing. Late in 1916, they formed the Montreal Clothing Manufacturers' Association to resist unionization with all of its demands. When Semi-Ready's management resisted the Amalgamated, a strike began on 20 December 1916. The Association charged that Joseph Schlossberg was a German agent whose goal was to undermine the Canadian war effort by interfering with the production of officers' uniforms. Semi-Ready began hiring strikebreakers, and its managing director boasted to the deputy minister of labour that 'we have been able to equip our factory without the strikers returning to work.' Peter Bercovitch, speaking for the union, labelled the charge against Schlossberg a 'baseless appeal to prejudice,' while Schlossberg wryly observed that 'in Germany he would have been known as a "d — d" Jew and it seemed strange to come to Canada to be called a German.' The union's New York attorney declared meanwhile that, in fact, Schlossberg was a Russian. Bercovitch called on Lyon Cohen, president of the Manufacturers' Association and probably Montreal's most prominent Jew, to publicly declare that Jewish union leaders were not Germans. Realizing that the charge was absurd and that it could seriously damage the image of the community in the heated wartime atmosphere of 1917, Cohen issued a strong denial: 'we, the manufacturers, disagree with you leaders and strikers in certain matters, but we agree with your protest against slander.' Cohen thus put an end to this form of mudslinging.

Emotions ran very high a few days later as strikebreakers, under massive police protection, entered the Semi-Ready plant. Picketers who attempted to stop these 'scabs' were arrested on charges of fighting and interfering with the police, while another was arrested for severely beating a strikebreaker.[84] Sidney Hillman, New York president of the Amalgamated, visited Montreal, where he witnessed 'scenes of uncommon hardship ... in temperatures of twenty below zero the picket lines were filled mostly by young girls who came out at six in the morning, only to be ridden down by the ... Police.'[85] Speaking of the mounting violence on the picketline, Bercovitch, recently elected to the Quebec Legislative Assembly, defended the union members at a bail hearing and asked, 'I would like to know under whose orders the police work, those of the city or of the Semi-Ready company,' and charged that the company had interfered in the legal process.

By early January 1917, the strike had spread to all of Montreal's major large clothing companies, which were determined to stop the Amalgamated's drive dead in its tracks, even if this jeopardized their profitable contracts for army uniforms. Industry leader Lyon Cohen precipitated the industry-wide shutdown. On December 30 he dismissed an employee, who was a union delegate, on the grounds that his union activity had reduced Cohen's Freedman Company's production by 30 per cent. Failing to get the worker rehired, the Amalgamated called a strike of the 300 Freedman employees on January 12. Cohen tried then to move his production to another firm, which had settled with the Amalgamated the previous October and had agreed to secretly manufacture for Cohen. However, when the cutters refused to handle Cohen's goods, they were dismissed, and a general strike erupted in the industry, bringing some 4,000 workers from the major firms out in sympathy; soon another 1,000 workers were affected when independent smaller firms were shut down as the strike spread. By February 12 virtually all men's clothing production in Montreal had stopped.

The real issues were union recognition and collective bargaining. Wage increases and the reduction of hours – and even the use of contractors – though highly important, would not likely have led to the shutdown. Indeed, some employers, including Cohen, were willing to increase wages, reduce hours, and even scale down or eliminate the use of contractors. Cohen believed in doing away with sub-contracting because, although profitable and convenient, it encouraged sweatshop conditions, which he genuinely deplored. His own premises were relatively clean, modern, airy, and, in comparison with most contractors' sweatshops, probably deluxe. Other employers like the Peck Company had modern factories.

But recognition of the union cut deeply into their perceived rights as businessmen. As an example, Cohen, their spokesman, recounted how the union had forced him to fire a highly productive but unpopular worker; he then explained that shop delegates (who came with union recognition) caused 'unrest ... and ... diminished production.' For him, the question was clearly 'who should control the shop floor, the fore-man or the shop delegate.' Other manufacturers argued that the real sticking point for them was protecting their right to fire incompetent workers.[86] Ultimately the question was one of power. This was the key to understanding 'the efforts of labouring people to assert some control over their working lives, and of the equal determination of American business to conserve the prerogatives of management.'[87] The concept that anyone but employers should share control of the workplace was completely foreign and totally unacceptable.[88]

Union recognition, which eventually brought the dreaded closed shop in its wake, meant sharing control of the workplace; it could bring interference with other aspects of management and, ultimately, with the pursuit of profits. Therefore, in the 1917 confrontation, factory owners were prepared to fight a long, bitter, and costly battle, and to use rough tactics against the very class of Jewish poor and underprivileged they were actively helping through the local charities. The union charged that 'besides alleging that union leaders were German agents,' the Manufacturers' Association, hoping to have Schlossberg deported, had asked the New York Police Department for his record. Some manufacturers who were shareholders in munitions plants, a reference to Mark Workman, president of Dominion Steel Corporation, blacklisted the striking clothing workers. The union also alleged that, as heads of Montreal Jewish charities like the 'Baron de Hirsch,' employers denied help to strikers who applied for it. Bitterness spilled over into other sectors of the city's Jewish life. When Lyon Cohen participated in the official opening of a new synagogue, a crowd of clothing workers hooted, jeered, and threatened violence to silence him.[89] Economic warfare thus penetrated into the sanctuary of the Lord.

The Amalgamated saw the 1917 Montreal struggle as a battle against some of the worst excesses of industrial capitalism. The union, their newspaper reported, 'brought to them a realization of the fact that they were not merely human tools for production of merchandise, rightless, hopeless and aimless, but that they were human beings entitled to the blessings of life, liberty and the pursuit of happiness.'[90] The Amalgamated was led by men with selfless dedication to social justice and industrial peace, and Hillman, Schlossberg, and Caiserman were undoubtedly sincere. Hillman would recount at the 1918 Baltimore convention the heartbreaking circumstances among Montreal's Jewish, Italian, and French-Canadian women clothing workers in 1917: 'little girls [victims] of the cannibalistic industrial system, which ... feeds upon helpless children.'[91] But not only humanitarian concerns had set the 1917 strike in motion; there were practical and strategic reasons, as well. The largest garment-manufacturing centre was Montreal, and if the union could secure recognition there, then Toronto and Hamilton would more easily follow suit. This, in turn, would stabilize the industry, and prevent the exploitation of workers.

For a significant number of clothing workers, who were influenced by left-wing reformist ideology, Poale Zion, or the more radical Bundist outlook, these struggles were more than simply bread-and-butter issues, more than Gompers-style progressivism.[92] However, there are indications that for many workers the idealistic concerns were less important than they had been only four years before. During the 1912 confrontation, the presence of intellectuals like Hananiah Caiserman and Reuben Brainin, the broad support of Poale Zion clubs, and the editorial backing of an independent though short-lived strikers' newspaper had together created an atmosphere of ideological conflict which was not evident in the 1917 contest. This was clearly an extension of an international organizing drive by the newly formed Amalgamated, whose leaders, Hillman and Schlossberg, were idealistic but pragmatic unionists, not ideologues. And their strategy found acceptance among most Canadian clothing workers.

Mediators soon appeared. In early January 1917, Sam Jacobs – a leading Montreal lawyer who was a personal friend of Lyon Cohen and other clothing manufacturers – suggested to Schlossberg and Cohen that the former minister of labour William Lyon Mackenzie King be appointed to arbitrate, but this idea went nowhere.[93] At the same time, Montreal's mayor, Médéric Martin, who was increasingly concerned about the implications of a strike of nearly 5,000 workers, was also trying to effect a settlement. The Businessmen's Strike Relief Committee invited him and other prominent Montrealers, including Professor Stephen Leacock of McGill, to help. He urged mediation 'in order that a basis of settlement, fair and equitable to both parties, shall be arrived at.' Though the union expressed interest in Martin's proposal, it was rejected by the employers on grounds that they 'have already conceded everything, with the exception of the right to control their own affairs which in their opinion is not a matter which may be arbitrated.' They offered instead to meet separately with their own employees. Martin's suggestion of a three-rnan arbitration board was also unacceptable, and by mid-February he concluded that the manufacturers were stonewalling and urged the strikers to 'act with calm, but energetically insist on the upholding and recognition of their rights. Their cause is just and will ultimately triumph.'

It was now a question of endurance. The manufacturers had chosen to fight during the slack season of January and February. At the end of this period, the workers' bellies would be empty, and with no alternative employment many would be tempted to go back to work. Some producers evaded the strike by employing non-union labour. The firm Rubin

Brothers, for example, boasted that they were overstocked anyway and could easily carry on reduced production with strikebreakers.[94] Atlas Clothing and Modern Boys Clothing reported to the Department of Labour that all their goods were produced by contractors; since they used non-union labour, these firms could continue business undisturbed.

Other small manufacturers, however, were desperate by the end of February. Heavily pressed to fill orders to keep up their cash flow and maintain their government contracts – lest they go out of business entirely – some settled with the union. On February 26 Harris and Sons, whose 175 employees had been on strike for two weeks, accepted the Amalgamated's terms, and College Brand Clothes capitulated two days later. These, however, were only small victories. The bigger firms continued to defy the union, and the pickets kept up their daily vigil at the factories. Meanwhile, financial support for the strikers came from the union's New York headquarters and from the Businessmen's Strike Relief Committee.

Violence on the picket line ensured continuing bitterness, while the Montreal Police Department was not impartial in handling these confrontations.[95] In early February, fifteen strikers were charged with preventing strikebreakers from entering several factories and for fighting with police officers.[96] A bomb exploded at the home of one strikebreaker, while another was so severely beaten up by assailants that he lost an eye. Some of this roughhouse was perpetrated by Jewish women; Rachel Black was arrested in mid-February,[97] while Annie Solovitsky, Mary Levine, and Annie Shuta were fined for beating up a strikebreaker. Demonstrations and marches included 'un grand nombre de jeunes filles,' and *Le Devoir* observed that 'a very large part of the demonstrators, especially the women, were by their appearance Israelites.' Despite an appeal for moderation from the police commissioner, the violence continued. Tony Calebro was arrested for carrying a revolver, which he brandished in the faces of strikebreakers. But all their court appearances did nothing to break the strikers' spirits. They were often attended by friends, who crowded into the courtrooms to give them moral support. 'The Recorder's Court was jam-packed this morning with Israelites of both sexes,' *Le Devoir* reported in early February, 'who came to learn the fate of their 32 striking compatriots, who appeared for sentencing.'

It was the longest, most bitter, and probably most violent strike in the history of the Canadian needle industry up to the 1930s. Before it was settled in May 1917, more than 4,500 workers were on strike against sixty-nine companies (including fifty-six small independent firms), completely shutting down the production of men's clothing and uniforms.[98] The issues of the strike illustrate important aspects of this industry; they also highlight major themes in the immigration and settlement of the rapidly increasing Jewish population.

It is difficult to estimate the effects of the strike on Montreal's Jewish population, which in 1917 could be described as a community only in the broadest sense. It is highly possible that some mediation efforts were started within established community organizations by major personalities associated with neither side of the dispute – like A. Lesser, who had been instrumental in settling the 1912 confrontation – or some of the city's prominent rabbis. But since Jews were involved on all sides of the disputes, the strike can only have sharpened the already deep intracommunal divisions. Other frequent, bitter, and lengthy labour conflicts involving hundreds of Jewish bakers and butchers during the early 1900s also accentuated those rifts within Montreal Jewry.[99]

Yet other stirring events of 1917 elicited a kind of unity among Jews in Europe and in North America. Reports of immense suffering among the Jewish masses of Poland and the Ukraine gave rise to separate fund-raising drives. By 1917, these were coordinated into one account to aid all afflicted Jews in the East European war zones. There was concern over the fate of the Jews in Palestine, suffering from the aftermath of the war. These and other issues filled the pages of the *Keneder Adler*, which reflected public opinion among the Yiddish-speaking segment of Montreal's population. Rallies, drives, benefits, campaigns, marches, and demonstrations occurred frequently in the Jewish quarter during these dramatic months. The Monument National, the Gésu Hall, and the Gaiety Theatre resounded with Yiddish speeches, songs, poetry readings, and eyewitness accounts of tragic events in Europe and the conquest of Palestine by General Allenby's armies. Synagogues, union halls, clubrooms, cafes, and private homes reverberated with animated discussions of the meaning of these matters.

A.M. Klein's poem 'Autobiographical'[100] suggests that many individual Jews felt personally involved in the dramatic events of those years. In the midst of these many momentous global concerns, the local clothing workers' strikes appeared to many, less important. And while it is understandable that their class conflict was not widely discussed in public, even the events of the strike and the conflicting positions were not examined in great detail in the *Keneder Adler*.

To be sure, the paper carried many reports on these bitter strikes,[101] but the issues and events were not described in nearly as much detail as they were in the Montreal English-language papers, the *Gazette*, *Star*, and *Herald*. More importantly, the *Adler*, which, after all, was the voice of Montreal's Yiddish-speakers, though generally supportive of the workers, published strong editorials only late in the dispute. Its strike-related editorializing was reserved for an antisemitic outburst by a magistrate in Recorders' Court, where a number of strikers were up on assault charges, claiming that Jewish witnesses were, because of their religion, less believable than Christian policemen.[102] On February 11 the *Adler* announced that it had learned of plans by manufacturers to bring in a large number of strikebreakers from the United States, and warned the Canadian government to stop them at the border.[103] Four days later, it proclaimed that support for the local schneiders' (tailors') strike was pouring in from all classes, including Mayor Martin, who was reported as saying that the union's cause was just. But the *Adler* refrained from making a strong commitment to the workers' cause. Frankness was sacrificed possibly in fear of alienating the community's kingpins, like Cohen, who headed the 1917 fundraising campaign to assist Jews in Eastern Europe. Most Jewish intellectuals remained silent on the incongruity of this situation, apparently even Caiserman, who was deeply involved in war relief. The irony was not lost on the beleaguered clothing workers. If the *Adler* was not supportive, they would publish their own Yiddish paper. This sheet, which ran for twenty issues during the eight weeks of the strike, encouraged the strikers.

The rabbis also were absent from the columns of the *Adler* or the *Canadian Jewish Chronicle*, which had succeeded the *Canadian Jewish Times* in 1914. The most prominent were rabbis Meldola de Sola of the Spanish and Portuguese synagogue, Herman Abramowitz of the Sha'ar Hashomayim, and Nathan Gordon of the Reform Temple Emanu-el. Conceivably, they could have wielded some influence on both parties to the strike by mediating in the traditional role of the East European rabbi.[104] Nor is there any evidence that they tried publicly to mediate, or discuss, the strike in Sabbath sermons.

In early March of 1917, a memorandum of agreement signed by Michael Hirsch for the Manufacturers' Association and Peter Bercovitch for the union established a committee to investigate causes and solutions to the dispute.[105] A board consisting of five members, two appointed by each side and a fifth by the other four, 'none of whom are to be connected either directly or indirectly with the clothing industry,' was to report within two months, while 'the employees are to return to work forthwith without reserve of any kind.' After lengthy hearings lasting nearly two months, the board's report recommended granting a forty-six-hour week, a salary increase, time-and-a-half for overtime, and recognition of the union. All these conditions were accepted. The last point had been vital to the Amalgamated; it appears that, despite the already considerable length of the battle, Hillman, Schlossberg, and the Amalgamated members probably would have held fast to win it.

Although the board refrained from recommending a union shop, it did urge that a 'conference committee' be elected in each factory by the workers. Union recognition was confirmed by 'the fact that the employers signed the agreement with the newly established Joint Board,' the central authority of the Amalgamated.[106] The report was approved by a mass meeting of union members on May 14, and the longest strike until then in the Canadian men's clothing industry came to an end. Settlement of a lengthy strike by the Amalgamated in Toronto had been concluded successfully in March; Hamilton factories were organized at the same time. The popularity of the union increased, membership soared, and – most important of all – a period of industrial peace ensued in that branch of the needle industry for the next four or five years.

Yet, this brief respite did not bring Montreal's Jewry lasting peace. The strike of 1916–17 was only one feature of internal tensions. The gulf between groups was an economic one. Enjoying pleasant homes in upper-class, English-speaking neighbourhoods, the Jewish *haute bourgeoisie* tended to absorb the lifestyle and values of the dominant Anglo culture. The sons played sports, attended McGill, and travelled; the daughters performed charity work, took voice lessons, 'visited,' taught Sunday school – and awaited marriage. The parents formed Jewish social, athletic, and philanthropic societies; they built impressive synagogues in the West End, supported the 'Baron de Hirsch' and many other local Jewish charities, and built a downtown Jewish businessmen's club, the Montefiore.

But although they strived for integration while still retaining their religion and cultural identity, these Jews encountered barriers to the complete social acceptance they so much desired. At the same time, they were estranged from their fellow Jews down in the quarter.

The clothing industry was vital to Montreal's Jews. Figures for the number of Jews employed in the industry before the 1931 Dominion census are not available; in that year, 16.49 per cent of all Jews gainfully employed worked in the industry (compared to 5.69 per cent of all other ethnic origins), while in Toronto, Winnipeg, and Vancouver the figures were 27.42 per cent, 11.88 per cent, and 8.76 per cent respectively. In previous decades, before Jews had achieved a significant degree of occupational mobility, the percentages were probably much higher.[107] Even so, in 1931 Jews still composed 31.2 per cent of all Canadian workers in the manufacture of women's ready-made clothing, 40.9 per cent of the workforce in ready-made men's clothing, 26.9 per cent in other clothing, and 34.9 per cent in hats and caps.[108] Absorbing such a high percentage of all Jews 'gainfully employed,' the needle industry, or the 'rag trade,' as it was sometimes affectionately called, was dominant in their economic life in Toronto and Montreal during the great migration before 1914, and, in diminishing degrees perhaps, for a generation thereafter. Thus it is central to an understanding of the broad pattern of Montreal's industrial development in the late nineteenth and early twentieth century.

The needle industry was also an important aspect of the Jewish intellectual scene. In the broadest sense, the goals of the labour militants in the UGWA and ACWA represent the universalistic pursuit of social justice. But this purpose of workers' betterment was a direct importation from Europe, where Jewish workers had been developing an ideology of class action, self-help, and industrial unionism that became widespread during the late nineteenth and early twentieth century.[109] The formation of the ILGWU and the ACWA, and the fervour and militancy of Jewish workers during these strikes, reflect the strength of these movements in their native countries. This intellectual baggage engendered union militancy when they found themselves in the sweatshops.

In a number of ways, the clothing industry was an 'intermediate zone' of Jewish economic, social, and cultural adjustment. 'At the corner of Pain and Anguish,' Jewish immigrants – as well as many others – received their first Canadian employment, and their first exposure to its industrial system, to urban life with its desperations and opportunities, and to an industry whose conditions aroused class consciousness and labour unionism. The needle industry was more than just a great Jewish metier; it was a principal focus of Jewish life itself. And with this came a deepening sensitivity to political realities and opportunities in Canada and in the Jewish world at large.

In the early 1900s, the Toronto local of the Socialist Party of Canada had a large number of Jewish members, including women, and the Social

Democratic Party's Toronto Jewish locals participated in 1911 in efforts to organize a socialist Sunday school.[110] Shortly after the start of the First World War, Jews of Austrian extraction were scrutinized as were the many thousands of other 'enemy aliens,' mainly Ukrainians, living in Canada.[111] Some were arrested, including one Russian Jew (believed to be a German) who was imprisoned in Kingston's Fort Henry in 1914; he was released on the intervention of local Jewish businessman, later an alderman, Isaac Cohen.

In September 1918, Dominion security officers wanted to outlaw the Jewish Social Democratic Party and monitor the *Israelite* and *Keneder Adler*. This was part of a general program of censorship and surveillance of ethnic workers and organizations which had been deemed unlawful under an Order-in-Council (PC 2384) and were believed to be 'saturated with the Socialist doctrines which have been proclaimed by the Bolsheviki faction of Russia.'[112] During Canada's 'Red Scare' of 1919, the Royal North-West Mounted Police reported that Jews were believed to be in leading positions of the Russian Workers' Party and 'that Jewish radicals were thought to be especially dangerous not only because of their prominence within the Social Bolshevik leadership, but also because they represented a cultural minority that manifested "the bitterest hostility" towards Anglo Canadians.' During anti-alien riots in Winnipeg in January and February of 1919, the business establishment of Sam Blumenberg, a prominent local socialist, was wrecked. A military intelligence report held that Becky and Michael Buhay, members of the Jewish Social Democratic in Montreal, were the city's 'cleverest and most outspoken' radicals. A few months later, three Jews were included among the five 'foreigners' rounded up under Section 41 of the Criminal Code, passed to punish sedition following the 1919 Winnipeg General Strike. Moses Almazov, Sam Blumenberg, and Michael Charitonoff were classified as dangerous enemy aliens, subjected to weeks of surveillance by the RNWMP, and charged with seditious conspiracy. They were threatened with deportation and sentenced to terms in Stoney Mountain Prison.[113] All were ultimately released, but the deportation threat hung over them for some months.

6 Zionism, Protest, and Reform

Jewish nationalism was brought to Canada in the 1880s and 1890s and became central to the debate on the Jewish future. A most interesting element in the intellectual dimensions of Canadian Jewish history is the fusion of Jewishness and Canadianness. The experience of the Canadian Zionist movement highlights the impact of local attitudes towards nationalism which would lead to the establishment of a Jewish national home in Palestine. Theodor Herzl's formulation of political Zionism and his appeal to local Jews for support was never intended to challenge their primary loyalty to Canada.

The aspiration for a revival in Israel had taken root in Canada long before. Indeed, one of its first Zionists was the Christian enthusiast Henry Wentworth Monk, who in the 1870s and 1880s advocated a Jewish homeland in Palestine and campaigned avidly.[1] In 1887 a branch of the Chovevei Zion (Lovers of Zion) organization was formed in Montreal by a local Hebrew teacher, Alexander Harkavy, who subsequently moved to New York, where he achieved great eminence as a Yiddish lexicographer.[2] Another Montreal Zionist group, formed five years later, was known as Shavei Zion (Return to Zion); in 1894 some of its members actually attempted to start an agricultural colony at Hauran, in the northeastern corner of what is now Jordan.[3] After a harrowing year, the Montrealers returned to Canada, much sadder and considerably poorer.

In 1898 Zionist groups sprang up in Montreal, Toronto, Winnipeg, Kingston, Hamilton, Ottawa, and Quebec.[4] In November 1899 a national organization of these groups – the Federation of Zionist Societies of Canada – was established, and over five hundred memberships (known as shekels, for the ancient Hebrew coin) in the world Zionist organization and nearly one thousand shares of the Jewish Colonial Trust were sold across Canada. Montreal businessman Clarence de Sola, supported by a devoted and growing group of followers, set about spreading the Zionist message from the Atlantic to the Pacific – even in the isolated farm colonies on the Prairies.

Similar to South Africa, another binational state,[5] where Jewish identity fused with Zionism, Canadian Zionism was stronger than the United States variety, where such a normative identification was not deemed possible. Zionism thus followed 'divergent paths' in the two countries because of several factors.[6] These mainly were: British chauvinism among Canada's Jews; the country's binational character and the absence of a countervailing pan-Canadian nationalism; the religious conservatism of Canadian Jews and their wide geographical dispersion; the organizational genius of Clarence de Sola himself; and the general 'conservatism' of Canadian society.[7] At any rate, the early movement was indeed moulded by de Sola, who for twenty years headed the Federation and was its titular leader, chief spokesman, and major ideologue.[8] Through the prism of his career, the movement evolved in a period of significant numerical growth and geographical spread, as well as one of far-reaching social and economic changes in the Canadian Jewish community.

Having launched their campaign in 1899 with the founding of the Federation, de Sola and his associates were tireless in spreading the message. Montreal rabbis, including Meldola de Sola of Shearith Israel and Rabbi Aaron Ashinsky of Shaar Hashomayin, delivered pro-Zionist messages from their pulpits. From Toronto, Dr John Shayne, Moses Gelber, and, later, Sam Kronick carried the cause to English- and Yiddish-speaking audiences across southern Ontario, and in Ottawa, Archie Freiman soon became deeply involved.[9] Youth and women's organizations flourished. In Toronto, Zionist clubs were so numerous and active that in 1910 they united to purchase a house for their meetings.[10]

From Winnipeg, M.J. Finklestein, Harry Weidman, and H.E. Wilder served in various capacities on the Federation's national executive. Finklestein was an important local lawyer, one of the few Manitoba Jews in that profession, while Wilder was one of the proprietors of *Dos Yiddishe Vort*, the Yiddish weekly which circulated to communities across the Prairies.[11] In these vibrant western centres, Zionism developed in other ideological directions. And in smaller western and Maritime localities, groups of men and women tirelessly ran local campaigns and attended national and regional conventions, selling the fifty-cent 'shekels' which denoted official membership, emptying Jewish National Fund boxes, and collecting funds. Montreal businessman Leon Goldman watched over the organization's daily affairs, while de Sola dealt with 'the big picture,' visited branches, and corresponded grandly with fellow 'world leaders.' In Montreal, the movement was backed by key intellectuals like Reuben Brainin, editor of the *Keneder Adler*, and Hirsch Wolofsky, the publisher, although they sometimes challenged de Sola's autocratic manner and lack of cultural depth.

By 1910 the Federation was growing steadily. Its total national membership rose from a few hundred in 1899 to 1,000 in 1903, over 2,000 in 1906, and nearly 6,600 in 1920,[12] one in every nine or ten adults and a significant proportion of the members of small communities. Of nearly 6,600 members in 1920, for example, the smaller places, with only 23 per cent of the Jewish population, supplied nearly half the national membership.[13] In many of these centres, support was close to total. Many leading members of these new communities, like Isaac Cohen of Kingston and Bernard Myers of Saint John, were East European immigrants of the 1890s or early 1900s who brought their Zionism from Europe. As immigrants, they were receptive to appeals from leaders like Clarence de Sola, an establishment figure who provided a Canadian stamp of approval to the movement. The federation, moreover, was the only sustained organizational link binding communities across Canada together and providing opportunities to meet.

While directing this expansion, Clarence de Sola and his Montreal associates distanced themselves from the American Zionists, who were beset, de Sola thought, by far too much internal dissension and bureaucracy. In December 1901 he advised Theodor Herzl to resolve this situation, while pointing out that, because of these problems, Zionist associations in several United States cities had recently asked to join the Canadian federation instead.[14] In a letter to Max Nordau in February 1910, de Sola underscored the greater success of Zionism in Canada as compared to Britain and the United States. According to de Sola, the 'larger contribution per capita of our population than in any other country' had been due 'to the fact that we have insisted all along on the strictest discipline in our ranks, with the result that our organization is strong and united, and schismatics have always found themselves in an utterly hopeless minority.'[15] Not long afterwards, he dispatched an acerbic letter to the Central Zionist Bureau in Cologne, sharply disagreeing with proposed constitutional changes to allow more than one central authority in a country: 'the greatest fault of the Jewish people to-day is their unwillingness to submit to discipline.' 'In Canada,' he boasted, 'we have had a rigid almost military discipline in our Federation.'[16]

De Sola's belief was shared by others. In 1903 Zionist official Jacob de Haas – who, after visiting Canada and the United States, had a good basis of comparison – wrote to Herzl that 'the movement here [in Canada] appears to be stronger and more solid than in the United States and altogether considerably different.' Implying a comparison with unnamed American Zionist figures, he continued, 'de Sola works very hard and is popular.'[17]

Right from the beginning, de Sola was determined to run his own show. In March 1899, in reply to a letter from the president of the Federation of American Zionists, requesting their cooperation, de Sola had stated that the Canadians felt strongly

> that the autonomy and individuality of [their] Federation should not be sunk or lost sight of ... the Canadian Jews have always maintained a very independent course in their communal affairs ... not ... from any lack of good feeling towards our neighbours, but [it] is simply the natural feeling of people living in a separate country, in which, to a certain degree, the sentiments and traditions are different from those of the neighbouring country.[18]

In 1919 the peppery Leon Goldman, indignant that the American Zionists had taken credit for Canadian contributions to the post-war Palestine Restoration Fund and shekel purchases, warned that this made it difficult to get 'wholehearted support in Canada.'[19] But while the centrist Federation and its successor, the Zionist Organization of Canada, maintained a jealous independence, the various left-wing Zionist organizations in Canada bonded with sister societies south of the border. These links thrived in several of the youth movements, branches of the American organizations.

Goldman was at pains to let world Zionist leaders know the limit of Canadian goodwill. In February 1920 he wrote to London requesting information about discussions at a recent session of the Actions Committee 'so as to enable us to be in a position to discuss intelligently the workings of our Organization, when we are dealing with our branches and affiliations in this Country...'[20] A few years later, in response to several dunning letters from headquarters, he insisted that fundraising would be conducted by Canadians aware of local conditions, seemingly not understood by the German officials: 'we cannot lose sight of the limitations of the Jewish community of this country,' whose 'material wealth ... cannot be compared in any degree with that of our brethren in the United States of America.'[21] Canadian Jews had been subjected to 'campaigns after campaigns' for Palestine, for Ukrainian pogrom relief, and for local purposes. Moreover, he protested against the propaganda employed in canvassing Canadians for money: 'It is not necessary to bring to our notice the report of the conditions in Eastern Europe in order to induce our organization to do their duty; for [we] are fully aware of those conditions and very much alive to the necessity of obtaining vast amounts of money for the work of reconstruction ...'

De Sola's philosophy of Zionism, as expressed in his addresses at Canadian Zionist conventions, adhered closely to the Basle program: the establishment of a Jewish national home in Palestine and the strategies adopted by the leaders of the world movement for its implementation. He was devoted to Herzl, perhaps responding to his personality and speeches, and moved by the honours he received in London at the Fourth Congress in the summer of 1900, and by his own private visit to Herzl in Vienna in the preceding June. Although encouraged by Herzl and Nordau to attend other congresses, de Sola declined and willingly bowed to strategical decisions made by others. At later congresses, the Canadian federation was usually represented by British or American delegates, or by any Canadian who happened to be travelling to Europe. After presenting perfunctory reports, Canadian delegates were never active in the debates.

To de Sola, who in his business regularly negotiated contracts with Cabinet ministers and senior civil servants, the discussions between Herzl and the Turkish sultan, the kaiser of Germany, Emperor Franz Joseph of Austria, and other European potentates were an entirely legitimate way of securing recognition of Palestine as the Jewish national home. He delighted in news of Herzl's high-level diplomacy, and frequently embellished his letters and speeches to Canadians with updates on these negotiations.

All the same, de Sola was well informed of events, through his correspondence not only with Rabbi Gaster in London but also with Zionist figures elsewhere – including, of course, those at the movement's headquarters in Vienna, Cologne, and Berlin. He read the English Zionist press, the Vienna-based organ *Die Welt*, and, initially, the *Maccabean*, the American Zionist monthly, which he circulated to Canadians to enhance their knowledge of developments abroad. Once the Montreal-based *Jewish Times* became more favourable to Zionism, de Sola favoured this publication.

De Sola and other Zionist spokesmen did not perceive any conflict between Zionism and patriotism. Even though the *Jewish Times* initially thought that Zionism might arouse antisemitism, this never seems to have concerned him.[22] In a letter to one supporter, he stated:

> The idea that the reestablishment of the Jewish state would throw suspicion upon the loyalty of Jews residing in other lands [is] too absurd to call for serious reply. To our minds, the Zionist movement aims at securing a home for Jews living in countries where they are suffering oppression. Those, who like ourselves, enjoy the same privileges as the other citizens of the countries we live in declare most emphatically our loyalty to the countries we live in notwithstanding that we are a nation.[23]

Despite these early concerns, the loyalty question did not become a major issue in Canada, as it did in the United States.

In addition, de Sola also conceived of Zionism in more practical terms. To a member in New Brunswick, he explained that the aim was not to 'restore the whole of the Hebrew race to Palestine. The object ... is simply to restore to that country that portion of our race who are at present suffering from persecution, and who, as a consequence, are emigrating and seeking new homes.' He argued that 'for an organized mass of people to flood these western countries under no direction, and with no proper training for agriculture, or other means of living, will be disastrous, and must naturally only produce misery.' The only feasible and businesslike solution was to settle these people in Palestine, where they could be self-supporting in agricultural or other pursuits. Thus, de Sola saw Zionism as a practical solution to the potential problems of vast European immigration to Canada.

From the beginning, with de Sola's support, the Federation gave priority to fundraising over education. In addition to the shekel, the basic membership fee, and the sale of Jewish Colonial Trust shares, the Jewish National Fund to purchase land in Palestine was a special Canadian cause. 'Mere ebullitions of sentiment would prove inadequate unless supported by concrete achievements,' de Sola told the national convention in January 1911.[24] 'When we gather in Convention annually, the first thing that interests us is to see how much we Zionists have contributed in hard cash to the funds of the Movement.' Although widely supported, there were some internal tensions regarding the emphasis on money-raising rather than education or, as one dissenter put it, 'the proper understanding of Zionist principles and institutions.'[25] But most members agreed that 'our Movement aims at an ideal but we are practical enough to recognize that it can only be attained through that which is material.'[26] In one confrontation, de Sola exclaimed that he would brook no opposition from one 'of no influence in the community, a comparatively recently arrived emigrant' who had dared to attack 'the leading Jews in Canada, and the power and authority that they represent.' Such leading Jews, he observed, contributed 'about four-fifths of the ... funds of the Movement every year in Canada [which] has been the cause of the success of Zionism in this country.'[27] De Sola thus was adamant that large donors kept the federation alive, and dissenters who wanted to enrich its cultural program were not welcome.

As a result Canada engaged in ambitious undertakings, which diverted energies and resources. This activity substituted for education, which might have laid the basis for a Jewish cultural renaissance in Canada. The only cultural dimensions were small ideological offshoots like Farband or Poale Zion (Labour Zionism) or Mizrachi (Religious Zionism), or in the youth movements. Perhaps given their backgrounds, the Russian and Polish Jews, who by 1920 predominated, needed little of this cultural stimulation. But there was little debate and exposition of Jewish culture within the Zionist movement. By the end of the First World War, Canadian Zionism had produced only a few intellectuals with the ability to energize the movement or even challenge the Federation's leadership.

Women were most active, forming their own associations and national connections (later Hadassah-WIZO), and supporting special projects in Palestine. Several groups had existed in a number of cities since the first of them, the Daughters of Zion, had been founded in Toronto in 1900.[28] Over the next eighteen years, numerous organizations were formed to help Jewish women in Palestine improve health and 'home craft' standards in the country (Jewish Women's League for Cultural Work in Palestine), assisting in hospital care (Palestinian Sewing Circle), and other causes. Anna Selick of Toronto had formed the nucleus of Canadian Hadassah in 1916. After a helpful visit from Henrietta Szold, then president of American Hadassah, an organization of women's chapters was established in Toronto, Hamilton, Brantford, London, and Windsor. Over the next few years, most of these groups came in under the umbrella of Canadian Hadassah, which spread across the country. This remarkable organization soon became the most continuously active arm of the movement in Canada, adding a sense of immediate and pressing concern. These women worked fervently for several

Palestinian causes – first for the Helping Hand Fund, and later for a girls' domestic and agricultural science school at Nahalal, a nurses' training school in Jerusalem, and a number of other major projects, such as a convalescent home and a tubercular hospital.[29] Innumerable raffles, bazaars, teas, and tag days kept members busy raising money for all of these projects. The leaders of Hadassah, such as Lillian Freiman, Rose Dunkleman, and Anna Raginsky, personified the cause which mobilized across Canada thousands of Jewish women who, along with the Pioneer Women and Mizrachi Women, performed veritable prodigies of fundraising for the health and welfare of women and children in Palestine.

Hadassah's achievements in Palestine were remarkable, and the energy, success, and emotional commitment of its members were attributable not only to their Jewish identity; the cause also appealed to 'their instincts as women – a love of cleanliness, an abhorrence of disease, [and] a solicitude for the welfare of children.'[30] Hadassah evolved from a women's auxiliary in the male-dominated Federation to a body supporting its chosen projects, sometimes in concert with the Hadassah organization in the United States, charting its own course early on with distinctive goals, separate fundraising efforts, and its own national office. Its early leading spirits were mostly young middle-class women anxious to provide a separate voice for women and promote social welfare in the Jewish national home.

Thus, Hadassah offered Canadian Jewish women an independent voice and an opportunity to choose their causes.[31] It served as an entrée into society, in both the Jewish and the non-Jewish world, raising their profile as Jews, as Canadians, and, above all, as women. Within the Jewish community, their moral influence and political power were of great significance. By 1920, it was the strongest, most coherent, and best-led national organization on the Canadian Jewish scene.

As the mainstream Zionist youth organization, Young Judaea emulated its parent, the Federation. In its structure and philosophy, it was a vehicle for the Canadianization of large numbers of Canadian Jewish youth, grooming them for leadership in the Zionist movement. Its leaders saw their role as educators of the youth who would 'serve in Jewish life on this continent ... [and] make a contribution to the perpetuation of the Jewish people, so that the Jew, who has not expended his creative ability, may contribute again to the culture of the world.' But another goal in Young Judaea was combatting assimilation. Jewish youth, according to this view, was adrift in North America because parents, schools, and synagogues were no longer able to adequately instil traditional values and culture. 'Young people ... have found it difficult to live as Jews,' wrote one commentator 'and their Jewishness for the most part has not meant enough to them to forgo the comforts and conveniences that could be theirs for the very easy task of forgetting that they are Jews ... And so they have sold their birthright for a mess of pottage.'[32] Thus, Jewish continuity was threatened, unless this trend could be arrested by a comprehensive educational program.

The desperate plight of East European Jewry during the First World War altered the Federation's role in communal affairs. Also, the war highlighted the influence of immigrants on the social and intellectual life of Canadian Jewry, vying with Zionism in attaining Jewish national aspirations. As well, the war gave rise to discontent among young intellectuals who, disenchanted with de Sola and his associates, preferred rival Zionist agendas.

The immigrants who had arrived after 1900 were focused on their close relations in towns and villages within the war zones. The Yiddish press, which by 1914 included three Canadian papers (and New York Yiddish dailies which circulated in Canada), carried news of starvation, forced migration, and pogroms, raising deep concerns and active relief campaigns.

The government's suppression and censoring of publications in enemy languages, chiefly German, did not affect the Jewish newspapers published in Canada, and this, in fact, led to some resentment. One newspaper editor commented in 1918 that Jews, who 'are hardly considered a desirable addition to the business life of any country, are permitted to retain their newspapers.'[33]

In 1914, the world was swept into the First World War. This, of course, brought Jews along with other Canadians into the burgeoning Canadian armed forces. Precise figures of Jewish enlistments are unobtainable, but they might well have been affected by the conflicting loyalties of the recent arrivals. Perceptions of antisemitism in the Army – which, after all, was a cross-section of Canadian society, where racial and religious prejudice were present – could also well have hampered volunteer enlistments. And it was believed, but impossible to prove, that significant numbers of Jews, anticipating antisemitism in the Army, attested on enlistment as Christians or as having no religion.

Nevertheless, considerable numbers of Jews rushed to the colours, and, in 1916 Captain Isidore Freedman of Montreal recruited over

400 men for Montreal's Jewish Reinforcement Company, a unit (underwritten by Sir Mortimer Davis) whose soldiers were dispersed among other Montreal battalions.[34] According to historian Louis Rosenberg, there were at least 2,712 Jews in the Canadian Expeditionary Force, including 56 officers and 2,655 non-coms, 1,213 of whom (39 officers and 1,174 non-coms) served overseas.[35] How many Jews served at the front, got overseas to Britain, or volunteered is not known, though in June 1917, 1,682 Canadians voluntarily reported themselves to Jewish chaplains of the British Army.[36] Moreover, an undetermined number – estimated by Rosenberg at 400 – served in the battalions of the Jewish Legion, which was recruited in 1917 and 1918 by the British Army for service in the conquest of Palestine from the Turks.

In the trenches on the western front, Jews did their duty along with their mates, and 123 of them died.[37] Seventy-six were decorated for acts of bravery, including Myer Tutzer Cohen, a lieutenant in the Black Watch, who won the Military Cross for his bravery at the Battle of Passchendaele in November 1917.[38] Herman Abramowitz, rabbi of Montreal's tony Shaar Hashomayim synagogue, served as honorary chaplain to the Jewish troops in Canada, but as there were not enough of them in any one base overseas, Army officials balked at appointing a chaplain for the Jewish soldiers over there.[39] Abramowitz noted in July 1917 that in view of the recent passage of the Military Service Act, 'the necessity of the appointment of a Jewish Chaplain will be evident.'[40] Jewish troops in Britain usually attended local synagogues and, on the western front, were served by Rabbi Michael Adler, a British Army chaplain.[41]

One soldier wrote to Rabbi Abramowitz in February 1917 from Bramshott Camp in England, where he was posted to the 25th Reserve Battalion, that he rejected an offer of a soft berth there for the rest of the war: 'that is not what I came over here for. I want to get with a unit that is going to France, or anywhere else ...'[42] He pleaded for a letter of introduction to London's chief rabbi for the next time he got there on leave. Another soldier in the line with the Third Canadian Siege Battery wrote in February 1917, during an early morning lull in the fighting, that after leaving the Somme he was living deep underground in a former wine cellar. 'Our troops have been on the go continually and together with the artillery have not given the Boche a moment's rest – no time to consolidate ... Tonight everything is uncannily quiet. I should not be surprised to see either a gas attack or a big strafe come off at daybreak.'[43] But his biggest news and greatest enthusiasm was in meeting up with several other Montreal Jewish boys: Harold Leavitt,

Marvin Workman, 'who has not yet been in the line' (but was later killed in action), and Edgar Goldstein. He reported that other Montreal boys were stationed in England and vowed to look them up – but might never have had the chance.

The war affected the program of the Canadian Zionists. They supported a recruiting campaign undertaken for the Jewish Legion, a five-thousand-man force in the British Army – the first Jewish military formation in modern times – organized to liberate Palestine from Turkish rule. Following the 1917 decision of the British government to recruit British and American Jews to this special force, the Canadian government agreed to allow hundreds of Jews already in the Canadian Expeditionary Force who had indicated a desire to transfer to the Legion,[44] and Jews who were 'not subject to conscription in Canada,' to join the Legion.[45] An officer from the British Army arrived late in 1917 to begin an enlistment drive across the country.

Meanwhile, Yitchak Ben-Zvi and David Ben-Gurion had been travelling throughout North America in 1915 and 1916 recruiting young Jewish men for a pioneer army to serve in Palestine once the war ended. The two-man mission had been warmly greeted by Jews in Toronto, although Ben-Gurion was disappointed that only seven men signed up.[46] In Hamilton, he found only one qualified man, a professional jockey, who wanted to join the *shomrim*, a force of mounted watchmen; the rest he rejected as 'not suitable material ... Most of them are forty or fifty years old and burdened with families.' A scheduled meeting in Montreal was cancelled for lack of interest, and a gathering in Winnipeg, according to one observer, produced 'a serious failure [because] ... Ben-Gurion is a very weak speaker and is no great agitator.' In 1918 both Ben-Gurion and Ben-Zvi joined the Legion, and sought recruits in the United States. American and Canadian volunteers – at least three hundred of the latter – were sent to Windsor, Nova Scotia, for basic training before being shipped overseas to British Army depots. Later that year, they were sent to Egypt as the 39th Battalion of the Royal Fusiliers.

Bernard Joseph, the McGill law student who had formed Young Judaea, participated in the Legion recruiting campaign and joined up himself. For him, as for a number of others, the experience served to reinforce an already deeply embedded Zionism. Joseph completed his law degree in Montreal and in 1921 returned to Palestine. Later, having adopted the Hebrew name of 'Dov,' he pursued an active political career in Jerusalem. After the war, a small colony of Canadian ex-Legionaires settled at Avichayil, a village north of Tel Aviv, though most eventually returned to Canada. Persistent harassment of the Jewish soldiers by British military police in Palestine in 1918 and 1919, and the complete ban on visitations to Jerusalem, contributed to their frustration and anger. Fifty-four soldiers, all of them from Canada and the United States, who loudly and physically objected to this discrimination – including four privates from Toronto – were court-martialled for disobedience and mutiny and served terms in military prison before being given amnesty.[47]

The Balfour Declaration of November 1917 had elicited widespread emotional responses, and not just from Zionists; Canadian Jews marched through the major cities, attended numerous emotional rallies, and listened to countless messianic speeches. Long-standing anglophiles such as de Sola waxed eloquent at this revolutionary new turn in Jewish history. At last there was to be a home for the Jews in their sacred ancient land. But would they regard Palestine as the national home for all Jews, themselves included, or continue to see it as a refuge for the persecuted? For most, the latter was true, and British sponsorship implied that the refuge would be larger, stronger, and much more secure. All Jews believed that, given Britain's imprimatur the dream would be fulfilled soon. Thus, Zionism in Canada attained a new intensity, largely because of the Balfour Declaration and, later, by the mandate of the League of Nations.

From the outset, the Federation received regular goodwill messages from all levels of government. Perhaps Liberal politicians were repaying a political debt by supporting their causes. But the Zionists needed this public attention because their movement emphasized world approval for their cause. Favourable editorial comment in the newspapers indicated at least some public acceptance.[48] In Canada, where identification with Britain remained, support for the mandate was considerable.

The First World War had disrupted much of the early Zionist reconstruction in Palestine. The Turkish authorities had expelled many Jews and interned others; meanwhile, development had languished and settlements had declined. Worst of all had been the immense human suffering, particularly in Jerusalem among the largely elderly population dependent on charity. While the Turks remained in control, little could be done directly by Canadian Zionists. Funds raised in Canada had usually been transferred directly to the international body in neutral Copenhagen so that Zionists on both sides could continue to communicate.

Even though the Federation of Canadian Zionist Societies was the only national Jewish body, it did not speak for everyone. The severe crisis in Europe united Canadian Jewry to perform unprecedented prodigies. And while developing this cooperation, culminating at the end of the war, the mandate of the Federation was challenged, and defeated, by the new-found collective action of the immigrants.

The war created serious political difficulties for all Zionists – especially in Canada, which was fighting against Germany and its ally Turkey. Sensitive to potential problems in Palestine if the Zionist cause was identified with either side, the world Zionist organization's executive had sought to remain neutral. De Sola was instructed that money could not be sent directly to Palestine, but had to be forwarded through American relief organizations. Still, the war did reduce Zionist fundraising until about 1917, because of the uncertainty of the fate of the *yishuv* (Jewish settlement) and the emergence of other, more pressing concerns.

This wartime hesitancy led to dissatisfaction among young intellectuals and professionals like Abraham Roback, Louis Fitch, and Hyman Edelstein, all of them contributors to Montreal's *Canadian Jewish Chronicle*, the successor to the *Jewish Times*, creating intracommunal economic conflict and serious structural problems.[49] To a growing number of Canadian Jews after the war, such as the average garment worker, the affairs of their union were more important than Zionism. And those working-class Jews drawn to a Zionist group would have been uncomfortable in the middle-class, English-language, fundraising-oriented Zionist societies, which included their employers.[50] They tended to support the more idealistic and intellectually satisfying programs of Labour Zionism and, for the Orthodox, Religious Zionism.

The end of hostilities following Allenby's conquest of Palestine opened opportunities for the reconstruction of the Jewish settlements there. Canadians were asked to contribute money through the Helping Hand Fund and the Palestine Restoration Fund, both of which were established in 1917. Before the Helping Hand Fund was wound up in 1918, the Canadians raised nearly $160,000, an amount far exceeding the aggregate proceeds of all previous Zionist campaigns. This success was aided by the full employment, prosperity, and emotions of wartime. In addition, a new and younger leadership had arisen in the communities, especially among women. Lillian Freiman – wife of Archie Freiman, a leading Zionist activist in Ottawa – campaigned extensively throughout Canada.[51] She spread word of the destitution in Palestine[52] during a self-funded coast-to-coast tour to appeal directly to as many of Canada's Jews as she could reach. Her eloquence opened hearts and purses as never before, and the fund collected $160,000 in cash and $40,000 in clothing, medicine, and foodstuffs, including significant contributions from many non-Jewish Canadians. It was the greatest fundraising drive ever mounted by Canadian Jews and set a new standard formerly unattainable. But the Palestine Restoration Fund, which followed almost immediately on the heels of this drive – and was also led by the Freimans – was even more successful; nearly $275,000 was collected by 1921.

The First World War accentuated differences between Canadian and American Jewry. For example, loyalty to Britain's cause provided Zionists with opportunities to identify their purposes with Britain's imperial mission. As far back as 1903, when the Uganda proposal (a temporary refuge for Jews in British East Africa) had been under consideration, de Sola had spoken on the subject of Zion's redemption under the British flag. Fourteen years later, when Allenby's armies were poised for an assault against Turkish Palestine, de Sola saw the British liberation of *Eretz Yisrael* (The land of Israel) as the dawning of a new messianic age. He even announced at the fourteenth convention of the Federation, in 1917, that it was time for the re-establishment of the Sanhedrin – the Jewish judicial body in ancient Palestine – as the supreme court of Jewish law and the governing council of the people of Israel.[53] Within this context of British Canadian nationalism, Zionists were free of any suggestion of dual loyalty.[54]

Amid considerable tension and acrimony within the organization, de Sola relinquished the presidency at the 1919 convention. He was replaced by a provisional committee, which later selected Archie Freiman as his successor. The Federation, renamed the Zionist Organization of Canada, went on to undertake even more ambitious fundraising ventures, continuing the Zionist activity that de Sola had pioneered decades beforehand.

Zionism provided Canadian Jewry with an 'ideology of survival,' as well as an identity, in spite of its flawed vision and leadership woes. The message from the European Zionist Federation and, ultimately, from Jerusalem was unchanged – 'send us more money, and more and still more.' World Zionist leaders, with few exceptions, were in full support. But it was unrealistic to expect de Sola to do much more than follow orders.

While resembling the American and British Zionist philosophy, Canadian Zionists did not have to compete with previously established organizations, or with national loyalty. To a much newer community, Zionism provided both an acceptable structure and an identity throughout the country, emerging as the normative form of Canadian Jewish identification even as early as 1914.

These developments coalesced in the movement to establish a Canadian Jewish Congress, which first convened on 16 March 1919, marking a watershed in Canadian Jewish history and a veritable revolution in the power structure within the community. In the Congress, the East Europeans served notice that they had arrived and would be heard as an important force.

They had a fundamentally different experience of political activism than the established community, who were already politically engaged. But the East Europeans abhorred this old-style *shtadlanut* (political influence by Jewish elite). The important deliberations over Jewish rights in the Montreal school system, for example, had excluded the input of the East Europeans, who strongly favoured a more democratic debate on relevant issues.

The idea of a 'parliament' of Canada's Jews had first been raised in 1908 by an early editor of the *Keneder Adler*. He called upon all Jews interested in convening such a body to write him; he lectured on the subject and publicized the idea in his columns. In February 1909, the question of establishing a Canadian Jewish board of deputies – modelled perhaps on the British board – was raised. But opposition came from the directors of the 'Baron de Hirsch,' who resisted sharing their power with new immigrants, and the idea was allowed to die.[55] The congress idea was revived in 1912, but broad support was aroused across the Dominion only after the outbreak of the First World War. Inspired by the American Poale Zion groups, who had summoned Jews in the United States to establish a democratic American Jewish Congress in 1914, Reuben Brainin began agitating for a Canadian counterpart to facilitate relief efforts and post-war planning.

The First World War had a catalytic effect on Canadian Jewry, motivating those with relatives in the war zones to raise considerable funds. In Montreal, some two hundred representatives of seventy synagogues and organizations united for this purpose in November 1914. Believing that 'uptowners' were not fully supportive, the 'downtowners' independently established a War Relief Conference on a democratic basis that would represent the majority's desire to give priority to overseas relief funding. 'It is our obligation to ensure that the cry of the hungry and of the suffering shall not be a voice calling in the desert.'[56] This conference laid down three essential principles on which the Canadian Jewish Congress was later founded: the immediate mobilization of relief for war-stricken European Jews, the affirmation of democratic principles, and a concern with immigration problems. Calling itself the Canadian Jewish Alliance, the group invited Jewish organizations to meet and discuss these and many other issues. The alliance would take the lead in the drive to establish a nationwide conference.

The Alliance met to draft a 'Declaration of Principles,' in which the solution of the sufferings of Jews in the European war zones 'must derive from the will of the awakened awareness of the entire Jewish people.' Representatives of numerous Montreal synagogues, labour unions, sick benefit societies, loan syndicates, cultural and political organizations, and charitable societies, representing the vast majority of the city's Jewry, were present. The congress idea was obviously very popular, and branches sprang up across the country.

At the March 28 meeting, Yehuda Kaufman, a leading left-wing Montreal Zionist, urged the community to press Britain to insist that Russia, its ally in the war, protect its Jews, who were suffering under severe persecution. He stressed, secondly, that Canada was a pioneer country with great colonization possibilities, a clear reference to concerns about possible limitations on Jewish immigration.[57] Kaufman argued further that the Jews of both Canada and the United States needed to establish a political body that could express what he called 'our national revindications' at a postwar peace conference. Labour activist Hananiah Caiserman, an active participant in these Montreal initiatives, recalled that 'the appeals of the Montreal Committee [the War Relief Conference] made an impression all over the country.' In response to them, local committees were organized, to supplement efforts already under way to collect money for war relief,[58] under the umbrella of the Canadian Jewish Alliance.

This push for a congress was opposed by the Federation of Zionist Societies of Canada, which held that the time was not 'opportune.'[59] Their president Clarence de Sola opposed a congress which would compete for financial contributions, fragment communal unity, and frustrate the Federation's claims of representing Canadian Jewry. Opposing the Montreal forces in the Alliance, the Zionist federation summoned its own national conclave – known as the Canadian Jewish Conference – in November 1915, although in Caiserman's eyes 'it was certainly not representative ... of the Jewish masses in the Dominion.' But the Federation and Alliance proposals differed only on who should prioritize the agenda and how leaders should be selected. Otherwise, as Caiserman shrewdly observed, there 'existed a striking similarity of purpose' between the two parties. However, the mounting European crisis forced a semblance of unity in preparing to present Jewish concerns at a peace conference after the war.

The interior of Montreal's Shearith Israel synagogue on Chenneville Street (built in 1838), showing the central bima, raised dais, and the women's gallery above. (Canadian Jewish Congress Charities Committee National Archives, Montreal)

A chicken warehouse next to the Warshawer Kosher Restaurant on Agnes Street, Toronto, 1910. (City of Toronto Archives, SC231-291)

For many Jews in the early 1900s, living conditions in 'The Ward' in Toronto were extremely poor. (City of Toronto Archives, RG 8-11-94)

Women of Toronto's Romanian Jewish Benevolent Society demonstrate (ca. 1918) in favour of Britain's mandate to establish a Jewish national home in Palestine. (City of Toronto Archives, S SC231-2206)

Jewish newsboys, Toronto, ca. 1910. (Ontario Jewish Archives, 6718)

Negotiating for a chicken in 'The Ward', ca. 1910. (Ontario Jewish Archives, 6723)

Teraulay Street in the heart of 'The Ward,' Toronto's Jewish quarter, ca. 1910. (Ontario Jewish Archives, 6714)

Observing the *taschlich*, Rosh Hashana, Toronto, ca. 1910. (Ontario Jewish Archives, 6721)

However, an invitation for Canadian Jews to be represented at the American Jewish Congress in September 1915 was a delicate issue. The United States was not yet a belligerent in the war, and the Canadians might be caught in the middle on differences of opinion between the United States and Great Britain.[60] The *Adler* called for a special conference – which would be addressed by Justice Louis D. Brandeis of the Supreme Court of the United States, Zionist leader and advocate of the American Jewish Congress – to discuss the issue before the forthcoming convention of the Federation in November. While pronouncing the Canadian congress desirable, 'indeed a necessity,' the *Adler* emphasized that it was vital 'to be extremely circumspect and to act with every reserve' because 'it is ... a very debatable point if, under such circumstances, Canadian Jews may be represented in this [American] Congress, ignorant as we are of what the Congress may do and how its measures may react upon ourselves living here on British soil.'

Ensuing *Adler* and the *Chronicle* editorials emphasized that the forthcoming conference to formulate an answer to the American Jews would benefit both the Zionist Federation and all of Canadian Jewry, which 'will acquire an experience of solidarity' – a subtle reminder to the Federation of their limited mandate.[61] It was clear, moreover, that the Federation's agenda – the building of Jewish settlement in Palestine – was much too narrow for most Canadians. In September a mass meeting in Winnipeg approved sending a telegram to Lord Reading, a prominent British Jew, asking him to use his influence to secure full civil rights for Jews at the end of the war. The meeting called also for 'the recognition of the claim of the Jewish people [for] unrestricted settlement in Palestine,' but this was a far less important demand than that for civil rights for the Jewish minorities in Europe. In Toronto, similar enthusiasm was expressed by both Zionists and others at their meetings.

But some differences of opinion had begun to surface. At one meeting in Toronto, Rabbi Dr Price denounced the attempts of certain self-appointed 'leaders' to create factions in the community, saying that they were 'a curse to Canadian Judaism.' He may have been referring to Clarence de Sola, who absolutely opposed establishing a congress, which could well detract from the centrality of the Zionist cause. The Federation did, at least officially, support the idea of a special conference. Leon Goldman, its executive secretary, toured the country together with Louis Fitch, pumping up enthusiasm for the idea. In Ottawa, however, Fitch made it clear that he saw the conference as a prelude to a congress which must be 'an organized Jewish representative body in Canada.'[62] The *Chronicle*'s editor, Hyman Edelstein, picked up on this point in his editorial on October 29: 'It is the first time in the history of Canadian Jewry that a body of new representatives of our entire community will assemble.'

Edelstein went on to articulate a broad agenda for the conference. The first was immigration; assuming the resumption of an 'inevitable vast influx of immigrants into this country on the conclusion of that war,' he believed that 'the best instrument to accomplish this happy end is the Conference.' Next, was the appointment of an observer, rather than a representative, to the American Jewish Congress, to attend and report back. Third was the need to attend to 'domestic questions' – requiring the solidarity of the Jews of Canada. Edelstein proposed the establishment of a Canadian Jewish Board of Deputies 'on a democratic basis ... to hold the reins of communal administration for the entire Jewry of this dominion.'

The conference opened on 14 November 1915, in Montreal, with virtually unanimous public support, including even the Federation's. An executive committee was elected to carry its efforts forward and to work with organizations not yet represented, 'with the object of calling a Congress of all Canadian Jews if necessary.' But even with that enthusiasm, the process stalled. The Zionists now balked, and Clarence de Sola withdrew his support. "The Zionists alone,' he told delegates, 'have ... a clearly defined plan for putting an end to Israel's woes. All others have yet no plan, no organization.' The ordinary Jew, however, 'the rank and file, the men who knew suffering,' did support Zionism, 'only the Zionists have ... a plan that would put an end of the Goluth [exile], that would realize our racial individuality, a plan that would enable us to develop to the utmost limit our religious teachings, our spiritual aspirations, our philosophy and our sacred Hebrew language.' De Sola could find little interest in the post-war concerns of a congress: poverty in Montreal, starvation in Eastern Europe, civil and political rights for Jewish minorities, the school question in Montreal. He saw only one solution to the 'Jewish problem': Zionism. No wonder, then, that with Zionist control of the Canadian Jewish Conference the congress idea went nowhere.

These differences reflected the divided state of Canadian Jewry at this critical time; the Alliance was eclectic and feisty, democratic and socialist, while the Federation was cautious and conservative, paternalistic, and traditional. And while both camps believed in the same causes – the presentation of Jewish minority rights to the peace conference, the relief of war sufferers in Eastern Europe, and the future of Jewish settlement in Palestine – there were wide gulfs over the order of priorities and methods of presentation.

In sharp contrast, American Zionists had pushed strongly for an American Jewish Congress in which immigrants could raise more money for Palestine. Moreover, a congress would be a vehicle to lead American Jewry. Thus they would outflank the 'establishment' in the American Jewish Committee, composed of aristocratic and rich Jews of German origin. They resented the East Europeans' attempt to form a new organization tinged with a strong nationalist flavour, which was at odds with their own conservative outlook.[63] Realizing that the East Europeans wanted a voice in American Jewish affairs, Zionists there took the lead in the campaign to establish the American Jewish Congress.

While the Federation's philosophy was a far cry from that of the American Jewish Committee, its leader, Clarence de Sola, was equally an establishment figure. He was uneasy with some of the downtown East Europeans and, though he made efforts to keep them within the ambit of the Federation,[64] he was only partly successful. The Poale Zion clubs had a separate national organization and fundraising campaigns, and their leaders had little to do with the Federation. The Zionists felt threatened in several ways. First, the broad scope and emotional appeal of a national congress would downgrade the Federation, and its role as a conduit to the non-Jewish world. Secondly, it would assume control of all Jewish relief efforts, including those in Palestine, and establish its own priorities. And thirdly, the program of such a congress would include authority over the Zionists at a peace conference or, possibly, radical solutions to contentious issues like the school question.

During the war, the tide of opinion, however, swung gradually in favour of the Alliance. The democratic elections to the newly formed American Jewish Congress in 1918 influenced Canadians, especially westerners, to demand the same system. The Alliance mounted a vigorous campaign in Winnipeg and in the farm colonies and villages where Winnipeg's *Dos Yiddishe Vort* circulated; its powerful editorials through 1917 and 1918 had demanded openness and democracy in the formation of the congress. In Toronto, as well, the Jewish press had become strongly favourable to a congress founded on broad democratic principles. Meanwhile in Montreal Reuben Brainin's short-lived daily *Der Veg* (The Way) tried to mobilize popular support for the proposal. At last, then, a provisional congress committee under Hananiah Caiserman was struck in December of 1918, with the mandate of convening all Jewish organizations – including the Zionist federation – to send representatives to the congress.[65]

Though still harbouring reservations, the Federation – headed from 1919 on by the genial and pliable Archie Freiman, who had succeeded the ailing Clarence de Sola – had agreed to participate in the movement. Newspapers had been ecstatic over the revival of congress proposals and the Zionists' willingness to cooperate. The *Chronicle* thanked them 'for having kept the Jewish national idea alive' and continued: 'Now that the idea is to become realized [through the Balfour Declaration of 1917], it can no longer remain in the hands of the few. It has become the personal problem of every Jew and Jewess the world over.'[66]

Thus the conclave which assembled in Montreal in January 1919 included 125 local organizations representing virtually all shades of opinion. A committee was struck to organize the congress on a democratic basis, with an agenda that included the most burning issues of the day: the establishment of a Jewish national home in Palestine, the recognition and legalization of Jewish national rights 'where they live in compact masses,' 'equal rights' with other minorities in Canada, affiliation with a world Jewish congress, relief of war-sufferers, assistance to Jewish immigration to Canada, and 'co-operation with the Canadian labour movement.'[67]

District conferences in Montreal, Toronto, and Winnipeg were assembled in early March of 1919 to discuss these issues and establish procedures for the election of delegates. Nearly 25,000 ballots were cast in these elections, an astonishingly high figure from the total Jewish population of about 125,000. When the Canadian Jewish Congress convened on March 16 at Montreal's Monument National (a site symbolically important in the emergence of French-Canadian nationalism), the immigrants had finally succeeded in setting up a national democratically elected body. The East European era had arrived. From all across the Dominion the delegates came, from Sault Ste Marie, Birch Hills, and Plum Coulee to Glace Bay, and from all the other cities and towns where Canada's Jews lived, they came to debate the momentous issues then facing the Jewish people in Canada, in Eastern Europe, and in Palestine.

The deliberations showed energy, vision, organizational skill, and understanding of Jewish interests among the leaders of the East Europeans. Several establishment figures were recruited to the leadership, most notably clothing manufacturer Lyon Cohen. His unopposed election to head the Congress deliberations, and, at its close, to the presidency of its permanent organization, indicated his standing, notwithstanding his controversial role in the 1916–17 strike. Cohen's exemplary leadership over the next few days justified this trust.

From these earnest discussions and debates came a remarkably clear statement of concern about the community's self-image and future, as well as about the pressing issues of Jewish minority rights in Eastern Europe, the future of the Jewish national home in Palestine, and, above all, the recognition due to the 'Jewish nation,' which should be 'admitted as a partner in the League of Nations' in order to protect these rights and claims.[68]

In several other resolutions, the Congress addressed the problems of the recent immigrants, including the perennial school question. After much debate on the latter, Louis Fitch and Hananiah Caiserman's resolution instructing the Congress executive 'to promote a system of separate Jewish schools ... wherever such is possible' was passed. Overwhelming support was given to a resolution favouring the five-day workweek, indicating the strength of pro-labour sentiment among the delegates. Protest was lodged against the recent massacres of Jews in Ukraine, Hungary, Poland, and Romania; the Congress directed its representatives at the Versailles Peace Conference to recommend that the countries in which these massacres were perpetrated be forced to grant minority rights.[69]

Thus, when the Congress adjourned late in the evening of March 19 after final words of assessment from Yehuda Kaufman and the distinguished Yiddish philosopher and writer Chaim Zhitlowsky, it had not only made major achievements but it had also established for itself a most formidable agenda.

The *Chronicle* had argued in January 1919, before the Congress was established, that instead of demanding a state immediately, Jews must press the Great Powers for 'opportunities and conditions to enable them to bring the Jews back to Palestine' in order to establish a Jewish majority – in time – under British trusteeship. But 'the Palestine question is [not] the only question [for] world Jewry to solve,' the *Chronicle* had continued. There were specifically Canadian problems, like immigration 'and the enactment of such laws as will insure the future of the Jewish immigrant to this great Canada of ours.' There was as well a need for 'compulsory education throughout the provinces ... that will enable the Jewish immigrant to imbibe the ideals of Canadian citizenship in the least possible time.' And the Congress must have the cooperation of Canadian Jewry's leaders to establish an organization 'representative of all classes.'[70]

But this appeal had yielded only disappointing results. At the meeting held in Montreal in January 1918 to set the congress going, few Montrealers had attended. 'So far the balance of power seems to be with the working classes rather than with the recognized leaders of the community,' the *Chronicle* had commented, lamenting that in comparison with other Jewish communities, Montreal's Jews were apathetic 'and indifferent to all matters that do not affect our own personal welfare ... The Jewish community of Montreal is sufficient unto itself and each little group into which it is divided worships its own particular "ism" and refuses to be drawn into a discussion of the "isms" of any other group.'[71] Essentially, then, Montreal's West End Jews had chosen to opt out. Even when the congress was an 'established fact,' as the *Chronicle* had called it on the eve of elections in late February 1919, 'certain classes in the community have been peculiarly apathetic.' The weekly pleaded with them to participate, or have the congress, which would speak for all of Canadian Jewry, dominated by the classes that were actively participating in the elections. 'We must see to it,' one editorial exhorted, 'that the voice of the Canadian Jewish Congress is not the voice of the radical, the reactionary or the extremists.' A week later, the *Chronicle* was more optimistic: 'the nominations for the ... Congress inspire us with hope. Those, so far chosen, are splendidly representative of the best in Montreal Jewry.'

When the Congress finally met in March 1919, the *Chronicle* hailed it as a most significant event: 'We are a peculiar people, all the more peculiar in that each one of us is an individualist in thought and in action, but WE CAN MEET on common ground and that ground is the welfare of the Jew.' It attributed this success partly to Lyon Cohen, and to the fact that 'every shade of opinion [was] represented except that of the assimilationists.'

Soon after the termination of the first Congress, it was clear that immigration would dominate because on this one topic the Congress could hope to have influence. Sam Jacobs took up this cause; elected MP for Montreal's Cartier riding in 1917, Jacobs was Canada's most important Jew in federal politics and in the ranks of the Liberal Party.[72] At one Congress session, he gave a speech in which he predicted that 'Jewish immigration is bound ... to occur in large numbers' now that the war was over.[73] Because 'these [people] will shortly be knocking at our doors for entry, and it behooves us to see that they are not turned away from our shores indiscriminately ...,' a committee ought to contact the government of Canada 'to ascertain how far restrictions will be made to prevent these people from coming into the country....' Jacobs suspected that the government might introduce a literacy test, as well as make changes to the immigration act to debar persons of questionable political ideas. He pointed out that 'it is at best extremely difficult to ascertain the political past of any immigrant' and noted the room for abuse among officials in determining an individual's political views. In any event, he added, most Jews belonged 'to the moderate parties in the countries from which they come, and these men after a short residence in Canada, enjoying Canadian treatment, eventually give to Canada a high type of citizen, conscious of his obligations, law-abiding and hard working.'

Caiserman, as the general secretary of the CJC, performed veritable prodigies of organization in the face of problems which, in a few short years, would terminate all Congress activities. But after his first year, he was communicating with the Jewish delegation at the Paris Peace Conference pledging Congress's support in attempting to secure recognition both for Jewish minority rights in the new nations of Eastern Europe and Jewish national representation to the League of Nations.

The main Congress activity, however, was to combat the government's strong anti-alien pressures during and after the war. The Winnipeg General Strike of May and June 1919 was attributed to the presence of 'foreigners,' the Austrians, Galicians, and Jews who lived in the city's North End.

A number of Jews had been active before the First World War in the Socialist Party of Canada and the Social Democratic Party.[74] The Mounties (the Royal North West Mounted Police, RNWMP) believed that Jewish-dominated trade unions like the ILGWU and the Amalgamated had connections with the radical and dreaded One Big Union, which was thought to have fomented the general strike. Articles in the Winnipeg press accused 'the Jews' of being 'financial supporters of the strike fulfilling a mission for the higher-up Bolsheviks.' One Jew, in particular, Louis Kon (alias Koniatski, Kohn, or Cohn), was described in police files as 'a rabid Socialist and Bolshevist ... very active during the first week of the strike, in spreading Bolsheviki propaganda among the foreign element of the East Kildonan district ... That Kon is in close connection with the Strike leaders now on trial for Seditious conspiracy is shown by the fact that during the strike the different leaders were constantly in communication with Kon on the telephone.'

A later report stated that 'Kone [sic] is very intimate with [strike leaders] R.B. Russell, Rev. Ivens, Alderman [A.A.] Heaps ... and W.A.

Pritchard. He does not do much public speaking and prefers to work "inside."'[75] There is some evidence that this ascription of an important 'backroom' role to Kon was part of a wider attempt by the Mounties to implicate Jews. On 27 May 1919, at the height of the strike, one officer reported: 'The Jewish element of Winnipeg are taking a very active interest in the strike, even those who have nothing in common with the labor movement are devoting their time in an endeavour to augment this movement.' Another RNWMP spy reported that 'two brothers named Oshenski (Jews) were agitating for the [postal workers] to remain on strike, one of them stating in my presence that "They were not going to swallow the 'Crap' handed out by the speakers."[76] On June 16, when the Mounties arrested eleven of the strike's leaders, three Jews were rounded up and interned, though subsequently released. Many rank-and-file Winnipeg Jews supported the strike, and M. Temensen and Max Tessler represented the Metal Workers on the General Committee. While there were also two Jews on the Citizens' Committee of One Thousand, which opposed the strike, they were punished with electoral defeats by Jewish and other voters in the 1920s.

One month later, Courtland Starnes, the RNWMP's senior officer in Manitoba and a man who believed that the strike marked the start of class war in Canada, observed that the country's welfare hinged on 'keeping away from Jewish Capitalists or Labor men.'[77] Meanwhile, an organization called the Jewish Labour League was named as one of eighteen groups spreading sedition on the Prairies. Other Jewish radical groups of the early 1920s, including the Jewish Socialist Party of Toronto and the Jewish Socialist Democratic Party of Canada, were equally active. The former organization was especially busy in October 1920, publicizing Russian communism and hosting the Winnipeg revolutionary Moses Almazoff, who had been victimized in the aftermath of the general strike. He called for the organization of 'a strong protection army with a dictatorship and discipline.' But the RCMP (as the RNWMP was renamed earlier that year) reported in November that of the approximately five thousand Jewish workers in Toronto, only about fifty had joined this group. Although the RCMP mounted special watch and maintained spies in ethnic communities they suspected of harbouring communists, they were not worried about links between Jews and communism. This report from an officer viewing the situation in Edmonton was probably typical: 'I have never received any information that the Jewish element of this district had any serious revolutionary aims ... [They] appear to be a quiet, law abiding people.'

The emergence of the Social Democratic Party and, in 1921, the Communist Party of Canada heightened nativist and anti-immigrant sentiments. Jews were the object of special resentment. A more immediate concern, however, was that regulations against the immigration of 'enemy aliens' implemented in 1919 would prohibit the landing of Austrian, German, Bulgarian, and Turkish Jews.[78] Jews were later exempted from this order, but the Congress remained deeply concerned about other orders concerning proper papers, minimum landing money, and continuous voyages, as well as the November 1919 revisions to the Dominion's immigration act that allowed wide discretionary powers to admitting officers. Restrictions on Doukhobors, Mennonites, and Hutterites also gave rise to serious concern, especially when, in November 1920, a new order-in-council raised the required amount needed by each immigrant to $250. In addition to dealing with broad Jewish interests, the Congress addressed the issue of family reunification.

The conditions of these displaced persons were especially serious in Ukraine, following terrible pogroms in 1918 and 1919 in the wake of the Russian Revolution and the ensuing civil war. Tens of thousands of Jews had been murdered, some of them in the most bestial fashion, by the armed forces of Simon Petlyura, leader of the short-lived Ukrainian republic, and by other pogromists,[79] while many thousands of others were dwelling as refugees in abominable conditions there and, in increasing numbers, in the eastern sectors of Romania. On 24 November 1919 a huge demonstration of 'mourning and protest' of 30,000 Jews took place in Montreal, while in Winnipeg and Toronto similar demonstrations were held. Several days later, the *Adler* carried detailed reports on the pogroms in Kiev, where in one day some four hundred Jews were murdered amid mayhem and widespread destruction.[80] On November 19, Congress officials requested of the government that an official commission, composed of Jewish Canadians, be sent over to investigate the condition of dependants of Canadian citizens in Ukraine, take them relief supplies, and begin bringing them to Canada. As Simon Belkin, a close observer of contemporary events, put it, 'it was no more a question of ... relief for stricken brethren overseas; it became a question of rescuing tens of thousands of homeless refugees ...'[81]

Belkin headed the Ukrainian Farband, a Dominion-wide organization of Jewish immigrants from Ukraine, which raised funds to send Caiserman to survey the situation there. Meanwhile, the government requested the CJC to supply the names of all Ukrainian dependants whom Canadian families intended to bring to Canada. Eight thousand persons across the country responded to a survey. The information was tabulated and presented to the government, and the Congress awaited its reaction.[82]

Parallel with these activities, the Congress revisited the Montreal school question. At the plenum, delegates like Louis Fitch had made this a special issue, even though non-Montreal delegates were unsure about the proposal to set up a Jewish separate school system there. In any case, the Congress failed to unite a badly divided Montreal community. They proposed to canvass the city's entire Jewish population to determine the aggregate Jewish school taxes – presumably to prove that the Jews were not sponging off the Protestants, who repeatedly alleged that Jewish school taxes did not cover the cost of educating Jewish children in their schools. The Congress's efforts to bring representatives of the three Jewish schools set up by local organizations together under a Congress school committee failed.

In another area, the Congress attempted to intervene with some steamship agents and bankers who, though entrusted with money to send to relations in Europe, were alleged to be dishonest. Caiserman took special interest in establishing an immigrant aid society to handle policy questions and problems of Jewish immigrants, especially those involving the Dominion government. He was successful in bringing several organizations together in 1919, and subsequently the Jewish Immigrant Aid Society was established, with its head office in Montreal and branch offices in Toronto and Winnipeg.[83]

But after such an auspicious beginning in 1919–20, these activities faltered, and in a few years the Congress was virtually defunct. Caiserman, who was apparently unpaid, warned that, despite immense enthusiasm at the first plenum, 'one very important matter escaped the attention of the delegates, namely, to secure the necessary money in order to install an office and conduct it in a businesslike manner.'[84] Lack of adequate finances thereafter proved to be 'a very serious handicap and at times paralyzed [Congress] activities.' But sufficient financial support was lacking, and the Congress agenda met with apathy. Why had a movement that had started with such enthusiasm in 1915 and convened such an impressive gathering in 1919 faltered badly just a year later?

There are several possible explanations. The war had ended, and within a year or two, the worst of the Ukrainian, Polish, and Romanian anti-Jewish outrages had abated. Leadership may have been a fairly serious problem; while Caiserman was an able worker, a cadre of community leaders was needed to energize Canadian Jewry and represent the organization to the public and to governments. Lyon Cohen was undoubtedly such an individual, but he seems to have lost interest after chairing most of the sessions at its first plenum. Perhaps he was too narrowly focused on problems in Montreal itself to take the organization in hand and develop it. Industrialist Mark Workman had been involved initially, but he was not interested, apparently, in carrying the Congress forward. Also, leaders like Cohen and Workman, and many lesser figures, may have been seriously affected by the business recession of the early 1920s, when the clothing industry experienced a serious shake-out. What the Congress needed was someone with Clarence de Sola's drive, single-mindedness, and financial resources. But de Sola was now dead.

The Congress itself was by 1921 crippled by a lack of leadership and funding. It languished for a year or two and then virtually disappeared as a force in Canadian Jewish life; it would not be revived until 1933. Through the 1920s, Canadian Jewry was without its parliament, without its forum of opinions from across the intellectual spectrum, and without a voice for its collective concerns. But it would be wrong to assume that even a stronger organization could have affected public policy on immigration. The exclusionist policies followed in the 1930s were pursued even after the Congress was re-established. A continuing Congress might, however, have achieved a unity of the sort envisioned by Caiserman, who would have carried it forward with his accustomed humanity, energy, and brilliance.

Even so, with the realization of the Congress ideal, Canadian Jewry had reached a watershed in its evolution within the fences of its communal life. The war had brought the community prolonged crisis, terrible disaster, and apparent triumph in perhaps equal measure, and had changed its structure in important ways. The East European immigrants had proved that they could circumvent old organizations like the Zionist federation, and create new ones that served their specific needs. This process had not originated with the war, but the compelling exigencies of wartime were so powerful that the immigrants had swept aside virtually all resistance.

By 1920 it was clear that Canadian Jewry – once again reasserting its distinctiveness from United States Jewry – had become so diversified and so complex that it was remarkable that a truly representative, democratic congress could ever have been created. But behind all the divisions and dissensions lay a vital and – considering the war and the pogroms – common ground. It was hope, even optimism, for the Jewish future. The Bolshevik Revolution, still being tested in 1920, promised reform and reconstruction for Jewish life in Russia. The Balfour Declaration promised a Jewish national home in Palestine. The freedom offered by North America promised material improvement and social equality. The Treaty of Versailles, with its provisions for minority rights in the new nations of Eastern Europe, promised equality for the Jews of Poland, Romania, and Hungary. Most of these promises were yet to be realized. But enough had been tasted and enjoyed to give substance to an optimism that, in years before, had been little more than a dream.

The year 1920 was a watershed in Canadian Jewish identity in this northern land of 'limited identities,' where region, culture, and class differ so significantly. It is clear that as early as the American Revolution, when loyalty to the Crown became a hallmark of British North American identity, the Jewish community was divided – as were the non-Jews in both Quebec and Nova Scotia – and that Britishness among Jews was just as pronounced as it was in the general population – perhaps even more so. In view of their minority status, most Jews likely would have been reluctant to utter dissent and thus attract attention (and even antisemitism) on the grounds of disloyalty. Yet it was not only fear that inspired their Britishness; it was also pride in Britain's accomplishments and the borrowed prestige of its imperial stature. In the mid-nineteenth century, Abraham de Sola noted the differences between his political context and those of his American counterparts, while his sons, Clarence and Meldola, were by 1900 fully fledged Canadian nationalists. To them, Zion's heritage would be redeemed through Albion's magnanimity and tolerance.

As well, the Canadian Jewish identity was now imprinted by the crude rawness of this enormous land, which stamped itself on those who struggled to make the living which conditions in their European homeland denied them. Intellectuals like Reuben Brainin noticed such coarseness immediately on reaching Montreal, in the early 1900s: 'No one asks whence or whither? why or wherefore? There are no wayfarers on the paths of the mind and no one turns the vessel to see its nether side. All but count and account, and merely pose the question, how much? ... There is much laboring and little of the song of labor.'[85] Brainin and other intellectuals, and Montreal Yiddish poets of the 1920s like Jacob I. Segal, understood instinctively the problem of maintaining a Jewish identity in Canada. Segal's haunting poem 'Fremd' (Strange) expressed his sense of ambivalence upon witnessing the transformations in the Jews around him, caught between rejoicing for the opportunity and freedom Canadian life offered and mourning the loss of a culture which had not fully survived the migration to the New World:

> And sometimes – a Sunday morning,
> When the houses are still sleeping here,
> It seems to me the spirit of the neighbourhood
> Is like a world of very long ago.
> Here lives another generation,
> That has nothing at all to do with Montreal.[86]

Longing for that 'other generation' of the past, Segal, in his poem 'A Jew,' becomes the quintessential Canadian Jew caught between the fading tradition of the past and the confusing modernity of the present and future:

> It's no use my turning east
> and it's no use my praying west,
> I'm forever on the road, in transit,
> dragging my baggage of exile.
> ...
> But it survives, my Jewish tree,
> like a talisman of homecoming
> and it longs to gather all us Jews
> from our spaceless boundaries of loss.[87]

The 'baggage of exile' was the past, the very burden of Jewish history: the challenge, on the one hand, of repairing the world, and the responsibility, on the other, of building a rampart around the Torah.

Modernity was also seen as threatening the continuity of Jewish religious tradition, the Halakha, which embodied the hallowed principles and practices of observant Jews. The openness and materialism of North American culture robbed those Jews who were drawn into its vortex of their own rich tradition. Rabbi Yudel Rosenberg, a Chassid known as the Skaryszewer Ilui (the Genius of Skaryszew), who had moved from his native Poland to Toronto in 1913 and to Montreal in 1919, lamented the widespread violation of the Sabbath among Canada's Jews, and concluded that Torah Judaism was in a state of siege.[88] In 1923 he published an eloquent plea, *A Brivele fun di Zisse Mamme Shabbes Malkese zu Ihre Zihn un Tekhter fun Idishn Folk* (A Letter from the Sweet Mother Sabbath Queen to Her Sons and Daughters of the Jewish People), in which he implored Canada's traditional Jews to return to Sabbath observance. Failure to do so, he implied, would prolong the already overlong exile of the Jewish people, and delay the coming of the Messiah. But who would hear the rabbi's urgent appeal amid the buzz of sweatshop sewing machines and the noise of the 'jargoning city'? And who would heed his call for Torah observance, forsaking the blandishments of North American culture? Indeed, how could Canadian modernity accommodate such a tradition as that of Eastern European Jews? Such questions cried out for answers, but the formulation of those answers had not yet begun.

History's message was at best ambiguous for Canadian Jewry in 1920. Their past was marked by massive migration to cities, towns, and farms, and by a European Judaic ghetto culture then being transformed amid revolution, nationalism, and modernization. By 1920 these forces were already radically altering the coordinates of East European Jewish existence. Thus the 'baggage of exile' brought to Canada by the Jewish immigrants to be admitted during the 1920s would typically be somewhat different from that of their pre-1914 counterparts. The newcomers had experienced first-hand a war of unparalleled bloodshed and destruction, the massive upheaval of the Russian Revolution, the ensuing devastating Russian civil war, the emergence of Polish and Romanian independence, and the terrible Ukrainian pogroms.

If the past was ambiguous, so was the present, and the future was an enigma. Canada's Jews were linked to Europe and the past, while they built new lives in Canada and contributed to the reconstruction of the old-new land in Palestine, thereby investing in the present and the future. Canadian Jewish history to 1920 – and well beyond – was shaped by a set of coordinates which were unique to the northern half of this continent, and which resulted in the evolution of a distinctive community: Canada's political structure and dual 'founding peoples,' its economic dependency and long-lasting constitutional colonial status, its own immigration patterns and urbanization processes, had together shaped a historical experience different from that of United States Jewry. But these were not the only elements that had moulded Canadian Jewish history, important though they were. There was also the past beyond Canada. Canada's Jews were not like Ireland's 'exiles' in the New World, who were 'involuntary' emigrants to America.[89] Jews were generally willing emigrants from their most recent sojourning places, though some of them may have seen themselves as exiles from an ancient home. Now taking root in the northern half of North America, they continued to exist – with still-worried glances over their shoulders – in both parochial and secular time, as well as in Canadian space, awaiting an uncertain future.

PART THREE

Between the Wars, 1919–1939

7 Jewish Geography of the 1920s and 1930s

The 1920s dawned amid widespread mourning for the terrible losses the nation had sustained on the Western Front, the Red Scare of the Winnipeg General Strike, and the economic uncertainties of a vulnerable staple economy. Just as Canada was in transition to a peacetime society, the Jewish community was undergoing its own transformations. Louis Rosenberg's book *Canada's Jews: A Social and Economic Study of the Jews in Canada* provides a superb portrait of the community's evolution in the 1920s,[1] surpassing any work then available on United States Jewry. Based on the Census of Canada data, it showed significant changes since 1911. Overall, the population had increased by 26 per cent, from 125,197 in 1921 to 155,614 in 1931, but with only a mere 8.3 per cent growth, to 168,585, in 1941. Compared with the total Canadian population, Jews were more urbanized, more concentrated in lower-middle-class occupations, and better educated; divorce rates were higher, while fertility, death, and natural-increase rates were lower; and the Jewish population was younger.

In Toronto the population rose by 34.5 per cent during the 1920s, exceeding Montreal's growth of 26.6 per cent and Winnipeg's 19.0 per cent.[2] Most Jewish residents still lived in centre-town wards: in Montreal's St Louis and Laurier wards (where Jews were a majority), as well as in St Michel and St Jean Baptiste (where they were more than a third); in Toronto's Wards 4 and 5; and in Winnipeg's Main Street area, north of the CPR yards. But suburbanization was under way as Toronto's Jews began moving into York Township and Forest Hill; Montrealers into Outremont, Westmount, and Notre Dame de Grace; and Winnipeggers north into newer areas of Ward 3.

Their numbers also increased in the smaller cities, such as Rouyn-Noranda, North Bay, Sudbury, Timmins, and Fort William, where resource-based industries created boom-town growth. In Cornwall, textile and paper factories had opened. St Catharines, Oshawa, and Windsor, centres of automobile manufacturing, attracted rising numbers of Jewish businessmen and professionals.[3] And economic expansion created by Sarnia's petrochemical works, Hamilton's steel and numerous secondary manufacturers, and Kitchener's beer, rubber, and furniture plants, all gave rise to larger Jewish communities.

While these places flourished, others dwindled.[4] In the Maritimes, the communities in Sydney, Moncton, and Fredericton grew, while those in Saint John, Halifax, and Glace Bay declined. Out west, Jewish numbers were growing in Melville, Selkirk, Medicine Hat, Calgary, Vancouver, Edmonton, Regina, Saskatoon, Lethbridge, and Prince Albert. But those in villages and towns, mostly in Saskatchewan, fell, as well as in several small towns and cities in Quebec and Ontario. And as Rosenberg's book emphasized, Jews were widely dispersed in Prairie towns and villages. In Saskatchewan, Jewish populations disappeared in thirty-four communities during the 1920s but turned up in sixty-four other small places, where life was very difficult. Rosenberg noted: 'The majority of Jews living isolated in [them] must either cease to be Jewish except by accident of birth or must eventually leave for larger Jewish centres as soon as their children reach the age when they require Jewish education to supplement the education given in the public schools.'

Over 55 per cent of Jews in 1931, in contrast to almost 51 per cent of Canadians of all origins, were in what Rosenberg called the 'productive age group,' between twenty and fifty-nine, 'who are assumed to possess the full capacity to work.' Jews had the highest marriage rates of all Canadians over the age of fifteen; 41.33 per cent were married, compared with 37.83 per cent of 'all origins,' reflecting the fact that 'Jews tended to immigrate as family units rather than as individuals.'

A higher marriage rate, however, did not result in higher-than-average fertility. Between 1926 and 1936, the ten-year average Jewish birth rate was 14.2 (per 1,000), compared with 22.1 for 'all origins,' and the Jewish death rate was 5.5, compared with 10.3, limiting the Jewish rate of natural increase to only two-thirds that of the national average. Meanwhile, intermarriage was inched up from 4.64 per cent in 1926 to 5.5 per cent in 1936, nearly twice as high for men as for women. Over time, then, with no new significant immigration, their numbers would likely diminish. As to the economic structure of Canadian Jewry, Rosenberg calculated that

47.54 per cent of its population were gainfully employed, just marginally less than that of Canada as a whole, possibly because Jews stayed in school longer than did most others.

As Jews moved out of the old inner-city areas into new suburbs, they built synagogues. In the early 1920s, Montreal's Reformers' Temple Emanu-el and the Conservatives' Shaar Hashomayim (Gates of Heaven) were erected in Westmount. In the meantime, Toronto Reformers were completing their new Holy Blossom Temple on Bathurst Street. Whether of Romanesque and Moorish design, like Holy Blossom, or modernistic, like most others, these substantial synagogues testified to the affluence, ambition, and self-confidence of their Jewish middle-class members. Some of these edifices included social and athletic facilities. They often displayed domes, always prominently showed the Star of David, and, usually, had large Hebrew lettering carved in stone over the entrance.

Most of the new synagogues were less pretentious, such as Toronto's Rodfei Sholem's (Pursuers of Peace), a modest structure in the Kensington Market area, or the Agudath Israel Anshei Sepharade (Organization of Israel, Sephardic People) on Palmerston Avenue, both of them in the heart of the less affluent Jewish community, which was moving westward from the older centre-town area of settlement.[5] Understated buildings were the norm in the smaller communities, too, although Windsor's Sha'ar Hashomayim (Gates of Heaven) congregation erected an impressive version of its Montreal namesake in 1931. Some communities added a degree of decoration, such as Knesset Israel (Congregation of Israel), an unimposing structure in Toronto's Junction area, which was adorned inside with depictions of scenes from the Ethics of the Fathers. As well, simple houses or former churches were converted for use, all a testimony to their members' commitment to Jewish continuity.

Jewish geography across Canada remained overwhelmingly urban. In nearly every city and town – as well as in many western villages – there was a Jewish presence, if only a general store. In some there was also a Jewish district, a group of stores constituting an ethnic sub-economy of delicatessens, bookstores, bakeries, groceries, butcher shops, clothing stores, pawnshops, and institutions. Such places were not 'ghettos' in any sense; they were areas like Montreal's The Main, Toronto's Kensington Market, and Winnipeg's North End – areas where there was a large Jewish community and with it the opportunity to buy Jewish food, books, and religious items and attend religious, social, and political gatherings. Even a small city like Brantford, Ontario, had a tiny Jewish centrepoint near the old shul on Palace Street, with about a dozen families living within a four-block radius, close to Harris's grocery.[6] And in nearby Hamilton, the community centred on Cannon Street, with Boleslavsky's delicatessen serving as a favourite meeting place.

These neighbourhoods were not coterminous with all Jewish-owned businesses, such as clothing stores, metal or upholstery workshops, and junkyards, which were not oriented specifically to a Jewish clientele and were spread widely. Those enterprises that were located in the 'Jewish area,' on the other hand, were intended for a recognized and usually sizeable population. These locales were often situated in close proximity to non-Jewish neighbourhoods, like those populated by French Canadians and Ukrainians in The Main, Italians and Chinese near Spadina, and Ukrainians and Germans in the North End.

Even in Montreal's St Louis and Laurier wards, where Jews were a majority, few streets or blocks were entirely Jewish; French-Canadian neighbours, stores, and churches were never far away. The same was true in the other cities. In Toronto, for example, while Harbord Collegiate and Central Tech were largely Jewish, the nearby Christie Pits baseball and football fields attracted a multi-ethnic presence.[7] In Winnipeg's St John's Collegiate, Jews, while numerous, rubbed shoulders with the diverse non-Jewish majority; together they shared the North End streets and parks.

In Vancouver, the immigrants who had settled first in the East End, and had built a new synagogue in 1921, began moving in large numbers towards the south and west very rapidly in the 1920s.[8] A new Jewish community centre was built, reflecting the current economic improvement. This continued during the 1930s, although the old East End, now home to Asian and European immigrants, continued to serve as home to the stores selling Jewish foods.

As the 'Gateway to the West,' Winnipeg had mushroomed in size during the great boom before the First World War. The Jewish population had increased more than eightfold between 1901 and 1911, and by over 50 per cent again to reach 14,837 in 1921.[9] It further grew to 17,435 in 1941. Thus, there was modest growth during the 1920s and 1930s, essentially mirroring the changes in the city as a whole. While almost 98 per cent of all Jews remained within city limits, and mainly in Ward 3, they migrated northward and eastward into newer and more commodious housing close to the older district.

Jews enjoyed a higher representation in Winnipeg's professional classes than others. This trend was accelerating. Although comprising only 7.5 per cent of the population, they were 11.2 per cent of its lawyers in 1931 and, in 1941, 19.6 per cent.[10] In these two census years, Jews were 11.5 and 18.3 per cent of the doctors and 18.5 and 11.4 per cent of that city's teachers. Meanwhile, by 1941, they made up more than a third of the city's retail merchants and more than two-thirds of its hawkers and pedlars. They were also strongly represented among skilled tradesmen such as furriers, electricians, sheetmetal workers, tailors, and teamsters. Among women, on the other hand, the only professionals were a few teachers and nurses. Others were sales people, bookkeepers and cashiers, and music teachers. A high proportion of Winnipeg's Jews attended school. More than a third of all males had nine to twelve years of education, second only to the 'Celto-Saxons' (Rosenberg's designation), while women were even more schooled than their male counterparts. Among male Winnipeggers having thirteen years or more of schooling, Jews led all other ethnic groups, although Jewish women lagged behind.

The Winnipeg community then centred mostly in the North End; that broad area, bisected by Main Street, was also an 'unenclosed ghetto' where immigrants of many origins found some solace from what appeared to be a hostile and exclusionist environment.[11] Their vibrancy made the district a unique and culturally rich place, a veritable Vilna – the lively Lithuanian city of unparalleled Jewish intellectual life – a landscape of restaurants, delicatessens, bakeries, barbershops, bookstores, photo studios, markets, synagogues, schools, and other centres set in this Prairie metropolis of frigid winters and scorching summers. Jack Ludwig's story 'Requiem for Bibul' recalls the flavour of Winnipeg's fruit pedlars in the district's smelly back alleys and run-down streets, with their horses, shnorrers, kibitzers, and rabbinical students, while Miriam Waddington's poems recount the sweetness of her youth amidst its special Yiddishkeit.[12]

Women's lives were governed by many of the traditional assumptions and rules – they should marry young, have children, and run a 'proper' Jewish home – even though circumstances had changed in the transformations from Europe to North America. Thus women who came of age in the interwar years remembered that in families with scarce resources education was usually reserved for boys, who were destined to be breadwinners in their own families; women were encouraged to attend business college, take secretarial jobs, and await marriage. Others clerked in stores, while a few trained as nurses, teachers or, worst of all jobs, clothing factory workers.[13] But there were some exceptions; Mildred Gutkin's parents 'simply assumed that education was for all,' an attitude that allowed her to attend both the Universities of Manitoba and Toronto. But she knew that she was privileged 'and that I was asking for something special.'[14]

The size of Jewish families was diminishing in the 1930s, but exceeded all other ethnic groups. In 1931, 41.6 per cent of all families had three or more children, compared with 37.7 per cent of East European, 27.2 per cent of Scandinavian, and 24.8 per cent of Celto-Saxon families.[15] Both in 1931 and 1936, the proportion of Jewish families in Winnipeg without children was lower than that among any other ethnic group.

Housing patterns indicated that Jews stood behind East Europeans in the owner-occupant category in 1936, Jews being likelier to live in rented quarters as tenants or sub-tenants, perhaps preferring to invest in business and education rather than in home ownership. Winnipeg Jews possessed twenty institutional buildings, including seven schools, eight synagogues, an old people's home, a sick-benefit hall, a fraternal lodge headquarters, a Zionist hall, and an orphanage. Berel and Bertha Miller's bookstore at 816 ½ Main Street was regarded as an informal cultural home, especially for the newest immigrants.[16] Most of these institutions were clustered near Main Street above Aberdeen and thus served numerous organizations, including *landsmanshaften*; free-loan, charitable, relief, and social service societies; and many political and cultural associations.[17] Of great pride were the schools, which were monuments to Jewish commitment to continuity and expressions of Jewish ethnicity.[18]

Meanwhile, the Jewish farm colonies began a slow decline. Louis Rosenberg, who had taught school in the Lipton, Saskatchewan, colony from 1915 to 1919 and served as Jewish Colonization Association director from 1919 to 1940, attributed this to 'the vagaries of drought, grasshoppers and world wheat prices.'[19] Interwar world wheat prices gyrated wildly, while farm mechanization and drought drove tens of thousands of bankrupt western farmers off the land. Similarly affected were the settlements near Winnipeg, where Jewish dairy farmers, known to some local wags as the *milkhike Yidn*, gradually succumbed to the Depression. The colonies had been declining since 1911, when they held a total of 1,316 persons. By 1921 there were 1,278, and in 1931 only 876.[20] The numbers of independent Jewish-owned farms had risen significantly, from 325 in 1911 to 1,290 in 1921 and 1,312 in 1931, but the heyday of the colonies was clearly gone.

This decrease was not entirely a result of 'climatic and economic conditions,' as Rosenberg stated, or of insufficient Jewish institutions.[21] The real problem was serious undercapitalization. The average value of a 'Jewish farm' in Saskatchewan in 1911 was $3,086, compared with $8,766 for all farms. This gap narrowed over the next ten years and disappeared by 1931, but even then, Jewish farmers grew significantly less wheat and oats than the average, had less improved land per farm, and invested less in implements. As late as 1931, one of every five Jewish farmers owned an automobile, and one in seven a tractor – compared with one of every two and one in every three non-Jewish farmers. The ratios for combine ownership were even worse. Except for those such as the Hoffers at Sonnenfeld and 'Uncle' Mike Usiskin at Edenbridge, Jews as a group had not succeeded at western farming.

The Jewish Colonization Association, the farmers' main support, encountered serious discontent in 1930 among some of the Hirsch colony settlers because of a dispute over land titles and other matters.[22] Immigration Department officials like F.C. Blair took note of these events, which enhanced his department's negative view of Jews as farmers and potential immigrants.

However, on a visit to the colonies in the early 1920s, Vladimir Grossman, a Montreal Yiddish journalist, reported prosperity, noting 'splendid farm equipment, ... expensive threshing machines and huge tractors ... splendid horses ... sleek cattle and yards full of chickens.' At Edenbridge, farmers concentrated on growing wheat, and while Hirsch farms were being ravaged by an infestation of locusts, farmers there nevertheless were 'looking forward to better times.' Grossman shrewdly concluded, however, that the JCA had made a serious mistake, because the colonies were so 'scattered and far flung.' In his book *The Soil's Calling*, he described what he saw and, very encouraged overall, suggested that farming offered an opportunity for Jewish 'young people with no future in the cities ... [who] should be directed land-ward.'

Still, there was no escaping the fact that Prairie farming was rough and demanding, especially during the lean years of the 1930s. No better insight can be gained than by reading Mike Usiskin's *Oksen Und Motoren* (translated as *Uncle Mike's Edenbridge*), about life on his colony north of Humbolt, in the Park Belt of Saskatchewan's north country. Written by a curmudgeon who had toiled a lifetime on his farmstead, this memoir speaks of his love for the land, the freedom he found in clearing it, the joy of harvesting and helping neighbours – Jew and Gentile alike – and of the contentment of a simple life far from the corrupting city.[23] He recorded with delight the numerous social gatherings: dances, musicals, plays, pageants, and addresses by visiting speakers.

Offsetting those rosy remembrances, there were social problems at Edenbridge.[24] The colonists were not homogeneous in origin, religious belief, or social outlook. Those like Usiskin who had hoped to emulate life in the new Jewish settlements in Palestine were disappointed by this discord. 'Our dreams were shattered,' he lamented. The colony lived on nevertheless, buttressed by stalwarts like him who worked the land until they died.

Land of Hope, the memoirs of Israel Hoffer, a pioneer farmer near the colony of Sonnenfeld, tells of poverty, confusion, jealousy, and discontent with JCA's policies that led to bitterness and, sometimes, to violence.[25] The hardships of life were overwhelming. 'My parents were thirteen years in Hirsch farming,' one daughter of colonists remembers. 'They had a hard time ... The last few years we were there the crops didn't yield so very good.' Lonely, poor, inexperienced, and uncertain of the future, Jewish farmers – like so many others during the Dirty Thirties – tended to give up and drift to the cities and towns. Many stuck it out at Sonnenfeld, however, while the arrival of a few new colonists brought over by the JCA rejuvenated the colony for a few years.

Justifiably, Jewish officials were concerned. L. Mallach, a writer for the *Keneder Adler*, travelled west in the summer of 1929 and did an on-site survey of troubled Edenbridge. 'Unless we encourage more people to go on the land in Western Canada,' he predicted, 'there is a great danger that the doors of Canada will close entirely upon the Jews.'[26] He warned the JCA against certain practices. Aware of the JCA's poor record in Argentina, Mallach thought the organization insensitive and arrogant, alleging that its new Canadian director had not even bothered to see Edenbridge for himself.[27] Consequently, the colonists were despondent. 'Out of the eyes of every one of [them] despair stared me in the face,' he wrote. 'Who is it that is going to reap the harvest of our toil?' they asked him. 'I looked at their hands, so much like the plowed up fields and they looked to me not like skin and flesh but rather like fossilized rock, their faces were brown and burnt and their lips a froth-like blue.'

The Jewish colonies declined as compared to those of the Mormons because of social, religious, and institutional reasons.[28] The Mormons built compact colonies of contiguous settlement, were committed to building 'a new Zion in the wilderness' as a refuge from persecution, and enjoyed the benefits of very substantial continuing material and moral support from their mother church in Utah. The Jews, on the other hand, did not establish such close-knit settlements, with the consequence that vital needs of social contact and religious requirements (a *mikveh* – ritual bath, kosher meat, and a synagogue) were very difficult to meet. Furthermore, the Jewish agricultural experience in the Canadian West lacked the intense religious idealism of the Mormons; though a few were idealists like Mike Usiskin, and few had adequate farming experience, Jews settled essentially for economic reasons. And finally, support form the JCA did not equal Mormon backing from Utah. Consequently, Jewish efforts were unsuccessful. Most other immigrant groups settling the West, including the Mormons, had an agricultural tradition. By contemporary standards, unlike Jews, many of the early Ukrainian settlers also arrived with substantial capital resources (being 'peasants of means'), and this too facilitated their adjustment to the demands of Prairie farming.[29]

In the towns and villages scattered across the Prairies, there were many Jewish storekeepers fluent enough in Ukrainian and German to serve the immigrant farmers better than their Anglo-Saxon competitors.[30] With its twenty to thirty Jewish families, Melville was typical, although larger than most. Here, these families – children especially – tried to balance their Canadian and Jewish identities. Ruth Bellan belonged to both Canadian Girls in Training (CGIT), puzzling over the Christian prayers, and to Young Judaea, stressing Jewish identity and pride in Zionism. In Birch Hills, Gretna, Plum Coulee, Altona, and Grandview, the towns where her father opened one ill-fated store after another, Fredelle Bruser felt the angst of being a Jewish child, the only one in her town, who was denied the experience of Christmas in her Prairie community. Out in these small places, where most Jews survived on mutual support, Anne Werb remembered going from the hamlet of Richard, Saskatchewan, to a nearby village for the High Holy Days.[31] Jewish accounts of relationships with neighbours usually stress conviviality and cooperation, although the persistent stereotyping provided an underlay of antisemitism.

After 1945 the JCA settled some Holocaust-survivor families on farms in the Niagara peninsula and southwestern Ontario. Mostly, it was a one-generation phenomenon. As in the West a generation earlier, most of the youth moved to the cities, where farm life was a distant memory. Nostalgia lingered, however. For many years, former residents of the Trochu colony in Alberta, now living in Los Angeles, formed their own club, met for dinner once a month, and reminisced about the good old days.[32]

Urban life presented other challenges. Toronto's commerce and industry in the 1920s and 1930s began to rival that of Montreal. Its Jewish community approached Montreal's in size and wealth, increasing from 34,770 in 1921 to 46,751 in 1931 and 49,046 in 1941.[33] Jews were the largest minority group in the city, where they were gradually moving westward in the belt between Queen and Bloor streets, towards Dovercourt. One scholar found that 'on many streets, such as Kensington Avenue, individual block[s] ... which had been entirely non-Jewish were eighty or even 100 per cent Jewish by 1931 and that 63 per cent of Jewish families were home owners.' But this was by no means a Jewish ghetto. In the areas known as St John Ward, the McCaul Street enclave, or Kensington Market, Jews had neighbours of many diverse origins.

Despite some segregation, self-imposed or otherwise, a degree of integration was taking place in the city's public schools. Immigrant parents fervently supported both education and maintaining Jewish identity.[34] Contrary to early years, immigrants sent their daughters to academic schools, like Harbord Collegiate, which promised status, secular culture, and a route to integration. Jewish children were doing well in Toronto's public schools, according to a 1926 report, where they constituted 80 per cent of the student body.[35] Even though Yiddish was usually spoken at home, they not only had higher scores on IQ tests than their classmates, but also excelled in silent reading and arithmetic, and, in general, had 'a greater per centage above the average,' and surpassed Gentiles in the 'superior' and 'very superior' categories. These results, the survey reported, accorded with those achieved in New York and California, although it was noted that, 'while Jews are fairly representative of their race as such, the Gentiles are of a lower social order than those of most Gentile school districts, and hence are scarcely representative of the Gentile race.'

Still composed overwhelmingly of immigrants, the Toronto Jewish community's occupational profile in the mid-1920s showed interesting diversity.[36] While many earned their living exclusively within its confines, as rabbis, cantors, Hebrew teachers, ritual slaughterers, and as suppliers of ethnic services such as butchers, bakers, delicatessen owners, grocers, poulterers, and fishmongers, there were also insurance and real estate agents, lawyers, accountants, doctors, and dentists, whose clientele was overwhelmingly Jewish. Carpenters, plumbers, painters, blacksmiths, and builders serviced Jewish customers; while in the clothing factories, thousands of operators and pressers worked within this ethnic economy. But there were also many Jews whose livelihoods bridged them to the wider Toronto world. Jewish-owned movie houses were spread across the city, as were numerous other establishments: cleaners and pressers, tailors, milliners, tobacconists, confectioners, and jewellers, while shops selling shoes and men's and ladies' wear proliferated. And by horse-drawn wagon or truck, dozens of Jewish junk dealers scoured the city and the countryside for industrial and household cast-offs for recycling.

This snapshot of Toronto's Jewish occupational diversity and enterprise taken in the relatively prosperous mid-1920s – and Montreal and Winnipeg were likely similar – could well have changed for the worse. There was undoubtedly much downward mobility during the Depression. But many immigrants had apparently arrived with substantial skills and experience – even some capital – that permitted them to adapt to the modernizing urban economy. In this environment, opportunity beckoned and many with humble skills – a tailor, say – might start as a modest clothing contractor. A carpenter, bricklayer, or tinsmith might build a house or two 'on spec.' Thus previously established class identity began to vanish in the open economy of Canada's cities. Immigrant entrepreneurs, once perhaps class-conscious workers, transformed themselves precariously into the middle class and, though some fell back, many were moving ahead in an environment where class lines were blurred.[37] Many Jews, nevertheless, had to scramble for a living, while trying to adjust to new cultural realities. Allan Grossman, later a member of the Ontario Legislature and a cabinet minister, remembered the family tensions ensuing from these circumstances: 'the struggle for existence engaged our attention so much that we missed a great deal ... Perhaps this spiritual separation of immigrant parents from their children is part of the price of migration.'[38]

Housing availability and opportunities for work in the Spadina district clothing factories influenced Jewish demography in Toronto. However, legally enforceable restrictive covenants prevented them and other ethnic 'undesirables' from buying property in certain areas.[39] Nevertheless, some Jewish grocers, tailors, pedlars, salesmen, contractors, butchers, and junk dealers dabbled in real estate, achieving modest success. Some itinerant pedlars of dry goods, for example, became small-scale storekeepers, proudly posing with their families for an opening-day portrait before the shop window.

Although largely law-abiding, criminality was not unknown in the community, notably bootlegging, which was sometimes combined with gambling, prizefighting, or prostitution.[40] Others specialized. In 1926, one Toronto Jewish bootlegger was doing $1.6 million business annually.[41] Some Jews were also members of certain 'mobs,' like that of Hamilton's Rocco Perri, who from the 1910s to the 1930s ran extensive bootlegging operations managed by his wife Bessie Starkman. She was murdered in 1930 and was succeeded as Perri's wife by Annie Newman. At the same time, in Montreal Anna Herscovitch, alias 'Madame Anita,' teamed up with mobster Tony Frank to run a string of notorious brothels on Cadieux Street, the city's main tenderloin.

In Toronto, which was still largely composed of immigrants, the local *landsmanshaften*, fraternal orders, and mutual-benefit and friendly societies functioned independently. With their welfare dimensions, provisions for burial, sickness or death benefits, familiarity, comfort, interest-free loans, friendly advice, and democratic character, the *landsmanshaften* possessed a *heymishe* (homelike) quality missing in the community-wide philanthropies. They provided also a 'wraparound culture' of social activities that involved their members in regular, almost familial, association.

The Workmen's Circle and the Jewish National Workers' Alliance, both of them political organizations, also provided life insurance as well as sickness and death benefits.[42] By 1945, Toronto also had twenty-eight mutual-benefit societies, with memberships ranging from 38 to 594, and Jewish lodges in fraternal orders like the Knights of Pythias, the Ancient Order of Foresters, and the Independent Order of Odd Fellows. Formed to meet practical needs, these associations grew from a total of 1,086 members in 1911 to 3,120 in 1921, 5,600 in 1931, 6,700 in 1941, and 9,500 in 1945, encompassing nearly half of all Jewish males between twenty and fifty-five years of age, mostly wage earners, artisans, and salaried employees. For example, the Peretz Branch of the Jewish National Workers' Alliance had thirty-four wage earners and fifteen artisans among its sixty-eight members in 1941. Of the radical left-wing United Jewish Peoples' Order (UJPO), 441 members in 1936, or 68 per cent, were wage earners, the vast majority of them needleworkers.

The names of the *landsmanshaften* proclaimed their founders' origins, most of them towns in the Kielce area of southwestern Poland, giving the community a distinctly Polish face. Other societies included Jews from Galicia, Kiev, Minsk, and Belarus.[43] Another society was named Anshei New York, honouring the city that was also a source of inspiration for North American Jews, while yet another was grandly entitled Hebrew Men of England, borrowing the prestige of the British Empire.

Other societies were based on Jewish tradition, such as Chevra Mishnaith (Students of the Mishnah), or were given names like the Hebrew Friendly, Judaean Benevolent, Sons of Abraham, Tifereth Israel (Glory of Israel), Hebrew Sick Benefit, Beth Aaron, Agudath Achim (Club of Brothers), or, grandly, Pride of Israel. Other associations, those with less formal structures usually, were attached to the few Hassidic rabbis, like the distinguished Rabbi Yehudah Yudel Rosenberg.

These associations owned and managed 40 per cent of all Jewish cemetery land – to keep their members' burial costs low.[44] Comparing Jewish and non-Jewish societies in Ontario, one study found that Jews had longer life expectancy and similar sickness rates, and roughly five to six times the hospitalization rates of non-Jews. On average, Jews, however, paid at least twice as much in dues to their societies for these benefits and support to local Jewish philanthropies. As well, doctors on long-term contracts treated members and families in return for an annual per capita payment. The societies paid out seven or eight times more than non-Jewish associations for medical attention.

Although the *landsmanshaften* provided small loans to their members, some cities, had separate lending societies that served the wider Jewish community.[45] In the 1918 annual statement of the Montreal Hebrew Loan Association's registry, of 1,090 applicants, 31 were classified as ritual slaughterers, Hebrew teachers, or Jewish booksellers; 24 as merchants or manufacturers; 46 as pedlars; 21 as shop owners and tradesmen; and 25 as agents. And there were many in more humble occupations: 16 farmers; 11 contractors; 38 custom tailors, tailor-shop owners, or contractors; and 44 milk, bread, fruit, or ginger-ale pedlars. There were owners of 47 shoe-repairing stores; 77 country, junk, rag, second-hand clothing, furniture, and fur pedlars; 54 small proprietors; 345 working men; and 239 store owners. While most of that group were seeking business loans, thirty-eight were for remittances to Europe and five to delighted parents (happily?) about 'to marry off a daughter.'

Activity was reportedly brisk during the 1930s. Loans usually ran from fifteen to twenty-five dollars for four-to-six-month periods; borrowers signed notes, which required one or two endorsers. Toronto's Association took no other forms of security, but Montreal's accepted jewellery and government bonds.[46] In the Depression year of 1932, with a capital of $53,849, the Montreal Association loaned $105,227 to 960 borrowers, but reported that due dates for one-third of its loans had to be extended and that it was difficult to get endorsers. In Toronto that year, virtually all of the $25,437 on loan to 653 borrowers was repaid, but more slowly than the year before. Then, in 1937, it was reported that while the Association was offering to defer repayments, the number of supporters for '[this] sorely needed Jewish aristocracy of true service was dropping.'

By 1935 loans in Montreal rose 23.5 per cent to $130,104 and in 1937 another 27.59 per cent to $166,000. Toronto loans, meanwhile, rose from $24,775 in 1935 to $37,235 in 1937, and the average loan nearly doubled.[47] Despite mounting pressures during the difficult 1930s, however, on the whole borrowers paid back their loans, although during these hard years some required extensions.

Home to nearly 40 per cent of Canada's Jews, Montreal* – the poet A.M. Klein's beloved 'City Metropole' – was undergoing change. From 52,287 persons in 1921, the Jewish population reached 63,721 in 1941.[48] By the 1920s, virtually the entire city section from the waterfront north in a belt along St Lawrence Boulevard ('the Main') to the lower reaches of Outremont constituted a huge, predominantly Jewish enclave of factories, shops, synagogues, and tightly packed housing. Although they lived in other districts, the fact that this 'Jewish quarter' was at the geographical centre of the city and divided the French and the English sections of Montreal was symbolic of the precarious marginality of the Jewish presence to both. The Jewish population in the suburbs of Outremont and Westmount grew by nearly 60 per cent each, while the city of Montreal's grew by 21.78 per cent. Clearly, the shifts out of the older areas of settlement along the St Laurent/Main axis to the western suburbs was well under way. Still, the vast bulk of the city's Jewish population lived on the eastern side of Mount Royal, though the movement there was northward and westward into the eastern fringes of Outremont.

A similar shift to the westernmost suburb of Notre Dame de Grace and, to a minor extent, to Lachine on the western tip of the Island of Montreal was also in progress. This migration, especially of Canadian-born, indicated the modest prosperity reached during the 1920s as families sought newer and more salubrious suburbs.[49] In the older areas and in parts of Outremont, the housing usually took the form of the traditional Montreal 'plex' model. This included two to six apartments, some of them accessible only by winding outside stairways, which were perilous during the city's ferocious winters.

---

* In the context outlined here, Montreal includes Greater Montreal and the municipalities of Outremont, Westmount, Verdun, and Lachine.

Suburbanization brought about a growing integration into the anglophone and, to a much lesser degree, francophone cultures. A sociological survey of 512 Jewish families in 1938 showed that while in 9.4 per cent of households French was spoken, English was used in all others, except for the 5.7 per cent of those that relied solely on Yiddish.[50] In nearly 80 per cent of homes, combinations of English, Yiddish, and French were spoken. Yiddish was the sole language used in 13 per cent of homes in the older areas, but was, at most, a second language in the suburbs. The same trend was evident where both English and Yiddish were employed, although overall this combination was used in 59.6 per cent of all homes in the survey. Thus, while English was their dominant language, Yiddish remained strong, and French was marginal. The survey also showed a preference for English newspapers and periodicals, although in the older areas, Yiddish dailies were popular, with, notably, those from New York preferred over the local *Keneder Adler*.[51] But among all children, English publications outsold Yiddish ones, while those in French and Hebrew ranked low. Thus the integration into English culture was well under way, curbed only by existing antisemitism.

Still, Montreal's Jews clung to their ethnic identity, judging by the survey's data on Jewish association membership; 44.3 per cent of all parents belonged to a Jewish organization. Children, however, preferred the recreational clubs like the Young Men's Hebrew Association (YMHA) and Young Women's Hebrew Association (YWHA); Jewish education was also stressed. Congress surveys revealed that 82.28 per cent of boys and 52.7 per cent of girls had some formal Jewish education, reflecting the stark reality that book learning for girls was considered of lesser importance than training in the domestic arts. However, children received very uneven instruction: after regular school hours and on Sundays, 53.2 per cent of them went to private schools, or heders (rooms), which were run by freelance teachers. Here they received private tutoring, which usually ended with bar mitzvah. Almost a third of Montreal Jewish children attended either Talmud Torah or the Peretz School, the former offering traditional studies, and the latter a national and progressive education as well as considerable instruction in Yiddish.

As for synagogue attendance, the 1938 survey showed that among males 27.9 per cent (in the suburbs only 17.6 per cent) of grandfathers attended synagogue daily, in comparison with just 6.5 per cent of fathers and 2.2 per cent of sons. Of course, the difference in time available for daily synagogue attendance was a factor. Among fathers, however, 27.5 per cent attended Sabbath services – though only 9.8 per cent in the suburbs – while 34.5 per cent of sons attended, with a remarkably high 43.1 per cent in the suburbs, where new synagogues featured special Oneg Shabbat services on Friday nights. On the three major holidays of Sukkot, Pesach, and Shavuot, 34.6 per cent of fathers attended and 22.6 per cent of sons, with slightly higher per centages in the suburbs. These data suggest that formal religious observance was fairly high among all three generations of Jewish males.

The survey's evidence on food-purchasing patterns adds to the impression of a traditional community. Almost 92 per cent of all those questioned, even a surprisingly high 82.3 per cent of suburban Jews, reported that they bought their meat from Jewish butchers. Fish and bread, too, were purchased in Jewish stores by 77.7 and 67.6 per cent of those surveyed. Adherence to *kashrut* (the rules governing kosher food), then, was fundamental. In all measures, including *kashrut*, synagogue attendance, education, and organizational affiliation, as well as in the use of Yiddish at home, Montreal Jewry remained a traditional community. But as shown, while religious life thrived, education efforts did not reach even half of all girls and concluded for most boys at age thirteen.

Governance was a seriously divisive issue in all three cities. Strong efforts in Montreal, Toronto, and Winnipeg to establish a *kehillah* (community) organization, essentially for the supervision of *kashrut*, were unsuccessful.[52] The providing of kosher meat created controversy. At issue was profit for the butchers, the *mashgichim* (inspectors), and the rabbis, who were the final authority in these matters. To the Orthodox Jews, *kashrut* was essential, and for the many non-observant, a matter of tradition and preference. However, the disputations, lawsuits, and appeals for political intervention served only to confuse and, probably, disgust the observant, while amusing the sceptics. At the same time, the entire Jewish community was exposed by this public display. Beyond this lay the fact that the internal unity was fragile, indeed. In the case of Toronto, acrimony existed between the Lithuanian, Russian, and Galician settlers, and the newly arrived Polish element. Among many Jews struggling to make ends meet and those on the left, moreover, the issue of *kashrut* may not have been of paramount importance.

Organized philanthropy in Montreal since 1863 had been dispensed by the Baron de Hirsch Society and other loosely associated organizations. In 1916 the newly formed Federation of Jewish Philanthropies combined all of them in one fundraising campaign.[53] Allocations to the individual charities were determined by the federation's executive, composed mainly of the big givers. Similar organizations were established in Toronto the same year and, later, in Winnipeg and Hamilton. While these federations had no legislative powers, they began to insist on 'scientific philanthropy,' which discouraged volunteerism and the old-fashioned spontaneous charity in favour of more formalized and efficient structures in the hands of professional social workers.[54] For example, in Montreal, the Federation of Jewish Philanthropies employed professional caseworkers to deal with a serious problem of juvenile delinquency. The federations also assumed such new responsibilities as the provision of old-age homes and of hospitals in Montreal and Toronto, as well as social and recreational facilities for youth. All of these institutions required boards of management and, increasingly, professional staff. Thus, a small Jewish civil service was formed – including growing numbers of women, like Toronto's Dora Wilensky, who headed Jewish Family Services.

Sports facilities, in the YMHAs and YWHAs, housed athletic teams and provided healthy outlets for Jewish youth, who may have felt unwelcome in the Christian venues. Besides serving as channels for youthful energy and competitiveness, and as places to socialize, these organizations were yet another form of acculturation in a society in which athleticism and sportsmanship were highly admired. Jewish teams competed in football, basketball, softball, and soccer in city and provincial leagues; the Winnipeg YMHA football team even won several city championships in the 1930s.[55] Professional boxers like Toronto's Baby Yack and Sammy Luftspring and amateur wrestlers like the Oberlander brothers of Montreal often wore the Star of David as an assertion, a challenge to opponents, and an emotional rallying emblem for the Jewish spectators at these events. Sports, then, besides serving as a valuable activity in their own right, provided an additional vehicle for the assertion of Jewish identity.

Connections with kinfolk still in *der alter heim* (the old home) continued. Immigrants corresponded with their families in Europe, sending news, remittances, and photographs of their spouses and children (often standing proudly in front of a house, a store, or a new car), and in return received news, gossip, and publications. Feelings of nostalgia were expressed in songs like 'Belz, my little town of Belz,' an enormously popular Yiddish theatre song 'that expressed longing for hometowns in Eastern Europe.'[56] This emotion was typical of the 'deep love' many immigrant Jews, still ambivalent in their new world, felt for their place of origin, which they represented as 'a nurturing, authentic Jewish space.'

Many other Yiddish songs reflected these sentiments, such as 'Bay dem Shtetle,' which reminisces about the 'little town ... a little house with a green roof, and around the house many trees grow,' and the days when 'Father and Mother and Khanele and I ... lived together there.' There were songs like 'Warshe,' about Warsaw, [57] and 'Die Roumanish Kretchme' (In a Romanian Inn). There was 'Galitsye' (Galicia) and the all-time favourite, the show-stopping 'Rumania, Rumania,' whose risqué lyrics recount the joys of life in a 'wonderful land, where it was a pleasure to live, and to delight in the joys of wine, women, and camaraderie.' 'Ay, s'iz a mekhaye, beser ken nit zayn, ay, afargenigin iz nor Rumenish veyn.'

Thus, recalling the dear old home in the dear old town by the dear old river in a life of simple pleasures – while tearfully recalling parents left behind – was integral to Jewish popular culture in the interwar years. In this landscape of memory, longing was mixed with pride in hometown greatness and in luminaries such as distinguished rabbis. Not yet fully comfortable in their new abode, many Jews still identified with *der alter heim* of vivid memory, making Eastern Europe, or at least their hometown, a continuing part of their mental and cultural map.

Other popular songs, tunes, and ballads that circulated through the Jewish quarter on song sheets and phonograph records told of love, romance, marital problems, immigrant adjustment, wronged women, loving mothers, death, and financial embarrassment, as well as coarse and vulgar material about gamblers, prostitutes, criminals, and other low-life elements.[58] Poignantly soulful songs like 'A Brivele der Mamen,' about an immigrant's lonely mother in the old country, and 'My Yidishe Momme,' about neglect of filial piety towards an abandoned mother in the old neighbourhood, were among the most popular songs. When itinerant actors and singers performed these soulful tunes and poignant dramas, there wasn't a dry eye in the house. Few, if any, of these songs were specifically Canadian in origin or content; along with the Yiddish theatre and, by the 1930s, Yiddish movies, they came north from the United States, usually from Warsaw and New York, whose Jewish community helped to set the cultural norms for Jews throughout North America in the interwar years.

Out east, home to many Jewish immigrants, most communities remained stable after the 1920s. Some, however, declined. Saint John, the largest, had grown from 642 persons in 1911 to 848 in 1921, but fell to 683 in 1931 and all the way down to 569 in 1941. Similarly, Halifax peaked and then declined, as did Yarmouth, Woodstock, Glace Bay, and New Glasgow, reflecting the general economic downturn in the region. But Sydney, with its busy steel mill, thrived during the 1930s, as did Moncton, a railway centre, and Fredericton, the New Brunswick provincial capital. But these were small communities, the largest roughly equal to Saskatoon, London, or Quebec City. Saint John before 1920 had boasted three synagogues, two of them catering to different social and economic groups and the third a small chapel close to the business district.

This division was typical of such communities. Immigrants of different origins followed varying rituals in prayer, special tunes, and pronunciation of Hebrew and Yiddish, or what some scholars have called 'the congregation's official liturgical rendition; the architecture of its sanctuary; the gestures, actions, dress and comportment of participants; role differentiation; any particular use made of the authorized prayer book; and many other things.'[59] These were serious matters. The Halifax Jewish community, which was organized as the Baron de Hirsch Hebrew Benevolent Society in 1890,[60] was beset by dissension which led to division, and another synagogue was formed. The first congregation's building was destroyed in the Halifax explosion of December 1917, and in 1920 a new structure was begun. By 1936, though acrimony continued, the two congregations reunited. Like Saint John, Halifax as a port city welcomed the new arrivals, assisting the distressed and, during the 1930s, helping some families to settle on farms in rural Nova Scotia. Meanwhile, congregations were also established in Moncton, Fredericton, Glace Bay, New Waterford, Sydney, and Yarmouth.

Jews who settled in St John's, Newfoundland, formed a community in 1909, and in 1931 built a synagogue. In the usual pattern, they earned their living through petty trade, many of them having started as pedlars in the colony's outports, where they sold goods to fishermen's families. By 1921 there were an estimated fourteen Jewish families, including sixty-four individuals living in St John's, which had become the hub of Jewish life in the Dominion.[61] Israel Perlin, a former pedlar who had arrived in the 1890s, operated a wholesale dry-goods store and supplied itinerant Jews with goods and, no doubt, ample advice about prospects for business. After purchasing a cemetery plot, the congregation hired a series of rabbis, but none stayed for long. Meanwhile, the community grew, and another started up in Corner Brook. Relationships between Jews and other Newfoundlanders were satisfactory. 'There was no such thing [in Newfoundland] as segregation,' one old-timer recalled. 'I must say, [they were] very friendly. Never turned around and called you by any name as they did in some parts of Canada, when they say "sheeny" or "bloody Jew" or something. Never heard that. Never had any [bad] experience of any description, the greatest respect. We never heard it once mentioned, "the Jew," to us.' The problems both of ensuring Jewish education in small centres and religious continuity hastened the departure of settlers once their children reached their late teens. Consequently, once vibrant communities declined and, in some cases, flickered out altogether. Such was the fate of St John's and Corner Brook, as of many others across Canada, especially those in northern Ontario.[62]

Thus, Jews were accommodating to urban life in a nation struggling with serious economic and political problems, inter-regional tensions, and cultural and constitutional transformations.[63] As noted above, all of these impinged on Jews in various ways. Communal life in the large cities expressed itself in many forms of 'limited identities.' Yiddish publications, both secular and religious, thrived. The local press included Montreal's *Keneder Adler*, Toronto's *Yiddisher Zhurnal*, and Winnipeg's *Yiddishe Vort*, as well as association bulletins, weeklies like *Der Kamf* for the communists, and periodicals for the Labour Zionists. At the same time, the *Canadian Jewish Chronicle*, the *Canadian Jewish Review*, the *Jewish Standard*, and the *Jewish Western Bulletin* served the growing number of English readers. And numerous pamphlets and books emerged, both religious and secular. The latter included Nachman Shemen's 1939 *Tsvishn Kreig Un Friden* (Between War and Peace),[64] a wide-ranging analysis of interwar world affairs. And poetry thrived, too, notably in the small Montreal group of Yiddish poets that included Yacov Yitzchak Segal along with numerous others who made this city a veritable 'utopia' of Jewish culture.[65]

Jewish culture possessed, as well, a growing consciousness of its historical roots in Canada. Engineer Martin Wolff published a pioneering survey in 1925, and a year later, Arthur D. Hart edited *The Jew in Canada: A Complete Record of Canadian Jewry from the Days of the French Regime to the Present Time*, overall a remarkable scholarly accomplishment that brought together significant articles on the community's history, current organizational structure, and leading citizens.[66] The search for a historical legitimacy included also *Looking back a Century*, a work by Abraham Rhinewine, editor of the *Yiddisher Zhurnal*, published posthumously in 1932, the one-hundredth anniversary of Jewish political equality in Canada. At the same time, Gutl Zack was writing scholarly pieces for the *Keneder Adler* on Canada's Jewish past, later incorporating them into an important book.

Immigration was an important dimension of Jewish geography. For eight years, Chaya Rivka Wolodarsky Forman, living in Rizshe, Ukraine, had not heard from her son, Joseph, who had immigrated to Winnipeg in 1913.[67] When she finally received a letter from him in March 1921, she could hardly contain her joy:

> My Dear Loving son, ... before I received your letter, Sarah-Malke's letter brought me news of your marriage. Mazel Tov, also the news that you have a daughter, mit Mazel. May she have a long and healthy life! I only hope that I will live to see all of you with my own eyes.[68]

Chaya Rivka finally arrived in Winnipeg on Dominion Day, 1922, to rejoin her family.

The greatest difficulty facing the Jewish community in the 1920s was enabling Jews like Chaya Rivka to enter the country. Post-war unrest in Poland and the Soviet Union was inducing Jews to seek new opportunities in Canada. At the same time, however, due to the 1920s depression, the community was limited in its ability to aid in relief efforts. Immigration was also bedevilled by the restrictive policy of the Dominion government, the prevailing perceptions of Jews, and the problems of handling new arrivals.

Equally fateful was the collapse of the young Canadian Jewish Congress, only a year after its founding amidst so much enthusiasm and hope. Hananiah Meir Caiserman, its general secretary, blamed a lack of funds, while Montreal businessmen Lyon Cohen and Mark Workman, the organization's chief elected officers, seemed to have lost enthusiasm for it.[69] Money was certainly a serious problem. In late March 1920, Caiserman criticized A.B. 'Archie' Bennett, secretary of the Ontario branch, for that group's failure to pay its obligation to the national office in Montreal.[70] Clearly, there was serious tension between Montreal and Toronto, and without Cohen, efforts to sustain enthusiasm for the Congress failed. A leaflet circulated in Toronto in March 1920 enjoined its Jews to register for Congress elections by pointing out that '[C]ongress organizations everywhere are the outcome of awakened Jewish pride, and the feeling that Jews can organize and look after their affairs through a representative body elected in a properly democratic manner.'[71] But it was of little help. Neither was its Yiddish appeal, though it was more dramatic: 'Help save the unfortunates in Poland and Ukraine.'

The sudden failure of Congress is ironic since immigration was so high on its agenda. Soon after Congress's formation in March 1919, the national executive challenged Ottawa on proposed amendments to the Immigration Act,[72] especially those that were intended to severely limit those of 'questionable political background,' and especially Jews who because of oppression 'feel a natural resentment for the countries of their origin.' It then asked 'that special provision shall be made in this section for the Jewish people,' or that officials be instructed to give Jews 'special consideration.'

In the wake of the 1919 Winnipeg General Strike and the accompanying 'red scare,' Ottawa moved decisively to plug certain 'gaps' in the inflow of 'undesirable' immigrants. Acting under the immigration law of 1910, the government passed orders-in-council to regulate immigration and activated the 1908 provision for continuous journey, which required immigrants to enter directly from their country of origin or citizenship 'on a through ticket purchased in that country.'[73] As well, they were required to possess valid passports and $250 in cash. This placed serious burdens on those who had fled war-ravaged Eastern Europe and resided temporarily in other countries. Faced with this restrictive atmosphere and the threat of new limitations, Congress appealed to the highest levels of government, hoping to keep Canada's doors open.

In June 1920 Sam Jacobs, a Liberal MP,[74] lambasted the Conservative government's restrictive immigration policy for placing 'stumbling blocks' in the way of 'proper immigrants.'[75] Meanwhile, picking up on the favouritism shown to farmers from Nordic countries, the *Keneder Adler* debunked some who claimed to be farmers and were 'not and never have been farmers.'[76] That April, Caiserman had complained to the immigration minister, saying, 'Your department regards Jewish immigration as undesirable' because of 'superficial knowledge of Jewish immigration to Canada.'[77] Cognizant of the official preference for farmers, he averred that there were indeed Jewish farmers who had 'proven to be a great success.' He pressed mainly for honesty. 'I should then know that by working to aid Jewish immigrants ..., I am working against the policy of our government, [even though] we had the right to expect that the Christian nations of the world would apply the great principles of Christianity in saving an innocent people from annihilation.'[78]

Policy changes were adversely affecting Jews, in particular, because the traditional preference for British subjects, Anglo-Saxons, North Europeans, and farmers was being enforced far more rigorously than ever before under the Immigration Act of 1919.[79] At the same time, tough-minded immigration officials were detaining and deporting Jews for the slightest of reasons. Moreover, the 'continuous journey' regulation stymied East European Jews because they did not have access to those shipping companies that reached Canadian ports, preventing 'the east European Jewish migrant who did not possess a prepaid ticket to Canada to comply with this regulation.'

An order-in-council in 1921, which required immigrants to have valid passports from their countries of origin, bewildered many Polish and Russian Jews. It was impossible for them to get passports unless they returned – a risk few would take. In 1922 a stiff occupational test accompanying yet another order-in-council was imposed, stipulating that Canadian, not British, consular officials examine all passports, a reasonable requirement, except that very few Canadian consular officials were posted anywhere near the East European Jewish migrants. Severe restrictions placed by the Johnson Immigration Act of 1921 and its refinements in 1924 on immigration into the United States, imposing strict quotas on specific ethnic groups, such as Jews, and an accompanying blockage on the reunification of families, forced many would-be entrants to the United States to turn to Canada.[80]

Laws were tightened still further in 1923 by yet another order-in-council, which ranked immigrants according to racial preferences into 'preferred,' 'non-preferred,' and 'special permit' classes. The last category included Jews, who were subject to even more severe restrictions, which were refined over the next few years (notably limiting the family members who could be considered first-degree relatives). In practice, Jews were now situated on the lowest level of priority, effectively barred from entry.

Complaints against such exclusions were noted in the Yiddish newspapers by recent immigrants who were desperate to bring over family members. Montreal's *Keneder Adler*, for example, commented often on the discrimination against non-British and non-Nordics, observing mordantly in a November 1927 editorial that Germans only ten years after the war were now among Canada's most preferred immigrants.[81] These policies were puzzling, but clarified by the 1927 Synod of Anglican Bishops, which voiced concern that an influx of Catholics, Orthodox, and Jews would disrupt Canadian society. Certainly the community could not rely on Jewish steamship agents in Canada or abroad to deal satisfactorily with immigrants' problems. While some agents had the reputation of being scrupulously honest, others did not. Allegations – whether true or not – of bribery and swindling of clients did not help.

Meanwhile, Sam Jacobs and various other Jewish 'notables' approached the problem of restrictions by undertaking *shtadlanut*, the old tradition of important Jews representing Jewish interests before the secular powers, which they combined with new-style ethnic brokerage politics. In this spirit, they went to Ottawa and made the rounds of Cabinet ministers, influential MPs and senators, and department officials. As well, Jacobs made speeches in the House of Commons, hoping to affect public opinion and government policy.

To plead, even beg, that Jews be exempted from this or that regulation, and hint at possible political or other 'benefits,' was all part of traditional *shtadlanut*. Success depended on employing all available resources, including using 'notables' such as Lyon Cohen. Lillian Freiman was an important participant. As the wife of Ottawa department store tycoon A.J. 'Archie' Freiman, she had gained personal connections with Mrs Arthur Meighen, the wife of the most powerful minister in the Borden Cabinet. Mrs Meighen happily agreed to support a project to bring Ukrainian orphans to Canada,[82] following Jacobs's success in securing entry of Jewish refugees from the Ukrainian pogroms, and his efforts to relieve other restrictions on entry. Mrs Meighen also intervened on various other occasions later in the 1920s.

Immigration, though, was a divisive issue even in a strongly supportive community. An unsigned memorandum (probably written by Caiserman)[83] asserted that organizing the protest meetings against the pogroms in Eastern Europe, and the necessary relief work, had exhausted the Congress's finances. When, in an effort to secure the admission of dependants, especially from Ukraine, the Canadian Federation of Ukrainian Jews, the Ukrainian Verband, chose to circumvent Congress, Caiserman complained. This independent action created ambivalence (especially in Winnipeg, where they were strongest) about unified allegiance to the Congress at the very time when it was conducting its 1920 registration.

In 1920 the Jewish Immigrant Aid Society (JIAS) was formed by Congress and other organizations specifically to address immigration. Led by Lyon Cohen and Sam Jacobs, JIAS became a major force able to appeal to government and respond to threats of further restrictions in a new act, which would 'control, select, and if found necessary, reduce or entirely suspend immigration of elements deemed undesirable by allowing the Minister to regulate the inflow.'[84]

Polish, Romanian, and Ukrainian Jews in Canada were desperately hoping to rescue the thousands of refugees from poverty, war, and revolution, many of them members of their own families. JIAS feared that the new act's provisions, which allowed the exclusion of a whole 'race or nationality,' might be used against Jews. While this fear proved to be unfounded, JIAS did encounter mounting antisemitism among Immigration Branch officials who were empowered to exclude Jews who did not qualify under criteria that favoured farmers.[85] JIAS also tried to outflank the Jewish middlemen who allegedly bamboozled clients and often failed to deliver permits they promised,[86] and thus eliminate the unseemly profiteering by steamship agents, influence pedlars, and lawyers. This would not only lower costs considerably, but also streamline the process of dealing with officials who had the ultimate authority to issue permits. The continuing contest between JIAS and the travel agents illustrates that migration was a complicated business, one in which some agents were believed to have profited not only from the commerce in permits, steamship tickets, and remittances, but also while serving as notaries or translating documents, and even from real-estate transactions.[87] These travel agents were, according to historian Harold Troper, 'the hub of the whole settlement process,' at least until Jewish professionals emerged and JIAS became known and fully trusted as the appropriate address for immigration matters.

From its headquarters in Montreal, JIAS dealt effectively with the Ottawa officials, who in turn preferred JIAS to the independent agents. In addition, JIAS branch offices in Toronto and Winnipeg, as well as volunteers across the country, provided local support for landed immigrants and for the screening of prospective sponsors. Despite successes, JIAS was criticized in early 1927 in the *Keneder Adler* for not doing enough to bring in Jewish farmers, for alleged improprieties,[88] and for its high-handed administration, excessive bureaucracy, exorbitant membership fees, and unfriendly employees. The most damaging complaint alleged favouritism in awarding permits. Worse was to follow. In March, the *Adler* alleged that JIAS officials were in fact selling these permits and mismanaging the organization's funds. Soon afterward, a gathering of concerned organizations heard that criminal charges of theft had been brought against two JIAS officials; it was recommended that the organization's structure be radically changed.

Meanwhile, in the wake of the Bolshevik Revolution and the ensuing civil war in Ukraine, widespread loss of life and destruction was taking place in the Jewish communities there. Caiserman observed conditions first-hand during his 1920 tour of Eastern Europe, which he undertook to survey the destruction and to estimate how Canada's Jews could help the victims of mass murder, rape, and pillage.[89] These disasters produced tens of thousands of Jewish orphans, who roamed the Ukrainian countryside searching for food and shelter. In the summer of 1920, it was reported that there were some 137,000 of these children, many 'practically living wild and semi-barbarous lives, ... eating such edible wild roots and herbs as were left in a territory ... sadly ravaged by war and post war excesses.'[90] The tragedy touched hearts everywhere. In late August 1920, some fifteen hundred Jews gathered in Saskatoon to propose sending the orphans to Palestine, for which they offered strong financial support,[91] one of many such demonstrations.

Back east, Lillian Freiman also responded. She was already deeply involved in helping immigrants, and on occasion went to Halifax to assist recent arrivals under threat of deportation. One witness remembered that during one of these missions, 'she put her motherly arms around the two or three closest to her [and] ... kept repeating these words, "Nisht vein, nisht vein" [Don't cry, don't cry]. An overflowing heart more than made up for her imperfect Yiddish.'[92] Alerted to the plight of the orphans in Ukraine, she rallied national financial support for her Committee for the Relief of Ukrainian Orphans, to bring some of them over to Canada and to feed and clothe others.[93]

Further exploiting her contacts with Mrs Meighen, Freiman negotiated an agreement with Frederick Charles Blair, a key official at Immigration, to admit two hundred of these orphans 'on humanitarian grounds,' as an experiment, with others allowable depending on the results. For many, this campaign was personal. Mrs S. Levine of Brantford wrote to Freiman, noting that her community had raised a thousand dollars,[94] and asked: 'As I have a sister-in-law with three orphans in Warsaw, I would like you to bring them with the two hundred. Their father is dead and they are suffering terribly. Two children of that family have already died of hunger. When they come they will have a good home and will be well taken care of.' But despite heroic efforts by Lillian Freiman and others,[95] the campaign did not reach its goals, even though in Western Canada communities outdid themselves in raising funds and taking in the children.[96]

In Montreal, surprisingly, the campaign failed utterly. The *Chronicle* complained bitterly that the local bigshots 'have established a reputation for "passing the buck," particularly heading up fundraising campaigns. One of the most popular games in this city is that of "Chairman, Chairman, who'll be the Chairman?"' Toronto was just as unenthusiastic, and the whole Ukrainian relief effort faltered. What the *Chronicle* saw as an opportunity to 'forge an unbreakable link between our Jewish people over here and our Jewish orphans over there – a link that will do much for the strengthening of our Judaism' was not taken up by the community at large.

And while the *Chronicle* extolled philanthropy, it was forced to conclude that the relief campaign was unsuccessful. Even appeals to history were of little avail. 'The present is a crisis in Jewish history,' the journal stated in late December 1920, 'a crisis that is taking physical toll in Europe and spiritual toll in America ... The simple act of living in America,' it continued, 'engenders a moral and spiritual responsibility to equalize the toll of blood and tears that is being exacted from our people on the other side.' In April 1921, the *Chronicle* announced sadly that only 'a very small proportion of Canadian Jewry is represented in the figures [of contributors].'

Lillian Freiman, however, was steadfast. Meanwhile, Montrealers Harry Hershman (a bookstore owner) and Dr Joseph Leavitt, along with William Farrar of Hamilton (a Christian who took a deep interest in Jewish religious and communal affairs), were dispatched to Europe in February 1921. Operating in the Polish Ukraine with the support of the American Jewish Joint Distribution Committee, a United States Jewish relief organization, the Canadian group established itself in Rovno and began to select suitable candidates from the thousands of orphaned children in the area.

Hershman's letters tell of the numerous practical problems his team encountered. 'It is almost impossible to do any work on account of the noise. You can imagine 90 kids or more running around the place,' he complained in one letter to Lillian Freiman.[97] As he was making arrangements for transport, Dr Leavitt, who was trying to improve the children's nutrition, urgently wired Hershman: 'INSIST FROM STEAMSHIP COMPANY THAT CHILDREN DO NOT IMMEDIATELY GO INTO QUARANTINE UNTIL I GET THERE AND SPEAK WITH LONDON OFFICE FIRST.' After appraising two orphan boys from the countryside, Hershman wrote to Leavitt: 'Send along one suit of clothing size 28 ... stockings and underwear for a boy of nine years the children are practically naked. I think I will have to take them to Rovno they have nothing in their home no beds, no food, no care but they are very nice boys.' Hershman's notes, written while searching for orphans in the countryside, are interesting: 'June 16 p.m. Arrived Wyzwa at 7:45. Solomon S. OK Rather small for age. Obtained release; Herschel P. 12–13. To see again and decide. Parents died but aunt who was keeping him was killed.' Lillian Freiman, meanwhile, had gone on her own to Antwerp, where 146 chosen children were eventually assembled. On August 21, she brought the first group of 108 to Quebec; the others followed within a few weeks.[98]

By that time, the campaign in Canada was faltering. A group of dissidents had circulated letters inexplicably demanding that the selected orphans come only from the Soviet Ukraine.[99] This protest further soured fundraising efforts. By early 1921, perhaps as a result of a severe business recession, of the hundreds of people who had been willing to house orphans, only 149 had actually applied, well short of what was needed. The effort by Freiman and her associates was symbolically important nevertheless. While awaiting the ship that would take her and the children to Canada, she had presided over a moving Sabbath celebration. Hershman remembered that after he chanted the kiddush (blessing) over the wine, Freiman 'carried the cup to each child to taste the kiddush [cup], and from her eyes flowed a stream of tears ... but through the tears we could see her great nachas [joy] that she derived from this experience.'[100] The image of her leading the children off the ship at Quebec after months of excitement made her the leading Canadian Jewish figure of her generation.

Harry Hershman's role in the project was also unique.[101] Not only had he spent several gruelling months inspecting the children in Poland with Dr Leavitt and William Farrar, but, up until his death in 1957, he constituted a one-man follow-up committee. He sent the children clothing and presents for birthdays and bar mitzvahs; he attended their weddings and rejoiced in the births of their children, as he corresponded with many of them and their foster parents. One foster parent reported to him: 'Dear friend Mr. Hershman, if you saw Sarah now, you would not recognize her. She has grown, and is fat and healthy – She gets on good in school and I am proud of her ... I am sending you my Sarah's picture as a remembrance.'[102] The correspondent informed him that 'as Sarah told me she has left a sister in Russia, we would like to have her address so Sarah and her sister can correspond so they will not lose tract [*sic*] of each other.' Hershman carefully answered all the letters he received. Some of his charges experienced difficulties and were a concern to him for many years; his files are a rich source on their adjustment to Canada, as well as a testament to his sustained devotion, himself childless, to the Ukrainian orphans. By the time they arrived, to be hailed by the *Chronicle* as 'Canadian citizens of the future,' concern for the orphans was overshadowed by the heart-rending stories of other refugees still overseas, which continued to attract notice in Canada.[103] Monies left over from the orphan project were used to set up a soup kitchen for Jews in Ukraine.

JIAS performed prodigious work during the 1920s, especially on behalf of immigrants reaching Halifax, Saint John, and Quebec, whose arrival was often precarious.[104] 'That happy period when immigrants generally were welcome guests in Canada is gone ... [and] each new arrival is looked upon with a thousand eyes and the stranger, the alien is sent back on the least pretext,' wrote one observer in the *Chronicle* in June 1920.[105] Those Jews who failed to pass rigorous inspection, or meet other requirements, faced deportation. The *Chronicle* reported that in spite of Freiman's intercessions, a large number were deported, while still others were threatened with it. On 2 July 1920 the *Chronicle* reported that 'only last Saturday, 350 Jewish immigrants landed in Quebec from the S.S. Grampian and were permitted to land only because of prompt intervention by several Quebec Jews. It is ridiculous to expect the small community of Quebec to undertake the whole burden for Canadian Jewry.'[106] Readers were reminded that 'the immigrant's present plight can only find its counterpart in our past or the past of our parents. Only a Jew can know the heart of a Jew. That is why the Jew is ready to take care of his own.'

Some immigrants allegedly were being treated brutally by officials. At Saint John, in February 1921, JIAS complained that one bureaucrat for several days had prevented the relatives of incoming immigrants to speak to them – some separated for many years – until after they had been released.[107] Officials had even refused to allow JIAS to send in kosher food. One little boy of eleven was so distraught at being separated from his family that he attempted to hang himself. He was cut down while still alive, quickly judged by officials to be insane, and immediately deported, all alone, back to Poland.

JIAS claimed that its representatives who tried to intervene were met with delays, obfuscation, and contempt by bureaucrats, who saw Jewish intercession as bothersome. One Quebec official complained to Ottawa that 'for the last 6 weeks or 2 months, this office has been experiencing considerable difficulties and no end of extra work due principally to the activity of a number of local residents of the Hebrew persuasion, who in their enthusiasm to assist the Jewish Detentions, are causing a lot of friction and injury to the discipline in Detention Quarters, and unrest generally amongst all the detentions.'[108] With 'each trifle that occurs to a Jewish detention, let it be imaginary or otherwise,' he continued, 'the supposed victim is ever anxious to request an investigation and every one of his countrymen detained with him is a willing witness to substantiate his storey [*sic*].' Without elaboration, he referred to the fact that 'contraversy [*sic*] and evident bitterness that exists between the factions of Jewish residents in Quebec' was also making his work difficult.

Officials of the Jewish Colonization Association also tried to alleviate immigrants' distress. Leon Rosenthal, a JCA administrator in Montreal, wrote to the minister of immigration in November 1920 on behalf of two hundred detainees, mostly young men aged twenty to twenty-eight who, because of ignorance, had failed to comply with various regulations.[109] Since these men were suitable for the western farm colonies, and would have had his organization's support, he pleaded their case, ending with a supplication 'on purely humanitarian grounds,' stating that 'it would be a pity, a great pity, to condemn these 200 or more young men in the very bloom of their life. It would be unfair, and therefore unbritish, to adhere to the letter of the law without permitting a liberal interpretation thereof.'

During its first year, JIAS attended to 1,788 cases of detention at the major eastern ports. Of these, 1,306 persons were released; but 232 were deported, 2 died in detention, 226 'escaped,' and 22 were further detained,[110] many of whom were planning to move to the United States. According to Caiserman, 'nearly 75% of all [Jewish] immigrants arriving to Canada through Quebec have as their destination United States of America.'[111] However, valid visas were required from an American consular officer in the country where the journey started. JIAS blamed steamship agents in Europe for misleading immigrants. They 'give immigrants wrong addresses and tell them that when they get to Canada they will have no difficulties of proceeding to United States.'

The financial strain on JIAS as a result of this kind of fraud was serious, and the human cost was worse. 'Hundreds of immigrants,' S.B. Haltrecht reported to New York's Hebrew Immigrant Aid Society (HIAS), the sister organization of JIAS, 'are walking through the streets of Montreal, puzzled as to what they should do and we can give them no satisfactory advice.' Now nearly desperate to stop this influx, Caiserman wrote to the Danzig offices of HIAS, complaining about 'criminal and irresponsible steamship agents.' He informed them that the United States prohibited entry to all but properly visaed immigrants,[112] advising them to enlighten the immigrants of this as well as the requirements of 'continuous journey.'

Sometimes JIAS officials in Montreal, unaware of regional problems, received peppery communiqués, as a Vancouver member responding to a request for funds wrote: 'Apparently in your haste to organize your society in the East you have paid little attention to Vancouver. Do you know how much money was spent on this work and do you know the number of men who have been engaged in the handling of these affairs without one single dollar of remuneration?'[113]

From the start, JIAS officials were aware that, because their resources were inadequate, they required money from abroad. They secured a twenty-thousand-dollar subsidy from the JCA and petitioned HIAS for information, advice, and money.[114] Caiserman wrote a begging letter to the president of HIAS in October 1920 to no avail. Within a month, the organization was in a desperate financial state. 'It is absolutely necessary,' its general manager wrote to New York, '[for HIAS] to come to [our] assistance, as far as United States immigrants are concerned.' HIAS could not help, offering only to warn European Jews not to try to enter the United States via Canada. Further appeals that year yielded nothing.

The following year, however, HIAS was more generous, recognizing the JIAS claim that 'a very large number of [Jewish] immigrants ... mostly young men of military age ... who arrive in Canada are actually destined to relatives in the United States, it is our duty to help these immigrants ... as ... if they arrive at any American port.' The Americans observed that JIAS had struggled during the spring and summer of 1921, when about 3,800 Jews had arrived in Canada. Many were detained 'upon almost any conceivable ground,' requiring appeals against about five hundred deportation orders (some requiring repeated appeals), the placement of guarantees with shipping companies, the cost of feeding and sheltering detainees, and the posting of substantial bonds.

The Jewish community was outraged by these detentions and deportations. Archie Freiman and the Montreal tobacco magnate Sir Mortimer Davis pressured the government to relax its enforcement. 'When advised yesterday that Jewish immigrants were released from detention[,] Freiman of Ottawa wired all [JIAS branches] commending your action and urging all Jews to work for and support you next Tuesday,' an organizer for the Conservative Party cabled Prime Minister Arthur Meighen in December 1921.[115] But interventions were needed to overcome the department's rigidity. 'Department's action resented by Jews as unjust discrimination and serious breach of faith,' the intervenor reported. 'Respectfully submit that you instruct Minister to review these twenty cases immediately and arrange release. Please advise me by wire as to action taken. Am endeavouring to hold Freiman's good will,' he concluded. Conservative candidates in constituencies with substantial Jewish populations also lobbied Prime Minister Meighen to release detained immigrants. A worried Montreal Conservative MP complained to Meighen that 'my life here has been made almost unbearable by the requests ... by prominent Jewish citizens ... to use whatever influence I may possess with the Minister of Immigration to have some of these [detainees] admitted. I was given no peace night or day ...' Concerned about his chances for re-election in his riding, he pleaded: 'These Jewish citizens ... will play an important part in my reelection, but in order to retain their enthusiasm and support it is up to me to demonstrate that I have been able to accomplish something for them. Unless I can do so I am afraid that I shall not get this large vote.'

Protests were also mounted by Jewish hoi polloi. H.D. Rosenbloom, manager of the Toronto Joint Board of the Amalgamated, cabled Meighen during the campaign on behalf of his three thousand members to 'protest most vigorously against the wholesale deportations ... and against restriction of immigration generally.' Meanwhile, individuals with influence on MPs tried their best to intervene, usually without success.

Once the Liberals returned to power in December 1921, the Jewish community hoped for favourable changes, such as the earlier 'open door' approach. Immigration, however, was not a major issue in Mackenzie King's successful campaign,[116] who recognized it as unpopular amidst the economic distress of a recession. Under the circumstances, King was typically circumspect before the election. But once in power with a minority government, he and his Cabinet were vulnerable to pressures from within his party, and Sam Jacobs, who was pressed by his Jewish constituents in Cartier, exploited the opportunity to force the issue.[117] Their collective voice, the *Keneder Adler*, which was closely attuned to the 'downtown' Montreal Jews, many of them immigrants who hoped for family reunification, instructed Jacobs in 1917 to 'remember that the support of this paper was given to you readily and gratuitously with the sole aim that we should have a representative and spokesman in the parliament of Ottawa.' Would he be up to the task at hand? was now the question.

He was, but he needed help. The most important JIAS intervention occurred in September 1923, when at the urging of HIAS and the JCA, Sam Jacobs, Lyon Cohen, and several others persuaded the minister of immigration and colonization, to allow one thousand Ukrainian Jewish refugees living in Romania to enter Canada.[118] Despite the opposition by some of his officials – F.C. Blair, in particular – the minister agreed to allow the refugees in at the rate of one hundred a week (later amended to three hundred a month).[119] All were aware that the minority Liberal government could not afford to alienate even the tiny Jewish community.

Discussion about Canada as a refuge for Jewish fugitives from the Soviet Union had begun in 1921, when the International Labour Organization made inquiries of the Canadian high commissioner in London.[120] Blair, however, was adamant, insisting that only 'a very small proportion of those who have emigrated to Canada are engaged in [farming] in this country ... The record of the Jewish Western colonies is not reassuring ... Young people have practically all left and gone to the cities ... [Land] brought under cultivation did not average ten acres per family. This does not look like real farming.' For his part, Calder was keenly aware of protests against repeating the generous pre-war policy of allowing 'an influx of Continentals ... [that] was larger than the country could afford.'

The matter was raised again the following summer by a senior British government official who at the behest of Fridtjof Nansen, the League of Nations high commissioner, was negotiating to try to admit Jewish and other Russian refugees.[121] Apparently aware of Canadian reluctance, he wrote to Mackenzie King suggesting that while 'perhaps the Canadian government does not wish to receive Jews, I believe that ... they are very sober and hardworking people, and that the whole of their transportation and installation expenses would be met by the Jewish organizations which are helping them.'[122] Three weeks later, King relayed the inquiry with his tacit approval to his minister for consideration.[123] Blair continued to resist, but, notwithstanding his and other criticisms, the prime minister's tacit consent to the refugee project provided the needed official approval.[124]

The various difficulties in moving this group, most without valid Russian passports, were overcome through the intercessions of Jacobs and the Freimans. Moreover, leaders of several American Jewish relief organizations promised financial assistance to the Canadians if they could secure a more generous quota,[125] leading to pressure for its enlargement. Finally, it was agreed to allow in a maximum of five thousand Russian Jews stranded in Romania.[126]

Over the next year, these Jews were organized by officials into groups for despatch to Canada. Ships were hired to take them from Constanza to Quebec, Montreal, or Halifax. The project was enormously complicated and costly, and involved transportation, provisions for kosher food, and medical assistance, as well as their maintenance as needed in Canada. Appeals for assistance from the Paris-based JCA and HIAS in New York brought in substantial subsidies. But even those sums, added to what could be raised in Canada, were insufficient. An unsigned letter (probably from Lyon Cohen) to the American Jewish activist Joseph Barondess, dated November 1924, after the last ship had arrived, blamed the lack of money for the failure to utilize the full quota.[127] 'It is my belief that if American Jewry had listened to you and me in our appeals and had come forth early in the year with substantial assistance, the entire quota would have been conserved.' Canadian Jews could not raise the rest of the money needed, perhaps owing to the continuing economic recession.

Meanwhile, local volunteers persevered. As hosts at the major reception centre, the Jews of Halifax outdid themselves. In Toronto and Montreal, emergency committees rented rooms and arranged jobs. In Winnipeg, Harry Wilder served as chairman of the committee that was responsible for distributing the newcomers to centres across the West Several of the men were sent to work on farms, not always with great success. 'In some cases the individuals left for [the] West quite willingly,' he reported, '[but] with others we had great difficulty. We had to use considerable pressure and met with strong opposition, while in one or two instances we were entirely [unsuccessful]. In these last instances ... the committee was advised to positively refuse to give either food or shelter.'[128]

Russian Jews aboard the S.S. *Madonna*, which reached Halifax from Constanza on 30 August 1924, were sent to Montreal, Toronto, and Winnipeg for dispersion across their respective regions, and Wilder was informed that '120 immigrants are expected to arrive in Winnipeg on ... September 2nd on the Madonna Special.' In fact, 121 arrived. Fifty of them were to remain in Winnipeg, while the others were distributed to Vancouver, Edmonton, Saskatoon, Regina, Calgary, and Sibbald. The relief effort in the West was enthusiastic. In November 1924, a Mrs Margulies of Ebenezer, Saskatchewan, was sent a letter to 'acknowledge receipt of six ducks and one turkey, which you have been good enough to contribute for the Refugees.' Mrs Margulies had previously contributed ten dozen eggs, a sum of five dollars, and a parcel of clothes. Although most of these refugees went to the cities, JIAS did succeed in distributing them across the country; 45 per cent settled in the Maritimes and Quebec, 30 per cent in Ontario, and 25 per cent in the West.[129]

By the end of the project in November 1924, however, only 3,400 of the 5,000 permits had been used. Efforts continued to rescue the remaining refugee Russian Jews stranded in Constantinople,[130] as a deputy minister of immigration tightened the screws. The unused permits tantalized Jacobs and others, who pressed the government for a 'quota' of three thousand Jews for 1925. It was granted, but that was the last of such arrangements.

Resistance to the admission of Jewish refugees was intensified during the late 1920s and 1930s by restrictionist bureaucrats who dominated the department. Sympathetic ministers had been replaced by tougher-minded ones, and antisemitic sentiment was mounting in Quebec, where Ernest Lapointe led a group of sixty Quebec MPs, nearly half of Mackenzie King's Liberal caucus;[131] his influence on the prime minister was paramount, especially on issues such as Jewish immigration. By 1925–6, Jewish political influence had terminated, and immigration to Canada slowed to a trickle. In his Ottawa office, bureaucrat Blair was 'determined never to be duped by Jews again.'[132]

Jacobs, however, persevered. In a letter to future prime minister Richard B. Bennett in October 1925, he deplored the change in official attitude: 'All our efforts during nearly a year have gone for naught. We were up against Egan and Black, a combination which was sufficient to break down the work over which we had toiled for so many months. Black – your former Party organizer – is preening himself on his success in outpointing US.'[133] The deputy minister of immigration, William Egan, while giving evidence before the House of Commons Select Standing Committee on Agriculture and Colonization in 1928, reacted sharply when he was asked whether there were 'any especially vigorous efforts on the part of certain people to get a large number of Jews admitted into the country.' He replied, 'There is a constant hammering from one end of Canada to the other ... I have been accused of introducing restrictive measures galore.'[134] In 1930 and 1931, two new orders-in-council were issued. One permitted only immigrants with enough capital to buy and operate their own farms. The other barred all non-agricultural immigrants, except those of British or American origin. While not totally ended, Jewish immigration –

except by those who could qualify for 'special permits' as first-degree family members – was effectively halted.

Advocates of increased Jewish immigration hoped to win points by expanding the existing farming colonies out West, but received no support among immigration officials. Since 1921, Blair, after closely examining the Jewish colonies, had decided against their expansion.[135] Once he became director in 1936, his surveillance increased, and he commissioned a special report.[136]

He was obviously gaining ammunition to reject Jewish appeals. He wanted a comprehensive assessment, including statistical data on the areas under cultivation, a detailed census, and numbers of those who had acquired title to their lands. He asked about the extent of relief given in the past five or six years, and wanted information on 'the young people still in the colonies, and some indication as to whether or not Jewish people have made, or are making, a success of land settlement in the several colonies.'[137]

A field officer visited the six major colonies in March and April 1937, and reported at length on the basis of JCA files, municipal and other records, as well as interviews with long-time non-Jewish neighbours, local bank managers, and the Jewish farmers themselves. He found that in Sonnenfeld, Hirsch, Lipton, and Edenbridge, 'the Jewish people cannot be considered outstanding as a farming class. A few of them are good. The majority are average or slightly below.' Farmsteads were unkempt. Jews, he found, practised poor farming methods and had put their spare cash into education Blair noted: 'One of the outstanding things noticed was the desire of the families to give their children the best education possible. To get money for this most everything else was let go.'

Such government concerns were not lost on Jewish officials who, when possible, attempted to encourage immigrants to settle on farms.[138] Vladimir Grossman's encouragement of Jewish farm settlement was motivated not only by the hope that it would help to obviate opposition to Jewish immigration but also because 'the land ... is the only way to a new Jewish life ... It is not a sacrifice but a great regenerative method by which we may gain security for the future.'[139] But with the collapse of western farming during the 1930s, this was romantic nonsense.

The government's compliance with the bigotry expressed by Blair and other Ottawa officials kept Jews out.[140] Despite his protestations of sympathy for the Jews in Germany, along with his willingness to receive Jewish delegations and meet with the Jewish MPs (Samuel Jacobs, Abraham Heaps, and Samuel Spector), Prime Minister Mackenzie King held fast to the established policy – inherited from the 1920s – of severely reducing Jewish immigration.[141] Thought by some to be a 'crusading opportunist,'[142] King was an extremely cautious politician. He knew that it was essential both for his government's survival and for national unity, precarious since the 1917 Conscription Crisis, to retain traditional Liberal support in Quebec. And while this support was strong, King – who harboured his own antisemitic bogeys – could not afford to succumb to Jewish demands for opening Canada's gates to refugees.

Further pressures to admit some Jewish refugees came from the Canadian National Committee on Refugees and Victims of Political Persecution (CNCR). Led by Senator Cairine Wilson and Constance Hayward, and backed by some sympathetic newspaper editorials following the Kristallnacht attacks on Jews in Germany in November 1938, this organization found no echo of Canadian public opinion in favour of refugee admissions.[143] Immigration was in bad odour with intellectuals such as the historian Arthur Lower, of Winnipeg's Wesley College. Through the 1920s and 1930s, he severely criticized previous immigration policies, which in his view had attracted many unsuitable immigrants. Worse yet, they created, in Lower's eyes, a situation in which Canada's Anglo-Saxon character and institutions were jeopardized because, like Gresham's law of bad coinage driving out good, 'bad' immigrants drove 'good' Canadians out of their own country.

Generally, the activities of the Jewish MPs or the CNCR were in vain, although the CNCR did save some lives and assisted the successful refugees.[144] Ironically, some of the admitted German and Czech refugees did indeed go into farming, like Samuel and Anne Sussel, who came to Canada in 1937 from Mainz. After spending four years in Edmonton with their two children, they bought a farm in 1941 near Chilliwack, British Columbia, and settled down there to run a small dairy herd, raise poultry, and grow raspberries.[145] A considerable number of Czech Jews farmed successfully in the Brantford area.

Thomas A. Crerar, one-time minister of immigration on four occasions in the late 1930s, urged his Cabinet colleagues to admit Jewish refugees. But each attempt failed, and he was forced to inform the petitioners that the policy would not be changed.[146] In the final analysis, it was Prime Minister Mackenzie King, by no means an antisemite (though he was prey to then-current attitudes about Jews) and by his own account sympathetic to the plight of Jews in Germany, who maintained the immigration policy. National unity required concession, conciliation, and compromise, and he had to meet the severe domestic problems of the 1930s.[147]

Thus, by 1931, immigration was less than one-fifth what it had been in 1930, only 649 compared with 3,421.[148] Figures rose somewhat over the next two years, then fell again in 1934. For the next twelve to thirteen years, despite desperate appeals from Jewish refugees and organizations, the government restricted Jewish entry on the theory that, as one official later put it, 'none is too many.' Most of those who got into the country did so under the 'permit system,' which was characterized by a certain amount of influence-peddling.[149] When the plight of Jewish refugees reached a crisis in 1938, King told his cabinet that 'the time has come when, as a Government, we would have to perform acts which were expressive of what we believe to be the conscience of the nation, and not what might be, at the moment, politically the most expedient.' But bowing to opposition from Quebec members, King agreed that provincial governments should decide on the admission of refugees.[150]

The provinces resented having to support unemployed immigrants on their relief rolls, and urged the Dominion government to 'curtail the activities of the Department of Immigration,' which they regarded as 'over-zealous.' Anxious to comply and still allow in the 'right sort' – that is, of farmers – King's government in 1927 had agreed to allow officials in the provincial governments, which were equally responsible for immigration, to 'see that the [Dominion] regulations were even more restrictive than before.' In other words, the provinces were to have the key responsibility for immigration, and the premiers the deciding voice on the provinces' absorptive capacity. Such considerations would determine how many immigrants would be admitted. Because of anti-immigrant sentiments and, in the 1930s, severely depressed economic conditions, the provincial governments probably were as unsympathetic as Ottawa officials like Blair to Jewish immigration.

Jews were becoming increasingly anxious about their brethren in Central and Eastern Europe. In Germany, by 1935, Hitler had begun the process of identifying and excluding them from society, while brutal persecution was taking place in the streets. In Poland, Marshal Pilsudski's death that same year unleashed antisemitic forces that seriously worsened the lot of that country's Jews. Meanwhile, in Hungary and Romania, antisemitic political parties contended for power. All the while, through newspapers and personal letters, the alarming news of deteriorating conditions in Europe arrived in Canada. European relatives pleaded to their families in North America for help in entering Canada. Letters to harried JIAS officials from Germany were increasingly desperate. An unemployed young father of a three-year-old child, writing from Dusseldorf in February 1939, asked officials to 'imagine my inner torture. Every morning, when I get up after a sleepless night, [there is] always the same sorrow, and there is no escape ... Please forgive my pestering, but help me.'[151] Urgent appeals were likewise made to government officials, to the Congress, and to MPs. A few appellants made it. The Neumann family from Brecla, Czechoslovakia, through a lucky contact with a Canadian Pacific Railway official who certified Oscar, the father, as an experienced farmer, and the family's conversion to Roman Catholicism, secured entry in September 1940.[152] But Canada's gates were all but locked to Jewish immigration.[153]

In fact, Canada's virtual exclusion of Jews was due primarily to the prevalence of antisemitism, particularly in French Canada, where priests, politicians, and intellectuals actively opposed Jewish immigration. Petitions circulated by the St-Jean-Baptiste Society drew tens of thousands of signatures. Power-broker Ernest Lapointe 'took a hard line with respect to refugees,' convincing King that to do otherwise would strengthen the Quebec nationalists and weaken the Liberal Party in Quebec. When a delegation of the three Jewish MPs pleaded with the prime minister in May 1938 for the admission of one thousand Jewish refugee families, King – conscious of the virulent antisemitism in Quebec – referred them to the Quebec members, like Lapointe, of the Cabinet, a polite, but definite, refusal.[154] As well, in Alberta, Social Creditors such as MP Norman Jaques issued statements attacking the prospect of Jewish refugee immigration.

Most Canadian intellectuals and opinion-makers said little in favour of accepting Jewish refugees. Academics Frank Underhill and Frank Scott, on the left, apparently kept silent on this issue, while many others let their anti-foreigner views be known. In the meantime, Jewish leaders lobbied unsuccessfully in Ottawa, although some prominent Jews disposed of special immigration permits for a fortunate few in the community.[155] Reflecting many years later on his own valiant efforts to secure more entry permits, the Congress's Saul Hayes said:

> When the survivors blame the Jewish communities of the free world for not having tried to force the hands of the Roosevelts, Churchills, MacKenzie [*sic*] Kings, etc., they're probably right. Actually I don't think we could possibly have even if we had marched on Ottawa every hour on the hour. But we can't have an easy conscience because we didn't try to the extent that we should have. We were too damned polite about it.

Blair scrutinized all applications for entry and determined to keep Jews out. He was aided in this by many other officials, including Vincent Massey, Canadian high commissioner in London, and by widespread public opinion in favour of a closed-door immigration policy. 'Canadians preferred almost anyone – including Germans – to Jews.'[156] Even after the horrors of Kristallnacht on the night of 10 and 11 November 1938, neither Mackenzie King nor the leader of the opposition, Dr Robert Manion, would change their policies on allowing Jewish refugees into Canada. In Montreal, the influential *Le Devoir* opposed 'making Canada the Jewish paradise' and the Société St-Jean-Baptiste collected 127,364 signatures on its petition against immigration of any kind, especially Jewish immigration. At a Montreal election campaign rally in November 1942, the youthful Pierre Trudeau stated that 'he feared the peaceful invasion of immigrants more than the armed invasion of the enemy,' an obvious reference to Jews.[157] On the other hand, there were loud public protests after Kristallnacht; in Toronto, seventeen thousand people mustered in Maple Leaf Gardens to hear former Ontario chief justice Sir William Mulock and former University of Toronto president Sir Robert Falconer denounce the atrocities.[158] Other protest meetings took place in Halifax, Kingston, and Montreal.

Meanwhile, a small group of Canadian churchmen – Anglicans, United churchmen, Presbyterians, Baptists, and Quakers – gathered in response to Rev. Claris E. Silcox's call for action in early 1936 and came out publicly for 'a reasonable number of selected refugees.'[159] This hedged appeal, which, oddly enough, did not specifically mention Jews, was only one of many denunciations of Nazism from churches – the Anglican and United churches were the most active – and from clergymen like Silcox and Tommy Shields of Toronto's Jarvis Street Baptist Church. A convention of Quebec and Ontario Baptists in June 1939 resolved that 'this Baptist Convention do urge upon proper governmental authorities the desirability of admitting to Canada carefully selected individuals or groups of refugees ...' That very month, upon hearing of the plight of the refugees on the *St. Louis* University of Toronto professor George M. Wrong begged King to allow them sanctuary in Canada 'as evidence of the true Christian charity of this most fortunate and blessed country.'

In 1943 the Baptist intellectual Watson Kirkconnell decried the mass murder of Jews in Europe in a moving poem inspired by Isaiah entitled 'The Agony of Israel.'[160] Though eloquent on the unfolding tragedy, Kirkconnell did not call for the admission of refugees. Neither did

Rev. Ernest M. Howse, of the United Church, when he delivered his stirring address 'I Speak for the Jew' in October 1942 at the Winnipeg Civic Auditorium:

> So I speak for the Jews. But I speak for someone not different from myself ... I think not of Jews and Jewesses; I think of men, women, and children, of young lovers and little babies, of homes and families. And when I plead for the Jew I plead for my own family and yours, and all the families of mankind.[161]

What is notable is that – however fragmented, weak, and inadequate – there was indeed a Canadian Christian witness to the worsening plight of European Jews in the 1930s and 1940s.

Meanwhile, Canadian Jewish response to the persecutions of Jews in Germany, besides boycotts, demonstrations, and petitions, also included numerous editorials in newspapers and in weekly publications like the *Chronicle*, where Abraham M. Klein excoriated the German persecutors of Jews. In a *Chronicle* editorial following the 1938 Kristallnacht pogroms, he called on Canadian Jewry to 'remember our flesh and blood in the land of the Hamaniac, and let our voice issue in sorrow, in anguish and protest.'[162] In 1942, Klein published his lengthy poem *The Hitleriad* in which he dealt with the power of Hitler's evil and listed his 'crimes and atrocities.'[163]

In 1940 Canada did receive some seventeen hundred 'accidental' Jewish (or half-Jewish) immigrants. These German and Austrian refugees were rounded up in Britain in 1940 as aliens from enemy countries, and were shipped off to detention in Canada and other Commonwealth countries.[164] About a third were teenagers, among them rabbinical-school and university students, artisans, and professors. After a week to ten days at sea in steerage – with the usual seasickness, salmonella poisoning, and food shortages – surrounded with barbed wire and machine guns, and on the same ships as Nazis and German prisoners of war, they disembarked in Canada amid tight security. Initially, camp conditions in the Eastern Townships were awful. Although officially categorized from the start of the war as 'friendly enemy aliens' (class B) or 'friendly aliens and refugees from Nazi oppression' (class C), the Jewish internees 'were treated as if they were prisoners of war' or potential spies, even though Canadian authorities were informed by the British of their status.[165] On arrival in Canada, some internees were robbed by soldiers of all their valuables and were locked up, some in the same camps with Nazis and other war prisoners.

Officials quickly separated the Jews from the prisoners of war. However, they initially enforced tight discipline, even making it difficult for Congress officials to visit. Two months after the internees' arrival, British authorities sent the Canadian government guidelines for their release. Some were to join auxiliary military units, participate in war work, or undertake further studies. The authorities balked, and the internees had to continue waiting in prison camps. Some seven hundred of them were so disheartened that they accepted an offer to return to Britain, with the assurance that they could join non-combat army labour battalions. Those remaining stayed on in the belief that, sooner or later, they would be released,[166] as some were in July 1941. An army officer in command of one of the camps warmly concurred: 'After nearly a year's experience with these people it is my opinion that this would be beneficial. They are highly temperamental and react very keenly to what they think are injustices and are very grateful for any favours given them.'

Those released went to the cities for further schooling or into war work. Others still in the camps readied themselves for civilian life. They studied English, and general interest and academic subjects in preparation for matriculation exams. 'Generally life is very bearable,' one of them wrote, and the commissioner of the camps, Colonel Reginald Fordham, 'was very sympathetic to the men under his care.' Some internees regarded the guards – mostly French Canadians – as lenient and humane, while others saw their treatment as degrading, inhumane, contrary to Geneva Convention rules, and worse than that accorded captured German officers.[167] The camp schools were run in cooperation with McGill University officials, and only four months after internment began, examinations were held.

At the same time, their lot was improved through the efforts of the Central Committee for Interned Refugees (CCIR), formed in 1941 by the National Council for Refugees (NCR) and the United Jewish Refugee and War Relief Agency (UJRA). Headed by Senator Cairine Wilson, the CCIR first laboured to have internees released and then arranged for jobs, support for them, and, sometimes, intervention with employers. Every petition was scrutinized by Blair, who 'proved to be a formidable obstacle to the smooth and quick release of the interned refugees.' Blair utilized every flaw in every file as an excuse to deny release. 'Blair ... found the means to interpret the immigration regulations in their most restrictive sense.' In early December 1943, the Canadian government issued an order-in-council (PC 9440) that closed the camps and freed the last of the internees. They were then free to find their way into Canadian life.[168]

These 'accidental immigrants' of 1940 adjusted to Canadian life and the Jewish community in various ways. In some cases, however, there was a certain cultural dissonance. One of them reported:

> When I told people I came from Austria, they'd say 'Oh, you're a landsmench of mine. You come from Galicia too' and I tell him no, I came from Vienna. 'You come from Austria, so, you must come from the same part that I come from.' So, after awhile, I say sure, I gave up ... I learned how to speak Yiddish. With my German background it wasn't too hard. I got along very nicely.

After their experiences, they were usually resourceful. Most of them adjusted well and developed considerable admiration for some aspects of Canadian norms, such as the absence of a stratified class system:

> What impressed me the most, coming to Canada, is the lack of the caste system. In Canada I learnt very soon that the only thing that counts was money, more or less, to determine your status. Another thing that I admired very much and that I was not used to from Europe was that Jewish people were workers here ... This impressed me very much in favour of this part of the world.

These 'accidental immigrants,' and the few thousand other Jews who had entered Canada during the Nazi era, were joined by many others when the war was over and contributed to the enormous changes that were to come in the 1950s. Meanwhile, as Canadian Jewry experienced these social transitions and organizational developments, the clothing industry was undergoing tension, disorder, and bitterness.

8 Clothing and Politics

Deep divisions existed between employers and workers in the burgeoning clothing industry, which created an economic frontier for Jewish entrepreneurs and a factory for Jewish workers, who were a large component of the industry's labour force in Montreal, Toronto, and Winnipeg. Both the leaders and the members of the major clothing trade unions were predominantly Jewish,[1] while Jews became some of the largest manufacturers.

After the First World War, the manufacture of women's ready-to-wear items boomed, creating a huge demand for cheap labour. Known among Jews informally as the *shmata* business, or the rag trade, it took on its own personality and attracted many daring (or foolish) entrepreneurs. Later, an even greater market emerged for inexpensive but stylish dresses for the growing numbers of women working in offices, banks, and stores.[2] For its workers, however, this industry created some of the worst labour conditions in Canada.

Dress manufacturing was a gambler's industry in which only the very shrewdest or luckiest survived. Owing to rapidly changing styles, producers were sometimes left with unsaleable stock. In the 1920s, it was said that for a factory owner to last for as long as ten years was a miracle. The bonanza mentality was also encouraged by the industry's relatively easy entry. The start-up costs – estimated at $1,500 to $2,000 – were relatively low, machines easily rented, inexpensive accommodation leased, and cheap labour readily hired. With increasing urbanization, changing tastes in clothing, and the expansion of the retail sector following the First World War, outlets were increasing and becoming more accessible as major department stores like Eaton's, Morgan's, Simpson's, the Hudson's Bay Company, and a number of smaller chains were expanding their branch stores and order offices. Meanwhile, numbers of stores were proliferating with some 104,000 in the 1920s. Twenty years later, there were 128,000.[3] Specialized dress shops were springing up everywhere – a high per centage of them Jewish-owned – featuring factory-made frocks in the latest styles and fabrics at modest prices.

In addition to the principal centres of Montreal and Toronto, Hamilton was a secondary production hub for men's clothing, as were Ottawa, London, Winnipeg, Edmonton, and Vancouver. After 1920, fur-processing and womenswear manufacturing developed in Winnipeg, while entrepreneurs in Edmonton and Vancouver produced clothing for the local market.

At the same time, the Jewish-dominated trade unions had emerged, including the Amalgamated Clothing Workers of America (Amalgamated), the International Ladies' Garment Workers' Union (ILGWU), and the United Hat, Cap and Millinery Workers' International Union, to be joined by the Industrial Union of Needle Trade Workers (IUNTW), an affiliate of the Workers' Unity League. These unions, as Ruth Frager's *Sweatshop Strife* records, were not concerned only with shop-floor struggles; their battles for better material conditions were linked to 'a broader social vision' of a classless, socialist society.[4] Such views, however, led in different political directions, creating severe tensions. And while such transcendent socialist values were held by many leaders and rank-and-file unionists, the struggle to make a living blunted much of the idealism. Certainly most union leaders concentrated on basic issues like the dispersion of the clothing factories, the improvement of wages and working conditions, and the establishment of union shops. Their goal was overall industrial stability, not revolution.

All of the unions, except for the National Clothing Workers of Canada, an affiliate of the All-Canadian Congress of Labour, and the IUNTW (a branch of the Workers' Unity League, which was in turn a wing of the Communist Party of Canada), were branches of internationals based in New York. Most of the strikes conducted by both the ILGWU and the Amalgamated were directed by organizers sent from the New York headquarters. Moreover, severe tension between the unions during the late 1920s and early 1930s nearly wrecked the ILGWU, and substantially weakened the Amalgamated. In Quebec, employer resistance to the ILGWU was particularly strong, and political opposition prevalent. French-Canadian workers faced pressure to join the accommodationist Catholic syndicates instead, thus weakening the ILGWU's general effectiveness in Montreal until the late 1930s.

The new dress-manufacturing business has been described as 'a trade for nervous men.'[5] The operation of the older and more stable cloak-and-suit factories resembled the menswear industry, encompassing all stages of production and maintaining quality control this way. Toronto's John Northway, a large-scale manufacturer, sold his ready-to-wear coats, mantles, suits, and skirts in his thriving chain of retail outlets in western Ontario, a vertically integrated operation that foreshadowed many others. Some did only the cutting in their own factories and let the sewing out to contractors, while others used contractors for all operations, and took delivery of finished goods ready for shipment to their customers. Still other large-scale retailers, such as Eaton's, manufactured goods in their own factories in Toronto.

Contractors were the marginal men, neither solely manufacturers nor workers. Often they were both. They were usually experienced tailors, designers, or cutters, but lacked capital or commercial connections in the retail sector. Most of them were Jews, working on the borders of the industry. They offered manufacturers a cheaper mode of production by operating in low-rent lofts, garrets, or the workers' own homes. In the worst of these shops, investigations reported crowding, poor ventilation, lack of sanitation, low wages, long hours, and the widespread use of child labour.[6] Contending with each other for work, contractors pushed costs down still further, eliminating those unable to compete. Some contractors prospered, morphing into manufacturers in their own right. They produced garments for sale to their own customers from the remnants of the cloth given them by manufacturers or, if their credit was good enough, entirely from their own goods. As in the menswear trade, this transition was clear evidence of upward mobility from the precarious margins of contracting.

Dress manufacturing by the 1920s exhibited the industry's worst problems, particularly the exploitation, or 'sweating,' of workers that had been prevalent in all branches of the needle trades.[7] The hard-won collective agreements reached in menswear after the bitter strikes in 1917 had mostly broken down by the early 1920s, owing to post-war readjustment. Employers then reduced wages, re-established piecework, and evaded unions and their 'unbearable demands' altogether by moving their plants to outlying centres, which the unions called runaway shops. Unresolved battles were fought throughout the 1920s, and the majority of strikes and lockouts were short. Most contractors were eventually brought into line, even though the number of these shops grew.

The predatory buying practices of the major department stores, described so graphically in the evidence given before the 1934 Royal Commission on Price Spreads and Mass Buying, helped turn the dress industry into a jungle where ruthless cost-cutting measures, including wage reduction, spelled survival. The trade was bedevilled by style piracy, unfair returns, predatory price-cutting, unethical practices by large buyers, and unconscionable labour exploitation.[8]

Clearly Quebec had traditionally lower wages than Ontario and a population influx from rural areas which created a huge pool of unskilled, cheap labour. The negative attitude of the Roman Catholic Church towards the international unions stymied organization of the workforce. The Catholic syndicates were organized in opposition to the 'internationals' and what the church considered their dangerous leftist ideologies.

One highly successful dress manufacturer was Abraham Sommer of Montreal. Born in 1878 in Lodz, Poland's textile manufacturing centre, he moved to Montreal in 1901, where he established the Queen Dress and Waist Company. During the 1920s, he and his brother Charles built it into one of the leading firms in the business.[9] He eventually constructed the Sommer Building, which was one of the major centres of the industry in the downtown Montreal garment district. Sommer also joined many of the leading social and charitable groups in the Jewish community. Successful manufacturers might develop buildings like Sommer, designed to accommodate the many and often transitory small-scale manufacturers. Some became importers of goods from New York or Paris. Most supported trade associations that were organized to regulate the industry. Sommer and Abraham Gittelson, another major manufacturer, organized the Ladies' Garment Manufacturers' Association of Canada to protect their interests in labour matters.

The major Toronto dress manufacturers were mostly pre-1914 immigrants with experience as salesmen, cutters, or designers who were willing to take the dangerous leap to manufacturing. Abraham Posluns founded Superior Cloak in 1916 and produced higher-end goods. Another was Charles Draimin, whose small-scale firm burgeoned in the 1920s. Elias Pullan specialized in the manufacture of suits and coats. Many others lasted in the business for varying lengths of time,[10] depending on their ability to keep their balance.

In Winnipeg, several manufacturers set up businesses to exploit the western market for ready-to-wear. Morris Haid, arriving in Canada from his native Austria in 1893, established the Western Shirt and Overall

Company around 1900. Haid and his partner, Harry Steinberg, prospered.[11] Benjamin Jacob, with partner John Crowley, founded a highly successful women's coat-and-suit manufacturing business during the 1920s, employing more than two hundred workers even in the depressed early 1930s. A number of Winnipeg Jews were active in the local fur-processing business.

By this time, in Montreal, Toronto, and Winnipeg, the new large downtown buildings housed increasing numbers of small dress factories. Producers located their offices, cutting rooms, and, often, factories there for the convenience of their buyers, who either worked in the local large department stores or were out-of-town retailers. These new buildings, each accommodating dozens of shops and two or three hundred workers, towered twelve or fourteen storeys – large for the time – on the fringes of the downtown core. The Blumenthal, Wilder, Jacobs, Sommer, and Mayor buildings, as well as other ungainly structures, ringed Montreal's Bleury–Ste-Catherine intersection and nearby streets. In Toronto, similar edifices stretched along Adelaide and King streets, and up Spadina Avenue, while Winnipeg's garment centre arose in the area northwest of the Main-Portage intersection.

Even as some of these businesses waxed and waned, the conditions of the workers worsened. The piecework system of payment bred severe competition among workers as well as among manufacturers and contractors. In 1925 a Jewish employee in a Montreal dress factory complained:

> You can never do enough for the boss. Every half hour the boss counts the number of dresses on our chairs. I am a finisher, and sometimes I feel like doing something desperate when I see the girls rushing the lives out of themselves, each to do more dresses than the others.[12]

Because of the volatility of the clothing industry, unions struggled to survive. In Montreal, the ILGWU found that French-Canadian workers, mostly women, were difficult to organize. Disruptions to the cloak-and-suit trade during the First World War had seriously disabled the union,[13] which, after nearly twenty years in Canada, had serious structural problems. The recession of 1920–2, volatility in dress manufacturing, and a well-managed open-shop campaign among manufacturers placed the ILGWU on the defensive, as piecework was reintroduced by Toronto manufacturers, hours increased, and new firms either ignored the union/employer agreements or kept the union out.

Conditions in Montreal were worse. In January 1925, the womenswear industry there was racked by a general strike that dragged on for months.[14] Although the ILGWU locals had a large combined membership of 1,500 to 1,600, the strike affected a total of 6,000. Recognizing its own vulnerability, the Toronto ILGWU soon joined in.

The leader and strike spokesman for the Montreal clothing unions was Joseph Schubert, a long-time city alderman and leading leftist. Jewish leadership in the clothing-trade unions was strong, even though Jews were not a majority of the workforce. Men like Schubert were usually selected to head the joint boards because virtually the entire leadership of the New York–based international was Jewish. Moreover, it was assumed that Jews could negotiate effectively with employers who were mainly Jews.

The presence of so many Jews in an increasingly militant workforce sometimes attracted adverse publicity. During the 1925 strike in Montreal, Schubert felt it necessary to deny rumours, intended to discredit the strikers, that the workforce was entirely Jewish.[15] In fact, he said there were four hundred French Canadians among the sixteen hundred picketers. The prominence of Jews among both the rank and file and the leadership was also an issue in the ILGWU strike, which began in Toronto in early February of that year. One leading Jewish Toronto manufacturer, who represented fourteen producers employing 65 per cent of the workers, alleged that the union was attempting to oust non-Jews. Replying for the union, Mary McNab noted, 'It was rather laughable to have a Jew manufacturer claim defence of Gentile girls.' Tim Buck, of the Communist Party of Canada, claimed that police were 'selectively harassing Christian pickets while leaving the Jews alone,' presumably acting on orders from the manufacturers to foment ethnic conflict.

While manufacturers deplored charges of preferential hiring of Jews, they did concede that 'the needle industry was largely in Jewish hands.'[16] All the chairmen of the Toronto, Montreal, and Winnipeg joint-boards of the ILGWU, the United Hat, Cap and Millinery Workers' International Union, the International Fur Workers, and the Amalgamated were Jews, while only the few union locals established for other ethnic groups were headed by non-Jews.

Meanwhile, in Montreal by 1931, there were more than 6,300 Jews working in all branches of the industry, from a total Jewish population of 57,997. Louis Rosenberg noted that nearly three-quarters of all gainfully employed Montreal Jews worked in the industry; they constituted 35 per cent of its workers, while more than 53 per cent were French

Canadian.[17] In the women's-clothing sector, Jews, half of them women, constituted 32 per cent of all workers. French Canadians were nearly 60 per cent of its workforce, and of that number nearly 92 per cent were women, the vast majority of them young.

The Montreal and Toronto strikes of 1925 were the spearhead of the ILGWU's drive for recognition, better sanitary conditions, an end to piecework, and an industry-wide forty-four-hour week. Most firms, especially the larger ones, chose to settle quickly; in early February, twenty-seven manufacturers employing seven hundred workers signed contracts with the ILGWU.[18] By early March, only 6 of the 115 shops that had been struck first were still holding out. They, too, gave up and signed.

For the next few years, these agreements held and the industry was stable. But in 1928 the ILGWU was beset by competition from a rival union, the Industrial Union of Needle Trade Workers, which recruited members from ILGWU locals and mounted left-wing attacks that diverted energies from the main tasks. Employers benefited from this friction, and the spirit of the 1925 collective agreements disappeared amid bitterness and tension.

By 1930 reports of Montreal dress manufacturers operating their plants seven days a week brought the ILGWU, the newly organized Catholic syndicates, and various other unions together to pressure them into reducing their hours and creating opportunities for some two hundred unemployed cloak-makers and four hundred dressmakers.[19] The unions targeted Sunday work and the sweatshops, some of which were fire traps, where workers were badly exploited. Manufacturers capitulated when threatened by possible strikes at seventy firms for a forty-two-hour week and wage increases. These conflicts were settled by an agreement and the establishment of a seven-person grievance board headed by Rabbi Harry Stern of Temple Emanu-el.

However, manufacturers continued to allow contracts to lapse, then hired new workers at lower wages. As well, the emergence of new non-union firms led to frequent strikes as the ILGWU tried frantically to organize them. While most disputes were resolved quickly, many firms avoided a settlement by contracting out or leaving town. In 1933, Gustave Francq, chairman of the Quebec Women's Minimum Wage Board, reported that 'owing to disrupted conditions in the clothing trade, many firms are not operating but letting their manufacturing out to subcontractors, who are in many cases "fly by night" factory owners.'[20]

Meanwhile, the Department of Labour statistics showed that by December 1931, 59.7 per cent of unionized garment workers were unemployed. While this picture improved in the spring, an average of more than 20 per cent were out of work during the busy summer months. This pattern continued for the rest of the decade.

To meet the needs of these workers, Jewish agencies were disbursing more than ever before on the unemployed. Social workers from Montreal's Baron de Hirsch Institute reported widespread hardship, including a significant increase in social and medical problems. By early 1931, poverty was so severe that the *Keneder Adler* and the *Canadian Jewish Chronicle* spearheaded a fundraising campaign for the unemployed. The *Chronicle* reported that 'the degree of unemployment in the Jewish community is very large. Thousands of family breadwinners are working either not at all, or only on part time, and earning mere pittances.'[21] By October, in anticipation of a hard winter, fifteen Montreal labour organizations established the Peoples' Kitchen to distribute soup, meat, and tea to the unemployed. Women and children also showed up at the Kitchen, leading a reporter for the *Chronicle* to comment: 'Even two or three days a week in a dress, millinery or cloak shop would be welcomed these days by the Jewish unemployed girl.' Meanwhile, the Jewish People's Restaurant for the Unemployed gave out ten thousand meals to the needy in 1931[22] and, in the first four months of 1932, distributed another thirty thousand meals. The Federation of Jewish Philanthropies struggled to meet the need. Throughout the early 1930s, the 'cry of the poor ... the sick, the aged and the orphan' was voiced frequently, and the Federation ran advertisements in the *Chronicle* appealing to employers to hire Jewish workers.

Even those with jobs could not make ends meet. Commenting on prevailing conditions generally in the needle trades the Royal Commission on Price Spreads reported in 1935 that 'aside from extreme variations in wages, the industry was afflicted by oppressively long hours, and violations of laws governing employment conditions, hours, and wages especially in the dress trade.'[23] Existing labour legislation could not protect workers.[24] Generally, inspections were rare and incomplete, and in rural areas the legislation was entirely ignored. The minimum wages in the dress industry ranged from $7.00 to $12.50 a week under Quebec law. If employers paid that, they forced their employees to work extremely long hours for it. When he arrived in Montreal from Chicago during the winter of 1934 to organize dressmakers' locals for the ILGWU, Bernard Shane found girls earning between $5 and $10 a week. But the Price

Spreads Commission heard harrowing stories of a few employers engaging in fraud to reduce wages in some of the shops outside Montreal.

By the 1930s, women and some girls of only ten, predominated as workers in the Montreal dress industry. Thousands of these operatives, known as *midinettes* (a contraction of the French words *midi* and *dinette*, meaning 'short lunch'), thronged the streets and squares of the factories and nearby commercial districts at midday as they came down from the large buildings.

Seasonal work created intensely active periods of several weeks, followed by long stretches of unemployment. During a busy period, a worker might earn a living wage in return for up to eighty or more hours of labour. But in slack times, it was very much less – or nothing at all. Testimony to the Price Spreads Commission indicated that, at best, a needleworker got forty weeks of work annually. Between jobs they either 'lived off their fat' or took other work. Statistics during the 1920s show that in April, May, and June, almost one-third of all them were out of work, while in some years unemployment ran as high as 60 per cent.[25]

Adding to the uncertainty of employment was the general volatility of the industry. Between 1916 and 1928, the average annual failure rate in dress manufacturing was 18.62 per cent; during the mid-1920s, the failure rates approached 30 per cent.[26] Despite such risks, by 1934 there were at least 693 manufacturers of women's apparel in Canada, almost doubled since 1924. Between 1922 and 1930, statistics for the Quebec women's clothing industry – numbers of employees, wages paid, and value of production – more than doubled.

Testifying before the Price Spreads Commission in January 1935, J.P. Levee, of the National Associated Women's Wear Bureau, reported that between 1932 and 1934, 232 new firms started up.[27] At the same time, however, the gross value of production fell to about two-thirds of the 1929 number, resulting in more firms chasing fewer sales. Many manufacturers were entering just as others were leaving, most likely unable to make ends meet. It was, perhaps, in this kind of volatile environment that one dress manufacturer asked another, 'How's business?' to which his interlocutor replied, 'How's business? Business is so bad that even the customers who don't intend to pay aren't buying.'

Meanwhile, workers were suddenly fired often without receiving their past-due wages. Even with an increase in companies and employees, total salaries and wages were falling drastically. As witnesses informed the Price Spreads Commission, the shops moved so frequently that it was impossible to keep track of them.[28] Leah Roback, then the educational director of the ILGWU in Montreal, recalled that conditions in most dress shops were 'vile.'[29] Even those in the big buildings (named after owners like Jacobs and Wilder) were known as 'cockroach shops.' In many of these, she noted the frequency of bosses favouring workers 'who were willing to give [them] the very fine intimate favours.'

By 1931 there were reports that rising poverty levels in Montreal were causing an increase in marital breakdowns.[30] A number of the free-loan syndicates, which 'include in their membership several thousand families of workmen or petty tradesmen,' were likewise in danger of foundering. The Montreal Federation of Jewish Charities admitted to being 'caught in the vicious circle of a condition of affairs which makes the maximum demands ... [when] revenues are likely to be at their very lowest ebb.' Its president, the businessman Allan Bronfman, feared that the Federation would be insolvent. Editorials in the *Chronicle* favourably noted the scheme of the American Jewish Agricultural Society to resettle underemployed workers as part-time farmers on the outskirts of the cities. 'The back-to-the-land movement on the part of our people serves many functions,' ran one such editorial. 'It not only tends toward a solution of the economic problems of surplusage and unemployment, but it also removes from our midst the ever-present and ever-unjust accusation that we are by psychology and habit a race of middlemen, a race of parasitic luftmenschen.' The Federation of Jewish Philanthropies in Toronto faced mounting pleas from the unemployed, many of whom were ineligible for municipal assistance and reluctant to apply for public charity.[31]

The Ligue du dimanche, reflecting religious orthodoxy and humane concern,[32] alleged that some owners professing benevolence were operating seven days a week whether employees were Jews or not. In response, the provincial government amended the Lord's Day Act to prevent all Sunday work, creating hardship for Sabbath-observing Jews.

A reaction to these worsening conditions was the drive to unionize all workers.[33] A series of strikes in 1934 and 1935 forced major women's apparel companies into line. In the charged atmosphere of Quebec, the activities of such international unions as the ILGWU or the Amalgamated aroused the enmity of the church and the competition of the Catholic syndicates. They also stimulated antisemitism. Recalling her attitude towards Shane and other leaders of the unions, one of the midinettes remembered that 'ils me semblaient bien aimables; mais ils étaient juifs comme les patrons et je ne comprenais pas en ce temps-là qu'ils puissent être de notre côté.'

The Catholic syndicates organized unions that competed with the ILGWU. Encouraged by the Quebec government and some Roman Catholic clerics, syndicate representatives opened negotiations with dress manufacturers in April and May 1934. As well, Quebec's premier, Louis Alexandre Taschereau, attacked the ILGWU, accusing its members of communism.[34]

These suspicions were overcome partly through the efforts of Claude Jodoin, later enlisted by Shane to act as a bridge to the French-Canadian workers, and Rose Pesotta, a Russian-born, Jewish anarchist, feminist, and seasoned veteran in organizing women workers in the United States.[35] While these victories for the ILGWU in Montreal indicated a rapprochement between French Canadians and Jewish workers and organizers, they remained members of separate locals which communicated through a governing council called a joint board.

However, taking a stand in 1934, the Communist IUNTW,[36] led by J.A. Guilbeault and Leah Roback, took some four thousand dressmakers out on strike and closed down 125 shops. This effort was to organize their fellow workers and to ensure a forty-four-hour week with a minimum weekly wage of $12.50 and benefits. Strikebreakers provoked serious violence in the Ste Catherine Street and Phillips Square clothing sector. The majority of the large owners held out, and the strike failed. The ILGWU's opposition to the IUNTW was also a factor, reflecting the bitter rivalries between the Social Democratic and Communist left.

Having bested the IUNTW, Charles Sommer, head of the Montreal Dress Manufacturers' Guild, continued discussions with more compliant syndicate representatives. In a March 1934 feature article, provocatively entitled 'A Disgraceful Climax in a Paralyzed Industry,' the *Chronicle*, then edited by Rabbi Charles Bender of She'arith Israel, had castigated him and other Jewish employers for 'engaging in a dispute with unionized Jewish wage earners ... [and] fleeing from ... Montreal, taking their shops with them to the small country towns.'[37] This trend had become 'epidemic in character,' the intention being to lower the Jewish 'wage standard to that of their "village" [French-Canadian] competitors.' The manufacturers all along believed 'that the quicker they dispensed with their Jewish employees, the less danger there would be for all organized unions [because] the natural trend for the Jewish worker is to be associated with a union.'

The *Chronicle* offered a sympathetic assessment of the competing French Canadians.[38] In contrast to the Jewish workers, they were 'sons and daughters of the farmers in the area ... willing to work for a pittance.

As little as they earned, it was pin money and savings.' Now these French-Canadian workers 'are no longer farmer's sons, but members of the proletariat ... now nursing bitterness in their hearts towards their employers, who are exploiting them, and the "juif" is mentally accused by the employees for all their personal difficulties.' Some Jewish employers in the villages were accused of ignoring women's minimum-wage laws. The *Chronicle* cited a report in *La Presse*, alleging that one manufacturer in Joliette 'was ... labelling pay envelopes of the women workers with a greater amount than is actually to be found when the envelope is opened.' Here was an opening for antisemites 'because so many non-Jews would like to hold up this type of manufacturer as the symbol of Jewish morals in business.'

So while Jewish unemployed clothing workers 'walk the streets in an endless search for work because in the name of justice and humanity, they sought to organize the worker, and better the lot of every employee, Jew or non-Jew, in the clothing industry, the Jewish populace in general will be held responsible for a situation that the Jewish workmen sought to avoid, and because of which they were punished with unemployment and starvation.' A letter to the *Canadian Jewish Review* commented that the business ethics of some manufacturers were 'a disgrace to the Jewish community at large and not worthy of the name of Jew.'[39] And in his weekly *Review* column, Rabbi Harry Stern expressed 'a great deal of sadness ... that among those alleged guilty of underpaying their help are listed the names of Jewish citizens ... The Jew who fails to deal ethically with his fellow man stands especially condemned ... The laborer must be given his just desserts.'

In late June, the *Chronicle*, concerned with protecting Jewish jobs, attacked both the Catholic unions and the Jewish employers for signing 'sweetheart contracts.'[40] 'The Jewish needle trade [is] confronted by [a] serious situation' because if the Catholic unions controlled the clothing industry, Jews would not be hired. 'The purpose of this article is to warn the Jewish needle workers of the ambitions of the Catholic unions, and to place them on guard against a situation that may become another "Notre Dame Hospital incident" [a reference to the 1937 strike by Catholic interns opposed to hiring a Jewish doctor] ... If they gain control over the "needle trade," and if a strike should occur, it will not be for higher wages or shorter hours, but for the same reason as led to the strike of the interns.'

In pursuit of profits, the *Chronicle* asked how many employers would resist reputed offers of no strikes or stoppages and the probability of lower wages? After Premier Taschereau publicly attacked the international unions as 'American agitators,' the writer, Israel Medresh, warned Jewish workers to be on their guard. In January 1935 the *Chronicle* published a statement by Joseph Schlossberg, the international head of the Amalgamated, attacking the discrimination practised by Jewish employers against Jewish employees.[41]

The behaviour of some Jewish manufacturers during the 1934 strike in Montreal was provocative. According to one reliable Jewish witness, 'they hired gangsters to beat up the union organizers and ... workers on the picket line ... Quite a number of ... the gangsters ... were Jewish boys, from ... the Main in Montreal.'[42] The most militant strikers were Jewish women, who sometimes had to endure physical violence from these employers' goon squads. This militancy reduced employment opportunities, and, desperate for work, some Jewish workers tried to disguise themselves by speaking French and wearing crosses around their necks.[43] As well as vicious class warfare within the community, some employers even fostered antisemitism among the French-Canadian workers. However, many of the latter showed stubborn solidarity with the Jewish strikers. A temporary agreement was reached, but the continuing behaviour of the manufacturers was becoming a public scandal.

The re-established Canadian Jewish Congress was aware of this situation. Executive director Hananiah Meir Caiserman (a successful strike leader in 1917) criticized the community for not supporting Jewish employees and put this issue forth on the Congress agenda. Two main concerns were the worsening plight of the Jewish unemployed and complaints of discrimination against Jewish workers in the Montreal dress industry by the local Manufacturers Protective Association.[44] The same complaints arose in Toronto, where unemployed Jewish clothing workers organized the Alle Far Einem (All for One) society and a Women's Consumers League for mutual assistance.

Caiserman even appealed to the influential Archie Freiman, president of the Zionist Organization of Canada, to settle a strike at one factory and protect the jobs of forty-five workers. In March 1935 the Arbeiter Ring (Workmen's Circle) in Hamilton wrote to Caiserman complaining of 'prominent industrialists who are prepared to sell the poor for a few cents' profit. They discriminate against Jewish workers no less cruelly than do the official anti-Semites.'[45]

However, all efforts at mediation failed. At the Congress's Dominion Council meeting in December 1936, it was reported that 270 Jewish workers were fired when a major Jewish-owned clothing factory was shut down and moved from Montreal to Sherbrooke.[46] And one ILGWU official confided that the Jewish employers' collaboration with the Catholic syndicates in the leather trades, some of whose leaders were activists in the antisemitic Achat Chez Nous movement, 'will result in the slow elimination ... of Jewish workers in these shops.'

In June 1936, Louis Rosenberg observed that the 'runaway shops' were creating vast unemployment, thus straining the Federation of Jewish Philanthropies. In a severe rebuke of the Jewish manufacturers, Rosenberg noted this was 'not only a demoralizing factor in industry generally, but strikes at the very basis of 30% of Canada's Jewish population, and further restricts the possibilities of Jewish employment.' He went on to say, 'Those who sow the wind of [seeking] increased profits by encouraging the flight of contractors' shops in search of cheaper operating costs, not only reap the whirlwind of increased Jewish unemployment and increased Federation budgets in the larger cities, but are pulling down about the ears of the entire Canadian Jewish population, that economic, cultural and educational life which has been built up by the Jewish pioneers of the past sixty years or more.'[47] The Jewish involvement with the Catholic syndicates would endanger the livelihoods of thousands of households.

Some rabbis urged the factory owners to show compassion for their Jewish workers. Rabbi Stern appealed directly to his congregant Charles Sommer 'not to throw them out onto the street.'[48] Attacking what he called Jewish antisemites, Rabbi Charles Bender condemned employers 'who barricade [the] door against Jewish help ... [and] make a specialty of engaging non-Jewish labour although the same work could be carried out as efficiently and as ably by Jewish hands.'

This controversy was taking place while labour conditions were unimproved, as the Price Spreads Commission reported in 1934. As late as 1937, observers noted overproduction and unhealthy competition within the industry. As profit margins fell, manufacturers boosted output to keep their businesses afloat. Surplus production was being dumped in cities across Canada. Meanwhile, some manufacturers were evading Quebec's minimum wage laws through the use of what the *Labour Gazette* called 'cunning schemes ... and we often read in the daily papers of manufacturers brought to court on charges laid by inspectors from the Minimum Wage Commission.' One had been fined in March 1934 for paying one girl $2.70 for a week's work of forty-eight hours.[49]

Meanwhile, the battle between the ILGWU and the Catholic syndicates continued. In January 1937, the *Chronicle* warned of 'Fascism in the needle trades,' arguing that the same French Canadians who fostered the Achat Chez Nous campaign had 'given birth on the fertile soil of this province with its bursting bag of Jew-baiting tricks ... [to a] Fascist union'[50] Promising to ensure 'no communism, no radicalism, no red-ism the idea is to inveigle the Jewish manufacturers into recognizing the Fascist union as the one most compatible with employers' interests.'

The outlook was bleak, unless Jewish employers would not be 'bamboozled.' The community faced 'another link in that devilish chain [with] which destructive forces are continually trying to encircle us.' In April the *Chronicle* warned of trouble for Jewish employers if they signed on with the Catholic syndicates, whose slogan was 'No foreigners [international unions] should interfere in Quebec affairs.' The paper hinted darkly at 'certain powers, other than those of employers and employees [who] are behind this latest effort to throw the industry into turmoil. The ILGWU will be the first to go. Who knows, maybe the Montreal Dress Manufacturers Guild will be next.'

The church prevailed upon French-Canadian workers – then about 80 per cent of the total – to join Catholic syndicates, although, according to the *Chronicle*, 'about sixty per cent of this number are all in favour of the [ILGWU].'[51] '[What] we have here was [the] first taste of the padlock law against Communism with its elastic interpretation.' Even worse was that Jewish manufacturers 'were boycotting Jewish labour.' 'The reprehensible feature about the present situation,' the *Chronicle* continued, 'is the attitude of the Jewish grandees of the dress industry' – no doubt, a slap at Charles Sommer. 'With one hand they deprive the Jews of their earning capabilities, and with the other hand they support charitable institutions to dole out relief.' There could be 'a boomerang of unpleasant consequences,' it predicted. Meanwhile, the *Keneder Adler* also condemned the manufacturers 'for raising a racial issue and creating an anti-Jewish worker movement.'[52] One manufacturer voiced his dissent: 'The bringing in of the religious issue in a conflict between capital and labour in a trade which lies mostly in the hands of Jewish manufacturers is terrible for the whole Jewish folk.'

By the spring of 1937, the Montreal dress industry was in the midst of a momentous strike. Leah Roback, who was fluent in French and Yiddish, was recruited by the ILGWU to help marshal the women workers in the ladies' ready-to-wear 'cockroach shops,' where, besides the sub-standard conditions, widespread sexual harassment and exploitation occurred.

Roback was highly effective as an organizer, earning enormous respect from francophone and Jewish women workers.[53] The ILGWU was determined to take charge and reverse the disastrous defeat of 1934. The union knew that instability in Montreal could spread to Toronto, tempting manufacturers to relocate to Quebec towns, possibly saving 40 per cent of their labour costs. ILGWU officials in New York were concerned, as some American manufacturers were moving across the border, and were determined to establish 'uniform industrial standards' across Ontario and Quebec. To help the Montrealers, Rose Pesotta, a first-class organizer, was dispatched in early 1937. As she observed in her autobiography, *Bread upon the Waters*, 'the dressmakers needed a woman's approach.' She sent women canvassers from house to house to recruit members and organized social gatherings and a radio broadcast. The union headquarters were improved with a re-equipped library and kitchen, while a stage, piano, radio, and phonograph were added. A celebration of Ste Catherine's Day, the holiday for 'old maids,' drew a huge crowd of dressmakers. The organizing drive became an enormous success.

But it also attracted notice from employers. When seven workers at one factory were fired for union activity in January, the plant was quickly struck. The owner capitulated, and as the effectiveness of the ILGWU increased, its headquarters were inundated by appeals for strikes in other shops too. In early April, the union decided to shut down the entire industry to force employers to sign contracts with them rather than the opposing Catholic syndicate. Within days, more than five thousand workers had struck in one hundred factories, and enthusiasm ran high. Improvising on a French march, the midinettes, along with Jewish women, sang their own composition 'We Will Win' out on the picket lines.

La Nation referred to the strike as a plot by 'la juiverie internationale,' and *Le Devoir* pointed to 'profiles sémitiques' on the picket lines.[54] But the midinettes and their allies stuck to their guns. Although half the dress manufacturers still favoured the Catholic union, by mid-June they reluctantly accepted the ILGWU – the so-called Jewish union – because it was clear that it had won over the vast majority of workers. Ultimately, most workers focused on their material well-being. One worker, Aldea Guillemette, recalled that 'when the midinettes of Montreal rejected ugly appeals to religious and racial prejudice ... they built ... a union so powerful that not even the combined efforts of politicians and unscrupulous bosses could destroy it ... because our purposes [were] the same, whether Catholic or Jew, French-Canadian or Italian.' This strike showed, among other things, that space and culture were not necessarily definitive aspects of Jewish identity – even in Montreal, where historians have stressed ethnic solitudes, not only French and English, but also Jewish. Clearly, the factory floor was what defined one form of identity, that of workers seeking improvement in working conditions, without regard for ethnicity and religion in the Quebec of that era. Culture, therefore, must yield to space, at least in this context, as the determinative factor for Jewish clothing workers in the 1930s.

The rejection by most of the midinettes of antisemitism was in stark contrast to the exploitation of this hatred by some Jewish employers. As well, some parish priests in Sunday sermons and an article in *Le Devoir*, which called Shane 'un Judéo-Américain,'[55] stirred up the animus. The irony was that while Congress was fighting antisemitism, some dress manufacturers were spreading it. As well, Rabbi Stern wrote in the *Canadian Jewish Review*, 'Are there not many even today despite minimum wage laws who keep the pay of their employees down to the lowest notch? And are not these often the persons who head [Jewish] charity lists.'

Intra-communal tensions persisted even though a favourable contract was won.[56] This deep animosity was further reflected in a letter that year from the secretary-treasurer of the Montreal Joint Board of the Amalgamated, to Allan Bronfman, the president of the Jewish General Hospital. White protested the appointment of Henry Weinfeld, a key legal adviser to the dress manufacturers, to the hospital's campaign council. 'Mr. Weinfeld's role in the recent silk dress industrial conflict amounted to an attempt to eliminate gradually every single Jewish worker from the industry.'

Thus, this serious class conflict persisted, with Jewish manufacturers – many formerly workers – and their associations pitted against Jewish workers and their unions, impacting on the livelihoods of all. The values of North American free enterprise, and entrepreneurial derring-do, clashed with the spirit of East European left-wing *chavershaft*, utopianism, and beliefs in the dignity of labour. But the industry also brought Jews and the majority French Canadians into conflict. The exploitation of workers by bosses had an ethnic face. Just as important, however, the unions provided avenues of cooperation between Jews and French Canadians in a deeply divided Quebec. It was not only 'the great Jewish metier,' to borrow the historian Moses Rischin's felicitous phrase, it was the central feature of their economic and social existence. By 1940, virtually all women's apparel factories in the Montreal region had signed contracts with the ILGWU, which by the 1950s had established significant health and welfare benefits for its members.

Clothing and Politics 259

In Toronto, as well, the womenswear sector was in flux. In response to attempts by the Communist IUNTW to organize the dressmakers, and in the aftermath of a disastrous strike in early February 1931, the rival ILGWU, already established among the city's cloak-makers, set up a dressmakers' local and called a general strike a few weeks later.[57] But this strike also failed, as employers refused to further increase the wage differentials between themselves and the Montreal manufacturers. 'We are willing to come to terms,' the employers stated, 'if they [the ILGWU] will organize Montreal at the same time.'

Toronto was chaotic with work stoppages and demonstrations over insufficient wages, especially those of the women, who vastly outnumbered men.[58] Employees at Delight Dress, who were affiliated with the IUNTW, struck unsuccessfully in May 1932, while experiencing picket-line violence and arrests. Again in March 1934 a strike resulted in failure. In the meantime, several bitter walkouts in cloak-and-suit shops, called by the ILGWU, created continuing tension on Spadina; in January and February 1934, some two thousand cloak-makers paralyzed that sector by downing tools until manufacturers settled.

The real watershed was the protracted confrontation of forty-nine days at Superior Cloak, which was called by the ILGWU in July 1934.[59] The owner, Samuel Posluns, determined to break the union's power, locked out his two hundred workers and, under a newly formed company, Popular Cloak, moved his production to Guelph, where he employed local non-union workers. Former employees drove up to Guelph and picketed Posluns's plant. Violence erupted and arrests of numerous strikers followed. Posluns was charged by police with firing a revolver at one worker, and several strikebreakers (who had moved to Guelph from Toronto) were taken to hospital with serious injuries after a bloody melee of stone-throwing, fisticuffs, and clubbing. Police called in the fire department to help control the fighting. Sam Kraisman, an ILGWU organizer, alleged he was threatened by the employer's goon squad bearing knives and lead pipes. In the aftermath of the fray, a magistrate ordered two picketers (described as 'foreigners'), both up on charges of causing a disturbance, to 'get out of town immediately and stay out.'[60] Meanwhile, the ILGWU called a general strike at all Toronto cloak factories. Kraisman alleged that 'bootlegging [union shopwork done by non-union labour], contracting and subcontracting ... in the cloak trade ... sweatshops ... is carried on under the most vicious conditions,' while some firms were withholding (and never paying) 10 per cent of workers' earnings on various pretexts.[61] Most companies settled within days. Posluns, however, held out until September, after a summer of violence and protracted mediation.

Meanwhile, in Winnipeg, by 1931, of nearly two thousand workers employed in the clothing industry, more than a quarter were Jews. Ten years later, they were a third of all Winnipeg needleworkers and engaged in organizing unions.[62] Sam Herbst successfully brought women's apparel workers into the ILGWU and fought several bitter strikes to create a very strong union, which achieved recognition and material benefits throughout that city's women's apparel trade.

As these struggles continued, the men's clothing industry was readjusting after its conversion from uniform to suit production during the early 1920s. New manufacturers, some formerly contractors, challenged older firms; many of the latter gave up business, ceding to upstarts who could produce good quality, ready-to-wear suits and coats at modest prices, having learned methods during the war for more precise standard sizing and mass production.[63]

David Dunkelman's Toronto firm, Tip Top Tailors, was a most successful new company.[64] Starting in 1910 with a modest initial investment, within ten years, he was operating on an immense scale. In 1930 he built a huge factory to produce tens of thousands of suits and coats for sale in his own retail outlets across Canada. Tip Top Tailors was by then one of the nation's biggest men's clothing manufacturers and retailers.

Sam Rubin in Montreal was another entrepreneur in men's ready-to-wear. He started out in 1920, and by the early 1930s his firm did $1,000,000 in annual business, producing 2,500 garments a week. By this time, in a standard tactic, he had moved part of his production to the village of Ste-Rose, claiming nevertheless that his entire workforce was unionized, and that 75 per cent of his three hundred employees were Jewish.

Some menswear manufacturers, pressured by competition, endeavoured to reduce labour costs by hiring non-unionized labour and contractors. Thus they broke their previous agreements with the Amalgamated which had established relative stability in the industry from 1917 to the early 1920s. When Montreal firms began reducing wages by about 15 per cent following similar wage reductions elsewhere,[65] a rash of strikes immediately broke out against the deteriorating conditions. Throughout the early 1920s, mostly in Montreal, repeated strikes and lockouts created chaos in the industry.

As well, owners increasingly resorted to contractors and moved their production to nearby towns. By the early 1920s, Fashion Craft had moved to Ste-Rose, the Elkin Company to Farnham, Rubin Brothers to St-Hyacinthe, and Crown Pant to Cornwall. The union responded by trying to organize the local French-Canadian workers. At the same time, they struggled to maintain standards in unionized shops and recruit workers in contractors' shops. Similar problems were experienced in the Toronto menswear trade, where the union demanded the same conditions as in Montreal.

On the educational front, the union organized study programs in its Workers' School, including classes in English and public speaking, discussion groups on issues and forms of organization regarding labour problems, and lectures by university professors on modern history, labour conditions, science and civilization, and education. Other unions, like the United Hat, Cap and Millinery Workers' Union, organized similar programs.[66]

Meanwhile, as industrial equilibrium was re-established in 1925 through labour agreements,[67] the union felt restored and confident about the future. But by the 1930s, the men's trades were again in disarray. The rivalry of Communist and Catholic unions in Montreal, layoffs, and the return to the use of contractors and 'runaway shops' greatly weakened the Amalgamated. In a critical *Chronicle* editorial in July 1932, A.M. Klein pointedly sided with the Communist affiliate New Clothing Workers of Canada (an offshoot of the Industrial Union of Needle Trades Workers) in its dispute with the Amalgamated because Jewish workers affiliated with the new formation were in danger of being ousted from the trade and 'the livelihood of families is in jeopardy.' As a result of the Depression, union membership dropped significantly, while unemployment increased and wage levels fell. In a trenchant study of the industry in Montreal and Toronto in 1934, professors Frank Scott and Harry Cassidy revealed widespread distress among workers as a result of employers' increasing use of contractors and runaway shops.

In Cassidy's evidence to the 1934 Price Spreads Commission, he testified that 'a great majority of [workers] in the industry are now close to or below the border line of abject poverty.'[68] Workers had been on half-time for years; many families were on relief, while others needed two or more wage earners to subsist. Some non-unionized workers were earning as little as four dollars for a sixty-hour week, while 'one young girl received $2 for 55 hours work before the [1933] strike.' There were rumours of even worse conditions in some Quebec home workshops.

Cassidy testified that, 'in both Ontario and Quebec, there has been an appalling degradation of labour standards during the depression. In both provinces labour in the men's clothing industry has been exploited and sweated ... The suits we are wearing to-day,' he told the commissioners, 'many of them, have been made in sweat shops, under disgraceful conditions.'

The wide variations in working conditions depended, Cassidy stressed, on factory location, union affiliation, and the employer's humanity. In general, workers in Toronto fared better than those in Montreal in unionized shops, and in the larger factories. But the insidious and destructive processes – especially severe in depressed economic conditions – of open competition in the industry drove manufacturers to cut costs any way they could. He stressed that even employers 'who have endeavoured to maintain fair conditions for labour have been severely affected by the competition of employers who have not been maintaining fair conditions.' Thus a vicious downward competitive spiral existed, with bad labour conditions driving out the good. As Cassidy observed: 'The burden of cutthroat competition ... has fallen more heavily upon the firms that have endeavoured to maintain fair conditions of work and wages and that have avoided sharp competitive practices. We were informed that firms of this sort had quite definitely lost business to lower standard concerns.'

The large department and chain stores relentlessly exploited this chaos, especially among the small, marginal firms whose 'uneconomically low prices eagerly sought by mass-buyers endanger the solvency of more reputable and stable establishments and contribute to the general disorganization of the industry.'[69] They forced struggling manufacturers to slash prices, offer generous inducements, accept large numbers of returns, and tolerate repeated contract violations. These terms were so advantageous that some large stores discontinued manufacturing goods in their own factories. They were the real titans of the apparel trades, indirectly deciding which firms would live or die – who by sudden bankruptcy, who by slow strangulation, who by labour strife, and who by despair. These appalling circumstances, in which both employers and employed were being exploited, seemed hopeless. To address these problems, both the Ontario and Quebec governments passed legislation. Quebec's Collective Labour Agreements Extension Act of 1934 provided a framework in which agreements were established and made obligatory throughout the entire clothing sector.[70] A year later, Ontario brought in the Industrial Standards Act, with similar provisions.

These were also years of serious political turmoil for many unionists. In the late 1920s, leftists affiliated with the Communist-led Workers' Unity League angled for control of some locals of the Amalgamated. In Montreal, the contest between these leftists and the majority, who were called rightists by the *Keneder Adler*, was sometimes bitter and violent.[71] Peace was eventually restored, but the differences simmered for years. The United Clothing Workers, an affiliate of the All-Canadian Congress of Labour, briefly drew off some of the Amalgamated's members. A general strike forced employers, some of whom had lengthened hours and moved production out of town, to accept the union shop and a 20 per cent wage hike. By the end of the decade there was a degree of stability, however, with only some minor disruptions.

Thus, the dress trade acted as a bonanza – almost a 'next year country' enticing ambitious would-be-manufacturers. Many of these so-called nervous men were ground down by the business and eventually extinguished. On the other hand, the labour sector was seriously disrupted by the hard-pressed manufacturers and contractors. Most Jewish workers suffered from these conditions, and were thus embittered towards Jewish capitalists.

Tensions sifted through Jewish life as the well-to-do clothing manufacturer who served as a Jewish community leader and philanthropist was disliked by both Jewish and French-Canadian workers. Clearly, for many Jews, class consciousness conflicted with, and sometimes overrode, ethnic identity.[72] Thus, while the clothing industry provided 'a zone of emergence' for Jewish business activity, it also created a launching pad for workers' militancy and a forum for the reconfirmation of the class consciousness that many Jewish workers had brought with them from the old country.

The Bolshevik Revolution of October 1917 reverberated around the world, drawing many Jews to Communism. In Canada, some saw this cause as the fulfilment of their Jewishness. 'I never had a conflict about being a Jew and a Communist,' reflected the long-time activist Joshua Gershman. 'I became a Communist because I am a Jew.'[73] Communism promised a new age of peace, freedom, and equality and, as its sayings went, a society 'from each according to his ability, to each according to his needs,' a message that carried with it 'the prophetic ring of the coming of the Messiah.' Jewish youth, dismayed by rapacious imperialism, brutal antisemitism, and exploitative international capitalism, joined with others of all races and nationalities in rallying around the red flag and the stirring 'Internationale,' the Communist anthem. Some, like Bill Walsh and Harvey Murphy, were ready to dedicate their very lives to this cause. They studied the works of Marx, Lenin, and Trotsky, and at countless meetings, legal or clandestine, throughout the world, they stood with clenched fists raised in salute to sing the anthem of their cause. In labour temples, union halls, and community buildings throughout Canada the Communist ideal was spread by publications and the fiery speeches of intellectuals and visitors from the Soviet Union. They were secular missionaries, traversing the country and preaching that the better world 'in birth' would be theirs to create and enjoy. Their life's cause was to overthrow capitalism, replacing it with a new social and economic order. 'By no means all communists ... in those days were Jews, but I think it a fact that it was the Jews who provided the passion,' wrote Hugh MacLennan in the 1930s. 'Who could blame them? For they knew, while the French and English blocs did not, exactly what Hitler was preparing for all of US.'

While comprising only a small minority of the whole community, Jewish Communists fervently supported what they believed was a brilliant new socialist experiment being created in the Soviet Union. A few Canadian Jews, Ukrainians, and Russians even moved there.[74]

One very active Jewish leader of the movement was Maurice Spector, a Ukrainian-born University of Toronto graduate and Osgoode Hall law student.[75] Well-versed in Marxist theory, he was a member of the Young Socialist League, editor of the *Varsity*, and a regular contributor to left-wing newspapers. He also taught classes at the Ontario Labour College. In 1918, as *Varsity* acting editor, Spector criticized the war and the Allies' role in it, allegedly violating wartime censorship laws. In 1921, he helped draft the first program of the Communist Party of Canada (CPC) and authored a lengthy report on the CPC convention in February 1922.

Spector was one of the movement's chief spokesmen. He was recognized as one of its leading minds, a man who developed a critical approach to the 'Comintern and Soviet politics.'[76] As editor of the *Worker* from 1922 to 1928, he toured Canada calling for disciplined work in the labour unions, agitation in election campaigns and in Parliament, mass demonstrations, organization of the unemployed, and participation in the everyday struggles of the working class. He spoke at meetings of the Young Jewish Socialist Club and the Young Communist League, which, according to the RCMP, were '90 percent ... Jewish,'[77] where he urged revolutionary activity.

He warned his listeners against corrupt union officials, urging them to be on the lookout for 'traitors.' He even believed 'that the Army and Navy would help the Canadian worker to overthrow the present system,'[78] including British imperialism. In his capacity as editor of the *Worker*, Spector attended the Third Congress of the Communist International in 1923 in Moscow, and subsequently visited Germany to observe its revolutionary situation. He influenced the CPC not to condemn Trotsky despite events in the USSR, and he even criticized the Communist Party of the Soviet Union, causing considerable internal Party debate. Several years later, in 1928, after attending the Sixth Congress in Moscow and continuing to espouse Trotsky's views, notably the critique of Stalin, he was expelled from the CPC. He resumed legal studies.[79] In 1929 he formed an active but ill-fated Trotskyist organization and maintained a lively correspondence with the American Trotskyists Max Shachtman and James P. Cannon. He also contributed articles to their weekly, the *Militant*, while his Toronto group was beset by serious factionalism.

Two Jewish women, Annie Buller and Becky Buhay, rose to leadership positions in the party throughout the 1920s and 1930s,[80] Buller as an organizer of the Montreal Labour College and the business manager of the *Worker*, and Buhay as an activist in the needle trades and as secretary of the Canadian Labour Defence League. Buller was arrested for her provocative role in the bloody Estevan, Saskatchewan, coal miners' strike in 1931 and was sentenced to a year in jail. Buoyed by their unbreakable faith in the cause and steeled by adversity, including the antisemitism directed at them, Buhay and Buller, in the historian Joan Sangster's words, 'occupied strategic positions' and 'commanded [a] lasting mythology' in the party throughout the interwar years.

Buhay's brother, Michael Buhay, was also a strong activist. An ardent advocate of the general strike, he spoke often at gatherings of the Montreal branch of the One Big Union and to Jewish Communists, while serving as the business agent of the Montreal locals of the Amalgamated Clothing Workers' Union.[81] Sometimes using the alias William Morris, he was described by the RCMP in 1923 as 'a well educated man and a very good propagandist of the Bolsheviki ... ' He ran for the party in the 1944 Quebec provincial election in the Montreal riding of St-Louis, speaking out against race discrimination and fascism in Quebec, and citing the recent burning of a Quebec City synagogue.

The CPC established the Jewish National Bureau, which employed a series of organizers and in 1926 began publishing the monthly Yiddish periodical *Der Kamf* (The Struggle). The 'Official Organ of the Jewish Propaganda Committee Communist Party of Canada,' *Der Kamf* (which was regularly scrutinized by the Mounties' agents) became a semi-weekly in October 1934 and was distributed at workers' mass meetings.[82] A Jewish Proletarian Authors' Circle was formed in Montreal and Winnipeg, providing Marxist writers with a formal venue to air their views on proletarian literature.

In Toronto, the Yiddisher Arbeiter Froyen Farein (Jewish Women's Labour League) was founded in 1923.[83] This association of Jewish working-class women, mostly housewives, organized a children's camp – the famous Camp Naivelt – in 1925, canvassed for Communist candidates, and raised money for *Der Kamf* and for ICOR, the Association for Jewish Colonization in the Soviet Union. Moreover, they worked for the Party's electoral campaigns and strike activity, and they were an essential feature of their movement's culture of radicalist education and social protest. In 1924 and 1933, the women of the Farein helped to organize kosher-meat boycotts to try to lower its exorbitant costs. While the Farein did not stress gender equality, the Jewish Communist movement provided a modest forum for women's self-expression, as well as offering a vehicle for the 'political mobilization of women for the class struggle.'

The Young Communist League (YCL) included many Jews,[84] according to the RCMP, with their eyes on Baron Byng School in Montreal, where the League's influence was 'particularly strong.' They usually tried to calculate Jewish numbers at Communist youth gatherings, such as one held by the Canadian Student Assembly in 1940, where the 'amount of Jews, ... mostly from the West and McGill, was remarkable.'

The Mounties, however, recognized that Finns comprised the largest ethnic component of the CPC, whose membership hovered around three thousand. Ukrainians were the second most numerous group, and Jews a distant third.[85] According to secret RCMP estimates, Jews made up less than 10 per cent of the membership, which in 1931 included some 400 Jews, 3,000 Finns, 800 Ukrainians, and 200 Anglo-Canadians, totalling 90 to 95 per cent of the Party's members.

Canada's Jewish Communists were also recruited to support a major project in the Soviet Union. ICOR, the Association for Jewish Colonization in the Soviet Union, was establishing Jewish farm colonies in Ukraine, Crimea, and, after 1934, in Birobidjan, an autonomous Jewish territory based on collectivist agriculture.[86] This American organization, founded in 1924, targeted Canada, mostly Jewish farmers in the

West, on the assumption that they were likelier to agree to live in this new frontier, or lend financial support, than those in the cities. Intended to thwart the Zionist endeavour in Palestine, ICOR also mounted vigorous propaganda campaigns in the 1930s to combat ethnic nationalism and link Jewish identity to the class struggle.

In early December 1931, Professor Charles Kuntz of California spoke in Edmonton about his recent trip to Birobidjan, pleading for help.[87] A Canadian section of ICOR was organized in March 1931 and began publishing a newsletter, *Kanader Icor*, for distribution among its chapters. A group of its members attended Moscow's November 1934 celebrations honouring the revolution. In 1935 an autonomous Canadian ICOR with some five thousand members was set up, with headquarters in Toronto. Harry Guralnick spoke on behalf of ICOR across the West, describing a thriving Jewish national autonomy in the Soviet Union.[88] In flourishing Birobidjan, resource rich in coal, gold, iron, forests, and fertile land, Jews, he proclaimed, could become a true nation in their own autonomous republic. But a vigilant RCMP reporter noted that 'not much interest is manifest in this particular move among the listeners.' Undercover Mounties maintained regular surveillance in western Jewish communities, producing interesting reports. 'The Saskatoon [ICOR] organization was not strong,' wrote one informant, because 'the Jews of this city lacked the true proletarian outlook. They all considered themselves capitalists and potentially at least wealthy. In a word, they were possessed of a strong bourjoisie [*sic*] psychology.'[89] The RCMP believed that ICOR had numerous active branches, but that there was little evidence of significant activity outside the West.

When Jewish Communists met in Edmonton on 21 October 1934, approximately eighty people heard Guralnick proclaim that in Birobidjan, Jewish workers were 'building socialism,' and that the Soviet system would eventually 'spread all over the world.'[90] But according to RCMP informers, even this audience was unmoved. Guralnick was interrupted several times, and the audience 'took very little interest in the speech.' The Edmonton commissioner of customs informed his superior that 'almost all of the membership of the "ICOR" Committee in Edmonton are of the lower class of Jew, small storekeepers and peddlers of a class who, while at the present time do not actually associate themselves with Communism, would in a second jump to which ever way they think would suit their purposes ... It is of note,' he continued, 'that as far as we can gather none of the wealthy Jews seem to associate themselves with this committee.'

The mainstream Jewish community and the Zionists, in particular, vehemently opposed ICOR's program and philosophy. The *Canadian Jewish Chronicle* was an outright opponent of Communism and even lauded Quebec premier Maurice Duplessis's attacks on Communists. While the CPC supported Jewish settlement in Palestine, it favoured 'the solidarity of the Jewish and Arab toiling masses ... There is room ... for both peoples, and ... a basis for their cooperation.'[91] In 1937, several months after the outbreak of the Arab Revolt in Palestine, Jewish Party members joined Montreal leaders of the Labour Zionists, the ILGWU, the Amalgamated, and the Workmen's Circle at a mass meeting to promote Jewish-Arab cooperation 'as an antidote against the poison of chauvinist propaganda.'

Emma Goldman, the renowned Socialist leader, spent considerable time in Canada in 1926 and 1927. A vociferous opponent of Soviet Communism, Goldman lectured frequently in Yiddish and English to appreciative audiences in Montreal and Toronto on topics like 'The Present Crisis in Russia and on Modern Drama'[92] and became involved in a public controversy over free speech and planned parenthood. During her stay, she was visited by family and friends (including her lover, Leon Melamed) and established considerable, though brief, contact with Canadian revolutionaries.

Goldman enjoyed the radical scene in Toronto. 'The comrades in [Toronto] are an exceptional bunch of people,' she wrote to a New York friend in February 1927. 'In all the years I do not remember having met with so much genuineness, so much sweet hospitality, such fine spirit.'[93] She soon moved on to Winnipeg to an equally enthusiastic reception and stayed on for another year, lecturing on a wide variety of political, social, and literary topics. By the early 1930s, her concerns had shifted to the threats of European fascism and Nazism, and when she returned to Canada, she lectured on these topics to well-attended meetings in Toronto and Winnipeg. She died in Toronto in May 1940.

These mavericks aside, most Canadian Jewish Communists in the 1930s adhered strongly to the Comintern's policies on capitalism and world peace. Along with the professional revolutionary Joshua Gershman, who led the radical labour movement in the needle trades and the IUNTW, Fred Rose (Rosenberg), a Polish-born Montreal electrician, was very active in CPC circles. Shortly after he entered the country from Poland in 1924, Rose joined the Young Communist League. He became its national secretary in 1929, attended a course of instruction in Russia in 1930, and served on its international executive committee.[94] Monitored closely by the RCMP, Rose was convicted in 1931 of sedition under Section 98 of the Criminal Code and served a year in jail. Upon his release, he served on the CPC's secret Central Control Commission.

Rose's real talents lay in political propaganda. In 1939 he published a well-documented pamphlet alleging that big companies in the Sudbury area employed professional investigators to ferret out union sympathizers among their workers. Those accused were then fired.[95] That same year, he reacted to the British and French sell-out of Czechoslovakia with another pamphlet: *Stop Hitler! The Nazis Have Struck Again!* He noted that 'the truth is that the second world imperialist war to redivide the world has been on for two years: in Spain, China, Ethiopia, Austria and now Czechoslovakia!' He then asked, 'Who will be next?' His most famous pamphlet was *Hitler's Fifth Column in Quebec.* Published in 1942, it was a damning indictment of clerico-fascism in the province and caused such a furore that Montreal's future mayor, Jean Drapeau, then a member of the Bloc Populaire Canadien, sued Rose for libel. The drawn-out action dragged on for years and was settled out of court only in February 1946. During the 1930s, Rose ran for office unsuccessfully both provincially and federally in Montreal ridings. Finally, in August 1943, he won Montreal Cartier in a by-election, and successfully defended his seat in 1945.

Rose was an effective campaigner. During the 1943 contest, he strongly attacked fascism, employing the endorsement of Fina Nelson, whose son Willie had been killed in action while serving with the RAF in 1940.[96] Rose published a large handout containing photographs taken in his riding of dirty and hungry-looking children, crowded and dilapidated housing, cluttered backyards, unpaved lanes, abandoned stores, and homes filled with bedraggled children and pregnant women staring vacantly into space.[97] Once elected, he regularly communicated with his constituents through pamphlets containing some of his numerous speeches in Parliament, including *Fred Rose in Parliament* (a fifty-page Yiddish translation of his speeches on domestic and foreign policy issues), *Le Masque tombé,* and *La Menace du chaos: Le Complot Tory contre le Canada* (on fascism in Quebec). Although popular in the Cartier riding, Rose was in serious trouble with the law. He had been arrested in September 1942 on charges of subversive activities as a member af the CPC. (The CPC was outlawed in 1940 and renamed itself the Labor Progressive Party in 1942.) He confessed to all of the charges, promised to withdraw from Party activities, and was released a few weeks later. However, he was soon engaged in serious espionage activities on behalf of the Soviet Union, and was arrested shortly after the revelations of the Soviet embassy clerk Igor Gouzenko were made in September 1945. The court found Rose guilty of espionage and sentenced him to six years' imprisonment. He was released in 1951 and spent the remainder of his life in Poland.

At least six other Jews, of a total of twenty-six individuals, were named in the Royal Commission investigations based on the Gouzenko documents.[98] One of them was Sam Carr (Schmil Kogan). Born in Ukraine, he arrived in Canada in 1924. Carr worked as a harvester and a labourer in Saskatchewan, joined the Young Communist League in Montreal, and became one of its organizers. In 1931, four years after moving to Toronto and joining the CPC, he became its organizing secretary and was soon up on charges laid under Section 98. Found guilty, he was sentenced to ten years imprisonment; but he was released in 1935, just in time to become one of the main activists of the On-to-Ottawa March of the unemployed.

Carr then helped to recruit Canadian volunteers to fight for the Republicans in Spain. He also edited the CPC's *Clarion* from 1938 to 1940, subsequently went 'underground,' and resurfaced in September 1942. The Mounties arrested him on a variety of charges, but let him go a few weeks later on condition that he cease all CPC activities. Like Rose, however, Carr also worked for Soviet intelligence. Both men, in fact, were agents of the NKVD (the precursor of the KGB) for years, reporting on the CPC and various political matters, and, on rare occasions, providing information on Canadian political, military, and diplomatic matters.[99] Active in the Soviet military intelligence network (GRU) since 1942, Rose and Carr successfully helped the Russians recruit a wide network of subagents in Ottawa, Toronto, and Montreal. Their spying continued until the Gouzenko revelations brought on the Royal Commission inquiry, which resulted in their prosecution and imprisonment.

Numerous Canadian Jews were seriously affected by the anti-Communist measures undertaken by the Government during the late 1940s and 1950s in the aftermath of the Gouzenko revelations. Morris Scher, who had arrived in Canada in 1951 after wartime service with the Free Polish Army and the Jewish Brigade in Italy, was denied Canadian citizenship until 1963 because of RCMP suspicions (unfounded) that he was a Communist.[100] Musicians, writers, film editors, television producers, poets, politicians, union officials, teachers, professors were all affected in this Canadian version of the McCarthy witch hunt in the United States.

The Jewish Communists agonized about the rise of fascism, especially after the Nazis came to power in Germany in 1933.[101] In this context, terms such as 'fascists' and 'Hitlerites' were routinely levelled against the Zionists. In 1936, Sam Carr asserted that Zionism was 'inspired by ... fascists.' Jewish Communists continued their anti-Nazi campaign through the Canadian League against War and Fascism. But because of their simultaneous attacks on Zionism and their charges that community activists such as Quebec MLA Peter Bercovitch were 'fascists,' they were ineffective against antisemitism, and their attempts at recruitment failed utterly. The bitterness between the Communists and the Jewish community heightened during election campaigns.

The Jewish Communists publicly attacked Jewish capitalists and tried to embarrass them in the community. Lyon Cohen, a prominent Montreal activist and men's clothing manufacturer, was the owner of the Cuthbert Company, a large brass foundry that workers struck in July 1937. Cohen refused to negotiate.[102] The local Communist Party Trade Union Commission tried to organize a concurrent strike at Cohen's clothing factory and threatened to distribute Yiddish leaflets and hold public protest meetings in the Jewish district to try to force Cohen to the bargaining table.

Epithets of 'social fascism' flung at the Canadian Jewish Congress generally ceased by the mid-1930s. The Communists then focused on creating a Jewish united front against the real fascist menace in Europe. In July 1935, *Der Kamf* even found Zionist socialists to be acceptable allies in the battle against fascism.[103] While the Congress was sceptical, the Communists persisted in their efforts. Yet after the German-Soviet non-aggression pact was signed in August 1939, many somewhat embarrassed Jewish Communists temporarily dropped their popular-front efforts, while still continuing to condemn fascism. Gershman, perhaps a maverick on this issue, believed that the Soviet Union had no alternative but to sign the agreement.

The infamous pact created what the Mounties labelled 'confusion among communists,' and it resulted in significant disaffection among many Jewish comrades.[104] In October 1939 the RCMP reported that 'a great number of erstwhile members, mostly of the Jewish faith, have left the ranks, disclaiming the "good intentions" of Russia in its fight against the Jew-baiting Nazis.' However, most leaders remained loyal to the

Party. Despite strong anti-Communist attacks, their candidates in the Winnipeg municipal elections of 1940 did relatively well in the Jewish polls. Joseph B. Salsberg, an activist in the United Hat, Cap and Millinery Workers' Union during the 1920s and 1930s and a member of the Toronto city council since 1938, was beaten in Toronto's Ward Four partly because of a decline in Jewish support. He entered provincial politics in 1943 and, aided by the fact that the Soviet Union was by then an ally, was elected to the Ontario legislature from Saint Andrew, a largely Jewish riding. Another Communist, Joe Zuken, served for many years on Winnipeg's city council.

The Communist cause attracted many other Jews to its messianic ideals. Bill Walsh (Moishe Wolofsky) – the son of Hirsch Wolofsky, who owned Montreal's influential *Kanader Adler* – believed fervently that 'socialism would open the door to a golden era for the people of the world, including me.'[105] He remained a Party member after Salsberg and many others resigned following the Kruschev revelations and the exposure of officially sanctioned antisemitism in the Soviet Union. Signing up in the Party in 1930 before his eighteenth birthday, Dave Kashtan was moved by the belief the 'we [Communists] had the alternative answers to the building of a better social system.'[106]

In their search for Communists, the RCMP paid special attention to the United Jewish People's Order (UJPO). It was formed in 1945 by defectors or expellees from the Arbeiter Ring[107] by an amalgamation of the Labour League of Toronto, the Jewish Aid Society of Montreal, and a Winnipeg group known as the Jewish Fraternal Order. With branches in many cities in the mid-1940s, it was principally centred in Montreal, Toronto, and Winnipeg.

The principal actor in the organization was Joshua Gershman, who also served as national Jewish organizer of the Labor Progressive Party.[108] By 1946 the UJPO had established branches in Hamilton, Windsor, Calgary, and Vancouver and ran a children's camp near Winnipeg, as well as a summer seminary for young leaders. The organization also sponsored lectures, choirs, and concert tours; the long-lived Toronto Jewish Folk Choir became an institution on the Toronto cultural scene. The youth wing was strongly supported, numbering five hundred members by 1947. Gershman, Salsberg, and Rose were frequent speakers at youth meetings on cultural and social themes, and often discussed 'new institution[s] for the welfare of the Jewish masses.'

While its agenda was progressive in the very broadest sense, the UJPO's principal concerns were Jewish issues based on the belief that the Jewish Communist movement accepted implicitly the premise that 'Jews did constitute a nation.'[109] At its 1945 founding convention in Montreal, the organization condemned the revival of antisemitism in Quebec 'as if nothing would have happened in the last 6–7 years.' Speakers attacked the restrictive admission policies of McGill University, and condemned British imperialism in Palestine and India; United States' and Britain's hostility against the Soviet Union; the return of fascism in Germany, Italy, and Greece; and widespread red-baiting in North America.

While not outspokenly anti-Zionist, the UJPO objected to what it regarded as the excessively Zionist character of the Canadian Jewish Congress prior to the Second World War. In January 1938 Gershman had lamented that the Congress was not 'a convention of the Jewish masses.'[110] After 1945, however, the UJPO – possibly because of the Holocaust – now an active component of the Congress, strongly favoured Jewish immigration to Palestine and the building of the *Yishuv* (settlement) there. On the eve of the 1948 Israeli war of independence, the *Vochenblatt* called upon Canadian Jews to mount 'a more mighty struggle against every sign of compromise [by the United States and Britain] ... to destroy and bury the decision of the UN to establish a Jewish state ... Not a single Jew must stay outside of this struggle! As Canadian citizens and as Jews we must not allow the Zionist leaders to be satisfied with a quiet and weak request to the Government [of Canada]. What is necessary is a complete mobilization of all for a demonstrative and active struggle.'[111]

Although the UJPO enjoyed considerable support, its actual numbers are unknown. The Mounties estimated that crowds of 'some eight hundred persons of Jewish racial origin' would turn out to hear its speakers.[112] Similar sized crowds attended banquets and other occasions, where a comradely spirit prevailed. Indeed, the 'constant usage of the term "comrade" whenever the participants addressed one another' caused the RCMP spies some concern. Police scrutiny of the UJPO also included very careful review of the *Vochenblatt*, which was translated by an unnamed person denoted only as 'MHA.' On one occasion, the election of a UJPO member to the executive of the Ostrovtzer Aid Society in Toronto led an RCMP officer to comment that 'this would seem to indicate how the Communists are penetrating the Jewish landsmanshaften with the ultimate object of turning them into the tools for their policies.'[113]

The RCMP was concerned that the organization gained representation in the Canadian Jewish Congress in 1945. A statement presented by the so-called Leftist Jewish Movement was signed by various members of the Labor Progressive Party, including Fred Rose, then a member of the Congress's Dominion Council.[114] It called on the Congress to combat antisemitism, to request the softening of immigration laws, to assist Jewish immigrants to Canada and other countries, to help in 'the upbuilding' of Palestine, and to provide 'moral support and sympathy' for the Jews in the Soviet Union. Although these ideas were mainstream Canadian Jewish Congress goals, an RCMP report noted worriedly about

> a nationally organized Jewish Order under complete Communist domination with ties growing ever closer and stronger with the International Workers' Order, I.W.O., with the ultimate object of gaining a stranglehold on Jewery [sic] throughout Canada in an effort to control and direct their activities along Communist lines.

Another contemporary RCMP report ascribed even darker purposes to the UJPO. It stated that 'each move [is] an attempt to infiltrate into the Canadian Jewish Congress with the ultimate object of splitting that organization or gaining a controlling hand.'[115] The UJPO, in fact, was powerless in the Congress, then firmly controlled by the Montreal whisky tycoon Samuel Bronfman and its executive director, the lawyer Saul Hayes. Like most Canadian Jews, these two men were not in the slightest way sympathetic to the CPC.

The UJPO's multifarious activities included charitable and cultural efforts as well as a fundraising campaign to help build orphanages in Poland and one to settle Jewish orphans in the Soviet Union.[116] By 1945 it supported two afternoon schools in Montreal, both named after the radical theoretician Morris Winchevsky, educating several hundred students. It also sponsored several children's summer camps founded by the Arbeiter Ring in the 1930s, such as Nitgedeiget (Don't Worry), which was also attended by French-Canadian children. Other camps included Kindervelt (Children's World), established near Toronto in 1925, and Naivelt (New World), which since the late 1930s gave instruction on the working-class struggles and the rising threat of fascism. A 'Spanish Week' was observed there in the summer of 1937, in support of that beleaguered republic's government. The Soviet theme was prominent at Kindervelt, which was dominated by a huge statue of a man and woman clenching a hammer and sickle.

Despite these substantial efforts, however, the UJPO struggled to recruit a second generation. First, socialism was eroded because few Canadian-born children of radical socialists became workers.[117] Second, the use of Yiddish diminished, replaced by English. Thus the ideas of Winchevsky and other Jewish Communist theoreticians were no longer easily accessible. And last, the Second World War and its ensuing prosperity made Communism, especially the repressive Stalinist variety, seem at worst repugnant and at best irrelevant. Nevertheless, the UJPO was significant to a generation nurtured by its values and critical of North American materialism, even while many enjoyed its rewards. The spirit lived on in the children's camps like Naivelt and in its adult colony, where discussions – heated debates even – took place on the burning issues of the future of socialism, imperialism, and (of course) the 'Jewish question' long into the summer nights.

While the radical left flowered, it must be stressed that the Jewish socialists, collectively, were far more numerous than the Communists. Certainly, the socialist platform blended with the mainstream Zionist ethos, and many socialists were active members of the Canadian Jewish Congress. A very rough chart of the Canadian Jewish left would look like the one on page 276.

Several points require explanation. The first is that while these organizations had defined identities that conformed to ideological beliefs, their affiliations developed in different ways. The split between left (*linke*) and right (*rechte*) Labour Zionists developed much more sharply in Toronto than elsewhere in Canada because of deep ideological differences over teaching Hebrew or Yiddish in the Nationale Radicale Schule (National Radical School), where instruction was given to children in the afternoons and on Sundays.[118] The left group in Toronto, though Marxist, was staunchly anti-Communist and, in fact, led the fight against Communist influence in the clothing-industry unions in the 1930s.

The UJPO, on the far left, sometimes attempted to mask its thoroughgoing Communist affiliation, despite its strict adherence to the Kremlin's policies and pronouncements. The Arbeiter Ring (Workmen's Circle) was a fraternal order with socialist ideas and programs that were dedicated to the promotion of progressive Yiddish culture.[119] Because the Arbeiter Ring members were influenced by East European Bundist ideas, which emphasized Jewish cultural autonomy in the Diaspora and were therefore non-Zionist, some wags called them 'Zionists with sea sickness.' Some of its members were inclined to be more radical politically in

Jewish Left in Canada

Poale Zion (Labour Zionists)		Arbeiter Ring (Workmen's Circle)	United Jewish People's Order
Right (*rechte*) Generally known as Labour Zionists Farband Sick-Benefit Yiddishists and Hebraists	Left (*linke*) Marxists – followers of Ber Borochov Known as Achdut-Avoda-Poale Zion Published *Proletarishe Gedank* (Workers' Thought); and *Unzer Vegg* (Our Way) Independent Arbeiter Ring Sick-Benefit Yiddishists	Bundists Included territorialist and anarchist wings in some cities Arbeiter Ring Sick-Benefit Yiddishists	Communists Anti-Zionists until 1948

smaller offshoot or affiliated wings, or in anarchist or territorialist groups in some cities. (Territorialists favoured a non-Zionist Jewish homeland.)

The left Poale Zion (sometimes known as Achdut-Avoda-Poale Zion) were followers of Ber Borochov, a Zionist socialist theorist who tried to mobilize the Jewish proletariat to support the Zionist national revival.[120] The organization's main publications, *Proletarishe Gedank* (Workers' Thought) and *Unzer Vegg* (Our Way), had a lot of Toronto content. Its sick-benefit offshoot was known as the Independent Arbeiter Ring (not be confused with the Arbeiter Ring).

The Labour Zionists raised money to aid workers' causes through the General Federation of Labour in Palestine. In 1938 a new umbrella organization, the Labour Zionist Movement of Canada, unified and strengthened these efforts.[121] There were other differences – some doctrinal, others personal – within these groups in Winnipeg and Montreal, and the future historian of the Jewish left has a fascinating, yet arduous, task. What needs full examination, besides the ideologies particular to these groups, are the political and social expressions of these manifestations of secular Judaism.

The ideas of the Jewish labour movement extended from Soviet communism to Zionist socialism, but all celebrated the liberation of the common people from the shackles of oppression. They trumpeted this goal in their publications, manifestos, and speeches with an almost religious zeal, especially on May Day, the international workers' holiday. In

Toronto, as Ben Lappin recalled in a touching memoir, May 1st was alive with preparations for the annual Jewish workers' march in honour of this festival.[122] Union locals marched in formation next to the Labour Lyceum, while the left and right Poale Zion and Arbeiter Ring organizations gathered separately on a nearby street. Fraternal orders, youth groups, schools, and sports clubs also came together to parade. And then, with gaudy banners in Yiddish, English, or Hebrew proclaiming the rights of working men and women on high, they set off in formation up Spadina to Bloor towards Christie Pits, where they would hear lengthy and flowery Yiddish speeches and proclamations on pioneering in Palestine and the strength of united Jewish labour. Meanwhile, the Communists conducted their own march towards Queen's Park, where they denounced capitalism and the brutal oppression of workers, under the scrutiny of RCMP informers and the steely watchfulness of mounted Toronto policemen, members of Chief Constable (who styled himself a General) Dennis Draper's so-called Red Squad, who were ready to wade into the crowd with truncheons flailing at the slightest provocation, 'paddy wagons' at the ready.

Leftist ideas influenced many Jews as the Depression bit even deeper into the souls of Canadians. In the Co-operative Commonwealth Federation (CCF), David Lewis, who became national secretary in 1936, was well versed in British Labour Party thought. 'My brand of socialism,' remembered Lewis, a Rhodes scholar from a Bundist family background that stressed Yiddish culture and socialism,[123] 'was of the rather harsh medicine variety, the only cure for an increasingly sick system. It was of working-class origin and [had] nothing but contempt for "hypocritical bourgeois morality." It was hard-nosed, derived from Marxism of the revisionist kind, and concentrated more on strategies to smash the capitalist system than on programs to build a more humane one.' But at McGill and at Oxford, he learned to temper these views under the influence of young professors associated with the League for Social Reconstruction who stressed 'the need for positive programs.'

Lewis, a Polish-born agnostic Jew, contributed enormously to making the CCF a party of democratic socialism similar to the British Labour Party. He combined the qualities of leadership, the penetrating mind of 'an intellectual deeply committed to matters of definition and policy,' and a brilliant capacity to organize.[124] He did not, however, attempt to follow the British model slavishly and understood that Canada, unlike Britain, depended heavily on exports of raw commodities and was thus seriously exposed to the vagaries of international markets. Lewis stressed the need for democratic planning to keep control of the sick Canadian economy.

Despite his radical socialist origins and his early cooperation as CCF national secretary with other working-class parties, Lewis was strongly anti-Communist.[125] He became aggravated by some of their 'slick [electoral] manoeuvre[s]' and their control over the committees to aid Spanish democracy during the Spanish Civil War. Lewis, allied with the Anglo-Protestant ex-clergyman and CCF leader J.S. Woodsworth, was a major builder of the democratic socialist party. Many of his early efforts were spent in establishing links with the labour movement, which he recognized 'was necessarily engaged on the economic front against the same forces which the party faced on the political front.' Here he developed even stronger suspicions of, and antipathies towards, the Communists. He struggled through the late 1930s to keep them from competing with the CCF's efforts to win union support.

The Spanish Civil War crystallized the significant political issues for Canadian radicals in 1936. The democratically elected Republican government in Spain was attacked by powerful fascist forces led by Gen. Francisco Franco, who was well supported by military advisers and air and ground units from Nazi Germany and fascist Italy. The Republicans, on the other hand, were boycotted by the Western democracies and were only weakly supported by the Soviet Union. To offset this imbalance, thousands of Communists and other radicals from Europe and North America volunteered to serve in the International Brigades, to defend Spanish democracy.

Among these forces was a Canadian contingent, the Mackenzie-Papineau Battalion, that comprised some twelve hundred men, including thirty-eight Canadian and thirteen American Jews.[126] These Canadians were in violation of the Foreign Enlistment Act, which was specifically designed to prevent them from serving in the Spanish conflict. While most used their own names, some assumed aliases as part of their 'underground' journeys to Spain. For example, Muni Erlick signed up as Jack Taylor, Paul Skup as Paul Scott, Matthew Kowalski as Jack Steele, and Alan Herman-Yermanov as Ted Allan.

In the wider Jewish community, there were some expressions of sympathy for the Spanish Republican cause. In 1937, Temple Emanuel's Rabbi Stern published a letter from a Mac-Pap volunteer, Samuel

Abramson, in his weekly column in the *Canadian Jewish Review*, but he prefaced it with the caution that 'we are not so sure about all the issues involved in the fratricide war raging in Spain.'[127] Marc Chagalle, who had received some letters from Canadian Jewish boys in Spain, wrote sympathetically in the June 1937 issue of Toronto's *Jewish Standard*: 'Powerful interests inside and outside of Spain, seeing their profits threatened because of the election of the democratic People's Front Government, declared war on the Government of the Spanish People. These interests started the war.'[128] Chagalle argued that 'if the letters that the Jewish boys write are any indication of the spirit and discipline of the loyalists, then we may rest assured that Fascism will be defeated in Spain.' *Der Kamf* reported regularly and published a lengthy entry on some of the Canadian Jewish volunteers after their return in 1939. It featured interviews with Mac-Pap volunteers Izzy Goldberg, Isaac Shatz, Sydney Cohen, and Victor Himmelfarb.

While only 25 per cent of all volunteers for the Spanish Republicans were Canadian-born, 65 per cent of the Jewish volunteers had been born in Canada.[129] Moreover, with one lawyer, two doctors, two pharmacists, a social worker, and a male nurse among them, the Jews had a higher level of education and skill than the average Canadian recruit. Their ranks also included an aviation mechanic, a fur cutter, a miner/prospector, two students, a musician, a warehouseman, two painters, two salesmen, two clothing workers, a driver, two seamen, and a barber. Eight of the Jewish volunteers (including the writer Ted Allan) served in non-combat roles, as medics and journalists, for example. Only seven, four of whom were veterans of the Canadian Expeditionary Force in the First World War, had previous military training. Of those whose fate is known, twenty left Spain alive, and seventeen returned to Canada or the United States. Two were prisoners of war, eight were wounded in action (some more than once), six were killed in action, and one was declared missing.

Most Jewish volunteers had belonged to the YCL and the CPC or the Communist Party in the United States or Spain. Commitment to the cause was generally strong. 'Being of Jewish origin, my hatred for fascism was so great as to compel me to leave a good home and fight these bastards,' wrote Isaac Shatz of Toronto in the questionnaire that all volunteers were asked to complete upon arrival in Spain. Some of the Jewish volunteers had colourful backgrounds. Muni Erlick was a Jewish Ukrainian, born in 1906. He joined the YCL in Paris in 1924, moved to Romania in 1925, then immigrated to the United States in 1926 and lived briefly in Detroit. In 1927 he moved to Montreal, where he joined the CPC and managed the Party's Jewish weekly. He also served as the national secretary of the Party's Jewish Bureau and worked in various other capacities until he shipped off to Spain in 1937. Following his return to Canada, he joined the Canadian Army in November 1942, served in the Armoured Corps, and was killed in action in France in August 1944.[130]

Hamilton native Bert 'Yank' Levy grew up in Cleveland. He served in the merchant navy and joined the Jewish Legion in 1918, serving as a machine-gunner. He went to Mexico in 1920–1, did some gun-running to Nicaragua in 1926, and spent six years in a United States jail for armed robbery. He joined the International Brigades in 1937, becoming an officer in the machine-gun company of the British battalion. Captured at the Battle of Jarama, he spent six months in one of Franco's prisons. Upon his release in 1940, he travelled to Britain and became a lecturer to the British Home Guard on guerrilla warfare, which was also the subject of a work he wrote for United States Army's infantry journal. The article was published as *Guerrilla Warfare* in 1942 and in its day served as the standard text on the subject.[131]

Sam Abramson, a Zionist activist, went to Spain in June 1937 and served as an ambulance driver. In a series of letters to Hananiah Caiserman, Abramson described the military situation in Spain, appealed for Canadian support of medical assistance to the Republicans, conveyed greetings (including regards from Emma Goldman), and stated his commitment to the battle against fascism. 'I have been doing all I can to get people back home to start a Jewish Committee for Medical Aid to Spain,' he wrote in March 1938.[132] 'We must all contribute to the defeat of fascism,' he continued. 'Will you give them your help[?]'

Two months later, Abramson urged Caiserman, who was battling fascism through the Congress, to 'treat the fascists like what they are, and when you strike, strike hard ... Fascism is more than an academic problem to you these days. Don't give way an inch for if you do you'll get no thanks from the enemy.'[133] Abramson advised Congress concerning a 1938 pamphlet entitled *Facts about the Jews*, which minimized the Jewish Communist presence. 'I can't say I was pleased with the general tone of the pamphlet.' Condemning its virtual apology for J.B. Salsberg, Abramson countered angrily: 'Isn't he a damn good civic representative? Should we [not] rather apologize for a Peter Bercovitch who voted for the Padlock law?'

Following the disbanding of the International Brigades in Barcelona in October 1938, Abramson's heart was bursting:

> Barcelona gave us a big farewell yesterday. It was simply magnificent, almost beyond words. Hundreds of thousands of people turned out, the streets were strewn with flowers, women kissed us as we marched along, everybody was quite overcome with emotion ... Our fight is not yet over. Spain must not become another fascist victim ... Salud y Victoria.[134]

A week later, he expressed his anguish over leaving Spain, whose 'fine people' he had come to love, and proclaimed his determinaton to continue his work for democracy there. 'If Fascism triumphs here,' he observed prophetically, 'then there will be a great offensive on the few countries still holding out. No Pasaran.'[135]

In spite of a growing 'concern with the threat from German-inspired Fascism' in 1943, Jews constituted only a tenth of CPC membership, although Joe Salsberg and Fred Rose successfully won election that year on the strength of their personalties and their stand on current issues. Nevertheless, in French Canada, and in the mind of Abbé Lionel Groulx, all Jews were Judeo-Bolshevists. On occasion – such as during rallies on behalf of the Spanish Republicans in 1937 – Université de Montréal students paraded through Montreal's main streets chanting, 'À bas, à bas. À bas les Communistes. À bas les juifs.'[136] To them, Jews were the purveyors of the modernization that threatened the very survival of French Canadians. Indeed, domestic fascism seemed a greater threat than it was in either the United States or Britain, and, as a result, Communism was possibly stronger among Canadian Jews. Some French-Canadian nationalists of that era even admired the politics of Salazar and Mussolini. Comparisons are difficult, but Communism seems to have registered a greater degree of electoral success in Canada than in the Jewish communities of the United States or Great Britain, principally for domestic reasons.

Certainly, the general public blamed Jews for much of the Communist agitation in Canada, especially in Quebec, where the Taschereau government tended to blame Communist activity on Jewish radicals.[137] When questioned in connection with the Gouzenko allegations in 1945, Gordon Lunan was asked, 'How could someone with your [British] background and education get mixed up with people like this – he read off some names – Rosenberg, Kogan, Gerson, Mazerall [sic]. The Z in

Mazerall's name was evidently enough to reclassify him from Gentile to outcast Jew.'[138] Recalled Lunan, 'A sizeable section of the movement ... was essentially [a] middle class Jewish association of well-informed, culture-oriented, freethinking people who did not or would not fit into conventional Montreal society ... For many, the odour of persecution and pogroms was still in their nostrils.'[139]

The association of Communism with Jews stirred up antisemitism throughout the world. In Britain, 'the belief that the October Revolution was a 'Jewish plot' gained currency even in sections of the 'respectable' press.'[140] As the historian Sharman Kadish observed, 'The charge of "Jewish Bolshevism," gave more mileage to antisemitism [in Britain] in the years after the First World War.' This held true in Canada and the United States too, even though Communism attracted only a tiny minority of Jews. Antisemitism, of course, did push some Jews to the CPC, the one party that openly rejected racism and discrimination. But yet another political movement, Zionism, had always held an important place in the cluster of Jewish political ideas, and in the interwar years it became even stronger. At the same time there were practical political problems in Montreal requiring immediate attention.

9 The Politics of Marginality

For many years, the Jewish community had endeavoured to gain equal rights within Quebec's Protestant school system, which since 1903 they could legally attend and were obligated to support through real-estate taxes. But Jews were in a 'catch-22'; they could not sit on the Protestant Board of School Commissioners, secure teaching jobs (except in schools where they were the majority), or be free of some discrimination – all because they were not Protestants. Eventually, some Jews started pressing for the right to establish a separate Jewish school system. But by 1920 positions were unchanged, and the controversy festered, foreshadowing darker days ahead. This community faced special challenges because of its place amidships – a double minority, in fact – in the unique linguistic and cultural duality of Quebec.[1]

The community was split into two major factions – those who desired a separate Jewish school system and those seeking equal rights within the Protestant system. Also involved were the Protestant Board of School Commissioners, the government of Quebec, the Roman Catholic hierarchy, French-Canadian nationalist extremists, and the general public of the province. This question was highly controversial, touching on other important matters, such as the English/French and Protestant/Catholic balance of forces and, to some, the undesirability of granting non-Christians equality. While constituting only 6.13 per cent of the population of Greater Montreal in 1921, the city's Jews were the third largest ethnic community and were dominant in clothing manufacturing. Living mostly in the St-Laurent Boulevard north-south corridor dividing the English and the French sections of the city, they constituted, geographically and culturally, a veritable 'third solitude' in this city of historical tensions between English and French. At the level of law, politics, and civil status, therefore, the Jews of Quebec were in an inferior position. This was unique in the Western world, since after 1919 most countries had established state school systems giving all citizens *de jure* equal rights.

By the early 1920s, Jewish pupils in certain inner-city areas outnumbered the Protestants.[2] In the few schools where the Jewish children formed a majority, the Protestants agreed to employ some Jewish teachers, although they were nevertheless officially required to teach the rudiments of the Protestant faith. The Protestants, however, firmly rejected Jews as members of their board, and as some Protestant spokesmen stated, if they were unhappy, they should seek to set up their own school structure.

Easier said than done. There were two serious impediments to that idea. The first was resistance to the very notion of a separate Jewish school set-up in a 'Christian society,' and the second was the lack of consensus among the city's Jews on the make-up of such a system. These two barriers challenged all of the involved parties, and periodically resulted in a flooding of the city's newspapers with reports of meetings held to stake out positions and explain them to an increasingly polarized Jewish community. The controversy also produced an angry and defensive Protestant school board. Expensive and lengthy court battles reached London's Judicial Committee of the Privy Council, Canada's final court of appeal. At numerous Jewish rallies, no eloquence was spared in enunciating the views of one party or another on this controversy, which dominated Montreal's communal politics throughout the decade. Moreover, the controversy reflected the economic and social tensions in a deeply fragmented community.[3]

This question aroused strong feelings in the Catholic and Protestant communities, as well. The Protestants insisted upon full control over their schools and compensation for the cost of teaching Jewish children. As well, as Reverend Canon Elson I. Rexford, a leading spokesman for the board, pointed out in a 1924 pamphlet entitled *Our Educational Problem: The Jewish Population and the Protestant Schools*,[4] the Jewish community's attempts to force the Protestant board to accept one Jewish representative would be stoutly resisted because 'the main object of our public school system is the formation of Christian character.'

Rexford and his associates were unwavering. They informed the Jewish community's representatives that if Jews were not prepared to accept the status quo, the board would consider 'withdraw[ing] the Jewish children'[5] – in effect, evict them. The integrity of Christian education was at stake. 'The Jewish population might rest assured,' Rexford stated, 'that the Protestant[s] ... would never consent to hand over to Jewish administration and control [our] splendid educational system.' In fact, he contended, the presence of 'large numbers of Jewish children [in] our Protestant schools has seriously impaired the value of these schools as institutions for Protestant education and has led many Protestants to withdraw their children from these schools.' The possibility of an eventual Jewish majority, given the rate of increase during the previous twenty years, was worrisome indeed.

To the Protestant board, Jewish presence was vexing on other grounds, as well. They had a large number of religious holidays, whose observance 'seriously interferes with the working efficiency of the ... schools.'[6] As for employing more Jewish teachers, Rexford stated that of the seventy Jewish women teachers already working, 'many of them [were] from a foreign population [and] speak English imperfectly, ... [and] in mixed [Jewish-Protestant] classes it does not seem reasonable to place Protestant children under [the] direction of these Jewish teachers.' In some of the centre-town schools, where Jews were the majority, 'it is most undesirable that [religious] instruction should be given to a few Protestant pupils in the presence of a large number of Jewish pupils who are simply listeners, and onlookers.' As well, Jews made unconscionable demands such as 'ask[ing] for special courses in the Hebrew language and literature under special teachers trained and appointed by themselves' – at the expense of the board, of course. These inconveniences, Rexford implied, were more than the Protestants should have to bear! However, the rejection of Jewish teachers, except in the schools where Jewish pupils were predominant, was particularly humiliating.[7] This problem was highlighted by the *Keneder Adler* – a newspaper more attuned than the *Chronicle* to the concerns of the Yiddish-speaking Jewish working class, whose ambitious daughters, having qualified as teachers, were excluded simply because they were Jews.

Just as problematic was the belief that the Jewish community failed to pay its way. Although 13,954 Jewish children attended Protestant schools in 1924, the school tax revenues on Jewish-owned property, according to Rexford's careful calculations, yielded less than half the annual cost of educating them.[8] The Protestants who had to pay the difference felt exploited and, in 1922, demanded a repeal of the 1903 act. This would be replaced by legislation that required Jews to pay their school taxes to the province's 'neutral panel' (an entity that received the school taxes levied on corporations and allocated these monies to the Protestant and

Catholic school boards) and permit the Protestants to claim from it the full cost of accommodating Jewish children in their schools. This neat solution would lower their own school taxes by almost a third. Their constitutional rights could be restored, and a bigger share of the 'neutral panel' monies could be acquired. If so, Jews, would be allowed to remain in the Protestant schools, being granted 'privileges,' not 'rights.' Clearly they would be without the advantages of Protestants.

In support of the community now readying itself for battle, the *Canadian Jewish Chronicle* countered the argument about financial losses by pointing out the irregularities by which some Jewish ratepayers were mysteriously registered on tax rolls as either Protestant or Catholic, thus diminishing Jewish contributions to education funding.[9] All Jewish Smiths and Millers were listed as Protestant, while Pascals were deemed Catholic. And some of the largest Jewish taxpayers were corporations whose taxes went to the 'neutral panel.'[10] Nevertheless, the financial issue persisted. Beleaguered and defensive, but ever aware of its constitutional rights which since Confederation enshrined the existence of Protestant and Catholic confessional school systems, the Protestant board and its community stood firm throughout the storm. It would countenance no Jewish representation, demurred at hiring more Jewish teachers, and demanded full compensation for its costs.

Within the Jewish community, there was little compromise among the parties in the dispute, a fact duly noted by the Protestants. The government of Quebec and the Catholic Church, to protect their interests, also became parties to this contretemps. Many Jews living in upscale west-end districts represented by the Jewish Educational Committee favoured an accommodation involving the continuation of the 1903 arrangement, with minor revisions. On the other hand, many downtown (or east-end) Jews represented by the Jewish Community Council wanted to dissolve the existing compact and establish a separate Jewish panel.

Montreal's west-end upper crust included both old wealth patrician figures, and nouveau-riche clothing manufacturers with wide-ranging industrial interests. These families constituted a plutocracy which strongly influenced the community's internal affairs and – through lawyers Samuel Jacobs and Peter Bercovitch, MLA since 1916 for the downtown St Louis riding – had a voice in both Dominion and Quebec politics. It was a group that commanded a certain respect, indeed awe, even in the Bronfman family, which, with a substantial fortune made in the whisky business, had settled in Montreal in 1924.[11] This group and the numerous supporters of the Jewish Educational Committee saw the school issue as a test of their acceptance into Montreal's anglophone world.

These uptowners had been led in many matters since the early 1900s by the lawyer Maxwell Goldstein, who had pressed for equality in the school system. By the early 1920s, even his and other personages' appeals that Jews be allowed to sit as 'advisory' members of the Protestant board, to assist in solving questions on Jewish matters, were firmly rejected. The Committee nevertheless believed that the majority wished to retain the status quo. Indeed, they felt, 'there is too much segregation already.'[12] Jews constituted 90 to 100 per cent of the students in twelve to fifteen of the large Protestant schools in the downtown area, Goldstein pointed out, and about 30 to 35 per cent of the total student body in the entire Montreal Protestant system.

Although Goldstein would have preferred a non-denominational system, he recognized this to be impossible and conceded that the Protestant system 'has been the most beneficial to the Jewish Community, and upon the whole has been fairly administered.' While ultimately seeking full equality, the integrationists continued to press for representation. But in 1922, Goldstein saw the Protestant move to repeal the 1903 act as a serious threat. He predicted the complete segregation of Jewish students in certain Protestant schools because they would be there only on sufferance, rather than as a right. While he was unhappy with Jewish inferiority under the 1903 compact, under no circumstances would he accept the Protestant proposal to scrap it altogether and put the Jewish community out on the street, bereft of any rights.

Other uptown voices joined the debate. In October 1923 Rabbi Max J. Merritt of Reform's Temple Emanu-el,[13] a leading member of the Jewish Educational Committee, strongly denounced the 'short-sighted and illiberal factions' in both the Protestant and Jewish camps, especially the latter.[14] The establishment of a separate Jewish school system would be 'a backward and deplorable step ... a fatal blow [to] ... the very heart of a genuine and all-inclusive national spirit which is as the very breath of life to this young commonwealth.' He warned that 'the ideal of a Canadian national unity will fade into mere nothingness [if] a group of Protestant extremists be permitted to join battle with a group of Jewish extremists to undermine secular and Canadian education.' Formerly holding a pulpit in Evansville, Indiana, the Nebraska-born Merritt was unfamiliar with Quebec political and social realities, and with Montreal's Jewish cultural dynamics. A few months earlier, he was quoted as saying at a public meeting that 'if our erratic, contentious, and short-sighted co-religionists of the East End [the downtowners] had had the wisdom to follow the wise, farsighted, and statesman like guidance of our legislative representatives at Quebec ... [and] the Jews of the West End, with their progressive, intelligent and truly Canadian vision,' a satisfactory arrangement could be made with the Protestants. The *Chronicle* labelled these remarks 'crude' and 'tactless' and called on the rabbi for a categorical denial or explanation. Merritt did not deign to respond.

But Merritt was not alone. Even the Conservative Shaar Hashomayim congregation, newly housed in a cathedral-like edifice in Westmount, opposed a separate Jewish school system – despite an appeal by the congregation's president, the esteemed community leader Lyon Cohen, that it remain temporarily neutral.[15]

Cohen, in fact, favoured a compromise allowing some Jewish cultural autonomy in the predominantly Jewish centre-town Protestant schools.[16] But his was a rare voice in the west end, where the majority feared the consequences of a separate Jewish school system. They valued political equality over public education in Jewish subjects, and they could afford private Jewish education, regardless. They argued that the intermingling of children was preferable to segregation in parochial schools.

The downtown Jews who adopted a nationalist position received the backing of the Jewish Workers' Conference, which represented some ten thousand members of the clothing workers' unions, the Arbeiter Ring (Workmen's Circle), the National Workers' Alliance, and a number of left-wing associations. Arguing for minority rights and for the protection of Jewish culture and tradition, they also asserted that the Jewish mentality is 'distinguished from those of the English-Canadian and French-Canadian population insofar as they have different racial characteristics, customs, and habits, resulting from a somewhat varied environment and upbringing, all of which makes the task of their education abstrusive to the Protestant teachers ...'[17]

They repeated the demand for a separate Jewish school system, a proposal by some members of the Poale Zion (Labour Zionists) at the 1919 meetings of the Canadian Jewish Congress.[18] Hananiah Meir Caiserman and Louis Fitch, leaders of this cause, argued not only that Jewish pupils were exposed to religious instruction in the New Testament (although in theory, they were exempt), but also that Jewish cultural interests were undermined. 'The Protestant school implanted in the hearts of the Jewish children a Christian spirit ... [and] the same Christian spirit has reached into many of our homes,' Caiserman asserted. 'A generation of children is lost to Judaism at a time when the Jewish youth of ... Canada is the greatest hope of Judaism.'

Caiserman and other separate school system supporters wished to remedy a situation where twelve thousand schoolchildren received no parochial education whatsoever. In their own schools, this trend towards ignorance and ultimate communal degeneration[19] could be reversed. William Nadler, executive secretary of the Jewish Community Council (JCC), argued that 'only by sending our children to school, where the teaching of Judaism will play a prominent role, can we give to this country, a good Jew and a good Canadian. Let us have Jewish separate schools, and we will contribute to Canada a finer and higher type of Canadian Jew ... [able] to make the synthesis between Canadianism, Judaism and HUMANITY.' The JCC hoped to set up about seven downtown Jewish schools, which would be supported by taxes and grants from the 'neutral panel' on the same basis as the Protestant and Catholic systems.

Hirsch Wolofsky, of the *Kender Adler*, supported this position and frequently attacked the opposition for bringing 'shame and ridicule' on the community.[20] Instead of complete independence, he proposed that these schools be entrusted to a Jewish committee acting under the Protestant board, with instruction in Judaism to replace Christian religious teaching and Jewish teachers to be employed. 'This ... plan would not affect the rights of the Reformed Jews in the West End,' Wolofsky argued. '[It] would satisfy the nationalistic and orthodox Jews who supply 90 percent of the Jewish children in the local schools and would provide a basis for the institution of a system of separate schools in the event of this plan not working out successfully.' This sensible compromise, however, went nowhere in the heated atmosphere of an embattled community.

In 1924 this issue was addressed by the Quebec provincial government, headed by Premier Louis-Alexandre Taschereau, who abhorred racial and religious prejudice.[21] Tutored by Peter Bercovitch and Joseph Cohen, fellow Liberal MLAs, Taschereau favoured an accommodation between moderate Protestants and Jews, but he insisted that Jewish children had the 'same rights as Catholics and Protestants to receive education in schools which would not wound their religious sentiments.' Still, he favoured compromise and had openly supported the nomination of Bercovitch, an integrationist, over that of Louis Fitch, a separatist, as Liberal Party candidate in the riding of St Louis during a recent election campaign.

Seeking both enlightenment and respite, Taschereau in early 1924 struck a Royal Commission, composed of three Protestants, three Jews, and three Catholics, and chaired by the former premier, Sir Lomer Gouin, to examine the question. The Jewish members of this Committee of Nine, as it came to be known, were Michael Hirsch, Samuel Cohen, and Joseph Schubert. Hirsch and Cohen were uptowners and wealthy businessmen, the former a cigar manufacturer and the latter a mining engineer with extensive interests in Quebec asbestos and gold properties.[22] Schubert was an alderman, a socialist, a trade unionist, and a downtowner committed to the idea of a Jewish separate school system.

These choices outraged major parts of the community, the *Chronicle* bristling: 'We cannot scare up even a breath of enthusiasm about the Jewish personnel of the School Commission.'[23] While its Protestant and Catholic members were 'giants,' the Jews were mere 'mice,' no doubt recommended by Peter Bercovitch, who advised Premier Taschereau on the selection. Hirsch was already *parti pris*, having taken a strong stand for a renewed deal with the Protestants (i.e., returning to the 1903 accord), while Cohen – a newcomer to Montreal – had taken no part whatever in Jewish community affairs: 'We seek in vain for Mr. Cohen's name among the leading members in cultural, spiritual or even philanthropic, organizations ...' Even Schubert, the socialist and labour spokesman, 'who may be said to be the only one who understands, and therefore "represents," a certain portion of that large majority of the Jewish community,' was questionable because most Jews, the 'traditionally orthodox both in ... national and religious viewpoint,' had no representative on the commission.

The Community Council, an essentially downtown organization led by lawyers Louis Fitch and Michael Garber, also protested. In an open letter to Premier Taschereau, they claimed that Hirsch was already committed to the status quo, while Cohen, an American, unfamiliar with the local scenes, was 'not ... an enthusiastic supporter of Jewish religious and national education for the mass of Jewish children.' Arguing that 'the School problem to Jews is essentially one of the preservation of national culture, language and those elements most dear to a self-respecting people,' Fitch and Garber asserted that 'the persons most fit to present these views, although recommended[,] have been ignored by the Government and its advisers.'[24]

Adding his voice to the contretemps, Caiserman protested that Peter Bercovitch 'does not appreciate the importance ... the gravity of the school problem and its effect on Jewish life in this province.' The Jewish

Community Council also protested to the premier that because Hirsch and Cohen both favoured the status quo, they would 'give an undue advantage to the views of the Jewish Educational Committee' to the detriment of 'the great majority of the Jewish people residing in the heart of the city [who] are Orthodox and desirous of procuring for their children some teaching for Jewish ... cultural and religious lines.'

Once the commission began its hearings, the conflicts surfaced. In an early session, the Protestant board spokesman Col. J.J. Creelman stated that aside from the financial question, the board considered Jewish holidays to be a serious problem, and that it was 'impossib[le] [to] teach to Protestant children Protestantism in a Protestant way with Jewish teachers and in the presence of Jewish children.'[25] For the downtown 'nationalists,' Louis Fitch retorted that this justified a separate Jewish school system, leaving 'the Protestants ... to educate their children as good Canadians, at the same time not forgetting their ancient heritage.'

Protestant spokesmen, however, were divided. Herbert Marler, MP for the Montreal riding of St Lawrence–St George, criticized Creelman for intolerance and argued for a friendly solution on the grounds that 'a large number of Protestants in this city are against the abrogation of the Act of 1903.' Another prominent Montreal Protestant, W.D. Lighthall, supported Marler's views. At the same time, Maxwell Goldstein proudly asserted: 'If the Protestants are insistent that they don't want us, then we are too proud to stay with them, and we will get out and make our own separate schools.' A former rabbi of Temple Emanu-el, Nathan Gordon, stated that 'we [Jews] will not tolerate any humiliation ... if we cannot get along with the Protestants, then let us have a panel of our own.' The *Chronicle* asserted that 'we Jews have no desire to de-Christianize the Protestant schools, just as we are absolutely opposed to having our children Christianized in the Protestant schools.'[26]

John Farthing, the Anglican bishop of Montreal, defended the superiority of Protestant Christian ethics and the letter of the law. As he stated: 'We have ... a distinct civilization to maintain which is based upon the Christian teaching ... and if we should in our schools weaken that influence ... we undermine the very civilization that is built upon that foundation.' Notwithstanding, then, the demurral of a few of its liberal members, the Jewish community could expect little from the Protestants. The *Chronicle* observed that 'should we succeed in keeping our children in the Protestant schools in spite of the aggressive attitude of the Protestant Commissioners ... they will be regarded as ... aliens to be segregated from the rest of the herd.'[27]

All the while, the Jewish street was alive with intense debate.[28] Spokesmen for various positions on the issue – and several individuals eager for a chance to make a speech – appeared before the three Jewish commissioners. Israel Rabinowitz observed these meetings and poked fun in his columns for the *Adler* at some of the pompous personages, including Rabbi Joseph Corcos of the Spanish and Portuguese synagogue and other uptown dignitaries, who gave their views. But there was pathos too. A recently graduated teacher stated that many Jewish women teachers were barred from the Protestant schools.

These meetings also provided opportunities for the rhetorical settling of old scores. Hirsch Wolofsky ridiculed the 'assimilationist' Jews, a not-too-subtle reference to the uptowners. Because their children were segregated into Jewish-only classes within the Protestant schools (so as not to disrupt the studies of the non-Jewish pupils), they reluctantly favoured Jewish separate schools. 'It has been the fate of our race,' Wolofsky stated, 'that those Jews who stand on the threshold between Judaism and Christianity will, when they realize that anti-Semitism does not spare them, either return to Judaism or else cross over the threshold altogether and pass over to the Christian fold.'[29]

In the Royal Commission's report of early 1925, its Protestant and Jewish members divided along predictable lines. The three Protestant members insisted on the unconstitutionality of the 1903 act and on keeping complete control of their schools regardless of the Jewish presence in them. 'The question of Jewish holidays, Jewish teachers and of segregation are questions of administration,' they stated, 'and as such must remain subject to the discretion and control of the Protestant Board.' But, in a spirit of concession and conciliation, they recommended that 'such questions should be ... dealt with by all those interested in the spirit of equity, fairness and toleration.'[30]

This was not good enough for the *Chronicle*. 'Once we admit that the idea of segregating Jewish children as if they were lepers or the breeders of contamination is purely an impersonal matter of administration, we admit that there [are no] Jewish school problems,' it commented. 'Once we say that it is all right for a Jewish girl to make all the sacrifices necessary for obtaining a teacher's diploma, ... but that her chances for obtaining a position are nil ... then we do admit that there is no Jewish School Question, and we can stop worrying about it here and now.'

Commissioners Hirsch and Cohen reported that there was no need for a separate Jewish school panel, 'providing there is no discrimination against Jews and other non-Protestants and non-Catholics,' a point, the *Chronicle* asserted, that was meaningless in view of the Protestant board's renewed discriminatory practices. It recommended that the provincial government establish a separate body to have full control over finances for all non-Catholic education in the Protestant schools, so that 'there would be no discrimination ... by the board or by principals or teachers, and that segregation because of religion, race, or creed be illegal.' In a minority report, Schubert recommended that a Jewish committee be set up by the Protestant board to administer those schools with overwhelming Jewish enrolment, and that religious instruction be carried out after hours.

Common to all three Jewish commissioners, however, was an insistence that, as Hirsch and Cohen put it, '[those in] the Jewish community ... have to extricate themselves and their children from the humiliating position in which they have been, and are being[,] placed.'[31] Seizing the moment, Hirsch Wolofsky invited all classes in the Jewish community to unite behind a demand for separate schools. He noted that 'different factions in the community were never closer to an understanding than they are at present.' He called for a conference chaired by Lyon Cohen and Samuel Jacobs to prepare a presentation to the provincial government.

Premier Taschereau, who had hoped for a compromise, was now faced with a problem. At the urgings of Jewish representatives, he referred the act of 1903 to the Quebec Court of Appeal for an advisory opinion. 'Are we to force Jewish children to go to Christian schools where they may be taught things repugnant to them?' he asked in the Legislative Assembly. 'Are we to leave these 13,000 children without education? Are we to say that the Jews have no status whatever in Quebec, that they are, in the words of one of the judges, outcasts? Is that the meaning of the British North America Act? ... It is necessary that the Jews should be able to determine their position. They have asked for this legislation so that they may go to the Supreme Court and the Privy Council, and we are permitting it. They had to find out what are their rights ...'[32]

In the advisory opinion handed down in March 1925, the court found the 1903 act *ultra vires* on the grounds that it violated article 93 of the British North America Act, which guaranteed Christian schools in Quebec.[33] Consequently, the court upheld the exclusion of Jews from the Board and from teaching positions, and ruled that the Protestant board had only 'as a matter of grace' to admit Jews, thus revoking their legal right to attend Protestant schools. Moreover, the court found that the Quebec legislature could not establish separate schools for Jews or other non-Protestants or non-Catholics, such as Greek Orthodox.

On appeal, the Supreme Court of Canada not only upheld the Quebec court, but also discovered further legal complications,[34] such as the finding that while the Jewish population of Montreal had the 'privilege' of attending either Protestant or Catholic schools at its option, this applied only to the city of Montreal as it existed at Confederation in 1867. This 'privilege,' therefore, would not extend to Jews living in suburbs that were annexed later, such as Notre Dame de Grace or those who lived in municipalities like Westmount, Outremont, and Lachine, precisely those districts to which Jews were moving.

While they were absorbing this bombshell, the school question surfaced in the May 1927 election, in which Taschereau's Liberal government was challenged by Camillien Houde's Conservatives. Championing the 'nationalist' cause, Louis Fitch opposed the well-ensconced Peter Bercovitch in the St Louis riding hoping to exploit the resentment many downtowners felt towards Bercovitch. Despite the support of both the *Keneder Adler* and the *Chronicle*, Fitch lost and Bercovitch continued arguing for a Jewish-Protestant compromise.

The contest continued, because the Supreme Court of Canada had found that the Quebec legislature could establish a third school panel, one for Jews. This judgment was upheld by the Judicial Committee of the Privy Council, which in 1928 concurred.

The ball was now back in the government's court, with an equal onus on the Jewish community to express its wishes. However, internal Jewish divisions had been inflamed by statements by lawyers representing uptown interests at the Privy Council hearings that 'the Jewish population, speaking generally, was very poor and made hardly any contribution to the local taxes and were not in a position to establish their own schools.'[35] This and comments that Jews who felt entitled to their own schools were 'ludicrous' and 'misguided' enraged the *Chronicle*. It was a dangerous kind of Jewish antisemitism that 'would have left the Jewish population without a single means of escape from an intolerable position, where they would have had no educational status except as may have been granted them by Protestant tolerance, and one lacking any sanction other than the good will of the latter.' A broad Jewish communal understanding of the Privy Council's judgment was now needed in order to utilize the opportunity presented. The question of the hour was this: Could the community unite and seize the moment by asking the premier for the separate school system that London said was legal? Alert to this opportunity, Wolofsky demanded the formation of a united Jewish committee to confer with the Protestant board and then with the government, 'so that when the next session of the legislature arrives we will at least be informed on the question and demand what is possible, just and within our powers.'

Intracommunal discussion abated for about a year, while some parleys with the Protestant board, initiated by Provincial Secretary Athanase David, were undertaken by Jewish representatives. Peter Bercovitch, who was apparently consulted by David,[36] tried unsuccessfully to reach an accommodation with the Protestants. Jewish communal unity on this issue was nowhere in sight.

By January 1929 the downtown 'nationalists' were up in arms over these negotiations. 'We are now faced with a bitter struggle,' Louis Fitch thundered at a late January mass meeting, 'with those of our own people who would teach Protestant culture to Jewish children – a fight against the assimilators, a civil war, a war between brothers.' The Maccabees who combated the nefarious influences of Hellenized Jews in ancient Israel, he stated, were engaged in no more momentous battles. The argumentation for a separate Jewish school system was becoming sharper. One speaker suggested that it would help Jews 'develop a culture centre in Quebec which would be unique,' a kind of centre of Jewish cultural creativity, possibly similar to Warsaw, Odessa, or New York.[37] Compromise between the two Jewish factions now seemed unattainable.

Deep dissension within the Jewish community probably contributed to the failure of these negotiations. Premier Taschereau again indicated his preference for a Protestant-Jewish accommodation. 'There are some Jews who ask for a separate panel,' he said in the assembly. 'I do not think it to be desirable. A third panel would mean perhaps a lesser Canadian spirit.' In Quebec, he continued, 'we have the greatest respect for minorities. French-Canadians in other provinces have suffered too much to be willing to sanction religious intolerance where they are in a majority.' Experienced politician that he was, Taschereau's strategy was clearly to strengthen the negotiating position of the Jewish community vis-à-vis the Protestants in order to bring about an arrangement acceptable to the majority on both sides. In late March, the Quebec legislature passed a bill allotting a portion of the neutral panel's proceeds for the education of mainly Jews and Greek Catholics who attended the Montreal Protestant schools.[38]

Further talks between Jewish and Protestant representatives followed, much to the annoyance of the Jewish 'nationalists' (or 'separatists,' as they now sometimes called themselves).[39] Efforts by Bercovitch and Cohen to secure Jewish representation on the Protestant board failed, despite the eloquent minority appeals that Jews should not be subjected to taxation without representation. Bercovitch, however, continued searching for a solution, reiterating that if the Protestants would not cooperate, he would be 'the first to ask for our own schools, despite the fact that I am opposed to separate schools.'

The 'nationalists,' with the support of the *Chronicle* and the *Keneder Adler*, had been demanding this for years; that is, to leave the Protestants alone and allow them to keep their precious schools to themselves. Their attitude continued to be 'They don't want us and we don't, or shouldn't, want them. Let us set up our own school system at long last and build a real Jewish culture in Montreal.' By January 1930, the now frustrated Bercovitch, true to his word, prepared the bill named the David Bill after its sponsor, Provincial Secretary Athanase David, which provided for the establishment of a five-person separate Jewish school board empowered to set up Jewish schools on the same taxation basis as the Catholic and Protestant ones. The Jewish board was also enabled 'to enter into arrangements with any other board of school commissioners or school trustees' for the education of Jewish children.[40]

This was an obvious opening for those like Bercovitch who still hoped for a last-minute deal with the reluctant Protestants, who, in the *Chronicle*'s words, 'are prepared to face [a Jewish withdrawal] with equanimity.'[41] It would take at least a year of planning to establish a Jewish school system. In the interim, Jewish children – who, according to the Privy Council's judgment, had no rights – would have to attend Protestant schools – on sufferance.

While concerned over appointments to the new Jewish school board, Caiserman doubted the government's will to follow through. Writing to the premier in late March, he pointed out that the bill needed amendments matching the powers of the Jewish school commission with the Protestant and Catholic committees of the Council of Public Instruction, which controlled education in Quebec. This was important, especially when the Catholic hierarchy insisted that, in the *Chronicle*'s words, 'it is the duty of the State to prevent teaching the child anything that may be considered anti-Christian or subversive to the social order.'[42] If this principle was accepted, Judaism could not be taught because it might be regarded as anti-Christian, he pointed out. The latitude needed in teaching history and social science might also run afoul of the prohibition on propagating revolutionary doctrine. This, of course, was nonsense. If Jewish schools were ever established, the *Chronicle* stated soothingly, 'nothing will ever be taught ... to bring into contempt the teachings of Christianity ... nor is there any possibility of Jewish public schools being employed for the propagation of revolutionary ideas.'

But such worries were just theoretical because the Jewish board included mostly prominent west-end rabbis and businessmen. Thoroughly outraged by these appointments, the *Chronicle* thundered that they had 'been chosen for the purpose not of undertaking to create a system of Jewish schools, but primarily [to] negotiate an honourable treaty with the Protestant School Board.'[43] The Jewish school board asked for four 'privileges' from the Protestants: the inclusion of Jewish history and Hebrew language and literature in the curriculum, positions for Jewish teachers in classes where Jewish children predominate, official recognition of Jewish holidays, and the termination of involuntary segregation of Jewish children. Moreover, they sought an end to 'the many instances of petty insults offered to Jewish children by teachers.'

Defeat, however, seemed guaranteed. By the end of 1930, the opposition of the Roman Catholic hierarchy, the rise of the antisemitic press, wavering by the Taschereau government, and the divisions within the Jewish community led most members of the Jewish board towards a compromise solution.[44]

In early December, without consulting the major community organizations, they made a contract with the Protestant boards of Montreal and Outremont providing for the acceptance of Jewish children as a right and the ending of segregation. But Jews, in turn, had to accept compulsory Christian devotional exercises, loss of credit for holidays, and continuing discrimination against hiring Jewish teachers.[45] The *Chronicle* conceded defeat bitterly, and 'those who seek to foster Jewish education amongst the masses and to arrest the forces of national and religious disintegration must seek other means to achieve their purpose.' No such arrangements existed, however, with the Protestant boards of Westmount, Verdun, and Lachine, where there were considerable Jewish populations and where further confrontations were possible.

The fourth party to this Jewish/Protestant dispute was the Catholic Church, which began to formulate its response to the ongoing debate by consulting with the Catholic committee of the Quebec Council of Public Instruction. While the provisions of a bill to permit a Jewish panel were under discussion in March 1930, Monseigneur Georges Gauthier, co-adjutor archbishop of Montreal, published an open letter in *L'Action Catholique* to warn Premier Taschereau of 'the most serious consequences' of this bill, which would apply to the whole province and 'would not fail to get us into trouble wherever one finds a group of Jews.'[46] His major concern, however, was that 'the favour granted to Jews today will perhaps be demanded tomorrow, under the same pretexts, by other religious denominations or even by anti-religious sects.'

In an emotional address at St Joseph's Oratory, Gauthier condemned the premier for extending to the Jews 'an entirely unwarranted sympathy' that would 'overturn an educational system which is for us [French Canadians] a safeguard and a security.'[47] At the same time, Jules Dorion in *L'Action Catholique* criticized the government for recognizing Quebec Jews 'as a distinct NATIONALITY, as considerable as the English or the French nationality of the province.' Dorion stressed that 'the Jewish children cannot nor must not be considered as being anything but English-speaking or French-speaking Canadians.' Raymond-Marie Cardinal Rouleau, archbishop of Quebec, warned that while the church had no objection to Jews getting the same educational privileges as Catholics and Protestants, there was serious danger of the 1930 bill leading to the creation of a religiously neutral school system in Quebec.

Other Catholic spokesmen held more extreme views. Abbé Antonio Huot, author of a 1914 tract on Jewish ritual murder, editor of *Semaine réligieuse de Québec*, and author of numerous anti-Masonic and antisemitic writings,[48] had strongly opposed a separate, publicly supported Jewish school system in editorials for *L'Action Catholique* in mid-May 1926. He demanded that the provincial legislature protect 'the interests of Christianity in the public schools of our province.' It would be a sad day for French Canadians, he said, to see Jews, 'the last immigrants to our country,' endowed with rights that 'have been refused to our French-Canadian compatriots in Manitoba,' where, in 1890, Roman Catholic schools were abolished, setting off powerful resentments in Quebec. If the existing arrangement was not satisfactory to the Jews, they could set up private schools, or, possibly, negotiate with the Protestants for distinct schools where the religious instruction would be appropriate.

Le Soleil, the daily French newspaper in Quebec City, expressed deep concern over the preservation of the province's Christian character and reminded readers that Jews were guests, not equal members, of Canadian society.[49] In early February 1926, *Le Soleil* informed its readers that 'being immigrants, and sons of immigrants, [Jews] have no special rights.' 'We owe nothing to the Jews,' the paper stated and concluded that 'moreover, as we are a Christian country, a Christian nation and not a neutral, unbelieving and materialistic one, to claim for non-Christians the best one can get indicates a strange broadness of outlook, an absence of judicial principles, a notorious inconsistency.'

One year before, Jules Dorion had written in *L'Action Catholique* that the best solution would be to give Jews their own separate school system.[50] This was a far more liberal position than that taken by Huot and the Catholic hierarchy, who were opposed to allowing Jews to sit on the provincial Council of Public Instruction lest they would undermine the Christian character of that body. Cardinal Rouleau wrote to Premier Taschereau on 28 February 1930, a few weeks after the David Bill passed the legislature, to express his concerns and keep the pressure on. He was joined in this campaign by the bishops of Montreal, Rimouski, Trois-Rivières, and Saint Hyacinthe, who maintained that while Jews should have their own schools, they would not admit Jews to the council.

Such high-level episcopal attacks drove Premier Taschereau to consult these religious authorities while the David Bill was being drafted.[51] Its implementation was delayed because some of the Jewish representatives were privately negotiating with the Protestant board for a return to the 1903 accord. Taschereau's government seized this opportunity to induce a compromise between Jews and Protestants. They repealed the David Bill and passed a new act – previously approved by Cardinal Rouleau and Monseigneur Gauthier – to establish instead a board of Jewish school commissioners for Montreal, with the purpose of negotiating a new deal with the Protestant board.

By this time, however, the whole controversy had aroused some virulent antisemitism. Camillien Houde, leader of the Conservative opposition in the Legislative Assembly, had been a supporter of the David Bill, but now, as a candidate in the Montreal mayoralty race, he thundered: 'If the Jews are not happy, they can leave.'[52] At the same time, an editorialist in *L'Action Catholique* commented, 'We must never forget ... that the Jews readily put up with neutral schools, divorce and in general every anti-Christian law.'

Meanwhile, Adrian Arcand, leader of the nascent Quebec Fascists and editor of *Le Goglu* – a Montreal weekly newspaper dedicated to publishing antisemitic articles and cartoons, and inspired by the German-Nazi organ *Der Sturmer* – exploited the controversy. In April 1930 he asserted 'that every religious or racial denomination other than the bilingual Christian denomination does not have any right to be recognized by our parliaments and our courts.'[53] Other expressions of antisemitism in Quebec were mounting during the early 1930s. The historian David Rome contends that 'the imagery of the Jews conveyed so successfully in the campaign about the school question became deeply rooted in the thinking and in the articulation of that nationalistic church-led portion of French Canada.'

The crisis was resolved by an agreement between Jewish representatives and the Protestant school board, but bitter, long-lasting communal divisions remained. The 'nationalists' lamented a lost opportunity to establish a separate Jewish school system, and the 'integrationists' regretted their failure to secure significant concessions within the system they were compelled now to support. They were now forced to integrate into the city's unyielding Anglo-Saxon society, perhaps weakening their own culture with this marginal status. At the same time, Catholic French Canada was now thoroughly aroused to a perceived 'Jewish menace.' 'There is no doubt,' the historian Cornelius Jaenen observed, 'that increasing antisemitic feeling and organization, the exclusion of Jewish refugees, the enforcement of Sunday observance legislation and the school question were all linked in some way to each other and were part of a sociocultural phenomenon.'[54] The Protestants of Montreal, meanwhile, although in full control of their schools, still had to cope with a large Jewish minority, who were now 'honorary Protestants,' for many Jews a distinct dishonour.

As a small minority, Jews had no choice but to accept a public humiliation, which left them apprehensive, defensive, and cynical. It was a bitter irony that, because of Jewish divisiveness and the lopsided compromise with the Protestants, Jews were officially relegated to second-class status in Quebec, which in 1832 had led the entire British Empire in extending them equal rights. Continuing antisemitic attacks in the press and the removal in 1936 of the Jewish exemption to the Quebec Sunday Observance Act (designed to protect workers against undue exploitation) increased their uncertainty. Meanwhile the *Chronicle* called for a Jewish Vigilance Committee,'to protect the good name of Jewry' in Montreal, where 'we have been made the object of libellous attacks by certain vigilant tabloids.'[55]

At one point in the struggle, the *Chronicle* commented on some unwelcome advice to Montreal Jewry that had appeared in one of the New York Yiddish dailies and concerned the injection of 'Jewish nationalism' into the 1927 Quebec provincial election campaign. 'It is futile for [the New York papers] to remind us that we are not living in Poland or Roumania,' the editorial stated, 'and that it is wrong to inject Jewish nationalism into the elections of a free country. If [Canada] is a free country, as the *Jewish Morning Journal* implies, it is precisely because its constitutional basis is the recognition of more than one national entity within its framework.'[56] The editorialist showed a clear understanding of the differences between two neighbouring, but highly distinctive, Jewish social and political contexts.

Perhaps the best statement of Canadian Jewish awareness of its unique situation, and of its distinctiveness from the American Jewish context, was yet another comment in the *Chronicle* late in the school controversy: 'The British Imperial policy derives its strength on the principle of the preservation of every individual culture within its realm.'[57]

The year 1931, then, was menacing, both economically and politically. The Depression was entering a desperate phase. And in Germany, the Nazi Party under Adolf Hitler had made enormous gains in the September 1930 elections for the Reichstag. For Quebec Jewry, the decade opened in abject defeat, deep disunity, and serious menace abroad. Humiliation, however, was fostering a steely resolve in the community that it must strengthen itself and marshal resources for what lay ahead.

Quebec's Jews also felt threatened by local antisemitism that emerged in virulent forms in the interwar years. The weekly *Canadian Jewish Chronicle* began reporting in the 1920s on the antisemitism (which it termed 'racial sadism') in *La Croix*, a Quebec Catholic weekly whose fulminations are 'so distinctly psychopathic that it really cannot bias any of its readers unless they are similarly degenerate and depraved ...'[58] *La Croix* continued its attacks on Jews until ceasing publication in 1936. Meanwhile, the *Chronicle* coverage of antisemitism in Europe and North America included examples appearing in the Quebec English and French press, such as the reprinting of excerpts from the fraudulent pamphlet *Protocols of the Elders of Zion* in the otherwise respectable *Quebec Chronicle*, in February 1922.

In francophone Quebec, Jews were held responsible for the Russian Revolution and the spread of international communism. Articles alleging these untruths frequently appeared in *La Semaine Commerciale*, *L'Action Catholique*, and *L'Action Française*, as well as, in milder form, in English dailies like the *Montreal Star*.[59] Taking note of this trend, the *Chronicle* argued that antisemitism was the fault of the 'Gentile environment,' which 'has created the modern Jew.' The paper was prepared to concede 'the truth of some of the accusations levelled against the Jews[,] and it is certainly stretching a point far to concede this, [but] there still remains no foundation for anger or hostility, because there can be no blame where there was no alternative ... The Ghetto developed the Ghetto Jew.'

Such arguments, however conciliatory, had no measurable effect, especially in Quebec, where a variety of socio-economic factors contributed to the rise of antisemitism.[60] The fear felt by the French owners of small businesses of competition from Jewish merchants gave rise to a boycott movement in the early 1920s in which French Canadians were advised to boycott Jewish businesses by following the slogan: 'Achat chez nous.'

By early 1924, *La Croix* was calling for a boycott of Jewish businesses 'to get rid of them either by elimination or by annihilation.'[61] A few months earlier, it had published excerpts from the *Protocols*, along with an editorial announcing that 'these documents are undoubtedly of Jewish origin ... It is a well-known fact that immigrant stations in the United States are filled with Jewish inspectors whose chief business it seems to be the insult and injury of incoming people other than Jews.'

The 'Achat chez nous' campaign was growing stronger. Writing in *L'Actualité économique* in June 1926, Henri Leroux urged 'Canadian retailers in Montreal, [to] fight against only one foreign race: the Jews.'[62] He alleged that the Jews were a more serious menace than all other ethnic competitors because they tried to 'take over the retail business by any means.' Jews were by nature commercial, Leroux continued, operating small grocery stores throughout Montreal and staying open day and night. With capital thus amassed, they entered clothing manufacturing. As both manufacturers and retailers, they drove French Canadians out of business. Jews also invaded the shoe, fur, meat, and fruit trades, employing French Canadians as their front men. In fact, Leroux asserted, Jews were successful because of their 'lack of sincerity and honesty.' They bought bankrupt stock and goods of poor quality, then sold them for lower prices. They cheated on weights and measures. They even saved by cutting expenses, including personal living expenses, and employing their families at home.

But French Canadians were retaliating, Leroux rejoiced, by advertising, just like the Jews, and 'by studying their ways of doing business, and by behaving honestly, by selling new items at reasonable price ... There is still enough time for Canadians to wake up.' In discussing other threats, such as department stores like Eaton's, Dupuis Frères, Dominion, and Piggly-Wiggly, Leroux avoided ethnic attacks entirely.

In an issue of *Le Detaillant* in May 1927, J.E. Sansregret, vice-president of the Retail Merchants Association of Canada, pointed out that in a survey of one Montreal suburb, 79.13 per cent of all stores were French-Canadian-owned, a figure roughly equal to their percentage of the population.[63] Still, the presence of Jews was vexatious: 'We notice that to dress the brother, the father, the husband, there is not one English, not one French Canadian, but 8 Jews are there to wait on you. There you go!' He pronounced that French Canadians must not stand still; 'rather, we must develop more, increase gains recently realized, with the risk of regressing.' French Canadians go into unprofitable lines, and 'we give to our fellow citizens of Hebrew origin the making of the supposedly profitable cloth.' And while French Canadians resisted hiring bilingual personnel in their stores, Jews had no hesitation, thus attracting a large and diverse clientele.

Are we masters in our own house? Sansregret wondered. Hardly! A French Canadian must understand his duty, 'which is to buy from his fellow countryman.' If he was to boycott the Jewish stores for six months, at least half of them would close up, 'and the business which puts all goods into circulation would be handed back to us and everyone would be better off.' This was a question of the very survival of French Canada, Sansregret stated. 'Today, the issue of nationalism has become an economic issue.' The vilification of the Jews was also included in Dupuis Frères's in-house publication, *Le Duprex*, which went chiefly to employees. In its February 1927 issue, it criticized French Canadians who purchased 'vile Jewish bric a brac.'[64]

Consequently, some Jews suffered considerable hardship. One general store owner, in Nicolet, Quebec, who boasted in April 1924 that 'my relations with my neighbours have always been of the very friendliest,' was told by a hostile townsman that 'it was the duty of good Christians ... to drive all the Jews out of the country.'[65] His 'friendly' neighbours showed him a copy of *La Croix* that informed its readers all about the Jews. 'My store is practically boycotted,' he wrote. 'The people won't come to buy. They only come in to ask me what would I do if my store was plundered or burnt down or if I was driven out of the country. Wherever I go, I hear them talking about Jews or I see them showing each other the paper.'

Much of this antisemitism was generated by writings in *L'Action Catholique*, whose wide clerical readership made it especially influential in Quebec, where it conveyed a powerful message to the priests, who spread the word to their parishioners.[66] Antisemitism was not incidental to the paper's editorial writers. In numerous articles, they conveyed the persistent message that Jews and Judaism were a dire menace, not just to Catholic Quebec, but also to the civilized world. 'Jews,' wrote Abbé Édouard Lavergne in 1922, 'as a race, are our enemies. Their goal is to destroy Christianity, but in order to achieve this goal, it was necessary to shed floods of blood.' Thus images of Jews attacking and killing Christians were employed to depict Jews as inhuman creatures who communed with the devil. In league with the Freemasons and the Bolsheviks, J. Albert Foissy wrote, the Jews wished to 'reverse the established social order' and establish Bolshevism, which is 'an episode of the battle involving fanatical Jews who, by the paths of international anarchy, pursue only the ruin of Christian and civilized nations.'

As stated in the *Protocols*, the Jews were determined to dominate the world. If the world press was still, it was, of course, because Jews also controlled that medium. *L'Action Catholique* stated that even the League of Nations was composed mainly of and manipulated by Jews. Thus they secured the League's mandate for Britain to establish a Jewish national home in Palestine, which Abbé Arsène-Louis-Phillipe Nadeau saw as 'a real challenge for all of Christianity' because the Jews 'would be able to erect factories or dumping grounds on Sacred Lands ... if they would not go as far as erect temples of debauchery.'[67]

Equally as bad, in the eyes of *L'Action Catholique*'s writers, was the Jewish domination of Poland, where three million 'parasites eat away at its exhausted body.' These 'Yid traitors, thieves, spies, crooks, howling Bolshevists, Hun-loving arrogants who go as far as insulting Polish emblems [are] full of hate, so much so that they attack Polish soldiers who have strayed, by mistake, into the ghetto districts.'[68] In the United States, Jews possessed an 'extraordinary power' in the press, the arts, the theatre, opera, jazz, and fashion, where morals were corrupted and decadence fostered.

In exposing these nefarious Jews, *L'Action Catholique* saw itself as protecting Christian interests. In fact, Abbé Lavergne said he wished Jews well, so long as they did not 'block the path, and by the exploitation of bad passions throw our people in hell, those we wish to meet in Eternal Bliss.'[69] And when persecutions of Jews commenced in Germany, *L'Action Catholique* extended both Christian charity and blame towards the victims. Thus writers like Jules Dorion complimented Hitler for giving Jews a little 'pull on the ears.' In general, though, they condemned the means but not the end – suppression of the world's 'undesirables,' the Jews.

At this same time, student activist leader André Laurendeau of Jeune-Canada, a group of French-Canadian intellectuals inspired by right-wing clerics and nationalists, stage-managed an antisemitic public rally at Montreal's Gésu Hall in April 1933.[70] Mounted to rebuke French-Canadian politicians who had attended a Jewish-sponsored mass meeting to protest German Nazism, the Jeune-Canada rally denounced Jews who 'represent ... the dream of Messianic mission [in which] Israelites aspire to dominate the world.' Jeune-Canada's leading spokesmen led the attack. Pierre Dagenais condemned 'the Jew [who] professes a spirit of proletariat internationalism,' while Pierre Dansereau announced that 'the Jewish element ... represents in Canada a power stronger than the voice of the blood.' Another speaker alleged that '150,000 Jews in Canada own a quarter of the Dominion's wealth and the 80,000 Jews in Montreal control two hundred million dollars worth of industry and commerce.' Stung by criticisms from Senator Raoul Dandurand, who condemned these remarks as 'the most cruel attack I've ever heard of,' and by vigorous Jewish reaction, which called Jeune-Canada members 'disciples of German Naziism,' Laurendeau responded by alleging that Quebec's Jews threatened the province's 'linguistic balance' and were carriers of both international communism and exploitative capitalism.

In May 1933, Adrien Arcand and his Parti national social chrétien launched the newspaper *Le Patriote*, which, the *Chronicle* reported, was initiated 'with the usual ... anti Jewish fulminations, and proves itself a worthy successor to *Le Goglu*.'[71] That paper, published by Joseph Menard, an associate of Adrian Arcand's, had alleged that Jews murdered the Lindbergh baby for ritual purposes. A month later, it announced that Jews were responsible for the downfall of the Roman Catholic Church in Spain, and that they 'have gobbled up the treasures of the Russian church.' In August, *Le Patriote* alleged to its readers that Sir Herbert Samuel, a prominent British Jew then visiting Vancouver, 'has been sent by the Elders of Zion to open up the gates of Canada to hundreds of thousands of German Jews.'

Dabbling also in theories of racial superiority, Jeune-Canada declared that while French Canadians could become 'a superior race,' the Jew was 'like a necessary canker for Christianity, and confirms the incompatibility between Israelites and Christians.'[72] Such verbiage, in all likelihood borrowed from Lionel Groulx or his intellectual mentors in France, inspired Laurendeau to proclaim that Jews '... represent a wild and dangerous dream that we must suppress at all cost: messianism. The Israelites aspire [to] ... the day when their race will dominate the world.'

Apart from the press, Jew-hatred also surfaced elsewhere. In 1931 aldermen in Montreal's Villeray Ward considered blocking off a Jewish cemetery in the north end with new streets to prevent its expansion. They also objected to a proposal to build a new Jewish hospital there.[73] That same year, Abbé Édouard Lavergne proclaimed, in radio broadcasts and in *L'Action Catholique,* his racist theories about a Jewish plot to corrupt good Christian morals, theories, he said, that were confirmed by the *Protocols of the Elders of Zion.* In September 1931 two Montreal aldermen led an attack on immigrants 'whom certain groups are endeavouring to bring to Canada [and who] are mostly Communists and propagandists of anti-Christian ideas.' Jewish meetings were interrupted by 'Fascist mobs ... with the battlecry of anticommunism and pro-clericalism ... with the police ... looking on benignly and – who knows – maybe indulgently.' A brave effort mounted by Peter Bercovitch, member of the Quebec Assembly, who introduced a bill in 1932 to make such defamations illegal, came to naught.

Meanwhile, J.A. Chalifoux, the leader of a brown-shirted fascist group, appealed to Premier Taschereau and proclaimed, 'We will fight the Jews on behalf of the merchants of Montreal.' At a meeting in St-Jerome in August 1933, Chalifoux and his followers threatened that 'they will tell [the Jews] to go to Palestine and if they refuse they will kill them.' He also threatened to lynch a local Jew. The city of Montreal, recognizing that many Jews were not yet naturalized, limited the street sale of newspapers, largely a Jewish trade, to 'British subjects' of at least five years. City officials also penalized Jews for opening bakeries and delicatessens on Sunday.

The Canadian Jewish Congress, dormant since 1920, was revived in 1933, principally because of this emergence of virulent antisemitism. It was not just that among contemporary opinion-makers, 'the Jew simply did not fit into their concept of Canada.'[74] Nazi-style uniformed 'storm troopers' also rallied and marched in several cities. Jews were denied professional, residential, and economic opportunities. Occasional antisemitic violence erupted. And enough open antisemitism was expressed in newspapers, political forums, the courts, and everyday life to convince Jews that they had to react to these hate-mongers. In 1935, Congress issued a pamphlet, *Jew Baiting in Canada,* describing the activities of twelve antisemitic organizations.[75]

Unique among ethnic groups, Jews were able, through the Congress, their three MPs, and several prominent individuals, to mitigate prejudice. Yet local antisemitism was part of an international campaign, including political parties in France and Germany and the Roman Catholic Church. In the United States, Henry Ford's daily newspaper, the *Dearborn Independent,* was filled with fulminations against the 'international Jew.' A pamphlet entitled *The International Jew* was circulated nationally in the millions, translated into several languages, and distributed throughout Europe.[76]

During the late 1930s, the Michigan-based hate-monger and Roman Catholic priest Father Charles Coughlin broadcast virulent Jew-baiting messages from his headquarters. In 1934 a Winnipeg anti-Jewish rag, the *Canadian Nationalist,* published the vile and venerable lie of Jewish ritual murder. Emulating Hitler's brownshirts and Britain's blackshirts, swastika clubs sprang up in Ontario during the 1930s. More genteel antisemitism was also in evidence. Universities limited Jewish admissions, especially into medical and dentistry programs, and restrictive covenants prevented Jews from living in certain urban areas, while insurance companies were believed to discriminate against Jews.[77] Bans existed on Jews at many resorts and private clubs, eliciting numerous jokes. One of them poses a Jew seeking admission to an exclusive Toronto club only to be rejected as 'pushy' by a member who proudly announces that one of his ancestors signed Magna Carta. 'Is that so?' replies the Jew. 'One of mine signed the Ten Commandments.' Many other wisecracks also deftly punctured antisemitic stereotypes, but all to little avail. Jew-baiting remained a popular Canadian pastime.

In Quebec, dedicated antisemitic weeklies such as *Le Goglu, Le Miroir,* and *Le Chameau,* which regularly featured cartoons caricaturing Jews as repulsive, vile, and filthy, and articles accusing Jews of foul crimes, were circulated by Adrian Arcand and his associates.[78] Arcand's blueshirts, modelled on their Italian Fascist and German Nazi counterparts, marched and organized. From his position at the Université de Montréal, Abbé Lionel Groulx published denunciations of Jewish materialism, communism, and capitalism. At the respected and influential newspaper *Le Devoir,* the editor, Georges Pelletier, regularly included antisemitic pieces, as did the editors of the monthly periodical *L'Action Française.* Students at the Université de Montréal demonstrated against 'Judeo-Bolshevism.' The interns at four Montreal francophone hospitals went on strike in 1934 to protest the hiring of a Jewish intern at L'Hôpital Notre Dame. As well, Quebec Jews were considered officially second-class citizens in elementary and secondary education by the Anglo-Protestant community. At McGill, meanwhile, Jews had problems gaining entry on the same basis as other Quebeckers. All of these unpleasant and menacing elements put the Jewish community on notice that, with respect to antisemitism, 'la province de Québec n'est pas une province comme les autres.'

As a reaction to these provocations, the Congress embarked on a program to educate Canadians about Jews and to enlist help from the Christian groups in these anti-defamation efforts. Sam Jacobs, the MP for Cartier, persuaded Henri Bourassa to support this campaign by strongly condemning antisemitism in two speeches in the House of Commons in the spring of 1934.[79] Similar lobbying with a leading Quebec liberal, Olivar Asselin, also bore fruit, while discussions with Bourassa and Father Paré of the Palestre National resulted in a meeting with high Catholic authorities and three lectures by Bourassa condemning antisemitism.

In responding to Hitler's persecution of Jews in Germany, the Congress adopted an aggressive policy of boycotting German goods and continued this drive through the 1930s. It also campaigned to prevent Canadian participation in the 1936 summer Olympic Games in Berlin. The Congress received backing from the Trades and Labour Congress of Canada, which supported a Germany boycott, called for the non-participation of Canadians at the Berlin games, and sent 'representations to the dominion Government ... to break off diplomatic relations with the Hitler Government until such time as [it] ceases [its] persecution of the organized working class of Germany, and to express abhorrence for the regime which has overthrown civil and religious freedom.' The Congress urged labour representatives throughout the country to form boycott committees 'which should make it a daily duty to visit friendly organizations ... [a]nd use any platform which will denounce Naziism and propagate the boycott.'[80]

The Congress's boycott committee received promises from businessmen to comply. Owners of Reitman's stores wrote in May 1934, 'We assure you that we feel the same towards Germany as you ... do and under the circumstances, we have ceased to do business [there].'[81] Congress general secretary Hananiah Caiserman also tried to warn Canadian manufacturers of the German practice of dumping goods in the Canadian market.

The responses to these efforts were mixed, even in the Jewish community. In one of his follow-up letters, the boycott committee chairman cautioned that 'we have learned that quite a number of Jewish merchants are continuing to buy and sell German merchandise. We express the sincere trust that you are not one of them.'[82] In a communiqué to eleven hundred wholesalers and retailers, he asked recipients to reply, 'in writing, that you are ready to cooperate wholeheartedly with the

Boycott, which every decent Jew in the world is compelled to conduct against Nazi Germany.' Although Canadian trade with Germany actually rose during the 1930s, by 1939 it had declined relative to Canada's total trade, and the fall in imports of German textiles, a sector in which Jews were especially prominent, was significant.

The Congress also reacted strongly to Canadian antisemitism. But this was like trying to wrestle an octopus. Often the Congress was in only an advisory role, as in the case of Alderman Max Siegler of Montreal. He was the object of a powerful campaign against his nomination for deputy mayor led by Le Club Ouvrier Maisonneuve, which protested that 'it is a shame to see that our French Canadian aldermen could not find anything else but a Jew as deputy mayor ... [and] that we must humble ourselves before the Jews ...'[83]

Besides protesting to politicians, the Congress tried to educate non-Jews by distributing literature explaining the dangers of Nazism, the falsehood of claims such as those in the *Protocols of the Elders of Zion*, and the need for vigilance against antisemitism at home.[84] Twenty different pieces of information were sent to public schools, theological colleges, universities, school boards, mechanics' institutes, provincial legislatures, and law schools throughout Canada. Nevertheless, antisemitism continued to rise. In September 1938 the Congress's eastern division was warning that 'Fascist and Nazi organizations in Canada are plotting to obtain political control of this province [Quebec] and to destroy the Jewish people.' Pointing to the assistance given to this 'Fascist machine' by a powerful press, as well as 'an avalanche of Nazi literature' emanating from 'French Canadian political, religious and economic groups,' the Congress asserted that 'these have during the last few years created an anti-Jewish atmosphere which is especially dangerous during elections.'

Literature circulated by the Congress in Quebec and the Maritime provinces stressed that 'the rising tide of anti-Semitism throughout the world is having its repercussions in Quebec, [where] the National Social Christian Party, led by Adrian Arcand, already boasts of having 15,000 members ... [and] uniformed "legions" hold weekly parades ... Scurrilous and malicious propaganda continues to pour out and poison the minds of innocent people.'[85] Photographs showing Canadian Fascists at a 'council of war' and ones depicting saluting Montreal adherents bore the captions 'Fascists hope to rule Canada in 1940,' 'It may happen here!' and 'Fascist legions are preparing to march in the streets of Montreal in the Spring of this year.'

There was genuine widespread fear in Eastern Canada of the fascist menace. Pamphlets circulated bearing titles such as *Canada under the Heel of the Jew, Why We Should Oppose the Jew, The Grave Diggers of Russia* (showing a face with exaggerated 'Jewish features'), *Politiciens et juifs, Fascisme ou socialisme,* and *National social chrétien.* Ideas derived from Hitler's *Der Stürmer* were widely distributed, as were such French slogans as 'Jews are the enemies of God and of all mankind. St-Paul'; 'The enemy of the JEW and of Communism is FASCISM!'; 'Fascism is the powerful weapon of the true Christian'; "The JEWISH rat gets richer with smuggling, drug trafficking and the white slave trade.' Antisemitic hate-mongering was serious.

Much of the counter-propaganda was conducted by the Committee on Jewish-Gentile Relations, a Toronto-based group headed by Dr Claris E. Silcox of the United Church of Canada and Rabbi Maurice N. Eisendrath of Holy Blossom Temple.[86] The committee boasted fifty permanent members drawn from the major Christian and Jewish organizations, and was mainly devoted to distributing literature such as James W. Parkes's *Judaism and Christianity* and Claris Silcox's *The Challenge of Anti-Semitism to Democracy.* In the fall of 1938, Parkes was brought from England for an extensive lecture tour at universities, churches, Canadian Clubs, and League of Nations societies. The Committee also distributed exposés of Father Charles Coughlin, the inventor of hate radio in Detroit. Coughlin apparently had some supporters in Canada, and his broadcasts had an audience here. A 1932 survey of radio-listening preferences in London, Ontario (where people were likely to tune in to American stations), revealed that his program, considered to be 'religious' in content, was well known. By 1938, his diatribes against Jews had grown increasingly virulent.

German Nazi antisemitism influenced some Canadians, especially in the Mennonite community, even though groups like Deutscher Bund Canada and the National Socialist Party (the NSDAP) had very few members – only eight-eight in 1937.[87] The distribution of antisemitic propaganda among Germans living in Canada was undertaken by the Nazis in the 1930s on a significant scale. In early 1935, Hans Seelheim, one of two German consuls in Canada, spoke to the Women's Conservative Club of Winnipeg about 'Jewish flesh merchants.' They, along with drug dealers, he said, 'are all Jews and the same goes for most boot-leggers.' He went on to Vancouver, where he delivered another antisemitic broadside to the Lions Club, drawing a vigorous protest from the local branch of the Congress. Such messages were also spread among German Canadians.

In Ontario, the Jews' response to antisemitism was weak initially, which was understandable given their minority status and immigrant make-up. But it strengthened as the community learned better methods of coping. In 1932, E. Frederick Singer, a Jewish Conservative MLA for the St Andrew riding in Toronto, introduced a bill to amend the Ontario Insurance Act to prohibit the practice of discriminating against minorities by charging higher premiums and providing inferior coverage.[88] Meanwhile, urged by Toronto Jewish community leaders, the municipal council prohibited discrimination in leases for the rental of city-owned land. However, in some of Ontario's provincial parks, cottagers were allowed to control access on the basis of race; in 1941, one official wrote that 'it has been [our] policy to prevent any infiltration of Jewish leaseholders ...'

The Congress also lobbied against antisemitic signs – such as those at various resorts that allegedly read, 'No Dogs or Jews Allowed' – as well as discrimination in employment and housing. Such efforts usually failed. During the Second World War, even with serious shortages of manpower in vital industries, discriminatory hiring continued. However, the Joint Public Relations Committee of Congress and B'nai B'rith did succeed, with the cooperation of the National Selective Service, in stopping such practices, and in 1944 they – along with J.B. Salsberg, the newly elected Labor Progressive member for St Andrew – encouraged the government of George Drew to pass the Racial Discrimination Bill, which outlawed some racist practices in Ontario.

The Congress's 1938 claim that its 'moral authority is recognized by our Federal, Provincial and Municipal Governments' was probably justified.[89] Through its public-relations efforts, it had established a unique relationship not only with governments, but also with the press, public bodies, churches, and labour in Quebec. Father Stéphane Valiquette, S.J., with the support of fellow Jesuit, Father Joseph Paré of Collège Ste Marie, and the encouragement of Rabbi Harry Stern of Temple Emanuel and Caiserman of the Congress, began in 1937 his efforts to convey his liberal views of Judaism to French-Canadian Catholics. With its status in the community, Congress had 'done away with the deplorable conditions which prevailed ... when any private individual spoke in the name of Canadian Jewry. Today only one organization speaks for and represents Canadian Jewry in an emergency, and that organization is the Canadian Jewish Congress.'

That view was not uncontested, and Congress warned against unnamed 'left labour organizations in Montreal [that] interfere with the authority of the Congress by duplicating activities, which will result in more harm than good.' However, the only serious rival, the Zionist Organization of Canada, had effectively yielded activities in this sphere to Congress, which, by 1939, had endured for more than five difficult years. It required new leadership and stronger financial backing to succeed both in combating antisemitism and lobbying for admission of more refugee Jews to Canada.[90] Samuel Bronfman, the Montreal whisky tycoon, was persuaded to accept the presidency, a post he filled with enormous dedication for the next twenty-two years.[91]

Bronfman was very much his own man. Injecting energy and financial resources into Congress affairs, he stressed the patriotism of Canadian Jewry and the need for public spiritedness to 'gain the respect of [its] fellow citizens – the non-Jewish citizens' (as he told Congress delegates shortly after his elevation to the presidency). With this attitude, Bronfman was not influenced by those who would press for a more favourable immigration policy. He therefore, in the view of historian Michael Marrus, 'sounded a particularly patriotic note while ignoring the burning Jewish concerns of the hour.'

Meanwhile, Abbé Groulx continued his attacks on Quebec's Jews. As a highly influential intellectual and teacher of Quebec history, he had a strong effect on his students at the Université de Montréal and readers of his voluminous writings. Some of these were published in *Le Devoir*, which was read by 'the clergy, the university community, civil servants, and the liberal professions.'[92]

Groulx was heavily influenced by the French racist nationalism of L'Action Française, a Paris-based movement whose major ideologues espoused extremist ideas of exclusivist racial purity, right-wing nationalism, and violent anti-liberalism.[93] Ever since he wrote *La Naissance d'une race* in 1919 to glorify the racial purity of the French-Canadian folk, Groulx was obsessed with the extreme racism which emphasized 'socio-psychological characteristics [that] are transmitted through the blood' and the 'degeneration' that comes from racial mixing. In his novel *L'Appel de la race* (1922), he emphasized the drawbacks arising from an English-French marriage. To him, the fusion of soul, blood, and soil were the true source of the race. Groulx's numerous writings emphasized 'the biological transmission of psychological characteristics,' ideas current among fascist and integral nationalist groups throughout Europe. Through his lectures, the pages of *L'Action Nationale*, and various historical works, Groulx's clerico-fascist, racist, and antisemitic ideas became the intellectual inspiration for Laurendeau's Jeune-Canada movement and for the writers of *Le Devoir*, including its editor, Georges Pelletier.

The McGill sociologist Everett C. Hughes observed in his seminal 1943 study of French Canada that antisemitism was a minor and symbolic aspect of French-Canadian nationalism in the 1920s and 1930s. It was, he said, a reflection of 'the more bitter attacks which the French Canadians would like to make upon the English or perhaps even upon some of their own leaders and institutions.' While most scholars do not identify antisemitism as a noteworthy theme in evolution of modern Québécois nationalism,[94] the historian Esther Delisle emphasizes that antisemitism was its 'primary focus.' The Jew, in the mind of Groulx, was racially inferior and, in his words, characterized by 'a fatal, invasive illness, one that no cordon sanitaire can artificially arrest.' To be sure, Groulx, Pelletier, and other antisemites were in a minority, as newspapers like *Le Jour*, *Le Canada*, and *L'Autorité* and journalists like Olivar Asselin and Henri Bourassa repeatedly condemned antisemitism. When interns at Montreal's francophone hospitals struck against the presence of Dr Samuel Rabinovitch at L'Hôpital Notre Dame in June 1934, Edmond Turcotte denounced them in *Le Canada*. Asselin, the editor of *L'Ordre*, in which he published an attack in March 1934 on Hitlerism and French-Canadian antisemitism, also condemned the walkout: 'The strike of the French Canadian interns could have only been motivated by racial hatred.' However forthright, this seems to have been the extent of editorial condemnation of antisemitism by French-Canadian journalists and intellectuals.

It is difficult to measure the level of activity against antisemitism within French Canada. While the province's most widely circulated newspapers, *La Presse*, *Le Soleil*, and *La Patrie*, were free of its poison, the antisemitism of Groulx and others still had enormous effect. One editorialist even averred that Jewish claims to public rights could bring 'violent reprisals.' *La Nation* editorialized: 'Communism, a Jewish invention, would thus become the most enormous lie to brutalize the working class and worsen the economic illnesses suffered by a world which waits for the future King of Israel to enthrone himself on top of a pyramid of corpses.'[95]

In the pantheon of perceived Jewish subversion of French Canada there was also capitalism, liberalism, the cinema, violence, vulgarity, and filth. Jews, according to articles appearing in *Le Devoir* during the 1930s, were 'aliens, circumcised, criminals, mentally ill, trash of nations,

Tartars infected with Semitism, malodorous – they smell of garlic, live in lice-ridden ghettos, have greasy hair and pot bellies, big crooked noses, and they are dirty.'[96] In September 1936, *Le Devoir* attacked the appointment of a Jew to the board of the Canadian Broadcasting Corporation.

Jews were also the subject of verbal attacks by prominent French-Canadian politicians. The Hon. Arthur Sauvé, postmaster general for Canada in R.B. Bennett's Conservative government, collaborated with a group that was affixing antisemitic stickers to letters. He also 'launched a tirade against the projected attempt to get an undesirable element ... which is hostile to the French Canadian people, to the French language and to their religion' into Canada.[97] Ernest Lapointe, Quebec lieutenant to Prime Minister Mackenzie King, privately insisted that his province could not be represented by a Jew, the MP Sam Jacobs, who had been designated to attend the 1937 coronation of George VI.

J.E. Grégoire, mayor of Quebec City, professor of economics, and key lieutenant to Maurice Duplessis, leader of the Union Nationale, praised the antisemitic newspaper *Le Patriote* before a crowd of twenty thousand in Montreal in July 1936.[98] Paul Gouin, leader of Action Libérale Nationale – a movement strongly influenced by Bourassa, Groulx, and *L'Action Française* – allowed his journal, *La Province*, 'to wander into an incoherent excursion the Jewish problem in such manner as to leave no doubt of the implications which this Fascist ideology holds for the Jews.'

When the Union Nationale won the 1936 provincial election, the *Chronicle* called upon Premier Duplessis to disavow the antisemitic views of 'a few judenfressers such as our old friend Saluste Lavery.' In March 1936, while bemoaning the fate of Quebec farmers, the MLA Laurent Barré announced, without any evidence, that some New York Jews had taken over a large milk concern in Montreal. Premier Duplessis saw fit to publicly link the Jewish MLA Peter Bercovitch, a Liberal, with the Communists, branding him their 'echo in the Legislature.'

Open violence against Jews was mounting. Premier Duplessis's public targeting of Communists as enemies of Quebec society occasionally encouraged street violence against Jews. 'The affinity between the two,' the *Chronicle* commented, 'has been drummed into their heads so persistently by certain elements that an anti-Communist riot immediately becomes an anti-Jewish riot.'[99]

This proclivity, coupled with negligible assistance from the Montreal police force, led to occasional Jewish self-protection. Street hooliganism in the guise of popular anti-Communism by Université de Montréal students was becoming a problem in October 1936, especially when the scholar-thugs received official approval and police protection.[100] Police also failed to protect Jews during an antisemitic riot in Ste-Adèle in mid-August 1937. Houses occupied by Jews had their windows broken, and two houses were torched. This came two years after a violent incident (alleged by Congress to have been inspired by a local Roman Catholic priest) in Val David, in which the synagogue and its Torah scrolls were destroyed and swastikas smeared on the walls. A Jewish summer colony in Ste-Rose had to be abandoned, and the Val Morin synagogue was also daubed with swastikas. The situation for Montreal Jews vacationing in the Laurentians (notably in Ste Agathe) in the late 1930s was so menacing that the *Keneder Adler* advised its readers to 'check with the [local] priest and mayor about their attitude towards Jews before renting.'

Such trends influenced political behaviour, with Jews overwhelmingly supporting Liberal candidates in provincial elections, largely because of Premier Taschereau's accommodationist stance towards the Jewish community. There were also widespread fears of Maurice Duplessis's reactionary Union Nationale policies, as well as of the presence of antisemitic elements within his party.[101] Solidarity with the Liberals faltered briefly when Jewish voters backed Louis Fitch in a 1938 by-election; he narrowly won for the Union Nationale. But it was ethnic politics pure and simple – 'Jews were willing to abandon the Liberal party in order to have a Jewish political representative' from the governing party. A year later, however, Jewish voters elected Liberal Maurice Hartt, mainly in protest against both the premier's anti-war stance and antisemitism among some of his supporters.

The most virulent expressions of Quebec antisemitism were to be found in the small-circulation weekly newspapers, *Le Goglu*, *Le Miroir*, and *Le Chameau*. They were largely devoted to disseminating lies, cartoons, innuendo, and accusations against Jews. They included not just the standard shibboleths of Judeo-Bolshevism but also, in Abraham M. Klein's words, 'all the Judaeophobic lampoons of the Dark Ages ... They filled their papers with slander as headline, garbled quotation as footnote, and forgery as space-filler.'[102]

Klein, editor of the *Chronicle*, called for a strong and immediate Jewish response to these lies. 'The situation is serious; it merits drastic action ... The battle is in our hands, and the law courts are open,' he wrote in a July 1931 *Chronicle* editorial, urging Jews libelled in these papers to 'take immediate action, if not in their own interests, then in the interest of the Jewish community in which they play a prominent part.'

Quebec antisemitism was hardly muted by the onset of the Second World War. In an October 1939 editorial in *Le Quartier Latin*, the Université de Montréal student newspaper, Jean Drapeau, a law student (and the future mayor of Montreal) stated that Jews are

> transforming the main business artery of our city ... into a filthy carnival where rotten meat sits stacked beside stale crusts of bread, and where the sidewalks too often serve as garbage pails for decomposing fruits and vegetables; ... by bestowing on our metropolis repulsive neighbourhoods we cannot pass through without our stomachs turning; ... [and by] ruining French-Canadian business by disloyal competition, based on immoral if not openly dishonest tactics.[103]

In 1942 the anti-conscriptionists in Montreal, many of them veteran ultranationalists and active antisemites, vented their anti-Jewish venom physically in several clashes in the streets.

Quebec City, the quiet and sleepy provincial capital, produced it own special contretemps. There, a tiny Jewish community of about one hundred families encountered the first attempt made in Canada to pass municipal legislation specifically against Jews. In 1932 the community purchased a property in the west end where they wished to build a synagogue to replace the old one, which was located in the former Jewish area of town. Municipal authorities approved their plans, which would fit in with the architectural style of the neighbourhood,[104] but because of protests by a small group, the city council passed a bylaw barring new structures other than private dwellings or stores. However, several schools and hospitals were subsequently built on the same street. The Jewish community acquiesced with barely a whimper.

In 1941 it tried again. After carefully consulting the mayor and the city's legal officials, it purchased another property and obtained a building permit. But again local opposition arose, and the proposed synagogue became an issue in the municipal elections of 1942, with one candidate promising to prevent its construction. Mayor Lucien Borne was presented with petitions signed by over 7,000 Quebeckers demanding action to stop construction, alleging that a synagogue would adversely affect pupils at the nearby Jesuit college.[105] In June 1943 the city council passed a bylaw prohibiting the building of a synagogue in that district.

The city also announced that it would expropriate the property (which had been for sale for ten years before being purchased by the

Jewish community) in order to extend an adjacent park. In city council, several aldermen indicated their intention to expropriate for parks and playgrounds any other land that the Jews might buy for a synagogue. One even suggested a resolution forbidding synagogues within city limits.[106] 'Are the councillors of Quebec City aware of the fact that a war is being fought for the four freedoms?' A.M. Klein, the *Chronicle*'s editor and later a distinguished poet, asked. 'Or does Quebec fight for only three of them?' Klein could not resist having some fun with this situation:

> We do not know whether the Municipal Council of the good City of Quebec has yet seen fit to pass a resolution of gratitude to its Jewish community for being instrumental, if only indirectly, in contributing towards the scenic embellishment of that fair metropolis, but certainly such a resolution has long been overdue ... No other group of citizens ... has recently done more towards the increasing of parks and playgrounds than the Jewish community ... in its futile quest for a site for its synagogue.

The Jewish community, now thoroughly intimidated, offered to turn the property over to the city in return for a building permit anywhere in Quebec suitable to the community. The city refused and, by a narrow majority, passed an expropriation bylaw. The entire Jewish community of the province was now on the alert and so were some of its leading public figures. Premier Adélard Godbout appealed several times for tolerance. Montreal's Cardinal Villeneuve and Abbé Maheux of Quebec pleaded in the same vein. The Jewish community, building permit in hand, decided to go ahead with construction while at the same time contesting the expropriation bylaw in court. In late May 1944 the new edifice, a modest one-storey building, was completed.

On the eve of its dedication and opening, on May 25, the building was torched and suffered severe damages. The arsonists were never found. The outrage was condemned in the press, with the *Montreal Star* saying the incident had a 'Nazi odour.' Reverend Dr Claris E. Silcox, of the Canadian Council of Christians and Jews, stated that 'the act of vandalism ... is the logical sequence of the "achat-chez-nous" movement, ... the bitter antisemitic propaganda before the war and the un-Christian petitions circulated by French Canadian organizations against allowing any Jewish refugees into Canada.'

However, not a word of disapproval was heard from the provincial government or the clergy. From the editor's desk at the *Chronicle*, Klein asserted that the 'dubious honour – the burning of synagogues – which hitherto characterized only Nazi cities is now shared by the capital of our province.'[107] Attorney General Léon Casgrain uttered the lame non sequitur that 'this Province is one where freedom of worship exists in its complete form,' but everyone else was silent. The synagogue was repaired and used for many years, but the municipal council's use of legal means to deprive Jews of their basic civil rights left a lingering aftertaste. As Caiserman put it, 'Never before in the history of our country had [the] right to erect a house of worship for the citizens of the Jewish faith ... been so openly or so unashamedly suppressed or challenged.'

Meanwhile, Jews experienced growing discrimination at some universities, especially at McGill, Montreal's only English-language university, which attracted the city's Jewish youth. But Ira Mackay, dean of arts, acted on the view that 'the simple obvious truth is that the Jewish people are of no use to us in this country,'[108] and that 'as a race of men their traditions and practices do not fit in with a high civilization in a very new country.' He convinced the university's administration to limit Jewish enrolment in his faculty to 20 per cent and to require Jews to have high-school averages of 75 per cent (in contrast to 60 per cent for Gentiles). Other faculties followed suit, and by 1939 the Jewish presence had declined to about 12 per cent in arts and medicine and 15 per cent in law.

At the University of Toronto medical school, the percentage of Jewish students rose rapidly after 1920; by 1930 they constituted more than one-quarter of its undergraduates.[109] This rising number became an issue among both its senior officials and the general public, who wrote letters to complain about it. One of them referred to the university's 'Hebrew problem' and, though there was no official quota, started to keep a yearly record of Jewish enrolments. By the early 1940s, Martin Friedland explains, the faculty's admissions committee was considering the serious problem of Jews in the medical school and adopted 'discriminatory practices' to limit their numbers.

Queen's was no exception. When a small group of Jewish students began to congregate regularly in an undergraduate common room in the early 1930s, a sign appeared that read: 'We gave you Palestine; now give us back this lounge.'[110] In reaction to the increasing numbers of Jews entering the University of Manitoba medical school in the early 1930s, the faculty imposed in 1936 a severe quota on Jews, ethnic minorities, and women, regardless of academic standing. After a group of students, who were supported by some members of the faculty, informed the university's governors of these facts, the practice was stopped. Nevertheless, by 1944 Jewish enrolments had dropped drastically, from twenty-eight to nine in the first-year class. At the same university, it was equally difficult for Jews to enter engineering. One undergraduate at Manitoba remembered feeling that 'Nazi and Fascist successes in Europe and the growth of similar movements closer to home brought out latent hostility among Gentiles and made Jews more worried and defensive.'

Interning, the vital training of medical-school graduates in hospitals, however, was so restricted for Jews and other non-preferred immigrant stock that access to the major hospitals, such as the Toronto General Hospital, was nearly impossible; no Jews were on the medical staff, and only one intern per year was accepted.[111] Jewish graduates of the University of Toronto's physiotherapy program were prohibited from the clinical training program at the TGH. Severe discrimination in Montreal's hospitals compelled the community in the late 1920s to build its own hospital. Most Jewish and other minority medical graduates from Canadian universities were forced to intern in the United States. Many of them stayed there.

Jews and other 'non-preferreds'[112] were excluded from fraternities and sororities, and those who had slipped in were suddenly dropped from the rolls. Such practices were ignored by university administrations, augmenting a hostile climate. The McMaster University student newspaper, the *Silhouette*, in a January 1936 commentary on antisemitic legislation in Nazi Germany, advised caution: 'We, on this side of the Atlantic, probably do not fully realize or understand the conditions existing in Europe.' While Jews have little influence in business or the professions in North America, it continued, 'in Europe the situation is different and this difference must naturally alter opinion on the subject.' The article was entitled 'The Case for Germany.'

Jews found it impossible to secure positions in medical research and teaching at the University of Toronto, 'an institution permeated with genteel antisemitism.' Here the discoverer of insulin, Frederick Banting, had openly expressed his anti-Jewish bias.[113] By the 1930s, however, a changed Banting had 'shed his antisemitism' and publicly supported aid to Jewish refugees and a liberal Canadian immigration policy.

Obtaining one of the scarce University teaching positions during the Depression was difficult, especially for Jewish applicants. But a German Jewish refugee scholar, the meteorologist Bernhard Haurwitz, was accepted by the University of Toronto for a Carnegie fellowship leading towards a permanent position, while Gerhard Herzberg, future Nobel laureate, was turned down.[114] Leopold Infeld, a distinguished scientist from Poland, was hired there in 1938. During the Second World War, one or two Jewish mathematicians and scientists were employed at other Canadian universities, and were among the approximately twenty Jewish refugee scholars who had been on the staffs of Canadian universities since the 1930s. But there was strong resistance at McGill to the hiring of German Jewish refugee scholars.

Meanwhile, even the most promising Jewish Canadian academics, like Lionel Gelber, were excluded. A Rhodes scholar, political scientist, and future prime ministerial adviser on foreign affairs, Gelber was denied a permanent teaching position at the University of Toronto, even though he was supported by the renowned political thinker Frank Underhills,[115] who wanted Gelber as the token Jew in the history department. However, even Underhill, liberal to the core, harboured antisemitic stereotypes; in a 1938 letter of recommendation for a student applying for a Rhodes scholarship (which the student, understandably, did not win), he wrote: 'he is a Jew with a good deal of the Jew's persecution complex and this makes him unduly aggressive and sarcastic in discussion and writing.' Leon Edel, eminent scholar of Henry James, also was unemployable, while the future chief justice of the Supreme Court, Bora Laskin, in 1940 received a lectureship in the law faculty at the University of Toronto, joining Jacob Finkelman, but only after making 'an extraordinary declaration of loyalty.'

Queen's University was mildly more liberal than either McGill or Toronto. In 1938 the medical scientist Benjamin Kropp – its first Jew – was recruited to the faculty, later joined by the mathematician Israel Halperin. But an issue arose in 1943 because Jewish enrolment had jumped from 45 to 127 students since 1938 and had doubled over the previous year.[116] In 1944, Jews constituted 15.1 per cent of arts enrolments and 13.4 per cent of those in medicine, leading Principal Robert C. Wallace to express the concern that restrictions on Jews at McGill were 'send[ing] the less competent Jewish students to Queen's.' Antisemitic views were voiced at a board of trustees meetings, and the question was referred to a committee, which recommended raising admission standards all around to solve the 'problem of Jewish students.'

McGill and the University of Toronto would not admit German Jewish refugees as students, but Queen's showed a more humanitarian attitude in this, allowing in a few, including Alfred Bader and Kurt Rothschild. Remembering his reception at Queen's, Bader recalled: 'The principal, the registrar and the professors treated me with care and respect; one family, that of Professor Norman and Grace Miller, treated me with love ... Norman was not one of my teachers, but he and his family treated me most kindly ... I have no idea why I was invited there so often.'[117] In August 1942 Carleton W. Stanley, president of Dalhousie University, tried to enrol three Austrian Jewish refugees in the medical school but was stymied by the faculty, most of them downtown practitioners.

Nevertheless, these universities were not hotbeds of antisemitism, although such feelings surely existed, as did prejudice against other minorities. Despite restrictions, universities were generally forums of integration for many Jewish students. Contacts made in sports, clubs, residences, and classes led, in some instances, to lasting friendships, and even business relationships, between Jews and non-Jews. More importantly, universities provided a generation of Jewish students with the incalculable benefits of higher education, a familiarity with the best of Western culture, a sense of accomplishment at the highest levels of learning, and an entrée, albeit sometimes a problematic one, to the professions. As well, the universities fostered secularization among the first-generation Jews, who aquired skills and confidence that enabled them to become leaders in the Jewish community and to take a slowly increasing part in Canadian public affairs during and after the Second World War.

Other forms of antisemitism were also current. The Ku Klux Klan surfaced briefly in Canada in the 1920s. Materials were circulated, some directed against specific individuals, like Archie Freiman, who sued an Ottawa policeman for libel.[118] Although more of a threat to Catholics than to Jews, the Klan carried powerful antisemitic messages warning of Jewish domination in industry, corruption, plots against Christianity, and vice. With the expected appearance of the Klan in Montreal, the Jewish community was warned of 'trouble in the future on account of the large proportion of Hebrews [here],' although nothing came of the scare. The Klan's greatest Canadian success was achieved in Saskatchewan in the late 1920s, but it never struck deep roots there.

Antisemitism was present in Western Canada as well, where Jewish stores were sometimes boycotted. In Winnipeg, local storekeepers' attempts in 1921–2 to regulate Sunday shopping resulted in conflict with Jewish retailers and some expression of antisemitism. Similar conflicts arose in Toronto.[119] The nationally organized Retail Merchants Association had a pronounced nativist ideology, but only in Quebec did this result in a campaign aimed almost exclusively at Jews. When the

Alberta Social Credit Party swept into power in 1935, it carried with it a considerable baggage of antisemitism inherited from its British intellectual father, Major Clifford H. Douglas, who, in his writings, employed the imagery of the *Protocols of the Elders of Zion* to depict high finance as part of a Jewish conspiracy to control the world. The Social Credit Party was intended to free society from the grip of these international Jewish financiers and establish a monetary system based on true values. Douglas's antisemitism combined traditional Christian views with modern varieties of Jew-hatred. Even after William 'Bible Bill' Aberhart became Alberta's premier, and publicly opposed antisemitism (denouncing the lie of an international Jewish conspiracy), he nevertheless harboured certain anti-Jewish attitudes derived from Christian beliefs. It should be noted, however, that Western farmers, who disliked Eastern financial and commercial domination, had absorbed a Prairie populism that vaguely associated these institutions with Eastern Jews.

This mild antisemitic strain was infected by Douglasite virulence against the Jews. 'Antisemitism emerged among some Social Crediters ... [because], for many Albertans, Douglas provided the key to unlock the mysteries of what had gone wrong with the world economic system.' But Aberhart, who 'could have turned anti-Semitism into a dangerous political dogma,' was highly ambivalent. On the one hand, he publicly denounced antisemitism, partly because his brand of Christian fundamentalism generally 'predisposed him towards a positive view of Jews' and partly because he had a special fondness for them. On the other hand, he believed that there was a tie between certain Jews and a world banking conspiracy. Thus, in the very statements in which he condemned antisemitism, he 'included comments that sounded implicitly antisemitic.'[120]

Some Alberta Social Creditors were outspokenly prejudiced against Jews. John Blackmore, long-time MP for Lethbridge and the first house leader of the Social Credit group in the House of Commons,[121] and Norman Jaques, MP for Westaskiwin from 1935 to 1949, were virulent. The party's national organ, the *Canadian Social Creditor*, was rife with antisemitic sentiments. Within the provincial administration, a Cabinet minister and a key official openly espoused Douglas's views. In Quebec, meanwhile, the Social Credit publication *Vers demain* printed similar diatribes. Other party organs continued to publish considerable amounts of such material during the Second World War. It was not until 1948 that provincial leader and premier Ernest Manning publicly rejected Douglas's antisemitism and ousted the extremists; they, nevertheless, continued to propagate their views and influence some people.

The Politics of Marginality 323

Jew-hatred flourished among some minorities. In Winkler, Manitoba, a mainly German-speaking Mennonite farming community, antisemitism deeply affected Ernest and Robert Sirluck, who were born and raised in the town. On his first day at school, Ernest was told by fellow pupils that he 'was a dirty Jew who had killed Christ.' 'Nor did things change a great deal as I was growing up,' he recalled. 'There was always someone willing to defend Christianity, and indeed racial purity, by hitting a smaller Jew, and since I was more lightly built and less developed by hard physical labour than these sturdy Mennonites and Lutherans, most of these encounters ended with my taking more and harder blows than I was able to give.'[122]

His brother, however, took up body-building, punched out the most aggressive bully, and was never picked on again. In the 1930s, as sympathy for German Nazism flourished in Winkler, Ernest acquired a handgun and rifle and engaged in target practice deliberately in full view of his neighbours, some of whom subscribed to and publicly displayed German Nazi publications like *Der Stürmer* and *Volkischer Beobachter*. 'Everyone in town knew that I had two guns, liked using them, and usually hit what I aimed at,' Sirluck reflected. Nevertheless, after Kristallnacht, on 9 November 1938, antisemitism grew 'more virulent and menacing.'

The same poison was present in the Ukrainian community, as well. A teacher for several years in rural Saskatchewan recalled: 'The terrible old story of the ritual murder of young Christians by the Jews at Passover is an oft-repeated legend ... told to him by a small Ruthenian [Ukrainian] child.'[123]

Nevertheless, one or two Jewish general stores could be found in most of the 230 towns in the Ukrainian areas of rural Manitoba and Saskatchewan,[124] and Jews were shopkeepers in Winnipeg's ethnically diverse North End. In this area, Jewish merchants, who often undercut their competitors, were regularly patronized by Ukrainians. Despite their continuing presence, Jews sometimes were portrayed by the intelligentsia of the Ukrainian movement and by their competitors as 'intruders.' They were 'accused of using false weights and measures, selling inferior merchandise at inflated prices, writing bogus cheques, and demoralizing settlers by selling alcoholic beverages, operating hotels with beverage rooms, distributing free beer to attract new customers, and criticizing Ukrainian reading clubs and co-operative stores.'

In 1912–13 boycotts were organized against the Jews, who, according to the weekly newspaper *Ukrainsky halos*, 'have been clinging to our national organism since time immemorial, gnawing and destroying it like maggots in their capacity of tavernkeepers, village usurers and agents of political demoralization during elections.' Jews usually were depicted in pageants and plays as ridiculous and contemptible figures and 'audiences were ... left with the simplistic impression that heartless Jews, devoid of all human qualities, were somehow singularly to blame for the Ukrainian peasantry's desperate condition.' They were condemned by some religious leaders as progenitors of socialism. An Edmonton Ukrainian-language newspaper, *Klych* (The Call), edited by Anthony Hlynka, the Social Credit MP for Vegreville, was noted by the Congress to be antisemitic and filled with 'traditional Ukrainian antipathies to Jews.'[125]

However, in such a diverse community, there was no single image of the Jews. The *Ukrainian Canadian*, a Winnipeg newspaper that represented the interests of working people, was inconsistent in its attitude towards Jews.[126] A sampling of its pages in the 1920s reveals no overt antisemitism. On the contrary, one article concerning a meeting of Western Canadian Jewish teachers was very positive, concluding that 'there is more than a little that we Ukrainians could learn from these Jewish "teacher patriots."' Frequent reports from Ukraine praised Jews fighting alongside Ukrainians against the Poles in Galicia and depicted Jews as fellow sufferers under Polish domination. On the other hand, once Bolshevism became firmly rooted in Eastern Ukraine, some Jews were seen as collaborators against the Ukrainians. Reports of Soviet persecutions of Jews, meanwhile, were often sympathetic to the Jews. The overall reaction of readers is impossible to measure, of course, but letters to the editor reflect little antisemitism.

Patriotic Polish community newspapers responded strongly to Jewish charges of Polish antisemitism and pogroms, as well as to Ukrainian allegations of brutality towards their countrymen in Galicia.[127] But while Ukrainian claims for cultural autonomy in Poland were viewed as legitimate, such demands by Jews were rejected and they were viewed 'as a non-Polish element,' guilty of 'disloyal conduct and criminal behaviour.' The journalistic stance protected Polish national honour against Jewish complaints of mistreatment, which were published in the international press. The Polish-Canadian newspapers expressed strong sympathy for the Jews in Germany, speaking of 'Jewish martyrdom' after Kristallnacht. However, later numerous brief entries indicate 'that the editors' anti-Jewish attitudes had not changed.' These antisemitic feelings were often suppressed, as their 'public posture was modified to fit the realities of Canadian life.' They feared that expressions of overt antisemitism might prejudice the Canadian anglophone establishment against Polish Canadians.

A community of about forty-five thousand people in a city of more than half a million, Jews constituted Toronto's largest ethnic minority after the Irish Roman Catholics. Italians lived in the same neighbourhoods – some, indeed, in the same houses – as the Jews in 'the Ward,' an area just north of city hall, or in the crowded west end, south of Bloor Street and east of Christie Street. Polish, Ukrainian, Irish Catholic, and other ethnic communities lived there too, amid the city's overwhelming majority of Protestants of British origin.

Baseball teams met frequently for tense, hard-fought games at a west-end park called Christie Pits. Jewish and Italian players dominated several teams and earned reputations for excellent play. But these games often degenerated into epithets, insults, and fisticuffs between members of competing teams. Jewish amateur and professional boxers Nat and Max Kadin, Sammy Luftspring, Davy and 'Baby' Yack, 'Spinney' Weinreb, 'Panco' Bergstein, and many others received much the same treatment in the ring.

In mid-August 1933, after a summer's harassment from 'swastika club' members in Toronto, Jews fought a bloody four-hour battle against a group of antisemitic Anglo toughs.[128] Hundreds of Jewish youths, assisted by Italians and Ukrainians, battled the Pit Gang, a crew with a long tradition of harassing minorities in Toronto's lower west end. After a baseball game one evening between local Jewish and church teams, the Pit Gang had unfurled a large banner bearing a swastika to well-orchestrated shouts of 'Hail Hitler.' Jewish players and spectators had tried to tear the banner down. Within minutes, axe handles, lead pipes, chains, and other weapons were wielded with terrible effect by both sides. Hurriedly summoned from pool halls, smoke shops, delicatessens, street corners, club rooms, assorted drinking and gambling joints, and front verandas, Jews in the district raced to join the fight. It took repeated charges by mounted police, motorcycle squads, and a substantial force of constables swinging nightsticks to separate the Jews from the Pit Gang. Nevertheless, reinforcements for both sides kept pouring in from surrounding neighbourhoods.

Despite pleas from the mayor, several aldermen, police, and Jewish community notables urging both sides to remain calm, tension continued to mount. The swastika clubs flourished, and more ugly antisemitic incidents occurred. Jewish resentment smouldered because of these humiliations, and was compounded by daily reports in Toronto's newspapers of the persecution of German Jews by Hitler's Nazis.

All of this antisemitism must be contextualized in the bleakness of the times – the aftermath of the First World War, which left Canada a nation mourning its 60,661 dead, the bitterness of the Depression, and the prevalence of worldwide antisemitism – not to mention the open hatred expressed towards other minorities in Canada. In England, Oswald Mosley's uniformed fascist phalanxes marched through the Jewish areas of London's east end, and in the United States, a variety of militant forces were outspokenly antisemitic, with the German-American Bund even mounting pro-Nazi rallies in New York City, in the very face of the largest Jewish community in the world.

While historian Irving Abella asserts that Canada between 1920 and 1940 'was a forboding place for Jews'[129], it is well to remember that the situation could have been worse, and immigrants from Eastern Europe knew this first-hand. Did antisemitism severely intrude on the daily lives of most Jews, and did it significantly impede their progress in business, the professions, or on the shop floor? Maybe. But antisemitism was one problem faced by Jews in the 1930s, along with massive unemployment, a poor economic outlook, an absence of cash, poverty, malnutrition, anger, restlessness, and a general long-standing resentment towards all foreigners, even Englishmen. In fact, many other groups experienced hatred and, sometimes, violence. Even the antisemitism present in French Canada was partially rhetorical and, although often extremely unpleasant, did not prevent most Jews from living amid francophones in generally 'correct' relationships and often genuine neighbourliness.[130] So, although their material conditions were not adversely affected by antisemitism, in the context of the European situation, Canadian Jews were understandably apprehensive and were subject to humiliations in Ontario, where restrictive covenants (which were upheld by the courts) limited Jewish residency and where 'Gentiles Only' and 'No Jews Wanted' signs were not uncommon at resorts and private recreational areas.

Overall, however, Jews got on with their lives despite humiliations and disabilities. As Barney Danson (battlefield soldier and, later, distinguished minister of national defence) remembered, 'We didn't go around wringing our hands in anguish.'[131] Jews attended school, fell in love, raised families, enjoyed celebrations, and endured the hard times, just like other Canadians – but knowing all the while that they were different. And that antisemitism, a poison that would never die, was threatening the very lives of their kinfolk across Europe. They yearned for better times; many saw hope in Jewish national revival in Palestine.

10 'Not Complex or Sophisticated': Interwar Zionism

Messianic dreams were not confined to the far left. The Zionist ideal of building a Jewish 'national home' in Palestine, which had flourished early in the century in the Federation of Zionist Societies of Canada and various labour and women's organizations, changed significantly in the interwar era as the community continued to diversify. In the Zionist Organization of Canada (ZOC) and the Hadassah-WIZO Organization of Canada (Hadassah), both affiliated with the World Zionist Organization, younger men and women had already assumed leadership roles. At the same time, Labour Zionism was gaining strength among Jewish socialists, members of the working class, and others who supported the collectivist values and projects of the Palestine workers' movement.

Although the ZOC had its headquarters in Montreal, the president through the 1920s and 1930s was A.J. Freiman, an Ottawa department store owner,[1] generally known as Archie, who was an excellent choice for president. He made friends easily, entertained heartily, and watched over the ZOC with unswerving commitment to the cause. During his twenty years in the chair, these qualities were tested often. He and his wife, Lillian, who headed Canadian Hadassah, gave themselves unstintingly to the movement.

However, Archie was unable to attend to the affairs of this growing organization on a daily basis, and so the Montreal headquarters needed more personnel.[2] Freiman also relied heavily on regional lieutenants, including Louis Fitch of Montreal and Harry Wilder in Winnipeg. Wilder served in various capacities on the ZOC national executive.[3] He was the proprietor of the *Israelite Press*, an English-language weekly, and a Yiddish daily (*Yiddishe Vort*) that circulated in the strongly Zionist Prairie communities. Wilder did not always support ZOC policies or

Freiman's leadership. In a candid letter to Chaim Weizmann, head of the World Zionist Organization, in January 1932, Wilder suggested that Freiman 'be relieved of his [ZOC] leadership ... The height to which we Canadian Zionists have raised him (and where his money kept him) – made him somewhat dizzy. The ascent was somewhat too rapid for him. He mistook the smoke of incense which we burned at his shrine (in a spirit of jubilation, not adoration) for real clouds, above which he was soaring. I am not speaking from rancour because, personally, I like Archie ...'

Montreal and Toronto were the largest centres of Zionist activity, but in the smaller towns and cities, devoted followers ran the local campaigns, attended the national and regional conventions, sold the fifty-cent shekels that denoted official membership in the ZOC, emptied the JNF blue boxes, and, most important, organized educational programs.[4] On a per capita basis, Jews in the non-metropolitan centres were Zionism's strongest backers. In 1923–4, 60 per cent of the contributors to Keren Hayesod, the Palestine Foundation Fund dedicated to building an infrastructure of Jewish settlements in Palestine, came from the 35 per cent of the Jewish population living outside Montreal and Toronto. Most came from the West, where Zionism took on an especially fervent and independent spirit. Shekel sales, a rough indicator of participation in the ZOC, suggest that membership was inversely proportional to the total number of Jews living in each place. In centres outside of Montreal, Toronto, and Winnipeg, an overwhelming majority of Jews bought the shekel, while in the metropolitan cities only a tiny fraction did.

Even as the only truly national Jewish body from 1920 until 1934, the ZOC did not represent all shades of Jewish opinion. Outside the ZOC, which though non-ideological was middle class in orientation, many Jews were drawn to labour and religious organizations within the Zionist movement, such as Poale Zion (both its left and right factions) and Mizrachi. Unlike the ZOC, which remained stoutly independent of its American counterpart, strong links were forged between Canadian and American members of Poale Zion and Mizrachi, especially in their youth movements.[5] Indeed, many immigrants, especially those living in the large cities, avoided any Zionist affiliations, because of the proliferation of alternative organizations.

The Balfour Declaration of 2 November 1917, while eliciting emotional support from Canadian Jews, raised an important question: Was Palestine to be the national home for all Jews or just a refuge for the persecuted? Because so few had moved there, most Canadian Zionists obviously believed the latter and continued their well-established focus on fundraising.

This point was underscored at the ZOC's 1924 biennial convention in Toronto,[6] where in welcoming Chaim Weizmann, chairman Moses Gelber assured the movement's world leader that he was 'amongst warm and loyal friends and supporters,' and that Canadians realized 'the great task you have before you but we are confident that you will be successful in your work.' Gelber continued that 'Canadian Jews ... would raise the necessary funds to rebuild.' This was to be achieved by a division of labour in which the world movement set general policy, the *halutzim* (pioneers) and others in Palestine performed the actual physical labour, and Canadian Jewry raised funds, theoretically uniting all Jews in a common endeavour.

This assertion of Jewish peoplehood[7] was clearly affirmed, judging by the success of Canadian Zionism over more than thirty years. The movement thrived because it provided an immigrant population with both Jewish and Canadian identity in a largely British country with a vibrant and sizeable French-Catholic minority. It also enjoyed the approval of prime ministers, who as early as the 1900s sent regular goodwill messages,[8] at the same time politely deflecting ZOC efforts to influence British authorities on Palestine mandate matters. Prime Minister Mackenzie King appeared only occasionally at the ZOC's biennial conventions, preferring to send Cabinet ministers or supportive telegrams. Reporting to Chaim Weizmann on King's address to a 1922 gathering, Freiman exulted, 'He gave us all an inspiring message, speaking in a most glowing way of the accomplishments of Jewry generally and particularly praising the great ideal which lies at the bottom of all our work.' Even this pretense of support to a largely immigrant community legitimized Zionism as a form of Canadian Jewish identity. This was strengthened by the imperial connection. In his opening address to the 1924 ZOC convention, Freiman waxed rhapsodic on this 'joint enterprise between the British people and the Jewish people,' emphasizing the benefits of a Jewish homeland to the British Empire.[9] Loyalty to Zionism, to the British Empire, and to Canada was an attractive package deal for Canadian Jews, with no apparent drawbacks.

Canadians since 1917 had raised huge sums for the Jewish settlements in Palestine, collectively known as the Yishuv, through the Helping Hand and Restoration funds. Because Palestine was administered until 1918 by Turkey, an enemy country, these monies were sent through

American organizations. Fundraising was thriving right after the war. Lillian Freiman campaigned strenuously throughout Canada and was largely responsible for the funds' successes.[10] Clothing, food, and money were collected and dispatched through the International Red Cross. The Restoration Fund, launched in 1919, set an unprecedented goal of $250,000, an enormous sum, considering an obligation under the newly organized Canadian Jewish Congress to also aid Jews in Eastern Europe.

The wartime experience helped Canadian Zionists to reaffirm their independence from the Americans and from the world headquarters' heavy-handed direction.[11] In late 1919, Leon Goldman expressed his indignation to Shmarya Levin that American Zionists had not informed him of Canadian contributions to the funds and of shekel purchases: 'You can easily imagine the hindrance which is caused to our efforts when we appeal for funds without being able to produce public recognition of funds already remitted.' Goldman and other ZOC officers also reminded world leaders of the limitations of Canadian goodwill. In 1919 he informed Levin that contradictory communications from Jerusalem were making it difficult to get 'wholehearted support in Canada.' He also demanded that the London Zionist office notify him of recent discussions of the Actions Committee (the executive of the World Zionist Organization), 'so as to enable us ... to discuss intelligently the workings of our Organization, when we are dealing with our branches and affiliations in this Country.'[12] After receiving letters from London dunning the ZOC for money, he replied that 'Canada's Jewish community [has] its limitations[,] and its material wealth ... cannot be compared in any degree with that of our brethren in the United States of America.' He also explained that Canadians were fully aware of conditions in Eastern Europe and resented being badgered for money. They would do their best. And that would be that.

His objections were not always acknowledged, and as a result some Zionist officials touring Canada did not appreciate Canadian assertions of independence.[13] But throughout the 1920s and 1930s, officers at ZOC headquarters in Montreal bluntly told overseas Zionist officials that shrill demands for more funds, however badly needed, were simply unacceptable. Fluctuating economic conditions and serious problems directing fundraising campaigns over vast spaces made it impossible for the organization to impose quotas.

Fundraisers from abroad recognized the distinctiveness of Canadian Jewry. One visitor in 1927 commented that he felt 'a completely different atmosphere, more friendliness, more intimacy ... [in] Winnipeg and Edmonton [than in the United States],' while another observed that 'in Potage-la-Prairie [*sic*], every Jew knows he is Jewish and in what way ...'[14] Vladimir Jabotinsky, head of the Zionist Revisionists, however, was apathetic towards Canada, and after a visit in 1924 'it was coupled in his mind with Manchuria,' although on a later visit he was more favourably impressed.

Schooled for a mere fundraising role by Clarence de Sola, the ZOC retained that orientation throughout the 1920s and 1930s. This suited Canadian Jews: as financial 'foot soldiers' in the Zionist 'army,' their obligations were essentially limited to writing cheques. And though they were badly in need of money to implement practical work in Palestine, the Zionist generals in Jerusalem and London never explicitly asked Canadian Jewry for a stronger commitment.

An implicit bargain – one that has lasted to this day – was struck: Canadian Jewry's role in Zionism was to provide cash. Freiman was clear: Canadians would raise the money, and the Jews of Palestine would build the homeland. After the First World War, North American Jews had a more important role in the Zionist cause, but Weizmann and his organization still directed the movement. Freiman and his associates discussed financial and organizational matters and spent little time examining ideas, education theories, world politics, or the general philosophy of the Zionist enterprise.

Chaim Weizmann understood the relationship. In a letter in 1923, he pointed out that in contrast to British Jewry's political utility in the Zionist cause, 'it is quite another matter ... with the Jews of America who are anxious to cooperate ... [They] are not complex or sophisticated, and they are ready to take a great share in the raising of funds ... Now the only way to deal with these people is with absolute candour, and ... simplicity.'[15] While these observations reflected a growing rift between himself and some Zionists in the United States Weizmann's patronizing attitude towards the Canadians, was essentially the same, though with one minor difference: he decreed that Canada could serve, on occasion, as a backdoor link to Britain.

Weizmann, in fact, was not above using Canadian Zionists as channels for petty espionage. In late 1922, he asked Freiman to gather 'interesting information with regard to Lord Beaverbrook's antecedents, which might, in certain circumstances, be of great value.'[16] Irritated by the anti-Zionist tirades in Beaverbrook's *Daily Express*, Weizmann wondered whether 'some of the leading Canadian Zionists ... could not ... intimate to Lord Beaverbrook that as Canadian Jews, they have watched the malevolent campaign which he is conducting with amazement and indignation.' Loyal to his chief, Freiman did his best to comply.

Weizmann also tried to exploit Canada's imperial connection to Britain. In 1928 he urgently requested that Freiman arrange a meeting between the president of the Zionist Organization of America, Louis Lipsky, and the British colonial secretary, Lord Amery.[17] In September 1936 he cabled Freiman requesting that he entreat Mackenzie King and Governor General Lord Tweedsmuir to protest British policy restricting Jewish immigration to Palestine. 'I spent over two hours with [King] at his summer residence. While it was obvious that he was extremely sympathetic towards our cause, for political reasons his hands were tied,' Freiman reported. On another occasion, Freiman briefly outlined 'the present political crisis in Zionism' and asked King to 'use his influence on our behalf.' Nothing came of these overtures.

While generous financial help was given, a deeper and more positive Zionist experience was disregarded by the leaders, thus discouraging any cultural renaissance. And so few cultural dimensions existed, except within Poale Zion, Mizrachi, and the youth movements. Consequently, Zionism in Canada produced only a handful of intellectuals able to influence the leadership of the ZOC.

The women who successfully ran the First World War campaigns were drawn largely from the Hadassah.[18] In centres large and small, these women worked fervently for several specific Palestine causes, such as the Girls' Domestic and Agricultural Science School at Nahalal, a nurses' training school in Jerusalem, a convalescent home, and a tubercular hospital. They held raffles, bazaars, teas, and tag days to raise money. With their practical work for Palestine and dedication to Jewish women and children, they united thousands of members across Canada to join in this work. Jewish women took up a specific female agenda within the movement for Jewish national revival.[19]

If Zionism in Canada ever had a vanguard, it was the women of Hadassah, especially in Western Canada.[20] At the 1924 ZOC convention, a Western delegate reported that

> in ... Winnipeg – and in many cities through the West – ... the women are almost frantically active. When it is considered that the two [Winnipeg] chapters, ... have some 600 members, embracing all classes and sections of our population, the wealthiest as well as the poorest; that they meet with religious regularity; that they display a degree of enthusiasm

and devotion heretofore unsuspected and unhoped for ... the 'mothers in Israel' have that future in their keeping.

Lillian Freiman, in the spirit of the 'new womanhood,' always referred to Hadassah members as 'sisters,' to their efforts as 'our hands joined in true sisterly love and endeavour,' and to the collectivity as 'our Jewish womanhood.' In her opening statement to the 1924 Hadassah convention, she linked Hadassah and other female expressions of Zionism to a broad embodiment of women's self-awareness. 'The flame,' she said, 'that has swept through the ranks of our womankind and sent them rallying round the standard of Zionism, is the same flame that has raised women the world over to the heights of martyrdom and of heroic achievement.'[21] She quoted Theodor Herzl's statement: 'When the women will be with us, then will our cause indeed be won.'

Rank-and-file members of Hadassah (renamed Hadassah-WIZO) in chapters across the country felt these bonds of sisterhood and saw themselves essentially as exponents of a new Jewish woman's identity.[22] Their dual role was to rebuild their national home in Palestine and to 'promote the health and welfare of women and children' there. With the slogan 'The Healing of the Daughter of My People' as its emblem, Hadassah devoted itself both to fundraising for women's health and educational and social welfare projects, and to elevating women's consciousness in Canada and Palestine.

In the late 1930s, reacting to the leaders' hesitation in bringing endangered Jewish children from Germany and Austria to Palestine, Hadassah women formed their very own rescue organization, called Youth Aliyah. Toronto's *Hadassah Reporter Magazine* complained in January 1939 that 'some infection must be drying up the channels of pity in Jewish life when Jewish fathers who could, with the stroke of a pen[,] lift a child from hopelessness to happiness have failed to do so.'[23] These women, together with sister groups around the world, aggressively raised money for Youth Aliyah and moved thousands of children to Palestine during the 1930s and 1940s. As mothers themselves, they knew the cause was indeed urgent. By 1938 three thousand children were arriving annually in Palestine, and in subsequent years numbers increased substantially.[24]

Youth Aliyah and numerous other health projects for women and children funded in part by Canadian Hadassah became models of dedication and efficiency. Because most members were middle-class, they had the resources to embark on fundraising campaigns, and an educational program which emphasized 'ideals of womanhood' and equal citizenship with men. In October 1939, the *Hadassah Reporter Magazine* observed: 'Both as women and as Jews we have had a long and hard struggle for equal rights as citizens. If this hard won position is not to be lost, we must assume with seriousness and sincerity our responsibilities as Jews and as citizens.'[25]

Labour Zionist women mobilized for their own causes. Pioneer Women, a group formed in Toronto in 1925 as a branch of an American organization, had an explicitly feminist and socialist-Zionist agenda. It drew a mostly young, secularist, working-class element, often recent immigrants, who, because they were poor and 'green,' felt uncomfortable with Hadassah.[26] Many were attracted to the collectivist outlook of the movement, which also 'provided its first generation of members and many of their daughters with an important social outlet and source for the learning and development of numerous skills.' Often drawn to the unionist cause, these women embraced this philosophy of Labour Zionism. 'We are socialists' one member wrote, 'not only in Palestine. We seek a life of social justice and equality, of creative living not only in Palestine, but in every land where human beings are conscious of society.' With a cultural program in Yiddish that included classes on literature, history, Yiddish and Hebrew folk-songs, Zionism, politics, medicine, children, and education, the Pioneer Women's movement became an important force on the Zionist left, advancing 'the creative activities of the working woman and working mother,' and promising that 'with the awakening of the will to create our own national life, there will come to the fore a tangible expression of the power and force of women.' More groups were formed in Toronto in the 1930s, and in 1939 its first English-speaking club emerged, consisting of daughters of the founders and graduates of the Farband (Labour Zionist) Folk Schule and Young Poale Zion. The movement spread to other cities, and Pioneer Women was the organization where immigrants found a comradely, family-like atmosphere.

Zionist enthusiasm flourished also in Young Judaea, essentially the youth branch of the ZOC. Despite having the example of its founder, Bernard (Dov) Joseph, who had joined the Jewish Legion in 1918 and immigrated to Palestine in the early 1920s, the organization never officially espoused *Aliyah* (emigration) as a goal for its members. Rather, it remained essentially what the ZOC hoped it would be: an educational force among Jewish youth, used – as one enthusiast wrote – 'to instil in the young a loyalty to the Jewish people and its glorious traditions; to inculcate a devotion to the Jewish homeland in Palestine and an appreciation of the Zionist aim and willingness to serve in the cause for the reestablishment of the Jewish Nation on its own soil.' Zionism, then, was seen as a broad educational vehicle 'to bring our Jewish youth under the influence of Jewish ideals and to improve them with sentiments of love and loyalty to all that is characteristically Jewish.'[27]

Some Judaeans, with the zeal and certainty of youth, believed Zionism required a deeper commitment. Phillip Joseph (brother of Bernard), when made president in 1924, told the ZOC convention that 'we haven't the money to contribute, and I do not know that we could raise it, but we have human lives to contribute, and these we have contributed. In the City of Montreal there were seventeen Young Judaeans, and they are already in Palestine, living there and,' he added for emphasis, 'not coming back.' This was the ultimate commitment – *Aliyah* to Palestine. 'There are others in Montreal who may leave within three months,' he continued. 'I do not know their value in dollars and cents, but to me they are worth more than dollars and cents, because you can't buy them.'[28] Phillip Joseph went to Palestine, like his brother Dov, to serve as an example to other Young Judaeans.

But to the ZOC leadership, Young Judaea's primary functions remained education and fundraising. Joseph thus found it necessary to defend his organization on those grounds alone. 'We are looking after the young,' he exulted at the convention. 'It is a good investment ... [because] the Young Judaeans are the future Canadian Jews ... good Canadian Zionists in [the] future.' Therefore, more money would be collected. 'Look what Young Judaea has done, what you have collected from them for Keren Hayesod ... Therefore I say give us $10,000 and we will give you $20,000.' This was the one statement that earned Joseph the applause of the delegates.

Abraham M. Klein, editor of Young Judaea's 1931 yearbook, searched for the middle ground. He carefully defined Young Judaeans as 'Canadian Jewish Youth consciously aware of [their] Jewishness ... concerned with that difficulty, which was proved to be the *pons asinorum* of twenty centuries, but which now for the first time seems to be nearing a definite solution: the ubiquitous Jewish Problem.'[29] Concerning *Aliyah*, he presciently recognized that 'due to the favorable economic conditions, and the mentality of Jewish Youth, a *Chalutz* (pioneering in Palestine) movement in America is so obviously futile that it needs no proof.'

Even so, Klein believed that Palestine's culture could be brought to Canada: 'The purpose of Young Judaea is thus an attempt to overlap, through education, the several thousand miles which separate us from Palestine.' Canada's Jewish youth had 'a curved ghetto spine.' Young Judaeans must become 'spiritual chalutzim' in Canada and create an appropriate environment for nurturing 'a race consciousness ... [to] be born out of a nation's will-to-live ... We must be the masters of our own fate!' He concluded, 'Jewish life, as at present constituted, with its barrenness, and emptiness, its utter meaninglessness, its haphazard activity, stands as an imperious challenge to Canadian Jewish Youth.'

By the mid-1920s, clubs had sprung up all over Canada; a national organization had been established in 1919, and a full-time director hired in 1924. Though in competition from *chalutz* movements which emphasized *Aliyah*, Young Judaea's undefined ideology was less demanding. Most Jewish youth could affiliate without causing parental concern that they would emigrate.

The weekly educational program consisted of lectures and discussions of Jewish history and current events, as well as 'readings from Jewish literature, the singing of national and traditional melodies, the celebration of Jewish festivals, dramatic presentations and debates' and some athletic events. But one early handbook distributed to group leaders advised that the teaching of Jewish history 'must be made to illustrate present day tendencies in Jewish life ... and must be made to give the clearest conception of the inherent instability and the tragic waste of Golus' [exile's] life.'[30] Largely financed by the ZOC, Young Judaea mirrored its organizational characteristics, including biennial and regional conferences, transnational social contact, and the aura of middle-class benevolence.

Fundraising soon became all-absorbing, most notably with Jewish National Fund (JNF) collection boxes. This excessive emphasis, however, soon gave rise to serious reservations. In 1927, Lionel M. Gelber of Toronto warned that if Young Judaea's principal educational role was to continue, it must not 'deflect its energies into the channels of practical Zionism ... Young Judaea must not lose sight of its main purpose.'[31]

Louis Rasminsky, the Young Judaea president in 1927 (and a future governor of the Bank of Canada), echoed Gelber's concerns. To him, the organization's role was to rescue an entire generation of Jewish youth from widespread indifference towards and ignorance of Jewish culture and history. 'It is tragic,' he wrote, 'that precisely at this time the Jewish youth should ... cease to be interested in its Jewish heritage and cut itself entirely adrift from any form of constructive Jewish life.' At a time when the detrimental forces of 'neglect by parents, the [North] American environment, the overwhelming spirit of the age – the weakening of all Jewish traditional bonds' were impacting on Jewish youth, fundraising should not overtake the main goal of education.

In Toronto and southwestern Ontario, these ideas were translated into intensive activity, with Young Judaeans raising money to buy books on Jewish history, culture, and religion for their libraries. By 1927, Toronto had thirty-three clubs, with some 650 members across the city. Hamilton, Brantford, Kitchener, and London, as well as other cities across the province, also had active groups. The organization flourished in Montreal, and throughout the Maritimes, Young Judaea clubs cemented ties among Jewish youth. Clubs in large and small western cities prospered. Young Judaea's impact on the isolated youth of the smaller centres was profound.

Other youth associations proliferated in the 1920s and 1930s, to reawaken a Jewish consciousness. The most prominent were Hashomer Hatzair (Young Guard), Hechalutz Hatzair (Young Pioneers), Zeire Zion (Young Zion), Young Mizrachi, and Gordonia (followers of the early pioneer A.D. Gordon).[32] In concert with their sister groups in Palestine, these organizations emphasized their own particular brand of Zionist ideology.

Hashomer Hatzair stands out in this respect. It espoused a Marxist ideology (which seemed at variance with its dedication to Zionism), rigid discipline, and a personal commitment to building a collectivist society in Palestine. Organized in Montreal in 1923, Hashomer Hatzair advertised itself as 'the Jewish Youth for the Jewish Nation ... defenders of the National Home ... a bulwark against assimilation ... Hashomer wants your souls.'[33] Its program proclaimed that 'the building up of Palestine is ... imposed on our youth of the present.' Rebelling against capitalism and materialism, the members, who called themselves *shomrim* (guards), were committed to *Aliyah* and saw themselves as the vanguard of a national renaissance, and as militant socialists living lives of selfless idealism and collectively rebuilding the homeland with their own sweat and blood.

The Montreal group was the strongest in North America. In 1931 it supplied five of the six *shomrim*, most of them women, going to Palestine. They were the first North Americans who were among the founders of Kibbutz Ein Hashofet.[34] A few years later, they were joined by nine other Montreal *shomrim*. 'We wanted to be pioneers. We wanted to build a country,' the early settler Celia Cohen recalled. 'It seemed then – and even now in memory – a nobler ideal than the desire to "make it" in America,' another *shomer* remembered. Propelled by Zionist and socialist zeal, Hashomer Hatzair also established groups in Toronto, Winnipeg, Hamilton, and Ottawa during the 1930s. In ensuing years, the movement sent hundreds of *shomrim*, mostly women, from Canada. Perhaps as women, without strong career concerns, they were better able to retain the integrity of Zionism's quasi-religious vision, and were attracted to this new egalitarian society. Their example stood as both a reminder and a reproach to cheque-book Zionists. Their songs evoked a romantic declaration of their zeal to make the world anew. Some of them, however, defeated by the Spartan conditions and extreme dangers, eventually returned home in disappointment.

Youth organizations committed to other ideologies also emerged, among them Betar (an acronym for Brith Trumpeldor, named in memory of Joseph Trumpeldor, who fell in defence of Tel Hai in 1921). This movement, which spread throughout Central and Western Europe during the 1920s under the inspiration of the intellectual and soldier Vladimir Jabotinsky, emphasized Jewish pride and military training, and intended to transform 'the Jew of the Diaspora into a fighter.'[35] Habonim (the builders), a youth branch of Poale Zion, established groups in Montreal, Toronto, and Winnipeg, where it became a thriving and influential organization that stressed *Aliyah* and *chalutziut* (kibbutz).

Zionist fundraising peaked in the 1920s. However, financial commitments to aid Eastern European Jews and support local projects competed with the Zionist endeavours. Canadian Jews gave generously and believed themselves to be ahead per capita of their American cousins. Just after the Keren Hayesod (Foundation Fund) was launched in 1921 to finance and coordinate the Jewish settlement in Palestine, Shmarya Levin, its chief spokesman in North America, visited Canada to help plan a vigorous national campaign.[36] He persuaded the ZOC to raise a million dollars with an appeal to 'Jews of Canada to rally to the glorious cause of laying the foundation of a true Jewish homeland in Palestine.' In the United States, however, the Zionist Organization of America (ZOA) sharply objected to the Keren Hayesod's mandate. ZOA president and United States Supreme Court Justice Louis D. Brandeis, who viewed Zionism as a progressive movement for American Jewry, objected to what he believed was the inefficient management of the Keren Hayesod. But these reservations found no echo in Canada. Unlike the United

States, Zionism had no organized opposition in Canada, although, occasionally, certain prominent Canadians publicly attacked specific features of Zionist philosophy.

One such opponent was Maurice Eisendrath, an American who had been rabbi of Toronto's Holy Blossom Temple since 1929 and was a prominent activist in the Canadian peace movement.[37] Like many Reform rabbis of his era, Eisendrath believed that Zionism weakened Jewish integration into Canadian life. His anti-Zionist sermons, public speeches, and articles in the *Canadian Jewish Review* – a weekly – asserted that Zionists were like 'our oppressors [who wish] to incarcerate us once more! ... The anti-Semite and the extreme and fanatical Jewish nationalist have much in common.' He later compared young Zionists with 'storm troopers or Komsomols' and asserted that 'Jewish nationalism [was] ... as dangerous to the essential spirit of the Jew as Fascism, Communism and Hitlerism are to the essence of Christianity.' These denouncements infuriated and sometimes outraged some of his congregants.[38] The Ontario Hadassah leader, Rose Dunkelman, decided to publish her own weekly newspaper, the *Jewish Standard*, to counter the *Review*, and hired Meyer Weisgal from New York as editor. Weisgal battled not only against Eisendrath in print and in weekly debates at Holy Blossom, but also against the Revisionists (opponents of Chaim Weizmann's policies), who were gaining strength in the late 1920s.

There were also persistent attacks on Zionism by Communists, who used terminology such as 'Jewish fascists' and 'Zionist fascists' to describe both members of the ZOC and Jewish socialists who were critical of the Soviet Union in the 1920s.[39] Such language was intended to highlight the association of Zionism with the Jewish bourgeoisie, as well as condemn rabbis whose class interests opposed those of the Jewish workers. As an editorial in *Der Kamf* stated in October 1929:

> In the Jewish milieux, we see a united front of the yarmulka (skull cap) with the Zionist and with the yellow 'socialist.' They hold their class interests under one roof ... The revolutionary worker rips the masks off both the parasitic rabbi and the laborite, and in their nakedness they lock hands against the only workers' republic where the workers are tearing off their earthly and heavenly chains. The rabbi and laborite and the Zionist decide on a fascist front against the conscious workers.

Sometimes Communists also linked Zionism together with British imperialism as collaborating opponents of the Palestinian Arab national liberation movement. Instead, the Jewish Communists supported 'a homeland' and settlement in the Soviet Union, in Birobidjan, to end the curse of Jewish homelessness. However, such anti-Zionist attacks ceased during the mid-1930s when the Communists focused on fighting fascism through the Popular Front, in which, they believed, all Jewish factions should stand united.

Such critiques of Zionism had little effect on the rank-and-file of the ZOC and Hadassah. They happily supported a movement that did not promote *Aliyah*. Among the few who departed for Palestine between the world wars, the most famous was Bernard (Dov) Joseph, who had become a prominent Jerusalem lawyer and rising star in the inner councils of the Jewish Agency. A few less-renowned individuals had gone up to Palestine. Some had bought small farms with the help of the Keren Kayemeth (Jewish National Fund) in Jerusalem. 'My thoughts frequently turn Eastward,' wrote Dr M.S. Rady from Winnipeg to the Keren Kayemeth's Menachem Ussishkin in 1929, 'wondering whether some day I will be able to emigrate there, and participate in the actual upbuilding of our Home Land ... Some day when I decide to take this step, I would like to feel that I am the owner of a small section of land, on which there is already a house where I could immediately go and live ... There in Palestine, you are enjoying the fairest of weather and bathing in the happy rays of the Eastern Sun.'[40] Thus a Jew living in the midst of Canada's own Eden dreamed of a rural arcadia in a promised land he barely knew.

Personally, however, the ZOC executive director, Rabbi Judah Zlotnick, thought many Canadian Jews should move to Palestine. After a visit in the summer of 1931, he wrote, 'it is time, I believe, for all lovers of Zion to come into closer contact with our country, or at least bring their children and their families closer to Eretz Israel [the land of Israel].'[41] He called on Canadian Jews to settle on orange farms in the Emek Hepher (an extensive area of Palestine that was purchased in 1927), both to build the national home and to secure their own financial position and that of their families. Only a very determined few followed Zlotnick's example, as the hardships of life in Palestine were daunting. In any event, the ZOC did little to encourage such enthusiasm. When several Montreal members of Hashomer Hatzair petitioned the ZOC to support their *Aliyah* in 1931, the sceptical National Council appointed a special committee 'to see that they are of the right and proper type.'

Whether they went as pioneers on the kibbutzim, as small farmers, or to the cities, there was only a trickle of Canadian immigrants to Palestine through the 1930s and early 1940s. Aside from members of Hashomer Hatzair who underwent a year of agricultural instruction on *hachshara* (special training farms) in the United States, the ZOC took little notice; as late as January 1936, it did not know how many Canadians were on these farms.[42] Even Hechalutz, the organizational arm that trained thousands of Diaspora youth for agricultural life in Palestine, did not establish a branch in Canada, probably aware of poor prospects. And the ZOC's focus on fundraising offset *Aliyah*.

However, the ZOC did support some individuals, like Max Adilman of Saskatoon, who had moved to Palestine. 'The fact that Adilman is settling [there] will have not only a moral effect on Canadian Jewry in general,' Zlotnick wrote to Menachem Ussishkin, the JNF head in Jerusalem, but he believed it would also influence some well-to-do Western Canadian Jews who might be persuaded to settle in Palestine.[43] The major Canadian investor in Palestine was Asher Pierce of Montreal. He believed that Canadian Jews – and those from other Western countries – should bring their ideas and capital to build up the Yishuv. In 1927 he established the Gan Chayim Corporation to develop orange plantations on the Sharon Plain, and also built a house on his own estate, which he called Tel Asher (Asher's Hill). Pierce was also involved in other development projects. Similar investments by Canadian Jews signalled a continuing financial interest well before the Second World War and foreshadowed their considerable investment after Israel's establishment in 1948.

While still not publicly encouraging it, the ZOC was helpful to those contemplating *Aliyah*. Indeed, emigration was hindered, especially during the late 1930s, as only a limited number of permits were issued. In April 1936, ZOC official Rabbi Jesse Schwartz wrote to the Jewish Agency asserting that 'Canada is entitled to a certain amount of consideration and we would ask you to do everything possible to give us the skilled labour certificate referred to.'[44] In view of the German refugee crisis, however, Canada's claims were ignored. The year before, Schwartz had tried to get two or three certificates for young women intending to make *Aliyah*. Seventeen-year-old Ben Dunkelman, understanding Zionism to mean *Aliyah*, moved to a kibbutz in 1931 and again in 1935, but eventually gave in to parental pressure and returned to Toronto. Though ardent Zionists, Rose and David Dunkelman obviously believed that Canadian Jews should contribute money, not their lives or their children, to the enterprise. Two women who went on *Aliyah* in the 1930s, Molly Lyons Bar-David and Sylvia Gelber, wrote superb memoirs of experiences during their transition to the difficult life of Palestine.[45]

The first Keren Hayesod campaign, which typified ZOC fundraising, was launched in May 1921 with considerable fanfare. Chaim Weizmann and Yiddish orator Shmarya Levin also visited several Canadian cities. Weizmann's memoirs provide a revealing account of his impressions:

> A big donor would often make his contribution to the fund conditional on my accepting an invitation to ... his house. Then I would have to face a large family gathering – three or four generations – talk, answer questions, listen to appeals and opinions, and watch my replies carefully, lest I inadvertently scare off a touchy prospect. I would sit through a lengthy meal and after it meet a select group of local celebrities; and again listen and answer till all hours of the night. Generally, I felt that I had fully earned that five thousand dollars[46]

While harrowing for Weizmann, his visit was a triumph for the cause. Wherever he went, masses of Jews congregated, moved by his personality and message. Yet even he could not breathe life into a campaign that faltered in the recession of the early 1920s. Only one-fifth of the million-dollar target was raised, and local campaign chairmen reported that economic conditions prevented further collections. Archie Freiman wrote Weizmann of his disappointment at being unable to collect on pledges because of the downturn in business.[47]

Zionist officials in London, however, were not sympathetic. 'The position in Palestine is exceedingly critical,' wrote one in November 1922, 'and for a country like Canada to discontinue its regular remittances for months at a time is a very bad sign.'[48] Long used to such reprimands, Leon Goldman dispatched a peppery reply, attacking these 'dunning methods,' objecting to excessive expectations, and warning London to back off. Circumstances in Canada were so critical, he cautioned, that many Jews were reduced 'to a condition of receiving, instead of giving.' Heavy pressure overseas, continued, however, and Freiman reluctantly agreed to mount a follow-up campaign. It began in early 1923 with a tour led by Colonel A.H. Patterson, who as commander of the Zion Mule Corps at Gallipoli and, later, a battalion of the Jewish Legion, was a hero to many Jews, who might open their wallets to him.

The Patterson tour was a success, especially in the West. Reporting from Winnipeg in February 1923, an official who was accompanying him wrote: 'If the big Jewish communities of Eastern Canada would contribute on the same proportion, the result would be an extraordinary one.'[49] But the East came up short. The economic situation there was so bad, an official reported, that 'the rich are keeping aloof from ... Jewish affairs. Even the local charitable institutions suffer very much ... In Zionist affairs one notices a mighty wave of pessimism and depression ... general apathy and indifference.'[50] So serious was the fall-off in philanthropy in Montreal that Rabbi Herman Abramowitz of Shaar Hashomayim synagogue publicly attacked the city's Jewish plutocrats (many of them his own congregants) for this lack of generosity. Montreal's leaders were, as Rabbi Abramowitz put it, like King Saul hiding in their tents, afraid to fight in defence of Israel. By late April, the campaign was still faltering. Weak leadership in Montreal not only bedevilled most campaigns throughout the 1920s but also, by poor example, affected the rest of the country. Montreal was so short of canvassers that Lillian Freiman came down from Ottawa to help out, but results rose only slightly, from disgraceful to merely poor. Even Louis Fitch and Michael Garber were unable to activate Montreal Zionists. Possibly, the ideological, class, and economic differences in that community affected the Zionist climate there.

Keren Hayesod's campaign in 1924 was no better, leading to an exchange of increasingly acrimonious letters between London officials and the ZOC.[51] This long-lasting tension was compounded by a dispute between the Keren Hayesod and the JNF over Canadian contributions. The ensuing debate between Montreal and London officials rapidly became abrasive. Behind all of this controversy was the perception among world Zionist leaders that Canadian Jews were underachieving. In early January 1924, Weizmann assessed the Canadian situation for the London directors of Keren Hayesod: 'Canada could raise for the *Keren Hayesod* much more than it has done; although trade is not flourishing they could certainly make a much better effort.' With quite astonishing hauteur and lack of understanding of current economic conditions, he claimed that Canadian Jews 'get their money in fairly easily,' and asserted that 'they could easily raise double if the three leading spirits of Canadian Zionism, Freiman, Levin, and Fitch[,] would apply themselves to the task. If Archie Freiman goes to Winnipeg he can raise double what Winnipeg gives now and it would be nothing but a pleasant trip for him. The same is applicable to any other city.'

Weizmann's expectations were shared by touring Keren Hayesod and JNF officials. David Rebelsky visited a number of Canadian cities on behalf of the Zeire Zion, a moderate socialist-labour movement, and reported to London in March 1925: 'I think like you that even under the present conditions, it is possible to obtain larger sums in Canada.'[52] The efforts, he asserted, were marginal in Montreal, Toronto, and Winnipeg, where 120,000 of the country's 130,000 Jews lived. He calculated that, comparatively, in the smaller places twenty-five times the amount was raised per capita. They needed better organization to tap the potential and handle the funds. Equally important, in Rebelsky's view, was the lack of Zionist propaganda, leaving local organizations floundering. But he stressed that 'the human material of Jews is better here than in any other country,' a compliment to the high level of Jewish culture in Canada.

The growth of the Canadian Keren Hayesod, however problematic, eclipsed the earlier prominence of the Jewish National Fund (JNF). By 1921 its Canadian receipts had fallen to only one-seventh of the 1918 figures.[53] The ensuing recession taxed these small, scattered communities to both meet their million-dollar commitment to the Keren Hayesod and support the JNF. Leon Goldman explained to JNF officials that in this situation, he had refrained from a campaign, 'owing to the destitute conditions of the poorer classes.'

Rabbi Zlotnick a few years later, however, increased receipts for the JNF, and exploited its use as a Zionist educational tool. But like Leon Goldman, he was forced to rebuke the head office, on their faulty perception both of Canada and its money-raising potential.[54] Undeterred by such reprimands, officials objected that Canadian Zionists had belittled the JNF. In February 1924, Goldman was forced, once again, to send a tart reply: 'You must leave the running of affairs in this Dominion, to the discretion of the Zionist Organization here and rely on its judgement as dependable ... instead of the repeated and unwelcome officious rebuke and faultfinding ... [and] over-frequent campaigning.'[55] Unconvinced, the JNF replied from Jerusalem that 'we cannot for a moment accept the view that Canadian conditions are so different that, alone of fifty-one countries, it must be allowed to carry on its JNF work independent of the Head Office.'

Until the 1920s, the JNF had collected modest sums from the sale of stamps and tree certificates, registrations in the JNF Golden Book, and contributions to the blue boxes in many homes. Rabbi Zlotnick, however, pitched appeals to the wealthy for large donations.[56] He emphasized the hundred-dollar Golden Book subscriptions and contributions to the Land Fund during a special High Holidays appeal in 1924 and 1925, with a modest success.

However, the blue boxes to collect money for land purchase remained the most popular and successful JNF activity.[57] The idea of buying land and planting trees in Palestine had both a practical and a sacred appeal. As well, it was an excellent device with which to explain Zionist ideals to the community, especially to children. Supported by Hadassah and Young Judaea, the boxes were placed all over the country; Zlotnick reported that the number of centres using them increased from twenty-six in 1923 to forty-two in 1925, and that the income from them rose threefold.

Enthusiasm was especially strong out West. In Winnipeg by the mid-1920s, a voluntary 'amusement tax' was levied on all Jewish dances, theatre performances, bridge parties, and other gatherings.[58] Blue boxes were circulated at weddings and bar mitzvahs, and placed in thousands of homes and businesses. Zionist educational material, mostly about pioneering in Palestine, was distributed, some of it written especially for Western Canadians. Dozens of small towns and villages with Jewish populations were canvassed. 'A Penny a Day Will Drive the Golus [Exile] Away' was one of the slogans printed on cards and circulars. In Winnipeg, teenagers initiated monthly collections and raised large amounts of money. So successful were these campaigns that suggestions were made that the Canadian JNF office be moved to Winnipeg. Eastern Zionists, however, were not amused.

Despite this general growth in JNF revenues, officials in Jerusalem continued to chastise Canadian Zionists.[59] The headquarters still set quotas and made invidious comparisons (Canada was usually matched with South Africa, which sent much higher per capita contributions) in an unrelenting barrage of letters directing Canadians to do their duty. Under this mounting pressure, Canadians became focused almost purely on fundraising. With the return of prosperity in Canada, by 1927, remittances surpassed $50,000 per year, with Winnipeg producing half of the national blue-box collections.

Encouraged by this improvement, Jerusalem officials campaigned to have Canada raise a million dollars to buy a block of land on the Sharon Plain north of Tel Aviv at Emek Hepher, a large tract of uninhabited sand and swamp. When the Freimans visited Palestine briefly in the spring of 1927, Menachem Ussishkin, head of the JNF, solicited and received their promise of help. Back in Canada, the Freimans lobbied other Zionists, and Ussishkin himself even appeared and persuaded the ZOC to commit themselves to raising a million dollars over the next seven years.[60] But the Depression intervened and by late 1929 the obligation had become overwhelming. While $300,000 had already been sent, most of these monies were bank loans to the ZOC advanced against future revenue from drives that were faltering now. Faced with commitments of $100,000 annually for seven years, the ZOC was in serious trouble. A 1928 campaign brought in a mere $230,000 in pledges. Of this, the JNF would get only two-fifths. By the spring of 1929, Ussishkin was desperately begging the Canadians to honour their commitment.[61] Some money was sent, but the Canadians, so deeply in debt to the banks, were 'finding [it] difficult to pay up, on account of the present depressing financial times.' Zlotnick wrote pointedly to Ussishkin that 'your continual urging us to make remittances is of no avail, and only serves to strain the relations existing between your office and our Zionists.'

The financial situation in Canada made it impossible to approach the banks for more loans. Zlotnick wrote, 'Our collections have been very poor.'[62] A year later, with the JNF still owing money on its bank loans and now $200,000 in arrears on its commitment, Archie Freiman informed Ussishkin: 'It is absolutely useless to talk about borrowing $100,000. There is not a bank in Canada that would advance us this amount at the present time, and even if we could get it, we have no moral right to accept it until we are more certain as to the results we will achieve in the near future.' The tension and bitterness between the financially strapped Canadians and the insistent Jerusalem officials continued until 1937 when, at last, the final payment was painfully made.

Unity was rare in Zionist ranks. Mizrachi, the religious Zionist organization that emerged in Canada in the interwar years, hampered the ZOC's fundraising campaigns. Displeased with the ZOC allocations, Mizrachi's Canadian supporters in 1920 demanded 'that a certain percentage of the total amount collected [in Canada] should go to the *Mizrachi* Fund, Keren Eretz Israel.'[63] Still unsatisfied, in 1928, Mizrachi inaugurated its own campaign, conflicting with the JNF and Keren Hayesod. The *Keneder Adler* observed that this was an inopportune time 'to institute a further campaign for Zionist purposes,' and that 'this would certainly prejudice the interests of the Keren Hayesod.' Worse still was that the Mizrachi leaders allegedly 'made a violent attack on the *Haluzim*, the builders of Palestine,' pointing out that they ate *trayf* (unkosher food) and violated the Sabbath.

Mizrachi's appeal was strong, given the belief, as expressed by one community leader, 'that the majority of Canadian Jewry are eager to see Palestine rebuilt in the spirit of Jewish traditions and along religious lines.'[64] Zlotnick, himself an Orthodox rabbi, believed that 'the greatest majority of Canadian Jewry are favoring the orthodox mode of life.' Mizrachi's ongoing independent fundraising campaigns elicited bitter comment in the Jewish press, as well as continuing resistance from the ZOC. But the ZOC wanted Mizrachi support for the Emek Hepher project and advised Jerusalem, 'It is our opinion that it would be most judicious and beneficial to our cause that as many as possible of the religiously inclined element should be settled there.' Noted Zlotnick: 'This is especially important from the point of view of propaganda in Canada ... [S]uch a Mizrachi settlement should be organized at the earliest possible moment.' In 1940 their representative in Canada tried to inaugurate a separate campaign on the eve of a nationwide drive for the United Palestine Appeal, which combined Keren Hayesod with other projects. But a Montreal ZOC leader complained: 'Discipline in the Zionist ranks was not to be expected from Mizrachi.'

Revisionists – followers of Vladimir Jabotinsky's breakaway from the World Zionist Organization – who opposed the WZO's gradualism and willingness to compromise, began organizing in Canada in 1926, during Jabotinsky's North American tour.[65] While the turnout to his lectures was small, a few enthusiasts were recruited. During a tour of Canada in 1935, however, he received a warmer reception and favourable comment in the Jewish press. Toronto's *Hebrew Journal* stated that Jabotinsky 'deserves to be heard with all due respect,' while the *Keneder Adler* regarded his criticisms of Weizmann as 'salutary and necessary.' The *Chronicle* argued that 'we should re-study the many important issues that the Revisionists have raised and decide for ourselves whether our present policy is the best one, the one most likely to succeed.' By 1931, a national conference of Revisionists was planned.

One 1932 Revisionist complaint to the ZOC about their inadequate efforts was answered patiently by Archie Freiman. 'I should imagine if you find our ... activities in Canada inadequate, if you feel that we are actually dead, and having the cause at heart, there is no reason why you should not make an effort to the things that your conscience dictates to you in the light with which you are blessed, rather than to ask me to do the work who may not see eye to eye with you.'[66]

Revisionist clubs were active in Toronto, Montreal, and, oddly, in the small communities of Newcastle, New Brunswick, and New Waterford,

Nova Scotia. In March 1932 a monthly bulletin, *Tel Hai*, began publication to distribute news and program guidelines, including instructions that 'it is necessary to participate in the general Zionist work [such] as National Fund [JNF] ... and Keren Hayesod ...'[67]

Only a few of the major Zionist leaders bothered to visit Palestine. Archie Freiman made the trip only once. Hirsch Wolofsky and Hananiah Caiserman went there on tour in the 1920s. Mordecai and Hiram Weidman of Winnipeg visited in 1923 and published a fascinating memoir of their trip.[68] And there were other occasional Canadian visitors, such as Rabbi Harry Stern of Temple Emanu-el in Montreal, who escorted a student study group in 1929. Nor did Canadians actively participate at World Zionist congresses. These international gatherings were a kind of world parliament of the Jewish people. Freiman appeared only once, although in 1929 he made an effort to send a 'real delegation' of ten persons.[69] The few Canadians who did attend were in Europe primarily on other business or on holiday. Thus, Canada had little input in these discussions; their delegates spoke only perfunctorily, reporting on their activities. The exception was Hananiah Caiserman, who, on the one occasion when he represented Canada, spoke with his characteristic emotional eloquence about the need for more educational efforts.

The emphasis on fundraising was rarely questioned openly, although Caiserman shrewdly observed the discomfort felt by many Zionists. After an extensive educational tour of Western Canada in 1925, he reported to the ZOC national executive that 'in the whole West ... nearly the whole correspondence which they receive is referring to the collection of funds ... Speakers who come to them are not coming to impart Zionist information ... but just to appeal for funds.' He warned that unless Zionists got substantial assistance for cultural programming, the movement would falter and the ZOC decline.[70] Caiserman observed that Young Judaea's successful programs were eliciting great interest. This cultural endeavour was essential, he said, 'in order that they are equipped to persuade the inhabitants of their communities to give liberally towards Zionist funds.' He gave a total of 103 lectures during his western tour on topics related to his trip to Palestine. He addressed groups of Hadassah, university students, Zionist societies, Young Judaea, B'nai Brith, and Talmud Torah classes, as well as non-Jewish groups and churches. But with the established pattern, even appeals for more cultural content from officials were disregarded. One of them thanked

Caiserman for giving him 'a clearer insight into prevailing conditions in Canada,' but then mused about 'the significant fact that the Funds for carrying on the campaign for Irish independence came very largely from the savings of Irish domestic servants in America,' obviously suggesting that Canadian Jews draw inspiration from that experience.[71]

While Jerusalem officials accepted Caiserman's assertion that Canada had suffered an 'economic decline,' they insisted 'that had we a stronger and more extensive organization [in Canada,] Palestine would not have suffered to the extent that it has done at the hand of Canadian Jewry.' As well, they stressed that 'educational activity should [not] be set up as [an] alternative to practical work. I am convinced that the two can and must go together ... We must eliminate the idea that cultural work is something opposed to collecting ... I think it would be an error if Young Judaea were to ignore this aspect of Jewish junior activity, because of exclusive concentration on the educational side of the movement.' These patronizing attitudes towards Canada prevailed throughout the interwar period.

Even the German and Austrian Jewish refugee question of the late 1930s did not deflect Canadian Zionists from their belief that Zionism came ahead of 'the emergency settlement of Jewish refugees now being deprived of livelihood and freedom.'[72] Officials of the ZOC, Poale Zion, and Mizrachi, meeting on 10 July 1938, unanimously rejected a proposal from the Canadian Jewish Committee for Refugees that they cooperate in a joint fundraising campaign with the United Palestine Appeal. While pledging support for 'any practical proposals that offer a chance of salvation for our stricken brethren,' the Zionists asserted that 'Jewish settlement in Palestine belongs in a different category ... Zionism strives to establish a Home for the Jewish people and not a refuge ... The task of the Zionist movement involves more than the settlement of refugees.'

Freiman had been encouraged to take this position by Weizmann, who in July 1934 wrote that 'during my recent visit to Palestine I had every opportunity of seeing at first hand the work that is being done there for the reestablishment of German refugees, and I came back more than ever convinced that it is only in Palestine that this work has any prospect of permanency. It would be a tragedy if this work were to be held up for lack of funds.'[73]

On the left, however, the much smaller Poale Zion pursued a program with more educational content. The ephemeral Mizrachi organization, meanwhile, tried to advance the cause of Torah in Zion. Small in number, these and a few similar organizations held strong beliefs in a specific philosophy, and focused on programs of self-improvement and on Zion's redemption.[74] But though dynamic, they were comparatively small and received very little press coverage.

Although the cities provided much of the ZOC's leadership, the strong support in smaller communities was reflected in its membership statistics and in the composition of the national executive, which was headed by Archie Freiman. As a generous donor to Jewish causes, Freiman was typical of the leaders and the rank-and-file ZOC members in the smaller cities. While the metropolitan centres contained an occupationally diverse Jewish population,[75] the Jews of the small cities were mostly small shopkeepers. They were decidedly middle-class in occupation, self-image, and aspiration, and inclined to identify with their leaders, mainly successful businessmen. Zionism, which stressed the redemption of Palestine, provided Canadian Jews with the responsibility to financially support those lofty purposes.

Thus, the fundamental objective of Zionism in Canada during the 1920s and 1930s continued to be an almost obsessive fundraising. And yet, the movement's youth wings were attracting growing numbers, who for the first time were studying Jewish culture. The leaders undertook immense obligations from 1918 until 1927, with the acceptance of the staggering million-dollar Emek Hepher project. Thus the pace of campaigning increased.

The ZOC and Hadassah provided a unifying framework for the community. Their biennial conventions and frequent regional gatherings were the forums for the expression of common attitudes and aspirations. Consequently, without any serious competition, their leaders fostered a Zionist identity for Canadian Jewry. This, however, was largely an invented identity with inherently extraterritorial goals. In the meanwhile, there were serious clouds on the world Jewry horizon to which Zionism was not an adequate response.

The acceleration of the genocide in Europe, in 1941, motivated Canadian Zionists to redouble their fundraising efforts. In addition, to popularize the movement, they organized diverse activities, under the leadership of Samuel Zacks, the dominant figure in the ZOC following the death of Archie Freiman in 1944. A forty-year-old wealthy Toronto stockbroker, he had for several years been involved in Jewish refugee work and Zionist activity in the Toronto area.[76] Dedicated and hard-working, he applied to his Zionist work the drive, initiative, and shrewdness that had gained him a fortune in Canadian mining promotions and great respect from a wide circle of friends.

Along with his organizational ability, Sam Zacks was gregarious and diplomatic. An avid fundraiser, he sometimes mixed his Zionism with business; in 1944 he promised one individual that he would double his money on a share purchase if he would increase his contribution to the ZOC.[77] Zacks was essentially a pragmatist who drew as many people as possible – even non-Jews – to the cause. Perhaps the keys to his success, however, were his open mind and the broad, conciliatory, and liberal approach he used to secure support for the entire movement.

Along with the appeals for more and more money for relief efforts in Europe, the Zionist campaigns for Palestine increased through the United Palestine Appeal. Labour, religious, and Revisionist organizations, however, conducted their own drives. By 1943 there was competition from some city welfare funds, which raised and allocated their funds as they saw fit. In this somewhat complex and confusing scene, the ZOC often felt frustrated.

Zacks spoke of these problems to Chaim Weizmann, who, in a separate endeavour, had been appealing to Canadian Jews throughout the war to support the Sieff Institute, his scientific research centre in Rehovoth, Palestine.[78] In responding to Weizmann in January 1943, Zacks showed polite exasperation. 'One of our main difficulties, in Canada,' he explained, 'as far as the Zionist movement is concerned has been the plethora of Campaigns ... In view of the fact that there is only a handful of workers, it places a heavy burden on the small group and the best results are not obtained.' He stressed that 'this country would be capable of much greater effort if things were not so chaotic and there was a greater coordination in the fund raising program.'[79] Weizmann, undeterred, continued to push his own private cause, demanding that the Canadians raise $150,000 to build a laboratory.[80]

In face of complexities such as these, Zacks believed that a comprehensive Zionist fundraising campaign would raise more money and also allow for independent rescue programs for European Jewry. In 1943 he calculated that United States Jewry contributed between fifty cents and one dollar per capita, but Canadian Jews gave approximately five dollars because, he believed, American Zionists had abandoned their own separate campaigns. If they had not, Zacks wrote to one associate, 'Zionism would have been many times more powerful there. Then they probably would have risen to the occasion and taken courageous steps to rescue European Jewry, instead of sleeping complacently, drugged by the opium of [broad-based] philanthropic appeals.'[81]

Zacks also had greater objectives. To an Halifax activist, he wrote: 'We should realize that fundraising is secondary to the other important work that faces us in the present crisis.'[82] 'My feeling is that we are making too much of a fuss about fundraising to-day,' he wrote to a Winnipeg supporter in early December 1943. 'Other work seems to be so much more important. I am losing patience with all the internal squabbles regarding fundraising.' He thought this bickering could be ended with a referendum allowing all subscribers to Zionist funds decide the matter.

The ZOC, cooperating with the United Zionist Council, attempted in 1943 to influence the media and politicians through a coordinated public-relations campaign.[83] Its major target was the British government, which many Zionists felt had betrayed its Palestine mandate with the 1938 White Paper which severely limited Jewish immigration and land purchases. London maintained this policy, even while millions of European Jews were being murdered.[84] In January 1941, at the urgings of Dov (Bernard) Joseph, the ZOC adopted a resolution calling for 'the establishment of Palestine as a Jewish Commonwealth within the British Commonwealth of Nations,' so that it could absorb distressed Jews from Europe.[85] In March 1941, David Ben-Gurion proposed that this Jewish Commonwealth allow rights for Arabs and Jews 'similar to that obtaining in Canada as regards the English and the French.'[86]

Public relations became the main Zionist activity. The urgent need to move Holocaust survivors to Palestine required an end to these British restrictions. Within the Canadian Jewish community, this struggle against Britain became increasingly popular. Except for some attacks from the radical left, anti-Zionism was rare.[87] In fact, membership in the ZOC jumped, and some young Jews championed *Aliyah* and *chalutziut* (kibbutz pioneering), making this dramatic period between 1943 and 1952 the most active in their fifty-year history.

Before 1943, attempts to stimulate pro-Zionist sentiments among non-Jews had been limited. Politicians were sometimes invited to Zionist conventions, and the Canadian press had been broadly supportive of the idea of a Jewish national home in Palestine.[88] But the sharp attack that Canadian Zionists mounted just after the British White Paper was published was so brief and uncoordinated that it attracted only passing attention in the nation's newspapers and resulted in little public debate.

When news of the mass murder of Jews by the Nazis began reaching the West in the summer of 1942, a mood of impatience and bitterness gripped North American Jewry. At a rally in New York's Madison Square Gardens in March 1943, Chaim Weizmann proclaimed that two million Jews had already been murdered and that 'the world can no longer plead that the ghastly facts are unknown or unconfirmed.'[89] Canadian Zionists, led by Sam Zacks, participated in efforts to rescue as many Jews as possible. Immigration to Palestine was essential, which meant either the suspension or the withdrawal of the White Paper. Canadian Jewry lacked influence, but the Zionists assuming that both government and Canadian public opinion might assist, formed a separate public-relations committee of the United Zionist Council.

The campaign of the Canadian Palestine Committee (referred to by Zionists as the Committee) and the Christian Council for Palestine, the latter to recruit clergymen to the Zionist cause, proved only a modest success. Established in the summer of 1943 under the direction of Henry F. Janes, a Toronto public-relations consultant who was later replaced by Herbert Mowat, the CPC was nominally headed by Sir Ellsworth Flavelle, a prominent Canadian businessman. (All three of these men were non-Jews.) The Committee first tried a direct approach at the highest political level. In December, Archie Freiman asked Prime Minister Mackenzie King to press the British government to lift the White Paper's immigration restrictions.[90]

A large delegation of Jewish and non-Jewish members of the Committee met with King in March 1944 to discuss the issues relating to Canada and the Palestine question.[91] They argued that as the friendship between the United States and Britain had been strained over Palestine, Canada serve as an 'interpreter' between them. Fully cognizant of the government's reluctance to admit Jews to Canada, the delegation reminded King that in the postwar years, when 'multitudes of uprooted people ... would be knocking on the doors of all countries,' Palestine could accommodate many of the Jews who might want to come to Canada.[92] In the end, King promised to support this view at an upcoming meeting of the Commonwealth prime ministers. But he would not challenge the White Paper. Committee delegations met with King and officials of the Department of External Affairs periodically thereafter to present position papers on the Palestine issue.[93]

But King's advisers at External counselled him to decline involvement, fearing that this would hinder eventual Jewish–Arab rapprochement. King refused Freiman's appeal, as well as Zacks's petitions. In the words of the historian David Bercuson, 'Canada ... stood smugly aloof' from the Palestine question, 'and no amount of Zionist public relations could change this fact.'[94] Nevertheless, while there was no discernible shift in the policies of the Canadian government concerning Palestine,[95] some newspapers began to publish sympathetic editorials and, more importantly, to give extensive coverage of anti–White Paper protests and Committee meetings.[96]

Frustrated at this level, the Committee began sending out informative literature, news releases, and speakers. Janes saw this activity not as publicity, but as goodwill, and he reported to the ZOC in early January 1944 that 'in his campaign, he touches on anti-semitism, [Jewish] achievements in Palestine, the White Paper and the plight of the Jewish people, the fact that the Arabs deserve no consideration because of their attitude in this war, whereas the Jews have suffered on one hand and served on the other.'[97]

The Western group of the Committee quickly established contacts in the major Prairie cities,[98] advising Zacks that a coordinated campaign to achieve their main objective 'of seeing the [Palestine question] brought up in Parliament' should be started immediately. 'Merely having the unorganized sympathy of a number of liberal minded non-Jews,' they explained, 'will get us nowhere.'[99] A series of separate committees was needed, one each for members of Parliament, the clergy, newspaper or radio persons, labour leaders, and major businessmen – all 'building up goodwill and public opinion until such time as the Parliamentary Committee is prepared to bring the matter up in Parliament.'[100]

The Westerners widely distributed pamphlets such as *His Terrible Swift Sword*, by Dr Norman Maclean – a former moderator of the Church of Scotland – as well as other write-ups that presented the Zionist case to non-Jewish local committee members, the press, business leaders, the clergy, and political figures. They also sent out speakers who awakened Christian sympathies for Zionism, while a large number of prominent Canadian public figures, including politicians, labour leaders, and university faculty members, were approached.

Rabbi Harry Stern of Montreal's Temple Emanu-el, a very active emissary in the 1943–4 campaign, was thought to be 'the best asset we have.' Janes wrote of Stern: '... his understanding of public relations is not equalled by any man I've met in a long time.'[101] Not only did Stern undertake several speaking tours, but he was also instrumental in setting up the Christian Council for Palestine, through which the Zionists hoped to influence Canadian clergy.[102] The council was organized in early 1944 by Janes.[103] He prepared a list of nearly eight thousand Protestant and Roman Catholic clergymen to whom pro-Zionist material was sent, including reviews of Pierre Van Paassen's *Forgotten Ally* – a book that detailed the contributions of Palestine Jews to British military efforts in the North African campaign – though any anti-British sentiments were carefully removed.[104] Groups of pro-Zionist Christian clergymen sprang up across the country. They disseminated information about Zionist achievements in Palestine, the Balfour Declaration, British immigration restrictions, and Jewish suffering in Europe.

By June 1944 the executive director of all these committees was Herbert Mowat, an effective spokesman and a highly efficient organizer. His speeches, like the one broadcast on 5 June 1944 over Halifax's CHNS, related some of the known facts of the Holocaust and discussed the need for a safe Jewish homeland where a million more refugees could be accommodated. The absorptive capacity of Palestine, which was greatly increased by Jewish agricultural innovations, was stressed, while British immigration restrictions were condemned as contrary to 'the humanitarian needs of our day.'[105]

These efforts succeeded, and by July 1944, supporters included sixteen MPs and many other prominent Canadians. By October 1945 the list included sixty-four MPs, twelve senators, various MLAs, and a handful of professors.[106] Mowat, a highly accomplished speaker, addressed meetings of service clubs, ministerial associations, and labour temples, and made radio broadcasts all across Ontario and the Prairies during the autumn of 1944. Although he usually included local Jewish communities in his tours, his main objective was to win the support of Christians for the moral, historical, and humanitarian Jewish claims for a national homeland in Palestine.

The Committee also lobbied newspaper publishers and editors for their support of Zionism. In November 1943 Zacks told a Winnipeg associate that Joseph Atkinson, publisher of the *Toronto Star,* was 'our main sponsor.'[107] In fact, after having spent many hours with various Ontario newspaper editors, Zacks reported a great deal of positive feedback.

Some of these efforts, however, failed. In the aftermath of the assassination of Lord Moyne, the former British high commissioner for Palestine, in Cairo in November 1944 by Jewish terrorists, *La Liberté et le patriote* of Winnipeg commented:

> The Congress Bulletin, organ of the Jewish minority in Canada, has made a fuss, as we recall, of the alleged persecution which the Jews of Quebec have to suffer. It freely accused French Canadians of persecuting the Hebrew minority. It swamped the newspapers of the country to spread these falsehoods. What will it say of the actions of the Jews of Palestine?[108]

The Committee received a lukewarm response in the media to the Zionist case, while the White Paper often got a noncommittal reaction.

Still, most editorial writers refrained from criticizing Britain except for some qualified reproaches during the War. After May 1945, editorialists saw less justification for excluding refugees from Palestine, but outright condemnation of British policy was still rare. Some newspapers even occasionally criticized the United States for 'interfering' with Britain's mandate for Palestine.[109] Thus the Committee refrained from being too stridently anti-British, and also distanced itself from the terrorist acts of Jewish extremists in Palestine.

J.M. Goldenberg of Saskatoon argued that Canadian Zionists should

> guard against excessive criticism of Britain ... because ... there exists in Canada such a strong pro-British attitude, that it will not tolerate violent British criticism ... It is not a case where large sections of the population like us less, but I think, they like Britain more, and they would not hesitate to sacrifice us, if they though it served Britain's interest best.[110]

While Revisionists were distributing stickers reading 'We will buy no English goods or services as long as England bars the Jews from Palestine,' the ZOC followed a more cautious course.[111] Following the assassination of Lord Moyne, Mowat urged Zacks not to challenge Churchill, who condemned the killing as an interference with the war effort. Instead, he pressed Zacks to advise an all-out effort against terrorists. He again warned that Zionists should be concerned about 'the bar of non-Jewish public opinion.'[112]

Although Zacks rejected the terrorists' methods, he also resented charges from some British officials that the terrorists were impeding the war effort, thus reflecting badly on Jews generally. 'The least [the British] could have done,' Zacks wrote, 'was to recognize the great contribution in this war by the Jews, which is greater than that of any other people.'[113]

Mowat, however, wanted to present to non-Jewish Canadians the traditional image of the Jew as passive victim and juxtapose it against that of the new Jew as progressive pioneer farmer in Palestine.[114] He remained vigilant on this aspect of Zionist public relations. In early 1947, Mowat reported that while in Calgary, he 'was informed that the flogging of the British officers in Palestine [by the Irgun Zvai Leumi (National Military Organization), the military wing of the Zionist Revisionists, in retaliation for the caning of several of their members in prison] had caused a greater deterioration of the Jewish cause in [Calgary] public opinion than all other factors combined in the last year ... At the bar of public opinion the cause of Zionism in Palestine touched an all time low.' The event had made a 'malignant impression' on the minds of Calgarians.[115]

After 1945 editorial writers generally were sympathetic to the Jewish 'victims of Hitlerism' and the partitioning of Palestine into Jewish and Arab states.[116] But there was also much sympathy for Britain. The *Toronto Telegram* stated in October 1946 that, while Zionists were putting pressure on Britain to admit Jews to Palestine, 'no Jew on this continent has asked for the admission of Jews here, which proves the political rather than the humanitarian nature of the Zionist movement.'[117] This was a nonsense. In spite of sustained official resistance to Jewish immigration, the Congress had tried to get some Holocaust survivors admitted to Canada. As well, President Truman's efforts on behalf of this cause had attracted widespread opposition in the Canadian press and some sympathy for Britain.[118]

Generally, the press supported the idea of Jewish emigration from Europe to Palestine after 1945, in large part, apparently, to forestall an influx of Jews to Canada.[119] In a public opinion poll in early 1946, 49 per cent of those responding favoured free Jewish access to Palestine; a few months later, the pollsters found that 49 per cent of those polled regarded Jews as the second least desirable immigrants to Canada (Japanese were first on the list). But the Irgun and Lehi (Stern Gang) anti-British terror campaign, which started with the bombing of the King David Hotel on 22 July 1946, 'almost completely derailed the Zionist campaign for public support in Canada.' The Zionist relationship with the government was further harmed when it was discovered that the *Haganah*, one of the ships used to run illegal Jewish immigrants to Palestine, was a former Royal Canadian Navy corvette sold as surplus by the War Assets Corporation 'to Jewish interests in New York.' These factors, and the hands-off government attitude towards the 'Palestine mess,' meant the Zionist public-relations campaign had attained only limited success.

Although Zacks understood the complex roots of Jewish terrorism, he and the ZOC actively condemned violence and the efforts by the American League for a Free Palestine (organized by the American novelist and playwright Ben Hecht) to form branches of the Irgun. In addition to finding terrorism morally repugnant, Zacks worried about a serious public relations backlash. In early 1947 he noted considerable media coverage given to Jewish terrorism and its backers in the United States and Canada. But the vast majority of Canada's Jews and the ZOC were opposed, categorizing terrorists as 'irresponsible sensationalists.' He appealed to the media to present this opinion.[120] Mowat felt that he was 'put on the defensive attempting to explain what is called Jewish terror ... It is my technique to attack the other side ... but it is a trying procedure in the teeth of the destructionist violent activities of the Irgun, which all regard as blatantly criminal.'[121]

In a letter to the *Windsor Daily Star*, one correspondent complained that a column referring to an advertisement of the American League for a Free Palestine 'can stir up a considerable amount of hatred against Canadian Jews who are in no way responsible for what Mr. Hecht does, and who in no way agree with his statements.' He urged the paper to 'at least ... [point out] that the ad admits it does not represent Jewish opinion ... All Jewry, American and Canadian and Palestinian, for that matter, are opposed to terrorist tactics.'[122]

After 1944, when the Jewish Brigade – a specially formed, Palestine-raised infantry unit of the British Eighth Army – went into action in Italy, the Zionists challenged the Jewish stereotype with the picture of the Palestinian Jew fighting on the side of Britain and the Western democracies. Before the brigade even got to Italy, however, Canadian Zionists were debating about the unit's creation, a British plan dating back to 1942,[123] and about encouraging Canadians to join up. The Jewish Agency in Palestine advised the Canadians to seek their own government's permission,[124] even though Zacks was 'getting inquiries almost every day from Jewish soldiers in the Canadian army asking if they would be allowed to join the Jewish Brigade ...' and the astonishing claim that 'it goes without saying that thousands of our boys would rather wear the Jewish uniform.' Zacks wisely let the matter drop.

Continuing an almost exclusive orientation to fundraising activities, world Zionist leadership gave education a low priority. But, to the contrary, Zacks and some other officers regarded education as Zionism's 'main work.' Zacks favoured establishing a publishing company to disseminate books, magazines, records, and music, and to arrange concert and lecture tours.[125] Supporting him were others like Halifax's Sam Jacobson, a regular correspondent about the movement. Jacobson saw Zionism as a 'mass humanitarian liberal movement, with the courage to arouse sympathy among Jew and non-Jew ... a movement that will be alive and growing; with a future, and not a narrow philanthropic movement using pussy-foot methods ... I believe [in] a strong [and] aggressive cultural program ...'[126]

By the early 1940s, small groups of Canadian Jewish teenagers were considering *chalutziut* in Palestine in a kibbutz, tilling the land and shouldering a rifle. The image of the rough-hewn pioneer living a frugal, communal-farming life on the ancient soil became a symbol of the renewal of both land and people. These young people were unconcerned that this life was dangerous and difficult, both physically and psychologically, or that their parents likely would object strenuously to their plans. Films, songs, dances, and visitors from Palestine all told them that any difficulties could be overcome, and that the sweet joy of Zion's redemption would compensate for any pain or loss.

The *chalutz* ideal grew in Montreal, Toronto, and Winnipeg, and by the spring of 1941, it was reported that five hundred members of various youth movements were committed to *Aliyah* while thirty *chalutzim* were prepared to leave for Palestine at the first opportunity. Many of them already had one or two years' agricultural training in the United States.[127] 'The Canadian Chalutzim are burning in their zeal to go to Palestine and participate in its defense at the present moment,' one writer claimed, and barriers to entering the United States during the war made 'a training farm for Canadian Chalutzim ... the demand of the hour.' A high percentage of those who went on *Aliyah*, had attended Jewish all-day schools, showing the influence of education on commitment.[128]

The activist Shalom Stern saw that because Canadian Jewry was part of the Jewish 'historical process,' it must 'recognize the fact that it is free to act in the interest of the Jewish masses ... for the purpose of salvaging the wreckage of Jewish life. It can also partake in the creation of the new living already preponderant on the soil of Palestine'[129] But Stern also emphasized that 'we are undoubtedly ... an integral part, of that particular cycle of history which embraces Jewry. In that sense Canadian Jewry must consider the Palestinian struggle a manifestation of our own battle.'

In 1944 the Hashomer Hatzair organization in Canada established a *hachshara* (training) farm near Prescott, Ontario, where about a dozen young people prepared for life on a kibbutz.[130] Although the Jewish Agency representative in New York was aware of the difficulties in attracting North American Jewish youth to *chalutz* life, he optimistically estimated that perhaps as many as one thousand would move to Palestine at the end of the war.[131] The Canadians from the Prescott farm would be part of this vanguard of pioneers. Badly in need of financial support, the group requested assistance from Zacks – the socialist youth asking the arch-capitalist for help in establishing a workers' commonwealth in Palestine.[132]

Zacks was urged to help by his friend Meyer Weisgal: 'I wished the General Zionists would make Chalutziut [settlement of kibbutzim] part of their program and enlarge the scope of their work.' Zacks not only wrote a big cheque, but also visited and warmly encouraged the young people in their endeavour.[133] Weisgal's wish was never realized, although Young Judaea struggled with the issue of *Aliyah*, unsuccessfully, for many years.[134]

While some members of youth movements like Hashomer Hatzair and Labour Zionist Habonim made *Aliyah* to kibbutzim, the agricultural life on Israel's embattled frontiers did not suit them all.[135] Indeed, some may not have had the loftiest of ideals. Mordecai Richler, for one, recalled:

> The truth is, I hadn't joined Habonim ... because of an overwhelming commitment to Zionism ... I longed to meet girls who could stay out after ten o'clock at night. And according to the disapproving gossip I heard in the Young Israel Synagogue, the girls in the movement, especially those who were allowed to sleep over at our Camp Kvutza, where there was no adult supervision, practised 'free love.'[136]

Some of the *chalutzim* eventually moved to the city or returned to Canada, often greatly disillusioned, but seldom regretful at having given their sweat and blood for the realization of the dream.

In the early 1940s, local Zionist groups began experimenting with various summer camps. Finally, in 1943, Camp Kadimah (Forward) was opened at Port Mouton, Nova Scotia, for forty-seven campers drawn mostly from Halifax.[137] By the time it moved three years later to a larger site, the camp had become a vibrant centre for Young Judaea activity and a continuing social bond for Jewish youth across the Maritimes.[138]

Around the same time, Camp Hagshama (Connection) was formed near Perth, Ontario; it was joined in 1948 by Camp Shalom (Peace) near Gravenhurst, Ontario, and Camp Hatikvah (Hope) near Oyawa, British Columbia. Other organizations established their own camps to perpetuate their Zionist ideals, while offering youth healthy outdoor activity away from the summer heat for a few weeks. But idealism was in the air, and many of Young Judaea's teenage leaders were swept away, though stymied by their parent organizations.

It was heady, intoxicating almost, for teenagers belonging to Zionist movements to mature within its rich atmosphere of socialism and worldly culture. 'You realized,' remembered the Hashomer Hatzair veteran Mesh Butovsky (who went on *Aliyah* in the early 1950s), 'that you were the vanguard of the Jewish people, transforming them through chalutziut to productive working class people ... The movement was our whole existence: In its relentless intensive atmosphere we were preparing for our new life in Palestine.'[139]

In the Zionist youth movements, the murder of European Jewry (since the 1960s called the Holocaust) was a significant element of the educational program. Prominently featured were examples of Jewish armed resistance, such as the 1943 Warsaw Ghetto uprising, the 1944 exploits of Jewish parachutists like Chanah Senesh, and the massive recruitment of Jews to units serving in the British Eighth Army's North African campaign and in the Jewish Brigade in Italy. These organizations' summer camp program also marked Tisha B'av, as the anniversary not only of the destruction of the Temple and the termination of the Second Jewish Commonwealth, but also of the obliteration of European Jewry: twenty-four-hour fasting, vigils, readings, and copious youthful tears were part of these memorials, in which the emphasis was on the redemptiveness of the resistance to Nazism rather than on the horror of the Holocaust. Thus treated, the Holocaust played in the Zionist narrative of the futility of Jewish continuity outside of Israel, the inevitability of anti-Semitism, and the possibility of further such horrors.

Local Zionist activities, especially in the smaller centres, originated with youth and Hadassah groups, thus curtailing men's involvement. There were no structured men's groups; they were organized solely to conduct the annual United Palestine Appeal campaign. At a general meeting, financial pledges were made in response to an outside speaker's appeal for funds. The organizers would follow through by collecting the pledged amounts and forwarding them to headquarters. A similar burst of activity took place every few years on the eve of the World Zionist congresses. Efforts were made to sell the shekel, a symbol of membership in one of the Zionist organizations, in order to broaden the base of support for the political parties with which these Canadian groups were affiliated.

The ZOC was in the best position to establish local men's associations. Most Jews in these smaller centers were already affiliated with the ZOC as contributors or shekel holders. There were few members of the Labour or religious Zionist organizations in these communities, not because of a lack of interest, but because establishing one broadly based organization proved easier.[140] Nevertheless, even the ZOC found it difficult to begin locals of its men's group, the Zionist Order of Habonim, in the smaller communities.

Always a pragmatist, Zacks realized that Habonim clubs – with their somewhat intensive cultural program – would not be suitable everywhere, and so he favoured establishing autonomous Zionist societies, ones with a 'provision for Zionist content,' in every community in Ontario, where he felt the movement was weakest.[141] 'We have had many speakers, spasmodically and without plan, go into the towns, in the past few years, but with no attempt to follow up or organize along Zionist lines.'

Most of Canada's Jews could participate only vicariously in the struggle for Israel's existence. But still the joy of involvement, especially among Zionist youth movement members, was one of the high points of their lives. Mordecai Richler recalled the scene in the St Urbain Street area when the United Nations General Assembly voted, on 29 November 1947, to partition Palestine and allow the establishment of a Jewish state:

> People charged out into the streets to embrace ... Men and women who hadn't been to a synagogue since last Yom Kippur surprised themselves, turning up to offer prayers of gratitude and then toss back glasses of schnapps with slices of schmaltz herring. Horns were honked. Photographs of Chaim Weizmann or Ben Gurion, torn from back issues of *Life* or *Look*, were pasted up in bay windows. Blue and white Star of David flags flapped in the wind on some balconies. Many wept as they sang 'Hatikvah,' the Zionist anthem ... We gathered at the [Habonim] house on Jeanne Mance Street, linked arms, and trooped downtown singing 'Am Yisrael Hai' ('The People of Israel Lives') and then danced the hora in the middle of St. Catherine Street, just outside the Forum, bringing traffic to a halt.[142]

Similar though more modest celebrations occurred elsewhere. In Brantford an impromptu party was called, bottles of schnapps produced, and traditional food proffered. Rabbi Gedaliah Felder solemnly pronounced the traditional blessing (Shehecheyanu) that marked major events in the Jewish calendar to honour this day, which foreshadowed the Jewish state. Toasts were drunk, embraces exchanged, declarations erupted, and tears flowed.

The security of the Yishuv was seriously threatened on the eve of the British departure from Palestine in the spring of 1948. At the urging of Ben Dunkelman and other Jewish war veterans, the ZOC cooperated by recruiting volunteers for Israel's defence and by sending over certain 'materials' – in fact, munitions and arms.[143] Zacks, frustrated by the

ZOC's administrative and financial problems, also pushed for action: 'I personally would like to see things proceed at a faster tempo because I feel it is the only way results can be obtained.'[144]

Leon Crestohl of Montreal, head of the United Zionist Purchasing Commission (which was assembling vital materials for the Yishuv) and later a Liberal MP for Montreal-Cartier, was another Zionist who actively supported recruitment.[145] RCMP informers who attended a mid-March 1948 meeting of the Montreal Jewish youth council, reported:

> Leon CRESTOHL then spoke very forcibly about 20 minutes on the emergency facing Jewry, claiming it to be the greatest the Jewish people had yet faced; he berated those who thought that it was not their concern ... He strongly urged all Jewish youth to give full support to this Appeal, then remarked 'I do not urge you to go to Palestine and fight, as I do not know the legality of such urging, however you all know what you should do.'[146]

As a result of such encouragement, and some direct recruitment campaigns, fifty-three Canadians, including fifteen non-Jewish flyers, enlisted in the Israeli Air Force during the War of Independence.[147] Six of these men, two of them non-Jews, were killed. Two hundred and thirty-two Canadian volunteers, all but a few of them veterans of the Canadian armed forces, joined the army.[148] Lionel Drucker served with distinction in the armoured corps and Ben Dunkelman as a senior officer in an infantry battalion. Some were put together with volunteers from other English-speaking countries in the so-called Anglo Saxon Battalion (the 72nd) of the Israel Defense Force (IDF) Seventh Brigade. Others were assigned to the so-called Canadian Platoon, which comprised about half of 2 Company of the Haganah's Givati Brigade.[149]

Not all the Canadian volunteers were happy with their assignments in the IDF. Hymie Klein of Vegreville, Alberta, who, possibly, wanted to be in a Hebrew-speaking formation, complained of being 'railroaded' and 'tricked' into an English-speaking unit, but he realized that 'Eretz is not to blame ... We must give it a chance.'[150] In general, however, the volunteers were happy serving the Jewish people in this way. They risked, and in some cases gave, their lives – a sacrifice far more substantial, obviously, than even the most generous donation made by the cheque-book Zionists back in Canada.

The experiences of the Young Judaeans who attended the one-year Machon (Institute) program in the early 1950s were probably typical of the few young Canadians who went to Israel as leadership trainees from the various youth movements. Their observations of the country at that crucial time in its history, when it was absorbing so many immigrants of diverse cultures, capture the contrasts and collisions that necessarily accompanied the ingathering of Holocaust survivors and Jews from Arab lands.

Their idealism was catching. For some of the youth, camp life provided forums for other types of discovery than those offered by the close proximity of both sexes. After a summer of intensive indoctrination from an Israeli *shaliach* (delegate) during Camp Biluim's first season in 1951, fifteen of its teenage leadership trainees solemnly resolved to form a *garin* (seed group) to prepare to build Young Judaea's first kibbutz.[151] There was a certain irony in this teenage earnestness, coming as it did through the efforts of Israeli educators who, in some cases, had themselves abandoned the collective life. A few members of the *garin* did make *Aliyah*, but they all eventually returned home, defeated by the demanding realities of Israeli life and the special circumstances of collective living.

Canadian Zionist activities in this period reached a level of intensity that was never to be equalled. Long-established fundraising programs were joined by a new interest in local political activity and a serious concern with *chalutziut*. In these respects, it might be said that the movement had matured. The vigorous political work undertaken by the Canadian Palestine Committee matched in intensity that of its American counterpart, though it probably had less effect on Canadian public opinion because of Canada's quasi-British identity. Nevertheless, though perhaps not critical in the formation of Canada's policy on Palestine between 1945 and 1948, the publicity drives and lobbying efforts undertaken by the Zionists can only have helped the cause.

The public-relations campaign initially attacked the British White Paper, and then it began to focus on Palestine partition and the full recognition of Israel by Canada. Finally, the campaign pushed for Israel's acceptance into the United Nations. Thus, between 1943 and 1948 the work of the Canadian lobby – mainly, but not exclusively, through the Canada Palestine Committee – was uninterrupted. This activity further united the pro-Zionist community in supporting the work of the Canada Palestine Committee, backed wholeheartedly by the Canadian Jewish Congress.

Even non-Zionists could get behind the cause. The Holocaust not only changed the course of modern Jewish history, but also reduced the intellectual options open to those concerned with the ongoing 'Jewish question.' Indeed, the very nature of the question was suddenly altered forever. From 1945 onward, Zionism moved slowly towards a position of legitimacy within the Jewish world.

Thus, by 1948, Zionism had become as close to being the universal credo and the normative identity of growing numbers of Canadian Jewry as any belief could. To be sure, the battle for its acceptance had never been as difficult as it was in the United States, where, in the minds of some Jews, there was a question of dual loyalty. Indeed, significant organized Jewish opposition to Zionism had never materialized in Canada, owing to a combination of historical circumstances that, in some respects, sharply distinguished Canadian and American Jewry. There were many non-Zionists and some anti-Zionists in the community, of course, but apart from sporadic and ambivalent attacks on Zionism by the Jewish Communists, no Jewish group set itself up in sustained opposition to Zionism. This is not to say, however, that the Canadian Zionist spirit was necessarily more intensive or profound than the American one.

Was Canadian Zionism at this time essentially just a philanthropic activity intended for Jews already in the land of Israel? The evidence is mixed, but this description is not really sufficient. For Canadian Jews, Zionism in the 1940s and early 1950s carried immense meaning, especially within the context of the Holocaust. Zionism kept many Jews close to their roots and deepened their sense of unity and common purpose with Jews around the world, while at the same time offering hope for survival and for national reconstruction. Like Zionists everywhere, Canadians believed themselves to be working under pressure, against dark forces that were destroying the Jewry of Europe and threatening their survival in Palestine. Resources were needed to rescue, to defend, and to build.

In the disorder of the wartime era, the Jews of the free world were the only ones in a position to provide resources. Canadian Jews accepted increasingly heavy financial responsibilities and put immense energy into urgent fundraising appeals in the belief that they also serve who write and gather cheques. To such people, the youthful enthusiasm for political ideologies and dubious settlement schemes was, at best, an unrealistic distraction from what they thought had to be the main goal of all Canadian Jewry: sending help.

Canadian Zionists also believed themselves to be an integral and vital part of Zionist labours. The fact that they themselves were not smuggling Jewish refugees illegally into Palestine, not building new settlements, not fighting off marauders, was less important than that they felt at one with their brother and sister Jews who were performing these heroic acts.

The support for Zionism in Canada did not end in 1948 when Israel was established. Indeed, the movement gradually became stronger from that point on because a growing number of Canada's Jews were Israel-centred. Ironically, though, success in establishing the state had, in some senses, lessened the urgency and the power of the Canadian Zionist work; Israel became the possession of all Jews, Zionist and non-Zionist alike.

By the mid-1950s, the Zionist organizations were becoming less significant for channelling Canadian Jewish engagement in the affairs of Israel. In part, this was a result of the growing strength of community fundraising activities through the new federations of Jewish charities, which decided how much to allocate to Israel and to other causes. Zacks lamented this transformation in a letter to Batshaw in December 1951.[152] But he also observed that

> there seems to be an awful lot of confusion. Many who do not want the ZOC to be political have succeeded in diluting it to such an extent that it is gradually losing its strength and vigor. There are also many who feel that it is no longer a general Zionist body ... It is painful to watch the disintegration.

Having lost its fundraising muscle to the United Israel Appeal (except in some small communities), the ZOC began to fade into insignificance. What emerged in place of it and its brother Zionist organizations – with the exception of those which, like Canadian Hadassah-WIZO, maintained fundraising autonomy – was a new and much broader Canadian Jewish partnership with the state of Israel and its people.

PART FOUR

The Second World War and Beyond, 1940–2008

11 Into Battle

The Second World War drew thousands of Jewish men and 279 Jewish women into Canada's armed forces, some of whom volunteered and were enthusiastic to fight the German Nazis, while others refrained from joining up and awaited conscription. Some of the latter – for their own reasons, no doubt – refused to sign on for duty overseas and preferred to sit out the war in uniform in Canada. But the war did not involve just sailors, soldiers, and airmen; it embraced almost the entire country. Let us look at how the Canadian Jewish Congress and the community responded to the war in 1939 and its various stages until 1945. How did the war affect the people and how did they react to it? What percentage of Jews of military age joined or were conscripted into the armed forces? What branches did they serve in? How well did they perform in the services? How were they treated as Jews, and what were their perceptions of antisemitism? Did they fight the war to settle an ethnic score with the German Nazis or as loyal Canadians? What efforts did they and the Congress make to establish an environment that facilitated Jewish cultural identity among servicemen, and how successful were they? These and other questions present themselves to historians seeking to understand the Canadian Jewish experience in the 1940s.

The Congress, since 1939 headed by Samuel Bronfman, monitored all aspects of the national war effort to inform Canadians that Jews were pulling their weight, contrary to the perception that their contribution during the First World War was inadequate. Bronfman was strongly patriotic and insisted from the beginning that Canada's Jews, united in the Congress, get fully behind the war effort.[1]

The Congress also understood that this was a fight against the German Nazis, who for six years had been trying to eliminate Jews from

Germany and all of Europe. This threat and Canadian antisemitism, which persisted during the war, were viewed as major concerns. The Congress also recognized – in part because of the First World War experience – that Jewish soldiers required an active support for their religious, social, and dietary needs; these were arranged through Jewish military chaplains working with the Congress to reach Jewish service personnel.[2]

The Congress formed the National War Efforts Committee (WEC) in late 1940 to direct these matters and to open military recruitment centres across the country. Bronfman paid particular attention to the figures of Jewish enlistments, directing WEC to do all it could to encourage Jews to join the colours.[3]

Until mid-summer 1942, the WEC concentrated on mobilizing the community behind the national war effort, while trying to organize services for Jewish personnel scattered in camps throughout Canada.[4] After more Jews enlisted – part of a general trend that year – and considerable numbers of Jewish men were stationed near major cities, the WEC sent out field workers to organize hospitality, recreation, and entertainment, although it often fell to the local communities and Jewish military chaplains to provide much of this outreach.

One might have expected a large Jewish enlistment, given the widespread newspaper coverage of the systematic harassment of Jews in Germany during the 1930s. After Hitler's accession to power in 1933, this persecution received detailed coverage in the mass media, especially in the *Toronto Star*,[5] whose Berlin correspondent, Pierre Van Paassen, sent back daily reports on the Nazi revolution. These were often given front-page coverage. The Yiddish press as well as English-language newspapers like the popular Canadian *Jewish Chronicle* reported these events, and the Bureau of Public Information, established by the Dominion government shortly after the outbreak of war, portrayed German Nazi massacres as 'deliberate instruments of Hitler's racial policy.'[6] Did this knowledge – not to mention the antisemitism current in Romania and in Poland – stimulate massive Jewish recruitment to the armed forces? The historian Jack Granatstein believes that 'the sons of Eastern European Jewish immigrants should have had a special urgency; ... they ought to have enlisted in what was unquestionably a just and necessary war, especially for Jews.'[7] Whether it is reasonable to expect Jews to have volunteered en masse for such units in a war against Nazism remains a question that only the soldiers themselves – and those eligible Jewish men who, along with many others, avoided military service altogether – can answer.

At a distance of fifty years, some Jewish veterans reflected on their own reasons for volunteering. 'As a Jew, you had to go,' veteran Aaron Palmer recalled. Barney Danson remembered that 'the evil of Nazism existed and we had to be in it, as Jews and as Canadians.' Edwin Goodman also believed that as a Jew he had a special responsibility to fight Nazism. On the other hand, Robert Rothschild, a regular army officer in 1939, did not feel an especially strong motivation because of his Jewishness. He did get that feeling after the war had started, however, and was proud of his four male cousins, who enlisted and fought in combat units. 'I felt better about them,' he remembered. Barney Danson felt some anger at the thought of the Jewish boys who did not join up and avoided military service altogether. 'I don't know how they could live with themselves. How could any [such] Jew look himself in the mirror?'[8]

Ernest Sirluck joined the Canadian Officers Training Corps and sought a combat posting because 'Jews had a special stake in this particular war and in the defeat of Nazism.'[9] He believed that '[Jewish] behaviour in this war would profoundly affect their status in the future, that any effort to avoid military service or get into its low risk branches ... would be closely monitored and unfavourably interpreted by a suspicious and often hostile population, among whom the antisemites had said from the beginning that the war was being fought for the sake of the Jews.' Sirluck later turned down a safe berth because 'as a Jew I should be in the dangerous shooting part of the war,' especially after his brother, Robert, was killed in action while serving with the Royal Canadian Air Force (RCAF). Seventeen-year-old Martin Roher tried to enlist in 1941, immediately after his older brother was killed in an RCAF training accident just before he was to have received his wings. Rejected for flight training, Roher joined as a physical-training instructor and was employed giving swimming lessons to commando troops.

Ben Dunkelman, an ardent Zionist, did not hesitate in 1939. 'My mind was made up,' he recalled. 'I wanted to get into the war ... It was quite clear to me that, as a loyal Canadian, it was my duty to volunteer to fight. Besides, as a Jew I had a special score to settle with Hitler ... The antisemitic persecutions raging in Germany and the other countries dominated by the Nazis had made it clear that these men were the implacable foes of my people.'[10] Harold Rubin 'began to picture [his] loved ones being subjected to ... horrible atrocities ... [and] found it difficult to get to sleep, even after an exhausting day at work.' He joined up a few days after the outbreak of war.

Monty Berger, the son of Montreal's Rabbi Julius Berger, had an 'acute consciousness' of why the war had to be fought. He tried to join the RCAF in May 1940 as aircrew, was rejected on medical grounds, and served as an intelligence officer with an RCAF Spitfire wing.[11] 'Not unlike other Jews in Canada,' he recalled, 'I had heard of cousins and relatives who had disappeared, or were killed in the nightmarish world that descended on Europe's Jewish population in the late 1930s ... My identity as a Jew ran deep. I felt fully the sense of frustration seeing Hitler and the Nazis go unchecked.'

Willie Nelson, who had joined the Royal Air Force in 1936 and was awarded the Distinguished Flying Cross in 1940 (the first Canadian Jew to be decorated), wrote home just before he was killed in action:

> I thank God that I shall be able to help crush the regime that persecuted the Jews ... I have never had such a desire to live as I do now; nevertheless, my feelings are so strong, that the personal element doesn't mean a thing ... and if I leave while flying ... it is the way I want ... I am happy in the thought of helping to crush Hitler.[12]

Judging, however, from some memoirs, there were those with little concern for the fate of European Jews and no strong enthusiasm for fighting Nazism. A young Toronto Conservative politician and insurance agent, Allan Grossman, thirty years old in 1940, offered to join the army if he could get a special berth with a political crony. When that did not work, he joined the reserves.[13] Irving Layton, twenty-eight years old in 1940, idealist, intellectual, and poet, applied to join the medical corps at the outbreak of war but was turned down. He subsequently joined the Canadian Officers Training Corps, washed out in 1943, and decided to sit out the rest of the war.

One intellectually precocious, nineteen-year-old Mount Allison University student, Nathan Cohen – who later became one of Canada's most important drama critics – wrote in May 1942 that 'Hitler and Mussolini precipitated no war, they are the products of our own sloth and shame.'[14] David Lewis, thirty-one years old in 1940, was national secretary of the Co-operative Commonwealth Federation (CCF) when war broke out. He felt no compulsion to object to his party's commitment to pacifism during the late 1930s. 'No one had any doubts,' he recalled, 'that war with Hitler was almost certain, yet we could not bring ourselves to support expenditures to improve Canada's preparedness.' His memoirs reflect no personal struggle over the question of enlistment in spite of his Polish birth. Lawrence Freiman, who was thirty, decided to enlist at the outbreak of the war but was dissuaded by his father's serious illness and the ensuing family responsibilities. 'It was one thing for a dental graduate to accept a commission in the medical corps,' Mordecai Richler recalled, but 'something else again for a boy to chuck law school for the infantry.'

From its beginnings in 1940, the WEC actively encouraged Jews to enlist, which was 'the primary duty of citizenship in the crisis which our country is now facing.'[15] Information on enlistment was widely distributed through speeches, pamphlets, and offices manned by Jewish First World War veterans. Special registration bureaus were opened on Spadina Avenue in Toronto and in the Jewish district of Montreal. As early as 1940, the *Canadian Jewish Chronicle* came out strongly in support of conscription and urged 'every citizen ... to contribute his share to the national defense.'

H.M. Myerson (who oversaw recruiting in Central Canada in 1940 and 1941) reported to the Congress that the Jewish contribution 'will be gauged in terms of able-bodied young men who have risked their all.'[16] Several obstacles to the recruitment of young Jews had already surfaced, including general indifference and apathy ('indolence of mind, ... desire to follow line of least resistance, ... having a good time, ... absence of pride in one's self, [or] in group [and] national life'). Parents, Myerson found, were reluctant to encourage or even permit their sons to join up, while young men feared they would not be able to get along with Gentiles. And the old Jewish hostility towards the military was still present. What to do? Myerson urged the Congress to promote military service by popularizing the idea in the Jewish press, making direct approaches to eligible young men, and giving appeals at meetings of all Jewish organizations, especially youth groups. He urged all the Congress top brass to get behind this campaign.

In 1942 the WEC launched a large-scale drive 'to awaken ... [the] realization of the gravity of our country's need and the necessity of making every possible sacrifice to enable all able-bodied Jewish Canadians to take their places in the ranks of Canada's fighting forces.' Rabbi David Monson of Toronto went out on recruiting drives, using the argument that 'if Hitler wins, Christians will be slaves. Jews will be committed to death.'[17] Monson encouraged men who had already signed up to bring in their friends and relations. He went to Toronto's Brunswick Avenue YMHA and to youth clubs, where he got a mixed reaction: some joined up right away; others said they would ask their families. The Jews he addressed during these recruiting drives, he believed, knew what Hitler stood for and were influenced by parents who in many cases had relations still living in Europe. Some parents reproached him, but he replied that service in the Canadian armed forces was necessary to ensure Jewish survival. Other Jewish recruiters did the same.

Strong support for a vigorous war effort also came from the far left, especially following the German attack on the USSR on 21 June 1941. Jewish Communists then redeployed the rhetoric of the Popular Front, which had been suspended since August 1939, the period of the German-Russian non-aggression pact. They issued calls for 'a second front now' to smash Nazi Germany. The Communists discouraged strikes and pressed for increased war productivity and for funds for Soviet medical relief. Above all, they appealed for unity among Jews, 'the first victims of fascism wherever it appears.'[18] They held marches and rallies such as the ones at Maple Leaf Gardens and the Montreal Forum in September 1943 for Shlomo Michoels, the head of the Soviet Jewish Anti-Fascist Committee, and Itzik Feffer, a distinguished Yiddish poet. Attended by Jews of all political persuasions, these meetings reiterated the Communists' support for a war against fascism, and for the gargantuan effort conducted by the Soviet Union. After the elections in August 1943 of J.B. Salsberg to the Ontario legislature and of Fred Rose to the House of Commons, the war effort was a major theme in their speeches.

According to the records of the Congress, 16,441 Jewish men and 279 women served in the Canadian armed services during the Second World War, and 163 Canadian Jews served in other Allied armed forces.[19] Jewish women constituted 0.55 per cent of all Canadian women who joined the forces, and women's nursing units. This was substantially lower than the percentage of Jewish women in the Canadian population in 1941 (1.46 per cent by religion). However, because of strong patriarchal values, families were likely resistant to the enlistment of their daughters. Not yet eighteen, Ziona Levin, of Winnipeg, joined the RCAF 'knowing of the horror that was going on ... I thought maybe I could do something.' But she kept it a secret until a week before leaving for training. One Jewish woman, Rose Goodman of the RCAF, was killed in a training accident in February 1943.

Only 39.1 per cent of Jewish men of military age (age eighteen to forty-five) were taken into the Canadian armed forces, as compared with 41.4 per cent of all Canadian men.[20] This included volunteers and conscripts drafted under the National Resources Mobilization Act (NRMA) of 1940. Of the 16,441 Jewish men enrolled, 3,479 (or 21.2 per cent) were NRMA men, or 'Zombies' (a term of contempt applied to draftees who refused to sign up for overseas service).[21] Although Jews constituted 1.46 per cent of Canada's total population, they were 2.2 per cent of its Zombies, the highest rate of any religious group in Canada relative to population. Interestingly, Jews apparently had a lower level of service in the combat arms than the general population. The death rate of all personnel in the Canadian armed forces during the Second World War was 4.08 per cent (42,042 of the total intake of 1,029,510 men). Using the same calculation for the Jewish community, the death rate was 2.61 per cent (429 deaths – recently raised to 431 – among 16,441 men). This was 62.25 per cent of the national average, lower by more than one-third.

Jews were less numerous in combat units probably because, with a higher level of education than the general population,[22] many could have been assigned to desk jobs and duties in rear-echelon units, where casualty rates were insignificant. Under the army's personnel selection policy, by contrast, men with the least education ordinarily were sent to infantry units, where casualties were highest. Jews presumably could have volunteered for service with the infantry, armour, engineers, and artillery, with the Royal Canadian Navy (RCN), or with RCAF aircrew. The lower than average death rate suggests that the majority did not do so.

However, some Jews had difficulty joining specific regiments as officers, even if they were qualified. After waiting to be posted to a combat role, Ernest Sirluck and a colleague applied to a regimental camp where the commander, unaware of his religion, said to him, 'You're just the kind of officers we want, not like those pesky Jews who keep trying to get in.' Sirluck, however, accepted an invitation to join the Royal Regiment of Canada.[23] In the early stages of the war, regimental commanders apparently could bar 'undesirables' from entering their units. A senior officer at National Defence reported in November 1941 that 'many young men of Jewish faith in Toronto ... have persistently and consistently been turned away from recruiting offices because of their race and religion.' He instructed that recruiters change course and let Jews into the army.[24]

Because Jewish conscripts had suffered severe persecution in the armies of the Eastern European countries – from which virtually all of Canada's Jews had originated – they traditionally tended to avoid military service. Though circumstances in Canada were very different, this fear of military service probably still continued in many Jewish families. Sirluck believed that there was much antisemitism in the armed forces, and when he enlisted in the army, he wrote 'none' for religion, fearing that if captured by Germans, 'it wouldn't be pleasant to have "Jew" on my name tag.'[25] Sirluck could have had O.D. (for 'other denominations') on his identification discs like other Jews. Such fears could well have discouraged many Jewish draftees from volunteering for general service.

Some Jews, keen on fighting Germans, may well have believed that, if taken prisoner, they would be subjected to special abuse, or even murdered. After all, even as teenagers, they must have heard the frequent press and radio reports of violent anti-Jewish measures in Germany before the Second World War and of the official confirmation by the Allied governments in late 1942 that the Jews of Europe were being systematically destroyed. Beliefs that as soldiers they would have been subjected to the same treatment, however, could not have been confirmed during the war. Indeed, the experiences of Jewish Canadian prisoners of war (POWs) varied considerably in this regard. Royal Canadian Air Force Sergeant-Pilot Sam Shapiro, who was held in several German POW camps – for nearly four years! – from 17 August 1941 to 16 April 1945, remembered experiencing much antisemetic abuse, and at one point with other Jewish service personnel, faced imminent death.[26] On the other hand, Pilot Officer Norman Shnier, whose Wellington bomber was shot down over Berlin in August 1943 (just one month after his brother, also in the RCAF, was killed in a bombing raid over Hamburg) experienced only minor antisemetic abuse in POW camps, though when captured, he had been asked by a German police captain: 'Jude? Jude?' To these questions he remained passive, and he wasn't bothered further. In one camp, the German commandant allowed Jewish personnel to hold Yom Kippur services. Astonishing as this seems, mid-gunner Manny Raber (whose bomber was shot down over Belgium in 1942) recorded in his memoir that he, too, attended a Yom Kippur service in a POW camp. And he makes no mention of antisemitism. Joe Sonshine's bomber was shot down over Belgium in June 1944, and he hid amongst partisans before his capture; he was shipped to Buchenwald, not because he was a Jew but because he was believed to be a spy.[27]

Though schooled in a strong pro-British environment, many Jews, like Canadians of other ethnic origins, may not have felt a deep enough personal loyalty to the British Empire to volunteer. Those on the far left initially regarded the war as imperialistic, at least until Germany attacked Russia on 21 June 1941. Early on, even Canadian Jews from

Eastern Europe did not believe that the Germans – who in the First World War generally had behaved decently towards them – were capable of mass murder.

Jews had served in all of Canada's wars, including the Canadian Expeditionary Force in the First World War, a few earning distinction for bravery in battle.[28] However, neither this nor the service of several hundred in the Jewish Legion in 1918–19 constituted a Canadian Jewish military tradition. It is perhaps not surprising, therefore, that the Jewish inclination to enlist did not exceed that of most other groups of Canadians. After the widespread revelations of the mass murders of Jews in late 1942, they could reasonably have been expected to volunteer, but available data do not reveal recruitment patterns at that point.

Perhaps Jews should have wanted to join armies in their adopted countries to express gratitude for having full civil rights, which most of Canada's Jews – except those in Quebec – enjoyed.[29] It might even be argued that Jews who believed Canada to be antisemitic should have been motivated to join in order to strengthen claims for full acceptance.

Non-Jewish perceptions of Jewish recruitment varied. In September 1940, the *Winnipeg Free Press* slammed those who were alleging that 'no Jews are joining the army, navy, or air force' as a 'Goebbels gang' of baseless liars.[30] Canadians should know, the editorial continued, that at a recent Canadian Jewish Congress meeting, Jews declared 'they were ready to dedicate their lives and all they possess to the cause of victory.' An RCMP report from Regina in December 1940 stated that 'despite anti-semitism in Saskatchewan, instigated by Nazi agents, Jews continue to enlist ... The military authorities in Ottawa know full well, Jewish-Canadians are enlisting away out of proportion to their quota of the population.' Another RCMP report, of July 1941, stated that out of the fifteen Jewish families in Kamsack, Saskatchewan, thirteen men had volunteered for active service overseas, with the Altman family contributing all five of their grown-up sons.

The Congress – always on the watch for antisemitism (such as allegations of black marketeering) – was very sensitive to the continuing allegations that the Jewish community was shirking its military duty. Since 1940 it compiled data on the names, addresses, regimental numbers, and next of kin of Jewish servicemen. This enabled them to refute such charges. When, in the spring of 1943, Toronto alderman Leslie Saunders – a leading Orangeman and first-class bigot – publicly alleged 'that the Jews of this country are not doing their duty in this war,' the Congress replied that there were 'well over 10,000 Jewish men and women in the service forces of Canada.'[31] Saunders, on the basis of what he said were 'official Government figures,' insisted that Jews constituted only 0.6 per cent of the 'active forces' (by which he would have meant 'general service' volunteers in the army, as well as RCAF and RCN personnel).

At this point in the war, the Congress claimed there were 4,677 Jews in the army, 4,009 in the RCAF, and 206 in the RCN, for a total of 8,892 Jewish personnel. This figure did not include draftees or others who might have missed its count, nor those who did not attest to being Jews, 'fearing the treatment that would be meted out to them by Nazis in the event of their being captured as prisoners.'

On behalf of the Congress, A.B. 'Archie' Bennett of Toronto challenged Saunders's assertions, stating that he would show the Congress's records to anyone prepared to tell the truth. While conceding that Saunders's figures could be true in the early stages of the war, Bennett stated that they were outdated by 23 July 1942. February 1942 data 'showed the Jews forming 1.7 per cent of the RCAF.' But a report published in 1943 by the Congress press officer, David Rome, stated that 'the problem of enlistments declined in importance as conscription was more generally put into effect,'[32] suggesting that Jews, unlike most other Canadians, had less of a propensity to volunteer for military service. This has now been confirmed.

The Congress's figures show that over the course of the war, Jews constituted 1.44 per cent of the army, 2.61 per cent of the RCAF, and 0.60 per cent of the navy.[33] Thus, only the Jewish contribution to the RCAF was larger than the Jewish percentage of the Canadian population (1.5 per cent in 1941). In all, Jews constituted 1.6 per cent of the total intake of personnel into the Canadian armed forces. It is not clear why many Jews preferred the RCAF, although it did have higher educational standards than the army, more glamour, less spit and polish, and earlier involvement in the fight against Nazism. As for the low number of Jewish volunteers for the RCN, the perceptions of snobbery and some early antisemitism within the navy were discouraging to all but the most ardent sailors.

The Congress encouraged Jewish enlistments through pamphlets, advertisements, and by a widely distributed series of illustrated booklets about Jewish war heroes. In 1940 the Congress published a large-format leaflet entitled *They Answered Hitler's Challenge*, which showed photographs of some 120 Jewish men serving in the forces and

Captain Isidore Freedman's Jewish Reinforcement Company, Montreal, 1917, before joining the Canadian Expeditionary Force in France. (A.D. Hart, ed., *The Jew in Canada* [Montreal 1926], 509)

Jewish orphans from Ukrainian pogroms in Rovno pose with Dr Joseph Leavitt (far left) and Harry Hershman (far right) in 1921. Some of these children may have been among those brought to Canada by Leavitt, Hershman, William Farrar, and Lillian Freiman. (Canadian Jewish Congress Charities Committee National Archives, Montreal)

Lillian Freiman seems never to have rested from strenuous efforts on behalf of Jewish immigrants to Canada, the building of the Jewish national home in Palestine, and the causes of Canadian Hadassah-WIZO. (Canadian Jewish Congress Charities Committee National Archives, Montreal)

A Jewish farm family at Lipton, Saskatchewan. (Canadian Jewish Congress Charities Committee National Archives, Montreal)

Like Millers' bookstore in Winnipeg, Hyman's Book and Art Shop on Toronto's Spadina Avenue was a favourite meeting place for many Jewish intellectuals. Benzion Hyman, an electrical engineering graduate of the University of Toronto, poses proudly in front of his store in 1925. (Ontario Jewish Archives, 1171)

Dedication of the new synagogue in Kirkland Lake, Ontario, 1 September 1929. Rabbi Rabin is carrying the Torah. (Library and Archives Canada, PA103552)

Discussion concerning the Ontario poultry strike, Kensington Market, Toronto, 1939. (Ontario Jewish Archives, 3875)

Certificate for Max Switzer, Jr, for a donation to the Polish Jewish Family Loan Association, Calgary, Alberta, December 1932. The photograph shows the founders and charter members. (Glenbow Museum and Archives)

Canadian Nationalist, a Nazi publication issued in Winnipeg, featured many cartoons and headlines linking Jews to Masonry and Communism. This one was published in February 1938. (Ontario Jewish Archives, 6158)

This sign, which was found near a resort northeast of Toronto, was typical of those posted at many places, before they became illegal. (Ontario Jewish Archives, 6161)

Women workers in a clothing industry shop in Montreal. (Canadian Jewish Congress Charities Committee National Archives, Montreal)

'Conducting honoured guest into synagogue': a procession, led by Rabbi Elizer Ebner and Cantor Morris Goldblum, for the dedication of a new Torah scroll at Congregation Beth Israel in Calgary, 1951. (Glenbow Archives, Calgary)

H/Captain Rabbi Samuel Cass, Canadian Army Jewish chaplain, and Canadian Jewish soldiers distributing gift bags to children at a Chanukah party in Antwerp, Belgium, 6 December 1944. (Library and Archives Canada, PA 202174)

Chanukah menorah at the Ontario Legislature, 1997. (Steven Tulchinsky)

'Collaborators and members of Dutch S.S. cleaning and repairing desecrated synagogue under supervision of Jewish members of 1st Canadian Division, Nijkirk, Netherlands, April 30, 1945': one of three photos taken by Canadian Army photographer Lieutenant G.B. Gilroy. Armed members of the Dutch resistance stand guard. (Library and Archives Canada, PA116329)

At the first of many rallies on *Simchat Torah* (Rejoicing with the Torah), Toronto Jewish youth show their solidarity with the Jews of the Soviet Union, 1967. (Ontario Jewish Archives, 1343)

The family of Haim Ben Haim from Morocco arrives at Montreal's Dorval airport in the early 1960s to add to Canada's growing Sephardic community. (Canadian Jewish Congress Charities Committee National Archives, Montreal)

offered regrets that it could not publish hundreds more.[34] Its western division distributed a lengthy questionnaire to communities to gather information on contributions to all manner of war work.

In mid-July 1941 the Congress's officials summoned community leaders to a conference in Montreal to discuss ways of increasing enlistments. Caiserman urged that 'an intensive and enthusiastic recruiting drive' be undertaken immediately:

> Jewish parents must explain to their sons that Jews were never, in their long and tragic history, in such jeopardy as they are now ... Jewish youth of military age must set an example of patriotism by enlisting in great numbers for active service. They must do so voluntarily and must not wait to be conscripted ... Enlist NOW. Enlist for ACTIVE SERVICE. ENLIST, IF YOU ARE A JEW.

Typical of these appeals was a candidly worded leaflet in Yiddish whose motto was 'Siz a koved tsu kemfen unter der britisher fon kegn undzer soynim' (It is an honour to fight under the British flag against our enemies). Addressed to 'brider und shvester' (brother and sister), the leaflet continued:

> What must be our stand both as Canadian citizens and as Jews? ... Jewish fathers and mothers! Encourage your children to join the Army! It is for you and for them an honour to fight for freedom, for Canada, for our people ... Jews! Take a rifle and sword in hand and go into battle for [your] country and people! [Translated by Ellen Tulchinsky]

The results of these recruiting efforts are not clear. The memoirs of several rabbis and other Jewish communal leaders include no mention of this and, indeed, very little about the war itself.

The Congress also urged Jews to vote 'yes' in the plebiscite that was held in April 1942 to free the Dominion government from its pledge not to conscript men for overseas duty. 'Canadian Jewry will most certainly vote Yes,' Abraham M. Klein prophesied in a *Chronicle* editorial.[35] 'A war against a ruthless foe cannot be fought with restrictive measures, and ... with one hand tied behind one's back. Against totalitarian aggression, the only answer is total resistance!' Hitler's persecution of Jews was also mentioned, but Klein's justification for a 'yes' vote was the government's need for a 'full and unrestricted mandate in the prosecution of the war ... and in that decision Canadian Jewry must play the part which both its Canadianism and its Judaism demand.' The call was heeded. Cartier – a densely Jewish area of Montreal – was one of Quebec's nine 'yes' ridings.

By mid-1942, reports were appearing in several Canadian newspapers about the mass murder of Jews in Europe. On June 16 the *Globe and Mail* published a front-page headline announcing that Lithuanian police had massacred sixty thousand Jews in Vilna. Two weeks later, the *Toronto Daily Star* published a story of another thirty thousand Jews being slaughtered in that country.[36] Soon reports were appearing regularly in the Canadian press, and by 1943 the destruction of the Jews of Europe was indisputable. And the knowledge that mass murder was under way affected Canada's Jews deeply. Rallies and memorials were held, especially to honour the uprising in the Warsaw ghetto in April 1943.

Antisemitism within the ranks was negligible. Jewish servicemen, when interviewed fifty years later, testify that manifestations of antisemitism, even casual remarks, were rare among the troops and officers during training and in wartime combat. In a rare account, A.M. Babb, the Saint John rabbi and unofficial chaplain to Jewish personnel stationed in southern New Brunswick, reported in June 1941 that six Jewish soldiers in the Dufferin and Haldimand Rifles, an NRMA unit composed of 'Zombies,' alleged that they had been subjected to humiliating treatment. Babb requested guidance 'for the sake of Jewish lads that will eventually come to the Regiment,' and five of the soldiers requested transfers to other units.[37] A young private in the 6th Light Anti-Aircraft Regiment complained to the army's chief rabbi, Gershon Levi, that his sergeant loaded him up with petty duties with the remark 'Let the Jew do it.' Harold Rubin, a sergeant in the Governor General's Foot Guards, recalled 'being subjected to a lot of embarrassment by some provocative Jew baiters,' but as a six-footer weighing 190 pounds, he found that 'after a few bouts with boxing gloves on, I gained the respect that was unobtainable in any other way.'

In letters from Jewish servicemen to their chaplains, there are very few complaints of antisemitism, but rather evidence of harmony and camaraderie, like those expressed by a naval rating on the HMCS *Unicorn* (the navy's shore establishment at Saskatoon), who wrote that he was lonely because 'at present I am the only Jewish boy on the Unicorn ... However, I can truly say that I have never met a finer bunch of men and officers than those serving with me.'[38] Robert Rothschild, a Royal Military College graduate of 1936 and a regular force officer in the Royal Canadian Horse

Artillery who later served as the key staff officer to Lieutenant-General Guy Simonds, stated that 'throughout my military career, I never experienced a semblance of discrimination,' though during the war he once overheard a fellow officer refer to another Jewish officer as 'that Jewboy,' for which the offender later apologized profusely to Rothschild. A corporal serving with the Royal Canadian Army Service Corps wrote to Rabbi Samuel Cass to say that in his unit, 'we [Jews] get along very well with our French Canadian camrades [sic],' and he wondered 'why can it not be so on civvy street?' The answer, he said, was 'we [must] not pretend to be better than they are ... [and] show them our good points, rather than allow them to think of us as scoundrels ...'

Edwin Goodman, who served through the war as an officer in the Fort Garry Horse, remembered that one Jewish trooper from Winnipeg punched out a sergeant who had called him a 'fucking Jew' (and was sentenced by a court martial to twenty-eight days in cells for the offence).[39] Major Goodman, an attack-minded squadron commander, overheard one of his sergeants say 'that fucking Jew will get us all killed if he keeps on this way.' Goodman let it pass. In 1939 he had tried to join the RCN's officer-training program, but the recruiting officer at its Toronto shore establishment, the HMCS *York*, asked him, 'By the way, are you Jewish?' When he answered 'yes,' the officer stated: 'I doubt that anyone who is Jewish will be an officer in this man's navy.' Ephraim Diamond, an RCN engineering officer, once overheard some of his fellow officers laughing about 'a funny Jew.' They quickly changed the subject when his presence was noted.

Ben Dunkelman applied to join the RCN in 1939 and was told that their officer quotas were full. He waited to be called, but was told by a Jewish friend that 'the navy would not accept Jewish officers.'[40] Barney Danson, a junior officer in the Queen's Own Rifles, remembered overhearing remarks that 'the Jews are running the country.' Rabbi Monson remembered being told by Jewish servicemen of antisemitism in the ranks of the Canadian army, especially remarks about Jews being the cause of the war. Still, such comments were relatively rare.

Some racial stereotyping, if not outright antisemitism, emerged nevertheless. A senior officer at National Defence headquarters in November 1941 suggested that Jewish 'temperament and characteristics are such that they would in many cases make them good "Operators Fire Control" in Artillery batteries,' a job involving good mathematical skills: in other words, Jews are smarter. This idea of a special Jewish unit was opposed and dropped because 'there is an undeniable racial angle to the matter which it would be best not to accentuate.'[41] Sam Finkelstein, an RCAF flight lieutenant attached to an RAF Pathfinder squadron in 1943, was asked by an English officer, Ray Hawken, to join him as navigator / bomb aimer in his Mosquito bomber. 'Why do you want me?' asked Finkelstein. 'You're Jewish, aren't you?' replied Hawken. 'Yeah, but so what?' said Finkelstein. 'Well, Jews are smart, and I want a smart navigator.'[42] After further discussion, Finkelstein agreed. He and Hawken flew fifty missions together (twenty more than the stipulated amount) without getting a scratch, and became lifelong friends. Barney Danson remembered that in his regiment, the Queen's Own Rifles, commanding officers 'often tried to push you into areas of perceived Jewish expertise. I recall at one time they wanted me to take over the running of the men's canteen. On another occasion they wanted me to become part of the group assessing individual capabilities, called Army Examiners.'

Some antisemitism was observed by non-Jewish soldiers. At a stand-easy before landing in Sicily in July 1943, Captain Ian Hodson of the Royal Canadian Regiment, which had several Jewish officers, was told by three of his subalterns, 'You've got to get rid of [name withheld].' 'Why?' said Hodson. 'Because he's a Jew,' they answered. 'Listen,' said Hodson, ending the informality, 'if I ever hear that stuff again, you'll be on your way back home so damn fast your head will spin.'[43] At the subsequent battle of Ortona in December, Lieutenants David Bindman and Mitchell Sterlin, both of them Jews – Sterlin giving his name to one of the regiment's key battles – gave distinguished service before being killed in action. Pilot Officer Dave McIntosh recalled hearing some nasty antisemitic remarks while serving in the RCAF.[44]

When possible, unit commanders cooperated with Jewish chaplains in allowing leaves for the High Holy Days or Passover. There was no resistance to Jewish personnel holding services during Sunday Church Parade. Chaplain David Monson, who asked for air transportation to visit a Jewish soldier stationed at a remote northern base, remembers an exchange with a senior officer: 'You want to go all that way for just one Jew?' 'Sir,' Monson replied, 'if there were more than one, I wouldn't ask.' The request was granted.[45]

The chief Jewish chaplain was Gershon Levi,[46] who served from March 1941 until the end of the war. Under him there were Rabbis Samuel Cass, Isaac Rose, E.F. Mandelcorn, H. Gevantman, and David Monson, who served for various periods. Jews in the RCAF were ministered to by Rabbis David Eisen, Julius Berger, and Wilfrid Gordon, all of whom held honorary military rank. In addition, there were a number of part-time Jewish chaplains, usually rabbis of small communities like Saint John, who were called upon to visit personnel on nearby bases or to arrange regular religious services, burials, home visits, and social events. There was no Jewish chaplain in the Royal Canadian Navy, though Rabbi Abraham Greenspan in Halifax served some of its Jewish personnel on occasion.

Levi and his associates tried to reach as many Jewish servicemen as possible. In 1941 they distributed copies of a prayer book, prepared for Jewish members of His Majesty's Forces by Joseph H. Hertz, chief rabbi of the British Empire. They also sent out *A Book of Jewish Thoughts* and a Jewish calendar showing sabbath candle-lighting times and significant dates. These publications were small enough to fit easily into the servicemen's battledress pockets. The prayer book contained English and Hebrew versions of some daily, sabbath, and festival prayers extracted from the Orthodox *siddur* (prayer book), as well as a group of special prayers for the sick and wounded, for the dying, for those going into battle, and for those going overseas.[47] The 'Prayer for Men on Active Service' appealed to 'God of the spirits of all flesh ... [to] endow us with courage and steadfastness loyal to do our duty as true Israelites to King and Country, and to take our full share in this War for Freedom and Righteousness.' *A Book of Jewish Thoughts* included some inspirational passages from the Bible, the Mishna, the Talmud, and some modern Jewish religious writing. Jews in the RCAF also received a book of psalms specially printed in Canada for this purpose.

These books were popular among Jewish personnel. Although wide distribution was attempted, those who were missed wrote to Levi asking for copies. Later, many expressed their appreciation. Ordinary Seaman Abe Halpern, serving on HMCS *Bytown* (the RCN's shore establishment in Ottawa), stated that 'the Prayer Book will be little used, [though] a Book of Jewish Thoughts and the Calendar will be of some value to me ... So far as religion is concerned, I am an agnostic.'[48]

To other servicemen, it meant a lot to have these books. Their Jewish identity and self-understanding were reinforced. Halpern, after declaring his agnosticism, stated:

> But so long as there exists a 'Jewish Problem'; so long as Jews are ridiculed, hated and discriminated against; so long as Jews are not given a country for themselves, in which they may prove their ability to build and create; so long as Jews remain disunited and tricked into complacency

by our so-called tolerant democracies; so long as conditions exist which breed antisemitism – I am a Jew.

Ordinary Seaman Louis Roter, serving aboard the HMCS *Orillia*, thanked Levi: 'It is very nice of you for thinking of us Jewish boy's [*sic*] in the fighting forces.'[49] Herbert Vineberg, of the RCAF, expressed his appreciation thus: 'when I received the siddur [prayer book] ... [I did] not [feel] a religious glow or even the sparkling of a dead or dormant religious philosophy. It was just a comfortable pick-up that indicates that my people do not forget their soldiers. I'd never have believed it.'

In letters received by Levi in 1942, some Jews expressed thanks because the books reinforced their faltering sense of Jewishness. S.S. Berlin, a Royal Canadian Navy Volunteer Reserve lieutenant, wrote, 'I was actually thrilled with the receipt of this gift ... This little [prayer] book is bound to provide the "lift" without which it sometimes becomes so difficult to carry on.' Others needed more. Pilot Officer John Marcus, posted to a night fighter squadron, wrote a long letter to Levi from 'somewhere in England' stating: 'Before I left Montreal I called you, but I also would have liked to have seen you, had a chat with you and asked you for your blessing ...'

Levi and Cass even received requests from Protestant chaplains for the prayer book and the *Book of Jewish Thoughts*. In the absence of a Jewish chaplain, the Protestants were officially responsible for Jewish personnel.[50] Levi routinely left a supply of the prayer books with Protestant chaplains for distribution. Some also wanted them for their own interest. One chaplain wrote to Levi, 'As Protestant Padre here I have given out the booklet to the best of my ability and will be pleased to continue doing so.' Sometimes requests came from other non-Jews. Occasionally, the base education officer or the commanding officer's adjutant would see to the distribution. The Presbyterian Protestant chaplain at the RCAF base near Goderich, wrote to Levi in March 1942 that he had not only 'distributed these three [prayer] books to the boys of the Jewish faith, [but also] called them together and spoke about getting together and reading the service with each other, and also promised them any help I was able to give them.'

Because they were living in barracks, eating army food, training to fight, and subject to tough discipline, recruits were grateful for sanctuary in a Jewish home, with friendly faces – and familiar food![51] The Halifax community, judging from the testimony of many servicemen and the records of its Servicemen's Centre, was exceptionally hospitable to the Jewish boys. One airman wrote Levi 'to tell you of the wonderful way in which the Jewish people of Halifax treated me along with many other Jewish servicemen ... Mrs. Finberg, along with her wonderful husband, treated many of us like her own children so it was no wonder she was "Mom" to us. It was swell to have a good Jewish meal for a change.' Ordinary Seaman Jack Bernstein echoed the same sentiment: 'The Jewish people of Halifax, led by the eminent Rabbi Greenspoon [Abraham Greenspan], are very hospitable to all the servicemen, and are doing all they possibly can, to make us feel at home.' The Halifax Jewish community, especially its women's organizations, responded generously to the needs of Jewish personnel who trained at nearby bases or had a layover there on their way to Britain. In February 1940, the Hebrew Community Council of Halifax was established for the war effort, and the local Jewish women welcomed Jewish service personnel to their homes for High Holy Day meals. They helped organize and staff the heavily used hostel for them, cooking kosher meals for hundreds of soldiers at a time.

Other communities were just as accommodating. From St John's, Newfoundland, an RCAF serviceman named Monson reported to Levi in March 1942 that he had 'met most of the Jewish families here and they are like all Newfoundlanders exceptionally hospitable. Mrs. Sheffman, about whom I am sure you have heard, has been very nice to me and [I] will be spending at least one Seder night at her home.'[52] Naval rating Bernard M. Saipe wrote from St John's that the local synagogue 'is indeed the meeting place for the boys in the various services that are stationed here and though the Jewish community is small they have certainly opened their hearts to us.' Jacob Feldman, a trainee on an airframe mechanic's course at an RCAF station near St Thomas, Ontario, reported in February 1942: 'I think you would be happy to know that the Jewish families in London, Ontario, have been treating the Jewish boys in uniform very decent and we really appreciate their hospitality.'

There was an apparent comfort factor in being with other Jews and in keeping rough track of them. Warrant Officer Sarah Lacle reported to Levi in November 1941 that 'Flt./Lieut. Durbin has left Paulson and is at Lethbridge. I would have been only too pleased to convey your regards, I also found him to be very nice.'[53] There are numerous references in the letters of thanks to Levi to the fact that the correspondent knows of other Jews on his base who had not received books and would like to, of Jewish servicemen posted elsewhere, and of Jewish friends and kinfolk elsewhere in the services.

Max Greenberg, on an RCAF station, wrote in April 1942: 'I believe that all the Jewish boys on this station have received the Prayer Book. If I hear of any new fellows that have not received one, I will ask them to write you.'[54] 'I am at present home on embarkation leave,' M. Charton wrote. 'I shall be only too glad to have any Jewish members of the Armed Forces not in receipt of this book write.' Levi, therefore, was at the centre of a vast Canada-wide network of information on what might be called Jewish military geography. He utilized these sources to reach as many Jews as he could – and not just to ensure that they received the books, but also to encourage them to attend services, to observe Passover and the High Holy Days, and to try to arrange family visits to nearby Jewish communities.

Interviews with ex-servicemen confirm that Jews often avidly sought out other Jews, especially relatives and hometown boys. Barney Danson looked out for his boyhood friend Fred Harris, also with the Queen's Own Rifles, until Harris was killed on D-Day. Aaron Palmer, a sergeant on the headquarters ordnance staff of the Third Canadian Division, recalled his joy in meeting another Jewish soldier from his hometown of Kingston just by accident at a depot in France. 'Wasn't that something!' he exclaimed in a letter to his mother.[55]

After Jewish servicemen reached bases in Britain, chaplains followed. Levi and Cass went over in 1943, and Rose and Monson in 1944. Overseas, they lacked the support system that was so available in Canada, but Jewish Canadians were being warmly welcomed by British Jews. In March 1942 Pilot Officer John Marcus wrote to Levi thanking him for the prayer book. He already had been given one by an English rabbi-chaplain named Marcovitch: 'He had organized a club at his synagogue of which you no doubt have already heard about from other members of the RCAF overseas. The Jewish women and girls come to entertain us and a jolly time is had. There are games and dancing, also refreshment.'[56] Manny Raber, an RCAF officer, visited some relations in Port Talbot, Wales, and Leeds who wanted him to meet some 'nice Jewish girls.'

In fact, Marcus had taken the initiative: 'I enquired a few days ago where I could find him from some Jewish people I went out of my way to meet, and they also told me that there are about 12 or more Canadian Jewish soldiers stationed near here, and I shall try to get to meet them.' The warm reception he got from one family embarrassed him. Some host families with marriage-age daughters especially welcomed single Canadian and American Jewish servicemen.[57] Barney Danson met his future wife at the home of one of these hospitable British Jews.

By late 1942, some Jews, most likely cognizant of the confirmed reports of mass murders in Eastern Europe, fought with extra fervour. Sam Finkelstein remembered having a special feeling when he released bombs over German targets. While on missions over Germany, much to his pilot's horror, Finkelstein would break radio silence, shout curses in Yiddish, and quickly switch off. Barney Danson remembered that as a Jew, he felt pressure to perform better, but he did not think he had to have special courage. When he was wounded, he thought, 'Oh, hell, I let the guys down.' Edwin Goodman, however, had mixed feelings: 'I knew that they [Germans] had killed my co-religionists and friends, but when I got the papers and personal effects of some of the Germans we killed, I felt compassion.'

Morris Lazarus, who served in the Italian campaign with the Canada–United States Special Service Force, an elite parachute unit, wanted to get at the enemy and volunteered for all the combat he could get.[58] RCAF Officer Sidney Saipe, who piloted a Mosquito bomber, informed his co-pilot Dave McIntosh that he wanted to kill as many Germans as possible. 'That's all I needed,' McIntosh recalled, 'a guy who wanted to win the Victoria Cross, ... a Jewish Billy Bishop with an unwilling occupant of the starboard seat.'[59] While not a Jewish Billy Bishop, Flight-Lieutenant Sydney Shulemson was awarded the Distinguished Service Order and the Distinguished Flying Cross, recognition second only to the Victoria Cross, for his 'inspiring leadership, great skill and courage' in battle.

Moe Usher, an RCAF wireless operator/gunner who flew on bombing missions from an RAF base in Northern Scotland, wrote to one of his brothers in Montreal: 'If ... my being over here helps to let youngsters like Danny [a nephew] soil their hands without fear of shadows overhead – it will be well worth fighting for ... I have often thought of the contrast between the kids over here and back home,' he continued. 'It is not very pleasant and the thought of my family going thru the suffering endured by civilians here makes me thank God you are all so far away.'[60] Cognizant of his short odds of surviving much longer, he sent money to a brother to buy a watch for his girlfriend, Shirley. Moe and his crewmates were killed soon afterwards, when their plane went down while they were returning from a mission in late March 1942.

Some Jewish servicemen took considerable pride in their performance. RCAF Corporal Fitterman, in training near Brantford, wrote proudly to Levi in August 1941:

> [You would be proud of] our men in the service ... it will please you to learn that at present we have 18 and their record is beyond reproach ... [It is] truly a good example to others, that whatever we do, we do well. Last week we had 'wings parade.' The two Jewish pupils, Sgt. Pilot Markus (Toronto) and Gasco (Montreal) finished very close to the 'top' and [were] posted for overseas duty, and these lads should be heard from, real fighting spirit and born leaders.[61]

Chaplains overseas kept in touch with some of the families of the wounded, the missing, and the prisoners of war. One mother with two sons in the army fighting in Italy wrote to Captain Isaac Rose, Jewish chaplain to the Canadian forces in Italy, in September 1944:

> I'm very anxious to hear which one you've seen as my youngest son was wounded while in action on Sept. 3rd & we just received the telegram ... I do understand that you are very busy but I am a mother & very anxious to know exactly how he is & your letter came at an opportune moment so if its Johny Levine, 5th Can. Infantry R.C.A.S.C. [Royal Canadian Army Service Corps] you've seen I wonder if you'd look in at the one in the Hospital for me. He's 0–191 SPR Lawrence Levine, 3rd Arm'd Reconnaissance Reg't, Governor General's Horse Guards. 'God' bless you for the good work your [sic] doing ...[62]

A sister wrote regarding Private Max Dankner: 'We received a telegram notifying us that he was severely wounded other than that we have not received word,'[63] A brother wrote regarding Private William Klein, of the Irish Regiment of Canada, 'I received a telegram last week stating William was wounded in action on Aug. 31. As yet I have not received any information as to the extent of his wounds ... My dad does not know about it, nor do I intend to let him know until Bill is quite well, and on his way home.'

Mrs A. Solway wrote to Rabbi Rose:

> My son has been wounded. The extent of the injury is as yet unknown and I'm terribly anxious. Please Sir, try to visit him as soon as possible as he is all alone and I am very concerned as to details ... I am a widow ... and my

three sons are in the Service, two being overseas. Gabriel is my youngest so please do your utmost to cheer him up and pray for my young son.[64]

Mrs S. Bach, of Hamilton, wrote at length concerning her son, Dave: 'My heart goes out to him, what would I not give to get a glimpse of his dear face, also my oldest son who is in Ireland somewhere ... Yes Sir we are very proud of our dear sons, as they are some of the very best, never think of themselves, but who they left behind.' She continued:

> I must tell you Sir that we are very Orthodox Jews ... My Hubby also Sons never ate trafe [non-kosher food] until the Boys went to the Army and Air Force, and the both boys and their Dad davened [prayed] untill they went into the Army, my Husband does yet; and I keep a very froom [religiously observant] House, you see my Grand Father – on my Dear Mothers side was Rove [distinguished rabbi] ... and I like to keep it up ... and my Dave writes to me that when he will please God come home safe and well he will begin where he left off ...

From Owen Sound, Mary Nidelman wrote to Rabbi David Eisen in July 1942 concerning her son, Bernard, 'our beloved and only son ... who has been reported missing in air operations overseas.'[65] She continued, 'We still cling to the hope that we may yet hear favourable news in the near future, but if that is not to be, we will bear up, and be proud that our son was bravely helping his country.' Mary Lozdon wrote to Cass about the loss of her husband, Morris Lozdon, who was with the Royal Regiment of Canada and whose body was never found after the Dieppe raid in August 1942: 'Until I hear further I shall keep on praying to God, as do our three little children ... To lose such a man is more than anyone can bear, & especially as young as he was, he was just 31 yrs & had ten hard lean years of marriage but we took it on the chin, & now this.'

The chaplains also visited Jewish personnel on their bases and kept up an active correspondence with many of them. In the process, of course, they received complaints and requests for support for compassionate leave, and provided moral support in cases of family problems back home. News of sickness, business reversals, delinquent children, and marriage breakdown were reported to the chaplains, who did their best to comfort the servicemen and limit the damage to their morale.

Cass also had to deal with 'matters involving extra-marital sex relationships of married men and the personal indulgences of non-married men and women ... very often leading to complicated and difficult situations.'[66] One can only guess what he could say to the trooper serving with the 28th Armoured Regiment who received this letter (known in the forces as a 'Dear John') from his Toronto fiancée:

> I am very sorry to have to say this, but it happened so, that I met a fellow and I find he is the one for me. Don't think that I was going out all this time with other fellows, though I met this fellow and I feel sure of myself in fact I know he is the one. Do you want me to send back the ring to you, if so let me know. It's up to yourself. I'm terribly sorry if this is going to hurt you, but it's better that it happened now then later. I'm sure you understand.

Or to this guardsman serving with the 21st Armoured Regiment, Governor General's Foot Guards, who reported to Cass that he had heard that his English wife 'wasn't behaving herself and ... refused to even treat me as a husband.' Other soldiers' letters were, no doubt, much easier to deal with. A private serving with the 4th Canadian Infantry Brigade, Royal Canadian Electrical and Mechanical Engineers, informed Cass that he planned to get married while on leave and wanted to know 'the dates when weddings are permitted according our law during ... April and May ... in case my leave should occur during the forbidden days [the period between Passover and Shavuot] for Chupes [weddings].'

The chaplains endeavoured to arrange services at the military bases on the high holidays of Rosh Hashana and Yom Kippur. At camps in British Columbia in August 1942, Cass tried to respond to entreaties from Pvt. Philip Levine of the Brockville Rifles (also an NRMA unit composed of 'Zombies'), who informed Cass that 'at yesterday's Jewish Church Parade in which the three regiments were present in force, a thorough discussion was held with a view to holding Rosh Hashana and Yom Kippur services here in Prince George. There is a keen desire by the greatest majority of the men concerned to hold these services.'[67] A cantor was needed, even though 'among us there are a few who could help out under the direction of a qualified reader, and these incidentally are the men who have been conducting our weekly service.' Levine had been searching for local Jewish religious resources and had found that 'there is a Jewish resident in town who has a "sefer torah" and a "shofer" which he has offered to us.' He stressed to Cass 'that there is the will of over 100 Jewish men to consider in this project and it is therefore deserving of your most earnest consideration.'

Unable to locate a rabbi to conduct the services, Cass wired the Protestant chaplain at the Prince George military camp, pleading, 'I must, therefore, ask of you that you supervise the arrangements for these services and encourage the men to take various parts of the service, which I am sure they can do.' He added:

> I know that you will do everything within your power as a Chaplain to make the men feel that they can carry on under their own power and experience the sacred traditions of their religion while carrying out the highest duty that they owe to their country and mankind ... I am sending you religious messages in the nature of sermonettes ... May I invite you personally to add to these services by giving them a message of your own.

Despite the chaplain's misgivings – probably because of his unfamiliarity with the Jewish faith – he apparently complied.

Similarly, at the RCAF station at Prince Rupert, Cass was informed by Flying Officer O. Fleishman that there were some twenty Jewish boys but no one capable of conducting the services.[68] Cass wired him saying that he was sending twenty-five sets of 'the Adler Mahzor' and a suggested outline for the various services by express, as well as some 'religious messages ... which may be read by yourself or someone you appoint.' He instructed Fleishman:

> In conducting the services, I would urge you to allocate different parts to several men so that everyone will have an opportunity to participate in them ... Although these arrangements may seem to be a very hasty makeshift, it is really not so. We cannot expect in the course of our duties in wartime to carry on as usual, and they will really experience all the more the sacredness of our High Holidays through their personal efforts on their behalf.

He wired also to Private A. Rosner of the Winnipeg Grenadiers, then stationed at Terrace, that Fleishman would be holding services at Prince Rupert. Cass urged that if he and other Jews there could not attend, 'your men will carry on under your own power, and will experience the sacredness of the traditions of the High Holidays all the more intensely because you have put forth every effort in personal participation.'[69]

The chaplains and the WEC could not monitor all the bases on which Jewish servicemen were located. Sometimes nearby communities took the initiative. In March 1943, Archie Dover, a member of Cornwall,

Ontario's, Beth-El congregation, informed the Congress that there were twenty-five Jewish soldiers at the local training centre:

> We are only too happy to take care of them in our synagogue, and have a service for them, but we are wondering if there would be some way of appointing our local Shochet [ritual slaughterer] to be an assistant Chaplain and have him conduct services at the Training Centre on Sundays for the Jewish boys.[70]

Cass discovered that 'there are fifteen boys from Toronto and several of them insisted that they attend Synagogue Parade only, [but] I don't believe it is wise to have Mr. Levine [Cornwall's shochet] conduct service in the Camp with such a small number ... if the boys still insist [on] attending Synagogue on Sunday.'

Gershon Levi organized weekly services wherever possible. In February 1942, he informed commanding officers of the RCAF stations in the Trenton area that 'arrangements have been made for the conduct, at the synagogue in Belleville, of Religious Services each week for RCAF personnel of the Jewish faith stationed at Mountain View, Belleville and Trenton. The services begin at 1100 hours, and last for 30 minutes.' He requested posting of notices and transportation for personnel attending.[71]

The Jewish chaplains, like others, had to bury the dead, see that graves were marked with the Star of David, and write to bereaved families. Gershon Levi was especially concerned that all Jews be identified. 'Charlet is definitely Jewish,' he wrote to Cass in January 1945, 'whatever the burial return may say, [but] Sgt. Kaughman does not appear in my records, nor in those of Congress, and does not look as if it should.'[72] Levi designed two different temporary Star of David markers made of boards and sticks for Jewish soldiers' graves.

Reuben Slonim, rabbi at Toronto's Beth Hamedrash Hagadol (McCaul Street Shul), conducted services every Sunday at the British Commonwealth Air Training station at St Thomas for about one hundred Jews. With the help of one of his 'parishioners,' and the shul's women's auxiliary, he provided elaborate Passover seder fare for the boys, including matzoh ball soup, gefilte fish, roast chicken, carrot tzimmes, prune compote, nuts, and sweets.[73] On his Sunday visits, Slonim brought salamis, pickles, corned beef, baked beans, 'and all the other marvellous kosher ambrosia from the Spadina Avenue delicatessens ... Nothing was too good for them: foile verenikes, kamish broit, knishes filled with potato or kasha, almond rolls and honey cake, pepper fish with plenty of sugar, according to the recipe of the Jews of Lodz and Warsaw.'

Parcels from home or from the many Jewish support groups were most welcome, especially if they contained food with a yiddish *tam* (that special Jewish flavour). Jewish veterans' eyes light up, even after fifty years, at the thought of food. Barney Danson and Edwin Goodman relished receiving *vurst*, which had to be specially packed in parafin wax. To this day, Danson remembers regretfully having to throw away one *vurst* that he wrongly thought had gone bad. (It had just 'matured,' he later realized.) In a letter to his mother in December 1944, Aaron Palmer wrote: 'Just received Aunt Hendah's parcel and the Voorsht that Aunt Leah sent. Everything came in fine condition.'[74] To another donor, he wrote: 'Received your lovely parcel ... Boy what a treat. All those fancy nuts, peanut brittle and chocolates.' Harold Rubin, along with another Ottawa Jewish soldier, went on a kosher delicatessen 'crawl' one night in Leeds. 'We couldn't help comparing these English establishments to Barney Weiss's delicatessen on Rideau Street,' he remembered.

One non-Jewish observer witnessed Jewish families visiting their servicemen at a camp north of Toronto just before the soldiers' departure:

> Every mother and grandmother had a huge food parcel for a son or grandson ... I have never seen such a feast in all my life. There was every kind of Jewish delicacy you can name ... Today I still remember the feeling of wonder and humility that hit me as I stood at that gate in front of those Jewish parents.[75]

Passover seders required elaborate arrangements. In early April 1944, Cass wrote to the commanding officer of the base at Debert, Nova Scotia, requesting 'adequate provisions for personnel of Jewish faith to celebrate the Feast of Passover.' He also wrote with elaborate instructions to the messing officer for the preparation of matzoh meal balls, charoseth, sponge cake, matzoh meal pancakes, matzoh fry, and matzohs with scrambled eggs.[76] He asked 'that Ordnance supply this mess with new dishes and cutlery, that have not been used before, as also pots, pans, etc. for preparing meals. In addition to the usual setting at table, wine goblets will be needed.' Prepared gefilte fish and smoked meat were sent by the WEC. For Passover observances in 1945, some 800 pounds of matzohs and 553 pounds of smoked meat were sent for Jewish servicemen in Canada.

Cass, recognizing the importance of Passover seders, took pains to organize these celebrations in the most difficult of circumstances:

> [Rabbi] Cass told me that as Passover in 1945 was about to begin, troops of the First Canadian Army were poised to cross the Rhine. Needless to say, all the troops – and especially the Jews – were apprehensive and jittery about entering Germany. Cass contacted General Crerar directly and stressed the importance of providing a seder and Crerar, bless his heart, immediately contacted CMHQ [Canadian Military Headquarters] in London and the necessary food was flown over from London. Cass said it did wonders for the morale of the Jewish troops.[77]

'I shall always remember,' Cass wrote in his war diary, 'the Passover Sedorim in the only structure left standing at Cleve where our men were marshalled to cross the Rhine and storm the east bank, taking matzohs and provisions with them from the Seder tables …'

Most service personnel were not likely to have access to information on the wider war and the disasters that had befallen European Jewry. In one book issued in 1944 for educational purposes, *The Battle of Brains: Canadian Citizenship and the Issues of the War*, soldiers were informed that small children were made to read *Der Stürmer*, 'which is full of abuse against Jews,' and that 'a systematic cultivation of a hatred of Jews has helped considerably to unite the German nation.'[78] By the time this work was published, most of Europe's Jews had been destroyed; but the book's readers were informed only that in the concentration camps, 'no Jews are accepted as sick; they could only be "well" or "dead."'

By late 1944, however, when the Canadian forces advanced into Holland, Jewish servicemen began providing assistance to Holocaust survivors in various locations. In December 1944, about five hundred children evacuated to Britain from German concentration camps were given food, chocolates, and toys at Chanukah parties, and supplies were sent to children still at Belsen.[79] Cass also reported to the principal chaplain (Protestant) that Chaplains Gevantman and Rose, then stationed in Holland, 'were very active in making the … Jewish festival a happy one for Jewish children … Through the Jewish Coordination Committee in Amsterdam, sweets were distributed to upwards of 3,000 children in the country.' Jewish communities in Amersfoort, Apeldoorn, Nijmegen, and Amsterdam were also given assistance, and 'troops were notified of all these functions and attended at the locality nearest their

Units.' Thirteen days after the town of Nijkerk was liberated by forces of Canada's 1st Division on 17 April 1945, Jewish soldiers happily observed armed members of the Dutch resistance supervising the clean-up of a local synagogue by captured local Nazi collaborators and SS men.

For the fifteen weeks immediately following the end of hostilities, Cass and Rose ran courses each week on Jewish history, religion, and culture for thirty men still in Holland.[80] They gave lectures that were intended 'to help the soldier refresh his knowledge of Judaism and ... to discuss the application of the ideals of Jewish religion and culture to the soldier's re-establishment in civil life.' Those who took these courses visited Jewish families in Amsterdam and toured its Jewish hospital, which housed many concentration camp survivors. Course discussions focused on antisemitism, Zionism, Holocaust survivors, and the post-war condition of Jews in Holland. Many highly appreciative letters were received from servicemen. One wrote that through this contact 'with Jewish men and women who witnessed and survived the Nazi bestiality, ... I have learned the meaning of life.'

For some Jewish service personnel, their Holocaust consciousness emerged when they searched for relatives in Eastern Europe at the end of the war. Private J. Chackowitz, who had not heard from his parents or any other family members in his Polish home town of Kosow-Telaki since 1940, applied to Cass for compassionate leave to try to find them.[81] In June 1945, Guardsman Julius Gosevitz wrote asking for Rose's help in getting information from the International Red Cross about his wife's family in Brest-Litovsk. Private W. Liebovitz requested permission to spend leave with an aunt and uncle living in Paris. A private serving in the Toronto Scottish Regiment in Holland asked Cass for help in locating a Jewish couple whose last known address was in Antwerp: 'The request was made in a letter received from an aunt in Toronto, that I do what I can to discover the fate of Mrs. Weiss and her children.' If successful in their applications, these soldiers would have learned all too well what happened to the Jews of Poland and France. But they were only a few, and the majority of servicemen returned to Canada very likely still unaware of the true dimensions of the Holocaust.

Some Jews serving with the Canadian army in Holland only saw firsthand what the Holocaust had wrought in that country. Only a day after Westerbork concentration camp was liberated by Canadian troops on 12 April 1945, Rabbi Cass was walking through it talking to as many of its surviving inmates as he could, and then conducting an emotional religious service.[82] A gunner serving with the 13th Field Regiment, Royal

Canadian Artillery, reported to Cass that when he was in Gorredojt, Friesland, he visited a synagogue: 'Sir the windows were broken but the ark was still up and there are five sefer torah in it ... and the Torahs are on the floor it is a shame to leave them like that.' A British Army gunner, serving with the 125 L.A.A. Regiment, Royal Artillery, reported that on seeing the 'disgusting mess' inside the synagogue in Nijmegen, he 'was shocked and filled with a deeper hatred of Naziism.' But when amid this devastation he saw the wall inscription *Da Lifne Mi Ata Omed* (Know Before Whom You Are Standing), he sensed that 'there still prevailed a spirit of holiness in this atmosphere.' In June, Rabbi Rose visited Displaced Persons camps in Germany and reported on the appaling conditions there.

Writing to the Congress's officials in January 1945, Cass reported on the Chanukah celebrations he had organized in several liberated Belgian and Dutch towns: 'Parties were arranged for hundreds of children ... and for adults too, for whom this was the first celebration in years.' In what must have been a most moving re-enactment of the first Chanukah, which marked the rededication of the Jerusalem Temple defiled by the ancient Greeks, Cass and scores of Jewish soldiers and civilians 'met in Synagogues which had been stripped and vandalized and rededicated them through the kindling of Hanukah lights.' He described how they 'met within front line areas under shell fire that seemed to burst just when an Amen was indicated in the Service.' Enthusiasm for these efforts ran high among Jewish soldiers. 'I am proud to say that our men contributed thousands of chocolate bars, bags of candy, and other delicacies as Channukah gifts to the children.'

Not content with organizing such celebrations, however, Cass stressed that rebuilding the Jewish communities in Holland required spiritual as well as physical resources. With no rabbis, teachers, or shochets, 'the reorganization of religious and communal life [here] is a task for generations,' and he urged the Congress to help fill the needs of thousands of children who were hidden during the war and were now looking in vain for their parents.[83]

Like many Jewish chaplains in Allied armies, Cass stayed on for almost another year in Holland and Germany, helping Holocaust survivors. His diary records his continuing encounters with them. He visited Bergen-Belsen in early December 1945, where he observed among the youthful Jewish inmates that 'Palestine is magic not only to their physical surroundings but to their entire spirit. It offers hope, pride, labor, creativity, a future, even in the depressing and dismal atmosphere of life in a military barracks.'[84]

Cass received many letters of gratitude. This one, from a sergeant in the First Canadian Army, Royal Canadian Electrical and Mechanical Engineers, who was about to leave for home, is worth quoting at length:

> I particularly remember your inspiring reconsecration of the little synagoge in Voghel, and your sermon last May in Almelo. I must confess that I was beginning to be discouraged and disappointed in our fellow Jews who had survived the horrors of the occupation. Your sermon showed me that I was wrong and led me to approach my fellow Jews with greatest sympathy and greatest understanding. As suggested in your bulletin, I have signed over my parcels to you.

With support from the WEC, chaplains also tried to make life easier for the families of Jewish service personnel. In July 1943, Cass wrote to the Montreal YMHA requesting a reduction in camp fees for children of servicemen. 'Please understand these families are not under normal circumstances, recipients of charity, nor do they wish to accept any now,' he wrote.[85] The chaplains and the WEC kept a list of the eighty-four Canadian Jewish prisoners of war, at least twenty-four of whom were RCAF personnel.

The chaplain–soldier relationship provides insight into the servicemen's level of Jewish education. Many of these sons of immigrants apparently had relatively little Jewish learning. Cass sadly noted 'an abyss of misinformation and of ignorance' about Judaism among the Jewish soldiers he encountered.[86] Whether they were typical of their generation is probably impossible to know. As they did constitute nearly 40 per cent of the men aged eighteen to forty-five, these soldiers were a good representative sample of the Canadian Jewish community's 'culture' in the interwar years. Many could not read the Yiddish letters they received from relatives. Perhaps the war changed some of them. Many of those Jews who enlisted already possessed a very strong sense that they were fighting for the Jewish people. One example of this attitude was that about 240 Canadian volunteers – including a number of non-Jews – followed Ben Dunkelman and joined the Israel Defence Force in 1948 to defend the new Jewish state. This was the second-highest per capita enlistment outside of Israel itself, surpassed only by the outstanding contribution of South African Jews.

The Second World War military experience occurred inside some emphatically Canadian institutions: the army, the RCAF, and the RCN. Sabbath observances took place on Sundays, not on the Jewish sabbath. Food was not kosher, except probably on Passover, when it was specially brought in (or possibly some mess officers attempted to follow Cass's elaborate instructions for preparing kosher food).* Services were of limited duration and, from a rigorous religious perspective, probably unsatisfying. Jewish servicemen and -women were thrown together, most of them probably for the first time in their lives, with non-Jews. Both would have seen each other in situations of mutual dependency. 'On the whole,' Cass reflected, 'relationships between Jew and non-Jew were of an excellent and wholesome character of comrades in arms.' Most Jews, he continued, made 'splendid adjustments to their non-Jewish buddies, considering the fact that many of them, particularly the large numbers enlisted from ... Montreal and Toronto, enjoyed only Jewish social relationships before enlistment.' He went on to say, 'Prejudices very often melted away in the flames of battle and fast friendships were formed between Jew and non-Jew.'[87]

In a sense, then, the services constituted a school for a type of Canadianization that went far beyond what most Jews had received previously. The servicemen and women, willy-nilly and probably unwittingly, absorbed the Canadian 'culture' of their military context. It might well be that the decline in antisemitism in Canada after 1945 was as much an outcome of this enforced togetherness and resulting camaraderie as it was a reaction to the horrors of the Holocaust and an offshoot of the prosperity that North America was enjoying. At the same time, for many Jews, service in the forces heightened their awareness of Judaism and deepened their identification with the Jewish people. The efforts of the Jewish chaplains, the soldiers' own war experiences, and a growing understanding of the evil intent of Nazism sharpened their dual identity.

At war's end, the troop ships brought the soldiers home to their loved ones. Some veterans, especially those who had seen combat, wandered confusedly, like Benny, the protagonist in one of Mordecai Richler's short stories, unable to adjust to civilian life and deeply unsettled for many years.[88] The vast majority, however, got on with their lives. But that is another story.

---

* Author's note: judging by my limited personal experience with RCN cooks in peacetime, I am doubtful.

12 Post-war Readjustments

'There ought to be a monument to each and every one of them,' commented Phillip Stuchen, a federal civil servant who spent nineteen months between 1945 and 1947 at displaced persons' (DP) camps in Landsberg and Heidelberg assisting Holocaust survivors. Stuchen was one of several Canadian Jews who worked for the United Nations Relief and Rescue Agency (UNRRA) and the American Jewish Joint Distribution Committee (the Joint). After a five-week orientation course in New York, he arrived in Germany in the summer of 1945 to join the health and welfare effort in the camps.[1]

Stuchen was impressed by the courage and determination of the survivors. In an article for the *Queen's Quarterly*, he described the strenuous efforts made by former concentration camp inmates to rebuild their lives by learning trades, producing goods for themselves and the occupation forces in Germany, and administering their camps. That this 'saving remnant' would be useful immigrants for Canada he had no doubt. The Holocaust survivors were 'well equipped with a trade or profession for that day when their emigration to ... Canada or elsewhere will take place. It may well happen, indeed, that a machine operator trained at Lampertheim or a tailor employed at Camp Landsberg will eventually find his way to Montreal or Toronto or Winnipeg.'[2]

Hananiah Meir Caiserman, accompanied by Sam Lipschitz (editor of *Vochenblatt*), dispatched by the Congress in 1946 to report on the condition of Jews in Poland and help locate surviving members of Canadian families, observed that 'all is dust and desolation.'[3] When he met some survivors in the ruins of Bialystok, Caiserman wrote: 'The twenty-five people (men and women) who had supper with us, each had a number burned on their arm while in the concentration camps. Each has a story of horror and slow death both physical and moral and one continues to wonder, "How could they stand it? How?"[4] Appealing to Canadian Jews to send over relief, he commented: 'I was not prepared to understand the real meaning of finding 65,000 Jews from 3 1/4 million who lived there before the war. Under the circumstances, I did not expect to find their loyalty as Jews unimpaired.'

In another communiqué, Caiserman reported a conversation with Yechiel Leben, a nine-year-old boy living at a children's home in a town near Warsaw. 'My father and mother were both burned alive. I only have my little brother, David, one year old, at the same children's home,' he said. He also has an uncle, Zigmund Leben, in Lodz, Poland. He knows he has another uncle named Leben who lives in Canada or in the United States. "Find him for me," he actually cried and I cried with him.' Especially moved by the plight of children who 'had escaped annihilation [and] wandered about the forests and fields of Poland, often dying friendless and without finding the peace of a grave,'[5] he adopted one of these orphans and urged Canadian Jews to open their homes to others whom the Congress was sponsoring.

When he arrived back in Canada in February with 1,500 letters and messages from survivors to their families, Caiserman was so emotionally overwrought that he was forced to rest for several days in Halifax before proceeding to Montreal. There he was deeply disappointed by the initial response to the project of bringing Holocaust orphans like Yechiel Leben to Canada, a response that, he commented, 'does not reflect honour on Montreal Jewry.' And he was outraged by the callous disregard of the Joint's appeal for assistance in placing Jewish women and girls whom the Canadian government was prepared to admit as domestics. Jewish housewives did not want them. 'I cannot believe that Jewish women would discriminate against Jewish girls and thereby deny them Canadian entry,' he thundered.

> Jews of Canada as elsewhere are living through the greatest crisis in our history. Each Jew must be aware of this and must draw conclusions of personal responsibility. Is there a greater humanitarian deed than the rescue from D.P. Camps of as many Jews as possible? ... How could there be a prejudice? ... It is a shameful prejudice against our own sisters. It is a matter of Jewish honour.

In the meantime, public attitudes remained strongly antisemitic, notwithstanding the newsreels showing horrific scenes from the recently liberated Belsen and Dachau concentration camps. In an October 1946

Gallup poll that asked respondents to list nationalities they would like to keep out of Canada, Jews were deemed the second least desirable immigrants.[6]

The attitude of some Canadian government officials was as bad or worse. One serving in the High Commission in London wrote of 'black marketing, dirty living habits and general slovenliness' of the Jewish Holocaust survivors in the German DP camps.[7] Nevertheless, Canada's antisemitic immigration policy softened in 1948, when the government recognized the need for an increased labour supply in a more buoyant economy and also gave in to 'irresistible pressure from her U.N. Allies.' Substantial numbers of Jews began arriving, starting with the 1,116 war orphans sponsored by the Congress.

Near Salzburg, Austria, Ethel Ostry Genkind (a Winnipeg native and a social worker with experience in Manitoba, Toronto, Montreal, and Palestine) handled the job of organizing the orphan children whom the Canadian government had allowed to enter the country. Witnessing Holocaust survivors in Austria, she wrote of 'hundreds of victims of the concentration camps, streamed in ... every day ... undernourished, sick, tortured, weary human beings ... sunken-eyed ragged adults and children with outstretched arms, begging hands and rickety bare legs, their chest bones sticking out from thin tattered bits of clothing.'[8] She warned of the problems ahead in the recovery and readjustment of these young people, most of them in their late teens: 'How can a child forget that his parents chose death that he might live or that he was forced to pull the trigger that killed his brothers and sisters? ... Integration of these young people is a slow process in which the whole community must play a part.'[9]

Enormous communal resources were mobilized by a committee headed by Samuel Bronfman, who took a special interest in this project. Reception centres were set up, and foster homes arranged in communities across the country.[10] In 1948, 1,800 Jews, including several hundred furriers and milliners, arrived under the so-called Tailor's Project, which arranged for experienced workers in the men's clothing industry to be admitted under the combined auspices of Congress, industry, labour unions, and the JIAS. In all, Canadian Jewry spent nearly three million dollars on the reception, resettlement, and rehabilitation of approximately 11,000 displaced persons and some 4,000 to 7,000 other survivors who entered Canada between 1946 and 1951.

Jean Gerber points out that 'Congress' post-war activities were overwhelmingly concerned with bringing survivors (who were often referred to dismissively as 'greener') into Canada, whereas in 1943 American Jewish organizations had already designated Palestine as the post-war haven for surviving Jews of Europe.'[11] From her key position in the German DP camps, Lottie Levinson, a former executive-secretary of the Congress in British Columbia, worked on the assumption that survivors would prefer to immigrate to Canada rather than to Palestine and deplored 'the fallacy of too much nationalism' among them.

Although overwhelmingly drawn from Eastern Europe, these migrants had experienced the Holocaust and had endured the destruction of both family and home; they had persevered through years of fear, hiding, and hunger, and had survived loss of childhood, values, and hope. The difficulty of their adjustment to Canadian life was observed by one Toronto social worker, Ben Lappin, who pointed out that the Canadian emphasis on 'positive ends [such] as the achievement of social and economic independence ... [evoked] bitter memories and suspicions among the orphaned children,' who might have expected a deeper understanding of their precarious mental state at that time.[12] Many Jewish professionals reported difficulties with the lay community, whose goodwill often surpassed their understanding of the need for a certain detachment in handling these cases. Although orphans and other immigrants benefited from this support, their difficulties in adjusting often created tensions.[13]

Some of them had intended to go to Palestine, but were forced by the delays in getting permits and by the conditions in the DP camps to go to Canada instead. One remembered:

> We lived in what had been a bathroom, in the barracks. The walls were mouldy. We lived there two years. I was sick – I lost a baby. One day my husband came home and said, 'Come on, we're going to Canada.' 'Wait a minute,' I said, 'that's not in the plan.' 'Look at you,' he said, 'we can't live like this. At least in Canada we can live.'[14]

Some immigrants, offended by what they perceived to be 'negative reactions and attitudes,' withdrew from the Jewish community. After a serious disagreement with a local union activist, one survivor realized 'that this person knew nothing about the ... Holocaust ... [and I] pledged never to discuss my experiences again with a non-survivor.'[15] Other survivors resented the established Jewish community. One commented, 'Maybe they were going around with the guilt they could not work out with themselves that they left us over there. They didn't put up here a big fuss.'

In Hamilton, where the community hosted twenty-five orphans and other survivors, social workers' inexperience and the 'problems of personality difficulties stemming from their concentration camp and other war-time experiences,' sometimes led to serious difficulties.[16] Even though their language training, clothing, loans, housing, recreation, and medical needs were provided for, the immigrants had difficulty connecting with community workers. For a variety of reasons, some did not feel comfortable at the Jewish Community Centre, where, as one of them put it, people were greeted coldly with '"Hello, how are you," and that's all.' And the social workers had their own complaints. One observed that the immigrants 'have adopted the "I have suffered and you owe me" concept.' In fact, many immigrants, alienated from North American Jews, were haunted by horrible memories, longed for lost loved ones, were fearful of antisemitism, and, in a few cases, had been morally corrupted by their wartime experiences. So, while the vast majority of them soon settled into jobs, families, and homes, others just drifted, alone, and permanently heartsick.

Survivors' adjustment depended mainly on the social norms in the host community. On the basis of extensive quantitative comparisons, Jean Gerber found that in Vancouver's small Jewish community, 'the fluid nature of the receiving ... Jewish society allowed survivors easy access to institutions and economic mobility.'[17] And because survivors had such diverse backgrounds, they easily 'integrated into existing patterns already established by the host Jewish group,' moving into the same neighbourhoods, occupational networks, and institutions. They strengthened the Vancouver Jewish community, contributing money, participating in its governance, and bringing 'a unique perspective on recent Jewish history, both in the realm of ideas and in ... teaching and documenting the Holocaust.'

In some cases, the new arrivals started off as labourers. One recalled working on a CPR construction crew near Penticton, British Columbia:

> There was [*sic*] nine Jewish boys in that railroad gang, so the Jewish community of Vancouver got permission, and they brought them down for Pesach and they had a seder for them and [one of us] decided when his contract expired that he's going to come to Vancouver and settle. Being a tailor by profession it was very easy for him to get a job here.

Even though she wanted to be with other Jews, one female survivor, at least initially, found it difficult to join the High Holiday services in a Vancouver synagogue:

> When I went to the synagogue here and I looked down and I've seen all the families, all of a sudden it was such a shock to me, I couldn't take it. I felt

that we had nobody, that I'm a piece of sand somewhere on an island, like [I had] no past. And I went out. I said, 'Am I jealous? No, I'm happy for the people,' but I couldn't take it. Then I said, 'I have to deal with it.' I bought some records of the famous Chazzanim, I took a few friends who didn't go to the holidays, and we would sit at home and listen. I couldn't face it for a long time.

By 1970, however, the vast majority of immigrant Jews had prospered and were employed alongside the native-born Jews, even occupying a higher percentage of the professional class.

In Toronto, one group calling itself Shearith Hapleta (Escaped Remnant), numbering 425 members, was formed for private cultural and social events, leading Rabbi Abraham Feinberg to comments: 'they tend to nourish themselves on the familiarity of their own colleagues.'[18] In Montreal, many survivors clubbed together in their own *landsmanshaft*, the Czenstochover Society, bonding in anguish, memory, and hope. A member reflected:

> We were very close, very, very close ... We used to tell stories. Do you remember this? As I said before, familiarity [with the past] is a very, very touching thing, which you can't buy for money. And we enjoyed it immensely, all through the years ...[19]

Another observed:

> I feel the closest to the people who came from the Zamosc roots ... It was very important for me, very important. Among these people, it was possible to reminisce about my home. This was a constant theme of our conversations. We used to remind ourselves of all the different things in our old home. This enriched my life very much.

A woman survivor who was crying at a Holocaust memorial service in 1949 was told by a Canadian-born Jew to stop. 'Enough is enough ... No more crying and no more talking about what happened. This is a new country and a new life.' But among themselves, survivors felt free to reminisce: 'Amongst our group, if we felt like talking about something, we could. We were listening to each other's stories, and it was just fine.' These small groups, dedicated to mutual aid, support for Israel, and Holocaust commemoration, thrived, helping survivors to adapt. Many married, started businesses, had children, and established homes. Some lapsed into a lifelong depression that affected even their children and grandchildren. Most felt the significant distance between themselves and the established Jewish community open up again over the proper response to the re-emergence of pro-Nazi organizations in the early 1960s.[20] Studying the life histories of survivors, Paula Draper concluded that 'their anguish and survival were ongoing, as they attempted to create new lives, new families, indeed new identities, in Canada. Yet the burden of memory keeps them forever strangers.' Reflecting on his childhood in Canada, Moses Znaimer, the son of survivors, remembered: 'I was not brought up to go out and conquer the world. I was brought up to be grateful that we weren't being killed in the streets or sent to the ovens.'[21]

But the very presence of survivors in the communities also contributed, in the words of Jean Gerber, to 'the emerging ideology of post-war North American Judaism, ... [which] sought to explain the Holocaust and the rise of the state of Israel as interconnected events.'[22] In a wider sense, the survivors, as 'eye-witnesses to the Holocaust, influenced the direction of community thinking about the nature and meaning of Jewish life ... They did this not only by appealing to a shared distant past, but by presenting a Judaism in which survivor and native-born could share a sense of history as well as a destiny.'

Though survivors formed the majority of post-war Jewish immigrants (some 30,000 to 35,000 of them and their children had come by 1956),[23] substantial numbers of Jews were arriving from the United States and the British Isles, and during the early 1950s, Israelis comprised the largest single component of arrivals. Three-quarters of the Israeli immigrants had moved to the homeland after the Second World War; only 11 per cent were born in that country. By 1963, nearly 11,739 Israelis had reached Canada, and many more were to follow. By that time, the five thousand Hungarians who had arrived in 1956 and 1957 had been absorbed, with large Congress assistance, and a substantial inflow was coming from Morocco, Egypt, and Tunisia. Meanwhile, the beginnings of what was to become a significant South African migration were already in evidence.

Life for Jews in Canada slowly became easier after 1945. Most of the nastiest and most public forms of antisemitism virtually disappeared, especially in Quebec. Human-rights and anti-discrimination legislation allowed for easier social and economic mobility, and general post-war Canadian prosperity facilitated an enormous expansion of the Jewish community's institutions. Jews united behind the Zionist banner as never before, joined in the dual objects of Jewish rescue and national revival. Some prominent Canadians harboured contemptuous attitudes towards Jews and there were antisemitic incidents, to be sure, some of them very serious.[24] Graves were desecrated, anti-Jewish literature was circulated, poisonous remarks were made by public figures, restrictive covenants prevented Jews from living in certain areas, and Jews still were barred from many resorts and private clubs. But all of these episodes were minor compared with the antisemitism current in Canada in the 1930s.

The change was particularly evident in Quebec.[25] David Rome, the Canadian Jewish Congress press officer who closely monitored the local scene, had reported in 1942 that 'the vigorous anti-conscription campaign in Quebec took a violently anti-Jewish form and was marked by several clashes in the streets of Montreal.' He observed the following year that only the Quebec City synagogue issue marred an otherwise quiet provincial scene. There was an upsurge of antisemitism in 1944, with the burning of the newly finished synagogue in Quebec City and the emergence of the 'Jewish issue' in the August provincial elections. But matters were generally improving. In 1945, Rome recorded only the damaging of several tombstones in a Montreal cemetery, while noting that Father Stephane Valiquette, S.J., had published an article in the influential Jesuit publication *Relations* that was sympathetic to the plight of the Jews, who, in his view, were in an inferior position in the Protestant school system. In 1954 Valiquette established a Quebec branch of the Council of Christians and Jews. Overall, Rome observed, 'there has been a diminution of anti-Jewish agitation ... in the province of Quebec ... and there have even emerged the beginnings of intergroup activity with the participation of the dominant Catholic Church.'

The Anglo-Protestants insisted that Jews had no rights in the Protestant school system. In 1945 the Protestant school board of Outremont – where some of Montreal's Jewish population was beginning to live – refused to renew the agreement allowing Jewish children to attend their schools. Premier Maurice Duplessis personally tried to persuade the Protestants to reconsider, but the issue took time to be resolved,[26] leaving the Jewish community sorely agitated. A few years later, similar problems arose in the suburb of Hampstead, which was experiencing a substantial Jewish influx. In this case, too, provincial authorities attempted to soften the position of the Protestant board towards the Jewish presence.

Despite these isolated incidents, something astonishing was taking place in Quebec. In Rome's words, it was 'the remarkable rapprochement between the Jewish community and the French-Canadian Catholic majority.' When Laurent Barré, the provincial minister of agriculture, made some antisemitic comments in the Legislative Assembly, he was publicly condemned by Mgr. Henri Jeannotte, a member of a special committee put together by Montreal's archbishop, Joseph Charbonneau, to deal with questions related to Jews. Jeannotte's statement met with approval in the French-language press. 'For the first time in the history of this province the Church condemned a public figure for his anti-Semitism,' David Rome exulted. Meanwhile, the committee began a systematic and widely noticed education campaign directed against antisemitism. It also played a key role in quashing the re-emergence of *Le Goglu*, the vicious antisemitic rag of the 1930s.[27] A Catholic youth publication that included antisemitic attacks was condemned, withdrawn, and reprinted with the offending passages excised. Archbishop Charbonneau even pressed *Le Devoir*, where antisemitic articles, so common in the 1930s, had completely disappeared, to employ younger, more progressive, and more humanistic editors. In a November 1952 issue of *Le Devoir*, none other than André Laurendeau, the leader of Jeune-Canada's antisemitic campaign of the 1930s, published a scathing critique of Senator Joseph McCarthy's antisemitic attacks: 'After the assassination of six million Jews under Hitler's reign, one must not have a too delicate stomach to swallow these fanatical denunciations without heaving. Such antisemitism is so stupid that it turned us into philosemites.'[28]

What explained this shift from what Rome called 'longstanding prejudice' to 'remarkable rapprochement'? David Rome believed that French Canadians, after a long resistance, finally had begun meeting with other groups 'to deal with common problems and to bring Canadians of various faiths together.' He pointed to the Council of Christians and Jews and the Quebec Federation of Youth as venues for the 'sympathetic appreciation of the intellectual and communal life of the Jewish and other groups in the country.'

This rapprochement was also apparent in the enthusiasm for works by the Quebec Jewish poet Abraham Moses Klein and the painters Norman Leibovitch and Louis Muhlstock in French-language periodicals. Several Montreal Catholic groups even initiated lectures by clerics on Jewish topics. In 1949 Rabbi Chaim Denburg was appointed a lecturer in medieval studies at the Université de Montréal, the first Jew to join the faculty of a Catholic university in Canada. While David Rome recognized that 'anti-Jewish prejudice was [not] destroyed in the province,' he believed 'it [had] distinctly lost the influence and the respectability which it once enjoyed.'

Meanwhile, it was noted that the medical school at the Université de Montréal, unlike McGill, had no Jewish quota and that Dominican and Jesuit priests were actively trying to dispel French-Canadian prejudice against Jews. 'French Canadians,' one journalist commented, 'are no more anti-semitic than their English compatriots and a greater frankness often makes them easier for many Jews to get along with than the more circumspect British.'[29]

Much was happening in Quebec to change traditional views. French Canada, as the sociologist Everett Hughes explained in his 1943 scholarly study, was still 'in transition,' influenced by massive industrialization wrought largely by American investment throughout the province. The battering ram of capitalism was destroying the old way of life, and the Second World War had accelerated the transformation from an essentially rural province to an increasingly urban, industrial society, which in turn brought a growing degree of secularization.

Some elements of the church became infused with ideas such as those espoused by Father Georges-Henri Lévesque, a Dominican priest-academic deeply committed to democratic norms and liberal values in transforming Quebec, who established the School of Social Sciences at Laval University in 1938.[30] The relationship of church and state and the definition of Quebec's very personality were undergoing significant revision. 'From 1945 on,' Pierre Elliott Trudeau observed, 'a series of events and movements had combined to relegate the traditional concepts of authority in Quebec to the scrap-heap.' Trudeau, only a few years earlier associated with clerical fascists and antisemites, was one of a small group of French-Canadian intellectuals with a new openness to ideas that rendered Quebec less isolated and inward-looking.[31] He was among those who led the 1949 Asbestos strike, which symbolized the end of the old Quebec and the dawning of the new. André Laurendeau and others began to meet French-speaking Jewish intellectuals and re-evaluate, and even repent, the antisemitism of their youth.

By the late 1940s, the Quebec Catholic Church was no longer as monolithic, parochial, and nationalistic as it had been between the wars and was beginning to shift its discourse to focus on more universalistic values. A more liberal clergy was emerging in Montreal, many of whom were attempting to enter into dialogue with non-Catholics. After the war, the Vatican also stressed to Quebec clergy the importance of the

European refugee crisis and the necessity of bringing an end to the traditional anti-immigration attitude in the province.

Antisemitism had by no means disappeared in *la belle province*. Canon Lionel Groulx, for one, did not change his views about Jews after the war. In 1954, when asked for his opinion on 'the Jewish problem,' he replied that while 'Christian kindness forbids us all forms of antisemitism, ... history and daily observations have only shown us [Judaism's] revolutionary tendency.' And because of the Jewish passion for money, he contended, one finds Jews at the bottom of 'every shady affair, of every pornographic enterprise: books, movies, plays, etc.' That's why, Groulx continued, Jews are prepared to sacrifice in business and the professions 'all moral scruples.'[32] *L'Action Catholique* continued to publish articles demonizing Jews just as it had in the 1930s.

Moreover, the idea of the mythical Jew as enemy of French Catholic communal purity continued to find public expression; the Custos report on the Asbestos strike of 1949 blamed the event on 'Judeobolshevists.'[33] In the late 1940s, an affair involving Comte Jacques Duge de Bernonville, who had been condemned to death by a French court for war crimes during the Vichy regime, indicated that, for a few at least, fascism was alive and well in 'la belle province.' This collaborator was illegally brought to Quebec and protected by local pro-fascist sympathizers, including the prominent historian Robert Rumilly. One provincial politician, René Chaloult, delivered a strong antisemitic statement in the National Assembly in defence of de Bernonville, and Montreal mayor Camillien Houde led the campaign to prevent his deportation. Accusations surfaced that as many as twenty more French war criminals were hiding out in Montreal.

Meanwhile, several prominent Québécois citizens wrote to Prime Minister Louis St Laurent, one describing de Bernonville as the victim of 'a well-organized plot by the Left which breathes hatred and dissension against those who would grant him shelter.'[34] Church officials described the count as an 'excellent citizen' and 'a Christian gentleman,' and the St-Jean Baptiste Society formed defence committees in Montreal, Quebec, and Trois-Rivières. While the controversy raged, unbeknownst to the public the Dominion government passed a special order-in-council that allowed five other former Vichyites, who were under sentence of death or being sought by French courts, to remain permanently in Canada, despite the fact that they had entered this country illegally.

Overall, however, the old clerico-fascism and its associated 'moral crusades' were out of favour, even among most of its former adherents.[35]

Although Adrian Arcand surfaced again in the mid-1950s to fulminate against Jews in his monthly journal, *L'Unité national*, he had little influence and soon disappeared from view. Undoubtedly, antisemitism was still present in Quebec and the rest of Canada, but the Holocaust and the post-war Nuremberg trials made public displays less respectable.

At this time, the Jewish community began to proactively reach out to francophone clerical and intellectual leaders.[36] Led by Congress officers Saul Hayes and David Rome, Quebec Jewry reactivated their public-relations committee and established the Cercle Juif de la Langue Française to demonstrate to French Canadians that Jews were not 'on the side of the English' in Quebec. In fact, a segment of Montreal Jewish intellectuals was genuinely interested in French culture and in establishing a dialogue in French with like-minded Québécois.

In 1954 Naim Kattan, a francophone Jewish immigrant from Iraq and a distinguished author, was employed by the Congress to direct the Cercle Juif's activities and edit its *Bulletin*, which stressed the duality of francophone Jews in a nationalizing Québécois culture which retained its links to religious particularism.[37] Kattan connected well with several leading francophone journalists, including André Laurendeau and Jean-Marc Leger of *Le Devoir*, Roger Duhamel of *La Patrie*, and René Lévesque of the CBC. However, they cautioned that the Quebec Jewish community should cease presenting 'an English facade, [and] airs of unilingual English-Canadians,' as Conrad Langlois of *La Patrie* put it. Though Congress could not abolish this English 'facade,' the Cercle Juif did provide a highly useful meeting ground for some Montreal intellectuals from two of Quebec's three solitudes.

Still, manifestations of antisemitism persisted. In 1965 the Quebec liberal thinker Claude Ryan expressed the astonishing view that if French Canadians and Jews were to achieve a full rapprochement, 'a certain updating of the Jewish religion might be in order.'[38] When faced with Jewish concerns about aspects of French-Canadian nationalism, Ryan also reacted strongly, asserting that the Jews put the questions to him

> in a rather aggressive tone, as if they were entitled to get firm assurance from a humble person like myself ... The only thing I can tell them ... is that to the extent that they associate with the search that is going on ... in the French Canadian mind, ... there is a greater chance that this search will end up in a happy way. But to the extent that they keep putting questions as if they were standing in an outside position, the dangers are extremely great that this might explode in their faces.

Jews must change, Ryan contended, to overcome the old antisemitic attitudes 'still very much alive in the minds of most French Canadians.' Among other things, Ryan asserted, many Québécois believe that the Jew 'will do practically anything in order to make a fast dollar'; that he has 'the reputation of paying low salaries and being not too scrupulous about working conditions'; that Jews in general 'are extremely important in the making of financial decisions' in Canada; that Jewish notaries 'have tended to specialize in practices that leave much to be desired'; that 'Jews will support one another to death'; that 'Jews killed Jesus Christ'; and that 'Jews do not care for morality.' Coming from one of Quebec's leading intellectuals, such statements were nothing short of nauseating.

Nevertheless, barriers were toppling. Dr Victor Goldbloom was appointed to the Cabinet in the Liberal government of Jean Lesage in the 1960s. As well, Jewish parochial schools were recognized and supported generously by the government, and the semi-independence of the Jewish social welfare network in Montreal was also upheld.[39] Growing numbers of Jews were even appointed to teaching posts in francophone universities. At the same time, however, they still felt vulnerable. The separatist upsurge in the 1960s, the language legislation of the 1970s, the October Crisis, and statements by some sovereigntists made Quebec Jews anxious, causing many young ones, concerned about success in future career choices, to leave the province.

Antisemitism survived elsewhere in Canada, too. Members of the Social Credit movement in Alberta (and in Quebec), for example, made their antisemitic views public on the platform and in print.[40] Alberta-based members of the Canadian Jewish Congress monitored the situation closely and regularly urged Montreal headquarters to institute countermeasures. By the late 1940s, however, Jew-hatred had become such an embarrassment to the Socred national organization that it repudiated those factions and 'dissociate[d] itself from the racial and religious intolerance which they are propagating.' Even so, these elements continued to put out antisemitic literature on a regular basis; the *Canadian Intelligence Service* was one such periodical. Occasionally, pamphlets like *Plans of the Synagogue of Satan*, by Colonel F.H.M. Colville, a British Columbia Socred member, appeared, but these were always repudiated by the movement's leaders.

Prejudice persisted in other forms. Restrictive covenants, for example, were contracts that prevented the sale of properties to Jews and other 'undesirables.' In one Ontario case, Bernard Wolfe of London agreed to purchase a summer cottage at nearby Beach O' Pines Resort, but he was prevented from taking possession by such a covenant, which barred sales to persons of 'Jewish, Hebrew, Semitic, Negro or colored race or blood.'[41] The Ontario Court of Appeal upheld a lower court decision declaring the covenant valid, but the Supreme Court of Canada overturned it in November 1950. Meanwhile, the Ontario legislature passed a bill prohibiting new restrictive covenants based on race or creed. Although these actions lifted the prohibition on residence, the Congress and B'nai B'rith still battled against racial, ethnic, and gender discrimination in the work world and the schools.[42] In the wake of the Beach O' Pines decision, the Ontario government discouraged summer resorts from advertising that their clientele was 'restricted' or 'selected.' It became increasingly difficult for racists to discriminate, and utterly impossible to restrict Jews from living in certain areas.

Ontario, which enacted the Racial Discrimination Act in 1944 and the Fair Employment Practices Act in 1951, led all levels of government in passing comprehensive bills to outlaw discrimination and the dissemination of hate literature. Joseph Salsberg, Rabbi Abraham Feinberg, various labour leaders, the Jewish Labour Committee, the Canadian Jewish Congress, Jewish activists in the Ontario Progressive Conservative Party, and the Canadian Jewish press were all leading advocates for human-rights legislation and spearheaded efforts to mobilize the province's ethnic communities and labour groups to support the campaign. With Jewish individuals and organizations in the lead, in 1947, Saskatchewan's CCF government enacted the Bill of Rights Act to protect civil liberties and human rights.[43]

The Congress official Ben Kayfetz recalled, 'When I was first employed by CJC in April 1947, the chairman of the Joint Public Relations Committee said my first priority was to plan and work towards the enactment of a Fair Employment law. It came much sooner than we expected, in 1951.'[44] The act received support from an increasingly sympathetic public, whose attitudes had been altered by the Holocaust. Ontario premier Leslie Frost took a special interest in this body of legislation, even though some of his constituents saw this bill as an infringement of their rights. One old friend of Frost's complained, 'I do not want a coon or Jew squatting beside me.'

The pursuit of civil rights allied Jews and blacks, who also faced discrimination in immigration, employment, and housing. The Negro Citizenship Association joined the Jewish-led Toronto Joint Labour

Committee for Human Rights and the Jewish Labour Committee for Human Rights in the 1950s and 1960s to secure legislation preventing such discrimination.[45]

Unfortunately, neither legislation nor embarrassment prevented continuing antisemitism. In 1949 the internationally recognized economist Louis Rasminsky on the staff of the Bank of Canada was passed over for the post of deputy governor and in 1955 for the governorship likely because of antisemitism (though he was promoted governor in 1961).[46] Admission to some medical schools was still severely restricted, as McGill, for example, limited Jewish admissions to a rigid 10 per cent until the 1960s and the University of Toronto required higher marks of Jews than other applicants. Jewish graduates had to leave the city for their year of internship because most of Toronto's hospitals would not accept them. It was also still difficult for qualified Jewish doctors to acquire admitting privileges at these hospitals. When Mount Sinai Hospital was completed in the late 1950s, it was denied status as a teaching hospital for the University of Toronto until 1962. Such discrimination forced the Toronto and Montreal Jewish communities to continue to support their own hospitals, whose campaigns raised roughly 25 per cent of all monies raised for Jewish capital projects in the 1950s and 1960s.

Undoubtedly, the persistence of antisemitism in post-war Canada influenced the Congress's submission to the 1949 Royal Commission on National Development in the Arts, Letters and Sciences (known as the Massey Commission). Congress argued that Canada's national cultural institutions (such as the National Library, the Public Archives, the National Gallery, the National Museum, the National Film Board, and the Canadian Broadcasting Corporation)[47] should 'search for the formula which will vouchsafe the creation of a vibrant and meaningful Canadianism.' Speaking on behalf of Congress, Saul Hayes insisted that if these bodies made Canadians aware of the contribution to the nation of the country's many different ethnic groups, Canadian democracy would be strengthened and 'the best of national characteristics of the people who inhabit Canada, through the catalyst of conditions here, [would] emerge as a distinctive element of North American civilization.'

This was an argument, in short, for multiculturalism.[48] But Hayes was forced to recognize that the theory had flaws. Should literature and artistic expression be rewarded along ethnic lines? 'Are you going to limit the form of those works?' Professor Hilda Neatby of the University of Saskatchewan asked. '[Do] you ... want to offer special incentives to the people to express themselves along particular ethnical lines?' Asserting that 'you cannot look at the Canadian scene without being aware of the existence of groups,' she appropriately suggested that 'general encouragement' of literature and the arts would be just as effective. In the end, Hayes's arguments had little impact. But his brief, which forecast the multicultural policies of the 1970s, was an attempt to address the new ethnic reality of Canada, and to prove that all forms of racism could be reduced through new approaches to the question of Canadian identity.

Jews were now able to leave the old, crowded centre-town districts and move into newer housing in the suburbs. In Montreal the biggest movement was up from Outremont over the mountain into Côte-des-Neiges, Notre Dame de Grace, and the western suburbs of Saint-Laurent, Côte St-Luc, Chomedy, and Dollard-des-Ormeaux. In Toronto the main Jewish migration pushed up Bathurst Street, past St Clair, Eglinton, and Lawrence.

In Winnipeg, Jews moved out of the old North End into adjacent West Kildonan and southward into River Heights.[49] They built synagogues, schools, and social facilities, replacing virtually all of the previously existing institutional network. In Vancouver, they shifted from the east-end immigrant quarter to the newer, lower-middle-class, west-side neighbourhoods, leaving behind the synagogues and kosher food shops that were later replaced by newer and more elaborate structures. Although by no means affluent, many were able to afford the down payments, modest under National Housing Act provisions, for these new bungalows and split-level homes.

The old Jewish neighbourhoods, meanwhile, remained. Many of the older generation of immigrants – now joined by Holocaust survivors – stayed on. Emotionally attached to their old synagogues and comfortable in their houses, they continued to walk the familiar streets and frequent the customary stores. Probably, they empathised with the recently arrived Italian, Greek, and Portuguese immigrants now buying houses and shops in their old neighbourhood. And, of course, not all Jews were financially able to move 'uptown' in the 1940s and 1950s; thus the inner-city neighbourhoods retained some Jewish families and the old hang-outs. The corner of College and Spadina in Toronto continued to draw people whose nicknames (Big Norm, Stok, Shacki, Feets, Applejack, Babe, Joe the Ball, Dapper, Dizzy, Jackriv, Fat Sam, Schvitzie, Gijik, Bagels, Baby, Piggie, Pork Chops, Oogie, and Butterballs) suggested the street smarts, derring-do, and post-war hipness of the Jewish would-be 'wise guys.'[50]

Some more affluent Toronto Jews moved away from the areas of first or second settlement up to swanky Forest Hill, but collided with its well-established Anglo-Saxon Protestants and a small pre-war Jewish group. The results, as reported in the 1956 sociological study *Crestwood Heights*, were interesting. Many of the new arrivals shed their 'old-fashioned' ways – abandoning Orthodox religious observances, for example – and adopted upper-middle-class norms. Both the Gentiles and the older Jewish settlers tended to regard the newcomers as 'vulgar, ostentatious, ignorant, and detrimental to the community.' In reaction to the rapidly increasing Jewish presence in Forest Hill public schools, in what was becoming a gilded ghetto, some of the long-settled Christians enrolled their children in private schools to avoid contact with Jewish students,[51] even though teaching standards were higher than in almost any other Toronto neighbourhood. Private schools, one Christian parent believed, were necessary because at Forest Hill Collegiate she thought her children would 'learn materialistic values ... mainly because of the insecurity of the Jews which has driven them to make a materialistic display of their position and wealth.'

With prosperity growing across Canada between 1945 and 1952, more than $31 million was spent on Jewish community buildings (including $11.5 million on hospitals, $8 million on synagogues, $5.24 million on YMHAs and community centres, and $4.18 million on schools).[52] New and expanded health and recreation facilities consumed more than half of the community's financial expenditures, while religious and educational institutions accounted for more than one-third. Social-welfare programs and general community administration took up the remainder.

Synagogues were springing up in the suburbs, and old shuls in many smaller communities were being replaced by new edifices that sometimes included community centres and athletic facilities. Typical of the latter were the Jewish centres in Halifax, Brantford, and Saskatoon.[53] A plot of land was purchased near the houses of the community's observant Jews, building and finance committees were struck, and a contractor engaged. Once the new building was completed (often after stormy meetings where members, now 'experts,' hotly debated plans for the new structure), the congregation took its leave of the old shul with prayer and rejoicing.

In Brantford the procession was led by children bearing the Union Jack and the Star of David; they preceded several elders carrying Torah scrolls and a newly acquired edition of the Talmud. Next came an aged but energetic fiddler, who led the congregants from the old shul to the new one as he lovingly played Yiddish tunes. Although the distance was only a hundred metres, symbolically it was one more major step away from the shtetl towards modernity.

In the bigger cities, many downtown congregations were re-established in new synagogues by members who had moved to the suburbs. In some cases, these new structures were built by amalgamations of two or three congregations that could not have afforded them individually. Other synagogues were built for entirely new congregations emerging on the city's outskirts. One, the Conservative Beth Am (House of the People) congregation, which was formed in 1954 by a group of working- and lower-middle-class Jews living in northwest Toronto, saw its fortunes fluctuate as Jewish geography changed.[54] It first assembled for services in a tent, then in a house, next in its own hall, and later, in a newly erected sanctuary. As numbers grew, Beth Am developed a large school, which flourished in the late 1950s and 1960s. However, a migration farther into the suburbs reduced membership in the 1970s, and the school's enrolment also declined sharply. By the mid-1970s, the congregation's long-range future was viewed as 'tenuous,' and in 1976 it amalgamated with another congregation.

Meanwhile, most of the old downtown synagogues were converted to churches or community halls for the new immigrants to the area. Only a few synagogues remained in use by the people unwilling or unable to move; others were kept going for the weekday convenience of businessmen whose stores or offices were located nearby.

Virtually abandoned, too, were the Jewish labour halls. Toronto's Labour Lyceum on Spadina, once home to the needle-trade unions and other left-wing organizations, and the major forum for debate for a generation of working men and women, struggled on with a rapidly diminishing and greying Jewish proletariat. By the mid-1950s, its May Day observances, once attended by hundreds of marchers proudly displaying their solidarity with workers everywhere, drew only a handful of the faithful. A story was read, labour songs were played, and a Yiddish speaker bitterly attacked the youth who had betrayed the movement and regarded their radical parents as 'simple-minded papas and blintz-frying mamas who cannot begin to fathom the *Weltschmerz* of our fine-cut intellectual offspring.'[55]

Such mordant views of ungrateful, non-comprehending, indeed self-absorbed youth, while understandable, were simplistic. As post-war Jewish geography changed, so did the community's ideals. The confusion and despair that gripped the Jewish radical left during trials of the Moscow doctors accused of plotting against the Soviet state and the treason charges against Rudolf Slansky in Czechoslovakia in the early 1950s – both clear evidence of antisemitism in Soviet-dominated Eastern Europe – drove long-time communist leader Joe Salsberg (affectionately known as Yossele or JB) out of the Party,[56] and destroyed the last vestiges of Communism's credibility for many Jews. Kruschev's revelations of Stalin's crimes at the 20th All-Union Party Congress in 1956 was the final straw. All that remained were a few cultural expressions of the movement's one-time fervour – the Toronto Jewish Folk Choir, for example, performed to full houses for years to come – and memories of the heyday of the Jewish left.

Some evidence of the type of Jewish family values that were current after the war can be found in a widely distributed cookbook and festival guide called *A Treasure for My Daughter*, published by a Montreal Canadian Hadassah-WIZO chapter in 1950.[57] This 'handbook for the Jewish Home' contains menus and recipes and explains the festivals and rituals through a conversation between a fictional mother and her daughter, Hadassah, who is soon to marry her sweetheart, David. It vividly depicts the 1950s assumption that the Jewish wife's basic role was to establish and maintain the Jewishness of home life by following *kashrut* and culinary tradition. 'Woman is to be the helpmate of man, socially, spiritually and physically,' Mother explains at one point, as if to underline the subservience expected. Regarding *nidah* (the period of separation between a husband and wife during the menstrual cycle), the mother adds that 'through the guidance in these vital matters which our laws afford, Jewish men have been taught respect for womanhood, moral discipline and ethical culture.' The daughter, portrayed as essentially ignorant of these matters and completely submissive to her family's wishes, asks questions about such fundamentals as betrothal and marriage, *mezuzah, kashrut*, sabbath, festivals, holidays, circumcision, *pidyon ha-ben*, bar mitzvah, and mourning – all the major events in the Jewish life cycle.

This book, and others like it, depicted the subservient and dependent role of the Jewish wife in the 1950s. Although portrayed as poorly educated in religious traditions, she was, however, responsible for the domestic observances of the holidays, including the laborious preparation of special foods. Assumed to be a 'housewife,' her responsibilities outside the domestic realm included an active role in Canadian Hadassah-WIZO, seen as the premier Jewish women's Zionist organization. Such volunteer groups were viewed as adjuncts to the main Jewish communal structure, which seldom allowed women into their higher councils.

These women became the 'matriarchs of Jewish suburbia,' fulfilling their roles both at home and in their cultural organizations and synagogues. Erna Paris, who grew up in Forest Hill, remembered:

> Our lives in the forties and fifties were insular and 'unreal' ... We knew almost nothing beyond the Village, the downtown department stores where we'd sometimes wander on Saturday afternoons and charge clothes to our father's accounts, and the bits of northern Ontario where we summered ... My friends were inordinately interested in clothes, encouraged by their mothers, who were grooming them as poised and beautiful Jewish Princesses (it must be said) from an early age.[58]

Paris and most of her contemporaries might have complied, but their younger sisters and, later, daughters were less likely to follow suit. More young Jewish women were pursuing higher education and entering the professions. By 1971 nearly 21 per cent of all Jewish working women were professionals, compared with 4.4 per cent in 1931.[59] Over the same period, the percentage of working Jewish women in blue-collar occupations fell from 33 per cent to less than 6 per cent. And increasing numbers of women entered the workforce, while still continuing to be homemakers.

But the status of women in the workforce was far from equal to that of men, largely because 'they enter later, often less prepared, and are often underpaid and overworked with their two jobs of paid work and homemaking.' For most working women, therefore, entry into the workforce was not a liberating experience, given that responsibilities at home were unchanged. A growing discontent raised the level of women's consciousness and led to the feminism that was to emerge in the 1970s and to flourish in the 1980s and 1990s.

These transformations were also reflected in shifting Jewish occupational patterns. The professional classes accounted for 5.62 per cent of the gainfully employed in 1941 and 8.57 per cent in 1951.[60] The percentage of Jews in commerce held steady, but in manufacturing it dropped almost 10 per cent. By 1961 the percentage of Jews in professions had risen to 13.59, while the number working in manufacturing had fallen dramatically. The number of Jewish university graduates was twice that of any other ethnic group. According to the 1961 census, Jewish males had the highest average income in Canada ($7,426, compared with $4,414 for all Canadians). This, perhaps, had much to do with the fact that 98.8 per cent of Jews lived in cities, the most highly urbanized of all Canadians.

A more important factor, however, was the Jewish proclivity for self-employment, a preference explained partly by job discrimination, which still persisted. Many Jews, anticipating anti-Jewish bias in fields like engineering and teaching, chose business or the professions instead. Consequently, 42 per cent of all Jewish males were self-employed, a rate nearly three times higher than that for any other ethnic group. This meant that more Jews were likely to remain in the labour force after age sixty-five, though they also entered it later because of a tendency to remain in school longer.

The face of Canadian Jewry was changing, and its numbers were growing. The population rose impressively from only 168,585 in 1941 to 204,836 in 1951 and 254,368 in 1961. It was registering its most significant growth rates in Alberta and British Columbia, even though the vast majority of immigrants moved to Montreal and Toronto.[61]

Edmonton, Calgary, and Vancouver showed the highest urban growth rates between 1951 and 1961; Winnipeg one of the lowest.[62] Its age profile and intermarriage rates were equally low. In 1931, Jews had made up a larger percentage of Winnipeg's fifteen-to forty-nine-year-olds than Canadians of all other origins, but in 1941 this cohort had shifted to ages twenty to fifty-nine, and in 1951 to ages twenty-five to sixty-four.

In 1931, 19.71 per cent of all Canadian Jews were between five and fourteen, but only 14.4 and 14.27 per cent were in that age group in 1941 and 1951. 'By 1951 average Jewish family size was the smallest of any among the eight largest ethnic groups in Canada,' Louis Rosenberg observed in his 1955 report on Canada in the *American Jewish Year Book*. As family size plummeted, marriages between Jews and non-Jews rose. They had skyrocketed from 4.9 per cent in 1926 to 12.4 per cent in 1944, declined to 10.4 per cent in 1946, and risen again to 12 per cent in 1953. Intermarriage rates continued their inexorable rise in the late 1950s and early 1960s. By 1963, they reached 18.5 per cent nationwide, and had doubled in the Atlantic provinces, British Columbia, Saskatchewan, and Alberta.

Regarded as a growing challenge to Jewish survival, intermarriage induced rising concern among community leaders, who viewed it as a serious threat to Jewish continuity.[63] 'A high rate of intermarriage weakens the norm of Jew marrying Jew and thus makes marriage to Gentiles more acceptable in the future,' sociologist Morton Weinfeld observed. Intermarriage rates rose even more rapidly in the 1960s, however, as post-war Baby Boomers came of age and a high percentage of them attended university.

The solutions to this problem were not readily apparent. Greater educational efforts and 'consciousness-raising' among the young were viewed as necessary measures by some, while Weinfeld suggested in 1981 that 'an open door policy [towards converts], in which every potential Jew counts, may do justice to both the diverse nature of Canadian Jewry and the need to minimize the population loss.' To add to the demographic conundrum, studies of the reproductivity of Canada's Jews in the early 1940s concluded that birth rates were so low that, barring changes to fertility or immigration levels, the community would ultimately die out.[64]

Between 1946 and 1960, Canada received some 46,000 Jewish immigrants, a figure equal to 27.3 per cent of the 1941 total Jewish population of 168,585.[65] This constituted a far higher proportion of post-war Jewish immigration than did the 160,000 who entered the United States.[66] It has been estimated that by 1990, Holocaust survivors comprised about 8 per cent of the United States Jewish community; in Canada they accounted for between 30 and 40 per cent of the total Jewish population by the same date.

In some respects, the face of Canadian Jewry was unchanged since its pre-war days. A survey taken in 1960 showed that established synagogue affiliations had not fundamentally altered since 1935. For example, 140 congregations out of 152 were Orthodox in 1935 (92.11 per cent), and 174 out of 206 were of that affiliation in 1960 (84.47 per cent).[67] The number of Conservative congregations had grown from 9 to 25 and Reform from 3 to 7.

Although before the war the majority of Orthodox rabbis serving Canadian congregations had been European-born and trained, by 1960 virtually all of them were graduates of yeshivas located in the United States, with a few from the four small yeshivas in Montreal and Toronto. Conservative congregations continued to draw their rabbis from the Jewish Theological Seminary in New York, and the Reform from Hebrew Union College in Cincinnati.

Membership levels in Conservative and Reform congregations had grown enormously, and their new synagogues and temples usually were large structures accommodating hundreds of people. In contrast, most

Orthodox congregations were much smaller, some unable even to afford their own rabbis.[68] In general, Louis Rosenberg noted, 'The rise in synagogue building and membership appeared to be motivated by a desire to "belong" rather than [by] strong religious conviction ... With the exception of the ultra-Orthodox, postwar active participation in Jewish religious life appeared to be limited to bar mitzvah and kaddish observance and synagogue attendance on Rosh Hashana and Yom Kippur.'

Relationships between rabbis and their congregations had changed, especially in Conservative and Reform congregations, where democratic norms prevailed. Speaking at the Rabbinical Assembly in 1975, Rabbi Wilfrid Schuchat of Montreal's Sha'ar Hashomayim observed mordantly that a rabbi can be popular with the synagogue's members and enjoy a big salary, but if he fails to hit it off with his board, 'he is ineffective in the congregation.'[69]

Traditional Judaism, nevertheless, experienced a revival in post-war Canada. Once sustained by the immigrant population, the Orthodox community soon had growing numbers of synagogues, most of them in the burgeoning suburbs, where sociologist Etan Diamond observes, they 'blended into the upwardly mobile, consumerist ... suburban culture, ... while retaining a strong sense of religious traditionalism and community cohesion.'[70] They still enjoyed, however, relatively little of the celebrity and social consciousness that were characteristic of rabbis in the much smaller Reform movement.

An Orthodox revival began in the autumn of 1941, when thirty-seven rabbinical students of the Lubavitch Hasidic movement arrived from Shanghai.[71] Refugees of the Lubavitch Yeshiva near Warsaw, these newcomers galvanized their nearly defunct community in Canada and served as forerunners for the Satmar, Belz, Klausenberg, and Tash Hasidim, whose communities formed in or near Montreal. Together they added a new vibrancy to Orthodoxy in Montreal. The Lubavitchers, who actively reached out to the rest of the Jewish community, most notably in the universities, also had a significant influence far beyond their own confines. The Hasidim and other Orthodox immigrants had a profound impact on religious education through the yeshivot they quickly established. By 1955 there were three Montreal yeshivot training young men in Torah studies, some of whom became the first Canadian-trained rabbis to serve in congregations.[72]

As well, a greater number of Canadians were pursuing advanced religious training in the United States. Between 1946 and 1955, twenty-three Canadian students graduated from American rabbinical seminaries, and forty-eight, three-quarters of them Orthodox, were still in training. These rabbis brought fervour and learning to their congregations, and an ability to relate well to young people. The Orthodox congregations, meanwhile, created more religious day-schools, offering instruction from kindergarten through high school. Jewish subjects were taught in Hebrew and Yiddish, secular subjects in English. Their constituency was drawn from the large infusion of ultra-Orthodox Jews, who accounted for about one-third of the 46,000 Jewish immigrants who had arrived in Canada between 1946 and 1960.[73]

Thanks mostly to increased immigration levels, Canadian Jewry did not falter, either in numbers or in spirit. Their philanthropic efforts were especially strong, and the community carried out enormous fundraising campaigns for both domestic needs and overseas projects. The greatest of these provided assistance to European Jews, who required massive aid. Canadian agencies operated mainly through the powerful American Jewish Joint Distribution Committee (Joint), to which the United Jewish Refugee Agency (UJRA) had contributed $350,000 in 1941 and 1942.[74]

In the spring of 1943, Canada sent another $100,000, along with shipments of food, blankets, and soap, to Russia, and provided subsidies to other aid programs. Huge relief shipments were also sent to Jews in Poland, France, Palestine, England, and Iran. In 1945 expenditures on these efforts reached one million dollars. The Congress employed Lottie Levinson, Ethel Ostry, and Phillip Stuchen to work in Europe with the United Nations Relief and Rescue Agency and the American Jewish Joint Distribution Committee. The Congress also marshalled the resources of various other organizations to help re-establish contact between Canadian Jews and their surviving family members in Europe and worked to facilitate good relationships between Jewish organizations and the UNRRA, efforts that were vitally important to advancing the welfare of Holocaust survivors.

Fundraising through the UJRA, which received money from intensive campaigning that reached out to every Jew in the Dominion, brought in $1.5 million in 1946. Virtually all synagogues made the Kol Nidrei appeal before the prayers ushering in Yom Kippur, when it was hard to ignore such a request. In addition, clothing and other supplies were collected and shipped to Yugoslavia, Poland, France, and Belgium, while several Torah scrolls were also dispatched. In 1947 one million pounds of kosher meat were sent to Eastern Europe, Italy, Germany, and France. European relief needs began to decline in the 1950s, but Canadian commitments to Israel had grown enormously.

Although assisting Holocaust victims in Europe was a conditioned response to tragedy, aid to the Jews of Palestine, known as the Yishuv, arose from millennia of hope. Both activities were deemed necessary, but one was inspired by a sense of closure, while the other was evoked by the Messianic hope of return to the ancient homeland and national revival.

This is not to say that the Holocaust and the rebirth of Israel were unrelated events, but the response of the Jewish world to each was inspired by different emotions. Consequently, by the early 1950s, fundraising campaigns for the Yishuv had assumed primacy over all else. In 1952 alone, of the $7.7 million raised for local and overseas needs, $3.8 million was allocated to Zionist endeavours. Another $1.3 million was provided for overseas and refugee aid, as well as all local Canadian social needs.[75] At the same time, State of Israel bonds were being sold in Canada.

Increasing numbers of Canadian Jews – proud of the military and economic successes of Israel, and curious about the country and its people – went there as tourists. Although often taken aback by the forthright, assertive behaviour shown to them by Israelis, Jewish tourists could take pride in having contributed a great deal to Israel. On a trip there in 1962, Mordecai Richler mused that

> these people, clearly dejected because not flowers but scorn was thrown in their path in Israel, had, it suddenly occurred to me, done more real good than I ever had. Tiresome, vulgar, rude they might be, but the flawed reality of Israel was testimony to their generosity. Evidence of their achievement was everywhere. Hospitals, factories, forests, libraries, schools, mostly paid for out of tin boxes in corner groceries as well as big donations pledged in the heady atmosphere of the country clubs.[76]

Fundraising campaigns were marked by considerable emotion, feelings usually heightened when eyewitnesses visited the European displaced persons' camps or viewed the success of the Yishuv. Less noticeable perhaps was the development of more skilled fundraising campaigns in the bigger communities by business and professional groups who targeted their own members for donations. Increasingly, too, professional fundraisers, many of them from the United States, were employed to manage the campaigns, while the federations who oversaw these efforts (such as the United Jewish Welfare Fund in Toronto and the Combined Jewish Appeal in Montreal) had the responsibility of distributing the monies among a variety of local institutions and organizations.[77]

Raising funds for Israeli and local requirements became a major preoccupation of Canadian Jewry in the 1950s, and one that necessitated continuing consultation between organizations. In 1951 the Congress, the ZOC, the Canadian Council of Jewish Welfare Funds, and B'nai Brith formed the National Conference for Israel and Jewish Rehabilitation to mobilize the community to meet rising demands more effectively. The United Jewish Appeal combined fundraising activities for all overseas needs and for local and national Jewish social services in one united drive.[78] Though most organizations cooperated, these increasingly efficient combined appeals were never able to bring all fundraising efforts in the community under their administrative control.

The one enduring umbrella organization during these years was the Canadian Jewish Congress. Presided over until 1962 by Samuel Bronfman and administered by a competent civil service headed by the executive director, Saul Hayes, the Congress had an authority unequalled by the American Jewish Congress. The Congress in Canada had several strengths. First, it was headquartered in Montreal, the country's premier metropolis and the home to about 40 per cent of Canada's Jews. Second, Samuel Bronfman's powerful personal involvement helped to give both focus and prestige. Above all, unlike its American counterpart, Canada's Congress effectively embraced Jewish organizations of nearly all political and social stripes in the country and was recognized as the voice of the entire community. This kind of catholicity and prestige, which derived from the dedication of officers like Hananiah Meir Caiserman, was not equalled anywhere else in the world and made of the Congress a true parliament of Canadian Jewry.

In the 1940s and 1950s, its gatherings were momentous events, and not just because of the pomp and ceremony so beloved by its elected leaders. The Congress's meetings informed Canada's Jews about crucial elements in their lives: the fate of less fortunate brothers and sisters around the world; the future of the state of Israel; and issues surrounding immigration, antisemitism, community relations, social changes, and education. Moreover, the Congress served as a forum for debate and a school for training new leaders. What also helped to strengthen its authority was the work of its brilliant director of research, Louis Rosenberg, whose numerous statistical reports, community studies, detailed investigations of the Jewish presence in Montreal schools, and historical documents in the Congress archives provided convincing evidence of the organization's sense of historical continuity and its commitment to addressing issues of vital concern to Canada's Jews.[79]

13 Jewish Ethnicity in Multicultural Canada, 1960–1980

When Herb Gray, member of Parliament for Essex West, was appointed minister without portfolio by Prime Minister Trudeau in October 1969, he was the first Jew ever to attain a federal cabinet position.[1] Others, such as Jack Austin, Robert Kaplan, and Barney Danson, followed Gray. By the late 1960s, a good number of Jews had been federal MPs, and many more had served as MLAs, provincial cabinet ministers, and as municipal councillors, mayors, and aldermen, while David Barrett headed an NDP government in British Columbia.

Although Gray's elevation was a significant political achievement, he was only one of many Jews who were 'making it' in Canadian public life. Pierre Trudeau created opportunities in federal politics that allowed Jews and other minorities to enter doors that were once tightly shut. By the late 1960s, some Jews were highly placed in the country's judiciary and civil service (the prestigious governorship of the Bank of Canada, for example, was held by Louis Rasminsky), and Jewish prominence in the professions was already noteworthy.

The rapid growth in appointments of Jews to university faculties was especially remarkable. After increasing slowly during the 1950s, Jewish appointments soared as universities expanded in the 1960s and 1970s. Faculty members were in short supply, and thus more Jews and other minorities were recruited. Political correctness and new laws that mandated fair-employment practices also helped to open doors. In 1961 there were 132 Jewish men and 19 women on university faculties; by 1971 those numbers had increased to 1,280 men and 225 women.[2]

At Queen's University, the number of Jewish faculty members rose rapidly during the 1960s, from about five to approximately thirty-five. At the University of Toronto, the increases were even greater. In the faculties of law and medicine, and in the departments of psychology and sociology, Jews were a high percentage of the total faculty, but there were few of them in modern languages, classics, and history, and fewer still in engineering. This acceptance of Jews extended even to the senior levels of university administration. The University of Toronto philosopher Emil Fackenheim and the law professors Bora Laskin of Toronto and Maxwell Cohen of McGill were notable not only in their professions but also for their participation in community affairs. Fackenheim, besides his eminence in German philosophy, wrote profound works on the Holocaust and modern Judaism.[3] Both within and outside the universities, scholarship on Jewish subjects was emerging. Soon, courses in Jewish subjects were introduced in some departments, providing a kind of breadth to the study of Judaism that had previously been strictly confined to texts at rabbinical academies.[4]

By the 1960s a number of Jewish business tycoons had emerged to take their places alongside the fabulously wealthy family of Samuel Bronfman. After his death in 1971, the fortune waxed and waned – and waned still further amidst controversy about a dubious turn to entertainment and other fields of investment.[5] For example, Sam Steinberg of Montreal parlayed a modest grocery store that was established by his mother in 1917 on St Lawrence Boulevard into a chain of supermarkets across Quebec and Ontario. He then successfully branched out into real estate, department stores, restaurants, and sugar refining to create a multi-billion-dollar empire before his death in 1978.[6] Steinberg's achievement was based on careful attention to detail and the understanding that to attract a large clientele in Quebec, it was essential to operate his businesses in French and to recruit able francophones for positions in his stores. By 1960 he had sixty stores in Montreal and thirty-two others across Quebec.

Real estate was an even more lucrative frontier of enterprise, and by the 1960s, Jewish firms were major players in the development of housing, industrial buildings, and inner-city skyscrapers. In Calgary and Vancouver, the Belzberg family was prominent. In Toronto, numerous Jewish-owned companies – Principal Investments, Cadillac-Fairview, and Olympia and York were among the leaders – helped to rebuild much of the downtown, while, as in the case of the Lebovic brothers, also constructing suburban developments.

The most dynamic of such real-estate firms was the Reichmann family's Olympia and York, which skyrocketed to astonishing success in the

1960s by developing small industrial buildings and housing estates, principally in Toronto and Montreal.[7] The family went on to erect major buildings in Toronto's burgeoning downtown financial core, with its tour de force being First Canadian Place, the headquarters of the Bank of Montreal.

By the mid-1970s, the Reichmanns – who were also major benefactors of Jewish religious institutions and generous donors to clinics and hospitals sponsored by other religious denominations – with perfect timing, made lucrative purchases in Manhattan just as property values started to skyrocket. Other profitable New York real-estate deals followed, capped by the World Financial Center, a skyscraper dramatically situated overlooking the Statue of Liberty at the entrance to New York harbour. After acquiring major shares of Gulf Canada and Abitibi-Price, the Reichmanns ventured into a major British development at Canary Wharf in London's Docklands area. Building on these successes, the Reichmanns became billionaires, though later business reverses somewhat reduced that lustre.

As well, the community was adjusting to new social realities outside its fences. Equality within Montreal's Protestant school system finally was successful. In hearings before the 1960 Quebec Royal Commission of Inquiry on Education, it was recommended that Jews be granted representation on the board.[8] In August 1962, Claude Ryan, a leading Quebec intellectual and later the editor of *Le Devoir*, urged the provincial government to concur because 'we will prove that what we ask for ourselves we also want for others.' The following year, Jews began to sit on Protestant school boards.

Meanwhile, a few provincial governments had begun to pay tuition grants to parents of children in the Jewish day-schools,[9] which, by the early 1960s, numbered no fewer than thirty, offering twelve to twenty-five hours per week of instruction in Jewish subjects in addition to the secular curriculum. Montreal had thirteen, Toronto eight, Winnipeg five, Calgary two, and Edmonton, Ottawa, Vancouver, and Hamilton one each. These schools, with 8,348 children, followed diverse programs. Some were *yeshivot*, which emphasized the study of sacred texts, while the modern schools taught courses in Hebrew language and literature, and Jewish history, religion, and customs. Schools with a left-wing orientation also offered Yiddish. In addition, some 14,500 pupils attended congregational afternoon schools, which gave about ten hours a week of Hebrew and religious instruction. Sunday schools, usually in

Reform congregations, offered three hours of instruction each week. Overall, about forty thousand elementary schoolchildren were enrolled, still only half to two-thirds of all Jewish children in the major cities.

However, the Jewish educational system was already severely strained. A shortage of qualified teachers was a serious problem, even though teachers' seminaries had been in operation in Montreal since 1946 and in Toronto since 1953. An equally vexing difficulty was the lack of resources for adequate teachers' salaries and expansion, forcing teachers out and increasing tuition fees. Moreover, the Congress officer responsible for education in the smaller Ontario communities noted 'a drop in enrolment of post–bar mitzvah age, and little interest in Jewish studies among university students and adults.'[10] Although these dilemmas were worrisome, it was unclear whether the Jewish community had the will to rectify this situation, leaving dedicated educationists, like the legendary Yaacov Zipper of Montreal, in deep despair. Beyond that lay the question of whether even a significant strengthening of Jewish education could nourish continuity.

As well as growing concern for the citizens of Israel, demonstrated by increased financial contributions, attention turned to the Jews in the Soviet Union. The Soviet government's campaign against Zionism was viewed as thinly veiled antisemitism and as an additional attempt to suppress Jewish cultural and religious expression, which had been revived in the Soviet Union following the Six Day War in 1967. Protests went into high gear across Canada in 1968. Speakers addressed public gatherings, and demonstrations took place on university campuses, on city squares, and in front of the Soviet embassy and its consulates.[11] At the urging of numerous synagogues and organizations, many Jews included a special prayer for Soviet Jewry in their Passover seders.

After meeting with a Congress delegation in the fall of 1970, Prime Minister Trudeau promised to strive during his forthcoming visit to the Soviet Union to persuade its government to 'allow Jews cultural freedom and permit some emigration to Israel.' Meanwhile, the Students for Soviet Jewry held a torchlight procession in downtown Toronto, and a large teach-in was held at McGill to denounce what Saul Hayes of the Canadian Jewish Congress called 'the Soviet denial of rights to Jews which are granted to other religious and ethnic minorities.'

At a Montreal gathering in November, Rabbi Gunther Plaut condemned 'outright antisemitism by government plan' in the Soviet Union. Perhaps recalling the alleged silence of Canadian churches during antisemitic persecutions of the 1930s and the subsequent Holocaust, he demanded to know: 'Where are the churches, where is the voice of organized Christian religion? Why are they silent? Why do they not help us mount a universal campaign to expose this latest example of cultural and religious genocide?' Answers from the churches were weak.

The campaign accelerated in 1971. When eleven Soviet Jews who hijacked a Russian airliner were convicted in Leningrad (two were sentenced to death, while the others were given very heavy prison sentences), the Congress called for mass demonstrations. In their thousands, Jews in Montreal, Toronto, Winnipeg, Vancouver, Edmonton, and Halifax complied by marching through the streets with placards proclaiming their indignation. The community, moved by a growing consciousness of the Holocaust – especially in the wake of the trial of Adolf Eichmann in Jerusalem – and of the threat to Israel posed by continuing Arab hostilities, responded with an emotive slogan: Never Again.[12]

Some eight thousand Jews assembled on Parliament Hill in Ottawa to demand justice for Soviet Jewry, while Minister for External Affairs Mitchell Sharp told a Congress delegation that the government of Canada had expressed concern. Even though he served as MP for the largely Jewish Toronto constituency of Eglinton, and acceded to some Jewish pressure to officially protest the Soviet mistreatment, Sharp nevertheless usually resisted. In his view, quiet diplomacy was better: 'Sometimes a public protest by the Canadian government made it more difficult for the Canadian ambassador to be successful ... on behalf of those who were being mistreated.'[13]

When Premier Alexei Kosygin paid a state visit to Canada in October 1971, Jews staged a massive peaceful demonstration demanding that Soviet Jews be given full rights to cultural expression and freedom to immigrate to Israel.[14] A group of sixty rabbis prayed in front of the Soviet embassy and on Parliament Hill while heading a mass demonstration of thousands. Similar rallies were held in Vancouver, and at Toronto's Science Centre some twelve thousand Jews protested again. This campaign continued through the 1970s. Similar efforts in the United States and Europe kept the issue alive. The Jewish community also pressured free-world governments like Canada's to force the Soviets to change their Jewish policy.

And they did. In 1971 Jewish emigration levels from the USSR were nearly three times the totals for 1968 to 1970. In 1972 immigration to Israel and North America more than doubled again, and it continued at high levels through the rest of the 1970s.[15] At the same time, Canadian Jewry was affirming not only that Jews were morally responsible for each other (in Hebrew: *kol yisrael arevim zeh bazeh*) but also that, in the post-Holocaust era, Jewish ethnic identity exuded new pride, assertiveness, commitment, and daring. A campaign to liberate the Jews of Syria from a horrifically oppressive regime, however, was not as successful. Tactics used on behalf of the Soviet Jews were redeployed, but the Syrian government was 'impervious to protest' and the campaign lagged for years, until, after the remarkable one-woman rescue efforts by Toronto's Judy Feld Carr through the 1970s and 1980s, the Syrian government allowed the remaining Jews to depart.[16]

Some Soviet Jews used Israel as a temporary refuge, migrating to Western countries as soon as possible; some chose Canada. Their initial adaptation was difficult. A study of about two thousand Soviet immigrants in Toronto conducted during the late 1970s found that their employment expectations far exceeded what JIAS or any other local agencies could offer. These immigrants, the study found, believed that Jews in Western countries could provide them with full support, indeed special treatment.[17] Frustration and bitterness emerged when these expectations were not met.

Most Soviets, contrary to the belief of many Canadian Jews, did not possess a passion to identify with other Jews. Arriving with the understandable expectation of better economic and educational opportunities, they also had 'a great desire to retain certain aspects of their Russian-Soviet cultural heritage, primarily the Russian language.'[18] Moreover, these generally highly educated people, with high self-esteem, rejected 'the status traditionally accorded to immigrants by the Jewish community.' Thus some time was required to attain mutual understanding. Assertions of solidarity were one thing; reality was another.

Canadian Jewish ethnic identity was tied to an increasingly strong association with Israel during the 1960s and 1970s. Always a Zionist community, Canadian Jews became immersed in pro-Israel activities during the Middle East crisis of 1967 and the subsequent Six Day War. The first response was more fundraising. A special nationwide campaign raised more than $25 million, and local committees canvassed as never before, during these highly emotional weeks, when Israel's very life seemed to be threatened. The country's victory in the Six Day War increased its popularity among Canadian Jews, just as it elicited awe and admiration from the Canadian public and press. Thus the emphasis on investment in building synagogues, community centres, and hospitals changed, and the community became 'Zionized' to an extent that must have surprised and pleased old-time Zionists. While the crisis in the Middle East mounted, North America's Jews eagerly followed events in the media. Emotions ran high, responding to an awareness of Israel's vulnerability. Spontaneous fundraising campaigns took place, and some volunteers flew over to offer help during the crisis.

Meanwhile, a group of Canadian Catholic and Protestant clergymen, profoundly conscious of historical precedents, wrote to the Soviet premier, Alexei Kosygin, who had supplied enormous amounts of weaponry to Egypt, and stated:

> Once before in this century the leader of a nation proclaimed the aim of destroying the Jews. The world did not believe him. The world stood by. Again the leader of a nation has proclaimed the aim of destroying Jews – this time the State of Israel. Let us not believe that the unbelievable cannot happen again. This time let us not stand by.[19]

Blood banks were set up, and material and medical supplies were collected by the Zionist Federation, the Congress, and B'nai Brith. Sensitive to the high 'costs of political impotence' during the Jewish refugee crisis of the 1930s and 1940s, Canadian Jewry mobilized for action in the belief, in Harold Waller's words, 'that the destiny of Canada's Jews was inextricably linked to the fate of Israel.'[20] The Canada-Israel Committee (CIC) was mobilized to solicit wider backing for Israel among all Canadians. Subsequent terrorist attacks and the Yom Kippur War of October 1973 renewed concern among Jews, who again demonstrated solidarity with Israel by large-scale fundraising initiatives and attendance at mass demonstrations in major cities. This outpouring of political support and material aid to Israel has continued to this day.

On a trip to Israel years later, the writer Mordecai Richler observed evidence of this generosity. He noted that 'just about every park, library, synagogue, operating theatre, yeshiva, or gym is tagged in celebration of one family or another.'[21] Rich Diaspora Jews, he noted, 'are expected to endow university chairs, and in return clothing manufacturers, real-estate mavens, and stock market gaons are flattered with honorary degrees and photo-ops with the prime minister. No issue of the *Jerusalem Post* is complete without its obligatory photograph of a middle-aged American or Canadian couple beaming in front of their gift: a bloodmobile, Talmud study room, tennis school, or intensive care ambulance.'

This support, however, did not end with material aid. Public-relations initiatives and pro-Israel lobbying gained increasing importance among community leaders, who worried about Israel's image in the media after her military successes and her occupation of the West Bank, Sinai, the Golan Heights, and the entire city of Jerusalem. The CIC, which was composed of representatives of the Congress, B'nai Brith, and the Canadian Zionist Federation, responded to the mounting criticisms of Israel. The CIC also dealt with the media's misrepresentations of Zionism and Judaism, as well as charges made by some members of the Canadian Arab community and several anti-Zionist Christian clergymen that Zionism was 'political Nazism.'[22]

One group of distinguished Christian clergymen in Toronto, who opposed such distortions, stated that 'Israel [was] the visible and tangible manifestation of both Jewish survival and Jewish security ... It is profoundly wrong to oppose Israel because of its Jewish foundations and to seek to dismantle its Jewish character as the anti-Zionists invariably desire.' Generally, however, such unqualified backing was absent from statements made by religious groups on Israeli/Arab relations. Despite the fact that the 1973 war was initiated by Egypt and Syria, there were no condemnations of those countries from the churches or the government of Canada, although several Catholic and United Church theologians issued a statement of concern which asserted that 'Christians must stand with Israel.' Indeed, the Canadian Council of Churches at this point adopted an 'even-handed' approach to the Middle East and manifested concern for both Arabs and Jews there, while the United Church essentially veered towards a position highly critical of Israel.[23]

At a special session of the House of Commons, External Affairs Minister Mitchell Sharp carefully stated that most Canadians preferred an even-handed approach to restoring peace to the Middle East, but that Egypt and Syria had violated the 1967 cease-fire lines. 'It may be neither appropriate nor possible,' he said, 'for Canada to maintain a perfect sense of balance in the present crisis.'

Sharp walked a fine line between an increasingly assertive Jewish community and a public that wanted him to maintain a balanced policy. Canada's support for United Nations Resolution 242, which called on Israel to withdraw from territories occupied in the Six Day War, was the keystone of this neutral position. 'It was my view and the view of my departmental officials,' Sharp reflected, 'that this difference will be resolved if and when Israel and its Arab neighbours (as Israel and Egypt were able to do eventually) get together to negotiate peace treaties.'[24]

Although they called for lasting peace in the Middle East and the right of Israel to exist within secure borders, the government and most of the non-Jewish community maintained a neutral stance on the Arab/Israeli conflict after 1967. Polls showed that in the late 1970s, the public was massively uninterested in these issues, though three-quarters of the 30 per cent who did have an opinion supported Israel.[25] The Trudeau government did bow to pressure from Jewish groups to cancel the Fifth United Nations Congress on the Prevention of Crime and the Treatment of Offenders, which was scheduled to take place in Toronto in September 1975, because the Palestine Liberation Organization (PLO) had been granted observer status. But the government did not block the May 1976 UN Habitat Conference, which PLO representatives attended. Meanwhile, the secretary of state for external affairs, Allan MacEachen, wanted to weaken connections between Canada and Israel and make contact with PLO 'moderates.' At an October 1975 meeting between MacEachen and the CIC, called to discuss Canada's abstention on the UN vote inviting PLO participation in the debate on the Palestinian issue, Jewish representatives received only a polite hearing. 'Canada,' the minister informed them, 'was not prepared to prejudge the PLO issue.'

Clearly the government was unmoved by the CIC's lobbying efforts, which up to that point had been deliberately and wisely low-key, as Rabbi Plaut put it, so as not to 'antagonize the government.' While Canada's policy of keeping up good relations with both Israel and the Palestinians made the CIC uneasy, Rabbi Plaut continued to be cautious: 'We cannot afford to throw our strength into a battle with our own government on the issue of the PLO,' he told his colleagues.[26] Because the Canadian government was entitled to formulate an independent policy, Plaut's restraint was entirely appropriate.

Criticisms of Israel's militancy spread in the 1970s. On university campuses, pro-Arab literature was circulated, while meetings and numerous demonstrations condemning Israel were held. Increasing numbers of radio and television broadcasts showed such an anti-Israel slant that both the Congress and the Zionist Federation felt it necessary to combat them vigorously.[27] In the late 1960s, a worrisome spate of articles written by Reverend Alfred C. Forrest began appearing in the *United Church Observer* condemning Israel's policies towards Palestinian refugees. Forrest was not the only churchman to be so critical. Deeply upset by Israel's occupation of the whole of Jerusalem in the Six Day War, Ernest M. Howse, a former United Church moderator, attacked the Jewish phrase 'next year in Jerusalem' as insincere and Israel's desire to hold on to the city as motivated solely by economic considerations.

But it was Forrest, with his widely read critiques of Israel appearing in the editorial columns of the *Observer*, who worried Zionists the most. As the official publication of Canada's largest Protestant denomination, the weekly reached approximately 300,000 homes and was obviously an important voice.[28] Forrest, perpetuating a view evident in the publication since 1948, blamed Israel for the Arab refugee crisis. At the same time, he stoutly resisted attempts to link criticisms of Israel with Christian indifference to the fate of the Jews of Europe during the Holocaust. Letters by Jewish luminaries, as well as meetings they initiated with leaders of the church, did nothing to change the paper's strong pro-Arab slant.

To M.J. Nurenberger, the editor of the *Canadian Jewish News* and not the most temperate editorialist himself, Forrest was 'the symbol of anti-Israelism in this country ... The most dangerous enemy of Israel because he is subtle and articulate.'[29] After a ten-month Middle East tour in 1968, Forrest published *The Unholy Land*, which included a description of Israel as 'a racist and aggressive state' and which further enraged the Jewish community. And he drew infuriated replies from them when he opposed Soviet Jewish immigration to Israel 'on the grounds that it was part of a sinister Zionist plot to expel the Palestinians,' and when he insisted that Christians did much to stop Hitler's murder of Jews.[30] Counter allegations of Zionist attempts to manipulate the news followed.

In December 1969 Forrest's exhortations to Christian clergymen to oppose Israeli government-subsidized 'study tours' to Israel as nothing more than 'propaganda' increased tensions.[31] Nurenberger excoriated Forrest, whom he said knew 'that any dissemination of hatred against the Jewish state is aimed indirectly at the Jewish people as well,' a charge that inappropriately put Forrest on the same level as Soviet antisemites. A few months later, Nurenberger held him up as an 'apostle of neo-antisemitism' and a disseminator 'of distrust and mutual suspicion among Jews and Christians.'

Thus Jewish leaders, viewing Forrest's critiques as antisemitism, felt their support for Israel to be embattled. Meanwhile, Forrest, who also felt besieged, continued, as Rabbi Gunther Plaut put it, 'on a one-way mission and no one could deter him.'[32] When, in the November 1971 issue of the *Observer*, Forrest implied that the Second World War was fought to save the Jews, he had passed into unreason. This outrageous comment angered even some members of the United Church, although delegates to its twenty-fifth general council gave him a standing ovation and protested against government of Canada loans to Israel.

It was only after the election of Bruce McLeod as United Church moderator and the murder of the Israeli athletes at the Munich Olympic Games in 1972 that Forrest's influence faded. Nevertheless, the seven-year contretemps severely damaged relations between the Jewish community and the United Church.[33] In his searching and balanced account of the conflict, which he labelled a 'family quarrel,' Rabbi Reuben Slonim pleaded for understanding on both sides, commenting, 'Only the most fervent partisan of the United Church or the Jewish community would maintain that all the right is on one side and all the wrong on the other.'

The Jewish community, led by the CIC, had only marginal influence on the Canadian government's Middle East policy.[34] For example, they failed to persuade the government to thwart the Arab boycott of Israel and of Jews working for Canadian companies that dealt with Arab countries. The Trudeau government minimized the importance of the boycott, and the federal Cabinet – bowing to business interests – was unwilling to pass anti-boycott legislation. In December 1977, the ministers of both trade and external affairs explained to the House of Commons that although the government opposed the Arab boycott, it would not publish a list of the Canadian firms that had been asked to take part.

The CIC did succeed in getting the government of Ontario to pass anti-boycott legislation in 1978[35] but failed to persuade the federal government to move the Canadian embassy in Israel from Tel Aviv to Jerusalem, an act that would signify Canada's approval of Jerusalem as the country's capital. Trudeau, who represented a heavily Jewish riding, had resisted pressure from Israel's prime minister, Menahem Begin, in November 1978. However, Conservative Party leader Joe Clark was anxious to gain Jewish support in the 1979 election campaign. Despite warnings from his officials, he pledged to make the move.

Clark stood firm on his promise. When he took office, however, he bowed to enormous counter-pressures from Arab governments, churches, Cabinet ministers, and government advisers, and rescinded his commitment. Upon re-election in 1980, Trudeau, who was resentful of the lobbying for Israel on the Arab boycott, shaped a new Middle Eastern policy. He emphasized, as expressed by External Affairs Minister Mark MacGuigan, that 'the legitimate rights and concerns of the Palestinians have to be realized.'

Similarly, Canada refused to soften its official criticism of Israel's invasion of Lebanon in 1982, in spite of the CIC's efforts. Broadly speaking, moreover, the media's response to Arab/Israeli issues clashed with Jewish positions, with the exception of occasional editorials in the *Globe and Mail*. In fact, opposition to Israel's policies accelerated sharply during the Gaza and West Bank disturbances, which started in December 1987.

By 1982 even some Jewish voices were raised against the Lebanon incursion, and the CIC was no longer widely accepted as their spokesman.[36] The unquestioning support of Israel by Canada's Jews began to be challenged by small but vocal groups who criticized the invasion and the shelling of Beirut and condemned the alleged complicity of Israel in the Sabra and Shattila massacres by Christian militiamen. Thus, while 'the organized Jewish community unconditionally supported Israel,' some of its followers were unwilling to accept that Israel could do no wrong, that Diaspora Jews had no right to criticize because they did not share Israel's real tax and security burdens, and that internal criticism only strengthened Israel's enemies and antisemites everywhere. While this belief served to stifle criticism on Middle East issues, there were independent thinkers.

The most dramatic manifestation of this mindset regarding Israel occurred in 1988, when fifteen Jews and fifteen Arabs participated in a government-sponsored seminar – a Jewish-Palestinian dialogue – on the Middle East at Chateau Montebello.[37] Critics of the seminar objected that the Jewish participants had been 'selected in a manner that produced greater support for the idea of a Palestinian state than existed in the community.' This exercise in Arab-Jewish dialogue was so controversial, in fact, that plans for holding a second seminar were shelved. This succeeded, however, only in angering those who believed in the necessity of such discussions to achieve peace in the Middle East.

Dissenting opinions also arose over Israeli policy on certain domestic issues, such as the emergence of liberal Judaism and the 'Who is a Jew?' debate of the 1980s. Challenges to the legitimacy of Reform and Conservative synagogues and their rabbis in Israel inspired the Canadian Reform movement to establish Kadima (Forward), a Zionist organization that was to support Reform Judaism in Israel, and launch a highly successful membership drive during the High Holy Days of 1977.[38] Kadima joined the Canadian Zionist Federation and sought representation at the World Zionist Congress so that it could articulate its position at the highest levels.

Both the Reform and Conservative movements were also reacting to antagonisms from some ultra-Orthodox in Toronto, where, they asserted, relationships between those three branches of Judaism were deteriorating. Rabbi Herbert Feder of Toronto's Conservative Beth Tikvah congregation complained that 'Orthodoxy has been ... boycotting meaningful dialogue with the Conservative and Reform movements to such an extent that we no longer meet. There is ... no arena in which individual rabbinic spokesmen talk as human beings. And that's a disgrace.' In response to criticisms from an Orthodox source of Kadima's effort to gain official status, Rabbi Plaut commented: 'If they [Orthodox Jews] are willing to dissolve Mizrachi [the religious Zionist organization], then we will dissolve Kadima.' He predicted that 'if Israel adopts a restrictive interpretation of what constitutes proper religious practice, that will bring about alienation in the Diaspora.'

Increasingly, Israel had become a central feature of Canadian Jewish identity. It was a source of enormous pride because of its many economic and military achievements; it replaced pre-1939 Eastern Europe as the wellspring of a new Jewish culture; and it served as a focal point for large-scale fundraising and organizational activities, which were motivated by the ongoing need to rescue Jews and rebuild the country. Perhaps a sense that greater efforts might have saved more brethren during the Holocaust was also fuelling their support.

Influenced by the climate of multiculturalism fostered by the Trudeau government after 1972, Canadian Jews found their ethnic identity increasingly shaped by Israeli paradigms and rhythms: the gathering of the persecuted, Independence Day, the pulse of Tel Aviv and Jerusalem, and Israeli music. As modern Hebrew was given ever stronger emphasis in schools, Israel entered the very souls of many Canadian Jews. What the historian Jack Wertheimer notes as the indelible impression that 'Israeli outlooks and practices' have made on the institutional life of Jews in the United States is no less true north of the forty-ninth parallel: 'Most synagogue-going Jews pronounce their prayers in Israeli Hebrew, listen and sing along to Israeli liturgical compositions, and wear and use religious articles imported from the Jewish state.'[39] Jewish schools focus heavily on Israeli culture, employ Israeli teachers, and send their students to spend a year of study in Israel. Through them, and American and Canadian yeshivah students, Israel has a 'radiating effect' on the whole community. 'I cannot explain,' Ruth Wisse reflected, 'the joy of Jerusalem in our lives. Many of us around the [Passover seder] table have lived in Israel, plan to live in Israel, want to live in Israel, or believe they ought to live in Israel, though we could not separate out these impulses or even account for all of them.'

Even with such Israel-centredness and the escalating financial contributions to Israel, higher per capita than anywhere except South Africa, *Aliyah* did not increase. Comfortable in their newly tolerant multicultural climate, Canadian Jews, in fact, have the second-lowest *Aliyah* rate in the free world.[40] Many Jews probably echo the sentiments of Mordecai Richler, who, after a 1992 trip, wrote:

> All at once, I ... was fed up with the tensions that have long been Israel's daily bread ... I was raised to proffer apologies because my ostensibly boring country was so short of history, but now, after five weeks in a land choked by the clinging vines of its past, a victim of its contrary mythologies, I considered the watery soup of my Canadian provenance a blessing.

There was also some growing discomfort with the policies of Israel's Likud government. Led since the 1977 election by Prime Minister Menahem Begin, Likud was viewed by many as excessively stringent and resistant to legitimate Palestinian claims.

Zionism had become so integral to Jewish identity that organizations such as the ZOC seemed irrelevant. With the financial power having shifted to the broadly based United Jewish Appeal, monies were allocated to both local and overseas causes, including Israel, except in a number of small communities, which, having few welfare needs, sent all their proceeds to Israel.

Even the left-wing associations, with their deep commitment to collectivist principles, experienced declining popularity. Their founding members aged, and their children were uninterested. By 1970, the recently formed Federated Zionist Organization of Canada, including all Zionist groups, was itself embroiled in a bitter dispute about the number of representatives allowed to its constituent parts.[41] Such bickering marked the nadir of these once proud organizations.

Israel was more than a fundraising project, especially to the youth of the rebellious 1960s, who had little patience for formal structures, banquets with their gowned and dinner-jacketed participants, and the shallowness of cheque-book Zionism. In rising numbers, these Jews were going to Israel to study, travel, and absorb the atmosphere. In 1969, Keren Hatarbut, the Canadian Association for Hebrew Education and Culture, undertook to send 250 Jewish boys and girls for summer sojourns on Israel kibbutzim to encourage them to go on *Aliyah*.[42] Synagogues were even more active, especially in sending youth over for summer programs meant to increase their Jewish consciousness. Meanwhile, tourism soared, and El Al's airliners carried hundreds of Canadians on its twice-weekly flights from Montreal and, later, Toronto to Israel.

Expressions of Jewish identity took on cultural dimensions, as well. Canadian Jews by the 1970s were being informed of their history in the republication of B.G. Sack's *The Jews in Canada*; a major two-volume illustrated survey by Rabbi Stuart E. Rosenberg; the publications issued by the Congress's national archives and written and edited by David Rome; the significant new scholarship published in the journal *Canadian Jewish Studies* (formerly the *Canadian Jewish Historical Society Journal*); and the activities of numerous local historians, who collected and stored documents, taped interviews, and wrote histories of their communities.

Their identity was also being expressed artistically, especially in literature, notably by such Montreal Yiddish poets as Ida Maza and Sholem Shtern. From the late 1930s to the early 1950s, A.M. Klein's poetry on Jewish themes embodied the culture of Yiddishkeit: the Talmud, festival observances, and the transforming rhythms and contexts of both the old shtetl and the new urban ghetto.[43] Klein's poetry after 1939 was profoundly influenced by the agony of the European Jews. His *Hitleriad* of 1942 and, perhaps most graphically, his 1951 *Second Scroll* – a powerful story of the search for a survivor – were the first English-language literary responses to the Holocaust by a Canadian Jew. In the glosses for *The Second Scroll*, his major opus, Klein reached deep into that parochial well to evoke memories and images of 'ghetto streets where a Jewboy dreamed pavement into pleasant Bible-land,' and praised God, who 'hast condescended to bestow upon history a shadow of the shadows of Thy radiance.' Klein was followed by the poets Irving Layton, Leonard Cohen, and Eli Mandel, who in the 1970s articulated both a response to and an awe of the Holocaust. After these poets burst on the scene, in the phrase of the literary scholar Michael Greenstein, 'words [were] in exile.'

Miriam Waddington's poetry contained echoes of the secular Yiddish culture she absorbed through her Winnipeg Peretz School education, and Jack Ludwig's stories reflected the struggles and the poignancy of living in that city's North End melting pot. Adele Wiseman's *The Sacrifice*, Mordecai Richler's *The Apprenticeship of Duddy Kravitz*, and the poetry of Irving Layton and Leonard Cohen shone as major literary achievements of that era. Wiseman explored the familiar anguish of intergenerational relationships, Richler the seldom-examined underside of Jewish economic upward mobility – he also displayed, in *St Urbain's Horseman*, a deep sensitivity to the Holocaust[44] – Layton, the ebullient awe of life and sexuality, and Cohen, 'love's solitary survivor.' These works reflected their lives spent growing up in Montreal and Winnipeg during the 1940s. Perhaps because it lacked those cities' internal tensions and ethnic diversity, Toronto did not produce Jewish literary figures of equal stature.

With these writings, Jews became highly regarded voices of Canadian ethnic diversity, major figures in Canada's literary canon, with their images, characterizations, and language now part of the national cultural landscape. Their popularity attested to a growing general interest in reading about the Jewish experience amongst non-Jews, as well.

Growing in confidence, in the 1960s, new immigrants and the younger generation began to challenge the Canadian Jewish Congress's all-too-pacific responses to the emergence of pro-Nazi groups. In May 1965 several thousand protesters demonstrated defiantly against a Nazi rally in Toronto's Allen Gardens. On the subject of aid to Soviet Jewry in the 1960s, Congress leaders had allegedly been 'lethargic, often passive.' But of greater concern was the CJC's opposition to government aid to denominational schools on the grounds that religious instruction did not belong in publicly funded schools. The Congress, conscious of differences of opinion among the rank and file, had reluctantly acquiesced to having a course in world religions taught in Ontario high schools but had opposed aid to denominational schools – even Jewish ones – in Quebec and Alberta.[45] Such a position was no longer acceptable. A new group, called the Ontario Committee for Government Aid to Jewish Day Schools, was formed in 1971 to lobby the provincial government. Although it was part of a growing grassroots movement, the committee failed to make any significant headway with the authorities. Nevertheless, it persisted until a 1996 decision of the Supreme Court of Canada effectively blocked all denominational claims for financial support.

Beyond school questions, the fundamental character of the organization was at issue. Rather than serving as an effective 'Jewish parliament,' the CJC had become more of 'an anti-defamation, civic-defense type of organization,' according to Rabbi Stuart Rosenberg, and it failed to keep abreast of the times. Its national religious affairs committee could not even resolve disagreements among Reform, Conservative, and Orthodox Jews on a variety of issues.

Local welfare organizations, moreover, objected to the Congress's assumption that it was the 'official' Jewish voice. In arguing that 'the problems facing us are serious [and] a different community is emerging,' the organization's detractors highlighted several features of the changing community profile: most Jews were Canadian-born; a high proportion was under thirty-five; the number of university graduates was much higher than in previous generations; the foreign-born included many Holocaust survivors; and there were now many Jews from Arab countries.[46]

The critics alleged, that religion, which pre-1940 had been a 'stabilizing influence' 'is significant by its very absence or by the markedly changed role of religion in the life of the ostensibly committed individuals.' This transformation was attributable to advancing cynicism, profound social changes, and 'a new, vigorous, and healthy diaspora Jewish posture and meaning.'

Thus the future of the CJC seemed shaky. Rabbi Rosenberg noted that in the United States, after the First World War, the American Jewish Congress lost credibility with that community's increasingly diverse constituents. In his view, Canadian Jewry, had perhaps also outgrown the need for the Congress. 'Could Congress,' he wondered, 'still retain its role in a larger, better educated, more ideologically diverse, and thus more complex Jewish community?' Indeed, in an age of so-called participatory democracy, could, or should, any single group purport to speak for all Jews? Even in Canada. The Congress, notwithstanding these and other caveats, continued to exist and even thrive under a series of dynamic presidents, as it was originally conceived: a parliament of Canadian Jewry, its voice to the increasingly diverse community and its major representative to the outside world.

In Quebec, the CJC viewed the separatist movement as potentially the greatest external challenge Canadian Jewry faced in this period. Though the Parti Québécois was not antisemitic, separation was seen as a significant threat, mainly due to the language issue. Except for a substantial francophone element from North Africa, Jews were overwhelmingly English-speaking. Though the Royal Commission on Bilingualism and Biculturalism reported that bilingualism among Quebec's Jews exceeded the anglophone community as a whole, separatism seemed dangerous. At the end of an illuminating review of the situation in 1972, Rabbi Rosenberg concluded that for Quebec Jewry, 'the road ahead is uncertain, fearful, even fraught with unknowable dangers.'[47]

Comparing the Jewish experience in Europe, where Jews were a minority in territories converting into national states, Rosenberg saw two problems emerging in Quebec. One arose from the emphasis the separatists placed on the pre-eminence of the French language. Legislation limiting parents' rights to choose the language of instruction for their children had been passed by the Union Nationale government in 1969. This law upset the traditional rights of English-speaking Jews and other non-francophones, and also seriously endangered the continuity of the English language in Quebec. The second problem was the separatist belief in *étatisme*, the view that the state was supreme, a poor portent for Jewish survival. Such pessimism was not lessened by the attitude of Quebec's most prominent nationalist, René Lévesque, who told a Toronto audience in December 1971:

> I know that eighty to ninety percent of the Jews of Quebec are nervous about the effects of separatism. I know that history shows that a rise of nationalism means Jews get it in the neck. But what can I do about it? I can't change your history. But I know that anti-Semitism is not a significant French-Canadian characteristic. The more serious problem for the Jews is that Jews in Quebec are closely related to the English community. If they choose to put in with them, what can I do?[48]

Food for thought this! What did the PQ have in mind for the English? And how could Quebec's Jews, most of whom indeed were closely identified with them, suddenly reverse nearly two hundred years of history and become 'pur laine' Québécois? Lévesque was in effect uttering a threat, the seriousness of which Jews had no trouble imagining. While there was no clear evidence of antisemitism in the Parti Québécois, statements made by the Front de Libération du Québec (FLQ), which was responsible for the bombings of the 1960s and the October Crisis of 1970, did contain some antisemitic references. Such sentiments can hardly have inspired Jewish confidence in their future in a separate Quebec. And while most Quebec separatists of the 1970s did not openly espouse antisemitism, some avowed and suspected antisemites among them attracted the notice of non-Jewish observers. The journalist Peter Desbarats noted that 'Jews in Quebec ... have a right to be concerned about nationalist developments in Quebec which would assume a chauvinist character and would create a tolerance for discrimination against non-French groups. There are two kinds of Jews in Quebec: the optimists who teach their children French and the pessimists who teach them Hebrew.'[49]

Some of the new antisemitism in Quebec was masked by anti-Israel rhetoric. The 1970 kidnapping and murder of Quebec's minister of labour and immigration, Pierre Laporte, for example, reportedly was preceded by an unsuccessful FLQ attempt to kidnap the Israeli trade attaché in Montreal.[50] In the separatist monthly, *ici Québec*, one writer called Zionism 'the cancer of the world' and alleged that Israelis injected mercury into oranges. In 1973 the president of the Montreal Council of the Confederation of National Trade Unions (CNTU) allegedly stated, before the Federation of Canadian Arab Societies, that

> the Jewish population of Quebec enjoys more privileges than any other minority in the world. We don't want them to poison the air of this country any further. Israel is now committing the same barbaric crimes against others that were committed against her in her previous history. We are sick and tired of being called antisemites.[51]

In addition, Quebec's Jews were alarmed by the remarks of Yvan Charbonneau, head of the Quebec French Catholic teachers' union, who, after returning from a meeting of the International Association against Racial Intolerance, stated that 'it was incumbent on Quebec teachers to instill anti-Zionist sentiments in the minds of their pupils.' To be sure, these remarks were vigorously repudiated by the archbishop of Montreal, Mgr. Paul Grégoire.[52] But in such an atmosphere, Charles Bronfman could hardly be blamed when, on the eve of the Parti Québécois victory in the 1976 provincial election, in remarks to Jewish community leaders, he was quoted as saying that the PQ was 'a bunch of bastards who are trying to kill us.' He also allegedly threatened to pull his family's enormous capital out of the province.

In the Jewish community, memories of pre-war antisemitism ran deep. The concept of francophone Jews serving as a bridge to French Quebeckers could not have encouraged the English-language Jewish community, especially in light of reports of very high rates of intermarriage between French-speaking Jews and non-Jews. The Parti Québécois victory therefore produced considerable anxiety in the Jewish community over what its future might be in what might well become a separate state.

In an article published in *Commentary* six months after the PQ victory, two McGill professors, Ruth Wisse and Irwin Cotler, wrote that Quebec's Jews had entered into a state of almost continuous caucus, 'in anxious discussion about their future under a government promising to aggressively pursue separation from the rest of Canada.'[53] While in the past 'Quebec's climate of candid ethnicity had made Montreal ... hospitable to groups (like the Jews) that could readily maintain their distinctiveness,' the authors argued that the situation had changed.

Although they sympathized with the strong French-Canadian desire for cultural distinctiveness, Wisse and Cotler asserted that 'Jews fear the inevitable fallout of these nationalistic impulses and oppose their repressive dimensions.' Even though the PQ was committed to both democracy and fair treatment of minorities, the McGill professors charged that there were already signals of authoritarianism and insensitivity – including the coercive features of Bill 101, which institutionalized the French language. Even more worrisome were some signs of racism and the fact that a labour leader's expressions of sympathy with the Palestinian cause suggested antisemitism was not repudiated by the French-Canadian elite.

According to some Quebec intellectuals, however, Wisse and Cotler misrepresented the true nature of the Parti Québécois's nationalist program – as well as erroneously depicting a previous lack of 'hospitality' towards minorities on the part of French Quebeckers.[54] Michel Laferrière, rebutting Wisse and Cotler in *Commentary*, asserted that if Jews had become increasingly bilingual, it was only 'because they had to ... [since] most of their income derived from the French Canadians, for Jews were often small shopkeepers and small landlords ... [and were] often perceived as direct exploiters.' Thus, he wrote, French-Canadian antisemitism was similar to black antisemitism in the United States; it was merely a legitimate response to 'Jewish exploitation.' And Laferrière rejected as outright defamation the suggestion that the Quebec nationalist song 'The Future Belongs to Us,' which was sung at Parti Québécois rallies, resembled a Nazi song from the movie *Cabaret*. The intention behind Bill 101, he continued, was to make French the only official language in Quebec, 'and corresponds to the legislation and practices of other provinces, which have made English the only language of social life, de facto or de jure.'

Another commentator observed that Jews prospered in Montreal, where, instead of seeking contacts with French Canadians, they had aligned themselves with the dominant anglophones. Thus, Jews regarded English as their only 'cultural gateway to Jewish self-expression.'[55] The Wisse-Cotler insistence that the French-Canadian elite should repudiate statements from radical leftists was also unacceptable. 'If Mrs. Wisse and Mr. Cotler already hear Nazi boots on the sidewalks of Montreal, that is really their personal problem,' the commentator asserted, and then claimed that they could not cite a single antisemitic action by the new government. Irwin Cotler surely had it right in recognizing that the use of French 'as the lingua franca of Quebec society,' had become 'a Jewish communal imperative – indeed a moral imperative.'[56] But if Quebec nationalism was exclusive rather than inclusive, and Jewish nationalism was becoming increasingly transnational and 'concerned with the indivisibility of Jewish peoplehood,' he observed, these Jewish and French-Canadian solitudes 'are likely to mis-read, if not misinterpret, each other's symbolic language.'

Although this was not quite a *dialogue des sourds*, clearly the two sides of this debate were miles apart. Jews, perhaps, did not fully comprehend the Québécois nationalists' sense of precarious marginality in a province whose economy was still dominated by non-francophones and a continent whose major language was English. Jews were unable, the scholar Pierre Anctil observed, 'to understand the language, the context, where the nationalists were coming from.'[57] At the same time, the nationalists did not fully grasp Jewish fears of authoritarian nationalism with racist undertones. Little understanding was possible in such an atmosphere.

Antisemitism could reappear anywhere in Canada, arguably, such as during the provincial referendum votes in 1980 and 1995. But the public expression of Jew-hatred was increasingly marginalized. Indeed, the community of Quebec, bolstered by a significant influx of francophone Jews from North Africa, had been enjoying a certain rapprochement with Québécois from the Quiet Revolution onward.

Perceptions of Jews by some French Canadians had changed significantly by the 1960s, perhaps partly as a result of the activities of Le Cercle Juif de la langue française in Montreal.[58] Antisemitism in Quebec was certainly waning and, as longtime editor of the Cercle's bulletin Naim Kattan observed, 'Relations between the two communities are only just beginning to be established on the social and human levels.' Jews even began to appear – perhaps for the first time – as sympathetic figures in French-Canadian novels of the 1960s. Finally, to French-Canadian writers like Yves Theriault, 'the Jew is no longer ... far-away ... but [is] the neighbour, someone nearer, the Jew who lives on the next street.' At last, the Jew was someone with whom it was possible to empathize, whose 'Jewish music, ... soul and ... spirit' Theriault might appreciate. The Jewish experience as a minority group, Kattan suggested, was seen almost as a model or symbol of the French-Canadian predicament, and served 'as an example, an encouragement, a confirmation.' Although most of these literary interpretations depicted the Jew only from the outside, never penetrating his soul, the generally favourable representation in literature was a watershed in French-Canadian attitudes towards the Jewish stranger.

Jewish perceptions of French Canada's distinctive personality were often decidedly sympathetic. The Royal Commission on Bilingualism and Biculturalism was a major forum for public debate on the future of Canada in the early 1960s. It held hearings across the country on the state of relations between English and French Canadians, while still recognizing the contributions made by other ethnic groups.[59] A submission from the Jewish Labour Committee (which represented trade unions with predominantly Jewish membership) expressed 'deep respect for the very survival of French-Canadian culture in an overwhelmingly Anglo-Saxon surrounding.' The committee asserted that rapprochement between the English and the French was essential for Canada's national survival, and that French and English must continue to be Canada's only official languages. Although it rejected official multilingualism, the committee argued that governments should support every ethnic group's right to assert its cultural distinctiveness.

In the long run, fears of Québécois nationalism generally proved to be ill-founded. The PQ record towards the Jewish community belied the concerns of Rabbi Rosenberg and others about an *étatist* denial of communal rights. In fact, the provincial government increased financial support for Jewish denominational schools and cultural projects.

Nevertheless, Jews, like other anglophones in Quebec, were worried. After the passage of a far-reaching law in 1977, language became the overriding issue for non-French minorities. This law required that people moving to Quebec send their children to French schools, a stipulation that effectively discouraged all but francophones from moving to the province.[60] While a 1984 Supreme Court decision guaranteed the right to an English education to persons from other parts of Canada, the children of immigrants from abroad were still required to attend French schools. This was emblematic of the Quebec government's determination to advance the French language à outrance.

In 1990 the Quebec National Assembly passed Bill 178 in an effort to regulate the size and placement of store signs in languages other than French. To enforce the law, 'language police' were hired to inspect business premises and fine offenders. Quite apart from the costs associated with enforcing the legislation, the Draconian nature of the law raised serious questions about the survival of civil rights for non-francophones in Quebec. If their language rights could be removed, what else might be threatened?

This law caused deep concern among both Jews and anglophones, although it was vigorously denounced in both *L'Actualité* and *Le Devoir*, the nationalistic and prestigious French daily.[61] The Jewish community was especially affected by the need for bilingually labelled kosher food products. Although this was done routinely on goods packaged in Canada, those from the United States, which carried English-only labels, violated the law. Efforts were made to have these items exempted, but as late as 1996 the issue – a minor blip, to be sure – occasionally cropped up, usually to the embarrassment of both the Jewish community and, apparently, the government of Quebec.

Montreal's Jewish community became more diversified during the 1960s, with the arrival of French-speaking immigrants from Morocco, Tunisia, Algeria, Egypt, Lebanon, and Syria. Some francophone Jews originated from Ashkenazim in Central or Eastern Europe, where French was the language of the elite.[62] Largely because they spoke French and had absorbed the culture of metropolitan France in the schools of the Alliance Israélite Universelle (Alliance), these immigrants were attracted to Montreal.

Finding comfort among themselves, these newcomers formed L'Association Sépharade Francophone, an umbrella organization of the francophone chapters of B'nai B'rith, Hadassah, and other organizations. It was renamed the Communauté Sépharade du Québec, both in recognition of the other languages besides French being spoken, including Judeo-Spanish (spoken by some Turkish Jews) and English (spoken by some Sephardim), and to emphasize its location in Quebec.

While they wanted to maintain their unique identity as both French speakers and Sephardim, they faced the problem of being a double minority: as Jews in a predominantly Christian province and francophones in a largely English-speaking community, both features of their identity were at risk. Their response was to seek a double integration into both francophone and Jewish cultures. In 1972 Rabbi Stuart Rosenberg observed that the francophone Jew 'has a choice of identifying either with the existing Anglophone Jewish community and probably losing his unique French Sephardi cultural heritage, or with a non-Jewish Francophone community and thus probably losing his Jewish religious connections.'[63]

The shortage of Jewish French-language services and institutions, especially schools, was problematic. Because of the confessional educational system, there were no French-language elementary schools for non-Catholics. Consequently, French-speaking Jewish children were forced to attend the Protestant English-language schools. Thus, until their language skills improved, they were placed in lower classes. A small number of Sephardi children did attend French-language Hebrew day-schools, which were associated for a few years with the Catholic school boards.[64] This situation presented a challenge, the *Canadian Jewish News* editorialized in December 1963, for both the Jewish community of Canada and the government of Quebec to keep the French culture of these students.[65] A special Sephardic day-school was opened with broad communal support in 1968. ''The assistance which the Ashkenazis [of Montreal] are giving us in terms of money,' the school's principal commented, '[has] amazed me ... This spirit of "Kol Yisrael chaverim" is a heartwarming thing and will do much to cement the ties of brotherhood and friendship between the two sections of our people.'[66]

As their numbers grew, the Sephardim formed their own synagogues, fourteen of them by 1979; these were supervised by the Rabbinat Sépharade du Québec. Even so, strong religious and family ties were not enough to stop the acculturation of young francophone Jews. A 1972 study of intermarriage in Montreal revealed that 50 per cent of North African Jews were marrying non-Jews.[67]

Eventually, two francophone Jewish day-schools were established in Montreal – École Maimonide and École Sépharade – and French-language classes in the anglophone Jewish day-schools were expanded with strong financial incentives from the Quebec government. During the 1980s the Sephardic presence was also becoming evident in Toronto, although the Ontario Sephardic Federation, in alliance with the Communauté Sépharade du Québec, was concerned because 'community organizations were not doing enough to integrate the Sephardim fully.' In Montreal, meanwhile, the Sephardim, previously focused on internal needs, 'began to make their presence felt in broader community settings,' forcing major Jewish organizations to use French and include more Sephardic representation.

In spite of these breakthroughs, the Sephardim often felt rejected by the existing Montreal Jewish community. New immigrants (once called greenhorns) had always encountered the patronizing attitude of some of the earlier arrivals, and the Sephardim were no exception. But as both French speakers and North Africans, they were viewed sceptically by Montreal Jewry for wanting to maintain a separate identity. While, even for them, 'separatism [was] an explosive political subject in Quebec,'[68] the Sephardim felt disconnected from the anglophone Jewish majority. A survey reported that the Sephardim considered certain groups to be more accommodating than others, starting with other francophone Jews, and followed by French Canadians, other North Africans, and Muslims. Canadian Jews were a distant fifth. Some 20 per cent of respondents expressed an outright dislike of the Ashkenazim.

The Sephardim resented the disparaging remarks made about their Arabic, and allegedly primitive origins by persons they perceived to be former residents of spindly one-room shacks in East European shtetls. Many Sephardim were proud of their roots and of the enlightened aspects of the Arabic culture of North Africa. As devotees of metropolitan French secular culture, they were resentful of being regarded as a threat by the rest of Montreal Jewry. Their École Maimonide was ignored by the local association for Jewish day-schools and received only minimal financial support from the Allied Jewish Community Services (AJCS). When other early requests for community assistance were rejected, Sephardic resentments towards Montreal Jewry mounted.

Occasionally, the community was warmly sympathetic. Having surveyed these complaints, the *Canadian Jewish News* asserted in early 1972 that 'the grievances reported must be dealt with in earnest for they concern fundamental issues.'[69] It called for Jewish employers to provide on-the-job training to upgrade the skills of these immigrants and urged Jewish agencies to recruit francophone personnel to meet the Sephardic community's needs. The following year, the sociologist Jean-Claude Lasry commented that Montreal Jewry, 'as a whole, was beginning to recognize the needs of Sephardim.' To overcome a general lack of understanding among most Jews, JIAS official Dr Joseph Kage called for a wide-ranging program of education on Sephardic culture. In 1979, at a meeting in Montreal of the General Assembly of Allied Jewish Federations, the AJCS responded to complaints of discrimination. They recommended ten major steps to strengthen Sephardi culture and proclaimed that 'Sephardic survival represents an important and urgent problem and a priority in the Jewish world.'

However, many Sephardim in Montreal maintained their isolation and their distinctive identity.[70] Settled mostly in the Côte-des-Neiges area and in the suburbs of Saint-Laurent, Laval, Côte St-Luc, and Dollard-des-Ormeaux, they attempted to navigate the turbulent waters of Montreal Jewish social politics and *le milieu Québécois* without compromising, and if possible strengthening, their identity. Their adherence to French led to an increased socialization with francophone Quebeckers, to the formation of synagogues with Sephardic rituals, to the retention of strong family ties, and to robust associational links. Apart from being shaped by local context, their identity was formulated also by poignant memories of the Maghreb: its French colonialism, Arab nationalism, and Jewish communal and family life. At the same time, the socialization of their kinfolk in Israel and France strengthened tendencies towards secularization and political assertiveness.

The community remained caught in the interstices of the three Quebec solitudes – the English, the French, and the Jews – and its intellectuals pondered their future. In a thoughtful article in Montreal's *La Voix Sepharade* in June 1987, Haim Hazan stressed the need for the Sephardic community's continuing adaptation to Jewish social and political realities in North America. In contrast to the North African respect for authority and hierarchical structures, he observed that '[in North America] freedom is absolute. For the first time in our history we face religious pluralism, something unknown to us ... Everyone is free to join the movement of his choice.'[71] To survive, Hazan asserted, they must offer something distinctively Sephardic to their youth. In a conclusion that voiced concerns remarkably similar to those of francophone Québécois, Hazan wrote:

> We are a small, vulnerable community, all the more vulnerable because we are isolated and because, in a continent of six million anglophone Jews, we, 25,000 francophones, want to remain Sephardic in a totally Ashkenazi milieu ... The status quo can only lead to suffocation and in time to our disappearance as a distinct community.

In the meantime, efforts to strengthen ties between the two segments of Montreal Jewry were continuing. They were at last learning to work together for common concerns.[72]

While Toronto's Sephardim were less numerous than Montreal's, their numbers were growing after 1957. Their adjustment, however, was even more difficult, in this English-language city. Although JIAS helped them find housing and employment, many reported that they felt confused by the process and alienated by the professional and 'businesslike' handling, which seemed uncaring and cold.[73] These newcomers, self-reliant and in some cases well-to-do in Morocco, which they had fled in the wake of rising Arab nationalism, felt ashamed of having to ask for assistance from 'strangers,' even though they were fellow Jews. They would rather have relied on the familiar family networks, as they had done in North Africa. Also disconcerting was the fact that besides being uncommunicative and unsympathetic, Canadian Jews seemed generally less religiously observant.

One study of the 350 Moroccan families who settled in Toronto between 1957 and 1965 found that their geographical dispersion across the city was a significant social disability.[74] The costs of transporting children to religious schools was prohibitive, forcing some families to withdraw and provide instruction at home. In addition to the problems associated with isolation in Spartan high-rises, low incomes, cultural uneasiness, and language barriers, generational dissonance was becoming an especially painful concern. Relationships between children seeking emancipation in a multicultural environment and old-fashioned parents were strained. But the greatest disappointment was their sense of rejection by Toronto Jewry. As one observer noted, 'What they are seeking is a Canadian identity within the Canadian Jewish community, the barriers to which seem hard to overcome.' Many felt a much stronger cultural and emotional affinity for Italians, while those from Tangier preferred to associate with local Portuguese.

The Sephardim formed a separate congregation using the Shomrei Shabbos synagogue in the city's former Jewish quarter. In 1967, 150 families who called themselves Petach Tikvah Anshei Castilia (Gates of Hope, People of Castille) bought this synagogue,[75] but they changed quarters several times thereafter. Wherever they moved, they continued to make their distinctive mark on the city's Jewish scene and gradually evoked some local empathy. Complaints from within the community continued, nevertheless, and were often lodged against JIAS for its perceived insensitivity and against professional bodies that refused to recognize qualifications earned abroad. The latter was a sore point with many Sephardic immigrants.

All the while, they continued to face the dilution of their distinctive culture within the predominantly Ashkenazi milieu, an erosion that affected even their own schools. In Toronto, one parent uttered this *cri de coeur*:

> It's tragic. All this money spent so our kids could get a Jewish education ... All these sacrifices on our part and for what? They're not learning what we sent them to school to learn. So, it's arguments, arguments, all the time. They are not Sephardim anymore, really[,] and that hurts a lot.[76]

Interesting changes took place in religious life from the 1960s onward. The Hasidim grew in numbers as some of the sects, notably the Lubavitchers, established an energetic, almost missionary, outreach program for all Jews, especially university students. In the same period, alternative Jewish religious expression took new forms, with egalitarian services offered by Conservative and even a few 'renegade' Orthodox groups.

While, on the whole, traditional Judaism remained dominant in Canada, there was a significant increase in the number of Reform congregations. One study revealed that Reform Judaism was growing because 'it was less demanding than either Orthodoxy [or] Conservativism from a sacramental point of view and because it emphasized associational ties.'[77]

This was especially evident, interestingly enough, in small university cities like Kingston and Kitchener-Waterloo. Newer arrivals to those cities – many of them academics – were unwilling to accept the established synagogues and the existing social institutions of the community. They opted instead to form their own more liberal congregations, which held services in borrowed or rented premises, often university buildings. Rabbis were brought in on a part-time basis, and teachers, some of them qualified university students, were hired locally.[78]

These new congregations were not always welcomed by the older ones, but the Reform groups nevertheless thrived, largely because they offered a flexible and warm alternative to what some perceived to be religiously stiff and socially unwelcoming communities. In 1965 in Kitchener-Waterloo, an informal Jewish fellowship of a dozen mostly professional and academic families began to meet in each other's homes for worship and discussion, 'because Orthodox Judaism did not suit them.'[79] Assisted by Reform synagogues and rabbis in Hamilton and Toronto, the fellowship, which named itself Temple Shalom, soon grew to thirty families, established an afternoon school, bought a building, and employed a series of student rabbis. In 1996, Temple Shalom established itself as joint occupant with a local United Church congregation in the Cedars Worship and Community Centre.

In Kingston nearly one-third of the members of the new Reform group, which called itself Iyr Hamelech (literally 'the city of the king'), were married to non-Jews, who in some cases were 'the decisive influence in the family's decision to join the congregation.'[80] Formed in 1975, Iyr Hamelech's membership grew from a small nucleus to fifty families by 1995, an increase of 163 per cent in two decades. It continues to thrive. Since its members are, on average, younger than those in the older congregation (and are still having children), Iyr Hamelech – like its sister Reform congregations in other cities – should continue to offer a viable Jewish religious alternative.

In the larger urban centres, meanwhile, some of the new synagogues formed in the prosperous 1950s were having financial difficulties. Temple Beth Sholom, in Montreal's west end, closed its doors in 1980 and merged with the venerable Temple Emanu-el. Others had to economize by operating joint educational programs and amalgamated afternoon schools with other congregations. Some even had to rent out space.[81]

In early 1977 Toronto's Rabbi Michael Stroh warned that congregations should build more modest structures, owing to mounting costs and the 'mobility of the Jewish population.' Ailing synagogues, he said, should qualify for broad community support. Some experts predicted a polarization between the super-sized synagogue / community centre, which offered a wide range of facilities (shuls with pools, as one wag put it), and the tiny local synagogues, which provided space for only prayer and study, much like the old-time immigrant *shtibl* or Eastern European *bes medresh*, from which the modern North American synagogue had emerged.[82] Perhaps there was some agreeable symbolism in this turn back to religious privatism and tradition.

Such a transformation was not acceptable, however, if it meant the development of a 'club mentality' and the sacrifice of communal responsibilities, at least as far as Rabbi Gunther Plaut was concerned.[83] He called for the congregations to restructure themselves to handle community service on a broad scale – not just for their members, but for all Jews – in conjunction with federations and other agencies. Plaut asserted that while many rabbis spoke out for social justice, they often encountered difficulty in bringing their congregations onside:

> They generally do not interfere with the rabbi's freedom of personal action, but they will often insist that the rabbi make clear to the community that he is undertaking these political activities on his own and not in the name of either the Jewish community or the congregation.

Only when the rabbis espoused popular causes, such as support for Israel or freedom for Soviet Jewry, were they certain to be completely backed by their entire congregation.

Jewish liberalism – a broad term describing opinion ranging from the moderate to the radical left – had also become more central in the larger Jewish community. The situation in Canada was perhaps healthier than in the United States, where the introduction of affirmative action programs (which effectively discriminated against Jews and other whites) had alienated many of the old Jewish left and turned some into conservatives.[84] Also, the persecution of alleged leftists, a disproportionately large number of whom were Jews, had been less severe in Canada than in the United States,[85] leaving behind less of a legacy of injury and mistrust.

The thriving secular wing of the Jewish school system is in itself testimony to the fact that the liberal and progressive philosophy on which it had been founded many years earlier is still alive. These schools affirm a 'Jewish identity that [is] positive, relevent and meaningful.' By emphasizing the prophetic tradition and Jewish history, they teach children 'the dynamics of ethnic group formation and development, [which] underscores the similarities as well as the distinctive characteristics common to all minority peoples.'[86] While both Zionism and Israel are recognized as important parts of the curriculum, supporters of these secular schools consider their 'primary purpose to be the continuity and development of a viable, meaningful, prideful Jewish cultural identity in [their] own countries.' Thus secular Judaism has embraced a broadly defined Jewish culture that does not exclude religion, but sees it and its universal values – 'love and reverence for life, human worth and dignity, humility, learning and joy' – as essential elements of identity in the modern world. 'Being a Jew among Jews is easy,' one observer said. 'It's being a Jew among Gentiles that's difficult.'

This secular perspective, of course, is not new. It harks back to the philosophy of the Bund, the Workmen's Circle, and the UJPO, whose members stressed their solidarity with the Jewish people and embraced Yiddish language and culture, while still seeking integration into the countries where they lived. They saw themselves as 'secularists ... who have emotionally and intellectually chosen to express their Jewish identity in less ritualistic, non-religious ways.'[87] This philosophy was based on a fundamental resistance to the Jewish establishment, the dominating monied clique. It implied a critique of Jewish politics, which were becoming increasingly conservative. As what might be called non-Jewish Jews, these liberals followed an unconventional agenda. They rejected the 'religious infusion of the Jewish community structure [which] has not only gained the upper hand, but it has become hegemonic in the sense that the organization of ethnicity, in this country and in the U.S., has assumed a religious colouring.'

Younger secular and progressive Jewish leftists, according to the sociologist Michael Bodemann, have rejected the idea that ethnicity is 'a thing of the past [that] universalistically minded progressives must strive to overcome.' They object to the 'non-leftists' who dominate the major Jewish organizations, arguing that the 'very substantial number of Jews who are disillusioned with the established structures [are left] outside the community and leaderless.' The progressives continue to attempt to mobilize these disaffected Jews 'to confront the monolithic-conservative domination of Jewry by this tiny group of haute bourgeoisie who have their names inscribed in the masthead of the *Canadian Jewish News* or the elevators of the Baycrest Geriatric Centre.' Bodemann continues, 'One thing seems clear, as leftists of one sort or another, we have to realize the political importance of the factor of ethnicity – especially in a country that decreed multiculturalism. Like it or not, ethnicity's a central building block of the Canadian state, an important tool of political control.'

Assertiveness can go only so far in this search for legitimacy for the Jewish left. One adherent asked whether 'we secular Jews can match that kind of cement that has bound the religious Jew to a heritage derived from a distant, imperceptible past? We may have to try if we want to have a continuation of what we have achieved to date.'[88] He called for 'the observance of as many Jewish events as possible in a way that denotes originality while simultaneously denoting sameness.' Not all would agree that this course of action was easy, or even possible. Certainly not the New York intellectual Irving Howe, a leading spokesman for the Jewish left. In a major address at the University of Toronto in March 1979, he forecast the end of secular Jewish culture. The Holocaust destroyed the cultural well that had fostered this tradition, he argued, and North American Jews had fallen victim to the 'enticements of liberal democracy,' namely, post–Second World War prosperity and materialism. Many Jews, he noted, observed religious externalities, 'though they are not actively engaged' in religious life. Others had become enthusiastic champions of Israel, but in his view this translated into only weak support for substantive Jewish continuity.

Times had changed. The old Yiddish-speaking leftists were slowly disappearing – although some of their institutions, UJPO, the Toronto Jewish Folk Choir, and Camp Naivelt continue remarkably to thrive – just as the social-economic conditions that had kept their cause alive had vanished. Sweatshops had long since given way to better working conditions, and very few children of old activists spoke the language of Yiddish dissent or shared the outlook and commitment to the cause of secular Judaism – if they even understood what it once had meant.[89] In its place, a new Jewish ethnicity firmly grounded on Canadian realities had emerged. This multi-faceted identity, which was still evolving in a context that was itself in transition, reflected the complexity of the Canadian-Jewish interface in a Canada that was now native ground to most Jews. Having in large numbers emerged through schools and universities, Second World War military service, active lives in arts and letters, deep engagement in politics, successful businesses, and, above all, the transforming energy of Israel, Canadian Jews were assertive, confident, and proud, although certainly not without serious concerns about the future.

14 Complexities and Uncertainties

A growing awareness of the Holocaust entered into Jewish life in Canada in the 1980s and 1990s. Memorials to its victims were being built in synagogues, cemeteries, and community centres, and even on the grounds of the Manitoba legislature. In addition to the many survivors' memoirs that were rolling off the presses, their accounts were frequently commited to film and audio tape. Rallies were convened to honour Raoul Wallenberg and other 'Righteous Gentiles,' and university courses on the Holocaust proliferated. Meanwhile conferences on teaching the Holocaust were held, and educators' kits were distributed to schools. In recent years, groups of Jews began to travel to Poland's death camps, mainly Auschwitz, to join the March of the Living and bear personal witness to the Holocaust's most infamous killing ground.

Every year, on the twenty-seventh day of the Hebrew month of Nisan (usually in April), Jews in communities small and large gather to light *yahrzeit* (memorial) candles; recite the kaddish and *El Moleh Rachamim*, prayers for the dead; listen to talks by survivors and stand in solemn collective remembrance and reflection. In Toronto, during 'Holocaust Education Week,' dozens of events are held in public venues across the city. Having been separated by many years from those events, Canadian Jewry now embrace them, recognizing that the Holocaust is part of their collective identity, although as yet few have pondered the long-term utility of such an emphasis. Yet, as Ruth Wisse, writing in *Commentary*, remarked, now that Jewish children have taken over the job of reciting the texts commemorating the ghetto martyrs, she sometimes wonders what effect this has on them – has already had on them.[1] Despite such reservations, most communities continue to hold these observances, which mark the Holocaust as a normative aspect of Canadian Jewish identity.

Today, some 40 per cent of the Canadian Jewish Community are Holocaust survivors or their descendants, probably the highest percentage outside Israel. As they began to enter old age in the 1980s, numerous survivors produced memoirs recounting their tragic lives in Eastern Europe,[2] seemingly anxious to record their experiences for succeeding generations. And when former concentration camp inmates, who led separate lives for over sixty years, reunite, the emotions are beyond description.[3]

In 1982 historians Irving Abella and Harold Troper published *None Is Too Many: Canada and the Jews of Europe, 1933–1948*, revealing that Canada's record in saving Jews was the poorest of any Western country. From 1933 to 1948, Canada kept Jewish immigration to a minimum in deference to widespread antisemitism, which, as we have seen, was especially strong in Quebec. The government also complied with the actions of its own overtly antisemitic officials who conspired to deny entry to Jews. As a result, fewer than five thousand Jews entered Canada during that entire period.

Holocaust denial and rising incidents of antisemitism also sharpened public awareness. Politicized in the late 1950s and early 1960s by an outburst of swastika-daubings across the country, the trial of Adolf Eichmann in Israel, and the re-emergence of neo-Nazi parties in Canada and the United States, groups of survivors urged the Canadian Jewish Congress to take action.[4] When the Congress refused, these groups formed the Association of Survivors of Nazi Oppression, staged a public march in Montreal in the spring of 1961, and issued their own newspaper, the *Voice of Survivors*, to draw attention to their concerns about Nazi activities in Canada.

In Toronto, they directly confronted Nazis who rallied in downtown parks, forcing the CJC to create an anti-Nazi committee including survivors on its councils. In 1965, at the Congress's urging, the government created a Special Committee on Hate Propaganda headed by McGill's dean of law, Maxwell Cohen. This committee, whose members included Pierre Elliott Trudeau and Saul Hayes, helped bring about federal anti-hate legislation in 1970.[5] When the CBC aired an interview with Eric Von Thadden, the leader of a German political party with links to former Nazis, survivors launched protests. Creating a link between Holocaust awareness and Israel's security, which was so often threatened in the 1970s and 1980s, became increasingly common among Canadian Jewry. In response to this, the Congress resolved in 1971 to establish a Holocaust memorial; it set up a Holocaust education committee a year later.

This new militancy, which was perhaps excessively parochial, Rabbi Plaut commented, marked the community's transition from old-style, polite, or 'whispering' diplomacy to an emphasis on mobilizing Canadian Jewry for some 'militant and even radical action (save physical violence).'[6] The same spirit infused the 1970s campaigns to free Soviet Jewry, to transfer Canada's Israeli embassy from Tel Aviv to Jerusalem, and to oppose shifts in Canadian foreign policy favouring the Palestinians. Inspired by a range of organizations and a dynamic and well-informed leadership, the Canadian Jewish community was prepared to engage in 'near confrontation' politics to achieve its goals. While successful in some instances, these tactics failed in others – such as the embassy issue – a clear signal of the limitations to, and the potentially significant downside of, political stridency, in view of the fact that public patience for such tactics is limited.

Congress's new militancy extended into federal politics. Besides pursuing a well-tuned public relations campaign to alter negative perceptions of Jews, Congress adopted an aggressive stance towards public discriminatory practices, including those directed at Jews. Following the Reform Party's expulsion in early 1992 of four of its members who belonged to the white-supremacist Heritage Front, Congress confronted Preston Manning about lingering racism in his party, receiving in reply his assurances that the old poison would not be tolerated. Congress had come a long way from its hesitancy of the 1930s and 1940s, Janine Stingel argues: it 'was now a powerful lobbying force on the Canadian political scene, committed to protecting and promoting the rights of all minority groups.'[7]

In this same spirit of assertiveness, many Jews confronted the allegations that among the numerous post–Second World War immigrants there were many war criminals. As early as the 1940s, the Congress had alerted government officials that the approximately 2,000 veterans of the Halychyna (Galicia) Waffen SS Division who were about to be admitted to Canada had committed war crimes. Although this complaint was set aside, the belief persisted that many war criminals (like Vichyite Comte Jacques de Bernonville, who found refuge in Quebec briefly) had entered the country as a result of the shockingly permissive attitudes of immigration officials, sloppy RCMP screening, and a Cold War hostility to the Soviets, who had made many of the initial charges.[8] The possibility of lingering antisemitism was also considered a reason for the government's lack of interest. But the Congress relented at this time, as it went about coping with urgent problems in the war's aftermath.

This unresolved question had a long history. Rumours had circulated since the 1940s about alleged war criminals like Dr Josef Kirschbaum, an official with the Hlinka Slovak People's Party during the Second World War.[9] 'We know who they are,' one survivor stated in 1973, though he admitted that naming names was a ticklish matter. One major legal obstacle was Canadian law, which made extradition of suspected persons difficult. But allegations continued to surface, some appearing in press releases from the Soviet embassy in Ottawa in 1974. Promises of action from Secretary of State Hugh Faulkner to a Congress delegation in 1975 came to nothing, very likely because of Prime Minister Trudeau's strong reluctance to open old wounds.

One of the alleged war criminals was Albert Helmut Rauca, who was wanted in West Germany for the murder of thousands of Jews in the Lithuanian city of Kaunas in October 1941.[10] Living quietly in suburban North Toronto, the seventy-three-year-old Rauca, who had immigrated to Canada in 1950 and gained citizenship in 1956, was arrested by the RCMP in June 1982. The following October a court ruled that he be extradited; after all appeals were denied, he was handed over to the German police in May 1983 and flown to Frankfurt. Charged the following September with the murder of 10,500 Jews, Rauca died in a prison hospital before the case was heard. Although he was the only accused Nazi war criminal to be extradited, a considerable number were named as a result of the activities of a small group of Nazi-hunters, notably Sol Littman, the Canadian director of the Simon Wiesenthal Center.

This issue festered, and the Congress urged several approaches, including trials, revocation of citizenship, deportation, and extradition.[11] Following very strong pressure for action, in February 1985 the Mulroney government asked Justice Jules Deschênes 'to inquire into the matter of alleged war criminals in Canada.' Hearings ran in Ottawa from April 1985 until early May 1986. Submissions were heard from Jewish individuals and organizations, and members of other interested ethnic communities. In his report, which was published on 30 December 1986, Justice Deschênes made eighty-two findings and recommendations, and noted several important factors that had affected Canada's post-1945 policy on war crimes. In 1948, for example, secret suggestions made by the British government to the Commonwealth countries influenced Canada's decision to drop war-crimes prosecutions. Nevertheless, Deschênes concluded, Canada's policy was no worse than that of several Western countries, 'which displayed an equal lack of interest.' He also determined that allegations that about six thousand war criminals were in the country were unfounded, that charges against the Halychyna (Galicia) Waffen SS Division members 'have never been substantiated,' although in a recent study, Sol Littman presents an important case for revisiting the matter.[12] Deschênes also found that, contrary to rumours, Joseph Mengele had never entered the country.

Justice Deschênes recommended that, of 774 suspects' files, 606 be closed, the remainder investigated further, and only twenty be given 'urgent attention' for possible revocation of citizenship and deportation or criminal prosecution. He further recommended that amendments be made to Canadian laws to tighten procedures. He also felt that the government should consider either giving the Department of Justice and the RCMP 'a specific mandate' and sufficient staff to continue their investigations, or renewing the commission's authority to summon suspects and other witnesses for interrogation.

One of the most startling of several revelations to surface was that an inter-departmental committee, which met in 1981 to consider taking action against former Nazis, had been unable to prove that some of the accused lied, partly because they were unaware of the existence of crucial immigration files, which subsequently were destroyed.[13] This act, Justice Minister John Crosbie claimed, prevented the government from prosecuting many suspected war criminals. Outraged, the CJC representative at the hearings, Irwin Cotler, protested that these missing documents, together with the 1948 cessation of prosecutions, the sanctuary provided to war criminals, and the quashing of deportation orders issued against alleged Nazi collaborators, constituted an obstruction of justice.

The Jewish community endured political fallout from the commission hearings. Ukrainian-Canadian groups complained to politicians such as Don Blenkarn, Conservative MP for the suburban Toronto riding of Mississauga South. Ukrainians in Canada were often accused of harbouring war criminals, and they feared the use of evidence from Soviet sources. Blenkarn said that he had received more than one hundred written protests and had numerous visits from angry constituents, who, he said, 'are coming out with lines that I hoped had disappeared from this country. What is coming out is racial hatred [his code word, presumably, for antisemitism].' He continued, 'I hope [Deschênes] can find some evidence that's incontrovertible against some individuals. If he can't the government is going to pay for it heavily politically ... And the Jewish community is going to suffer.'

Congress responded forcefully that 'bringing Nazi war criminals to justice, is not a "Jewish issue," nor is it an ethnic one. Rather it is a case of fidelity to law and justice. And that makes it of concern to all Canadians.'[14] An insistence that 'no one ethnic or national group had a monopoly on Nazi collaboration, and it is wrong and counterproductive to assert that any one ethnic group is now to be singled out for investigation' did not, however, smooth feelings in some sectors of the affected communities. Angry controversy erupted from time to time between Ukrainians and Jews over wartime events in Eastern Europe.

The Ukrainian community was outraged by statements made by Sol Littman alleging that 'the Ukrainians, by reason of their larger numbers and historic hatred of Poles and Jews, proved themselves pernicious collaborationists ...'[15] The future Supreme Court justice John Sopinka, spokesman for the Ukrainian Canadian Committee, claimed that 'comments such as these put Ukrainians in the position of either having to denounce these groups and their leaders or accepting the stain of complicity in Nazi atrocities.' He pointed out that Second World War Ukrainian nationalist figures 'were the leaders of the Ukrainian people. They represent a chapter of Ukrainian history which is still cherished today. That is why attacks on [them] are seen as attacks on the cultural heritage of which Ukrainians are proud.'

Sopinka insisted that suspected individuals be differentiated from the Ukrainian community as a whole. 'Failure to make this distinction,' he argued, 'will only serve to perpetuate the unquestioned acceptance by future generations of the myth of Ukrainian collaboration with the Nazis.' Faced with the question of proper procedure, Sopinka admitted that 'the prospect of up to 3,000 war criminals of Joseph Mengele's ilk remaining at large in Canada calls for stern measures,' but that for the rest, mostly old men who had only a minor role in Nazi war crimes, he recommended less radical or no action be taken, especially if 'allegations against them are founded primarily upon unreliable Soviet evidence.'

In the end, Deschênes's specific and clear exoneration of the Galician Division may have been influenced by Sopinka's representations. Once the report was out, however, Rabbi Plaut commented that the 'anxiety in the Ukrainian community ... had exacerbated the tension between Canadian Jews and Ukrainians, and now that it has been allayed we may all return to a relaxed relationship.'[16]

The Congress's Manuel Prutschi believed that the Ukrainians' approach had backfired, however, and asserted that the Ukrainian Canadian Committee, and possibly the statements made by Sopinka, '[have] linked Ukrainians with war crimes in the public's mind.' Irwin Cotler saw a greater danger. 'If we convert this into an "ethnic" quarrel or, worse, a Jewish versus Ukrainian configuration, we not only trivialize but [also] distort the issue ... We seek justice, not labels; criminals, not communities; individuals, not nationalities.'

The controversy simmered, fuelled by the discoveries of historian Alti Rodal, who had been hired by the commission to review Canada's postwar record on the admission of alleged war criminals. Her report was not made public at the same time as the commission's because it contained highly sensitive material on various European political groups who collaborated with the Nazis. Nevertheless, bits and pieces leaked out.[17] Upon publication, her study revealed that as late as 1983, two alleged Nazi war criminals were allowed into Canada by a senior mountie 'who regarded the war criminals issue as blown out of all proportion by the Jewish lobby.' This officer was aided by several key officials who destroyed records and disregarded regulations.

Rodal not only documented official Canadian laxity, if not outright antisemitism, but also suggested that the United States had protected and employed alleged Nazis and key collaborators like Klaus Barbie – the infamous 'Butcher of Lyons' – in exchange for intelligence about the Soviet Union. She also revealed that in 1949, Pope Pius XII had pressured Prime Minister Louis St Laurent to admit Slovakia's Hlinka Guard commander, Karol Sidor. St Laurent, she charged, also participated in letting in four Vichy collaborators, including Comte Jacques de Bernonville, who was saved from probable deportation by yet another prime ministerial intervention in 1951. Finally, Rodal revealed that while in office, Pierre Trudeau had opposed action on these matters.

To some extent, Rodal absolved the RCMP of blame in these actions. Government officials, as a matter of policy, withheld lists of suspected war criminals from officers charged with screening immigrants. In some instances, these officials even overlooked the applicant's SS tattoo. An enraged editorialist in the *Canadian Jewish News* called for criminal prosecutions of any officials who destroyed documents and of the RCMP for contravening immigration laws.[18]

Ultimately, the government accepted only Deschênes's recommendation that the Criminal Code be amended to allow for the prosecution of alleged Nazi war criminals in Canada. By narrowing the path of justice to this single avenue, it would take considerable time to bring anyone to trial.

Moreover, the controversy left some bitterness. One distinguished Ukrainian-Canadian scholar of multiculturalism felt that there had been 'an indiscriminate Jewish vendetta' against innocent former displaced persons who had also suffered greatly during the Second World War.[19] One prosecution, however, did occur fairly quickly: that of a retired Toronto restauranteur, Imre Finta, who was arrested and charged with forcible confinement, kidnapping, and manslaughter in connection with the deportation of about 8,617 Hungarian Jews to Auschwitz-Birkenau in 1944.[20] His arrest followed a successful libel action brought against him by Sabina Citron, the founder of the Canadian Holocaust Remembrance Association. He had accused Citron of lying when she alleged that he took part in the deportation. Because of weak evidence, however, Finta was found not guilty in 1989. The government changed tactics; further criminal prosecutions against these persons were abandoned in favour of stripping them of their Canadian citizenship and deporting them.

The government also followed Deschênes's suggestion that it sign bilateral agreements with Israel, the Netherlands, and the Soviet Union to allow Canadian investigators to 'gather evidence there that would be admissible in Canadian courts.'[21] But the wheels of justice turned slowly, even in dealing with the twenty urgent cases. Despite the prodding from Jewish officials, Justice Department investigators moved cautiously; they did, however, strip Canadian citizenship from a convicted Dutch collaborator. Frustrated by the slow pace, David Matas of B'nai Brith reacted angrily. 'Unless the Government moves at once against war criminals in our midst,' he said, 'the verdict of history will stand. Canada will remain guilty, as charged, on every count – as an accessory after the fact of murder, of obstructing justice, and of providing sanctuary to cold-blooded killers.'

Charges were laid in several other cases, but the difficulties involved in gathering credible evidence after a lapse of more than forty years stymied convictions. Meanwhile, some Ottawa officials, Irving Abella later discovered, 'were determined to delay, indeed even thwart prosecutions.'[22] In 1989 the Simon Wiesenthal Center provided the Department of Justice with a list of twenty-one Lithuanian immigrants who were believed to be members of a police battalion that participated in the mass murder of Jews. In June 1995 charges were laid against five elderly men, two of them Latvian, two German, and one Slovakian.

The Congress continued their entreaties, and in early February 1995, Justice Minister Allan Rock promised quick action against twelve alleged war criminals residing in Canada. But eighteen months later, only eight had been charged, leaving Congress president, Irving Abella, to criticize the authorities for proceeding too slowly. 'Why have they not named the other four?' he asked.[23] Meanwhile, widely publicized revelations by Steve Rambam, an American private investigator, caused a sensation. Rambam claimed in late 1996 that he had interviewed 60 out of 157 alleged war criminals living in Canada and had secretly recorded some of them actually confessing to murdering Jews. With continuing charges that 'war crimes cases [are] crawling ahead at [a] snail's pace,' the issue continues to fester, and one commentator pointed out that Canada's choosing 'not to deal with Nazi-era enablers [still living in the country] sends a message to today's *genocidaires* that our country may be a safe haven as they try to escape justice.' Also seeking justice, in 2005, the Ukrainian Civil Liberties Association demanded an investigation into the wartime activities of alleged collaborators, some of them Jewish, in Soviet war crimes during the Second World War. The decision of the government in 2007 to strip two accused Nazi war criminals of their citizenship suggests that these issues will remain alive for sometime.

Holocaust awareness was also heightened by the deniers like Toronto's Ernst Zundel and the Eckville, Alberta, schoolteacher James Keegstra. Zundel was publishing and distributing antisemitic and Holocaust-denial literature in Canada and abroad. He was first charged in 1984 after a complaint was made under Section 177 of the Criminal Code, which makes it a crime to wilfully publish a 'false statement likely to cause injury to a public interest.'[24] However, some observers believed it was misguided to prosecute Zundel. Alan Borovoy, of the Canadian Civil Liberties Association, stated that the trial lent 'legitimacy ... to a very illegitimate organization. Legitimacy has been conferred on garbage.' Others believed that prosecuting Zundel, North America's leading publisher of hate propaganda, would declare that such activity would not be tolerated.

Zundel's trial opened in Toronto in 1985, but it was really the Holocaust that was on the stand. The prosecution had first to prove that the Holocaust had actually happened. Raul Hilberg, a distinguished scholar on the subject, and Rudolph Vrba, a former inmate at Birkenau, gave testimony. For the defence, several well-known Holocaust-deniers, including Robert Faurnisson of France, who claimed that Auschwitz-Birkenau inmates enjoyed a theatre, a ballroom, and a swimming pool and that it was scientifically impossible for Zyklon B gas to have killed so many people.[25] The prosecution won, and Zundel was sentenced to fifteen months in jail and three years' probation. This conviction was later overturned on appeal, and a second trial was held in 1988.

Zundel's new trial attracted widespread attention both from the Canadian media and abroad. This coverage pleased the defendant, who gloated that he had enjoyed a million dollars worth of publicity. But the trial's effect on the Canadian public was ambiguous because, while it enhanced public knowledge, it also encouraged the view that one could reasonably doubt that the Holocaust had happened.

In Red Deer, meanwhile, the trial of James Keegstra, town mayor and an experienced teacher of social studies at the Eckville high school, began. The carrier of a blend of ancient and modern antisemitic notions, Keegstra was accused of using his classroom to propagate his hatred of Jews.[26] Former students testified that Keegstra instructed them 'about Jewish control of the media and governments, and the Jewish role in fomenting wars and revolution and fomenting communism.' Students were given pamphlets that described the Talmud as containing 'vicious libelous blasphemies of Jesus, of Christianity and the Christian faith.' Keegstra allegedly expressed his agreement with claims that Jews were linked to a mysterious order called the Illuminati (a radical group of Masons in the eighteenth century), and that Jews had assassinated U.S. presidents Abraham Lincoln and Franklin Delano Roosevelt.

Several former students testified that Keegstra rewarded students who regurgitated these beliefs in their essays and produced notebooks filled with virulent antisemitic statements copied verbatim from Keegstra's classroom 'lessons.' Despite a rigorous defence, Keegstra was found guilty, given a one-year suspended sentence, ordered to perform two hundred hours of community service, and fined. His teaching job had already been terminated, and he never entered a classroom again. Even so, he enjoyed a certain local sympathy. The foreman of the jury that found him guilty even offered to pay his fine.[27] Still, an analysis of the effect of the trial on the Canadian public concluded that editorials and opinion columns had 'condemned Keegstra and what he represented.' Keegstra appealed his conviction all the way to the Supreme Court, where he lost.

Another active anti-Jewish publicist who surfaced in the late 1980s was Malcolm Ross, a Moncton schoolteacher. He was charged with promoting hatred against Jews by distributing original antisemitic material that both denied the Holocaust and posited the existence of a Jewish conspiracy to dominate the world. Authorities were reluctant to prosecute the case because 'there was little chance of getting a conviction in view of the fact that unlike Keegstra, Ross had not disseminated his views in class.' Ross was removed from his teaching position, but he appealed.

Although these were the most dramatic cases, surveys done during the 1980s indicated that a more subtle form of antisemitism was strongly present in Canadian society. A 1986 study concluded that 'anti-Jewish prejudice and admitted ignorance of Jewish issues are serious problems in Canada.'[28] Although 63 per cent of respondents were found to be entirely free of anti-Jewish prejudice, 'young people were strikingly ignorant of the Holocaust and were twice as likely as people in their middle years to blame Jews for their own victimization.' It further determined that about half of the 'poorly educated Roman Catholic francophones in Quebec or New Brunswick, were prejudiced against Jews.'

On the positive side, however, the study found that university graduates, especially women, were free of prejudice; that Christian belief was not a factor; and that 'francophones revealed a remarkable ability to jettison [antisemitic] prejudice once they encountered their first Jew.' Another study, conducted by B'nai Brith, concluded that 16 per cent of Canada's population and 22 per cent of Quebec's were antisemitic.

One dramatic anti-Jewish incident occurred in 1988 in the Montreal suburb of Outremont, where the Vishnitzer Hasidim's petitions for rezoning an empty lot to allow the construction of a synagogue were turned down.[29] The opposition was led by a city council member who feared further Hasidic incursion – the Vishnitzer were one of seven Hasidic groups there – into this quiet, largely French-Canadian, middle-class area. Allegations that there was a 'Jewish problem' in Outremont, and that the Hasidim were unfriendly people, who ignored parking laws and bought up too many homes, only exacerbated the tension.

Because it arose at a time of increased French-Canadian nationalism, the Outremont affair can be seen as a symptom of a general malaise that likely involved more than just antisemitism. In the words of one scholar, 'the Outremont affair was a multi-faceted and complex incident that involved a variety of groups.'[30] One *La Presse* columnist blamed Jews for the problem because he said they failed to integrate into 'the Quebec milieu.' He also criticized anglophone Jews 'for allegedly opposing the survival and protection of the French society.' In the end, two provincial Cabinet ministers defended the Hasidim as upstanding citizens, and a continuing dialogue eventually ended the contretemps. (In a series of incidents that were perhaps unrelated, but nevertheless indicated that antisemitism remained strongly present in Outremont, a gang of youths attacked some local Hasidim. A radio commentator blamed the Jews.)

In November 2006, another kerfuffle erupted in Outremont when some Montrealers took exception to the Hasidim who had objected to the appearance of scantily clad persons in the windows of a YMCA near their synagogue and school, even though the Hasidim had paid for opaque glass. But it raises the question of just how far a small minority's particularisms should be allowed to override the values espoused by the majority in a liberal democratic society.[31] But arson attacks in June 2007 on cottages owned by Hasidic Jews in Val David, the scene of similar violence in the 1930s, though condemned by officials, raises the related and still festering issue of limits to toleration of cultural differences in this society.

Antisemitism in Quebec, though muted, has nevertheless remained a public issue. Esther Delisle, a history PhD student at Université Laval, examined in her thesis 1930s antisemitism in the *Le Devoir* and in the writings of the father of modern French-Canadian nationalism, Abbé Lionel Groulx. She was stonewalled for two years with administrative delays before being examined on her thesis. When her study was published in 1992, bitter denunciations appeared in the Quebec press.[32]

Has antisemitism been worse in Quebec than elsewhere in Canada? A *New Yorker* exposé of the 'absurdities' of Quebec's language laws by Mordecai Richler in September 1991 drew attacks on his personal integrity by outraged Québécois journalists.[33] But a study conducted in the wake of his claim that anti-Jewish bigotry is 'a prominent feature of the contemporary Quebec outlook' demonstrated that he was essentially correct.[34] Other surveys found that Quebeckers 'exhibit higher levels of anti-Semitism than English-speaking Canadians, ... in part [because of] the special importance that Quebeckers attach to the value of conformity ... [Nevertheless,] the weight of the evidence runs against the suggestion that most Quebeckers are antisemitic.'

In fact, antisemitic incidents were occurring during these decades coast to coast. Cemeteries were vandalized, with gravestones overturned and painted with swastikas and slogans. The worst attacks took place in Western Canada. In Edmonton a synagogue was burned to the ground. One in Vancouver was firebombed and seriously damaged, and elsewhere others were daubed with hate messages. Threatening telephone calls were made to community leaders. A more serious menace was the rise of neo-Nazi organizations, which pushed old claims of alleged Jewish-Zionist 'domination' and advocated the 'elimination' of all Jews. A 1989 hate rally in Minden, Ontario, met with strong resistance from war veterans, Holocaust survivors, B'nai Brith members, and local citizens, and another one was stopped altogether.[35]

Some incidents were believed to be of neo-Nazi origin; others were related to Arab-Israeli tensions. There was even evidence that some incidents were coordinated. An inclination among skinheads to adopt white supremacist and neo-Nazi beliefs was of serious concern. The Heritage Front, led by Wolfgang Droege, was the most threatening of these groups. It operated a racist telephone hotline and plotted attacks on individuals.

A brief but bitter controversy in 1993 over the staging of the musical *Showboat* raised concerns when some spokespersons for the black community made baldly antisemitic charges.[36] A Nation of Islam representative, barred from entry into Canada, delivered anti-white and anti-Jewish attacks over the telephone from the United States. Another speaker fulminated about the alleged Jewish subjugation of blacks. Meanwhile, in August of that year, a Polish-language newspaper in Edmonton published excerpts from the fictitious *Protocols of the Elders of Zion*, a long-discredited diatribe against Jews. Three years later, antisemitic articles appeared in a Toronto Arabic-language newspaper.

Many Jews were worried. Some 70 to 80 per cent of Toronto's Jews, according to one scholar, continued to view antisemitism as a 'potential danger,' and have 'a sense of foreboding and a pessimistic assessment of the potential for future anti-Semitism in North America.'[37] However, a 1984 scholarly survey of the social geography of antisemitism found 'surprisingly warm feelings towards Jews on the part of Canadians,' 86 per cent of whom held positive or neutral opinions. In this survey, antisemitism was found to be highest in Newfoundland, New Brunswick, and Quebec – and lowest in Alberta. Although it was more pronounced among Catholics than in the general population, 'it was mainly Catholics of French origin who accounted for the tendency of Catholics to be more antisemitic than Protestants.' Paradoxically, antisemitism was stronger among the irreligious than among the more observant French-speaking Catholics, especially in Quebec, where a study conducted in 2002 found that antisemitic attitudes were strongest among the educated elite.

The report's authors recognized that while other studies lent 'no support to the view that Quebec nationalists were more antisemitic than non-nationalists,' there were probably historical and cultural factors that affected their attitudes towards Jews. French-Canadian antisemitism, according to historian Pierre Anctil, may be partly explained by their lack of contact with Jews – plain ignorance, in other words, of Jewish culture and history.[38] Since the 1980s, Anctil has published several major French-language books on Quebec's Jewish history and has translated several classics of Montreal Yiddish literature into French, all in a remarkable scholarly effort to educate francophones about this important dimension of their province's past.

Not surprisingly, social class determined antisemitic attitudes more than religion or francophone background, and the study found that 'irrespective of religion, the lower one descends in the socio-economic hierarchy, ... the more antisemitism one finds.'[39] For reasons unexplained, men had stronger tendencies than women towards antisemitism.

These results confirmed a conclusion reached in an earlier study: antisemitism was marginal in Canada.[40] Nevertheless, there was 'a positive correlation between antisemitic attitudes and opposition to Israel.' So 'an individual may well be free of anti-Semitism and still favour the Arab cause over Israel, [but] the proportion of anti-Semites is greater among those opposing Israel than among those favouring the Jewish state.' Generally, English Canadians were more likely to back Israel than French Canadians, although support among educated French Canadians was close to English levels.

A reputable overview of antisemitism in Canada in 1994 concluded that it was 'a marginal phenomenon, ... represented most visibly by isolated individuals ... or by fringe groups ... [It] remains unacceptable in mainstream society.' The report concluded that 'there is little likelihood of a serious outbreak ... [partly because] Jews have found a number of allies in the struggle against racism in Canada, a fact which in itself strengthens the sense of security of the community.'

However, what remains troublesome to Jews is the government's failure to make lower-court convictions of racists like Zundel stick, and the recent emergence of some manifestations of antisemitism among blacks and some new Canadians. In 2003, 30 per cent of Canadian Jews reported experiencing public antisemitism in the previous three years.[41] Other manifestations of the anti-Jewish disease continued to surface during the 1990s and into the twenty-first century in the form of vandalism, desecration, paint-daubing, and firebombing against synagogues, schools, and cemeteries, along with threats, harassment, assaults, and murder against persons. Occasionally, an ethnic newspaper will publish an antisemitic piece and a public person will engage in ethnic stereotyping, Israel-bashing, or Holocaust denial that leaves nothing to the imagination. First Nations leader David Ahenakew let loose some particularly virulent antisemitism in December 2002, though he later issued an apology, while deeply embarrassed members of his community expressed regret. Meanwhile, in cyberspace Jew-hatred is the stated mission of certain Web sites and chatrooms, and a 2006 survey indicated that antisemitic incidents were at 'their highest level in twenty-five years.'

Observers are justly concerned about the 'new antisemitism,' which includes a subtle but pernicious attempt to portray Zionism as racism.[42] In this new antisemitism, Irving Abella points out, 'Israel has become the collective Jew among the nations,' which implies 'the denial of Jewish peoplehood and Jewish statehood, ... rights granted to every other people on earth.' This, coupled with what he called the 'canard ... [of] the dual loyalty of Jews', the free use of Holocaust terminology to describe the plight of the Palestinians, and the fact that this new antisemitism is pervasive, subtle, and growing (making it 'very difficult for pollsters to measure') causes Abella – and no doubt many others – to be both worried and vigilant. Because Israel has become a cardinal feature of Canadian Jewish identity, threats to its safety – and, more recently, Iran's search for nuclear weapons – cause even deeper concerns. Sociologist Morton Weinfield suggests changing terminologies from 'Canadian antisemitism' to 'antisemitism in Canada' in recognition of the fact that much Jew-hatred is now in various ways imported from abroad and dispersed among Muslims, some new Canadians, some native born.

A B'nai B'rith survey showed, however, that antisemitic incidents in Canada registered a very sharp decline in 1996.[43] But in the multicultural context of today's university classrooms, according to historian Harold Troper, many non-Jews, especially members of the visible minorities, see 'racism directed against others [as] more immediate and threatening ... Non-Jewish students could not relate to the notion that negative press reports on Israel, if excessive, might well be manifestations of antisemitism. Jewish students engaged in the battle of comparative and competitive victimization to ensure themselves oppressed minority status inevitably lose ground to others.'

By the late 1990s, the war criminals issue was still a dominant one for Jewish organizations. One Latvian former concentration camp guard was deported in 1997, but several others died before their denaturalization cases could be heard and deportation carried out. While the War Crimes Section of the Department of Justice was proceeding at what seemed like a snail's pace, they countered that they were making progress.[44] But in 1998 two of the accused were exonerated because the judges believed their stories that even though they were members of the deadly police battalions, they were not murderers. Another left the country while his process was under way, and a fourth was facing deportation. Other cases were pending. But the problems of sufficient evidence and the aging of witnesses in these cases would delay resolutions, even though funding had increased significantly. Eleven years after the

Deschênes Commission's report, only fifteen cases had been started and fourteen were pending, while the files on all of the other cases were either inactive or closed. The prosecutions moved at a snail's pace in ensuing years, with most of the accused able to escape deportation or, if found to have lied about their wartime background, delay the process indefinitely. By 2002 a mere seventeen cases had been mounted,[45] though Justice officials promised more prosecutions soon. Meanwhile Nazi-hunter Steve Rambam proclaimed from New York that there were as many as 500 war criminals safely enjoying refuge in Canada, 'an old-age home for Nazi war criminals.' In the few cases in which deportations were ordered by the courts, the federal Cabinet stalled on enforcement. Given their ages and the lengthy appeal process, these men – and many others whose files were in legal limbo – were unlikely to meet justice.

Still, the battle against antisemitism in whatever form it takes can never relax. Warren Kinsella, author of *The Web of Hate*, an exhaustive account of Canadian hate groups, warned that people should be on guard against white supremacists, neo-Nazis, and Holocaust-deniers. 'When they suffer setbacks or legal challenges,' he warned, 'they go underground or form support networks across the country. Sometimes, they turn to foreign governments – or foreign neo-Nazi groups – for funding and support. And they grow.'[46]

The Heritage Front and other antisemitic groups remain active, particularly in Western Canada. In 1992 they were especially busy spreading hate through Okanagan Valley towns in British Columbia.[47] Two years later, neo-Nazi groups were reportedly targeting university and college campuses for new members. Clearly, vigilance on this front must remain a priority for the Congress, the B'nai B'rith, and the Simon Wiesenthal Center. With the emergence of virulent antisemitism in the Arab world in recent years and of its inevitable seepage into Canada, Jews have become nervous – again. In light of this trend and of the threat of international terrorism, Ruth Wisse warns that the West cannot ignore or underestimate the seriousness of 'the Arab war against Israel and the Jews.' In this new environment in which antisemitism is linked to anti-Zionism, sociologist Morton Weinfeld concludes that despite evident prosperity and enormous progress in integration into virtually all levels of Canadian society, many Canadian Jews feel 'threatened and besieged.' In July 2005, Irwin Cottler, Canada's minister of justice, condemned the 'delegitimization of Israel ... and the double standard in the singling out of the Jewish people and their discriminatory treatment in the international arena.'

University campuses, perceived to be a bastion of free speech, have become the new battleground where anti-Israel verbal and physical violence is especially pronounced. Since the second Intifada, pro-Palestinian radical students at Montreal's Concordia University have created an atmosphere of anti-Israel hatred and intimidation. In September 2002, a speech by Israel's prime minister, Benjamin Netanyahu, who had been invited by the Hillel organization on campus, was prevented by violent protesters, who rioted and assaulted police and students going to the lecture.[48] The university's timorous administration immediately declared a moratorium, which lasted for nearly two months, on public events on campus related to the Middle East and refused to reinvite Netanyahu! A more courageous response to campus anti-Israel intimidation was mounted by York University's president a few months later when a lecture by Middle East scholar Daniel Pipes was cancelled for security reasons. She reinvited Pipes, who gave his lecture surrounded by exceptionally strong security. The battle of the campuses may not be over, especially if aggressive anti-Israel bullying is met with weak and irresolute responses from university officials.

Activities within the Jewish community were just as important as these external factors. Structural changes in several organizations resulted in a reallocation of responsibilities in some of the larger centres. In Toronto, for example, the United Jewish Welfare Fund (UJWF) had partially merged with the Central Region branch of the Canadian Jewish Congress, forming a new body, the Toronto Jewish Congress, in January 1976. This new group assumed responsibility for some cultural initiatives, while the Congress continued to direct the Ontario region's 'external affairs,' its activities for smaller communities, and its formal Jewish education program.[49]

Winnipeg had carried out similar changes in 1974, when it amalgamated the local welfare fund with the Western Region branch of the Congress.[50] This new body, the Winnipeg Community Council, hoped to streamline operations and eliminate tensions between competing organizations. In this way, both local communities and the Congress, which retained many regional responsibilities, would be strengthened.

Such changes were undertaken to use resources more efficiently to meet new commitments and adjust to the local federations, who now managed the fundraising drives for all local, national, and Israeli causes. The last of these was funded by the United Israel Appeal (UIA), which, though under the umbrella of other federations in large communities, ran its own fundraising campaigns in small centres. The federations were supposed to allocate funds to all organizational claimants depending on need, but politics and personalities undoubtedly played a part in the deliberations.

The Council of Jewish Federations was to allocate funds to the Congress, the UJRA, and JIAS. For correctness, local groups agreed in 1974 to establish the National Budgeting Conference (NBC), which would decide annually on each community's contribution. The UIA is also a member of the NBC; it contributes to the Canada-wide organizations on behalf of smaller communities, where it is the major fundraiser. Thus the NBC has a central role to play in the national Jewish community. Its decisions have met with widespread approval – except from the UIA, which has seen its funding levels decline as local needs took priority.

The NBC's highly intricate cooperative structure for allocating donations was in place by the late 1970s. This financial federalism worked, despite major regional differences, because all its affiliates appreciated the significant improvement. Political scientist Harold Waller pointed out that the NBC is 'a uniquely Canadian phenomenon' that reflects 'the strong countrywide organization of Canadian Jewry.' That there is no comparable organization in the United States is an indication that Canada's national Jewish bodies have historically had more moral authority. This was also true of virtually all country-wide organizations. The large Toronto and Montreal communities and their respective federations also had great influence in the NBC, in effect making them 'national forces.' Waller concluded that 'any analysis of the politics of the Jewish community in Canada [today] must include the impact of the major federations.' Such financial federalism reflects a strong, nation-wide similarity of values, assumptions, and goals, despite regional and socio-economic differences.

From the 1970s onwards, the Jewish community was facing new and pressing local needs. Foremost was the plight of the poor (most of them elderly). In the mid-1970s, it was estimated that some eighteen thousand Montreal Jews were living in poverty, with families of four existing on an annual income of five thousand dollars.[51] One community activist attributed this to the high costs of kosher food and Jewish education and the difficulties accessing services. The Allied Jewish Community Services had to increase direct cash assistance to these families by 25 per cent in one year. An investigation the following year indicated an even more widespread problem that involved 18 per cent of the city's Jews. It was forecast that by 1987 'the aged [among whom poverty was widespread] would constitute anywhere from 27 to 37 percent of the Jewish population, or 25,000–30,000 persons.' This was, however, excessively pessimistic; the 2001 Census of Canada put the percentage at 22.

Toronto, with its growing and comparatively young population, was not as seriously affected, but its Jewish Family and Child Services estimated in 1979 that 'about 13,000 people, or 13 per cent [of its] population, were living at or below poverty level.'[52] About one-quarter of the poor were teenagers, and there were many Jews between fifty and sixty-five who 'fell into the displaced skills category in millinery, sales, and the fur and textile trades,' including many Sephardic immigrants with low employment qualifications. It was estimated that the number of Jewish elderly in Toronto – increasing numbers of whom were being abandoned by younger family members – would rise to eighteen thousand by 1986, and that the community needed to provide basic services. Other welfare responsibilities were increasing, caused by growing rates of marital breakdown creating single-parent families that needed various social services.

By 1981, Toronto had 42 per cent of the country's Jews, compared with Montreal's 34 per cent,[53] a shift of possible significance for the future. Montreal's Jewish population between 1971 and 1981 fell by more than eight thousand, primarily because young persons were leaving, 'thereby ensuring that the already distorted age distribution of the city's Jews, with its large proportion of elderly, would continue.' Forecasts of population loss varied widely. In 1982 the Allied Jewish Community Services had estimated the decline between 1971 and 1981 at twenty thousand persons and projected a further loss of ten thousand persons by 1987. Thus, the elderly, who once amounted to 20 to 27 per cent of the Jewish population, would rise 27 to 37 per cent.

A later study asserted that 'Montreal's Jews faced specific demographic problems related in part to the political-economic environment in ... Quebec.' In 1989 political scientist Harold Waller pointed out that nine thousand Jews aged fifteen to thirty-four and five thousand aged thirty-six to forty-five had departed the city between 1971 and 1981, leaving those 'age cohorts badly depleted.'[54] Aside from the social problems, this distortion placed a very serious financial burden on the rest of Montreal Jewry. A special committee struck by the AJCS in 1984 recommended that the community try to keep its youth, attract immigrants from overseas, and economize on elder care – though prospects for success were dim.

Winnipeg, meanwhile, faced even worse age distortions. Like Montreal, the young were moving out, seeking better economic opportunities elsewhere. Consequently, 27 per cent of its Jews were over sixty-five (compared with 20 per cent in Montreal and 15 per cent for all Canadian Jewry). Moreover, many of the young who remained in the city had abandoned the North End neighbourhoods, where Jewish community institutions were located.[55]

Across the nation, budgetary appropriations for elder care and other social programs mounted rapidly. In 1981 the Toronto Jewish Congress, which allocated funds for all community welfare agencies, reported that some twelve thousand to fourteen thousand disabled Jewish persons resided in the city. These agencies were also concerned about the mentally handicapped and an 'increasing number of impoverished elderly, ... (mostly women) abandoned by younger family members.'[56] The community's welfare budget was strained. By 1984, Montreal's AJCS called the demographic situation 'urgent' and demanded action lest the community's viability falter and services for the aging population be further restricted.

By the early 1980s, as the founders died off and their offspring left for the cities, the decline of Jewish life in small outlying centres was evident. This was especially poignant in the centuries-old community of Quebec City, where the remaining thirty-five families, now unable to meet expenses, were forced to put their embattled synagogue up for sale. St John's, with only twenty-eight families, could no longer support its rabbi and sold part of its building. Shawinigan's last Jewish family moved away. Out west, the towns of Medicine Hat, Prince Albert, Moose Jaw, and Lethbridge were no longer able to sustain either rabbis or synagogues. In Ontario, Brantford, Cornwall, and Guelph were just getting by, while Belleville, once a lively centre, had only a handful of Jews. Synagogues were sold off as these communities waned and vital religious and educational activities withered. Small-town Jewish life that had once been so vibrant was flickering out, leaving behind only cemeteries as physical reminders of the past. Meanwhile, this migration of people from many of the smaller centres to Toronto, Ottawa, Calgary, and Vancouver required those communities to adapt to the influx.[57]

Through the 1990s, the post-war trend towards smaller families and later marriages has persisted, and the percentage of elderly has continued to grow. As early as the 1950s, the birthrate for Jews was the lowest of all ethnic groups in Canada.[58] Other facts were just as startling. In the mid-1970s, 'persons over 65 accounted for 8 percent of the Canadian population, but 11.5 percent of the Jewish population.' The median age for Jews was 33.8 years, while the national mean was 26.3 years. Twenty years later, those over sixty-five were an even larger component of the community's population. At the same time, the rise of single-parent families – estimated in the late 1980s at 12 per cent of the Toronto Jewish population – 'delayed parenthood, unmarried couples, dual career families, and other developments' led to the need for 'a re-examination of conventional assumptions concerning the nature of Jewish families.' A growing recognition in recent years that gays and lesbians are part of the community hopefully suggests those assumptions have changed radically.

Higher levels of education and a deeper social awareness have been transforming the perspectives of many Jewish women.[59] By the early 1980s, eloquent and moving feminist expressions such as those in the acclaimed film *Half the Kingdom* were raising searching and significant questions about the virtual exclusion of women from some of traditional Judaism's most important prayers and rituals. Relegated to the balconies or screened off behind curtains in Orthodox synagogues, women felt like observers of the men, who led prayers, read the Torah, and studied the sacred texts. Modern, educated, articulate, and assertive women were now expressing anguish and resentment over this secondary role. They were also seeking a new openness in Judaism that would allow them full and equal access to, as the filmmaker Francine Zuckerman put it, 'the pleasure of community [and] the joy of the Jewish spirit.' In Michele Landsberg's prophetic words, 'one day we will re-nurture Judaism so that it becomes whole.'

Pursuing greater knowledge of the traditions that excluded them for so long, Jewish women have organized groups for study and prayer. Their movement shows signs of spreading its important message of equity, wholeness, and renewal in Judaism, though differences exist among its advocates. The traditional physical division, the *mechitzah* (the divider) between men and women in Orthodox synagogues, for example, does not offend the feminist Norma Joseph, who regards it as an opportunity for private prayer and 'the challenge of loving God.' 'The autonomy the mechitzah creates,' she comments, 'makes it possible for women to stand alone on [their] own merits to try to meet God.' The feminist perspective and its pursuit of a larger and more recognized role for women in Judaism promises to bear rich rewards for the entire community. The fact that many synagogue constitutions adopted in the

1980s and 1990s consider women as well as men to have full voting rights is clear recognition of this promise.[60] Further progress on this front is essential, warns the sociologist-feminist Sheva Medjuck: 'If Jewish women's voices are not heard [in communal affairs], the ... community runs the risk of losing large numbers of young, well-educated, potential leaders.'

Still, trends such as these led one expert to predict that Canadian Jewry's very survival was at risk because the core group, those who identified themselves as Jews by ethnicity rather than by religion, was shrinking.[61] Those who identified themselves as Jews by religion included many assimilated Jews who would eventually lapse. Meanwhile, intermarriage with non-Jews was rising to levels considered alarming. But a mid-1980s report for the Ontario Region branch of the Congress indicated that about 25 per cent of Jews married outside the faith, a rate only slightly higher than that of the late 1960s. Like all such studies, it had no conclusive evidence of the reasons for intermarriage, except that Jews who were unaffiliated with synagogues or Jewish organizations were more likely to intermarry. Also, those in Ontario and Quebec were less likely to intermarry, presumably because of a greater availability of Jewish marriage partners within their larger populations.

Concerns about Canadian Jewry's future were not alleviated by the continuing arrival of immigrants – Sephardic North Africans, Israelis, Russians, and South Africans – some of whom were perceived as 'problems,' in particular, the FSUs (officially, Jews from the Former Soviet Union) who had come over in two post-war waves (1973–80 and 1988–96). One official observed that the 5,500 then living in Toronto in 1982, for example, 'know nothing of our system ... of Jewishness'; he also noted that only half of them had any Jewish affiliation. Only 205 children were receiving any formal Jewish education, and only one hundred families attended holiday celebrations at synagogues, according to one survey.[62] Success rates for integrating FSUs, however, differed by region. In Edmonton, by 1982, some three hundred families were 'absorbed ... and on the whole ... established and gainfully employed,' but in Calgary, difficulties were reported (partly because of staff 'burnout' in handling the one thousand cases). In smaller centres like Halifax and Regina there were mixed results. Because of limited employment opportunities, integration in Halifax proved more difficult than in Regina. Hamilton, meanwhile, found that 'the Russian Jews tend to socialize among themselves, but are slowly coming into the community framework.' A later study based on 1996 data pointed out that a higher percentage of over 20,000 FSUs had post-secondary education than Canadian Jews, although their average incomes were lower. Nevertheless, their contribution to national income is double that of all immigrants, and they experience a higher rate of upward mobility.[63]

While the integration of the Russians was initially thought to be difficult, that of some other immigrant groups proceeded far more smoothly. The South Africans, for example, came from a richly developed society endowed with a full range of thriving Jewish institutions. Having abandoned a country sunk into a hatefully oppressive, and socially and economically uncertain, regime, the South Africans were delighted to migrate to a more peaceful land. One professor thought that he had arrived in 'the promised land,' while another who had spent two years in the southern United States before moving to Canada remembered that 'we immediately liked the calmness and order of Canadian society ... Everything and everyone seemed to have their rightful place with great respect for each other ... I also liked the "British influence" as I was used to that in South Africa ... Everyone was so well-mannered and helpful.'[64] By the mid-1990s, an estimated ten thousand South African Jews were living in Toronto, where they had adapted very well. Among them, however, were many who felt more comfortable socializing mainly with other South Africans. There were two Toronto synagogues primarily made up of South African immigrants.

The Israeli migration to Canada continued. By 1975 it was estimated that they numbered twenty-five thousand, mostly living in Toronto and Montreal.[65] By 1989 there were more than forty thousand, and they constituted nearly 11.5 per cent of the country's Jews. While these rapidly rising numbers were a concern and an embarrassment to both the Israeli government and the Canadian Jewish community, which was so strongly committed to the Zionist endeavour, this emigration (called *Yeridah* [going down], as opposed to *Aliyah* [going up]) continued apace. These Israeli migrants, reported to be 'completely alienated' from the organized Jewish communities, were the objects of continuing interest to Jewish communal leaders and, to some, of barely disguised disapproval for their abandonment of Israel, an act that earned them the name *yordim* (those who go down).

Israelis, unlike the other immigrants, held the general expectation, or declared intention, of eventually returning 'home.'[66] This mindset helps to explain their non-involvement in Jewish community organizations, while their secularism ruled out synagogue membership. 'The shared ethnicity does not entail unanimity of vision,' one recent analysis contended, 'as Israelis and Jews perceive each other as different in regard to values, mentality, culture and definition of Jewishness.' And what is especially important, the report continued, is that no matter how long they live in Canada, 'most do not give up their emotional and legal membership in Israel [and] rarely reconcile themselves to the factors that ultimately make their immigration permanent.' Once they realize that their intended temporary stay is permanent, Israelis find themselves torn, their 'imaginary suitcases' disappearing even though they have not yet fully adjusted to the new reality. Most participants in one study 'reported oscillating emotionally between the poles of connectedness and separatedness.'

Canadian Jewry, however, was even more troubled by the fact that considerable numbers of immigrants from Israel were originally from the Soviet Union. Many Russian Jews who had settled in Israel later requested refugee status in Canada, claiming that they had been persecuted because, as children of mixed marriages, they were not recognized as Jews in Israel.[67] Between 1992 and 1995, government tribunals granted refugee status to 726 Israelis; between January and October 1996, a further 710 Israeli 'refugees' applied. Even though most claims were denied, this trend was embarrassing for the Jewish community, not to mention Israeli consular officials in Canada. This trend continued in the early 2000s. In January 2007, it was reported that at least 3,000 Israelis had filed asylum applications with Canadian authorities since and that 500 had been approved.

Yet another serious communal challenge in the 1980s and 1990s was Jewish education. In spite of the community's growing investment in this sector, days-chools were becoming increasingly expensive, and conditions for teachers were in need of significant improvement. Indeed, low salaries had long been a scandal in Jewish parochial schools. As far back as 1964, the *Canadian Jewish News* commented mordantly:

> There definitely is a discrepancy between the living standard of the average family in our affluent society and our teachers. Especially is this difference noticeable when one compares the salary of a Hebrew teacher who carries the responsibility of molding the future Jewish generation to the income of the so-called Jewish civil servant.[68]

Because of its low status and poor remuneration (as well as the lack of fringe benefits, job security, and full-time employment), the job attracted few high-level professionals. One expert noted that 'until the Jewish mother can exclaim with pride "my son, the Jewish teacher" as she does "my son, the doctor," the status of Jewish education will not change.'[69] In such an environment, the persons attracted to teaching ranged from 'the well-intentioned but untrained housewife to the Israeli whose only qualification is that he speaks Hebrew.' It was only in October 1976 that a contract covering tenure, grievance procedures, and fringe benefits was agreed to by some of the Toronto schools and their general-subject teachers. Other schools refused such concessions and were threatened with job action. But there was just not enough funding. Unprecedented deficits in 1977 – some schools actually went bankrupt – resulted in a 10 per cent tuition increase. The situation was so serious in Montreal that in 1984 administrations were trying to force teachers to give up gains made in previous contracts. When the teachers resisted, a lockout ensued, and some four thousand students were forced to end their school year two months early. Extreme bitterness developed on both sides, and fears were expressed about the long-term effects of the dispute on the quality of Jewish education. Low salaries remained a sore point for years.

Public funding was usually not available. Instead, financing was secured almost exclusively through the Jewish community. Quebec was easily the most generous of all provinces, especially with the Parti Québécois government, which between 1976 and 1984 subsidized up to 80 per cent of general education, provided that a designated portion of it was in French. This requirement, while entirely reasonable, resulted in a lengthening of the school day and a reduction in the time allocated to Hebrew and English instruction, a development that raised questions about the efficacy of the subsidy system.[70] In addition to strengthening Jewish institutions in Montreal, this financial support fostered a promising new relationship between the community and the provincial government, whose agenda included 'the francisization of private and public schools.' Quebec's liberal attitude to Jewish and other private education came under criticism in 2006 as being so lax as to allow Hasidic schools, which enjoy public funding, to evade provincial standards, again raising questions about minority 'rights.'[71]

Ontario, on the other hand, adamantly refused to extend funding to Jewish day-schools – as well as those of any other religious denomination – even though the government of Premier William Davis increased financial support for the Roman Catholic school system far beyond what was required under the existing law. In Alberta, financial aid was available to

Jewish day-schools that hired approved teachers and followed the provincial curriculum, subject to the approval of local school boards.[72] In most cases, though, the problem of finding adequate funds forced day-schools to raise tuition fees to such levels that only the well-to-do – or those who qualified for subsidies – could afford to enrol their children.

The pressure for Ontario government support continued through the 1980s and 1990s. The Jewish community (backed by other groups) contended that under the Charter of Rights and Freedoms, it was as entitled as the Roman Catholic community to public monies. In February 1986, however, the Ontario Court of Appeals found against them; and in 1996 the Supreme Court of Canada wisely upheld that judgment. The issue was closed – though not for long. In 2000 a coalition of Jewish and other groups in Ontario brought an action to the International Court, which ruled that their cause was just. In 2002 the Ontario government decided to allow public support for private schools (in the form a tax credit). But the decision was reversed by the McGuinty Cabinet soon afterwards, and the matter remains in limbo.

The prevailing assumption that Jewish day-school education strengthened continuity was challenged by Sidney Harris, Congress president in 1975.[73] He asked (unsuccessfully) for a study to be conducted on the relationship between levels of Jewish education and intermarriage rates. Until that is known, the belief that Jewish education will immunize youth against intermarriage continues to dominate, although sociologist Morton Weinfeld wisely cautions against this 'vaccination approach' in which 'education is the vaccine and intermarriage the "disease."'

The Jewish parochial day-school movement has continued to grow, so enduring is the faith in its important role. In 1979 it was reported that a larger percentage of Jewish children attended these schools in Toronto than in any other North American city.[74] The commitment of the community was reflected in the financial backing provided by local federations. In Montreal in the late 1980s, the AJCS increased the amounts to the schools, especially for scholarships.

Jewish education became a subject of endless examination and commentary, periodic investigation, and widespread interest. The *Canadian Jewish News* often carried editorials pointing to perilous conditions and the urgent need for reform and improved financing. Other observers correctly stated that better results depended upon decent salaries for teachers.

Most observers had long noted that Jewish education must involve the entire family as part of an all-encompassing way of life. The central question had become 'How could a "Jewishly-illiterate" community survive?'[75] The answer was that it could not, various experts noted, if, as was often the case, children who attended Jewish schools 'knew more about Judaism than their parents and insisted on a greater degree of observance.' Only education would ensure harmony between parents and children. If that education was to be a preparation for life, it not only had to be conveyed by adequately rewarded teachers and encouraged by knowledgeable parents, but also had to take place within a committed family and community structure.

As M.J. Nurenberger, the editor of the *Canadian Jewish News*, shrewdly observed, 'There never was, and there never will be a substitute for the traditional upbringing of a Jewish child.'[76] At conferences, experts debated how education could be improved, whether it be through the encouragement of 'attitudes that will lead [children] back to Yiddishkeit,' an emphasis on survival, the imposition of higher standards for bar and bat mitzvah boys and girls, or better teacher training. One rabbi noted that it would be wrong to hark back to the shtetl, reminding listeners that 'our goal is not a recreation of Eastern Europe in Canada.'

Out in the struggling smaller communities, where there was usually only one synagogue conducting an afternoon school (i.e., after public school), the problems of teacher shortages and turnovers were even worse.[77] Moreover, in the usually nominally Orthodox synagogue, most members were not fully observant. In many cases, parents were not supportive of the religious instruction their children received, a situation leading to apathy and cynicism among both children and parents, as well as the effective termination of Jewish education in most cases at age thirteen, immediately after bar and bat mitzvah celebrations.

Task forces and special study groups continued to grapple with these issues, including staffing, visual aids, expert consultants, management practices, in-service training, space, salaries, benefits, and curricula.[78] Meanwhile, surveys proved that while most Jewish parents took a keen interest in and favoured improved education for their children, experts like the late Rabbi Irwin Witty, formerly Toronto's head of Jewish education, continued to emphasize that schooling was only part of the solution. At a conference in Kitchener in 1975, he informed delegates that 'it is not what is poured into the student at school that counts, but what is planted in him at home.' Indeed, family played a far more important role than Jewish schools in forming identity. A study by the sociologist Yakov Glickman showed that 'the mammoth resources poured into the Jewish school experience by the community seems, according to data, to have produced meagre results.' Adult education and 'family life' programs were likely to be far more effective, he believed.

The most challenging, and potentially most rewarding, parts of the Jewish agenda as the community observes its 240th anniversary lie within the confines of the community itself: education programs and social service for seniors. By themselves, Holocaust memorials, the now futile pursuit of alleged war criminals, the legitimate concern over antisemitism, and mounting worries about intermarriage offer little support for future enhancement of Jewish life. But Jewish schools do offer hope and can activate the real possibility that Jewish culture, in its many forms, will thrive in the future.

Although they were growing in every major community, the problems facing Jewish parochial education in day and afternoon schools persisted. Tuition fees remained out of reach for many families. The terms of the teachers' employment generally were not equal to those in the public sector. Thus the serious shortage of competent teachers continued. Even though community welfare funds were supporting the schools with ever larger grants, this was still not enough to keep them afloat.[79] Still, as sociologists Morton Weinfeld and Susan Zelkowitz observe, this growing dependency may involve communal interference in the 'goals, orientations, and content of Jewish schools.'

Ironically, the growing popularity of these schools created serious difficulties. Winnipeg educators reported that 'we are getting killed by our own success. The ... high school program is bursting at the seams and there is no more money left for expansion.'[80] Without improvements in funding, teaching, and the students' home atmosphere, the outlook is one of only qualified hope. Meanwhile, the question of the long-term effectiveness of these schools in countering current concerns about the continuity of Canadian Jewry begs answering. Part of that continuity involves the preservation of the Jewish family, which, as noted, faces many of the same threats as in the general population.

If the early years of the new millennium were marked by the complexities arising from the new immigration, the structural changes in the fundraising organizations, the new demographics of an aging population, the challenges of feminism, and the rise of Toronto as Canada's Jewish metropolis in place of Montreal, the uncertainties were mounting too. Antisemitism's re-emergence in more virulent forms – bombings seemed to have replaced synagogue daubing and cemetery desecration as the most dangerous threat – was the chief worry. And the belief that while not all anti-Israel expression was necessarily antisemitism, all antisemites were against Israel, was even more of a concern, because the existence of Israel had become, to most Jews, the necessary condition of Jewish continuity itself. This perception coincided with an assertiveness ('Never Again') stemming from the Holocaust, that Jews could not be 'sha shtill' (humble and quiet) in the face of this new antisemitism, and that in the wake of the Deschênes inquiry, alleged perpetrators living in Canada be finally brought to justice. But within the fences of the community, other uncertainties abounded, such as the fate of the smaller centres, teetering on the edge of closure. As well, what was to be done about education, that perennial problem which was the biggest challenge of all?

All the while, there loomed the question of Canada's future: would the country survive, would the nation continue in the face of a possible separation by Quebec? Such anxieties were in part carry-overs from earlier decades, but no less disquieting.

Epilogue: *Oyfn Veg* (On the Road)

On the eve of its 240th birthday, Canada's Jewish community is completely different in size, composition, and character from its modest origins. According to the 2001 Census, there are some 370,520 Jews in Canada, an increase of 3.5 per cent over the previous decade. While 70 per cent are Canadian-born,[1] immigrants are coming from a variety of countries, not just Eastern Europe. Toronto, rather than Montreal, is now the great Jewish metropolis, and Winnipeg, once third in importance, has given way to Vancouver, while the Jewish communities in Ottawa and Calgary have also grown enormously. The Jewish farm colonies on the Prairies have disappeared. Meanwhile, many of the smaller communities are heading towards oblivion, and much of the important regional presence in the Maritimes and in northern Ontario is rapidly disappearing. Unused synagogues, some with prayer shawls still ready for service, stand virtually vacant, occupied only for funerals or, possibly, High Holy Day observances.[2] Soon, even that vestige will end, and only the cemeteries will remain to host the yearly visits of the descendants who place stones on the monuments of the pioneer parents and grandparents buried there.

Canadian Jews live different lives than their grandparents did. As a collectivity, they are far better off and have the highest average incomes, the best levels of education, and the greatest rates of participation in the professions of all ethnic groups. They are some of the richest and the most learned Canadians. Above all other achievements, Jews have been fully absorbed into mainstream Canadian society. They are prominent in universities, the arts, and the media. Barriers no longer impede the entry of qualified Jews into any of these fields. Serious antisemitism has virtually disappeared from mainstream Canadian life. In recent years, even the federal Cabinet and the Bank of Canada have included Jews, while the Supreme Court, at last count, has had three sitting Jewish members. Such attainments, once so rare, are now commonplace and hardly merit notice.

New-found confidence and assertiveness sprang from a variety of sources, though the most important was simply that Canada, now happily multicultural, has become native ground for most Canadian Jews. About one-tenth of the community, almost 40 per cent of men of military age, were in uniform during the Second World War and, like all Canadians who served in the armed forces, were bonded by this dangerous form of national service. The war united the community again, as it had a generation earlier, to the fate of the remaining Jews of Europe and Palestine, since 1948 the State of Israel, and endowed Canadians with the responsibility of providing massive assistance for both. And they understood that because the Jewish world of Eastern Europe had been destroyed, they could no longer draw intellectual sustenance from it. A once vital heartland of Jewish life had disappeared. Only the memory remains, and that, too, is rapidly fading.

Meanwhile, the suburbanization of Jewish life continues, with expansion of synagogues and major new community centres – like those in Ottawa and Winnipeg, while another is planned for Toronto. Along with all the usual recreational and athletic facilities, these elaborate centres include a telling new component – substantial senior-citizen residences. Old-folks homes always existed, but most Jewish communities, with a disproportiate number of elderly members, are forced to devote ever larger resources to their needs.

Canadian Jewry has been transformed from a mostly insecure, poor, lower middle- to working-class community living in downtown urban enclaves to an assertive, well-off, confident, and middle-class group generally residing in the better urban areas and fully able to participate in all sectors of Canada's life. Indeed, some super-rich Jews now rank amongst the country's most powerful tycoons, though significant pockets of poverty continue to exist, especially among the elderly.

In spite of these successes, some Canadian Jewish prophets of doom (taking their cue from Bernard Wasserstein and Alan Dershowitz, who forecast the gradual disappearance of European and American Jews through intermarriage and assimilation) have become deeply concerned. Intermarriage rates in Canada, at 27–9 per cent, though not matching the alarming 47 per cent in the United States, are indeed growing, giving rise to serious concerns about the 'continuity,' or survival, of Canadian Jewish life.[3] This apprehension is based on the knowledge that children of intermarried parents are far less likely to identify themselves as Jews than children of two Jewish parents. The worry is a real one because, as sociologist Morton Weinfeld observes, 'almost no non-Orthodox Jewish family – and many Orthodox Jewish families – remains untouched.'[4]

Programs to enhance the Jewish identity among the community's youth – and reduce the propensity for intermarriage – have proliferated in recent years, but it is too early to measure their results. One of these important initiatives, the 'March of the Living,' sends hundreds of well-prepared teenagers on a tour to Poland and Auschwitz, where they are shown the notorious locale of the destruction of European Jewry, and then flown to Israel for a tour of the major sites of Jewish national revival. Thus Israel and the Holocaust are posited as the touchstones of a Jewish identity that is supposed to inspire youth to continue as Jews and marry Jewish spouses.

It remains to be seen if this will work, but thoughtful observers may wonder whether the messianic national dream (now realized) and the horrific mass murder (now fading from living memory) can be expected to provide a young adult with enough substance to sustain a lasting commitment to Jewish 'continuity.' Paralleling this emphasis, there is concern among some community leaders that Holocaust memorials may seriously distort priorities and sap energies needed to address more pressing needs, such as the challenge of enrolling more children in Jewish education.[5] As long as substantive Jewish education is a reality for only a minority of the community's youth – and this, sadly, is still the case in the metropolitan centres – continuity may continue to be elusive, while Jewish studies programs at a few universities are so new that their effects cannot yet be assessed. Meanwhile, as the debate on this sensitive subject continues, some detailed studies which conclude that, overall, Canadian Jewry is 'robust and vigorous,' and the wise judgment by Morton Weinfeld, as to its future that 'Jews should take a collective valium and think positively,' strongly suggest that Canadian Jewry should not panic.[6] But while Weinfeld sees the Jewish experience as 'a comparative success story' with an unsurpassed degree of integration into the Canadian mainstream combined with a high degree of 'Jewish cultural retention,' he worries that it remains unclear how or if the relatively high levels of Jewish identity will persist deep into the twenty-first century.'[7]

Much has been lost in the transformations of Canadian Jewish culture. The general use of Yiddish has virtually disappeared, though it survives among the ultra-Orthodox and a few devotees. The daily newspapers have folded, and their keen readers have died off. Although the Yiddish language may be fading, the music, literature, history, and cuisine of the Jewish communities of Eastern Europe have come alive in celebrations like Toronto's popular Ashkenaz festival.

The Jewish-dominated trade unions, whose feisty leaders led their militant rank-and-file members through the nasty strikes of the interwar period, are now bereft of Jews. The sons and daughters of the petty tradesmen and storekeepers and the toiling and striking operators, pressers, cutters, shippers, contractors, and small-scale manufacturers, went to university, to professional schools, or into business, as the Canadian clothing industry faded under the effects of cheaper production offshore – the ultimate runaway shop. Many of the younger generation prospered, moved uptown or to the tony outlying suburbs, and now drive BMWs, shop at Holt Renfrew, dine at La Gioconda (or places with similar names), and holiday in expensive locales. The former Jewish neighbourhoods of Montreal's Main, Toronto's Kensington Market, and Winnipeg's old North End are now home to only tiny numbers of Jewish residents, while the buildings in the 'Fashion Districts' sit bereft of sewing machines and racks of garments. Struggling and upwardly mobile immigrants from other parts of the world live in the houses once inhabited by Jews, and the little synagogues – many with their Hebrew lettering still in place – have been lovingly converted to Baptist and Pentecostal chapels for new Asian or South American Canadians. Most of the downtown spicy-smelling delicatessens with their delectable offerings – often referred to as 'heart attack of a plate' – have disappeared or changed into fashionable ethnic eateries where stylish uptowners occasionally drop in for Jewish 'soul food' (now usually Asian) or stroll through the old neighbourhoods remembering life as it was in the old days.[8]

The Jewish street corner guys – the ones who could get it for you wholesale, the punchy ex-boxers, the hulking ex-wrestlers, the pool-hall sharks, the bewildered war veterans who fought the good fight in Spain, Europe, and Israel, the racing touts, the gamblers, the bookies who drove chartreuse-coloured Cadillacs, smoked stogies, wore loud suits, and sported various *noms de guerre* – have all vanished. The rude waiters in delis and restaurants – a Jewish speciality, to be sure – no longer wait on tables. Gone, too, is the ephemeral 'Yiddishn Gass' (the Jewish street), meeting places, often street corners, restaurants, or club rooms, where Jews spontaneously gathered and vigorously debated – without adhering to *Roberts Rules of Order* – the issues of the day and the eternal, burning question of 'what is to be done?'

Meanwhile, a new generation of Canadian Jewish writers whose works reflect changing perceptions of current Jewish realities and their ethnic identity is beginning to appear. They will follow those who have superbly recorded the words and music of Canadian Jewish memory. It has been more than fifty years since the prince of Canadian Jewish letters, Abraham Moses Klein – may his memory serve as a blessing – wrote his poignant verses on the Jewish soul caught in the unyielding web of modernity, while looking back to the past and remembering the sweet smells and Oriental sounds of the olden days. Will the new writers replace him now? If some have the words, do they have the music of his yearning soul? Will they, like him, give voice, by the waters of Canada, to the Jewish longing for the coming of the Messiah? How will they link the Canadian Jewish experience to the Holocaust? To what extent will Israel, North Africa, the former Soviet Union, Argentina, and South Africa – the sources of Canada's newer Jewish immigrants – be reflected in the Canadian Jewish literature of future years? And how will these writings resonate in the hearts of its people?

While these literary works continue to enrich the Canadian Jewish canon, the historical record is being greatly enhanced by the publication of memoirs (including a good number by Holocaust survivors), family histories, synagogue and community memorial books, and regional collections.[9] Such works, it is hoped, will multiply; they provide invaluable material for future historians – and are an informative and entertaining perspective on the past for contemporary readers. Meanwhile, ongoing academic studies by historians, yiddishists, sociologists, and political scientists, most of them affiliated with the Association for Canadian Jewish Studies, provide rich new insights into the Jewish experience in this country.[10]

As Canadian Jewry now observes the 240th anniversary of the founding of its first organized Jewish community, the basic question remains: How can Judaism survive if, as present worrisome trends seem to suggest, there might not be enough committed Jews to form a strong community? Will the realm of the sacred perhaps redeem the failings of the secular? Those who diligently follow the path of the Almighty are growing rapidly, to be sure. The ultra-Orthodox can easily be seen on the streets of Outremont, Snowdon, and Thornhill, with their many children. A survey of the ten thousand Hasidim in Montreal, however, revealed a serious economic crunch in a community where poverty and unemployment are rife.[11]

Will the emergence of a constructive Jewish feminism, be it in Reform and Conservative synagogues or in private prayer groups, succeed in reviving Judaism while fulfilling women's eminently just claims for 'half the kingdom'? And what will be the effect of immigration, as more new Canadians arrive from the former Soviet Union, South Africa, Argentina, and Israel?

What is clear, as these pages, I hope, have shown, is that while Canadian Jewish history has been shaped by domestic and international events, these elements have never been sufficient for understanding the Jewish past, for Judaism exists in time as well as in space. It is collective memory, religious observances, and historical reconstruction that activate Jewish echoes of the covenant at Mount Moriah and its renewal at Sinai, of the continuity of the law, the reality of Diaspora, and the march towards Zion. It is, as well, a sense of peoplehood, however that is understood amidst the continuing 'enigmas of modern Jewish identity.'[12]

Over the past twenty-four decades, the interplay between Jewish culture and Canadian context has fostered an advancement – indeed, an abundance – for both. Jews have added the richness of their chant eternal to the sometimes discordant multicultural chorus of Canada, and have received in return the ample rewards of peace, freedom, and opportunity in a generous land. To be sure, the passage has not been an easy one. As the twenty-first century begins, however, it appears that the major external battles – those for toleration and acceptance – have been won, though vigilance is still needed in a world where dangerous new forms of Jew-hatred are emerging, as occurred at the World Conference against Racism in Durban in September 2001, which turned, in Irwin Cotler's words, into 'a festival of racism against Israel and the Jewish people.' The Jewish community rightfully worries when major political figures associate with supporters of Israel's avowed enemies, as happened in Montreal in August 2006, when prominent separatist politicians marched in a demonstration marked by a decidedly anti-Israel tone and plenty of Hezbollah flags. Reflecting on the displays of virulent antisemitism at Durban shortly after the Montreal demonstration, Cotler noted, 'Antisemitism – both old and new – is the canary in evil's mineshaft ... while it begins with Jews it does not end with Jews.'[13] Attempts to boycott Israel and insistance that Israel change policies regarding security matters are equally troubling.

It might be said that if Canadian Jewry was taking root until about 1920, the community has spent the last eighty-plus years branching out into the Canadian mainstream. Canadian Jewry is now perhaps in mid-passage, halfway between its past and Klein's 'fabled city,' an ever-receding messianic ideal that will never die as long as there is one

Jew looking for nine others to form a minyan (quorum for prayer). It is the past that defines a people, a nation, a culture. History tells us how we got to where we are and provides hints of how our future might evolve. The Canadian Jewish experience evolved at the interface between Jewish culture and Canadian context, a process that took 240 years and that, though challenged, will continue for generations to come. Jewish culture must be strengthened and meaningfully lived, and for that to happen, the community needs to recognize that its real frontier of opportunity lies within its own boundaries.

Indeed, there are challenging issues ahead, especially if Quebec separates from Canada. This would, initially at least, put even more pressure on Jews and other anglophones – though not likely on francophone Jews – to leave the province, out of concern for their personal and communal well-being. This would be a sad turn of events, given the centuries-old Jewish presence in Quebec and the fact that, in the words of the writer Merrily Weisbord, 'we live here, ... tied to the soil, having, for better or for worse, taken root.'[14] The result of the 1995 referendum suggests that the next referendum – or the one after that – may carry separatism to victory. In that unfortunate event, the Jewish community, like Canada as a whole, would be sundered.

This is all, of course, speculation on the future, not the province of the historian, except insofar as the Canadian past helps to shape current realities in this country's Jewish life. At the same time, this experience has always been deeply affected by the Jewish world beyond Canada and will increasingly be absorbed into what the historian Zvi Gittelman calls 'the global shtetl,' a political and technological process drawing Jews around the world into greater contact with each other, while activating confrontation and fragmentation over sensitive questions like: 'Who is a Jew?'[15]

Meanwhile, the road is open and the journey continues.

Appendix

Jewish Population of Major Canadian Cities, 1891–2001 (by Religion)

City	1891	1901	1911	1921	1931	1941	1951	1961	1971	1981	1991	2001
Montreal	2,473	6,941	28,807	45,802	57,997	63,721	80,829	102,724	109,480	101,365	96,155	88,765
Toronto	1,425	3,090	18,300	34,770	46,751	49,046	66,773	88,648	103,730	123,725	150,100	164,510
Winnipeg	645	1,156	9,023	14,837	17,660	17,027	18,514	19,376	18,351	15,350	13,160	12,760
Ottawa	46	398	1,781	3,041	3,482	3,809	4,558	5,533	6,385	8,470	9,665	11,325
Hamilton	316	485	1,763	2,592	2,667	2,597	3,236	3,858	4,115	4,300	4,370	3,855
Windsor	16	141	309	1,118	2,517	2,226	2,444	2,419	2,420	2,025	1,575	1,335
Vancouver	85	205	982	1,399	2,458	2,812	5,467	7,301	8,940	12,865	14,160	17,270
Calgary	6	1	604	1,247	1,622	1,794	2,110	2,881	3,275	5,580	5,355	6,530
Edmonton	1	–	171	821	1,057	1,449	1,753	2,495	2,475	4,250	3,930	3,980
Regina	9	–	130	860	1,010	944	740	817	759	710	490	375
Saskatoon	–	–	77	599	691	703	687	793	490	540	585	325
Saint John	34	292	642	848	683	569	580	514	320	–	195	120
London	144	206	571	703	683	731	969	1,315	1,565	2,095	2,165	1,880
Halifax	18	102	254	585	582	756	1,012	1,186	1,315	1,220	1,440	1,575
Quebec	45	302	398	375	436	376	408	495	365	–	145	105

Note: Figures for 1911 through 1941 are from Rosenberg, *Canada's Jews*, 308-9 (see also Louis Rosenberg, 'The Jewish Population of Canada: A Statistical Summary from 1850 to 1943,' *AJYB* 48 [1946-7]: 35); and the Census of Canada from 1951 to 2001 (after the 1961 Census, Metropolitan Area figures are quoted).

Notes

Abbreviations

ACWA	*Documentary History of the Amalgamated Clothing Workers of America*
AHR	*American Historical Review*
AJA	*American Jewish Archives*
AJH	*American Jewish History*
AJHSA	American Jewish Historical Society Archives, New York
AJYB	*American Jewish Year Book*
AO	Archives of Ontario
CES/EEC	*Canadian Ethnic Studies / Études ethniques au Canada*
CHA	Canadian Historical Association
CHR	*Canadian Historical Review*
CJA	*Canadian Jewish Archives*
CJC	*Canadian Jewish Chronicle*
CJCCCNA	Canadian Jewish Congress Charities Committee National Archives, Montreal
CJE	*Canadian Journal of Economics*
CJHSJ	*Canadian Jewish Historical Society Journal*
CJN	*Canadian Jewish News*
CJO	*Canadian Jewish Outlook*
CJR	*Canadian Jewish Review*
CJS	*Canadian Journal of Sociology*
CJS/EJC	*Canadian Jewish Studies / Études Juives Canadiennes*
CRSA/RCSA	*Canadian Review of Sociology and Anthropology / Revue Canadienne de Sociologie et d'Anthropologie*
CSIS	Canadian Security Intelligence Service
CWS/CF	*Canadian Woman Studies / Cahiers de la Femme*
CZA	Central Zionist Archives, Jerusalem, Israel

DCB	*Dictionary of Canadian Biography*
EJ	*Encyclopedia Judaica*
Glen.	Glenbow Museum and Archives, Calgary
HS/SH	*Histoire sociale / Social History*
JCS/REC	*Journal of Canadian Studies / Revue d'Études Canadiennes*
JHSWC	Jewish Historical Society of Western Canada
JPLM	Jewish Public Library, Montreal
JSS	*Jewish Social Studies*
JT	*Jewish Times*
JWB	*Jewish Western Bulletin*
KA	*Keneder Adler*
LAC	Library and Archives Canada
LG	*Labour Gazette*
MBHP	Montreal Business History Project
McGill	McGill University Archives
MHSO	Multicultural History Society of Ontario, Toronto
OJA	Ontario Jewish Archives, Toronto
PABC	Public Archives of British Columbia
PAM	Public Archives of Manitoba, Winnipeg
PANS	Public Archives of Nova Scotia, Halifax
QQ	*Queen's Quarterly*
RCPSMB	*Report of the Royal Commission on Price Spreads and Mass Buying*
TJHSE	*Transactions of the Jewish Historical Society of England*
WA	Weizmann Archives, Rehovot, Israel

Introduction

1 See Todd M. Endelman, *The Jews of Britain, 1656 to 2000* (Los Angeles, 2002), 1–13.
2 Robert Harney, 'Ethnic Studies: Handmaiden of Multiculturalism,' unpublished paper presented to the Canadian Historical Association, June 1984.

1. Foundations in the Colonial Era

1 Benjamin G. Sack, *History of the Jews in Canada* (Montreal, 1965), 7–11; Irving Abella, *A Coat of Many Colours* (Toronto, 1990); JPLM, Louis Rosenberg Manuscripts, Louis Rosenberg, 'The Earliest Jewish Settlers in Canada: Facts vs. Myths' (unpublished manuscript), 2.
2 The most recent and thorough work on this subject is Richard Menkis, 'The Gradis Family of Eighteenth-Century Bordeaux: A Social and Economic

Study' (Ph.D. diss., Brandeis University, 1988). See also his 'Historiography, Myth and Group Relations: Jewish and Non-Jewish Québécois on Jews and New France,' *CES/EEC* 23 (1991): 24–38.
3 Jacob R. Marcus, *The Colonial American Jew, 1492–1776*, 3 vols (Detroit, 1970), 1:381–2.
4 Gérard Malchelosse, 'Les juifs dans l'histoire canadienne,' in *Cahiers des Dix* (Montreal, 1939), 170; Louis Rosenberg, 'Some Aspects of the Historical Development of the Canadian Jewish Community,' *AJH* 50, no. 2 (1960): 121–42, 123–4; Solomon Frank, *Two Centuries in the Life of a Synagogue* (Montreal, 1968), 40.
5 A.J.B. Johnston, 'The People of Eighteenth Century Louisbourg,' in *Aspects of Louisbourg: Essays on the History of an Eighteenth Century French Community in North America Published to Commemorate the 275th Anniversary of the Founding of Louisbourg*, ed. Eric Krause, Carol Corbin, and William O'Shea (Sydney, 1995), 150–61, 159.
6 Leo Hershkowitz and Isidore S. Meyer, eds., *The Lee Max Friedman Collection of American Jewish Colonial Correspondence: Letters of the Franks Family (1733–1748)* (Waltham, 1968), 124, 136.
7 Marcus, *Colonial American Jew*, 1:363, 2:752.
8 Quoted in Jan Goeb, 'The Maritimes,' *Viewpoints* 7, nos. 3/4 (1973): 9–23, 13.
9 Rosenberg, 'The Earliest Jewish Settlers in Canada: Facts vs. Myths,' 1.
10 Jacob R. Marcus, *Early American Jewry: The Jews of New York, New England and Canada, 1649–1794*, 2 vols (Philadelphia, 1951), 1:200.
11 Marcus, *Colonial American Jew*, 1:380; C. Bruce Fergusson, 'Jewish History in Nova Scotia Dates Back to 1752,' in *Canadian Jewish Reference Book and Directory*, ed. Eli Gottesman (Ottawa, 1963), 290.
12 Denis Vaugeois, 'Samuel Jacobs,' in *DCB*, 4:384–6, 384; Marcus, *Colonial American Jew*, 2:681; Frances Dublin, 'Jewish Colonial Enterprise in the Light of the Amherst Papers (1758–1763),' *AJH* 29, no. 35 (1939): 1–25, 5; Marcus, *Colonial American Jew*, 2:681; Fergusson, 'Jewish History in Nova Scotia,' 290; Morris A. Gutstein, *The Story of the Jews of Newport: Two and a Half Centuries of Judaism, 1658–1908* (New York, 1936), 163–4.
13 Stanley F. Chyet, *Lopez of Newport: Colonial American Merchant Prince* (Detroit, 1970), 58, 82, 118, 128, 134, 213; Fergusson, 'Jewish History in Nova Scotia,' 290; Marcus, *Colonial American Jew*, 3:1294; Goeb, 'Maritimes,' 13; Cecil Roth, 'Some Jewish Loyalists in the War of American Independence,' *AJH* 38, no. 3 (1936): 99.
14 David A. Sutherland, 'Samuel Hart,' in *DCB*, 5:409–10.
15 Rosenberg, 'Some Aspects,' 122.

16 Sack, *History of the Jews in Canada*, 70.
17 Letter from Jonathan Sarna to the author, 6 Feb. 1992. See Jacob R. Marcus, *American Jewry: Documents – Eighteenth-Century* (Cincinnati, 1959), 90; Marcus, *Colonial American Jew*, 2:632, 733–7, 3:1054–5.
18 Charles P. Stacey, *Quebec, 1759: The Siege and the Battle*, rev. ed., ed. with new materials by Donald E. Graves (Toronto, 2002), 107, 178. On Alexander Schomberg, see *Oxford Dictionary of National Biography* (on-line edition), article by J.K. Laughton and Philip MacDougall, 49:241–2; Dublin, 'Jewish Colonial Enterprise in the Light of the Amherst Papers (1758–1763);' Marcus, *Colonial American Jew*, 1:381.
19 See Jose Igartua, 'A Change of Climate: The Conquest and the Marchands of Montreal,' CHA, *Annual Report* (1974).
20 Marcus, *Colonial American Jew*, 1:311, 2:727–8; Walter Dunn, Jr, 'Ezekiel Solomons,' in *DCB*, 4:718–9. See also Sheldon J. Godfrey and Judith C. Godfrey, *Search Out the Land: the Jews and the Growth of Equality in British Colonial America, 1740–1867* (Montreal, 1995), 82–92, and 115, for an extended discussion of Jewish commercial activity in the interior; and Robert A. Rockway, *The Jews of Detroit: From the Beginning, 1762–1914* (Detroit, 1986), 3–4.
21 Marcus, *Early American Jewry*, 1:230; see also Marcus, *Documents – Eighteenth Century*, 227–32, 457–9, 464–5, 474–5.
22 Allan Greer, *Peasant, Lord and Merchant: Rural Society in Three Quebec Parishes, 1740–1840* (Toronto, 1985), ch. 6.
23 Denis Vaugeois, 'Aaron Hart,' in *DCB*, 4:331–3; Raymond Douville, *Aaron Hart, récit historique* (Trois-Rivières, 1938), 30.
24 Marcus, *Colonial American Jew*, 1:382, 377, 379.
25 See Marcus, *Documents – Eighteenth Century*, 106; 'Minutes of the Shearith Israel Congregation in Montreal, 1778 to 1780,' *CJA* 1, no. 4 (1959): 10; Jacob Neusner, 'Anglo-Jewry and the Development of American Jewish Life, 1775–1850,' *TJHSE* 18 (1958): 231–42.
26 Marcus, *Early American Jewry*, 1:224.
27 'Minutes,' *CJA* 1, no. 4 (1959): 12, 14, 16.
28 Documents 1–10, *CJA* 1, no. 5 (1959).
29 Frank, *Two Centuries*, 40, 41; Doris G. Daniels, 'Colonial Jewry: Religion, Domestic and Social Relations,' *AJH* 66 (March 1977): 385. See Steven Singer, 'Jewish Religious Observance in Early Victorian London, 1840–1860,' *Jewish Journal of Sociology* 28, no. 2 (1986): 117–37.
30 Marcus, *Colonial American Jew* 2:711; 3:1267–78, 1287. For fascinating documents on Franks's later career, see Marcus, *Documents – Eighteenth Century*, 274–7; and Jacob R. Marcus, *Memoirs of American Jews*, 3 vols (Philadelphia, 1955), 1:45–9.

31 There was at least one Jewish Loyalist who fled from New York to Nova Scotia in 1782. See Marcus, *Documents – Eighteenth Century*, 282–3; Marcus, *Colonial American Jew* 3:1294–5.

32 Sylvia Van Kirk, '"Women in Between": Women in Fur Trade Society in Western Canada,' in *Readings in Canadian Social History*, ed. M. Cross and G. Kealey (Toronto, 1982), 191–211.

33 Malcolm H. Stern, 'Jewish Marriage and Intermarriage in the Federal Period, 1776–1840,' *AJA* 19, no. 2 (1967), 142–3.

34 *Le Bien Public*, 23 March 1939.

35 Marcus, *Documents – Eighteenth Century*, 429–31; Robert Cohen, 'The Demography of the Jews in Early America,' in *Modern Jewish Fertility*, ed. Paul Rittenband, Studies in Judaism in Modern Times, ed. Jacob Neusner (Leiden, 1981), 144–59, 145.

36 Alfred L. Burt, *The Old Province of Quebec* (Toronto, 1933), 194.

37 Bernard Blumenkranz, 'From the Expulsion from Provence to the Eve of the Revolution,' in 'France,' in *EJ*, 7:21–2; Marcus, *Colonial American Jew*, 1:388, 478.

38 See William Pencak, *Jews and Gentiles in Early America, 1654–1800* (Ann Arbor, 2005), esp. 62–82.

39 Nathan Glazer, *American Judaism*, 2nd ed. (Chicago, 1972, ch. 3.

40 Fernand Ouellet, 'Pierre-Stanislas Bedard,' in *DCB*, 6:41–9, 46.

41 Benjamin Sulte, 'Les miettes de l'histoire,' *Revue canadienne* (Montreal, 1870), 427–43, 43; W. Wallace, *The Macmillan Dictionary of Canadian Biography* (Toronto, 1963), 242; *Quebec Mercury*, 20 April 1807.

42 Abraham J. Arnold, 'Ezekiel Hart and the Oath Problem in the Assembly of Lower Canada,' *CJHSJ* 3, no. 1 (1979): 10–26, 13; *Le Canadien*, 18 April 1807. Abraham Rhinewine, *Looking Back a Century on the Centennial of Jewish Political Equality in Canada* (Toronto, 1932) contains much useful detail.

43 *Le Canadien*, 18 April 1807.

44 Ibid., 13 Feb. 1808. Coffin petitioned the House that 'Ezekiel Hart, étant Juif ne pourrait prêter le serment requis de la part des membres et par conséquent ne pourrait être admis à la Chambre' – that Hart, being a Jew, was unable to take the prescribed oath and was thus ineligible (ibid., 17 and 20 Feb., and 2 March 1808; *Quebec Mercury*, 15 Feb. 1808).

45 *Le Canadien*, 21 May 1808; *Quebec Mercury*, 21 March 1808; *Le Canadien*, 20 May 1808.

46 Quoted in Joseph Tassé, 'Droits politiques des juifs en Canada,' *Revue Canadienne* (June 1870), 411, 416; cited in Arnold, 'Ezekiel Hart,' 25.

47 See Jean-Pierre Wallot, 'Les canadiens français et les juifs (1808–1809): L'affaire Hart,' in *Juifs et canadiens: Deuxième cahier du Cercle juif de la langue française*, ed. Naim Kattan (Montreal, 1967), 113–21.

48 Helen T. Manning, *The Revolt of French Canada, 1800–1835: A Chapter of the History of the British Commonwealth* (Toronto, 1962), 84.
49 David Rome, 'Adolphus Mordecai Hart,' in *DCB*, 10:337.
50 *CJA* 1, no. 3 (1957): 8. See also Rhinewine, *Looking Back a Century*, 80–1.
51 Richard Menkis, 'Antisemitism and Anti-Judaism in Pre-Confederation Canada,' in *Antisemitism in Canada: History and Interpretation*, ed. Alan Davies (Waterloo, 1992), 11–38, 17; letter from Fernand Ouellet to the author, 1 Oct. 1990.
52 Menkis, 'Antisemitism and Anti-Judaism,' 11; Rome, 'Adolphus Mordecai Hart,' 337; D. Vaugeois, 'Aaron Ezekiel Hart,' in *DCB* 8:363–5. See Israel Feinstein, 'Anglo Jewish Opinion during the Struggle for Emancipation (1828–1858),' *TJHSE* 20 (1964): 113–43.
53 Denis Vaugeois, 'Bécancour et les Hart,' in *Les juifs et la communauté française*, ed. Naim Kattan (Montreal, 1965), 108–9; Denis Vaugeois, 'Moses Hart,' in *DCB*, 8:367–70.
54 Elinor K. Senior and James H. Lambert, 'David David,' in *DCB*, 6:179–81; MBHP, assignment of David David, Notary Griffin, 25 Jan. 1825, no. 5538.
55 Carman Miller, 'Moses Judah Hayes,' in *DCB*, 6:379–81.
56 MBHP, N.B. Doucet, nos. 10275, 10055, 11136, 11529, 8728, 13015, 13404; Crawford, no. 147; Carman Miller, 'Benjamin Hart,' in *DCB*, 8:365–7.
57 Paul-André Linteau and Jean-Claude Robert, 'Propriété foncière et société à Montréal: Une hypothèse,' *Revue d'histoire de l'amérique française* 28, no. 1 (1974): 45–6.
58 Michel De Lorimier, 'Louis Marchand,' in *DCB*, 11:585–7, 585.
59 See Françoise Noël, *Family Life and Sociability in Upper and Lower Canada, 1780–1870* (Montreal, 2003), 29–44, for a fascinating account of Joseph's social life; Elinor K. Senior, 'Eleazar David David,' in *DCB*, 11:234–5.
60 'Extract from the Register Kept by the Prothonotary of His Majesty's Court of King's Bench for the District of Montreal under the Provincial Statutes 9 & 10 Geo. IV chap: 75,' *CJA* 1, no. 1 (1955): 3; 'Sale of Seats in New Synagogue 31st August 1838,' *CJA* 1, no. 1 (1955): 16; Frank, *Two Centuries*, 42.
61 Esther I. Blaustein, Rachel A. Esar, and Evelyn Miller, 'Spanish and Portuguese Synagogue (Shearith Israel) Montreal, 1768–1968,' *TJHSE* 23 (1969–70): 111; 'Abraham Hart, Jr., London, to the Trustees of the Montreal Synagogue, Montreal, Lower Canada, 13 Dec., 1838,' *CJA* 1, no.1 (1955): 12. In June of 1835 a lot on Chenneville Street was purchased for a new synagogue. Frank, *Two Centuries*, 43; 'Deed of Sale of Lot for Synagogue on Chenneville Street from Representatives of M. Gabriel Cotte to the Trustees of the Israelitish Congregation in Montreal, Dated June 30th, 1835,' *CJA* 1, no. 2 (1956): 6–8; MBHP, Notary G.D. Arnoldi, nos. 4040, 4041, 4 and 9 March 1835;

Newton Bosworth, *Hochelaga Depicta: The Early History and Present State of the City and Island of Montreal* (Montreal, 1839), 112–13.
62 *CJA* 1, no. 2 (1956): 12–13.
63 *CJA* 1, no. 1 (1955): 6–7, ch. 2, article 1.
64 'H.B. Doucet, Notary Public, to Benjamin Hart and Aaron H. David, 2 Sept. 1839,' *CJA* 1, no.1 (1955): 13.
65 'An Act to Amend the Act of Lower Canada Therein Mentioned, Extending Certain Privileges to Persons of the Jewish Persuasion,' ch. 96, 9 June 1846, *CJA* 1, no. 6 (1962).
66 *The Occident*, no. 4 (1 July 1843).
67 Moses Hart, *Modern Religion* (New York, 1816); Denis Vaugeois, 'Moses Hart,' in *DCB*, 8:367–70.
68 Jacob R. Marcus, 'The Modern Religion of Moses Hart,' *Hebrew Union College Annual* 20 (1947): 585–616, 612; Hart also wrote diatribes against Roman Catholicism. Denis Vaugeois, 'Les positions religieuses de Moses Hart,' *Canadian Catholic Historical Association* (1966), 41–6; Malcolm H. Stern, 'The 1820s: American Jewry Comes of Age,' in *The American Jewish Experience*, ed. Jonathan Sarna (New York, 1986), 34–5.
69 A highly wonky individual, Noah had by this time experienced a personal clash with the equally idiosyncratic reformer William Lyon Mackenzie and hoped that Canada would continue under British rule. Jonathan D. Sarna, *Jacksonian Jew: The Two Worlds of Mordecai Noah* (New York, 1981), 123.
70 See Hasia Diner, *A Time for Gathering: The Second Migration 1820–1880* (Baltimore, 1992), 150; Mason Wade, *The French Canadians, 1760–1945* (Toronto, 1956), 189–90. I have not been able to find other confirmation of this assertion.
71 See Jonathan Sarna, *American Judaism: A History* (New Haven, 2004), 52–61.

2. Pedlars and Settlers on the Urban Frontiers

1 Harvard University, Baker Library, R.G. Dun and Company, credit ledgers, Montreal, 1846–76, 3 vols.
2 Ibid., 1:251.
3 Charles Cole, 'The Montreal Jewish Community in 1861 and 1871' (Honours undergraduate thesis, McGill University, Dept. of Geography, 1983), Appendices A (1861) and B (1871).
4 Carman Miller, 'Moses Judah Hayes,' in *DCB*, 9:379–81. See also Christopher Armstrong and H.V. Nelles, *Monopoly's Moment: The Organization and Regulation of Canadian Utilities, 1830–1930* (Philadelphia, 1986) 13, 14, 15. Miller, 'Hayes,' 380; Gerald Tulchinsky; 'Studies of Businessmen in the Development of

Transportation and Industry in Montreal, 1837 to 1853' (Ph.D. diss., University of Toronto, 1971), 465; Armstrong and Nelles, *Monopoly's Moment*, 78.

5 Steven Hertzberg, *Strangers within the City: The Jews of Atlanta, 1845–1915* (Philadelphia, 1978); Elliott Ashkenazi, *The Business of Jews in Louisiana 1840–1875* (Tuscaloosa, 1988); William Toll, *The Making of an Ethnic Middle Class: Portland Jewry over Four Generations* (Albany, 1982); David A. Gerber, 'Cutting Out Shylock: Elite Anti-Semitism and the Quest for Moral Order in the Mid-Nineteenth Century American Marketplace,' in *Anti-Semitism in American History*, ed. David A. Gerber (Urbana, 1986), 201–32. See also Rowena Olegario, 'That Mysterious People: Jewish Merchants, Transparency, and Community in Mid-Nineteenth Century America,' *Business History Review* 73 (Summer 1999): 161–89.

6 D. McCalla, *The Upper Canada Trade, 1834–1872: A Study of the Buchanans' Business* (Toronto, 1979); Gerald J. Tulchinsky, *The River Barons: Montreal Businessmen and the Growth of Industry and Transportation 1837–53* (Toronto, 1977).

7 Dun, Montreal, 1:193, 262.

8 Benjamin G. Sack, *History of the Jews in Canada* (Montreal, 1965), 154, 156.

9 Dun, Montreal, 1:232, 231, 255, 125.

10 Ibid., 2:105.

11 Ibid., 1:138, 256.

12 Ibid., 2:217.

13 Sack, *Jews in Canada*, passim.

14 Arthur D. Hart, ed., *The Jew in Canada* (Montreal, 1926).

15 Dun, Montreal, 1:192.

16 Hart, *Jew in Canada*, 330.

17 J.D. Borthwick, *History and Biographical Gazetteer of Montreal to the Year 1892* (Montreal, 1892), 471–2.

18 Dun, Montreal, 2:33.

19 Hart, *Jew in Canada*, 133.

20 Dun, Montreal, 1:192.

21 Ibid., 2:84.

22 Ibid., 1:409, 12, 177.

23 Ibid., 434.

24 Ibid., 2:84.

25 Ibid., 1:28, 137; 2:38.

26 Tulchinsky, *River Barons*, 219–20.

27 *Montreal in 1856: A Sketch Prepared for the Opening of the Grand Trunk Railway of Canada* (Montreal, 1856), 46.

28 Dun, Montreal, 1:84.

29 Ibid., 2:70.

30 Gerald Tulchinsky, 'Aspects of the Clothing Manufacturing Industry in Canada, 1850s-1914,' unpublished paper presented to the Business History Conference, Trent University, 1984, pp. 18–20.
31 Gerald Tulchinsky, 'Hollis Shorey,' in *DCB*, 12:968–70.
32 LAC, R.G. Dun and Company Credit Ledgers, XXVI, microfilm reel M-7760, 258. Hereafter cited as 'Dun, Toronto.'
33 Dun, Montreal, 1:261.
34 Dun, Toronto, 127.
35 Ibid., 231.
36 Ibid., 332.
37 Stephen Speisman, *The Jews of Toronto: A History to 1937* (Toronto, 1979), 12.
38 Dun, Toronto, 202.
39 Ibid., 339. Altogether, the Rossins owned 27 properties in Toronto in 1860 (City of Toronto Archives, Assessment Rolls, 1860, St George Ward, 6, 17, 12, 36; St James Ward, 25, 26).
40 Speisman, *Jews of Toronto*, 14.
41 Hugh Grant, 'The Mysterious Jacob L. Englehart and the Secret of Accumulation in the Early Ontario Petroleum Industry, unpublished paper, University of Winnipeg, Dept. of Economics, unpublished paper, 1990, p. 6.
42 Speisman, *Jews of Toronto*, 23.
43 Sigmund Samuel, *In Return: The Autobiography of Sigmund Samuel* (Toronto, 1963), 7–9.
44 Dun, Toronto, 136.
45 See Joy L. Santink, *Timothy Eaton and the Rise of His Department Store* (Toronto, 1990), 58–89.
46 Samuel, *In Return*, 17; McCalla, *Buchanans*, passim.
47 Samuel, *In Return*, 24, 18.
48 LAC, Dun, XXV, microfilm reel M-7759, 115.
49 Ibid.
50 Ibid., 220.
51 Brian S. Osborne, 'Trading on a Frontier: The Function of Peddlers, Markets, and Fairs in Nineteenth Century Ontario,' in *Canadian Papers in Rural History, II*, ed. Donald H. Akenson (Gananoque, 1980), 60.
52 LAC, Dun, XIII, 73.
53 Ibid. XV, 111.
54 Ibid. XIX, 35; microfilm reel M-7758, 36, 100.
55 Ibid. XXII, 50; XVIII, 106; Dun, Montreal, 1:402, 457.
56 See Sheldon and Judith Godfrey, *'Burn This Gossip': The True Story of George Benjamin of Belleville, Canada's First Jewish Member of Parliament 1857–1863* (Toronto, 1991).

57 Helmut Kallman, 'Abraham Nordheimer,' in *DCB*, 9:600–1.
58 Marian E. Meyer, *The Jews of Kingston: A Microcosm of Canadian Jewry* (Kingston, 1983), 15.
59 Hart, *Jew in Canada*, 96, 102, 98, 342.
60 Dun, Montreal, 4076.
61 Michael Bliss, *Northern Enterprise: Five Centuries of Canadian Business* (Toronto, 1987), 156, 187.
62 Shmuel Ettinger, 'The Modern Period,' in *A History of the Jewish People*, ed. H.H. Ben Sasson (Cambridge, 1976), 727–1096, 807.
63 Ashkenazi, *Jews in Louisiana*, 160.
64 Robin McGrath, *Salt Fish and Shmattes: A History of the Jews in Newfoundland and Labrador from 1770* (St John's, 2006), 18–33; LAC, R.G. Dun and Company Credit Ledgers, II, microfilm reel M-7756, n.pag.
65 Jan Goeb, 'The Maritimes,' *Viewpoints* 7, nos. 3–4 (1973): 12.
66 James A. Fraser, *By Favorable Winds: A History of Chatham, New Brunswick* (Chatham, 1975), 258, 289–91.
67 Goeb, 'Maritimes,' 13.
68 Hart, *Jew in Canada*, 552; Sheva Medjuck, *The Jews of Atlantic Canada* (St John's, 1986), 23; Marcia Koven, *Weaving the Past into the Present: A Glimpse into the 130 Year History of the Saint John Jewish Community* (Saint John, 1989), 1–3.
69 Eli Boyaner, 'The Settlement and Development of the Jewish Community of Saint John,' *New Brunswick Historical Society*, 15 (1959): 79–86, 84.
70 Medjuck, *Atlantic Canada*, 23–4.
71 Louis Rosenberg, *Canada's Jews: A Social and Economic Study of the Jews in Canada* (Montreal, 1939), 308.
72 D.O. Carrigan, 'The Immigrant Experience in Halifax, 1881–1931,' unpublished paper.
73 Quoted in David Rome, *The First Two Years: A Record of the Jewish Pioneers on Canada's Pacific Coast, 1858–1860* (Montreal, 1942), 3.
74 J.M.S. Careless, 'The Business Community in the Early Development of Victoria, British Columbia,' in *Canadian Business History: Selected Studies*, ed. David S. Macmillan (Toronto, 1972), 104–23.
75 Cyril E. Leonoff, *Pioneers, Pedlars and Prayer Shawl: The Jewish Communities in British Columbia and the Yukon* (Vancouver, 1978), 15.
76 David Rome, 'First Jews in Western Canada,' *JWB*, 30 June 1958.
77 Ibid.
78 Rabbi Jack A. Levey, 'A Message from Your Own Home Town,' n.pag.; D. Rome, 'Jews in the Cariboo,' *JWB*, 30 June 1958.
79 Careless, 'Business Community,' 108.

80 C. Leonoff, 'The Centennial of Jewish Life in Vancouver, 1886–1986,' paper presented to the CHA and Jewish Historical Society of Western Canada, Winnipeg, 8 June 1986, p. 3.
81 I.J. Benjamin, *Three Years in America 1859–1862*, 2 vols (Philadelphia, 1956).
82 David Rome, 'Early British Columbia Jewry: A Reconstructed "Census,"' *Canadian Ethnic Studies / Études ethniques du Canada* 3, no. 1 (1971): 57–62, 61.
83 Christine Wisenthal, 'Insiders and Outsiders: Two Waves of Jewish Settlement in British Columbia, 1858–1914' (MA thesis, University of British Columbia, 1987), 17, 14, 30, 59, 41, 47.
84 Cyril E. Leonoff, 'Pioneer Jewish Merchants of Vancouver Island and British Columbia,' *CJHSJ* 1 (1984): 12–43, 12.
85 PABC, 'Congregation Emanuel Victoria,' guide; PABC, 'Constitution and By-Laws of Congregation Emanu-El of Victoria,' VI (Victoria, 1893), 2.
86 PABC, File 7b, 'Documents re Hebrew Synagogue Emanuel 1862–63,' letter from Robert Bishop, 13 Nov. 1862.
87 Ibid., A. Hoffman to the Board of Trustees and Members of the Congregation Emanuel, 22 Nov. 1862.
88 Ibid., Hoffman to Rev. Dr N. Adler, 5 May 1863.
89 J.K. Unsworth, 'Victoria Synagogue Is the Second Oldest House of Worship,' *JWB*, 30 June 1958.
90 Alan Klenman, 'British Columbia Pioneers Contribute to Build Western Canada's First Synagogue, 1862–1863,' *Western States Jewish History* 22, no. 3 (1990): 258–64.
91 Wisenthal, 'Insiders and Outsiders,' 21, 19.
92 PABC, File 7b, 'Documents,' M.R. Cohen to the President of the Congregation, 9 Nov. 1863.
93 Leonoff, 'Centennial,' 5.
94 Leonoff, *Pioneers*, 168.
95 Peter Liddell and Patricia G. Roy, 'David Oppenheimer,' in *DCB*, 12:803–6.
96 Leonoff, 'Centennial,' 13.
97 See Michael B. Katz, *The People of Hamilton, Canada West: Family and Class in a Mid-Nineteenth-Century City* (Cambridge, 1975).
98 Barry M. Gough, 'The Character of the British Columbia Frontier,' *British Columbia Historical Readings*, ed. W. Peter Ward and Robert A.J. McDonald (Vancouver, 1981), 232–44, 240.
99 Robert A.J. McDonald, 'Victoria, Vancouver, and Economic Development of British Columbia, 1886–1914,' in ibid., 369–95, 372.

3. Victorian Montreal and Western Settlement

1 Henry Feingold, *Zion in America: The Jewish Experience from Colonial Times to the Present* (New York, 1974), 1–51; Arthur Hertzberg, *The Jews in America: Four Centuries of an Uneasy Encounter* (New York, 1989), 91–2.
2 Richard Menkis, '"In This Great, Happy and Enlightened Colony": Abraham De Sola on Jews, Judaism and Emancipation in Victorian Montreal,' in *L'Antisemitisme éclairé. Inclusion et exclusion depuis L'Epoque des Lumières jusqu'à l'affaire Dreyfus / Inclusion and Exclusion: Perspectives on Jews from the Enlightenment to the Dreyfus Affair*, ed. Ilana Zinguer and Sam W. Bloom (Leiden, Boston, 2003), 315–31; Carman Miller, 'Abraham de Sola,' in DCB, 11:253–6; Evelyn Miller, 'The "Learned Hazan" of Montreal: Reverend Abraham de Sola, LL.D.: 1825–1882,' *American Sephardi* 7–8, (1975): 23–42; *The Occident* 4, no. 11 (Feb. 1847).
3 John I. Cooper, *History of St. George's Lodge, No.1, G.R.Q.* (Montreal, 1955), 1; Benjamin G. Sack, *History of the Jews in Canada* (Montreal, 1965), ch. 9.
4 Edwin Wolf and Maxwell Whiteman, *The History of the Jews of Philadelphia* (Philadelphia, 1975), 373; Leonardo Hellemberg, 'Rebecca Gratz,' in *EJ*, 6:860; Stanley B. Frost, *McGill University for the Advancement of Learning*, Vol. 1, 1801–1895 (Montreal, 1980), 118.
5 Abigail Green, 'Rethinking Sir Moses Montefiore: Religion, Nationhood, and International Philanthropy in the Nineteenth Century,' *AHR* 110, no. 3 (June 2005): 631–59, 634; Isidore S. Meyer, 'Jacques Judah Lyons,' in *EJ* 11:626; Michael Brown, 'The Empire's Best Known Jew and Little Known Jewry,' in *The Canadian Jewish Studies Reader*, ed. Richard Menkis and Norman Ravvin (Red Deer, 2004), 73–89. See also Menkis, '"In This Great, Happy and Enlightened Colony"' 320–1 and passim, for an insightful examination of this aspect of de Sola's thinking and preaching.
6 See Yvon Lamonde, *Gens de parole: Conférences publiques, essais, et débats à l'Institut Canadien de Montréal, 1845–1871* (Montreal, 1990), 19–33, 115–120.
7 H. Blair Neatby, *Laurier and a Liberal Quebec: A Study in Political Management* (Toronto, 1973).
8 Jacques J. Lyons and Abraham de Sola, *A Jewish Calendar for Fifty Years, from A.M. 5614 to A.M. 5664: Together with an Introductory Essay on the Jewish Calendar System, etc.* (Cincinnati, 1854). Besides a small income, these literary efforts brought de Sola a considerable reputation as one of North America's leading Jewish scholars. On Lyons, see Hyman G. Grinstein, *The Rise of the Jewish Community of New York, 1654–1860* (Philadelphia, 1945), passim. See Carl Berger, *Science, God and Nature in Victorian Canada* (Toronto, 1983); *British American Journal of Medical and Physical Science*, 1849–50: 227–9, 259–62,

290–3; *Canadian Medical Journal and Monthly Record of Medical and Surgical Science*, 1852–3: 135–54, 203–11, 325–40, 464–8, 529–32, 589–99, 654–6, 728–41, later published as *The Sanatory Institutions of the Hebrews* ... (Montreal: 1861); Geoffrey Cantor, *Quakers, Jews, and Science: Religious Responses to Modernity and the Sciences in Britain, 1650–1900* (New York, 2005), 180–6, 197–203, 215–24.

9 See Lance J. Sussman, *Isaac Leeser and the Making of American Judaism* (Detroit, 1995), 161, 163, 287; Dropsie College, Philadelphia, Isaac Leeser Papers, letters from de Sola to Leeser, 6 Dec. 1848, 11 May 1856.

10 See Walter J. Fischel, 'Persia,' in *EJ*, 11:301–19, 316; Leeser Papers, de Sola to Leeser, 29 Oct. and 7 Dec. 1848, 16 April 1849.

11 Leeser Papers, de Sola to Leeser, 10 Jan. 1860, 19 April 1864.

12 Frost, *McGill University*, 118; Leeser Papers, de Sola to Leeser, 12 May 1864, 8 May 1865.

13 Ramsay Cook, *The Regenerators: Social Criticism in Late Victorian English Canada* (Toronto, 1985), 58–9, 245.

14 See Jack Riemer, 'Isaac Leeser,' in EJ, 10:1561–2; Feingold, *Zion in America*, 66.

15 Leeser Papers, de Sola to Leeser, 24 Nov. 1847, 12 June 1855.

16 Ibid., 10 Jan. 1860, 24 June 1866, 15 Aug. 1865.

17 See McGill, Abraham de Sola Papers, Evelyn Miller, ed., 'A Guide to the Microfilm' (1970); Leeser Papers, de Sola to Leeser, 15 Aug. 1865, 17 Aug. 1857.

18 Ibid., 8 and 15 Aug. 1865.

19 Ibid., 22 Feb. 1848, 12 May 1864.

20 *The Occident 6*, (October 1848): 368–70, quoted in Sack, *Jews in Canada*, 139–40. 'Baron de Hirsch Institute,' in *The Jew in Canada*, ed. Arthur D. Hart (Montreal, 1926), 201–5, 201; *Montreal Gazette*, 8 Jan. 1856.

21 David A. Ansell's reminiscences, quoted in Sack, *Jews in Canada*, 169.

22 LAC, MG 28, vol. 86, Jewish Family Services of the Baron de Hirsch Institute (est. 1863), Montreal, Minutes of the Board, Baron de Hirsch Institute of Montreal, 1863–1914 (hereafter cited as Minutes), Vol. 1, 23 July 1863. The qualification that members be unmarried was changed in November 1864 to allow 'any member of the Hebrew faith over the age of 13 years and unmarried of good reputation ... but in the event of their marrying while members, they still retain their membership' (ibid., 27 Nov. 1864).

23 Louis Rosenberg, *Canada's Jews: A Social and Economic Study of the Jews in Canada* (Montreal, 1939), 308.

24 Minutes 1, 18 Oct. 1874; *Montreal Gazette*, 7 Jan. 1875, 4 Jan. 1864, 25 Feb. 1872. See also *Montreal Gazette*, 4 and 11 Feb. 1873.

25 Minutes 1, 1862. Levey persisted in his efforts to limit the society's relief activities by giving notice of a motion in 1868 – which he apparently did not push any further – that would have limited annual relief payments to a maximum of $15 per applicant (Minutes 1, 12 July 1868); 'The Young Men's Hebrew Benevolent Society of Montreal,' Revised By-Laws, Art. II, Object, Section 1, included in Minutes 1, 13 Aug. 1871.
26 Ibid., 1 Feb. 1864.
27 Charles Cole, 'The Montreal Jewish Community in 1861 and 1871' (McGill University, Dept. of Geography, 1983), 12–13, 20.
28 See Judith Fingard, 'The Winter's Tale: The Seasonal Contours of Pre-industrial Poverty in British North America,' *CHA, Historical Papers* (1974): 65–94; Minutes 1, 25 March 1876, March 1878.
29 *London Jewish Chronicle*, 22 Oct. 1875. See also Minutes 1, 14 Nov. 1875, 4 Nov. 1877.
30 Ansell, 'Reminiscences,' quoted in Sack, *Jews in Canada*, 169; Hart, ed., *Jew in Canada*, 83–5, 93–5, 121–2.
31 LAC, MG 29, C95, microfilm reel A913, Clarence de Sola diaries, 23 July 1874.
32 *The Occident* 7 (April–Sept. 1849).
33 Gerald Tulchinsky, 'Clarence Isaac de Sola,' in *DCB*, 14:291–2.
34 Rosenberg, *Canada's Jews*, 12; LAC, MG 29, C95, microfilm reel A913, Clarence de Sola diaries, 21 April and 13 Dec. 1882.
35 Cecil Roth, 'Anglo-Jewish Association,' in *EJ*, 2:977–8. See also Eugene C. Black, *The Social Politics of Anglo-Jewry, 1880–1920* (London, 1988), 44–50; Todd Endelman, 'Communal Solidarity among the Jewish Elite of Victorian London,' *Victorian Studies* 28, no. 3 (Spring 1985): 491–526.
36 Bertram Korn, *American Jewry and the Civil War* (New York, 1979), 2; Michael Brown, 'The Beginnings of Reform Judaism in Canada,' *JSS* 34 (Oct. 1972): 322–42.
37 Rosenberg, *Canada's Jews*, 10.
38 Hertzberg, *Jews in America*, 103, ch. 7. See Avraham Barkai, *Branching Out: German Jewish Immigration to the United States, 1820–1914* (New York, 1994).
39 See Jacques Monet, *The Last Cannon Shot: A Study of French-Canadian Nationalism, 1837 to 1850* (Toronto, 1969); Brian Young, *In Its Corporate Capacity: The Seminary of Montreal as a Business Institution, 1816–1876* (Montreal, 1986); W.P.M. Kennedy, *Documents of the Canadian Constitution, 1759–1915* (Toronto, 1917), 665.
40 Usiel O. Schmelz, 'Migrations,' in *EJ*, 16:1519–20.
41 Jonathan D. Sarna, 'The Myth of No Return: Jewish Return Migration to Eastern Europe, 1881–1914,' in *Labor Migration in the Atlantic Economies:*

The European and North American Working Classes during the Period of Industrialization, ed. Dirk Hoerder (Westport, 1985), 423–34; Simon Kuznets, 'Immigration of Russian Jews to the United States: Background and Structure,' in *Perspectives in American History* (Cambridge, 1975), 40.

42 The figure of 10,000 is based on the estimates in Arthur Ruppin's *The Jews in the Modern World* (London, 1934), 52. Ruppin was regarded as the foremost scholar of Jewish society in history. However, estimates vary. Ronald Sanders, in his *Shores of Refuge: A Hundred Years of Jewish Emigration* (New York, 1988), puts the figure of new Jewish arrivals at 'about twelve thousand' (168).
43 See Rosenberg, *Canada's Jews*, 10, 13–15.
44 Marcus L. Hansen and John B. Brebner, *The Mingling of the Canadian and American Peoples* (New Haven, 1940).
45 See Harold M. Troper, *Only Farmers Need Apply: Official Canadian Government Encouragement of American Immigration, 1896–1911* (Toronto, 1972).
46 *Montreal Gazette*, 18 Jan., 1 Feb., and 14 and 22 May 1882.
47 Irving Howe, *World of Our Fathers: The Journey of the East European Jews to America and the Life They Found and Made* (New York, 1976), 47.
48 *Montreal Gazette*, 16 and 22 May, and 21 June 1882, 12 March 1883; *Manitoba Free Press*, 27 May and 2 June 1882. Cited in Norman Hillmer and J.L. Granatstein, eds, *The Land Newly Found: Eyewitness Accounts of the Canadian Immigrant Experience* (Toronto, 2006), 99–100.
49 Stephen Speisman, *The Jews of Toronto: A History to 1937* (Toronto, 1979), 58; Simon I. Belkin, *Through Narrow Gates: A Review of Jewish Immigration, Colonization and Immigrant Aid Work in Canada (1840–1940)* (Montreal, 1966), 31.
50 Belkin, *Through Narrow Gates*, 51.
51 Gerald Friesen, *The Canadian Prairies: A History* (Toronto, 1984), 183.
52 *Montreal Gazette*, 18 Jan. 1882; Oscar D. Skelton, *The Life and Times of Sir Alexander Tilloch Galt* (Toronto, 1920), 544.
53 Andrew A. Den Otter, *Civilizing the West: The Galts and the Development of Western Canada* (Edmonton, 1982), 11.
54 Quoted in Henry Trachtenberg, 'Opportunism, Humanitarianism and Revulsion: The "Old Clo Move" Comes to Winnipeg, 1882–3,' unpublished paper presented to the Canadian Historical Association Meetings, Winnipeg, 1986, pp. 2–3.
55 LAC, MG 26, John A. Macdonald Papers, A I, 524, Letterbook 21, 684–86, Macdonald to Galt, 26 Feb. 1882.
56 Quoted in Trachtenberg, 'Opportunism,' 3.
57 LAC, MG 27, 108, Galt Papers, 93316, Galt to Macdonald, 25 Jan. 1882.
58 See Abraham J. Arnold, 'Jewish Immigration to Western Canada in the 1880s,' *CJHSJ* 1, no. 2 (1977): 82–95. In the early 1890s, the Berlin Jewish

Conference on Emigration considered Canada a suitable destination for refugee Russians; Jonathan D. Sarna, 'Jewish Immigration to North America: The Canadian Experience (1870–1900),' *Jewish Journal of Sociology* 18, no. I (1976): 31–41; PAM, JHSWC Collections, MG 10 F3 (MGI, EI), 31998–99.
59 Trachtenberg, 'Opportunism,' 3.
60 *Montreal Gazette*, 18 and 23 Jan. 1882.
61 Joel Geffen, 'Jewish Agricultural Colonies as Reported in the Pages of the Russian Hebrew Press *Ha-Melitz* and *Ha-Yom*: Annotated Documentary,' *AJH*, June 1971, 355–81.
62 Ibid., 377. See Arthur A. Chiel, *The Jews in Manitoba: A Social History* (Toronto, 1961), 37–8, and Sack, *Jews in Canada*, 198–9, for fuller renditions and slightly different translations of this letter.
63 Sack, *Jews in Canada*, 200–1.
64 See Eugene C. Black, *The Social Politics of Anglo-Jewry, 1880–1920* (London, 1988), 254.
65 LAC, RG 15, Department of Interior, 318, file 73568(1), Galt to Burgess, 1 April 1884; Hall to Galt, 7 April 1884; Galt to Burgess, 5 May 1884. See also Trachtenberg, 'Opportunism,' 5.
66 Abraham J. Arnold, 'The Jewish Farm Settlements of Saskatchewan: From New Jerusalem to Edenbridge,' *CJHSJ* 4, no. 1 (1980): 25–43, and 'The Contribution of Jews to the Opening and Development of the West,' *Historical and Scientific Society of Manitoba Papers* 3, no. 25 (1968–9): 23–37, 36. See also Cyril E. Leonoff, *The Jewish Farmers of Western Canada* (Vancouver, 1984).
67 Belkin, *Through Narrow Gates*, 56. But see PAM, JHSWC Collections, MG 10, F3, declaration of William A. Thompson, 13 May 1886, indicating average loans of $500.
68 Belkin, *Through Narrow Gates*, 57.
69 Norbert Macdonald, *Canada: Immigration and Colonization, 1841–1903* (Toronto, 1966), 222.
70 'Report of Minister of Agriculture for 1887,' in *Sessional Papers* (Ottawa, 1888), 97.
71 PAM, JHSWC Collections, MG 10, F3, Galt to Hon. Thomas White, minister of interior, 6 May 1886; H. Parke to H.H. Smith, Dominion Lands Commission, Winnipeg, 23 Feb. 1892.
72 Belkin, *Through Narrow Gates*, 58.
73 Chiel, *Jews in Manitoba*, 47.
74 Cyril E. Leonoff, *Wapella Farm Settlement (The First Successful Jewish Farm Settlement in Canada): A Pictorial History* (Winnipeg, 1970), 2, 12–13, 16.
75 Michael R. Marrus, *Mr. Sam: The Life and Times of Samuel Bronfman* (Toronto, 1991), 37–8.

76 Skelton, *Galt*, 544.
77 LAC, RG 15, Department of Interior, 318, file 73568(1), Galt to Burgess, 30 Jan. 1888, p. 16751.
78 See Theodore Norman, *An Outstretched Arm: A History of the Jewish Colonization Association* (London, 1985).
79 One member of the board of directors favoured using the grant to establish a colony of some of the Russian Romanian Jewish refugees. See Minutes 1, 29 Aug. 1890, and 29 March, 12 Aug., 16 Aug., and 29 Sept. 1891.
80 See Timothy R. Neufeld, 'A Study of Jewish Philanthropic Company Colonization in Canada's Northwest during the Late Nineteenth Century' (MA thesis, University of Saskatchewan, 1982), 46.
81 Minutes, 1, 16 Nov. and 30 Dec. 1891; 7 Jan., 11 Feb., 24 Feb., and 21 March 1892.
82 Simon Belkin, 'Jewish Colonization in Canada,' in Hart, ed., *Jew in Canada*, 485.
83 Nine teams of horses were selected by William Jacobs 'free of cost or commission ... for about $120.00 the team'; Minutes, 1, 13 April 1892; 27 April 1893; 24 Sept. 1893; 19 April 1892; 24 April 1892; 14 Aug. 1892; 31 Oct. 1892; 27 Nov. 1892; 14 Aug. 1892; 31 Aug. 1892; 5 Feb. 1893; 18 Feb. 1893; 15 May 1892; 14 Aug. 1892.
84 *Montreal Gazette*, 18 July 1892.
85 Minutes, 1, 14 Aug., 2 Oct., 16 Oct., 27 Nov., and 30 Nov. 1892; 7 Feb., 13 Feb., 2 July, 15 Aug., 18 Oct., and 25 Oct. 1893.
86 *Montreal Gazette*, 20 Nov. 1893.
87 Minutes, 1, 22 Jan., 21 Feb., 18 March, and 12 Sept. 1894.
88 Belkin, 'Jewish Colonization in Canada,' 485–6.
89 Minutes, 1, 18 Feb. 1893.
90 Macdonald, *Immigration and Colonization*, 210, 224.
91 M.C. Urquhart and K.A.H. Buckley, *Historical Statistics of Canada* (Toronto, 1965), 320.
92 See C.A. Dawson, *Group Settlement: Ethnic Communities in Western Canada* (Toronto, 1936), 377.
93 Judith L. Elkin, *Jews of the Latin American Republics* (Chapel Hill, 1980).
94 Uri D. Herscher, *Jewish Agricultural Utopias in America, 1880–1910* (Detroit, 1981), 109–13.
95 See Robert Weisbrot, *The Jews of Argentina: From the Inquisition to Peron* (Philadelphia, 1979), ch. 1.
96 LAC, MG 30, H 94, vol. 24, 44.
97 Neufeld, 'Jewish Philanthropic Company Colonization,' 132–3.
98 Gary D. Best, *To Free a People: American Jewish Leaders and the Jewish Problem in Eastern Europe* (Westport, 1982), 144.

4. Travails of Urbanization

1 Paul-André Linteau, René Durocher, and Jean-Claude Robert, *Quebec: A History, 1867–1929* (Toronto, 1983), 130; Louis Rosenberg, 'A Study of the Growth and Changes in the Distribution of the Jewish Population of Montreal,' *Canadian Jewish Population Studies* [Montreal], no. 4 (1955): 13.
2 McGill University, Department of Geography, Shared Spaces Project.
3 Abraham J. Heschel, *The Earth Is the Lord's & The Sabbath* (New York, 1966), 98.
4 Rebecca E. Margolis, 'A Tempest in Three Teapots: Yom Kippur Balls in London, New York and Montreal,' in *The Canadian Jewish Studies Reader*, ed. Richard Menkis and Norman Ravvin (Calgary, 2004), 141–63, 149–50.
5 Michael R. Weisser, *A Brotherhood of Memory: Jewish Landsmanshaftn in the New World* (New York, 1985).
6 See Sylvie Taschereau, 'Les sociétés de prêt juives à Montréal, 1911–1945,' *Urban History Review / Revue d'histoire urbaine* 33, no. 2 (Spring 2005): 3–16.
7 John Benson, 'Hawking and Peddling in Canada 1867–1914,' *HS/SH* 18 (May 1985): 75–83; I.M. Rubinow, 'Economic Condition of the Jews in Russia,' *Bulletin of the Bureau of Labour* [Washington, DC], no. 72 (1907): 500.
8 Jean Hamelin and Yves Roby, *Histoire économique de Québec, 1851–1896* (Montreal, 1971), 267.
9 Gerald J. Tulchinsky, *The River Barons: Montreal Businessmen and the Growth of Industry and Transportation, 1837–53* (Toronto, 1977), 224.
10 Gerald Tulchinsky; 'Hollis Shorey,' in *DCB*, 12:968–70.
11 Moses Rischin, *Promised City: New York's Jews, 1870–1914* (New York, 1964); Todd M. Endelman, *Englishmen and Jews: Social Relations and Political Culture, 1840–1914* (New Haven, 1994), 190–204.
12 Arthur D. Hart, ed., *The Jew in Canada* (Montreal, 1926), 100–3, 342; R.P. Sparks, 'The Garment and Clothing Industries, History and Organization,' in *Manual of the Textile Industry in Canada* (Ottawa, 1930), 109.
13 Canada, Royal Commission on the Relations of Labour and Capital, *Report* (Ottawa: Queen's Printer, 1889), Quebec Evidence, Part 1, 295, 557–60; Lorna F. Hurl, 'Restricting Child Factory Labour in Late Nineteenth Century Ontario,' *Labour / Le Travail* 21 (Spring 1988): 101–2; LAC, MG 26, William Lyon Mackenzie King Papers, H, XXVII, C-19161.
14 Canada, House of Commons, *Sessional Papers*, no. 51 (1896): 23–5; *JT*, 4 Feb. 1898.
15 King Papers, XXVII, C-19162; XXVI, C-18556, 18558.
16 *KA*, 21 Feb. 1913.

17 Bettina Bradbury, 'The Family Economy and Work in an Industrializing City: Montreal in the 1870s,' in *Cities and Urbanization: Historical Perspectives*, ed. Gilbert A. Stelter (Toronto, 1990), 138–40; Irving Abella and David Miller, eds, *The Canadian Worker in the Twentieth Century* (Toronto, 1978), 154–5; Mercedes Steedman, 'Skill and Gender in the Canadian Clothing Industry, 1890–1940,' in *On the Job: Confronting the Labour Process in Canada*, ed. Craig Heron and Robert Story (Montreal, 1986), 156.
18 *JT*, 4 Feb. 1898, 17 Feb. 1899.
19 JPLM, Rosenberg Manuscripts, 'Minutes of the School Committee of the Corporation of Portuguese Jews of Montreal' (typescript), p. 40. In March of 1891 the issue of redistributing Jewish school tax monies was raised with the congregation, but the matter was shelved (ibid., 49–50).
20 LAC, MG 28, vol. 86, Jewish Family Services of the Baron de Hirsch Institute (est. 1863), Montreal, Minutes of the Board, Baron de Hirsch Institute of Montreal, 1863–1914 hereafter cited as Minutes), Vol. 1, 29 March 1891, 15 and 17 May 1892.
21 Ibid., 'Re Jewish School Tax, City of Montreal. Memorial of the Young Mens Hebrew Benevolent Society of Montreal, a Body Corporate, 4 May 1892'; Minutes, 1, 29 May 1892; CJCCCNA, School Question, unnumbered file, G. De Sola to H. Vineberg, 30 May 1892. Ansell's reasons were the same as those given in the memorial, namely, the distance the children would have to travel to get to the Spanish and Portugese synagogue (ibid., D. Ansell to G. De Sola, 12 July 1892).
22 CJCCCNA, School Question, Louis Pelletier to Rabbi M. de Sola, 1892; J. Boivin to Rabbi M. de Sola, 14 Oct. 1892.
23 See *Montreal Gazette*, 18 May, 1 June, and 10 Dec. 1892; 13 Jan., 10 Nov., and 19 Dec. 1893; Minutes 1, 2 Oct. 1892.
24 CJCCCNA, G. de Sola to Pelletier, 30 Dec. 1892.
25 JPLM, 'School Committee ... Portuguese Jews,' 67.
26 Louis Rosenberg, 'Jewish Children in the Protestant Schools of Greater Montreal in the Period from 1878 to 1958,' in *Research Papers*, Series E, no. 1 (Montreal, 16 March 1959), 6.
27 *Montreal Star*, 15 Feb. 1898.
28 P. Senese, 'Antisemitism in Late Nineteenth Century Quebec and Montreal: The Catholic Militants of *La Verité* and *La Croix*,' unpublished paper presented to the Canadian Historical Association, Victoria, 1990, p. 34.
29 Louis Rosenberg, *Canada's Jews: A Social and Economic Study of the Jews in Canada* (Montreal, 1939), 135. See LAC, MG 28, vol. 86, Jewish Family Services of the Baron de Hirsch Institute, Annual Reports, 1890–1900.

30 James Smart, Department of Interior, 21 July 1900; quoted in Jill Culiner, *Finding Home: In the Footsteps of the Jewish Fusgeyers* (Toronto, 2004), 230.
31 See annual balance sheet of Board of Directors, 1900, pp. 10–11.
32 Veronica J. Strong-Boag, *The Parliament of Women: The National Council of Women of Canada, 1893–1929* (Ottawa, 1976), 101–2; Stephen Speisman, *The Jews of Toronto: A History to 1937* (Toronto, 1979), 60.
33 Senese, 'Antisemitism,' 23–4, 28, 29, 30.
34 Phyllis M. Senese, '*La Croix de Montréal* (1893–95): A Link to the French Radical Right,' Canadian Catholic Historical Association, *Historical Studies* 53 (1986): 81–95. See also her 'Antisemetic Dreyfusards: The Confused Western Canadian Press,' in *Antisemitism in Canada: History and Interpretation*, ed. Alan Davies (Waterloo, 1992), 93–111.
35 Michael Brown, *Jew or Juif? Jews, French Canadians, and Anglo-Canadians, 1759–1914* (Philadelphia, 1987), 136–7.
36 *La Presse*, 23 Aug. 1899; see David Rome, *On Jules Helbronner*, CJA New Series, no. 11 (Montreal: CJCCNA, 1978).
37 *True Witness*, 11 Dec. 1897; 22 Jan., 26 Feb., 11 Sept., and 24 Sept. 1898; 11 Sept. 1899.
38 *La Minerve*, 12 June, 16 and 24 Sept., and 17 and 18 Nov. 1890.
39 See Patricia E. Roy, *White Man's Province: British Columbia Politicians and Chinese and Japanese Immigrants, 1858–1914* (Vancouver, 1989).
40 *JT*, 10 Dec. 1897.
41 For these insights and many others, I am indebted to Gordon Dueck. See his 'The Salamander and the Chameleon: Religion, Race, and Evolutionism in the Anglo-Jewish Press, Montreal, 1897–1914' (PhD diss., Queen's University, 2000).
42 *JT*, 4 Jan., 16 Feb., and 17 Aug. 1900. See also Frances Molino and Bernard Wasserstein, eds, *The Jews in Modern France* (Hanover, 1985), 107–13.
43 *JT*, 28 Oct. and 9 Dec. 1898; 20 Jan. and 15 Sept. 1899.
44 I. Goldstick, 'The Jews of London, Ontario: The First One Hundred Years,' in *Canadian Jewish Reference Book and Directory*, ed. Eli Gottesman (Toronto, 1963), 323.
45 Rosenberg, *Canada's Jews*, 308. See Max Bookman, 'Excerpts from the History of the Jew in Canada's Capital,' in Gottesman, ed. *Jewish Reference Book*, 387–405.
46 Harvey H. Herstein, 'The Growth of the Winnipeg Jewish Community and the Evolution of Its Educational Institutions,' *Transactions of the Historical and Scientific Society of Manitoba*, series 3, no. 22 (1965–6): 29; Henry Trachtenberg, 'Peddling, Politics, and Winnipeg's Jews, 1891–95: The Political Acculturation of an Urban Immigrant Community,' unpublished

paper presented to the Canadian Jewish Historical Society meetings, June 1991, Queen's University.

47 Speisman, *Jews of Toronto*, 50, 67; Rosenberg, *Canada's Jews*, 308; Sigmund Samuel, *In Return: The Autobiography of Sigmund Samuel* (Toronto, 1963), 45–50.
48 Rosenberg, *Canada's Jews*, 10; Jonathan Frankel, 'The Crisis of 1881–2 as a Turning Point in Modern Jewish History,' in *The Legacy of Jewish Migration: 1881 and Its Impact*, ed. David Berger (New York, 1983), 9–22. See also Uri D. Herscher, *Jewish Agricultural Utopias in America, 1880–1910* (Detroit, 1981), passim.
49 Rosenberg, *Canada's Jews*, 308.
50 See Lise C Hansen, 'The Decline of the Jewish Community in Thunder Bay: An Explanation' (MA thesis, University of Manitoba, 1977).
51 Rosenberg, *Canada's Jews*, 308–10.
52 Sheva Medjuck, *The Jews of Atlantic Canada* (St John's, 1986), ch. 2.
53 See Lee S. Weisbach, *Jewish Life in Small-Town America: A History* (New Haven, 2005), 4–5.
54 Rosenberg, *Canada's Jews*, 19.
55 Sheldon Levitt, Lynn Milstone, and Sidney T. Tenenbaum, *Treasures of a People: The Synagogues of Canada* (Toronto, 1985), 57.
56 Beth Israel Archives, Kingston, ON, unnumbered file of early congregational documents, 15 April 1902.
57 Ruth Bellan, 'Growing Up in a Small Saskatchewan Town,' in *Jewish Life and Times: A Collection of Essays* (Winnipeg, 1983), 116.
58 For an excellent description of the humble economic beginnings of the Ottawa Jewish community, see Laurelle Lo, 'The Path from Peddling: Jewish Economic Activity in Ottawa Prior to 1939,' in *Construire une capitale: Ottawa: Making a Capital*, ed. Jeff Keshen and Nicole St-Onge (Ottawa, 2001), 239–50.
59 Robert H. Babcock, 'A Jewish Immigrant in the Maritimes: The Memoirs of Max Vanger,' *Acadiensis* 16, no. 1 (Autumn 1986): 136–48.
60 Edmund Bradwin, *The Bunkhouse Man: A Study of Work and Pay in the Camps of Canada, 1903–1914* (Toronto, 1972), 108–9.
61 Rosenberg, *Canada's Jews*, 308.
62 Harry Gutkin, *Journey into Our Heritage* (Toronto, 1980), 179–81.
63 James S. Woodsworth, *My Neighbour: A Study of City Conditions a Plea for Social Justice* (Toronto, 1911), 66.
64 See Ol'ha Woycenko, 'Community Organizations,' in *A Heritage in Transition: Essays in the History of Ukrainians in Canada*, ed. Manoly R. Lupul (Toronto, 1982), 173–94, 174–5; Henry Trachtenberg, 'Benjamin Zimmerman,' in *DCB*, 15:1090–2.

65 Louis Rosenberg, *The Jewish Community of Winnipeg* (Montreal, 1946), 12, 22, 23.
66 Henry Trachtenberg, 'Unfriendly Competitors: Jews, Ukrainians, and Municipal Politics in Winnipeg's Ward 5, 1911–1914,' unpublished paper presented at the Canadian Association of Slavists, Learned Societies Conference, 1986, pp. 2, 4, 10–11, 14.
67 See Harvey Herstein, 'The Evolution of Jewish Schools in Winnipeg,' in *Jewish Life and Times: A Collection of Essays* (Winnipeg, 1983), 8, 9, 13, 17. See also Roz Usiskin, 'The Winnipeg Jewish Radical Community,' in ibid., 155–68.
68 Roz Usiskin, 'Continuity and Change: The Jewish Experience in Winnipeg's North End, 1900–1914,' *CJHSJ* 4, no. 1 (1980): 71–94, 84.
69 Mel Fenson, 'A History of the Jews in Alberta'; and Harold Hyman, 'The Jews in Saskatchewan,' in Gottesman, ed., *Jewish Reference Book*, 281, 293.
70 PAM, MG 10, F3 (MGIB, 3–1), Arthur J. Field, 'The Jewish Community of Saskatoon, Canada,' unpublished manuscript. See also J.M. Goldenberg, 'History of the Jewish Community of Saskatoon,' in *Agudas Israel Dedication Volume, 1905–1963* (Saskatoon, 1963).
71 PAM, MG 1O, F3 (MGI, BI-2), Louis Rosenberg, 'The History of the Regina Jewish Community' (manuscript).
72 Abraham J. Arnold, 'The Jewish Farm Settlements of Saskatchewan: From New Jerusalem to Edenbridge,' *CJHSJ* 4, no. 1 (1980): 37.
73 Simon I. Belkin, *Through Narrow Gates: A Review of Jewish Immigration, Colonization and Immigrant Aid Work in Canada (1840–1940)* (Montreal, 1966), 77.
74 See Anna Feldman, 'Sonnenfeld – Elements of Survival and Success of a Jewish Community on the Prairies 1905–1939,' *CJHSJ* 6, no. 1 (Spring 1982): 33–53.
75 Clara Hoffer and FH. Kahan, *Land of Hope* (Saskatoon, 1960), 29, 32, 91–3.
76 Michael Usiskin, *Uncle Mike's Edenbridge: Memoirs of a Jewish Pioneer Farmer*, translated from Yiddish by Marcia Usiskin Basman (Winnipeg, 1983), 11, 27.
77 LAC, MG 28, vol. 86, Jewish Family Services of the Baron de Hirsch Institute, Report of Baron de Hirsch Institute, 1908.
78 See Taschereau, 'Les sociétés de prêt juives à Montréal, 1911–1945'; Frank M. Guttman, 'The Hebrew Free Loan Association of Montreal,' *CJS* 12 (2004): 45–72.
79 Stephen A. Speisman, 'St. John's Shtetl: The Ward in 1911,' in *Gathering Place: Peoples and Neighbourhoods of Toronto, 1834–1945*, ed. Robert F Harney (Toronto, 1985), 107–20; S.B. Rohold, *The Jews in Canada* (Toronto, 1912), 13.
80 George Quinn, 'Impact of European Immigration upon the Elementary Schools of Central Toronto, 1815–1915' (MA thesis, University of Toronto, 1968), 95, 108.

Notes to pages 118–22   523

81 Speisman, 'St. John's Shtetl,' 113.
82 Lynne Marks, 'Jewish Mutual Benefit Societies in Toronto, 1900–1930' (University of Toronto, Dept. of History, undergraduate paper, 1978), 2. See *The Toronto Jewish City and Information Directory* (Toronto, 1925), 8–9.
83 Speisman, *Jews of Toronto*, 145–51.
84 Arthur A. Chiel, *The Jews in Manitoba: A Social History* (Toronto, 1961), 131, 135, 136.
85 Edward J. Bristow, *Prostitution and the Jewish Fight against White Slavery, 1870–1939* (New York, 1983).
86 Bernard Figler, *Lillian and Archie Freiman: Biographies* (Ottawa, 1962), 45. For an interesting overview, see Lloyd P. Gartner, 'Anglo Jewry and the International Traffic in Prostitution, 1885–1914,' *Association for Jewish Studies Review* 7–8 (1982–3): 129–78, 129.
87 Bristow, *Prostitution*, 170.
88 LAC, RG 76, vol. 542, file 804221.
89 Carolyn Strange, 'From Modern Babylon to a City upon a Hill: The Toronto Social Survey Commission of 1915 and the Search for Sexual Order in the City,' in *Patterns of the Past: Interpreting Ontario's History*, ed. Roger Hall, William Westfall, and Laurel Sefton MacDowell (Toronto, 1988), 265; Greg Marquis, 'The Early Twentieth Century Toronto Police Institution' (PhD diss., Queen's University, 1986), 72.
90 See Andrée Lévesque, 'Putting It Out: Social Reformers' Efforts to Extinguish the Red Light in Montreal,' *Urban History Review* 17, no. 3 (1989): 191–202.
91 See John McLaren, '"White Slavers": The Reform of Canada's Prostitution Laws and Patterns of Enforcement, 1900–1920s,' unpublished paper presented at the meeting of American Society for Legal History, Toronto, 1986.
92 'History and Development of the Big Brother Movement, Toronto Jewish Branch,' in Hart, ed., *Jew in Canada*, 450.
93 Peter Oliver, *Unlikely Tory: The Life and Politics of Allan Grossman* (Toronto, 1985), 2, 3.
94 Elspeth Cameron, *Irving Layton: A Portrait* (Toronto, 1985), 17–18, 25.
95 Doug Smith, *Joe Zuken, Citizen and Socialist* (Toronto, 1990), 8–9.
96 Irving Abella, 'Portrait of a Jewish Professional Revolutionary: The Recollections of Joshua Gershman,' *Labour / Le Travail* 2 (1977): 189–91.
97 Usher Caplan, *Like One That Dreamed: A Portrait of A.M. Klein* (Toronto, 1982), 18–19.
98 David Lewis, *The Good Fight: Political Memoirs, 1909–1958* (Toronto, 1981), 14.
99 Ari L. Fridkis, 'Desertion in the American Jewish Immigrant Family: The Work of the National Desertion Bureau in Cooperation with the Industrial Removal Office,' *AJH* 71 (1981): 293.

100 American Jewish Historical Society Archives, Waltham, MA (Brandeis University), IRO, Box 80, Winnipeg ICA, 1905–1913, File, Assistant Manager to Max Heppner, 3 Jan. 1913; Heppner to David Bressler, 7 April 1908; Heppner to IRO, 24 Aug. 1908; A. Samuel to David Bressler, 12 and 13 Sept. 1906.
101 Ibid., Box 70, Toronto 1912–1914, Associated Hebrew Charities File, P. Shulman to D.M. Bressler, 6 Aug. 1913.
102 CJCCCNA, JCA, L 7e, 'Report of Baron de Hirsch Labor and Immigration Bureau,' 11 Dec. 1907.
103 Baycrest Terrace Memoirs Group, *From Our Lives: Memoirs, Life Stories, Episodes and Recollections* (Toronto, 1979), 2–4, 21, 23, 46, 48, 40, 123.
104 Paula J. Draper and Janice B. Karlinsky; 'Abraham's Daughters: Women, Charity and Power in the Canadian Jewish Community,' in *Looking into My Sister's Eyes: An Exploration in Women's History*, ed. Jean Burnet (Toronto, 1986), 77, 78–9.
105 Ruth A. Frager, 'Uncloaking Vested Interests: Class, Ethnicity, and Gender in the Jewish Labour Movement in Toronto, 1900–1939' (PhD diss., York University, 1986), iv.
106 Roz Usiskin 'Winnipeg's Jewish Women of the Left: Traditional and Radical,' *Jewish Life and Times* 8 (2003) in *Jewish Radicalism in Winnipeg 1905–1960*, ed. Daniel Stone (Winnipeg, 2003), 106–21, 112.

5. 'Corner of Pain and Anguish'

1 See Jaroslav Petryshyn, *Peasants in the Promised Land: Canada and the Ukrainians, 1896–1914* (Toronto, 1985), ch. 7; James S. Woodsworth, *Strangers within Our Gates; Or, Coming Canadians* (Toronto, 1909), 111–59; David J. Bercuson, *Confrontation at Winnipeg: Labour, Industrial Relations and the General Strike* (Montreal, 1974), 126–7; Kenneth McNaught, *A Prophet in Politics: A Biography of J.S. Woodsworth* (Toronto, 1959), 119, 135–6; Henry Trachtenberg, 'The Winnipeg Jewish Community and Politics: The Interwar Years, 1919–1939,' *Historical and Scientific Society of Manitoba, Transactions*, Ser. 3, nos. 34 and 35 (1977–8, 1978–9): 115–53, 119–20.
2 See W. Peter Ward, *White Canada Forever: Popular Attitudes and Public Policy toward Orientals in British Columbia* (Montreal, 1978), 197, passim; Louis Rosenberg, *Canada's Jews: A Social and Economic Study of the Jews in Canada* (Montreal, 1939); Stephen A. Speisman, *The Jews of Toronto: A History to 1937* (Toronto, 1979), 67, 251; Gerald Tulchinsky, 'Immigration and Charity in the Montreal Jewish Community to 1890,' *HS/SH* 16, no. 33 (November 1983): 370–1; Simon I. Belkin, *Through Narrow Gates: A Review of Jewish*

Immigration, Colonization and Immigrant Aid Work in Canada (Montreal, 1966), passim; John Zucchi, *The Italians in Toronto* (Montreal, 1989); Anthony W. Rasporich, *For a Better Life: A History of the Croatians in Canada* (Toronto, 1982); Bernard Figler, *Biography of Sam Jacobs, Member of Parliament* (Ottawa, 1959).

3 Arnold Haultain, *Goldwin Smith, His Life and Opinions* (Toronto, 1910), 68, 125, 146, 189, 206.

4 See Goldwin Smith, *Essays on Questions of the Day: Political and Social* (New York, 1893), 183–220, 263–308; 'England's Abandonment of the Protectorate of Turkey,' *Contemporary Review*, 31 Feb. 1878, 603–21; 'The Jews: A Deferred Rejoinder,' *Nineteenth Century*, Nov. 1882, 708–9.

5 Todd M. Endelman, *The Jews of Georgian England, 1714–1830: Tradition and Change in a Liberal Society* (Philadelphia, 1979), 86–7.

6 Goldwin Smith, *Reminiscences*, ed. Arnold Haultain (New York, 1910), 380; 'England's Abandonment of the Protectorate of Turkey,' 619.

7 Goldwin Smith, 'Can Jews Be Patriots?' *Nineteenth Century* May 1878, pp. 877, 884.

8 Bryan Cheyette, *Constructions of 'The Jew' in English Literature and Society: Racial Representations, 1875–1945* (Cambridge, 1993), 15.

9 *The Bystander*, 3 July 1883, pp. 250–2.

10 *Weekly Sun*, 29 July 1897; Arnold Haultain, ed., *A Selection from Goldwin Smith's Correspondence* (Toronto, 1910), 462.

11 See *The Bystander*, 3 July 1883, pp. 250–2; 'The Jews: A Deferred Rejoinder,' 706.

12 See Kenneth Bourne and D. Cameron Watt, gen. eds, *British Documents on Foreign Affairs: Reports and Papers from the Mid-Nineteenth Century to the First World War*, Series A, *Russia, 1859–1914*, ed. Dominic Lieven, vol. 2, *Russia, 1881–1905* (Washington, 1983), 1–65; 'The Jews: A Deferred Rejoinder,' 692; *Bystander*, 1 Aug. 1880, 445–6; 1 March 1880, 156; *Weekly Sun*, 15 July 1897.

13 *The Bystander*, 3 July 1883, p. 251; 'The Jews: A Deferred Rejoinder,' 688–94; Goldwin Smith, 'New Light on the Jewish Question,' Part 2, *North American Review* 153 (Aug. 1891): 129–43, 131, 133; *Weekly Sun*, 27 March 1907.

14 Goldwin Smith, 'Is It Religious Persecution?' *The Independent* 60 (1906): 1474–8, 1476–7.

15 *The Week*, 24 Feb. 1894, 18 Feb. 1897; *Farmers Sun*, 18 May, 1 June, and 28 Sept. 1904; John Higham, *Strangers in the Land: Patterns of American Nativism, 1869–1925* (New York, 1975), ch. 4; *Weekly Sun*, 29 July 1897, 28 Aug. 1907.

16 Naomi Cohen, *Encounter with Emancipation: The German Jews in the United States, 1830–1914* (Philadelphia, 1984), 278.

17 LAC, Mackenzie King Diary, 20 Feb. 1946. I am indebted to Professor Jack Granatstein for this reference.

18 *Morning Chronicle*, 20 Dec. 1878. In reporting this story, the *Chronicle* stated that one of these 'Jews and Shavers' was employed by the Nova Scotia government, and another was appointed to the Provincial Legislative Council. See Phyllis M. Senese, 'Antisemitic Dreyfusards: The Confused Western Canadian Press,' in *Antisemitism in Canada: History and Interpretation*, ed. Alan T. Davies (Waterloo, 1992), 93–112; *Chronicle*, 8 Aug. 1903; *Halifax Herald*, 30 June 1904.

19 Mariana Valverde, *The Age of Light, Soap, and Water: Moral Reform in English Canada, 1885–1925* (Toronto, 1991), 56, 106; AO, Attorney General's Department, RG4–32, 1915, f.503, Clara Brett Martin to Edward Bayly, 26 March 1915, appended to Lita-Rose Betcherman, 'Clara Brett Martin's Anti-Semitism' (manuscript, 1991).

20 Valverde, *Age of Light, Soap, Water*, 56, 106.

21 *Halifax Herald*, 10 June 1913.

22 Terence Craig, *Racial Attitudes in English Canadian Fiction, 1905–1980* (Waterloo, 1987), 34.

23 Hilda Neatby, *Queen's University*, Vol. 1, *1841–1917: And Not to Yield*, ed. Frederick W. Gibson and Roger Graham (Montreal, 1978), 265; *CJC*, 18 April 1919.

24 University of Toronto Archives, A67–0007, Arthur L. Smith to Godfrey J.H. Lloyd, 5 July 1911; Godfrey J.H. Lloyd to Falconer, 13 July 1911; James H. Mavor to Falconer, 20 July 1911.

25 Martin L. Friedland, *The University of Toronto: A History* (Toronto, 2000), 235.

26 A.I. Willinsky, *A Doctor's Memoirs* (Toronto, 1960), 25. He was forced to travel abroad in order to qualify; though by 1918 he became a department head at the Toronto Western Hospital. See Stanley B. Frost, *McGill University: For the Advancement of Learning*, Vol. 2, *1895–1971* (Montreal, 1980), 128.

27 Paul R. Dekar, 'From Jewish Mission to Inner City Mission: The Scott Mission and Its Antecedents in Toronto, 1908 to 1964,' in *Canadian Protestant and Catholic Missions, 1820–1860s: Historical Essays in Honour of John Webster Grant*, ed. John S. Moir and C.T. McIntire, Toronto Studies in Religion, Vol. 3 (New York, 1988), 247; Speisman, *Jews of Toronto*, ch. 9; quoted in Dekar, 'Jewish Mission,' 248, 250.

28 Paul-André Linteau, René Durocher, and Jean-Claude Robert, *Quebec: A History, 1867–1929* (Toronto, 1983), 44, 47.

29 M. Brown, 'France, the Catholic Church, the French Canadians and Jews before 1914' (unpublished paper); Ernest Nolte, *Three Faces of Fascism: Action Française, Italian Fascism, and National Socialism* (New York, 1969), 77.

30 Jean de Bonville, 'Jules Helbronner,' in *DCB*, 15:468–70.

31 See Gordon N. Emery, 'The Lord's Day Act of 1906 and the Sabbath Observance Question,' in *Documentary Problems in Canadian History*, ed. J.M. Bumsted, 2 vols (Georgetown, 1968), 2:37–40; Canada, House of Commons, *Debates* (1906), 5637–8; Pierre Anctil, *Le Devoir: Les juifs et l'immigration de Bourassa à Laurendeau* (Montreal, 1988), 25; *Le Devoir*, 25 Feb. 1913, 15 April 1914, 29 Jan. 1913, 7 Feb. 1916.
32 Arthur D. Hart, ed., *The Jew in Canada* (Montreal, 1926), 499–500.
33 CJCCCNA, William Nadler, 'The Jewish-Protestant School Question' (manuscript, 1925).
34 *JT*, 6 Dec. 1901; Linteau et al., *Quebec: A History*, 209.
35 Quoted in Nadler, 'School Question,' 9.
36 Maxwell Goldstein, 'The Status of the Jew in the Schools of Canada,' in Hart, ed., *Jew in Canada*, 497.
37 Quoted in Nadler, 'School Question,' 10.
38 *Statutes of Quebec*, 3 Edward vii, ch. 16; Nadler, 'School Question,' 12.
39 Hart, ed., *Jew in Canada*, 497; Nadler, 'School Question,' 13.
40 *JT*, 30 July 1909.
41 Ibid., 2 April 1905.
42 Ibid., 7 Jan. 1910; 12 and 20 June 1913.
43 *KA*, 1 July 1913; *JT*, 27 Aug. 1909; *KA*, 12 Aug. 1913.
44 *JT*, 27 Aug. 1909.
45 David Rome, comp., 'The Plamondon Case and S.W. Jacobs,' Part 1, *CJA*, new series, no. 26 (Montreal, 1982): 7–18.
46 *La Libre Parole*, 31 July, 30 Oct., and 4 Dec. 1909; 1 Jan., 12 and 26 Feb., and 26 March 1910.
47 Ibid., 12 and 26 Feb. and 26 March 1910.
48 Rome, 'Plamondon,' 14; LAC, RG 13, CLXI, S. Glazer to A.D. Ellsworth, 29 March 1910; Joshua D. MacFadyen '"Nip the Noxious Growth in the Bud": Ortenberg v. Plamondon and the Roots of Canadian Anti-hate Activism,' *CJS/EJC* 12 (2004): 73–96.
49 Cited in Rome, 'Plamondon,' 86.
50 *JT*, 30 May 1913.
51 Shmuel Ettinger, 'The Modern Period,' in *A History of the Jewish People*, ed. H.H. Ben Sasson (Cambridge, 1976), 887–8.
52 *JT*, 27 June and 11 July 1913.
53 See David Rome, 'The Plamondon Case and S.W. Jacobs,' Part 2, *CJA* new series, no. 27 (Montreal, 1982).
54 *JT*, 22 Oct. 1913.
55 Wiliam D. Rubinstein and Hilary L. Rubinstein, *Philosemitism: Admiration and Support in the English-Speaking World for Jews, 1840–1939* (London, 1999), 72.

56 Antonio Huot, *La Question juive: Quelques observations sur la question de meurtre rituel* (Quebec, 1914), 20.
57 Rubinstein and Rubinstein, *Philosemitism*, 41, 57.
58 *Toronto Daily Star*, 28 July 1913, cited in Lita-Rose Betcherman, 'Clara Brett Martin's Anti-Semitism,' *Canadian Journal of Women and the Law* 5 (1992): 280–97, 290.
59 *Journal of Commerce*, 23 Feb. 1906.
60 See Jacques Rouillard, 'Les travailleurs juifs de la confection (1910–1980),' *Labour / Le Travailleur* 8/9 (1981/82): 253–9; Jean Hamelin, *Repertoire des grèves dans la Province de Québec au dix-neuvième siècle* (Montreal, 1970), 165–6; *Montreal Daily Star*, 7 and 8 Sept. 1900.
61 Hamelin, *Repertoire des grèves*, 165–6; LAC, RG 27, Department of Labour, Vol. 301, file 37.
62 *La Presse*, 12 March and 11 April 1904; 11 Feb. to 20 April 1910; Hart, ed., *Jew in Canada*, 343.
63 The Quebec government's Royal Commission on Tuberculosis in 1910 found that 'a great many Jews are ... tuberculous because they work in small unventilated, dirty and crowded shops' (cited in Katherine McCuaig, *The Weariness, the Fever, and the Fret: The Campaign against Tuberculosis in Canada, 1900–1950* [Montreal, 1999], 270). In 1940, one expert reported that Jewish mortality rates in Quebec were only 40 per cent of the general rate (ibid, 271). See *Montreal Star*, 7 March, 10 May, 11 May, and 13 May 1904.
64 The UGWA participated in Socialist Labour Party meetings in Montreal as early as 1907. *Montreal Daily Star*, 11 and 29 April 1907; Meyer London Branch (No. 151) of the New York–based Arbeiter Ring; Meyer Semiatycki, 'Communism in One Constituency: The Communist Party and Jewish Community of Montreal, with Particular Reference to the Election of Fred Rose to Parliament in 1943 and 1945' (York University, unpublished paper, 1977), 17; LAC, RG 27, Vol. 295, file 298; *Montreal Star*, 31 Aug. 1907; LAC, RG 27, Vol. 297, file 3199; *Montreal Star*, 6 and 13 March 1908; LAC, RG 27, Vol. 298, files 1123, 3309, 3310, 3392, 3402, 3434; Harry Gale, 'The Jewish Labour Movement in Winnipeg,' *JHSWC* 1 (June 1970): 3.
65 Susan Gelman, 'Anatomy of a Failed Strike: The T. Eaton Co. Lockout of Cloakmakers – 1912,' *CJHSJ* 9 (1985): 93–119; Hart, ed., *Jew in Canada*, 339.
66 *Montreal Gazette*, 11 June 1912.
67 *Montreal Witness*, 29 May 1912; *Montreal Star*, 6 June 1912; *Montreal Gazette*, 18 May 1912; *Montreal Star*, 13 June 1912; *Montreal Gazette*, 11 June 1912; *Montreal Witness*, 3 July 1912. See Marcus L. Hansen and John B. Brebner, *The Mingling of the Canadian and American Peoples* (New Haven, 1940), 217, 241, 262; *Montreal Gazette*, 11 June 1912.

68 Bernard Figler and David Rome, *Hananiah Meier Caiserman: A Biography* (Montreal, 1962), 28, 37; Rouillard, 'Travailleurs juifs,' 254.
69 'Labour Zionist Organization of Canada,' in *Canadian Jewish Reference Book and Directory*, ed. Eli Gottesman (Toronto, 1963), 378, 39. See Morris Winchevsky, *Stories of the Struggle* (Chicago, 1908).
70 LAC, RG 27, Vol. 300, file 3509, newspaper clipping, n.d.; Simon Belkin, 'Reuben Brainin's Memories,' in *Canadian Jewish Year Book* (Montreal, 1940–1). See also Eisig Silberschlag, 'Reuben Brainin,' in *EJ*, 4:1291–3; and Ali Mohamed Abd El-Rahman Attia, *The Hebrew Periodical Ha-Shiloah (1896–1919): Its Role in the Development of Modern Hebrew Literature* (Jerusalem, 1991), 105–6.
71 During a very bitter and protracted strike against Vineberg & Co., in 1914, Brainin acted as chairman of an all-Jewish arbitration board, which brought the dispute to an end. See LAC, RG 27, Vol. 303, file 112, newspaper clipping, *Montreal Herald*, 8 Jan. 1914.
72 LAC, RG 27, Dept. of Labour, Strike files, Vol. 300, no. 3509, *Gazette* clipping, 4 July 1912.
73 Hubert S. Nelli, 'Ethnic Group Assimilation: The Italian Experience,' ed. Kenneth T. Jackson and Stanley K. Schultz in *Cities in American History*, (New York, 1972), 199–215, 200.
74 See H. Noveck, *Fun Meine Yunge Yorn* (New York, 1957), 180–2.
75 See *Les Midinettes 1937–1962: Union des ouvriers de la robe* (Montreal, 1962).
76 LAC, RG 27, Vol. 299, files 3455, 3495.
77 Daniel Hiebert, 'Discontinuity and the Emergence of Flexible Production: Garment Production in Toronto, 1901–1931,' *Economic Geography* 66 (July 1990): 225, 242; interview with Max Enkin, Cambridge Clothing, 15 July 1976. See J. Terry Copp, *The Anatomy of Poverty: The Condition of the Working Class in Montreal, 1897–1929* (Toronto, 1974), 140–1; Henry Trachtenberg, 'The 1912 Lockout-Strike at the T. Eaton Company Limited, Toronto' (PhD research paper, York University, 1973), 1.
78 LAC, RG 27, Vol. 301, files 8, 26, 37.
79 Ibid., Vol. 297, file 3221; Lewis L. Lorwin, *The Women's Garment Workers: A History of the International Ladies' Garment Workers Union* (New York, 1925), 222, 587; LAC, RG 27, Vol. 299, file 3439.
80 Henry Pelling, *American Labor* (Chicago, 1960), 121; New York Office of the Amalgamated Clothing Workers of America, *Documentary History 1914–16* (New York, 1916), 104; Harold A. Logan, *Trade Unions in Canada* (Toronto, 1948), 214.
81 Steven Fraser, *Labor Will Rule: Sidney Hillman and the Rise of American Labor* (New York, 1991), 200–1.

82 *Montreal Joint Board ACWA: From Drudgery to Dignity 1915–1955* (Montreal, 1955), 12; Logan, *Trade Unions in Canada*, 214.
83 LAC, RG 27, Vol. 304, files 16, 17, 18, 19, 18a; newspaper clipping, *Montreal Mail*, 22 Dec. 1916; Brownlee to Brown, 6 Jan. 1917; newspaper clipping, *Montreal Gazette*, 16 Jan. 1917.
84 *Montreal Mail*, 22 Dec. 1916; *Montreal Gazette*, 5 Jan. 1917; LAC, RG 27, Vol. 304, file 18A, newspaper clipping, *Montreal Star*, 5 Jan. 1919; file 17 (35).
85 Mathew Josephson, *Sidney Hillman: Statesman of American Labor* (New York, 1952), 141.
86 *La Presse*, 20 Feb. 1917.
87 David Brody, *Workers in Industrial America: Essays on the Twentieth Century Struggle* (New York, 1980), viii.
88 See New York Office of the Amalgamated Clothing Workers of America, *Documentary History, 1918–20* (New York, 1920), 98, for list of employers' complaints against the union.
89 Hirsh Wolofsky, *Journey of My Life* (Montreal, 1945), 80.
90 See *Documentary History, 1918–20*, 88.
91 Josephson, *Sidney Hillman*, 88.
92 See Robert H. Babcock, *Gompers in Canada: A Study in American Continentalism before the First World War* (Toronto, 1974); Gregory S. Kealey, *Toronto Workers Respond to Industrial Capitalism, 1867–1892* (Toronto, 1980), passim; Bryan D. Palmer, *A Culture in Conflict: Skilled Workers and Industrial Capitalism in Hamilton Ontario, 1860–1914* (Montreal, 1979), 243–4; Henry J. Tobias, *The Jewish Bund in Russia, from Its Origins to 1905* (Stanford, 1972).
93 *Documentary History, 1918–20*, 94, 96, 97, 101–2.
94 LAC, RG 27, Vol. 306, file 17 (35), Report to Dept. of Labour, 27 Feb. 1917.
95 *Documentary History, 1918–20*, 102.
96 *La Presse*, 2 Feb. 1917.
97 *Le Devoir*, 22 and 30 Jan., 9, 12, 21, and 22 Feb. 1917.
98 N. Maurice Davidson, 'Montreal's Dominance of the Men's Fine Clothing Industry' (MA thesis, University of Western Ontario, 1969), 2–4.
99 *La Presse*, 3 April 1903, 24 March 1908, 2 Aug. 1909, 11 May 1912.
100 Miriam Waddington, Comp., *The Collected Poems of A.M. Klein* (Toronto, 1974), 272.
101 *KA*, 24 Dec. 1916; 11, 12, 13, 14, 18, 19, 21, 26, and 30 Jan. and 1, 2, 5, 6, and 11 Feb. 1917.
102 Ibid., 11, and 13 Jan. 1917. See *Documentary History, 1918–20*, 90.
103 *KA*, 3 Jan., and 11, 15, and 16 Feb. 1917.
104 See Mark Zborowski and Elizabeth Herzen, *Life Is with People: The Culture of the Shtetl* (New York, 1972).

105 *Documentary History, 1918–20*, 103.
106 M. Brecher, 'Patterns of Accommodation in the Men's Garment Industry of Quebec, 1914–1954,' in *Patterns of Industrial Dispute Settlement in Five Canadian Industries*, ed. W.D. Woods (Montreal, 1958), 100.
107 Rosenberg, *Canada's Jews*, 176.
108 Ibid., 177.
109 Ezra Mendelsohn, *The Class Struggle in the Pale: The Formative Years of Jewish Workers' Movements in Tsarist Russia* (London, 1970).
110 Linda Kealey, 'Canadian Socialism and the Woman Question, 1900–1914,' *Labour / Le Travail* 13 (Spring 1984): 81, 91, 94.
111 Lubomyr Luciuk, *In Fear of the Wire Fence: Canada's First National Internment Operations, 1914–1920* (Toronto, 2001), 69, 75, 90, 105, 108.
112 Donald Avery, *'Dangerous Foreigners': European Immigrant Workers and Labour Radicalism in Canada, 1896–1932* (Toronto, 1979), 75, 80, 82, 88.
113 Barbara Roberts, *Whence They Came: Deportation from Canada, 1900–1935* (Ottawa, 1988), 95.

6. Zionism, Protest, and Reform

1 Irving Abella, *A Coat of Many Colours: Two Centuries of Jewish Life in Canada* (Toronto, 1990), 149; http://wikipedia.org/wiki/Henry_Wentworth_Monk. See also Richard S. Lambert, *For the Time Is at Hand: An Account of the Prophesies of Henry Wentworth Monk of Ottawa, Friend of the Jews, and Pioneer of World Peace* (London: Andrew Melrose, n.d.); Peter A. Russell, 'Henry Wentworth Monk,' in *DCB*, 12:751–2.
2 Benjamin G. Sack, *The History of the Jews in Canada* (Montreal, 1965), 218–20.
3 Leon Goldman, 'History of Zionism in Canada,' in *The Jew in Canada*, ed. Arthur D. Hart (Montreal, 1926), 291; *EJ*, 14:343, 8:1475.
4 Goldman, 'History of Zionism in Canada,' 291–2; Stephen Speisman, *The Jews of Toronto: A History to 1937* (Toronto, 1979), 201; Arthur A. Chiel, *The Jews in Manitoba: A Social History* (Toronto, 1961), 154; Gerald Tulchinsky, 'Clarence Isaac de Sola,' in *DCB*, 14:291–2.
5 Gideon Shimoni, *Jews and Zionism: The South African Experience (1910–1967)* (Capetown, 1980), 2.
6 See Yonathan Shapiro, *Leadership of the American Zionist Organization, 1897–1930* (Urbana, 1971), 6.
7 Michael Brown, 'Divergent Paths: Early Zionism in Canada and the United States,' *JSS* 44 (Spring 1982): 149–68.
8 Hart, ed., *Jew in Canada*, 314.

9 Bernard Figler, *Lillian and Archie Freiman: Biographies* (Ottawa, 1962), 202–3.
10 See 'Early Zionism in Toronto,' in *Hadassah Jubilee Volume, Tenth Anniversary Toronto*, ed. Louis Rasminsky (Toronto, 1927), 135–48, 174–8; Dov Joseph, interview with the author, 2 Jan. 1980; Hart, ed., *Jew in Canada*, 319.
11 Harry Gutkin, *Journey into Our Heritage* (Toronto, 1980), 179; Hart, ed., *Jew in Canada*, 318.
12 CZA, KKL 5/359, 'Federation of Zionist Societies of Canada, Financial Statements and Record of Zionist Achievement in Canada, Submitted to the Seventeenth Convention' [1921].
13 Louis Rosenberg, *Canada's Jews: A Social and Economic Study of the Jews in Canada* (Montreal, 1939), 308.
14 LAC, MG 28, U81, Zionist Organization of Canada, Vol. 5, 473–4.
15 CZA, A 119/200–2, de Sola to Nordau, 28 Feb. 1910.
16 CZA, Z2/39, Clarence de Sola to Zionistisches Centralbureau, 8 Nov. 1910.
17 CZA, Z1/244, Jacob de Haas to Theodore Herzl, 14 April 1903.
18 LAC, MG 28, U81, Vol. 5, 94–5, Richard Gottheil to Clarence de Sola, March 1899.
19 CZA, Z4/1405, Goldman to Levin, 17 Dec. 1919. When similar temporary cooperation of Canadian with American Zionists was undertaken during the Second World War, the Canadian leaders and officials were reluctant partners and, when conditions changed, immediately broke the ties.
20 CZA, Z4/1405, Goldman to Zionist Organization, Central Office, London, 25 Feb. 1920.
21 Ibid., Goldman to B. Goldberg, 24 Dec. 1919.
22 *JT*, 30 Sept. 1898.
23 LAC, MG 28, U81, Vol. 5, 19, 201.
24 *Maccabean*, 20 Jan. 1911.
25 CZA, KKL 1/20 (1907–1913), A. Fallick to de Sola, 18 Oct. 1908.
26 *Maccabean*, 20 Jan. 1911.
27 CZA, KKL 1/21, de Sola to the Chief Bureau of the Jewish National Fund, Cologne, 13 July 1908.
28 George G. Greene, 'The Hadassah Organization in Canada,' in Rasminsky, ed., *Hadassah Jubilee*, 136. See also Esther Waterman, ed., *Golden Jubilee: Canadian Hadassah – WIZO 1917–1967* (Montreal, 1967), 30–1.
29 CZA, Z4/1402, Leon Goldman to Chaim Weizmann, 8 April 1919.
30 Rasminsky, ed., *Hadassah Jubilee*, 3.
31 See Veronica Strong-Boag, *The Parliament of Women: The National Council of Women of Canada, 1893–1929* (Ottawa, 1976).
32 Rasminsky, ed., *Hadassah Jubilee*, 169.

33 LAC, Chief Press Censor, file 119–N-1, Mareu to Chambers, 29 Sept. 1918, cited in Jeffrey A. Keshen, *Propaganda and Censorship during Canada's Great War* (Edmonton, 1996), 83–4.
34 Hart, ed., *Jew in Canada*, 506, 209; JPLM Archives, Allan Raymond Collection, Box 26, 'Mortimer B. Davis Congratulatory Letters,' #1, Captain Isidore Freedman to Sir Mortimer B. Davis, 14 Feb. 1917.
35 In an unpublished paper, 'Jewish Men of Gideon' (JPLM, Rosenberg Papers), Rosenberg cites no sources for his number nor, according to historian Duff Crerar (see note 41 below), do other books such as Will Bird's *Communication Trench* (Amherst 1933), 83, which puts the number of Jews at 2,574. The number of recruits to the CEF over the entire war was 619,636 men. Thus, there were at least 1,859 Jews in the CEF, and probably more, given the infusion of conscripts from April to November 1918 under the Military Service Act of August 1917.
36 LAC, RG9, III, c15, vol. 4,637 (Canadian Chaplain Service), 'Statistics File: Memo' reports that of the volunteers, 851, about 0.2 per cent, were Jews. This figure was, presumably, based on attestation upon enlistment. At the end of 1917, 1,033 CEF soldiers were Jews. Further research might provide greater clarity on these complicated matters.
37 The Canadian Jewish Congress Charities Committee National Archives has compiled a complete list ('Canadian Jewish Casualties in the Canadian Armed Forces') of Jewish soldiers who died while serving with the Canadian Expeditionary Force during the First World War, in the Canadian Armed Forces during Second World War, and during the Korean War.
38 'The CBC "Ventures in Citizenship" Broadcast of 9 November 1938 (Kristallnacht),' *CJS/EJC* (2002): 109–22, 116–17.
39 JPLM, Abramowitz Fonds, box 26, 'Miliataria,' Colonel A.J. Palmer for A/Adjutant-General to Rev. Dr H. Abramowitz, 18 March 1918.
40 Ibid., Abramowitz to Major Wm. Schonfield, Jewish War Services Committee, 16 July 1917.
41 Duff Crerar, *Padres in No Man's Land: Canadian Chaplains and the Great War* (Montreal, 1995), 38, 68, 276, 301; JPLM Abramowitz Fonds, Michael Adler to Dr Abramowitz, 10 Sept. 1918.
42 JPLM, Abramowitz Fonds, box 26, 'Militaria,' Leo [surname unclear] to Rabbi Abramowitz, 15 Feb. 1917.
43 Ibid., Shel A [?] to Rabbi Abramowitz, 26 Feb. [1917].
44 CZA, Z4/1 8, undated and unsigned letter to Nahum Sokolff, London.
45 A letter from Col. C.S. Macinnes to General Officer Commanding, Military District No.4, Montreal, PK, 5 March 1918, quoted in Zachariah Kay, 'A Note on Canada and the Formation of the Jewish Legion,' *JSS* 29, no. 3 (July 1967): 173.

46 Bereskin Myer, a former Winnipegger who had moved to Palestine in 1908, was dispatched to Britain and Canada to encourage volunteering for the Legion. Martin Watts, *The Jewish Legion and the First World War* (London, 2004), 157, 222; Shabtai Teveth, 'The "Two Sons" in America: David Ben-Gurion, Yitchak Ben-Zvi, and the formation of Hechalutz, 1915–1916,' in *Studies in the American Jewish Experience*, ed. Jacob R. Marcus and Abrahamm J. Peck, 2 vols (Cincinnati, 1981), 2:127–201, 144, 151, 164.
47 Joseph Ben-Shlomo, 'Jewish Legion,' in *EJ* 10:74, Watt, *Jewish Legion*, 229.
48 Zachariah Kay, *Canada and Palestine: The Politics of Non-Commitment* (Jerusalem, 1978), 41.
49 *KA*, 22 Dec. 1908.
50 For the history of the Poale Zion in Canada, see Simon Belkin's *Di Poale Zion Bavegung in Kanada: 1904–1920* (Montreal, 1956). The Mizrachi movement was begun in Toronto in 1911 and spread to other parts of Canada. See Bernard Figler, 'Zionism in Canada,' in *An Encyclopedia of Zionism and Israel*, ed. Raphael Patai, 2 vols (New York, 1971), 1:174–9, 175. A Mizrachi convention of delegates from across North America took place in Montreal in December 1919 (*KA*, 5 Dec. 1919).
51 Greene, 'Hadassah,' 145.
52 George G. Greene, 'The Hadassah Organization in Canada,' in Hart, ed., *Jew in Canada*, 285, 287.
53 *CJC*, 16 Nov. 1917.
54 Carl Berger, *The Sense of Power: Studies in Ideas of Canadian Imperialism, 1867–1914* (Toronto, 1970), passim.
55 Belkin, *Die Poale Zion Bavegung in Kanada*, 162–3, 132.
56 David Rome, *Early Documents in the Canadian Jewish Congress 1914–21* (Montreal, 1974), 2–3, 11; *Congress Bulletin*, April 1968, p. 2.
57 Simon I. Belkin, *Through Narrow Gates: A Review of Jewish Immigration, Colonization and Immigrant Aid Work in Canada (1840–1940)* (Montreal, 1939), 100; H.M. Caiserman, 'The History of the First Canadian Jewish Congress,' in Hart, ed., *Jew in Canada*, 465–82, 465.
58 Gutkin, *Journey into Our Heritage*, 195.
59 Goldman, 'History of Zionism in Canada'; Hart, ed., *Jew in Canada*, 360; LAC, MG 29, C95, Diaries of Clarence de Sola, 16 March 1919 (microfilm reel A915); Caiserman, 'First Canadian Jewish Congress,' 466.
60 *CJC*, 17 Sept. 1915; *KA*, 13 Sept. 1915, translated and reprinted in *CJC*, 17 Sept. 1915.
61 *CJC*, 8 Oct. 1915.
62 Ibid., 23 and 29 Oct., and 19 Nov. 1915.

63 Melvin I. Urofsky, *American Zionism from Herzl to the Holocaust* (New York: Doubleday, Anchor Books, 1976), 159–60.
64 Brown, 'Divergent Paths,' 159.
65 Caiserman, 'First Canadian Jewish Congress,' 468.
66 *CJC*, 17 Jan. 1919.
67 Caiserman, 'First Canadian Jewish Congress,' 469.
68 Ibid., 476.
69 Ibid., 477.
70 *CJC*, 17 Jan. 1919.
71 Ibid., 31 Jan., 21 Feb., and 21 March 1919.
72 See J. Keith Johnson, *Canadian Directory of Parliament 1867–1967* (Ottawa, 1968), 289–90; and Bernard Figler, *Biography of Sam Jacobs, Member of Parliament* (Ottawa, 1959).
73 *CJC*, 18 April and 16 May 1919.
74 Donald Avery, *Reluctant Host: Canada's Response to Immigrant Workers, 1896–1994* (Toronto, 1995), 65; LAC, RG 146, CSIS, Mike Buhay, 021, RCMP, 'Secret and Confidential Re: O.B.U. General Conditions in Montreal, 18 Dec. 1920.' The report stated that 'several members of this organization [the Amalgamated] are also very active members in the O.B.U. movement.' See also David Bercuson, *Confrontation at Winnipeg: Labour, Industrial Relations and the General Strike* (Montreal, 1990); H. Trachtenberg, 'The Winnipeg Jewish Community in the Interwar Period, 1919–1939: Antisemitism and Politics,' in *Jewish Life and Times: A Collection of Essays* (Winnipeg, 1983); LAC, RG 146, CSIS, Kon, 39, RNWMP, 'Secret and Confidential Report Re: Louis Kon-Suspect, 5 Sept. 1919.'
75 Ibid., 139, 'CrB. Memorandum Ottawa, 17 May 1921. Re: Louis Kon alias Louis Cohen'; LAC, RG 18, vol. 1314, file W.G.5 and Riot 1919, I, W.H.M. McLaughlin, 'Report Re: General Conditions of Winnipeg Strike, 27 May 1919.'
76 Ibid., Albert Reames, 'Report Re: General Strike in Winnipeg, 25 May 1919.' See Henry Trachtenberg, 'The Winnipeg Jewish Community and Politics: The Interwar Years, 1919–1939,' *Historical and Scientific Society of Manitoba, Transactions*, Ser. 3, nos. 34 and 35 (1977–8, 1978–9): 115–53.
77 LAC, RG 18, Vol. 1314, file W.G. 5 and Riot 1919, Courtland Starnes, 'Crime Report Re: General Strike in Winnipeg, 23 Jun. 1919' and 'Secret Memorandum on Revolutionary Tendencies in Western Canada'; Gregory S. Kealey and Reg Whitaker, eds, *R.CM.P Security Bulletins: The Early Years 1919–1929* (St John's, 1994), 47, 233, 267. See Lorme and Caroline Brown, *An Unauthorized History of the RCMP* (Toronto, 1973), 50–86; Kealey and Whitaker, eds, *R.C.M.P. Security Bulletins: Early Years*, 316.

78 Belkin, *Through Narrow Gates*, 95, 102.
79 See Nora Levin, *The Jews in the Soviet Union since 1917: Paradox of Survival*, 2 vols (New York, 1990) 1:43.
80 *KA*, 19 and 28 Nov. 1919.
81 Belkin, *Through Narrow Gates*, 95.
82 Caiserman, 'First Canadian Jewish Congress,' 479.
83 See Belkin, *Through Narrow Gates*, 102–4; and Joseph Kage, *With Faith and Thanksgiving: The Story of Two Hundred Years of Jewish Immigration and Immigrant Aid Work in Canada (1760–1960)* (Montreal, 1962).
84 Caiserman, 'First Canadian Jewish Congress,' 478.
85 Simon Belkin, 'Reuben Brainin's Memories,' in *Canadian Jewish Year Book (1940–41)*, 138.
86 Shari Cooper Friedman, 'Between Two Worlds: The Works of J.I. Segal,' in *An Everyday Miracle: Yiddish Culture in Montreal*, ed. Ira Robinson et al. (Montreal, 1990), 122; poem translated by Miriam Waddington.
87 Irving Howe and Eliezer Greenberg, eds, *A Treasury of Yiddish Poetry* (New York, 1969), 156–7; poem translated by Miriam Waddington.
88 Ira Robinson, '"A Letter from the Sabbath Queen": Rabbi Yudel Rosenberg Addresses Montreal Jewry,' in Robinson et al., eds, *An Everyday Miracle*, 101–14. On Rabbi Rosenberg, see Leah Rosenberg, *The Errand Runner: Reflections of a Rabbi's Daughter* (Toronto, 1981).
89 Kerby A. Miller, *Emigrants and Exiles: Ireland and the Irish Exodus to North America* (New York, 1985).

7. Jewish Geography of the 1920s and 1930s

1 Louis Rosenberg, *Canada's Jews: A Social and Economic Study of the Jews in Canada* (Montreal, 1939). A photo-reproduction of the book was published in 1993 by McGill-Queen's University Press as *Canada's Jews: A Social and Economic Study of Jews in Canada in the 1930s*, edited and with an introduction by Morton Weinfeld. The addition of 'in the 1930s' is misleading because, except for scattered data on immigration and criminality during the 1930s, no use was made of the 1941 census, which would have provided a statistical portrait of Canadian Jewry in the 1930s. The book is really about the 1920s.
2 Ibid., 31–4.
3 Concerning one northern Ontario community, see Lise C. Hansen, 'The Decline of the Jewish Community in Thunder Bay: An Explanation' (MA thesis, University of Manitoba, 1977).
4 Rosenberg, *Canada's Jews*, 16, 17, 43, 31, 19, 45, 47, 59, 83, 86, 100–1, 153, 308.

5 Sheldon Levitt, Lynn Milstone, and Sidney T. Tenenbaum, *Treasures of a People: The Synagogues of Canada* (Toronto, 1985), 58, 66, 53, 61.
6 Similar patterns of Jewish residential clustering existed in Thunder Bay. See Hansen, 'Thunder Bay,' 17.
7 See Cyril H. Levitt and William Shaffir, *The Riot at Christie Pits* (Toronto, 1987).
8 Avi Aharon Habinski, 'Assimilation and Residential Location: Jews in Vancouver' (M.A. thesis, Simon Fraser University, 1973), 33. See also Myer Freedman, 'Growing Up in Vancouver's East End,' *The Scribe* 11, no. 2 (1989): 4–7, 34–41.
9 See Alan F.J. Artibise, *Winnipeg: A Social History of Urban Growth, 1874–1914* (Montreal, 1975); Louis Rosenberg, *A Population Study of the Winnipeg Jewish Community* (Montreal, 1946), 14; Alan Artibise, *Winnipeg: An Illustrated History* (Toronto, 1977), 202.
10 Rosenberg, *Winnipeg*, 45, 69.
11 Harry Gutkin, with Mildred Gutkin, *The Worst of Times, the Best of Times: Growing Up in Winnipeg's North End* (Toronto, 1987), 268.
12 Jack Ludwig, 'Requiem for Bibul,' in *Ten for Wednesday Night: A Collection of Short Stories Presented for Broadcast by CBC Wednesday Night*, ed. Robert Weaver, (Toronto, 1961), 107–20.
13 *Women's Voices: Personal Recollections*, Vol. 7 of *Jewish Life and Times* (Winnipeg, 1998), 11.
14 Ibid., 14.
15 Rosenberg, *Winnipeg*, 72, 73, 75.
16 PAM, MG 10, F 3 (MG6A6), 'Memoirs of Berel Miller.'
17 JHSWC, List of Winnipeg Jewish Organizations, compiled January 1986.
18 See Harvey H. Herstein, 'The Growth of the Winnipeg Jewish Community and the Evolution of Its Educational Institutions,' *Transactions of the Historical and Scientific Society of Manitoba*, 3d ser., no. 22 (1965–6): 28–66.
19 Rosenberg, *Canada's Jews*, 225. See Gerald Friesen, *The Canadian Prairies: A History* (Toronto, 1984), 382–417; Rosenberg, *Canada's Jews*, 227; Arthur A. Chiel, *The Jews in Manitoba: A Social History* (Toronto, 1961), 56.
20 Rosenberg, *Canada's Jews*, 227. Some, like the tiny colony of Trochu, Alberta, had disappeared by 1926. See Max Bercovitch, 'I Stayed Here: 85 Years in Southern Alberta,' *Western States Jewish History* 26, no. 3 (1994): 259–63; Rosenberg, *Canada's Jews*, 227.
21 Y. Katz and J. Lehr, 'Jewish and Mormon Agricultural Settlement in Western Canada: A Comparative Analysis,' *Canadian Geographer / Geographie canadienne* 35, no. 2 (1991): 128–42. See also the works of Cyril E. Leonoff: *The Jewish Farmers of Western Canada* (Vancouver, 1948); *The Architecture of Jewish*

Settlements in the Prairies: A Pictorial History (Winnipeg, 1975); *Wapella Farm Settlement (The First Successful Jewish Farm Settlement in Canada)* (Winnipeg, 1975); and Rosenberg, *Canada's Jews*, 240. These figures were based on 'total gross assets' (ibid., 243).

22 LAC, RG 76, Records of the Immigration Branch, vol. 82, F.C.B. [Blair] to Gillmour, 22 April 1930; Vladimir Grossman, *The Soil's Calling* (Montreal, 1938), 42, 47, 48.

23 Michael Usiskin, *Uncle Mike's Edenbridge: Memoirs of a Jewish Pioneer Farmer*, trans. Marcia Usiskin Basman (Winnipeg, 1983). See Anna Feldman, 'Yiddish Songs of the Jewish Farm Colonists in Saskatchewan, 1917–1939' (MA thesis, Carleton University, Institute of Canadian Studies, 1983).

24 Usiskin, *Uncle Mike's Edenbridge*, 140.

25 Clara Hoffer and F.H. Kahan, *Land of Hope*, illustrated by William Perehudoff (Saskatoon, 1960), 131ff; *Personal Recollections: The Jewish Pioneer Past on the Prairies*, Vol. 6 of *Jewish Life and Times* (Winnipeg, 1993), 13; Anna Feldman, 'Sonnenfeld Elements of Survival and Success of a Jewish Farming Community on the Prairies, 1905–1939,' *CJHSJ* 6, no. 1 (1982): 33–53, 45. See also Esther Ghan, 'The Hoffer Colony: A Memoir,' *The Scribe* 9, no. 3 (1987): 5, for a fascinating account of a suitor who shot his beloved for failing to return his affections. She recovered and married another man, who demonstrated his love for her in more traditional ways.

26 LAC, RG 76, Records of the Immigration Branch, vol. 82, Enclosure 'Jewish Colonization and the Work of the Jewish Colonization Association in Western Canada,' June 8/30, F.C. Blair memorandum, 12 June 1930. The article was identified as being from the *Canadian Jewish Eagle* of 21 Nov. 1929.

27 *KA*, 27 Nov. 1929; LAC, RG 76, Records of the Immigration Branch, vol. 82, I, Finestone to F.C. Blair, 9 July 1930; *KA*, 19 Nov. 1929.

28 Katz and Lehr, 'Jewish and Mormon Agricultural Settlement in Western Canada.'

29 Stella Hryniuk, '"Sifton's Pets": Who Were They?' in *Canada's Ukrainians: Negotiating an Identity*, ed. Lubomyr Luciuk and Stella Hryniuk (Toronto, 1991), 15.

30 *Jewish Pioneer Past*, 27; Ruth Bellan, 'Growing Up in a Small Saskatchewan Town,' in *Jewish Life and Times: A Collection of Essays* (Winnipeg, 1983), 199. See Fredelle Bruser Maynard, *The Tree of Life* (Toronto, 1989) and *Raisins and Almonds* (Toronto, 1985).

31 Anna Feldman, '"Her Voice Is Full of Wisdom": Jewish Saskatchewan Women in a Small Urban Setting,' *CWS/CF* 16, no. 4 (1996): 100–2. See Molly Lyons Bar-David, *My Promised Land* (New York, 1953), 3–30; Robert England, *The Central European Immigrant in Canada* (Toronto, 1929), 92.

32 Bercovitch, 'I Stayed Here,' 263; Becky L. Cohen, 'Jewish Pioneers of Alberta, Canada, Sharing Their Personal Memories, 1891–1999,' *Western States Jewish History* 33 (2000): 4–29.

33 For general background, see James Lemon, *Toronto since 1918: An Illustrated History* (Toronto, 1985). The most thorough study of Toronto's Jewish history is Stephen A. Speisman, *The Jews of Toronto: A History to 1937* (Toronto, 1979). Insight into the community can be gained from a delightful essay by Ben Kayfetz, 'The Toronto Yiddish Press,' *CJHSJ/SHJCJ* 7, no. 1 (1983): 39–54; Rosenberg, *Canada's Jews*, 308; and Louis Rosenberg, *The Jewish Population of Canada: A Statistical Summary from 1851 to 1941 Containing Statistical Supplement for Period 1951 and 1954* (Montreal, 1954), 17. See also Louis Rosenberg, 'Population Characteristics of the Jewish Community of Toronto,' in *Canadian Jewish Population Studies*, Jewish Community Series, no. 3 (Montreal, 1955), 1; Daniel Joseph Hiebert, 'The Geography of Jewish Immigrants and the Garment Industry in Toronto, 1901–1931: A Study of Ethnic and Class Relations' (Ph.D. diss., University of Toronto, 1987), 289ff, 328.

34 Lynne Marks, 'Kale Meydelach or Shulamith Girls: Cultural Change and Continuity among Jewish Parents and Daughters – a Case Study of Toronto's Harbord Collegiate Institute in the 1920s,' *CWS/CF* 7, no. 3 (1986): 85–9, 88.

35 P.F. Munro, *An Experimental Investigation of the Mentality of the Jew in Ryerson Public School, Toronto* (Toronto, 1926), 10, 22, 23, 36, 40, 44, 54.

36 *The Toronto Jewish City and Information Directory 1925.*

37 See Daniel Soyer, 'Class Conscious Workers as Immigrant Entrepreneurs: The Ambiguity of Class among Eastern European Jewish Immigrants to the United States at the Turn of the Twentieth Century,' *Labor History* 42, no. 1 (2001): 45–59.

38 Peter Oliver, *Unlikely Tory: The Life and Politics of Allan Grossman* (Toronto, 1985), 11.

39 Levitt and Shaffir, *Christie Pits*, 34; Speisman, *Jews of Toronto*, 90; Richard Dennis, 'Property and Propriety: Jewish Landlords in Early Twentieth-Century Toronto' (unpublished manuscript), table 2, 'Summary statistics from probate for Jewish landlords in Toronto.' See also Richard Dennis, 'Landlords and Housing in Depression,' *Housing Studies*, no. 3 (1995): 305–24, 317; Deena Nathanson, 'A Social Profile of Peddlers in the Jewish Community of Toronto, 1891–1930,' *CJS/EJC* 1 (1993): 27–40.

40 See Sammy Luftspring, *Call Me Sammy* (Scarborough, 1975).

41 James Dubro and Robin F. Rowland, *King of the Mob: Rocco Perri and the Women Who Ran His Rackets* (Toronto, 1987), 192.

42 LAC, MG 30, C 119, Louis Rosenberg Papers, vol. 26, no. 19, 'Jewish Mutual Benefit and Friendly Societies in Toronto: The First Fifty Years, 1896–1945,' 21, 22, 33, 35.
43 Ben Kayfetz to the author, 16 July 1997. See Leah Rosenberg, *The Errand Runner: Reflections of a Rabbi's Daughter* (Toronto, 1981).
44 LAC, MG 30, C 119, Louis Rosenberg Papers, vol. 26, no. 19, 'Jewish Mutual Benefit and Friendly Societies in Toronto,' 39, 41, 41a, 44.
45 See Shelly Tenenbaum, *A Credit to Their Community: Jewish Loan Societies in the United States, 1850–1945* (Detroit, 1994); 'Hebrew Free Loan Association: Seventh Annual Report, Montreal, 1 May 1918,' p. 8 (photocopy supplied by Dr Shelly Tenenbaum).
46 'Resources, Operation, and Policies of 14 Free Loan Societies, 1932' (photocopy supplied by Dr Shelly Tenenbaum); *CJR*, 9 July 1937.
47 'Summary 1925–1937' (photocopy supplied by Dr Shelly Tenenbaum); Isidore Sobeloff, Detroit, to Lillian G. Ledeen, Los Angeles, 9 Nov. 1938 (photocopy supplied by Dr Shelly Tenenbaum).
48 Rosenberg, *The Jewish Population of Canada*, 17; Gerald Tulchinsky, 'The Contours of Canadian Jewish History,' *JCS/REC* 17, no. 4 (1982–3): 46–56, 48.
49 Paul-André Linteau, *Histoire de Montréal depuis la Confederation* (Montreal, 1992), 361ff, 366–7.
50 Judith Seidel, 'The Development and Social Adjustment of the Jewish Community in Montreal' (MA thesis, McGill University, 1939), table 37A.
51 Ibid., table 39A, 'Percent which each type of newspaper forms of reading material of three generations, for four areas, 1938'; and tables 50A, 53A, 54A, 63, 34A.
52 See Speisman, *Jews of Toronto*, 276–303; PAM, NG 10, F 3 (MG5D29), H.E. Wilder, 'The Maturing of Winnipeg Jewry,' *Israelite Press: 50th Jubilee Edition*, 23 June 1961; Ira Robinson, 'Towards a History of Kashrut in Montreal: The Fight over Municipal Bylaw 828 (1922–1924),' in *Renewing Our Days: Montreal Jews in the Twentieth Century*, ed. Ira Robinson and Mervin Butovsky (Montreal, 1995), 10–29; Moshe S. Stern, 'Communal Problem Solving: The Winnipeg VA'AD HA'IR 1946,' *CJHSJ* 4, no. 1 (1980): 4–24.
53 Daniel J. Elazar and Harold Waller, *Maintaining Consensus: The Canadian Jewish Polity in the Postwar World* (New York, 1990), 70.
54 Speisman, *Jews of Toronto*, 265. See also Jack Lipinsky, 'The Progressive Wedge: The Organizational Behaviour of Toronto Jewry, 1933–1948' (Ph.D. diss., University of Toronto, 2003); Tamara Myers, 'On Probation: The Rise and Fall of Jewish Women's Antidelinquency Work in Interwar Montreal,' in *Negotiating Identities in 19th and 20th-Century Montreal*, ed. Bettina Bradbury and Tamara Myers (Vancouver, 2005), 175–201, 176.

55 PAM, MG 10, F3 (MG2K6), 'The History of the YMHA,' n.pag. On Winnipeg Jewish sports activity, see also Leible Hershfield, 'The Contribution of Jews to Sports in Winnipeg and Western Canada,' in *Jewish Life and Times: A Collection of Essays*, 84–9.

56 Eleanor Gordon Mlotek and Joseph Mlotek, *Pearls of Yiddish Song: Favorite Folk, Art and Theatre Songs* (New York, 1988), 260; Rebecca Kobrin, 'Rewriting the Diaspora: Images of Eastern Europe in the Bialystok Landsmanshaft Press, 1921–1945,' *JSS* 12 (2006): 1–38, 3.

57 *Kammen Folio of Famous Jewish Songs: A Collection of Favorite Old Time Song Hits*, vol. 2 (New York, 1953), 15–17; *Kammen Folio of Famous Jewish Theatre Songs: A Collection of Popular Song Hits of Yesteryear*, vol. 1 (New York, n.d.), 4–8; Norman H. Warembud, ed., *The New York Times Great Songs of the Yiddish Theatre* (New York, 1957), 175–81.

58 Mark Slobin, *Tenement Songs: The Popular Music of the Jewish Immigrants* (Urbana, 1982), 99–103. To date there is no study of Jewish 'low life' in Canada, though some tantalizing possibilities for such investigations exist See Andrée Lévesque, *Making and Breaking the Rules: Women in Quebec, 1919–1939* (Toronto, 1989), 122; Slobin, *Tenement Songs*, 125; Stephen Speisman, 'Yiddish Theatre in Toronto,' *Polyphony* 5, no. 2 (1983): 95–8; and Jean-Marc Larrue, *Le monument inattendu: Le Monument-National 1893–1993* (Lasalle, 1993), 183–94. Le Monument-National was the most popular venue for Yiddish theatre in Montreal in the interwar years. On the history of Yiddish theatre in Montreal, see Jean-Marc Larrue, *Le théâtre yiddish à Montreal* (Montréal, 1996); Rosenberg, *Canada's Jews*, 308.

59 These and other matters have been examined recently in Jack N. Lightstone and Frederick B. Bird, *Ritual and Ethnic Identity: A Comparative Study of the Social Meaning of Liturgical Ritual in Synagogues* (Waterloo, 1995).

60 *Baron de Hirsch Congregation, 1890 to 1990: 100th Anniversary Commemorative Book* (Halifax, 1990), 25–6; Sheva Medjuck, *The Jews of Atlantic Canada*, (St John's, 1986), 33.

61 Alison Kahn, *Listen While I Tell You: A Story of the Jews of St. John's, Newfoundland* (St John's, 1987), 19, 36.

62 See Samuel Rothschild, 'A Reminiscence by Samuel Rothschild,' *Polyphony* 5, no. 1 (1983): 93–9.

63 See John H. Thompson, with Allen Seager, *Canada, 1922–1939: Decades of Discord* (Toronto, 1985).

64 Nachman Shemen, *Tsvishn Kreig Un Friden* (Toronto, 1939).

65 Pierre Anctil, *Yidishe Lideri: Poèmes yiddish, de Jacob Isaac Segal* (Montreal, 1992).

66 Martin Wolf, 'The Jews of Canada,' *AJYB* (1925), 154–229; Arthur D. Hart, ed., *The Jew in Canada: A Complete Record of Canadian Jewry from the Days of the French Regime to the Present Time* (Montreal, 1926); Abraham Rhinewine, *Looking back a Century on the Centennial of Jewish Political Equality in Canada* (Toronto, 1932).

67 Roz Wolodarsky Usiskin, ed., *A Lifetime of Letters: The Wolodarsky Family: The Period of Separation, 1913–1922* (Winnipeg, 1995).

68 Ibid., 124.

69 Gerald Tulchinsky, *Taking Root: The Origins of the Canadian Jewish Community* (Toronto, 1992), 274.

70 CJCCCNA, ZA 1920, 12/11, H.M. Caiserman to A.B. Bennett, 23 March 1920.

71 Ibid., 12/7.

72 Ibid., 12/4.

73 Valerie Knowles, *Strangers at Our Gates: Canadian Immigration and Immigration Policy, 1540–1990* (Toronto, 1992), 88.

74 J.K. Johnson, ed., *The Canadian Directory of Parliament 1867–1967* (Ottawa, 1968), 289–90; Bernard Figler, *Biography of Sam Jacobs (Samuel William Jacobs, K.C., M.P.)* (Montreal, 1959).

75 *CJC*, 18 June 1920.

76 *KA*, 14 April 1927.

77 LAC, RG 76, Records of the Immigration Branch, vol. 54, file 2240, H.M. Caiserman to J.A. Calder, 13 April 1921.

78 Ibid.

79 Deena Nathanson, 'The Role of the Jewish Immigration Aid Society in the Immigration Process, 1919–1931' (unpublished manuscript), ch. 1, pp. 7, 13, 18.

80 Henry L. Feingold, *A Time for Searching: Entering the Mainstream, 1920–1945*, Jewish People in America Series (Baltimore, 1992), 25–9. Many Jews, desperate to rejoin their families, turned to Canada.

81 *KA*, 13 Nov. 1927.

82 Bernard Figler, *Lillian and Archie Freiman: Biographies* (Montreal, 1962), 50.

83 CJCCCNA, ZA 1920, 12/7.

84 Simon I. Belkin, *Through Narrow Gates: A Review of Jewish Immigration, Colonization and Immigrant Aid Work in Canada (1840–1940)* (Montreal, 1966), 94–8.

85 See Harold M. Troper, *Only Farmers Need Apply: Official Canadian Government Encouragement of Immigration from the United States, 1896–1911* (Toronto, 1972).

86 Jack Lipinsky, 'The Apprenticeship of an Executive Director: M.A. Solkin, A.J. Paul and the Jewish Immigrant Aid Society of Canada,' *CJHSJ* 9, no. 2 (1985): 67–81, 72ff, 82.

87 Robert Harney, 'The Commerce of Migration,' in *If One Were to Write a History: Selected Writings by Robert Harney* (Toronto, 1991), 19–36.
88 *KA*, 12 Dec. 1926; 5 Jan., 6 March, and 15 May 1927.
89 See 'La politique antijuive du gouvernement de Denikine,' *Bulletin du comité des délégations juives auprès de la conférence de la paix* (Paris, 19 Feb. 1920); CJCCCNA, ZA 1920, 12/9, 'Facts about the Pogroms,' *CJC*, undated.
90 'Jewish War Orphans Committee,' in Hart, ed., *The Jew in Canada*, 513. See also *CJC*, 12 April 1922.
91 PAM, MG I0, F3 (MG2J24), F. Shnay, Prince Albert, to Leon Goldman, 10 Sept. 1920.
92 Quoted in Lawrence Freiman, *Don't Fall Off the Rocking Horse* (Toronto, 1978), 33.
93 *CJC*, 17 Sept. 1920; see 'Jewish War Orphans Committee,' 513–20, for the most complete account of this amazing rescue effort.
94 CJCCCNA, Hershman Papers, S. Levine to Mrs Freiman, n.d.
95 Nathanson, 'Role of the Jewish Immigrant Aid Society,' ch. 3, pp. 1–27.
96 *CJC*, 1 Oct., 15 Oct., 22 Oct., 26 Nov., 10 Dec., and 24 Dec. 1920; and 28 April 1921.
97 CJCCCNA, ZA 1921,13/4, Hershman to Freiman, 8 July 1921; Leavitt to Hershman, n.d.; Hershman to Leavitt, 5 July 1921, 'Itinery [*sic*] of Journey,' n.d.
98 'Jewish War Orphans Committee,' 518.
99 *CJC*, 28 April and 21 Jan. 1921.
100 Quoted in Figler, *Freiman Biographies*, 60.
101 CJCCCNA, Belkin Papers, Belkin to Lappin, 21 July 1959.
102 Ibid., Hershman Papers, name of correspondent withheld.
103 *CJC*, 20 Oct. and 28 April 1922; 15 June and 13 July 1923.
104 Belkin, *Through Narrow Gates*, 105–6.
105 A. Ulmy, 'Helpless Jewish Immigrants in Canada,' *CJC*, 25 June 1920.
106 *CJC*, 2 July 1920, 6 Aug. 1922.
107 CJCCCNA, ZA 1921, 13/11, 'In the Matter of Certain Complaints Made against J.L. Lunney, Dominion Immigration Officer, Saint John, N.B.,' 3 March 1921.
108 Ibid., ZA 1920, 12/2, E.J. O'Connell to W.I. Little, 13 Oct. 1920.
109 Ibid., A.C. Kaplansky to F.C. Blair, 20 Dec. 1920; Leon J. Rosenthal to minister of colonization and immigration, 26 Nov. 1920.
110 Belkin, *Through Narrow Gates*, 108.
111 CJCCCNA, ZA 1920, 12/6, Caiserman to president, HIAS, 8 Oct. 1920; James L. Rodgers to JIAS, 14 Oct. 1920; S.B. Haltrecht to HIAS, 15 Oct. 1920; Haltrecht to Fain, 28 Oct. 1920.

112 Ibid., ZA 1920, 12/5, Caiserman to HIAS, Danzig, Europe [*sic*], 2 Nov. 1920.
113 Ibid., JIAS Papers, Isadore Stein to H.M. Caiserman, 27 May 1921, CA1303, quoted in Nathanson, 'Role of the Jewish Immigrant Aid Society,' ch. 2, pp. 29–30.
114 Ibid., ZA 1920, 12/6, S.B. Haltrecht to John L. Bernstein, 16 Sept. 1920; Caiserman to president, HIAS, 8 Oct. 1920; John L. Bernstein to JIAS, 24 Nov. 1920; secretary, JIAS, to J.R. Fain, 29 Nov. 1920; 12/4, 'Jewish Immigration into Canada: H.I.A.S. Takes Steps to Remedy Conditions,' Report of Max Meyerson and Dr B.B. Berkowitz.
115 LAC, MG 261, Arthur Meighen Papers, vol. 30, file 96, J.F. Boyce to Arthur Meighen, 1 Dec. 1921, 017478; see telegrams from H.A. Drapeau, Major Paquet, and Charles C. Ballantyne; Ballantyne to Meighen, 1 Nov. 1921, 017436–8; Rosenbloom to Meighen, 11 Nov. 1921, 017398–9.
116 R. MacGregor Dawson, *William Lyon Mackenzie King: A Political Biography*, vol. 1, *1874–1923* (Toronto, 1958), 350.
117 Henry Paetkau, 'Particular or National Interests? Refugees and Immigration Policy in Canada in the 1920s' (University of Western Ontario, Department of History research paper, History 509, April 1978), 16.
118 Belkin, *Through Narrow Gates*, 132–43, and app. 4, p. 214.
119 Harold Troper, 'Jews and Canadian Immigration Policy, 1900–1950,' in *The Jews of North America*, ed. Moses Rischin (Detroit, 1987), 44–58, 53.
120 LAC, RG 76, Records of the Immigration Branch, vol. 51, file 2183, part 3, F.C. Blair to Larkin, 2 Dec. 1921. See Belkin, *Through Narrow Gates*, 111–21.
121 Michael R. Marrus, *The Unwanted: European Refugees in the Twentieth Century* (New York, 1985), 89.
122 LAC, RG 76, vol. 51, file 2183, part 4, Philip Baker to W.L. Mackenzie King, 27 July 1923; King to Robb, 18 Aug. 1923.
123 Ibid., MG 26J, King Papers, W.L.M. King to Philip Baker, 18 Aug. 1923, 70449–70550.
124 Ibid., RG 76, vol. 51, file 2183, part 4, quoted in Blair to Black, 17 July 1923. See Kristi Corlett, 'Arthur Lower's National Vision and Its Relationship to Immigration in Canada, 1920–1946' (M.A. thesis, Queen's University, 1995).
125 See Belkin, *Through Narrow Gates*, 137–8.
126 But see Nathanson, 'Role of the Jewish Immigrant Aid Society,' ch. 7, pp. 4–5.
127 CJCCCNA, ZA 1924, 17/6, [Lyon Cohen?] to Barondess, 7 Nov. 1924; general secretary to M. Kozlovsky, 14 Jan. 1925.
128 PAM, MG 2, 11 (J), 'Report of Distribution Committee' n.d.; general secretary to H.E. Wilder, 1 Sept. 1924; general secretary to Mrs M. Margulies, 12 Nov. 1924.

129 CJCCCNA, Belkin Papers, box 1, JIAS Reports, 9.
130 Troper, 'Jews and Canadian Immigration Policy,' 53.
131 J. Murray Beck, *Pendulum of Power: Canada's Federal Elections* (Toronto, 1968), 188.
132 Troper, 'Jews and Canadian Immigration Policy,' 55.
133 Jacobs to Bennett, 7 Oct. 1925, quoted in David Rome, ed., *Our Archival Record of 1933: Hitler's Year*, Canadian Jewish Archives, New Series, no. 5 (Montreal, 1976), 21.
134 House of Commons, Select Standing Committee on Agriculture and Colonization, *Minutes of Proceedings and Evidence and Report* (Ottawa, 1928), app. 8, p. 77.
135 F.C. Blair to Edouard Oungre, Jewish Colonization Association, 30 July 1921, quoted in Rome, ed., *Our Archival Record of 1933*, 21.
136 See Irving Abella and Harold Troper, *None Is Too Many: Canada and the Jews of Europe 1933–1948* (Toronto, 1982), 7–10.
137 LAC, RG 76, Records of the Immigration Branch, vol. 83, memorandum (signature illegible) to F.C. Blair, 2 June 1937; H. Allam to director, Soldier Settlement of Canada, 24 March 1937.
138 Abella and Troper, *None Is Too Many*, 12.
139 Grossman, *The Soil's Calling*, 42.
140 Abella and Troper, *None Is Too Many*, 9.
141 See Paula Draper and Harold Troper, eds, *National Archives of Canada, Ottawa, Canadian Jewish Congress Archives, Montreal*, Vol. 15 of *Archives of the Holocaust: An International Collection of Selected Documents* (New York, 1991).
142 My late colleague Frederick W. Gibson often used this phrase in describing Mackenzie King. King was worried that Ottawa, Sandy Hill district, where he lived in Laurier House, was becoming inundated with Jews. See Norman Hillmer and J.L. Granatstein, eds, *The Land Newly Found* (Toronto, 2006), 204–5.
143 See Valerie Knowles, *First Person: A Biography of Cairine Wilson, Canada's First Woman Senator* (Toronto, 1988), 195–224.
144 Kenneth Craft, 'Canada's Righteous: A History of the Canadian National Committee on Refugees and Victims of Political Persecution' (MA thesis, Carleton University, 1987), 23, 73, 119.
145 Cyril E. Leonoff, 'Farming in the 40s: The Sussels' Experience,' *The Scribe* 12, no. 2 (1991): 5–11.
146 J.E. Rea, *T.A. Crerar: A Political Life* (Montreal, 1997), 185.
147 On King as Canada's best prime minister since Confederation, see Norman Hillmer and J.L. Granatstein, 'Historians Rank the Best and the Worst Canadian Prime Ministers,' *Maclean's*, 21 April 1997, p. 34.

148 Rosenberg, *Canada's Jews*, 134.
149 See Abella and Troper, *None Is Too Many*, 34.
150 H. Blair Neatby, *William Lyon Mackenzie King*, vol. 3, *1932–1939: The Prism of Unity* (Toronto, 1976), 305, 2, 242, 249.
151 Ute Eichler, 'Between Despair and Hope: The Work of the Jewish Immigrant Aid Society in the 1930s and 1940s' (MA thesis, Queen's University, 1988), 29.
152 Peter Newman, *Here Be Dragons: Telling Tales of People, Passion and Power* (Toronto, 2004), 37–48.
153 See Abella and Troper, *None Is Too Many*, 18–19, 41–42. See also the heart-rending collection of documents edited by Draper and Troper cited in note 141 above.
154 Lita-Rose Betcherman, *Ernest Lapointe: Mackenzie King's Great Quebec Lieutenant* (Toronto, 2002), 242. Lapointe did nothing to stop the flood of antisemitic hate literature circulating in the late 1930s. In 1940 he vetoed the appointment of MP Sam Factor to the Cabinet, an appointment that King had initially favoured (ibid, 243, 304).
155 Frank Bialystok and Irving Abella, 'Canada,' *The World Reacts to the Holocaust*, ed. David S. Wyman (Baltimore, 1996), 749–81.
156 Ibid., 758.
157 Betcherman, *Lapointe*, 253; *Le Devoir*, 26 Nov. 1942, quoted in John English, *Citizen of the World: The Life of Pierre Elliott Trudeau*, vol. 1, *1919–1968* (Toronto, 2006), 96.
158 William D. Rubinstein and Hilary L. Rubinstein, *Philosemitism: Admiration and Support in the English-Speaking World for Jews, 1840–1939* (London, 1999), 103–4.
159 Alan Davies and Marilyn F. Nefsky, *How Silent Were the Churches? Canadian Protestantism and the Jewish Plight during the Nazi Era* (Waterloo, 1997), 37. See also Davies and Nefsky, 'The United Church and the Jewish Plight during the Nazi Era 1933–1945,' *CJHSJ/SHJCJ* 8, no. 2 (1984): 55–71; George M. Wrong et al., telegram to Mackenzie King (from http://www.virtualmuseum.ca), quoted in Hillmer and Granatstein, eds, *Land Newly Found*, 210–11.
160 Cited in Jack Lipinsky, '"The Agony of Israel": Watson Kirkconnell and Canadian Jewry,' *CJHSJ* 6, no. 2 (1982): 57–72, 58.
161 Quoted in Reuben Slonim, *Family Quarrel: The United Church and the Jews* (Toronto, 1977), 2.
162 A.M. Klein, *Beyond Sambation: Selected Essays and Editorials, 1928–1955*, ed. M.W. Steinberg and Usher Caplan (Toronto, 1982), 37.
163 Zailig Pollock, *A.M. Klein: The Story of the Poet* (Toronto, 1994), 111.
164 See Paula Draper, 'The Accidental Immigrants: Canada and the Interned Refugees: Part 1,' *CJHSJ* 2, no. 1 (1978): 1–38; 'Part 2,' *CJHSJ* 2, no. 2

(1978): 80–112; and 'The Politics of Refugee Immigration: The Pro-Refugee Lobby and the Interned Refugees 1940– 1944,' *CJHSJ* 7, no. 2 (1983): 74–88. See also Paula Draper, 'The Accidental Immigrants: Canada and the Interned Refugees' (Ph.D. diss., Ontario Institute for Studies in Education, 1983); and Eric Koch, *Deemed Suspect: A Wartime Blunder* (Toronto, 1980).
165 Draper, 'Accidental Immigrants, Part 1,' 21, 29.
166 Draper, 'Accidental Immigrants, Part 2,' 82, 84, 85, 90, 99.
167 See Walter W. Igersheimer, *Blatant Injustice: The Story of a Jewish Refugee from Nazi Germany Imprisoned in Britain and Canada during World War II*, edited and with a foreword by Ian Darragh (Montreal, 2005).
168 See Koch, *Deemed Suspect*, app. 'Who's Who,' 264–72, for a history of many of the detainees and their occupations.

8. Clothing and Politics

1 See Jacques Rouillard, 'Les travailleurs juifs de la confection à Montréal (1910–1980),' *L/Let* 8/9 (1981/82): 253–9.
2 See Veronica Strong-Boag, *The New Day Recalled: Lives of Girls and Women in English Canada, 1919–1939* (Toronto, 1988), especially 61–3, 85–6, 14–5. See also Graham S. Lowe, 'Women, Work, and the Office: The Feminization of Clerical Occupations in Canada, 1901–1931,' in *Rethinking Canada: The Promise of Women's History*, ed. Veronica Strong-Boag and Anita Clair Fellman, 2d ed. (Toronto, 1991), 269–85.
3 David Monod, 'Store Wars: Canadian Retailing in Transition, 1919–1939' (Ph.D. diss., University of Toronto, 1988), 5.
4 Ruth Frager, *Sweatshop Strife: Class, Ethnicity, and Gender in the Jewish Labour Movement of Toronto 1900–1939* (Toronto, 1992), 43.
5 I am indebted to L.G. Laviolette, former director of the Montreal Men's Clothing Manufacturers' Association, for this memorable phrase. See Mercedes Steedman, 'Skill and Gender in the Canadian Clothing Industry,' in *On the Job: Confronting the Labour Process in Canada*, ed. Craig Heron and Robert Storey (Montreal, 1986), 152–76, 153; Alan Wilson, *John Northway: A Blue Serge Canadian* (Toronto, 1965); *Report of the Royal Commission on Price Spreads and Mass Buying* (hereafter *RCPSMB*) (Ottawa, 1935), passim; Gerald Tulchinsky, 'Hidden among the Smokestacks,' in *Essays in Honour of J.M.S. Careless*, ed. David Keane (Toronto, 1990), 257–84.
6 *RCPSMB*, passim.
7 See Robert Mcintosh, 'Sweated Labour: Female Workers in Industrializing Canada,' *Labour/Le travail* 32 (1993): 105–38; LAC, DLP, V, 333, folder 24

(81), S. Gariepy to deputy minister of labour, 29 Dec. 1924, quoted in Veronica Strong-Boag, 'The Girl of the New Day: Canadian Working Women in the 1920s,' *Labour/Le Travail* 4, no. 4 (1979): 131–64, 154; Michael Brecher, 'Patterns of Accommodation in the Men's Garment Industry of Quebec, 1914–1950 (with Special Reference to the Urban Sector of the Industry),' in *Patterns of Industrial Dispute Settlement in Five Canadian Industries*, ed. H.D. Woods (Montreal, 1958).

8 *RCPSMB*, Evidence, 4315.
9 Arthur D. Hart, ed., *The Jew in Canada: A Complete Record of Canadian Jewry from the Days of the French Regime to the Present Time* (Montreal, 1926), 343, 357, 199; Zvi Cohen, ed., *Canadian Jewry: Prominent Jews of Canada – a History of Canadian Jewry, Especially of the Present Time, through Reviews and Biographical Sketches* (Toronto, 1933), 255.
10 Cohen, ed., *Prominent Jews*, 124, 126; Hart, ed., *Jew in Canada*, 565, 134.
11 Arthur A. Chiel, *The Jews in Manitoba* (Toronto, 1961), 60, 61.
12 'In a Dress Factory,' *The Worker*, 12 Sept. 1925, quoted in Strong-Boag, 'Girl of the New Day,' 141.
13 *Minutes of ILGWU Convention, Philadelphia, 1916*, 46–7; *Minutes of ILGWU Convention, Cleveland, 1914*, 162; Lewis Levitzki Lorwin, *The Women's Garment Workers: A History of the International Ladies' Garment Workers Union* (New York, 1925), 320–9, 351.
14 *Montreal Star*, 23 Jan. 1925; *La Presse*, 3 Feb. 1925.
15 Ibid., 20 Feb. 1925; *Mail and Empire*, 5 Feb. 1925; *Toronto Telegram*, 6 Feb. 1925.
16 *Globe*, 9 Feb. 1925.
17 According to Louis Rosenberg, *Canada's Jews: A Social and Economic Study of the Jews in Canada in the 1930s*, ed. Morton Weinfeld (Montreal and Kingston, 1993), 365, there was a total of 5,059 Jewish workers in the whole Montreal 'textile goods and clothing' industry; or 28.68 per cent of all workers. Jacques Rouillard estimated Jewish participation at around 30 per cent in 'Les travailleurs juifs,' 254. But, as Ruth Frager points out, Rosenberg lumped together textile goods and clothing 'despite the fact that relatively few Jews were involved in the production of textile goods' (*Sweatshop Strife*, 233n25). She calculates that Jewish participation in the Toronto clothing industry (not including the textile-goods industry) in 1931 was 46.04 per cent (compared with Rosenberg's estimate of 36.09 per cent for clothing and textile goods, a significant difference). A careful calculation of disaggregated census data supplied by Statistics Canada shows that male and female Jews constituted 35.3 per cent of all workers in the Montreal clothing industry (Statistics Canada, microfilm 11–016–107).

18 *Montreal Star*, 6 Feb. 1925; *La Presse*, 2 March 1925.
19 *La Patrie*, 17 Feb. 1930; *Montreal Star*, 14 Feb. 1930; *Montreal Star*, 25 and 27 Feb. 1930; *Toronto Telegram*, 13 March 1930; see also *LG* (1930): 379, 447.
20 *LG* (1933): 217, 627.
21 *CJC*, 2 Jan., 30 Oct., and 13 Nov. 1931.
22 David Rome, ed., *Our Archival Record of 1933: Hitler's Year*, Canadian Jewish Archives, New Series, no. 5 (Montreal, 1976), 61, 64; *CJC*, 23 Nov. 1934; *CJR*, 16 Nov. 1934; *CJC*, 23 Jan. 1931.
23 *RCPSMB*, 109, 112.
24 Bernard Vigod, *Quebec before Duplessis: The Political Career of Louis-Alexandre Taschereau* (Montreal, 1986), 132–5; Bernard Shane, 'Great Moments,' in *Les Midinettes 1937–1962* (Montreal, 1961), 110.
25 *LG* (1926): 167; (1927): 204; (1929): 215.
26 *RCPSMB*, Evidence, 4313; *Statistical Yearbook of Quebec* (1924), 359; (1932), 356.
27 *RCPSMB*, Evidence, 4311.
28 Among the manufacturers of higher-quality men's clothing, the use of these contractors was limited and the controlled 'inside shop' was prevalent (*RCPSMB*, 115–16).
29 'Interview by B. Ferneyhough with Leah Roback,' in *The Canadian Worker in the Twentieth Century*, ed. Irving Abella and David Millar (Toronto, 1978), 198–203.
30 *CJC*, 6 Feb., 13 March, 24 April, and 23 Oct. 1931; 27 July 1934.
31 Stephen A. Speisman, *The Jews of Toronto: A History to 1937* (Toronto, 1979), 336.
32 I am grateful to Profesor Paul André Linteau for this information.
33 See Mercedes Steedman, 'The Promise: Communist Organizing in the Needle Trades – the Dressmakers' Campaign, 1928–1937,' *Labour/Le Travail* 34 (Fall 1994): 37–73; Mercedes Steedman, *Angels of the Workplace: Women and the Construction of Gender Relations in the Canadian Clothing Industry, 1890–1940* (Toronto, 1997), 142–89; *LG* (1935): passim; Yvette Charpentier, 'Emancipation,' in *Midinettes*, 18, 80.
34 *CJC*, 6 July 1934.
35 See Rose Pesotta, *Bread upon the Waters* (New York, 1941), 253–77; and Rose Pesotta, 'The Beginning,' in *Midinettes*, 70–1.
36 Andrée Levesque, *Virage à gauche interdit: Les communistes, les socialistes et leurs ennemis au Québec 1929–1939* (Montreal, 1984), 54. On the Workers' Unity League, see Bryan D. Palmer, *Working Class Experience: Rethinking the History of Canadian Labour, 1800–1991* (Toronto, 1992), 228–9, 253–5; *The History of the Labour Movement in Québec* (Montreal, 1987), 129.
37 *CJC*, 9 March 1934.

38 Eli Gottesman, ed., *Who's Who in Canadian Jewry* (Montreal, 1965), 95. Rabbi Bender was the editor of the *Chronicle* from 1931 to 1936. But see Lewis Levendel, *A Century of the Canadian Jewish Press: 1880s-1980s* (Ottawa, 1989), 59; *CJC*, 9 March 1934.
39 *CJR*, 2 March 1934; see also 'Every Friday' and 'More about Jewish Anti-Semitism,' *CJR*, 23 Feb. and 9 March 1934.
40 *CJC*, 29 June 1934.
41 Ibid., 11 Jan. 1935.
42 Irving Abella, ed., 'Portrait of a Jewish Professional Revolutionary: The Recollections of Joshua Gershman,' *Labour/Le Travail* 2 (1977): 201.
43 Jack Cohen, 'Shmatas, Syndicates and Strikes: The Organization of the Dress Industry in Montreal between 1930 and 1940' (BA Honours thesis, Concordia University, 1984), 35, 45, 48; *CJC*, 11 Jan. and 27 Sept. 1935.
44 David Rome, ed., *The Jewish Congress Archival Record of 1934*, Canadian Jewish Archives, New Series, no. 6 (Montreal, 1976), 13, 18, 21.
45 Workmen's Circle of Hamilton to Caiserman, 18 March 1935, quoted in ibid., 63, 80.
46 David Rome, ed., *The Jewish Congress Archival Record of 1936*, Canadian Jewish Archives, New Series, no. 8 (Montreal, 1978), 5, 28, 105.
47 *CJC*, 5 June 1936; Louis Rosenberg, 'Montreal Jews in Industry,' *CJC*, 17 Jan. 1936. See also Louis Rosenberg, 'How Montreal Jews Earn a Living,' *CJC*, 27 Dec. 1935.
48 Interview with Rabbi Harry J Stern in Montreal, July 1981; *CJC*, 17 March 1933, 23 April 1937.
49 *LG* (1934): 302.
50 *CJC*, 8 Jan. and 23 April 1937.
51 Ibid., 30 April 1937.
52 'Dressmakers Strike Is on the Verge of Being Settled,' *KA*, 18 April 1937, quoted in Cohen, 'Shmatas, Syndicates and Strikes,' 71; 'Why I Left the Manufacturers' Guild,' *KA*, 28 April 1937, quoted in ibid., 79.
53 See Allen Gotheil, *Les Juifs progessistes au Québec* (Montreal, 1988), 67–103; Ghila Benesty-Sroka, 'Entrevue avec Lea Roback, une femme engagée dans de justes causes: Une mémoire contemporaine,' *CWS/CF* 16, no. 4 (1996): 81–5; Abella and Millar, eds, *The Canadian Worker in the Twentieth Century*, 198–203; Gemma Gagnon, 'La Syndicalisation des femmes dans l'industrie Montréalaise du vêtement, 1936–1937' (MA thesis, Université du Québec à Montréal, 1990), 23; Evelyn Dumas, *The Bitter Thirties in Quebec* (Montreal, 1975), 58, 59; Pesotta, *Bread*, 253, 261, 266–7.
54 Ibid., 161; Gagnon, 'Syndicalisation,' 123; *CJC*, 30 April 1937; Aldea Guillemette, Foreword, in *Midinettes*, 65, 66.

55 Pesotta, *Bread*, 261; *CJR*, 1 Jan. 1937.
56 Shane, 'Great Moments,' in *Midinettes*, 118; CJCCCNA, Caiserman Papers, vol. 2, 2/13, 'Amalgamated Clothing Workers Union, 1936–1943,' F. White to Allan Bronfman, 11 May 1937.
57 Catherine Macleod, 'Women in Production: The Toronto Dressmakers' Strike of 1931,' in *Women at Work in Ontario, 1850–1930*, ed. Janice Acton, Penny Goldsmith, and Bonnie Shepard (Toronto, 1974), 309–29, 310. On the Toronto clothing industry, see Daniel Hiebert, 'Discontinuity and the Emergence of Flexible Production: Garment Production in Toronto, 1901–1931,' *Economic Geography*, July 1990, pp. 229–53; Macleod, 'Women in Production,' p. 312.
58 Ibid., 314; LAC, RG 27, vol. 351, file 79, microfilm T-2762; ibid., vol. 361, file 62, microfilm T-2971; ibid., vol. 359, file 6, microfilm T-2969.
59 Ibid., vol. 363, files 165, 166, 171, 173, 174, microfilm T-2974; Erna Paris, *Jews: An Account of Their Experience in Canada* (Toronto, 1980), 140–1.
60 *Toronto Telegram*, 21 July 1934.
61 *Toronto Weekly Sun*, 28 July 1934.
62 James D. Mochoruk and Donna Webber, 'Women in the Winnipeg Garment Trade, 1929–1945,' in *First Days Fighting Days: Women in Manitoba History*, ed. Mary Kinnear (Regina: University of Regina, Canadian Plains Research Center, 1987), 134–48, 139–40; Louis Rosenberg, *The Jewish Community of Winnipeg* (Montreal, 1946), 59; H. Trachtenberg, 'The Role of the Manitoba Jewish Community in Canadian Politics and Labour, 1900–1975' (unpublished paper), 2–3; H. Trachtenberg, 'The Winnipeg Jewish Community and Politics: The Interwar Years, 1919–1939,' *Historical and Scientific Society of Manitoba Transactions*, ser. 3, nos. 34 and 35 (1977–8 and 1978–9): 138. See also Bruce F. Donaldson, 'Sam Herbst, the I.L.G.W.U., and Winnipeg' (undergraduate essay, University of Manitoba, 1976); and Harry Gale, 'The Jewish Labour Movement in Winnipeg,' in *A Selection of Papers Presented in 1968–69* (Winnipeg, 1970), 1–14.
63 Interview with Max Enkin, Toronto, 15 July 1976.
64 Ben Dunkelman, *Dual Allegiance* (Toronto, 1977), ch. 2.
65 *ACWA* (1920–2), 210, 217, 266.
66 Max Swerdlow, *Brother Max: Labour Organizer and Educator*, ed. Gregory S. Kealey (St John's, 1990), 11–3.
67 LAC, RG 146, CSIS, file on Mike Buhay, p.o. 21 RCMP, 'Secret and Confidential Re – O.B.U. – General Conditions in Montreal. 18 Dec. 1920.' RCMP observers thought that the Amalgamated was 'the most radical of all unions' on the continent, and that it included 'several members [who] are also very active ... in the O.B.U. movement ...'; *ACWA* (1922–4), 130–41; (1924–6),

114–19; *Programme of Seventh Biennial Convention: Amalgamated Clothing Workers of America (10–15 May 1926)*, 12; *ACWA* (1926–8), 48–54, 72–9; (1928–30), 79–86. See also Adhemar Duquette, 'French Canadian Workers Join the Union,' in *From Drudgery to Dignity 1915–1955: Montreal Joint Board Fortieth Anniversary* (Montreal, 1955); *CJC*, 22 July 1932; F.R. Scott and H.M. Cassidy, *Labour Conditions in the Men's Clothing Industry* (Toronto, 1935), 5–36.
68 *RCPSMB*, Evidence, 107, 114–17, 121, 122, 125.
69 Ibid., 109.
70 A.E. Grauer, *Labour Legislation* (Ottawa, 1941), 50. See also *ACWA* (1934–6), 216–22.
71 *KA*, 17 June and 25 Aug. 1927; *ACWA* (1932–4), 76–83.
72 See Bruno Ramirez, 'Ethnic Studies and Working-Class History,' *Labour/Le Travail* 19 (1987): 45–8.
73 Abella, ed., 'Portrait of a Jewish Professional Revolutionary,' 185–213, 204; Hugh MacLennan, 'Canada and the Spanish Civil War,' in *Canadian History since Confederation: Essays and Interpretations*, ed. Bruce Hodgins and Robert Page (Georgetown, 1979), 549. See Cy Gonick, *A Very Red Life: The Story of Bill Walsh* (St John's, 2001).
74 Suzanne Rosenberg, *A Soviet Odyssey* (Toronto, 1988), 3ff.
75 Lita-Rose Betcherman, *The Little Band: The Clashes between the Communists and the Political and Legal Establishments in Canada, 1928–1932* (Ottawa, 1982), 7–8; Ian Angus, *Canadian Bolsheviks: The Early Years of the Communist Party of Canada* (Montreal, 1981), 77. See also William Rodney, *Soldiers of the International: A History of the Communist Party of Canada 1919–1929* (Toronto, 1968), passim; *Toronto Daily Star*, 13 Aug. 1968; LAC, RG 146, CSIS, file on Spector, 427; Bryan D. Palmer, *Working Class Experience: Rethinking the History of Canadian Labour, 1800–1991* (Toronto, 1992); 227; Tim Buck, *Yours in the Struggle: Reminiscences of Tim Buck* (Toronto, 1977), 99, 104; Angus, *Canadian Bolsheviks*, 339–56.
76 Ivan Avakumovic, *The Communist Party in Canada: A History* (Toronto, 1975), 23; Angus, *Canadian Bolsheviks*, 104, 178.
77 LAC, RG 146, CSIS, Spector, 193, E.G. Frere 'Secret Report Re YCL – Toronto, Ont. International Youth Day, 8 Sept. 1924,' 193; ibid., 053, A.W. Duffus, 'Secret and Confidential Report Re Young Jewish Socialist Club 216 Beverley Street, Toronto,' 22 Nov. 1921.
78 Ibid., 072, E.G. Frere 'Secret Report Re YCL'; Avakumovic, *Communist Party*, 55, 57; Buck, *Yours in the Struggle*, 99, 104, 130–1; *Workers Vanguard*, 26 Aug. 1968; LAC, RG 146, CSIS, Spector, 433.
79 LAC, RG 146, CSIS, Spector, 193; C.D. LaNauze, 'Secret Re Maurice Spector,' 3 Dec. 1929; Spector to Shachtman, Oct. 1932, Max Shachtman Papers, Tamiment Institute, New York University, passim.

80 This paragraph is based on Joan Sangster, *Dreams of Equality: Women on the Canadian Left, 1920–1950* (Toronto, 1989), and Louise Watson, *She Never Was Afraid: The Biography of Annie Buller* (Toronto, 1976). See Catherine Vance, *Not by Gods but by People: The Story of Bella Hall Gauld* (Toronto, 1968).
81 LAC, RG 146, CSIS, Mike Buhay, 103, RCMP Toronto, 10 June 1923, 'Report Re M Buhay – Communist Party of Canada – Montreal, Quebec; ibid., 031, F.S. Belsher, 'Crime Report Re: – Communist Party – Ottawa, Ont., 7 Sept. 1921.' See also Gregory S. Kealey and Reg Whitaker, eds, *RCMP Security Bulletins: The War Series, Part 2, 1942–45* (St John's, 1993), 150, 359–61.
82 Ibid., 361. See also Gregory S. Kealey and Reg Whitaker, eds, *RCMP Security Bulletins: The Depression Years, Part 2, 1935* (St John's, 1995), 84–5.
83 Ruth A. Frager, *Sweatshop Strife: Class, Ethnicity, and Gender in the Jewish Labour Movement of Toronto 1900–1939* (Toronto, 1992), 160, 174–6; Ruth A. Frager, 'Politicized Housewives in the Jewish Communist Movement of Toronto, 1923–1933,' in *Beyond the Vote: Canadian Women and Politics*, ed. Linda Kealey and Joan Sangster (Toronto, 1989), 258–75, 260–1; Ester Reiter, 'Camp Naivelt and the Daughters of the Jewish Left,' in *Sister or Strangers? Immigrant, Ethnic, and Radicalized Women in Canadian History*, ed. Marlene Epp, Franca Iacovetta, and Frances Swyripa (Toronto, 2004), 365–80.
84 See Swerdlow, *Brother Max*, 1–18; Gregory S. Kealey and Reg Whitaker, eds, *RCMP Security Bulletins: The Depression Years, Part 1, 1933–34* (St John's, 1993), 290–1, 298; LAC, RG 146, CSIS, 85–A-88, H.A.R. Gagnon to Commissioner, 15 Feb. 1940, quoted in Paul Axelrod, 'Spying on the Young in Depression and War: Students, Youth Groups and the RCMP, 1935–1942,' *L/Let* 35 (Spring 1995): 43–63, 54.
85 Avakumovic, *Communist Party*, 35; Betcherman, *The Little Band*, 164.
86 LAC, RG 146, CSIS, lCOR, S.T. Wood, 'Secret Memorandum Re Edmonton "ICOR" Committee,' 13 Dec. 1934. See also Robert Weinberg, *Stalin's Forgotten Zion: Birobidjan and the Making of a Soviet Jewish Homeland: An Illustrated History, 1928–1956* (Berkeley, 1998); Henry Srebrnik, 'Red Star over Birobidjan: Canadian Communists and the "Jewish Autonomous Region" in the Soviet Union,' paper delivered to the Canadian Jewish History Conference, York University, June 1998, p. 2; LAC, RG 146, CSIS, ICOR, 497, 'R.C.M.P., "0" Division. Manitoba district. Winnipeg, Man., 14 Oct. 1927. Secret: Man. Dist. 100 W-28. Report Re Workmen's Circle-Jewish Organization Winnipeg. Re Article taken from the Israelite Press of 7 Oct. 1927,' 480.
87 LAC, RG 146, CSIS, Society to Aid Jewish Colonization to the USSR, ICOR file, Wm. MacDonald, 'Report Re ICOR Committee Edmonton, Alberta,' 10 Dec. 1931; Srebrnik, 'Red Star,' 4; Kealey and Whitaker, eds, *Security Bulletins: Depression, Part 1*, 175; Henry Srebrnik, 'Birobidzhan on the Prairies:

Two Decades of Pro-Soviet Jewish Movements in Winnipeg,' in *Jewish Radicalism in Winnipeg, 1905–1960*, Vol. 8 of *Jewish Life and Times*, proceedings of a conference organized by the Jewish Heritage Centre of Western Canada, 8–10 September 2001, ed. Daniel Stone (Winnipeg, 2003), 172–91, 174–5.

88 LAC, RG 146, CSIS, Society to Aid Jewish Colonization to USSR, ICOR, S.T. Wood, Secret Memorandum Re ICOR Jewish Colonization Organization in Russia, 14 Nov. 1935; ibid., F.W. Davis, Secret Re ICOR, 6 Nov. 1935; ibid., J.C. Bain, Secret Re ICOR Jewish Colonization Organization in Russia, 11 Nov. 1935; ibid., R.W. Buchanan, Secret Re ICOR Jewish Colonization Organization in Russia, 12 Nov. 1935.

89 Ibid., R.R. Tait, 'Secret Re Edmonton ICOR Committee,' 13 Dec. 1934; ibid., S.T. Wood, 'Secret Re Edmonton ICOR Committee,' 13 Dec. 1934.

90 Ibid., S.C. Coggles, 'Secret Re Edmonton ICOR Committee,' 24 Oct. 1934; ibid., J.H. McBrien, 'Secret and Personal Re ICOR Committee,' to commissioner of customs, Department of National Revenue, Ottawa, 28 Dec. 1931; Irwin Pollock, 'Civil Rights and the Anglo-Jewish Press in Canada: 1930–1970' (MA thesis, Wilfrid Laurier University, 1979), 56–7.

91 LAC, RG 146, CSIS, Spector, 367.

92 Candace Falk, ed., *Emma Goldman: A Guide to Her Life and Documentary Sources* (Cambridge, 1995), 93; Ben Kayfetz to the author, 17 July 1997; Richard Drinnan, *Rebel in Paradise: A Biography of Emma Goldman* (Chicago, 1961), 261.

93 Quoted in Alice Wexler, *Emma Goldman in Exile: From the Russian Revolution to the Spanish Civil War* (Boston, 1989), 120; Falk, ed., *Emma Goldman*, 94.

94 Justice Robert Taschereau and Justice R.L. Kellock, *Report of the Royal Commission Appointed under Order-in-Council Pc. 411 of February 5, 1946, to Investigate the Facts Relating to and the Circumstances Surrounding the Communication, by Public Officials and Other Persons in Positions of Trust, of Secret and Confidential Information to Agents of a Foreign Power, June 27, 1946* (Ottawa, 1946), 112.

95 Fred Rose, *Spying on Labor* (Toronto, 1939) and *Hitler's Fifth Column in Quebec* (Toronto, 1942). The French edition, *La Cinquième colonne d'Hitler dans Québec* (Progres de Villeray, n.d.), included a lengthy, detailed letter from Rose rebutting an editorial in *Le Devoir* (7 Dec. 1942) that denied Rose's charges. He had published an earlier pamphlet, *Fascism over Canada*, covering the subject in the 1930s (*CJC*, 15 Feb. 1946). See Myer Smiatycki, 'Communism in One Constituency: The Election of Fred Rose in Montreal-Cartier, 1943 and 1945' (graduate essay, York University, 1978); and J.K. Johnson, ed., *The Canadian Directory of Parliament, 1867–1967* (Ottawa, 1968), 505.

96 CJCCCNA, Fred Rose Papers, 'Letter from a Hero's Mother to the Mothers and Fathers of Cartier' (leaflet, 1943).
97 Ibid., 'You and Fred Rose Can Build a Better Cartier' (1943), *Fred Rose in Parliament* (in Yiddish), *Le Masque tombé*, and *La Menace du chaos: Le Complot Tory contre le Canada*; Taschereau and Kellock, *Royal Commission*, 116; Johnson, ed., *Canadian Directory of Parliament*, 505.
98 For the case of Professor Israel Halperin of the Department of Mathematics at Queen's University, see Frederick W. Gibson, *Queen's University*, vol. 2, *1917–1961: To Serve and Yet Be Free* (Kingston and Montreal, 1983), 277–84; Taschereau and Kellock, *Royal Commission*, 97, 98, 102–3.
99 J.L. Granatstein and David Stafford, *Spy Wars: Espionage and Canada from Gouzenko to Glasnost* (Toronto, 1990), 48. See Reg Whitaker and Gary Marcuse, *Cold War Canada: The Making of a National Insecurity State, 1945–1957* (Toronto, 1994), 71–3, 97, 209, 239.
100 Len Scher, *The Un-Canadians: True Stories of the Blacklist Era* (Toronto, 1992), 5.
101 Gregory S. Kealey and Reg Whitaker, eds., *RCMP Security Bulletins: The Depression Years, Part 3, 1936* (St John's, 1996), 210, 52, 66, 180, 361, 396, 434, 296, 319, 344, 354; Shloime Perel, 'History of the UJPO in Canada, 1926–1949,' ch. 12, p. 2. The latter work is part of a PhD thesis in progress at McMaster University, Department of Sociology.
102 Gregory S. Kealey and Reg Whitaker, eds, *RCMP Security Bulletins: The Depression Years, Part 4, 1937* (St John's, 1997), 10, 17, 291–2.
103 Perel, 'UJPO in Canada,' ch. 13, p. 5, ch. 16, p. 16; Abella, ed., 'Jewish Professional Revolutionary,' 204, 208.
104 Gregory S. Kealey and Reg Whitaker, eds, *RCMP Security Bulletins: The War Series, 1939–1941* (St John's, 1989), 27, 106, 120; Eli Gottesman, ed., *Who's Who in Canadian Jewry* (Montreal, 1965), 335. See Doug Smith, *Joe Zuken: Citizen and Socialist* (Toronto, 1990).
105 Cy Gonick, *A Very Red Life: The Story of Bill Walsh* (St John's Canadian Committee on Labour History, Memorial University of Newfoundland, 2001), 11.
106 Dave Kashtan, 'Living in One's Own Time: A Memoir from the Left,' and Kirk Niergarth, 'Fight for Life: Dave Kashtan's Memories of Depression-Era Communist Youth Work,' *Labour/Le Travail* 56 (Fall 2005): 199–236, 205.
107 LAC, RG 146, CSIS, LNPO, 51, 'Jewish Aid Society of Montreal, 23–9–46, Re: *Canadian Jewish Weekly*, vol. 6, no. 308, Toronto, Ont., 19 Sept. 1946'; LAC, RG 146, CSIS, UJPO, 'Second National Convention of the United Jewish People's Order. Held in Montreal, Que., 20–22 Jun. 1947. Convention Book ... Editor: H. Guralnick.'
108 Abella, ed., 'Jewish Professional Revolutionary,' 185–213. See Helmut Kallman, Gilles Potvin, and Kenneth Winters, eds, *Encyclopedia of Music in*

Canada (Toronto, 1981), 921; LAC, RG 146, CSIS, UJPO, 51, 'Jewish Aid Society of Montreal, 23–9–46, Re: *Canadian Jewish Weekly*, vol. 6, no. 308, Toronto, Ont., 19 Sept. 1946.'

109 Perel, 'UJPO in Canada,' Conclusion, pp. 4, 5; LAC, RG 146, CSIS, UJPO, 51, 'Jewish Aid Society of Montreal, 23–9–46, Re: *Canadian Jewish Weekly*, vol. 6, no. 308, Toronto, Ont., 19 Sept. 1946'; 'United Jewish People's Order Re: *Canadian Jewish Weekly*, vol. 7, no. 322, Toronto, Ont., 26 Dec. 1946'; Ibid., 43, N. Courtois, 'Re Albert E. Kahn, Speaker at Meeting of the United Jewish People's Order Montreal, P.Q., 8–10–46.'

110 Ibid., 331, 'Yiddish language, Summarized by MHA at R.C.M.P. Headquarters, News 665, 20–1–39. *Der Kamf* (The Struggle), vol. 14, no. 735, Toronto, 27 Jan. 1938.'

111 Ibid., 380, 'Yiddish language, Summarized by MHA at R.C.M.P. Headquarters, News 1911, 6–5–48. *Canadian Jewish Weekly*, vol. 8, no. 392, Toronto, 29 Apr. 1948.'

112 Ibid., 42, 'United Jewish People's Order, Re: Albert E. Kahn (Speaker at Meeting of United Jewish People's Order, Montreal, P.Q., 8–10–46)'; ibid., 53, J.E.M. Barrette, 'United Jewish People's Order, 7–9–46, Re: Laurentian Vacation Club, Lac des Quartoze [*sic*] lies, Terrebonne Co., P.Q.'

113 Ibid., 70, 'Memorandum for File Re: United Jewish People's Order, Canada General, 6–4–45.'

114 Ibid., 78, 'Communists Organize National Jewish Order.'

115 Ibid., 89, N.E. McFadyen, 'Memorandum to Inspector Leopold Re: United Jewish People's Order, 19–1–45.'

116 Ibid., 55, 'Yiddish language, Summarized by MHA at R.CM.P. Headquarters, News 1911, 18–6–46. *Canadian Jewish Weekly*, vol. 6, no. 294, Toronto, 13 Jun. 1946'; ibid., 261, 'Yiddish language, Summarized by MHA at R.C.M.P. Headquarters, *Der Kamf* (The Struggle), vol. 13, no. 655, 13 Aug. 1937'; Kealey and Whitaker, eds, *Security Bulletins: Depression Years, Part 3*, 330.

117 Perel, 'UJPO in Canada,' ch. 23, p. 5.

118 Ben Kayfetz to the author, 5 June 1998.

119 See Maximilian Hurwitz, *The Workmen's Circle: Its History, Ideals, Organization and Institutions* (New York, 1936); and C Bezdel Sherman, 'Workmen's Circle,' *EJ*, 16:635.

120 Raphael Patai, *Encyclopedia of Zionism and Israel* (New York, 1971), 1:151–2; 2:893–4.

121 Bernard Figler, 'Zionism in Canada,' in *Encyclopedia of Zionism*, 1:174–9, 176.

122 Ben Lappin, 'May Day in Toronto in the 1930s,' *Commentary* 19, no. 5 (1955): 476–9.

123 David Lewis, *The Good Fight* (Toronto, 1981), 27, 198.
124 Charles Taylor, 'Introduction,' in ibid., xi; David Lewis and Frank Scott, *Make This Your Canada: A Review of C.C.F History and Policy* (Toronto, 1943).
125 Lewis, The *Good Fight*, 107–8, 143, 151.
126 See Mark Zuehlke, *The Gallant Cause: Canadians and the Spanish Civil War, 1936–1939* (Vancouver, 1996); Myron Momryk, '"Canadian Jewish Boys in Spain": Jewish Volunteers from Canada in the Spanish Civil War 1936–39: A Profile' (unpublished paper, 1995), 6, 39, fn 34; Myron Momryk, 'Jewish Volunteers from Canada in Loyalist Armed Forces, Including the International Brigades, Spain, 1936–39,' paper for Canadian Jewish Historical Association meetings in Montreal, 1995.
127 *CJR*, 8 Oct. 1937.
128 *Jewish Standard*, June 1937; 'Mit Der Kanader Yiddisher Volunteer fun Shpania,' *Der Kamf*, n.d. Goldberg fought with the Dimitrov Battalion, which was composed of volunteers from the Balkans.
129 Momryk, 'Jewish Boys in Spain,' 6, 19, 27.
130 David Rome, ed., *Canadian Jews in World War II, Part 2: Casualties* (Montreal, 1948), 22.
131 Yank Levy, *Guerrilla Warfare* (New York, 1942); *CJN*, 9 March 1981.
132 CJCNA, Series ZB, S.H. Abramson Papers, Abramson to H.M. Caiserman, 10 March 1938.
133 Ibid., Abramson to Caiserman, 9 May 1938; Abramson to Caiserman, 4 Oct. 1938.
134 Ibid., Abramson to Caiserman, 29 Oct. 1938.
135 Ibid., Abramson to Caiserman, 7 Nov. 1938.
136 Sandra Djwa, *A life of F.R. Scott: The politics of the imagination* (Vancouver, 1971), 173.
137 Donald H. Avery, *Reluctant Host: Canada's Response to Immigrant Workers, 1896–1914* (Toronto, 1995), 114.
138 Gordon Lunan, *The Making of a Spy: A Political Odyssey* (Montreal, 1995), 29.
139 Ibid., 98. See also 100, 103, 109, 133 and 139 on the Jewish radical left in Montreal during the 1930s and 1940s.
140 Sharman Kadish, *Bolsheviks and British Jews: The Anglo-Jewish Community, Britain and the Russian Revolution* (London, 1992), 243.

9. The Politics of Marginality

1 See Leon D. Crestohl, 'The Open Forum on the School Question,' *CJC*, 26 March, 2 April, 9 April, 16 April, and 14 May 1926.

2 Gerald Tulchinsky, *Taking Root: The Origins of the Canadian Jewish Community* (Toronto, 1992), 138–44, 243–8.
3 See Ira Robinson, 'Kabbalist and Community Leader: Rabbi Yudel Rosenberg and the Canadian Jewish Community,' *CJS/EJC* (1993): 41–58.
4 Elson I. Rexford, *Our Educational Problem: The Jewish Population and the Protestant Schools* (Montreal, 1924), 29. Cited in George E. Fowler, 'A Study of the Contributions of Dr. E.I. Rexford to Education in the Province of Quebec' (MA thesis, McGill University, 1939), 196.
5 Rexford, *Our Educational Problem*, 32, 34, 35; *KA*, 5 Dec. 1927.
6 Ibid., 40, 41.
7 In August 1924, the *Chronicle* pointed out that while thirty-seven qualified Jewish teachers could not get jobs in Montreal, the Protestant board was importing teachers from England (*CJC*, 29 Aug. 1924; 3 and 5 Sept. 1924).
8 Rexford, *Our Educational Problem*, 35. Rexford's data did not go uncontested, however. Various Jewish spokesmen pointed out that taxes paid indirectly by Jewish renters in Protestant-owned buildings were disregarded (Michael Brown to the author, 15 Nov. 1997).
9 *CJC*, 28 Sept. 1923.
10 Rexford, *Our Educational Problem*, 42. Jewish-owned property in Montreal was worth about $36 million (*CJC*, 5 Oct. 1923, 27 Feb. 1925, 29 March 1929).
11 Michael R. Marrus, *Mr. Sam: The Life and Times of Samuel Bronfman* (Toronto, 1991), 113, 245–7.
12 Maxwell Goldstein, 'The Status of the Jew in the Schools of Canada,' in *The Jew in Canada: A Complete Record of Canadian Jewry from the Days of the French Regime to the Present Time*, ed. Arthur D. Hart (Montreal, 1926), 498.
13 Ibid., 120.
14 *CJC*, 5 Oct. 1923, 29 Dec. 1922, 27 May 1927.
15 Ibid., 9 Nov. 1923.
16 Ibid., 18 April 1924; William Nadler, 'Jewish-Protestant School Question' (manuscript, 1925), 24, 28.
17 Ibid., 347–9.
18 Bernard Figler and David Rome, *Hananiah Meir Caiserman: A Biography with an Essay on Modern Jewish Times by David Rome* (Montreal, 1962), 153, 157; Bernard Figler, *Biography of Louis Fitch, Q.C., Canadian Jewish Profiles* (Ottawa, 1968).
19 Nadler, 'Jewish-Protestant School Question,' 30–2.
20 See *KA*, 26 Feb. 1928; *CJC*, 29 Aug. 1924.
21 Bernard L. Vigod, *Quebec before Duplessis: The Political Career of Louis-Alexandre Taschereau* (Montreal, 1986), 254; Nadler, 'Jewish-Protestant School Question,' 23, 157–8.
22 Hart, ed. *The Jew in Canada*, 194, 429; *CJC*, 14 March 1952.

23 Ibid., 1 Aug. 1924.
24 Ibid.
25 Ibid., 3 Oct. 1924.
26 Ibid., 10 and 17 Oct. 1924.
27 Ibid., 3 Oct. 1924.
28 Ibid, 5 Sept. 1924.
29 Ibid., 12 Sept. 1924.
30 Ibid., 9 Jan. 1925.
31 Ibid., 16 Jan. 1925.
32 Ibid., 27 March 1925.
33 Goldstein, 'Status of the Jew,' 498. See *CJC*, 27 Feb. and 13 March 1925, for a lengthy report on an extended analysis of the court's decision.
34 See ibid., 13 Nov. 1925; 5 Feb. 1926.
35 *CJC*, 2 Dec. 1927, 10 and 24 Feb. 1928.
36 See ibid., 1 Feb. 1929.
37 See David Roskies, 'Yiddish in Montreal: The Utopian Experiment,' in *An Everyday Miracle: Yiddish Culture in Montreal*, ed. Ira Robinson, Pierre Anctil, and Mervin Butovsky (Montreal, 1990), 22–38; *CJC*, 1 Feb. 1929.
38 Ibid., 29 March 1929.
39 Ibid., 10 Jan. 1930.
40 Ibid., 24 Jan. 1931.
41 Ibid., 28 Feb. 1930.
42 Ibid., 25 April 1930.
43 Ibid., 2 May 1930.
44 Ibid., 5 Dec. 1930.
45 Ibid., 6 Feb. 1931, 12 and 19 Dec. 1930.
46 Quoted in Antonin Dupont, *Les Relations entre l'église et l'état sous Louis-Alexandre Taschereau* (Montreal, 1972), 259.
47 *La Semaine religieuse de Montréal* 89 (March 1930): 180; quoted in ibid., 259, 261, 262–3.
48 Richard Jones, *L'Idéologie de l'Action Catholique (1917–1939)*, Histoire et sociologie de la culture, no. 9 (Quebec, 1974), 26. See also Jean Hulliger, *L'Enseignement social des évêques canadiens de 1891 à 1950* (Montreal, 1957). The third of these editorials, from 19 May 1926, was reprinted as 'Questions des écoles à Montréal,' *L'Action Française* 15, no. 6 (1926): 379–81. See also Antonio Huot, *La Question juive: Quelques observations sur la question du meurtre rituel* (Quebec, 1914); 'Questions des écoles,' 380.
49 Marc Hébert, 'La Presse de Québec et les juifs 1925-1939: Le cas du *Soleil* et du *Quebec Chronicle Telegraph*' (MA thesis, l'Université Laval, 1994), 23; *Le Soleil*, 3 Feb. 1926 (quoted in ibid., 23) and 5 Feb. 1926 (quoted in ibid., 25).

50 Jones, *Action Catholique*, 293, 295.
51 Dupont, *Les Relations*, 261.
52 Quoted in Jones, *Action Catholique*, 295.
53 Quoted in ibid., 264; Vigod, *Taschereau*, 160; David Rome, 'The Political Consequences of the Jewish School Question, Montreal, 1925–1933,' *CJHSJ* 1, no. 1 (1977): 3–15, 12–13.
54 Cornelius J. Jaenen, 'Thoughts on French and Catholic Anti-Semitism,' *CJHSJ* 1, no. 1 (1977): 16–23, 22–3.
55 *CJC*, 17 April 1931. See Louis Rosenberg, *Canada's Jews* (Montreal, 1939), 270; Dupont, *Les Relations*, 272–3.
56 *CJC*, 27 May 1927.
57 Ibid., 10 Jan. 1930.
58 Ibid., 26 June 1925; 2 July 1920; 1 April 1927; 30 Sept. 1927; 1 July 1921; 31 Dec. 1926; 17 Feb. 1922.
59 Ibid., 17 June 1921; 1 July 1921; 4 May 1923; 12 Nov. 1920.
60 See Pierre Anctil, 'Interlude of Hostility: Judeo-Christian Relations in Quebec in the Interwar Period, 1919-1939,' in *Quebec since 1800: Selected Readings*, ed. Michael D. Behiels (Toronto, 2002), 396–423; *CJC*, 15 Dec. 1923.
61 Ibid., 2 Nov. 1923, 1 Feb. 1924.
62 Henri Leroux, *L'Actualité économique* 2, no. 3 (1926): 9–11.
63 J.E. Sansregret, 'La Part des canadiens-français dans le commerce et l'industrie,' *Le Détaillant* 1, no. 12 (1927): 14, 15, 16.
64 *Le Duprex* 1, no. 5 (1927): 4.
65 *CJC*, 11 April 1924.
66 See David Rome, ed., *The Jewish Congress Archival Record of 1936*, Canadian Jewish Archives, New Series, no. 8 (Montreal, 1978), passim; Jones, *L'Idéologie de l'Action Catholique*; Édouard V. Lavergne, 'Haine aux juifs,' *L'Action Catholique*, 21 Sept. 1921, quoted in ibid., 71, 91; J. Albert Foissy, 'Autour du monde,' *L'Action Catholique*, 4 Feb. 1921, quoted in ibid., 73; J. Albert Foissy, 'Impressions d'un veteran,' *L'Action Catholique*, 23 Aug. 1920, quoted in ibid., 74, 76, 80.
67 Abbé Nadeau, 'Chronique de la guerre,' *L'Action Catholique*, 19 May 1917, quoted in ibid., 81.
68 'La Pologne livrée aux juifs,' *L'Action Catholique*, 25 Sept. 1919, quoted in ibid., 83.
69 Lavergne, 'Haine aux juifs,' quoted in ibid., 85; Jules Dorion, 'Le Fascisme: Il lui faut quelqu'un, et une situation,' *L'Action Catholique*, 26 Aug. 1933, quoted in ibid., 87.
70 Donald J. Horton, *André Laurendeau: French Canadian Nationalist* (Toronto, 1992), 36–7; *CJR*, 28 April 1933; *CJC*, 28 April 1933. This *Chronicle* editorial

blasted *Le Devoir,* 'in whom the germs of the Goglu are multiplying at a fast rate,' for its 'meticulous devotion to the cause of Jeune-Canada' (Horton, *André Laurendeau,* 37).

71 *CJC,* 26 May, 2 June, 30 June, and 11 Aug. 1933.

72 André-J. Belanger, 'L'Apolitisme des idéologies québécoises: Le grand tournant de 1934–1936,' *Histoire et Sociologie de la Culture* [Québec], no. 7 (1974): 263; André Laurendeau, *Politiciens et juifs,* Les Cahiers de Jeune-Canada, no. 1 (Montreal, 1933), quoted in ibid., 264.

73 *CJR,* 10 Jan. 1931; *CJC,* 10 April 1931, 8 Dec. 1931; *CJR,* 29 Sept. 1931; *CJC,* 28 July, 29 Sept., 6 Oct., 25 Aug., 12 May, and 30 June 1933.

74 *AJYB* 39 (1936–7): 243; Irving Abella and Frank Bialystok, 'Canada,' in *The World Reacts to the Holocaust,* ed. David Wyman (Baltimore, 1996), 749–81, 752. See Irving Abella, 'Anti-Semitism in Canada in the Interwar Years,' in *The Jews of North America,* ed. Robert F. Harney and Moses Rischin (Detroit, 1987), 235–46; Stephen Speisman, 'Antisemitism in Ontario: The Twentieth Century,' in *Antisemitism in Canada: History and Interpretation,* ed. Alan Davies (Waterloo, 1992), 113–33.

75 *AJYB* 38 (1936–7): 243.

76 Norman Cohn, *Warrant for Genocide: The Myth of the Jewish World Conspiracy and the Protocols of the Elders of Zion* (New York, 1969), 158–62.

77 See Michael Doucet and John Weaver, *Housing the North American City* (Montreal, 1991), 123; *AJYB* 33 (1931–2): 59–60; 35 (1933–4): 64; 38 (1935–6): 168.

78 The *Canadian Jewish Chronicle* carefully reported on these publications, whose writers A.M. Klein labelled 'sewer denizens' (*CJC,* 22 July, 1932).

79 Dominion of Canada, *Debates of the House of Commons* (Fifth Session, Seventeenth Parliament), vol. 2, 1934 (Ottawa, 1934), 1661; CJCCCNA, Caiserman Papers, vol. 2, Membership Campaign, 1935–7; Caiserman to Bernard Gardner, 21 June 1935; Pascale Ryan, *Penser la nation. La Ligue d'action nationale 1917–1960* (Montreal, 2006), 139.

80 CJCCCNA, Caiserman Papers, vol. 2, Boycott of German Products, 1936–7, Caiserman circular letter, 10 Oct. 1935. The letter was marked 'Very Important, Very Urgent.'

81 Ibid., Reitman to Congress, 16 May 1934; Boycott Committee, 1933–5, Caiserman circular letter, 20 Aug. 1935.

82 Ibid., S.D. Cohen circular letter, 28 Jan. 1935; Cohen and Mrs Florence Levy, Chairman, Vigilance Committee, n.d.; Boycott Committee bulletin, April 1939.

83 Ibid., 2/2, Correspondence with Government Bodies, 1937–9, Club Ouvrier Maisonneuve.

84 Ibid., vol. 1, 1/6, Membership Campaign, Eastern Division, Books and Pamphlets, Caiserman circular letter, 25 Oct. 1937; Congress circular, 22 Sept. 1938.
85 Ibid., vol. 1, 1/3, Membership Drive, 1938, Congress circular.
86 See Avi M. Schulman, *Like a Raging Fire: A Biography of Maurice N. Eisendrath* (New York, 1993), 15–25. See also *The Never Failing Stream* (Toronto, 1939); CJCCCNA, Caiserman Papers, vol. 2, 2/21, Boycott Committee, 1938–9, Mimeographed Material, printed circular of the Committee on Jewish-Gentile Relations; Donald Warren, *Radio Priest: Charles Coughlin, the Father of Hate Radio* (New York, 1996), 237; Mary Vipond, 'London Listens: The Popularity of Radio in the Depression,' *Ontario History* 88, no. 1 (1996): 49–63, 52; Geoffrey S. Smith, *To Save a Nation: American Extremism, the New Deal, and the Coming of World War II*, rev. ed. (Chicago, 1992), passim.
87 Jonathan Wagner, 'Nazi Party Membership in Canada: A Profile' *HS/SH* 14, no. 27 (1981): 233–8, 234; Jonathan F. Wagner, *Brothers beyond the Sea: National Socialism in Canada* (Waterloo, 1981), 30, 38, 73; Jean Gerber, 'Canadian Jewish Congress: Pacific Region, Part I,' *The Scribe* 10, no. 2 (1988): 4–8, 13–14, 5.
88 Herbert A. Sohn, 'Human Rights Laws in Ontario: The Role of the Jewish Community,' *CJHSJ* 4, no. 2 (1980): 99–116, 104, 106; quoted in Gerald Killan, *Protected Places: A History of Ontario's Provincial Parks System* (Toronto, 1993), 56, 86.
89 CJCCCNA, Caiserman Papers, vol. 1, 1/7, Membership Campaign, Eastern Division, 1938, Address for members of the Speakers' Committee, mimeographed; Jacques Langlais and David Rome, *Jews and French Quebecers: Two Hundred Years of Shared History* (Waterloo, 1991), 123–4.
90 Irving Abella, *A Coat of Many Colours: Two Centuries of Jewish Life in Canada* (Toronto, 1990), 190–1.
91 Marrus, *Mr. Sam: The Life and Times of Samuel Bronfman*, 261, 264, 271.
92 Esther Delisle, *The Traitor and the Jew: Anti-Semitism and the Delirium of Extremist Right-Wing Nationalism in French Canada from 1929 to 1939*, trans. Madelaine Hébert (Montreal, 1993), 36; Michael Oliver, *The Passionate Debate: The Social and Political Ideas of Quebec Nationalism* (Montreal, 1991), 180–95.
93 Delisle, *Traitor and Jew*, 25–9, 26. See 'Lionel-Adolphe Groulx,' in *The Oxford Companion to Canadian History and Literature*, ed. Norah Storey (Toronto, 1967), 332–3; Susan M. Trofimenkoff, 'Lionel-Adolphe Groulx,' in *Canadian Encyclopedia*, vol. 2 (Edmonton, 1988), 941–2; and Susan Mann Trofimenkoff, *Action Française: French Canadian Nationalism in the Twenties* (Toronto, 1975), 23, 78–9.

94 See Ramsay Cook's discussion of Canon Groulx in *Watching Quebec: Selected Essays* (Toronto, 2006), passim; Everett C. Hughes, *French Canada in Transition* (Chicago, 1963), 216–18; Delisle, *Traitor and Jew*, 39, 41; Oliver, *Passionate Debate*, 181; Lita-Rose Betcherman, *The Swastika and the Maple Leaf: Fascist Movements in Canada in the Thirties* (Toronto, 1975), 131; Edmond Turcotte, 'Sur la voie patriote,' *Le Canada*, 20 June 1934, quoted in Pierre Anctil, *Le Rendez-vous manqué: Les juifs de Montréal face au Québec de l'entre deux guerres* (Montreal, 1988), 137–8; Olivar Asselin, 'La Grève de l'internat,' *L'Ordre*, 22 and 23 June 1934, quoted in ibid., 137.

95 Marcel Hamel, 'Tu mens, juif,' *La Nation*, 12 Nov. 1936, quoted in Oliver, *Passionate Debate*, 184–5.

96 Delisle, *Traitor and Jew*, 43; Lita-Rose Betcherman, *Ernest Lapoint: Mackenzie King's Great Quebec Lieutenant* (Toronto, 2002), 221.

97 J. Keith Johnson, ed., *The Canadian Directory of Parliament 1867–1967* (Ottawa, 1968), 519; *CJC*, 22 Sept. 1933; Betcherman, *Lapointe*, 231.

98 Herbert F. Quinn, *The Union Nationale: A Study in Quebec Nationalism* (Toronto, 1963), 38, 49; *CJC*, 24 July 1936; 7 and 21 Aug. 1936; 19 March and 2 April 1937.

99 *CJC*, 23 and 30 Oct. 1936.

100 Ibid., 30 Oct. 1936, 16 Aug. 1937; *KA*, 1 May 1927; *AJYB* 38 (1936–7): 243.

101 Jack Jedwab, 'Uniting Uptowners and Downtowners: The Jewish Electorate and Quebec Provincial Politics 1927–39,' *CES/EEC* 18, no. 2 (1986): 7–19, 12, 14; *Répertoire des parlementaires québécois 1867–1978* (Quebec, 1980), 207–8.

102 Abraham M. Klein, 'The Twin Racketeers of Journalism,' *CJC*, 8 July 1932, quoted in A.M. Klein, *Beyond Sambation: Selected Essays and Editorials 1928–1955*, ed. M.W. Steinberg and Usher Caplan (Toronto, 1982), 26–9, 27, 29.

103 Brian McKenna and Susan Purcell, *Drapeau* (Toronto, 1980), 37; David Rome, 'Canada,' *AJYB* 44 (1942): 181.

104 *Congress Bulletin*, Aug. 1943, p. 7.

105 Guy W.-Richard, *Le Cimetière juif de Québec: Beth Israel Ohev Sholom* (Sillery, 2000), xxiv.

106 Abraham M. Klein, 'Quebec City Gets Another Park,' *CJC*, 18 June 1943, quoted in Steinberg and Caplan, eds, *Beyond Sambation*: 190–1. See Ruth R. Wisse, *The Modern Jewish Canon: A Journey through Language and Culture* (New York, 2000), 260.

107 Abraham M. Klein, 'Incendiary Antisemitism,' *CJC*, 26 May 1944, quoted in Steinberg and Caplan, eds, *Beyond Sambation*, 219, 220; CZA, Z4/1O/74, 'Quebec. Authorities Charged with Indifference to Acts of Violence Against Jews,' Jewish Telegraphic Agency, 25 June 1944; *Congress Bulletin*, Aug. 1943, p. 7.

108 Quoted in Paul Axelrod, *Making a Middle Class: Student Life in English Canada during the Thirties* (Montreal, 1990), 33.
109 R.D. Gidney and W.P.J. Millar, 'Medical Students at the University of Toronto, 1910–40: A Profile,' *Canadian Bulletin of Medical History* 13 (1996): 40, and 'We Wanted Our Children to Have It Better: Jewish Medical Students at the University of Toronto, 1910–1951,' *CHA Journal* 11 (2000): 109–24; A. Brian McKillop, *Matters of the Mind: The University in Ontario 1791–1951* (Toronto, 1994), 360; Martin L. Friedland, *The University of Toronto: A History* (Toronto, 2002), 352.
110 Interview with Phillip Stuchen, 29 Oct. 1996; Percy Barsky, 'How "Numerus Clausus" Was Ended in the Manitoba Medical School,' *CJHSJ* 1, no. 2 (1977): 75–81, 76; Axelrod, *Making a Middle Class*, 33; Ernest Sirluck, *First Generation: An Autobiography* (Toronto, 1996), 32, 33.
111 Lesley Marrus-Barsky, 'History of Mount Sinai Hospital' (unpublished manuscript), 27–8, 43–5; Friedland, *University of Toronto*, 352; Axelrod, *Making a Middle Class*, 34; *KA*, 21 and 27 Dec. 1927.
112 Peter B. Waite, *The Lives of Dalhousie University*, vol. 2, *1925–1980: The Old College Transformed* (Montreal, 1998), 83; Sirluck, *First Generation*, 35, 42; *Silhouette*, 30 Jan. 1936.
113 Michael Bliss, *Banting: A Biography* (Toronto, 1984), 101, 159, 179, 252.
114 Lawrence D. Stokes, 'Canada and an Academic Refugee from Nazi Germany: The Case of Gerhard Herzberg,' *CHR* 57, no. 2 (1976): 150–70, 159; Friedland, *University of Toronto*, 343; Leopold Infeld, *Why I Left Canada: Reflections on Science and Politics* (Montreal, 1978); Eli Gottesman, ed., *Who's Who in Canadian Jewry* (Montreal, 1965), 354–9; Michiel Horn, 'The Exclusive University' (unpublished manuscript), ch. 18; Axelrod, *Making a Middle Class*, 33.
115 Michael Brown, 'Lionel Gelber,' in *New Encyclopedia of Zionism and Israel*, vol. 1, ed. Geoffrey Wigoder (Madison, 1994), 460; Donald Wright, *The Professionalization of History in English Canada* (Toronto, 2005), 96. In a letter recommending Gelber for a position at United College in Winnipeg, Underhill pointed out that 'he is a Jew who comes from a cultured and well-to-do family in Toronto' (LAC, Underhill Papers, MG 30, D204, Vol. 5, file A.R.M. Lower, Underhill to Lower, 28 Feb. 1939). I am grateful to Donald Wright for sending me a photocopy of this letter; cited in ibid., 210. Regarding Bora Laskin, see Jerome E. Bickenbach, 'Lawyers, Law Professors, and Racism in Ontario,' *QQ* 96, no. 3 (1989): 585–98, 595; and Philip Girard, *Bora Laskin: Bringing Law to Life* (Toronto, 2005), 121–3.
116 Frederick W. Gibson, *1917–1961: To Serve and Yet Be Free* (Montreal, 1983), 199, 200, 202.

117 Alfred Bader, *Adventures of a Chemist Collector* (London, 1995), 43; Waite, *Lives of Dalhousie University*, vol. 2, 119. Stanley responded sympathetically to a letter from the Jewish Immigrant Aid Society of Canada, whose director, R. Kanigsberg, had written asking for Jewish refugee academic placements (Queen's University, A.R.M. Lower Papers, Box 1, file 1939, R. Kanigsberg to Carleton Stanley, 21 Jan. 1939). Stanley had copies of the letter sent to each department asking for comments or suggestions (ibid., C.B. Nickerson to all departments). See *CJC*, 7 Oct. 1921; Martin Robin, *Shades of Right: Nativist and Fascist Politics in Canada, 1920–1940* (Toronto, 1992), 85.
118 *CJR*, 11 Oct. 1935; Robin, *Shades of Right*, 14.
119 David Monod, *Store Wars: Shopkeepers and the Culture of Mass Marketing, 1890–1939* (Toronto, 1996), 92–4; Janine Stingel, *Social Discredit: Anti-Semitism, Social Credit, and the Jewish Response* (Montreal, 2000), 4, 20, 11–12, 18–19. See also Alvin Finkel, *The Social Credit Phenomenon in Alberta* (Toronto, 1989), 82; Howard Palmer, *Patterns of Prejudice: A History of Nativism in Alberta* (Toronto, 1982), 152, 153, 155–6.
120 Ibid., 157. See also Janine Stingel, 'From Father to Son: Canadian Jewry's Response to the Alberta Social Credit Party and the Reform Party of Canada,' *CJS/EJC* 9 (2001): 1–37.
121 Johnson, ed., *Canadian Directory of Parliament*, 48, 291; Finkel, *Social Credit*, 105; Michael B. Stein, *The Dynamics of Right-Wing Protest: A Political Analysis of Social Credit in Quebec* (Toronto, 1973), 50–2; See David Bercuson and Douglas Wertheimer, *A Trust Betrayed: The Keegstra Affair* (Toronto, 1985), 2–44, passim.
122 Sirluck, *First Generation*, 8, 21, 23, 60, 67.
123 Robert England, *The Central European Immigrant in Canada* (Toronto, 1929), 92.
124 Orest T. Martynowych, *Ukrainians in Canada: The Formative Period, 1891–1924* (Edmonton, 1991), 89, 91, 238, 294, 204.
125 Stingel, Social Discredit, 199; Johnson, ed. *Canadian Directory of Parliament*, 272.
126 Sonia Riddoch to author, 15 July 1997; *Ukrainian Canadian*, 29 Aug. 1923.
127 Daniel Stone, 'Winnipeg's Polish-Language Newspapers and Their Attitude towards Jews and Ukrainians between the Two World Wars,' *CES/EEC* 21, no. 2 (1989): 27–37, 38, 29–30, 30–1.
128 This account is based on Cyril H. Levitt and William Shaffir, *The Riot at Christie Pits* (Toronto, 1987).
129 Irving Abella, 'Jews, Human Rights, and the Making of a New Canada,' *Journal of the Canadian Historical Association* (Ottawa, 2000), 3–15, 4.

130 See Sam A. Sharon, 'Tolerance Was Common in Rural Quebec,' *Montreal Gazette*, 6 March 1997; Mordecai Richler, *Oh Canada! Oh Quebec! Requiem for a Divided Country* (Toronto, 1992), 79–80; Anctil, 'Interlude of Hostility: Judeo-Christian Relations in Quebec in the Interwar Period, 1919–1939,' in Behiels, ed., *Quebec since 1800: Selected Readings*, 398–424; Speisman, 'Anti-semitism in Ontario: The Twentieth Century,' in Davies, ed., *Antisemitism in Canada*, 113–33, 121.

131 Barney Danson, *Not Bad for a Sergeant: The Memoirs of Barney Danson* (Toronto, 2002), 24.

10. 'Not Complex or Sophisticated': Interwar Zionism

1 See Bernard Figler, *Lillian and Archie Freiman: Biographies* (Montreal, 1962); Arthur D. Hart, ed., *The Jew in Canada: A Complete Record of Canadian Jewry from the Days of the French Regime to the Present Time* (Montreal, 1926), 276.

2 Hart, ed., *Jew in Canada*, 317.

3 Ibid., 318; PAM, MG 10, F3 (MG2J2), Harry Wilder to Chaim Weizmann, 20 Jan. 1932.

4 See Joseph B. Glass, 'Isolation and Alienation: Factors in the Growth of Zionism in the Canadian Prairies, 1917–1939,' *CJS* 9 (2001): 85–123; CZA, KKL5/365, 'Minutes of ZOC Convention, 1924,' 30; Louis Rosenberg, *Canada's Jews: A Social and Economic Study of the Jews in Canada* (Montreal, 1939), 197.

5 See Michael Brown, 'The Americanization of Canadian Zionism, 1917–1982,' in *Contemporary Jewry: Studies in Honor of Moshe Davis*, ed. Geoffrey Wigoder (Jerusalem, 1984), 129–58; 'Divergent Paths: Early Zionism in Canada and the United States,' *JSS* 44, no. 2 (1982): 149–68; and 'Canada and the Holy Land: Some North American Similarities and Differences,' in *With Eyes towards Zion III: Western Societies and the Holy Land*, ed. Moshe Davis and Yehoshua Ben-Arieh (New York, 1991), 77–91.

6 See Michael Berkowitz, *Western Jewry and the Zionist Project, 1914–1933* (Cambridge, 1997), iii; CZA, KKL5/365, 'Minutes of the Nineteenth Convention Zionist Organization of Canada Inc., 1924.'

7 See Gideon Shimoni, *The Zionist Ideology* (Hanover, 1995).

8 Zachariah Kay, *Canada and Palestine: The Politics of Non-Commitment* (Jerusalem, 1978), 34; WA, 10.7.22, Freiman to Joseph Cowen, 10 July 1922.

9 CZA, KKL5/365, 'Minutes, 1924,' 3.

10 CZA, Z4/1402, Leon Goldman to Chaim Weizmann, 8 April 1919.

11 CZA, KKL5/L5/318, Menachem M. Ussishkin to Zlotnick, 11 March 1929; Z4/1405, Goldman to Levin, 17 Dec. 1919.

12 Ibid., Goldman to Zionist Organization, Central Office, London, 25 Feb. 1920; Goldman to B. Goldberg, 24 Dec. 1919.
13 CZA, KKL5/3 19/2, Julius Berger to KKL, 27 Dec. 1927; KKL5/379, JNF (New York) to KKL (Jerusalem), 9 and 21 April 1926 (translated from the German by Tom Wien).
14 Quoted in Michael Brown, 'A Case of Limited Vision: Jabotinsky on Canada and the United States' *CJS* 1 (1993): 1–25, 3–4.
15 WA, Weizmann to Dr D. Feiwel, London, 21 Dec. 1923.
16 WA, Weizmann to Freiman, 14 Dec. 1922; Weizmann to Freiman, 5 Feb. 1923. Weizmann later wrote, 'I might add that [Beaverbrook] has somewhat moderated his activities since I wrote to you before, but at the same time, it is very desirable that we should have authentic information about him in reserve, to be used as occasion may demand.'
17 WA, Freiman to Weizmann, 27 Feb. 1928; Freiman to Weizmann, 8 Sept. 1936; Freiman to Weizmann, 14 Aug. 1936.
18 Bernard Figler, *History of the Zionist Ideal in Canada* (n.p., 1962), reprinted from *CJC*, 3–17 Nov. 1961; George G. Greene, 'The Hadassah Organization in Canada,' in *Hadassah Jubilee, Tenth Anniversary Toronto: Hadassah Achievement in Palestine*, ed. Louis Rasminsky (Toronto, 1927), 136, 145; 'Activities of Hadassah: Girl's Domestic and Agricultural Science School,' in Hart, ed., *Jew in Canada*, 282–7.
19 See Frances Swyripa, *Wedded to the Cause: Ukrainian-Canadian Women and Ethnic Identity, 1891–1991* (Toronto, 1993), 13–19.
20 PAM, MG10, F3 (MG2J31), *Canadian Hadassah Silver Jubilee, Western Division 1917–1942* (Winnipeg, 1942); CZA, KKL5/365, 'Minutes, 1924,' 41.
21 LAC, MG 28, V74, vol. 1, 'Minutes of the Third Convention of the Hadassah Organization of Canada. Toronto, 9 Jan. 1924. King Edward Hotel.'
22 Rachel Schlesinger, 'Volunteers for a Dream,' *CJHSJ* 10, no. 1 (1988): 20–33; LAC, MG 28, V74, vol. 15, 'General Correspondence, Hadassah-WIZO, Jan.-May 1935.'
23 Quoted in Schlesinger, 'Volunteers,' 25.
24 LAC, MG 28, V74, vol. 15, 'National Executive, 1939,' Minutes, 14 March 1939.
25 Quoted in Schlesinger, 'Volunteers,' 29.
26 Paula J. Draper and Janice B. Karlinsky, 'Jewish Women as Volunteers,' *Polyphony* 8, nos. 1–2 (1986): 37–9; Janice B. Karlinsky, 'The Pioneer Women's Organization: A Case Study of Jewish Women in Toronto' (MA thesis, University of Toronto, 1979), 18, 21, 106, 117; 145; *Pioneer Women* (Oct. 1935), quoted in Karlinsky, 'Pioneer Women's Organization,' 47, 51, 56, 76, 62.

27 Moe Levitt, 'The Federation of Young Judaea of Canada,' in Hart, ed., *Jew in Canada*, 289.
28 CZA, KKL5/365 'Minutes, 1924,' 43.
29 PAM, MG 10, F3 (MG2J6), *Year Book of Young Judaea, 1931* (Montreal, 1931), 7, 10.
30 *Jewish History Must Centre on Palestine: A Handbook on Club Leadership for Leaders of Young Judaea and Other Jewish Youth Clubs*, rev. ed. (Montreal, 1927), 22.
31 Lionel M. Gelber, 'Young Judaea in Canada,' in Rasminsky, ed., *Hadassah Jubilee*, 177.
32 See Samuel Grand, 'A History of Zionist Youth Organizations in the United States from Their Inception to 1940' (PhD diss., Columbia University, 1958); Ezra Mendelsohn, *Zionism in Poland: The Formative Years, 1915–1926* (New Haven, 1981), 72, 278–9, 285–99.
33 CJCCCNA, Souvenir Program, Second Annual Dance: Hashomer Clubs of Montreal, 19 Oct. 1924.
34 CJCCCNA, CJN clipping, 1980; Ariel Hurwitz, ed., *Against the Stream: Seven Decades of Hashomer Hatzair in North America* (Tel Aviv, 1994), 7, 51–2, 256.
35 Mendelsohn, *Zionism in Poland*, 320. See Moshe Cohen, 'An American Labor Zionist Youth Movement: Yunge Poalei Zion, the "Young Workers of Zion,"' in *Builders and Dreamers: Habonim Labor Zionist Youth in North America*, ed. B.J. Goldberg and Elliot King (New York, 1993), 39.
36 *EJ*, 11:109–11; CZA, KH1/15/1, Report to Congress, Sept. 1921, 'Canada'; ibid., Keren Hayesod Resolutions of the Convention of the Canadian Zionists in Montreal, 31/1/21; Melvin Urofsky, *American Zionism from Herzl to the Holocaust* (Garden City, NJ, 1976), 268–9.
37 See Thomas P. Socknat, *Witness against War: Pacificism in Canada, 1900–1945* (Toronto, 1987), 125–6; Maurice Eisendrath, *The Never Failing Stream* (Toronto, 1939), 232.
38 Stephen A. Speisman, *The Jews of Toronto: A History to 1937* (Toronto, 1979), 242; Meyer Weisgal, *So Far: An Autobiography* (Jerusalem, 1971), 92.
39 Shloime Perel, 'History of the UJPO in Canada, 1926–1949,' unpublished manuscript, ch. 9, p. 8; Philip Halperin, 'Down with the Religious Mold,' *Der Kamf* 11 (1929), quoted in ibid., ch. 10, pp. 5, 10.
40 CZA, KKL5/318, Dr M.S. Rady to M. Ussishkin, 20 Feb. 1929.
41 CZA, KKL5/466, J.L. Zlotnick to M. Ussishkin, 11 Aug. 1931; National Council of the ZOC, 5 Jan. 1931.
42 CZA, S6/1758, Rabbi Schwartz to A. Dobkin, Immigration Department of the Jewish Agency, Jerusalem, 10 Jan. 1936; Walter Laqueur, *A History of Zionism* (London, 1972), 326–7.

43 CZA, KKL5/318, Zlotnick to Ussishkin, 9 Feb. 1928. In 1923, Rabbi Brickner was reported to have told Arthur Ruppin 'that there is a favourable disposition for investments [in Palestine] in Toronto' (WA, Arthur Ruppin to Chaim Weizmann, 15 March 1923). See Zvi Cohen, ed., *Canadian Jewry: Prominent Jews of Canada – a History of Canadian Jewry, Especially of the Present Time, through Reviews and Biographical Sketches* (Toronto, 1933), 258; Irit Amit, 'Business and Zionism,' paper presented to the Jewish Geography Conference, University of Maryland, April 1995; Yossi Katz, *The Business of Settlement: Private Entrepreneurship in the Jewish Settlement of Palestine, 1900–1914* (Jerusalem, 1994), 208, 214.
44 CZA, S6/3814, Jesse Schwartz to J.N. Behar, 30 April 1936; Jesse Schwartz to C. Barlas, 25 Oct. and 1 Nov. 1935; Ben Dunkelman, *Dual Allegiance: An Autobiography* (Toronto, 1976), 35, 39.
45 See Molly Lyon Bar-David, *My Promised Land* (1953), and Sylvia M. Gelber, *No Balm in Gilead: A Personal Retrospective of Mandate Days in Palestine* (Ottawa, 1989).
46 Chaim Weizmann, *Trial and Error: The Autobiography of Chaim Weizmann* (London, 1949), 272.
47 WA, Freiman to Weizmann, 22 Dec. 1921.
48 CZA, KH1/15/1, Secretary of Board of Directors, KH to ZOC, 7 Nov. 1922; Goldman to KH, London, 20 Nov. 1922.
49 CZA, KH4/15/2, Goldstein to KH, London, 7 March 1923; KH1/15/1, Goldstein to KH, London, 13 April 1923.
50 Ibid., Goldstein to KH, London, 23 March 1923; *CJC*, 6 April 1923; KH4/15/2, minutes of Executive Committee, ZOC, 26 March 1923.
51 CZA, KH4C/763, Goldman to KH, London, 11 March 1924; KH to ZOC, 19 March 1924; Leon Goldman to KH, 7 April 1924; KH1/15/A2.
52 CZA, KH4C/763, Rebelsky to KH, London, 19 March 1925, translated from the Hebrew.
53 CZA, KH1/1511, Dr Zweig, KKL, The Hague, to KH, London, 3 March 1922; Leon Goldman to JNF, The Hague, 22 March 1922.
54 Ibid., Leon Goldman to KH, London, 10 April 1922; KKL5/364, KKL to Zlotnick, 14 Feb. 1924.
55 Ibid., Goldman to JNF, Jerusalem, 12 March 1924; Head Office of KKL to Leon Goldman, 18 March 1924.
56 Ibid., Zlotnick to JNF, Jerusalem, 29 July 1924; KKL5/366, 'Report of the Jewish National Fund in Canada for the Period 7 Dec. 1923–8 Dec. 1925'; 'Report to the XIV Congress of the Zionist Organization of Canada, Inc., for the Period 1 Jun. 1923 to 31 May 1925.'
57 CZA, KKL5/364, 'Jewish National Fund Activities in Canada for the First Three Months of 1924.'

58 CZA, KKL, Norman Shiffer to Dr Julius Berger, JNF Bureau, New York, 2 March 1926; KKL5/375, Shiffer to JNF Bureau, Jerusalem, 8 May 1927; 'Jewish National Fund Conference: Resolutions Adopted at the Second Annual Conference Held in Watrous, Sask., 1 and 2 Aug. 1926'; Shiffer to JNF Bureau, Jerusalem, 30 Nov. 1926; KKL5/379, Zlotnick to Berger, New York, 16 March 1926.
59 CZA, KKL5/366, Epstein, Jerusalem, to Caiserman, Montreal, 29 June 1925; KKL5/367 and KKL5/366, JNF Bureau, Jerusalem, to Zlotnick, 11 Nov. 1925; KKL5/368, printed reports of Zionist activity in Canada for Winnipeg Convention of ZOC.
60 CZA, Z4/3589, vol. 6, memorandum to the members of the Executive from Colonel Kisch, 28 Aug. 1927.
61 CZA, KKL5/319, Ussishkin to ZOC, 3 May 1929; KKL5/466, Zlotnick to JNF, Jerusalem, n.d.
62 CZA, KKL5/465, Zlotnick to Elias Epstein, New York, 31 Dec. 1930; KKL5/466, Freiman to Ussishkin, 7 April 1932.
63 CZA, Z4/1405, Leon Goldman to Zionist Organization, Central Office, London, 9 June 1920; KH4, B/1548, note to Mr Hermann.
64 CZA, KKL5/318, 'Minutes of the Meeting of the National Council of the Zionist Organization of Canada, 19 Dec. 1927'; KKL5/3192; A.B.B., 'The Mizrachi Holdup,' *CJR*, 22 March 1929; KKL5/3192, Zlotnick to Ussishkin, Jerusalem, 23 April 1929; KH4, B/555, Samuel Schwisberg to Leib Yaffe, London, 9 March 1940.
65 Brown, 'Case of Limited Vision,' 9–10; CZA, KH4, B/555, extracts from *Jewish Daily Bulletin*, 9 March 1936; Beit Jabotinsky Archives (Tel Aviv), 2/1/40 G, Executive Committee, World Union of Zionist Revisionists to Union of Zionist-Revisionists Canada, 9 Oct. 1931.
66 Beit Jabotinsky Archives, 2/1/40 G, A.J.E to Zionist Revisionists of Canada, 29 Dec. 1932.
67 Beit Jabotinsky Archives, 1/1/40 G, 'Programme for the Winter Activities,' Zionist Revisionists of Canada, Central Committee.
68 PAM, MG10, F3 (MG6AtO), extracts from the diary of H.L. and M. Wiedman, *Impressions of Eretz Israel 1923* (Winnipeg, 1923); Kenneth I. Cleator and Harry J. Stern, *Harry Joshua Stern: A Rabbi's Journey* (New York, 1981), 97.
69 WA, Freiman to Weizmann, 10 June 1929; Cleator and Stern, *Harry Joshua Stern*, 97.
70 CZA, KKL5/366, 'Summary of Report Western Trip. 6 Aug. to 13 Dec. 1925,' enclosed by Hananiah Caiserman to Mr Epstein, Jerusalem, 25 Dec. 1925.
71 CZA, KKL5/374, E.M. Epstein, Jerusalem, to H. Caiserman, 20 Aug. 1925.

72 CZA, S5/468, 'Joint Statement of the Zionist Organizations in Canada,' Special Meeting of the National Council of the ZOC and the National Executives of the Poale-Zion-Zeire Zion Organization of Canada and the Mizrachi Organization of Canada, 10 July 1938.
73 WA, Weizmann to Freiman, 8 July 1934.
74 See Jacob Katzman, *Commitment: The Labor Zionist Lifestyle in America* (New York, 1976).
75 See Rosenberg, *Canada's Jews*, 160 and ch. 19.
76 Michael Brown, 'Samuel Jacob Zacks,' in *New Encyclopedia of Zionism and Israel*, vol. 2, ed. Geoffrey Wigoder (Madison, 1994), 1429.
77 Christopher Armstrong, 'Moose Pastures and Mergers: The Ontario Securities Commission and the Evolution of Share Markets in Canada, 1940–1980,' unpublished manuscript, pp. 17–18.
78 LAC, MG 31, H113, Steven Barber Papers, vol. 27, file 9, Weizmann to Harry Batshaw, 19 May 1941.
79 LAC, MG 30, C144, Samuel J. Zacks Papers, vol. 5, 'Chaim Weizmann,' Zacks to Weizmann, 25 Jan. 1943.
80 Ibid., Weizmann to Zacks, 16 April 1943.
81 Ibid., vol. 2, 'Sam Drache, Winnipeg 1943,' Zacks to Drache, 22 Sept. 1943.
82 Ibid., vol. 3, 'Sam Jacobson, 1943,' Zacks to Jacobson, 22 Dec. 1943.
83 Michael Brown, 'Zionism in Canada: World War II and the War of Independence,' in Wigoder, ed., *Encyclopedia of Zionism*, 1:245.
84 See Bernard Wasserstein, *Britain and the Jews of Europe 1933–1945* (Oxford, 1979).
85 Alon Gal, *David Ben-Gurion and the American Alignment for a Jewish State* (Jerusalem, 1991), 180.
86 Ibid., 249.
87 Dr I.M. Rabinovitch, who gave a lecture to the Canadian Club of Montreal in October 1946 entitled 'The Menace of Political Zionism,' was condemned by the local rabbinical association for attacking 'the greatest recreative force in Jewish life today.' The rabbis claimed to 'speak in the name of all our colleagues when we express our determination to continue espousing the cause of a legally and publicly recognized national home for the Jews in Palestine as inspired by our Torah and reaffirmed by the Zionist ideal' (LAC, MG 30, C144, Samuel J. Zacks Papers, vol. 7, 'Oct.–Dec. 1946,' statement by Montreal Rabbinical Association).
88 See Kay, *Canada and Palestine: The Politics of Non-Commitment*; and David J. Bercuson, *Canada and the Birth of Israel: A Study in Canadian Foreign Policy* (Toronto, 1985), which provides a comprehensive treatment of this subject.
89 Walter Laqueur, *History of Zionism* (New York, 1978), 551.

90 Bercuson, *Canada and the Birth of Israel*, 23.
91 LAC, MG 30, C144, Samuel J. Zacks Papers, vol. 6, 'Henry F. Janes, Canada-Palestine Committee, 1943–46,' confidential report from Henry F. Janes – The Rt. Hon. W.L.M. King's meeting with delegation from the Canadian Palestine Committee, the Canadian Christian Council, and the Zionist Organization of Canada on 31 March 1944.
92 Ibid.
93 Ibid., 'Memorandum on the Jewish National Home in Palestine,' 14 July 1945.
94 Bercuson, *Canada and the Birth of Israel*, 23.
95 Kay, *Canada and Palestine*, 88.
96 LAC, MG 30, C144, Samuel J. Zacks Papers, passim and especially vol. 10, 'Henry F. Janes.' Janes's reports to Zacks carefully documented press coverage.
97 Ibid., vol. 1, 'Harry Batshaw 1944,' minutes of Public Relations Committee meeting, 13 Jan. 1944, p. 2.
98 Ibid., vol. 2, 'Irwin Dorfman, Winnipeg,' Irwin Dorfman to Zacks, 24 Nov. 1943.
99 Ibid.
100 Ibid.
101 Ibid., Henry F. Janes to Zacks, 13 Jan. 1944. Rabbi Stern, the spiritual leader of Temple Emanu-el in Montreal since 1928, was an ardent and active Zionist, unlike most of the Reform rabbinate. See his book *The Jewish Spirit Triumphant: A Collection of Addresses* (New York, 1943); and Cleator and Stern, *Harry Joshua Stern: A Rabbi's Journey*.
102 LAC, MG 30, C144, Samuel J. Zacks Papers, vol. 2, Zacks to Dorfman, 16 Dec. 1943.
103 Ibid., vol. 10, 'Canadian Palestine Committee, 1944.'
104 Ibid., 'Henry F. Janes,' Janes to Rabbi Schwartz, 9 Dec. 1943.
105 Ibid., 'Canadian Palestine Committee, 1944.'
106 LAC, MG 26, 14, William Lyon Mackenzie King Papers, Ellsworth Flavelle to King, 9 Oct. 1945, 321723 (microfilm C-9873).
107 LAC, MG 30, C144, Samuel J. Zacks Papers, vol. 2, 'Sam J. Drache,' Zacks to Sam Drache, 9 Nov. 1943.
108 Ibid., vol. 1, 'Harry Batshaw, 1944,' David Rome to Harry Batshaw, 10 Nov. 1944.
109 Ibid., 'Harry Batshaw, Montreal 1946–47,' Report #4 on Palestine and Zionism.
110 Ibid., vol. 3, 'J.M. Goldenberg,' J.M. Goldenberg to Zacks, 20 June 1946.
111 Ibid., 'I.M. Gringorten,' Gringorten to Zacks, 11 Oct. 1945.

112 Ibid., Mowat to Zacks, 21 Nov. 1944.
113 Ibid., Zacks to Mowat, 23 Nov. 1944.
114 Ibid., Mowat to Zacks, 26 Nov. 1944.
115 Ibid., vol. 2, 'Canadian Palestine Com. 1947,' Mowat to Harry Batshaw, 21 Feb. 1947.
116 Ibid., vol. 1, 'Harry Batshaw, 1945,' 'Canadian Editors Look at Palestine,' 2 Oct. 1946, memorandum from Harry Batshaw, K.C, no. 2.
117 Ibid.
118 Ibid., 'Canadian Editors Look at Palestine,' 25 Oct. 1946, memorandum on publicity, no. 5.
119 Bercuson, *Canada and the Birth of Israel*, 37, 41, 43, 47.
120 LAC, MG 30, C144, Samuel J. Zacks Papers, vol. 7, Jan.–March 1947.
121 Ibid., vol. 1, 'Canadian Palestine Committee,' Mowat to Zacks, 7 April 1948.
122 Ibid., vol. 4, 'Harry Rosenthal, Windsor,' Harry Rosenthal to R.M. Harrison, 28 May 1947.
123 Shabtai Teveth, *Ben-Gurion: The Burning Ground, 1886–1948* (Boston, 1987), 764.
124 LAC, MG 30, C144, Samuel J. Zacks Papers, vol. 6, 'Oct.–Dec. 1944,' Jesse Schwartz to S.J. Zacks, 4 Oct. 1943; Zacks to Schwisberg, 4 Nov. 1944; Schwisberg to Zacks, 6 Nov. 1944.
125 Ibid., 'Samuel Jacobson, 1946,' Sam Jacobson to Zacks, 3 Jan. 1944.
126 Ibid., vol. 3, 'Samuel Jacobson, 1943,' Jacobson to Zacks, 26 July 1943.
127 CJCCCNA, 'Hechalutz Bulletin,' March 1941, n.p.
128 Chaim I. Waxman, *American Aliyah: Portrait of an Innovative Migration Movement* (Detroit, 1989), 83.
129 CJCCCNA, *Toward a Positive Zionism* (Hashomer Hatzair, Canadian Region, n.d.), 11.
130 CJCCCNA, 'Genesis ... the First Month at the Shomria Farm, Prescott, Ontario.'
131 CZA, S6/2 1 69, Joseph Israeli, New York, to Abe Herman, Jerusalem, 15 Feb. 1944.
132 LAC, MG 30, C144, Samuel J. Zacks Papers, vol. 9, 'National Executive Board,' minutes, 17 July 1944.
133 Ibid., 'Meyer Weisgal,' 3 Sept. 1944.
134 For an extended discussion of the turmoil in Young Judaea over *Aliyah*, see my *Branching Out: The Transformation of the Canadian Jewish Community* (Toronto, 1998), 249–52.
135 See Mordecai Richler, 'Montreal, 1947: "We Danced the Hora in the Middle of the Street,"' from 'My Sort of War,' *New Statesman*, 4 Sept. 1964, in Goldberg and King, eds, *Builders and Dreamers*, 126–9.
136 Mordecai Richler, *This Year in Jerusalem* (Toronto, 1994), 31.

137 *Camp Kadimah: The First Fifty Years 1943–1993* (Halifax, 1993), 6.
138 Sheva Medjuck, *The Jews of Atlantic Canada* (St John's, 1986), passim.
139 Interview with Professor Mervin Butovsky, 27 Nov. 1996.
140 There were exceptional small communities in which organizations other than the ZOC or Hadassah existed briefly. During the 1940s, Welland had a Labour Zionist group for some years, and Kingston had a Mizrachi nucleus at the same time.
141 LAC, MG 30, C144, Samuel J. Zacks Papers, vol. 2, 'Joseph N. Frank, Montreal,' Zacks to Frank, 12 Nov. 1946.
142 Richler, *This Year in Jerusalem*, 33–4.
143 See David J. Bercuson, *The Secret Army* (Toronto, 1983), and 'Illegal Corvettes: Canadian Blockade Runners to Palestine, 1946–1949,' *CJHSJ* 6, no. 1 (1982): 3–16; Dunkelman, *Dual Allegiance*; and LAC, MG 30, C144, Samuel J. Zacks Papers, vol. 12, File 'Israel Supply, 1948–56,' Teddy Kollek to Sam Zacks, 14 Sept. 1948.
144 LAC, MG 30, C144, Samuel J. Zacks Papers, vol. 1, 'Leon D. Crestohl,' Zacks to Leon D. Crestohl, 26 Aug. 1948.
145 Bercuson, *The Secret Army*, 45, J.K. Johnson, ed., *The Canadian Directory of Parliament 1867–1967* (Ottawa, 1968), 143.
146 LAC, RG 146, CSIS file on UJPO, 179–80, W.M. Brady Re Montreal Jewish Youth Council 'United Palestine Appeal,' 15 March 1948.
147 Eddy Kaplansky, *The First Flyers: Aircrew Personnel in the War of Independence* (Israel Defence Forces, Air Force History Branch, 1993), 24–5, 34–5.
148 See Bercuson, *The Secret Army*, passim; and Dunkelman, *Dual Allegiance*, passim.
149 Bercuson, *The Secret Army*, 103.
150 LAC, MG 30, C144, Samuel J. Zacks Papers, vol. 8, H. Olyan to Appel, 7 Oct. 1948 (enclosure).
151 Ben-Zion Shapiro Papers (on loan to author), 'Resolution of the Formation of Garin Aleph shel Yehuda Hatzair B'Canada, 22 Aug. 1951.'
152 LAC, MG 30, C144, Samuel J. Zacks Papers, vol. 1, 'Harry Batshaw,' Zacks to Batshaw, 10 Dec. 1951.

11. Into Battle

1 Michael R. Marrus, *Mr. Sam: The Life and Times of Samuel Bronfman* (Toronto, 1991), 279–80.
2 Jeffrey A. Keshen, *Saint, Sinners and Soldiers* (Vancouver, 2004), 39–40; Duff Crerar, *Padres in No Man's Land: Canadian Chaplains and the Great War* (Montreal, 1995), 38, 68, 276, 301.

3 Marrus, *Mr. Sam*, 281–4.
4 CJCCCNA, DA 18/ 318/, memorandum to War Efforts Committee from William Abrams, 14 July 1942.
5 Cyril Levitt and William Shaffir, 'The Press Reports: Toronto Learns about Nazi Atrocities in 1933,' in *False Havens: The British Empire and the Holocaust*, ed. Paul R. Bartrop (New York, 1995), 21–51, 21.
6 Quoted in William R. Young, 'Building Citizenship: English Canada and Propaganda during the Second War,' *JCS* 16, nos. 3–4 (Fall/Winter 1981): 121–32, 122.
7 J.L. Granatstein, 'A Half Century On: The Veteran's Experience,' in *The Veterans' Charter and Post-World War II Canada*, ed. Peter Neary and J.L. Granatstein (Montreal, 1998), 224–34, 227.
8 Interviw with Barney Danson, 30 June 1994. See his *Not Bad for a Sergeant* (Toronto, 2002).
9 Ernest Sirluck, *First Generation: An Autobiography* (Toronto, 1996), 97, 104; Martin Roher, *Days of Living: The Journal of Martin Roher* (Toronto, 1959), v.
10 Ben Dunkelman, *Dual Allegiance* (Toronto, 1976), 45–6; Harold Rubin, *Those Pesky Weeds: An Autobiography* (Ottawa, 1992), 101.
11 Monty Berger, with Brian J. Street, *Invasion without Tears: The Story of Canada's Top-Scoring Spitfire Wing in Europe during the Second World War* (Toronto, 1994), 209.
12 CJCCCNA, Fred Rose Papers, 'Letter from a Hero's Mother to the Mothers and Fathers of Cartier' (leaflet, 1943).
13 Peter Oliver, *Unlikely Tory: The Life and Politics of Allan Grossman* (Toronto, 1985), 32; Irving Layton, *Waiting for the Messiah* (Don Mills, 1985), 207–8, 213–14.
14 Wayne E. Edmonstone, *Nathan Cohen: The Making of a Critic* (Toronto, 1977), 17; David Lewis, *The Good Fight: Political Memoirs, 1909–1958* (Toronto, 1981), 168; Lawrence Freiman, *Don't Fall Off the Rocking Horse* (Toronto, 1978), 75; Mordecai Richler, 'Montreal, 1947: "We Danced the Hora in the Middle of the Street,"' from 'My Sort of War,' *New Statesman*, 4 Sept. 1964, reprinted in *Builders and Dreamers: Habonim Labor Zionist Youth in North America*, ed. B.J. Goldberg and Elliot King (New York, 1993), 126–9, 127.
15 'The War Efforts Committee of Canadian Jewish Congress,' ed. Vladimir Grossman, in *Canadian Jewish Year Book III, 1941–1942* (Montreal, 1941), 68; Irwin Pollock, 'Civil Rights and the Anglo-Jewish Press in Canada: 1930–1970,' (MA thesis, Wilfrid Laurier University, 1979), 16.
16 Glen., A.I. Shumiatcher Papers, 'Report Submitted by Mr. M.H. Myerson, Director of Recruiting Activities, Eastern Division,' n.d. [1941?].
17 Interview with Rabbi David Monson, June 1995.

18 Shloime Perel, 'History of the UJPO in Canada, 1926–1949,' unpublished manuscript, ch. 17, p. 4. See also Irving Abella, ed., 'Portrait of a Jewish Professional Revolutionary: The Recollections of Joshua Gershman,' *Labour / Le Travailleur* 2 (1977): 185–213, 208; Ben Lappin, 'When Michoels and Feffer Came to Toronto,' *Viewpoints* 7, no. 2 (1972): 43–64, 55–6.
19 CJCCCNA, Finding Aid to War Efforts Committee Records, Statistical Highlights, CJC 'Yearboxes,' ZA 1945, box 3, file 46. See also David Rome, 'Canada,' *AJYB* 49 (1948): 288; Charles P. Stacey, *Arms, Men and Governments* (Ottawa, 1971), 416; *Women's Voices: Personal Recollections,* Jewish Life and Times, no. 7 (1998), 91.
20 *Census of Canada* (1941), vol. 3, 14, 204; Stacey, *Arms, Men and Governments,* 590; Max Bookman, 'Canadian Jews in Uniform,' in *Canadian Jewish Reference Book and Directory,* ed. Eli Gottesman (Ottawa, 1963), 111.
21 See Daniel Byers, 'Canada's "Zombies": A Portrait of Canadian Conscripts and Their Experiences during the Second World War,' in *Forging A Nation: Canadian Military Experience,* ed. Bernd Horn (St Catharines, 2002), 155–76; Stacey, *Arms, Men and Governments,* 66.
22 See Louis Rosenberg, *Canada's Jews: A Social and Economic Study of the Jews in Canada* (Montreal, 1939), 265; Brian Nolan, *King's War: Mackenzie King and the Politics of War* (Toronto, 1988), 117.
23 Sirluck, *First Generation,* 93.
24 Department of National Defence, Directorate of History and Heritage, File #112.3S2009 (D262), 'Reinforcements and Recruiting – Generally – Oct. 1940 / Feb. 1941,' Colonel, director of staff duties to director of mobilization and recruiting, 20 Nov. 1941. I am grateful to Professor Larry Stokes, who discovered this letter and kindly photocopied it for me.
25 Sirluck, *First Generation,* 68, 83.
26 Interview with Sam Shapiro, 2 Feb. 2006; telephone interview with Norman Shnier, 4 Jan. 2006; Manuel Raber, *Manny Goes to War: The War Memoir of Manuel Raber* (Medicine Hat, 1999), 223. This rare and wonderfully descriptive memoir describes the training, social life (!), combat, and prisoner-of-war experiences of this young RCAF volunteer from Medicine Hat, Alberta.
27 *Globe and Mail,* 27 Sept. 2006.
28 LAC, MG 30, Louis Rosenberg Papers, vol. 26 'Jews in Canada's Defence Forces.'
29 'Military Service,' *EJ,* 2:1550–68.
30 Glen., A.I. Shumiatcher Papers, box 6, file 49, *Winnipeg Free Press,* 6 Sept. 1940; Gregory S. Kealey and Reg Whitaker, eds, *RCMP Security Bulletins: The War Series, 1939–1941* (St John's, 1989), 311, 312, 381–2.

31 Young, 'Building Citizenship,' 124; CJCCCNA, DA 18, 5/3B, Saul Hayes to CJC members, n.d.
32 David Rome, 'Canada,' *AJYB* 45 (1943): 225; Byers, 'Canada's "Zombies",' app. 5.
33 There were an additional 163 Canadian Jewish personnel in the Allied forces. See Bookman, 'Canadian Jews in Uniform,' 111; and Stacey, *Arms, Men and Governments*, 590.
34 Glen., A.I. Shumiatcher Papers, box 7, files 49, 50; CJCCCNA, Caiserman Papers, vol. 4, reports about immigration (1920–50), antisemitism (1949), education (1934); CJCCCNA, Pamphlet Collection.
35 Abraham M. Klein, 'The Plebiscite,' *CJC*, 24 April 1942, quoted in A.M. Klein, *Beyond Sambation: Selected Essays and Editorials 1928–1955*, ed. M.W. Steinberg and Usher Caplan (Toronto, 1982), 141–3, 142; J.L. Granatstein, *Canada's War: The Politics of the Mackenzie King Government, 1939–1945* (Toronto, 1975), 227.
36 W. Victor Sefton, 'The European Holocaust – Who Knew What and When – a Canadian Aspect,' *CJHSJ* 2, no. 2 (1978): 121–33, 128–9; Barbara Schober, 'Holocaust Commemoration in Vancouver, B.C., 1943–75' (MA thesis, University of British Columbia, 2001), p. 29..
37 CJCCCNA, DA 18, 3/14A, Rabbi Babb to H/Capt. Cass, 21 June 1943; 6/6, Levy to H/Capt. H.H. MacSween, Chaplain (P) HQ Command, 2 Corps, Tpt. Coln. RCASC, 7 March 1944; Rubin, *Pesky Weeds*, 104.
38 CJCCCNA, DA 18, 1/3, N.J. Direnfeld to Gershon Levi, 22 Nov. 1942; J.L. Granatstein, *The Generals: The Canadian Army's Senior Commanders in the Second World War* (Toronto, 1993), 153; interview with Maj.-Gen. Robert Rothschild, 18 July 1994; LAC, MG 30, 0225, Rabbi Cass Papers, vol. 9, app. 3, section I, 25.
39 Interview with Edwin A. Goodman, Q.C., 30 June 1994; Edwin A. Goodman, *Life of the Party: The Memoirs of Eddie Goodman* (Toronto, 1988), 18; interview with Ephraim Diamond, 19 June 1995.
40 Dunkelman, *Dual Allegiance*, 46.
41 Department of National Defence, Directorate of History and Heritage, File #112.3S2009 (D262), 'Reinforcements and Recruiting – Generally – Oct. 1940 / Feb. 1941,' Colonel, director of staff duties to director of mobilization and recruiting, 20 Nov. 1941.
42 Interview with Sam Finkelstein, 29 June 1994; Barney Danson to the author, 28 Aug. 1994.
43 Interview with Lt. Col. Ian Hodson, RCR (Retired), 25 Feb. 1997. See also 'The Jewish Captain,' in Barry Broadfoot, *Six War Years: Memories of Canadians at Home and Abroad* (Toronto, 1974), 326–7.
44 Dave McIntosh, *Terror in the Starboard Seat* (Don Mills, 1980), 105.

45 Interview with Rabbi David Monson, June 1995.
46 See Rabbi S. Gershon Levi, *Breaking New Ground: The Struggle for a Jewish Chaplaincy in Canada* (Montreal, 1994).
47 *Prayer Book for Jewish Members of H. M.* Forces (London, 1940), 4.
48 CJCCCNA, DA 18, 3/3, Abe Halpern to Gershon Levi, 11 Nov. 1942.
49 Ibid., Louis Roter to Gershon Levi, 2 Oct. 1942; Herbert Vineberg to Gershon Levi, 6 Feb. 1942; S.S. Berlin to Gershon Levi, 3 Feb. 1942; John Marcus to Gershon Levi, 23 March 1942.
50 Ibid., J.M. Roe to Gershon Levi, 12 Aug. 1942; Levi to commanding officer, No. 5 Equipment Depot, RCAF, Moncton, 7 April 1942; Levi to Flt./Lieut. David J. Lane, 7 April 1942; Harry R. Nobles to senior Jewish chaplain, 7 April 1942; H.A.R. Keith to Gershon Levi, n.d.; Levi to Flt./Lieut. L.B. Merrell, C.O., No. 16 'X' Depot, RCAF, 7 April 1942; M.C.P. Macintosh to Levi, 31 March 1942; Flt./Lieut. J.N. Smith, adjutant for commanding officer, No. 5 Equipment Depot, to Gershon Levi, 26 March 1942; David J. Lane to Gershon Levi, 24 March 1942.
51 For a poignant story of one encounter between a Jewish RCAF officer and a host family, see Norman Levine, 'In Quebec City,' in *The Spice Box: An Anthology of Jewish Canadian Writing*, ed. Gerri Sinclair and Morris Wolfe (Toronto, 1981), 166–76; CJCCCNA, DA 18, 3/3, unsigned to Gershon Levi, 14 April 1942; Jack Bernstein to Gershon Levi, 8 Sept. 1942; Deborah Osmond, 'Tzedakah: Jewish Women and Charity in Halifax, 1920–1945' (undergraduate essay, Department of History, Dalhousie University, 1996), 63.
52 CJCCCNA, DA 18, 3/3, Monson to Gershon Levi, 24 March 1942; Bernard Saipe to Gershon Levi, 14 Feb. 1942; Jacob Feldman, 2 Sqd., 2 Wing, ITS, RCAF, to Gershon Levi, 10 Feb. 1942;
53 Ibid., Sarah Lacle to Gershon Levi, 28 Nov. 1941; Gershon Levi to B.R. Woloshin, No. 3 B&G School, RCAF; Levi to Rfm. J. Fogelbaum, 'C' Coy, Royal Rifles of Canada, Vernon, BC, 26 May 1942; L./Cpl. I. Capland to Levi, 30 April 1942.
54 Ibid., Max Greenberg to Gershon Levi, 29 April 1942; M. Charton to Gershon Levi, 1 April 1942.
55 Interview with Aaron Palmer, 23 June 1994.
56 CJCCCNA, DA 18, 3/3, John Marcus to Gershon Levi, 23 March 1942; Raber, *Manny Goes to War*, 49–50, 62.
57 Rubin, *Pesky Weeds*, 127; interview with Barney Danson, 30 June 1994.
58 Interview with Morris Lazarus, 30 June 1994.
59 McIntosh, *Terror in the Starboard Seat*, 4; Gerald Tulchinsky, *Branching Out: The Transformation of the Canadian Jewish Community* (Toronto, 1998), 244; *Globe and Mail*, 3 Feb. 2007.

60 CJCCCNA, Moses Usher Papers, Moe Usher to Abe and Rose Usher, 8 June 1941.
61 CJCCCNA, DA 18, 3/6A, Fitterman to Gershon Levi, 12 Aug. 1941.
62 CJCCCNA, DA 18, 517, Mrs F. Levine to Isaac Rose, 18 Sept. 1944.
63 Ibid., Ruth Dankner to Isaac Rose, 15 Sept. 1944; Morris Klein to Isaac Rose, 12 Sept. 1944.
64 Ibid., Mrs A. Solway to Isaac Rose, 11 Sept. 1944; Mrs S. Bach to Isaac Rose, 3 Oct. 1944.
65 CJCCCNA, DA 18, 6/4, Mary Nidelman to Rabbi David Eisen, 9 July 1942; 6/3, Mary Lozdon to Rabbi Samuel Cass, 12 Jan. 1942 [1943].
66 LAC, MG 30, 0225, Rabbi Samuel Cass Papers, vol. 9, app. 1, 25; app. 3, section 1, 14, 17, 18.
67 CJCCCNA, DA 18, 3/9, Levine to Canadian Chaplain Service, 31 Aug. 1942; 3/10, Cass to H/Capt. and Chaplain E.E. Brandt, 2 Sept. 1942; Brandt to Cass, 2 Sept. 1942.
68 Ibid., Fleishman to Cass, 31 Aug. 1942.
69 Ibid., Cass to Rosner, 2 Sept. 1942.
70 CJCCCNA, 3/6 B, Archie Dover to CJC, Montreal, 11 March 1943; 2/Lt. Gordon Miller to Samuel Cass, 19 March 1943.
71 Ibid., Gershon Levi to officer commanding, RCAF Station, Mountain View, Ont., 2 Feb. 1942.
72 CJCCCNA, DA 18, 3/13, Gershon Levi to Sam Cass, 22 Jan. 1945.
73 Reuben Slonim, *To Kill a Rabbi*, (Toronto, 1987), 154–6.
74 Aaron Palmer to Mrs S. Palmer, 22 Dec. 1944; Aaron Palmer to Mary [name illegible], 13 Sept. 1944; Rubin, *Pesky Weeds*, 140.
75 Doug Wilkinson to the author, 25 Sept. 1995.
76 CJCCCNA, DA 18, 311O, Cass to OC Infantry Training Brigade, Debert, NS, 3 April 1944; H. Gevantman to B. Wollow, War Efforts Committee, 26 March 1945.
77 Barbara Wilson to the author, 17 Nov. 1995; LAC, MG 30, 0225, Samuel Cass Papers, vol. 9, app. 1, 14. Cass brought a considerable supply of Passover food into Germany for this special seder. See J.L. Granatstein and Norman Hilmer, eds. *Battle Lines: Eyewitness Accounts from Canada's Military History* (Toronto, 2004), 366–7.
78 *The Battle of Brains: Canadian Citizenship and the Issues of the War* (Ottawa, 1944), 80, 83, 84.
79 CJCCCNA, DA 18, 6/7, Chaplain, (O/S) (P), Canadian Military Headquarters, 8 Jan. 1945; LAC, photo Collection, DND 1937–52, PA 116331, photo by Lt. G.B. Gilroy, 30 April 1945.
80 CJCCCNA, DA 18, 6/7, Cass to principal chaplain, (O/S) (P), Canadian Military Headquarters, 8 Jan. 1945, 'Report on Activities of Canadian Jewish

Chaplains Centre Submitted to H/Capt. I.B. Rose, Resident Dean'; LAC, MG 30, 0225, Samuel Cass Papers, vol. 9, app. 2, section 2, 6/6, 2.
81 CJCCCNA, DA 18,6/6, Cass to officer commanding AAG (Pers), 7 Nov. 1945; file 5/6, Guardsman Julius Gosevitz, 21 CAR, (GGHG), 1 Sqdn., to Isaac Rose, 6 June 1945; Cass to officer commanding, No.1 Canadian Vehicle Company, RCOC Canadian Army, England, 30 Oct. 1945; LAC, MG 30, 0225, Samuel Cass Papers, vol. 9, app. 3, section 1, 32.
82 Draper and Troper, *Canadian Jewish Congress*, 356–7; Robert Engel, 'My First Canadian Rabbi,' preface to Cecil Law, 'Camp Westerbork, Transit Camp to Eternity: The Liberation Story' (unpublished manuscript). Engel, a Westerbork survivor, recalled, 'I'll never forget [Rabbi Cass's] sermon, the sincerity of warmth. He spoke in Yiddish and English; we loved him. He was one of us' (LAC, MG 30, 0225, Samuel Cass Papers, vol. 9, app. 3, section 1, 27–8).
83 LAC, MG 30, 0225, Samuel Cass Papers, vol. 16, Cass to H. Abramowitz, 16 Jan. 1945. See Alex Grobman, *Rekindling the Flame: American Jewish Chaplains and the Survivors of European Jewry, 1944–1948* (Detroit, 1993).
84 LAC, MG 30, 0225, Samuel Cass Papers, vol. 9, app. 1, Daily Record, 685, 5 Dec. 1945, app. 3, section 1, 37.
85 CJCCCNA, DA 18, 3/8, Cass to H. Bud Weiser, 6 July 1943; Bookman, 'Canadian Jews in Uniform,' 111; Jonathan Vance to the author, 12 Feb. 2006.
86 LAC, MG 30, 0225, Samuel Cass Papers, vol. 9, app. 1, 18; Rubin, *Pesky Weeds*, 142. See David J. Bercuson, *The Secret Army* (Toronto, 1983), 60–4.
87 LAC, MG 30, 0225, Samuel Cass Papers, vol. 9, app. 1, 35.
88 Mordecai Richler, 'Benny, the War in Europe, and Myerson's Daughter Bella,' in *The Good Fight: Canadians and World War II*, ed. J.L. Granatstein and Peter Neary (Toronto, 1995), 426–30.

12. Post-war Readjustments

1 Interview with Phillip Stuchen, 29 Oct. 1996.
2 Phillip Stuchen, 'Mass Employment for Displaced Persons,' *QQ* 54, no. 3 (1947): 360–5, 365.
3 Bernard Figler and David Rome, *Hananiah Meir Caiserman: A Biography with an Essay on Modern Jewish Times by David Rome* (Montreal, 1962), 290; Hananiah Meir Caiserman, 'H.M. Caiserman's Report on Poland,' *Congress Bulletin*, March 1946, p. 6. Caiserman was accompanied on this mission by Sam Lipshitz of the UJPO, who reported for Toronto's *Yiddisher Zhurnal*.
4 CJCCCNA, Caiserman Papers, vol. 4, 'Jews in Poland, 1946,' Bialystok, 16 Jan. 1946, Typescript, 2.
5 Figler and Rome, *Caiserman*, 272, 291.

6 Nancy Tienhaara, *Canadian Views on Immigration and Population: An Analysis of Post-War Gallup Polls* (Ottawa, 1974), 59.
7 LAC, RG 76, vol. 443, file 673831, pt. 12, Molson to Immigration, microfilm C-10323; quoted in Jean Gerber, 'Immigration and Integration in Post-War Canada: A Case Study of Holocaust Survivors in Vancouver, 1947–1970' (M.A. thesis, University of British Columbia, 1989), 26; and Jean Gerber, 'Opening the Door: Immigration and Integration of Holocaust Survivors in Vancouver, 1947–1970,' *CJS/EJC* 4/5 (1996–7): 63–86. See Harold Troper's 'Canada and the Survivors of the Holocaust: The Crisis of the Displaced Persons,' in *'She'erith Hapleta, 1944–1948: Rehabilitation and Political Struggle* ed. Y. Gutman and Avital Saf (Jerusalem, 1990), 261–85; Irving Abella and Frank Bialystok, 'Canada,' in *The World Reacts to the Holocaust*, ed. David Wyman (Baltimore, 1996), 749–81, 759; Ben Lappin, *The Redeemed Children: The Story of the Rescue of War Orphans by the Jewish Community of Canada* (Toronto, 1963); Greta Fischer and Pearl Switzer, 'The Refugee Youth Program in Montreal 1947–1952' (M.S.W. thesis, McGill University, 1955); CJCCCNA, UJRA Collection, vol. 27, War Orphans Immigration Project, E. Ostry Correspondence, 1947–8. A most affecting overview of the project is provided in Fraidie Martz's *Open Your Hearts: The Story of the Jewish War Orphans in Canada* (Toronto, 1996).
8 Ethel Ostry Genkind, 'Children from Europe,' *Canadian Welfare* 25, nos. 1–2 (1949): 31–4; cited in Franca Iacovetta, *The Gatekeepers: Shaping Immigrant Lives in Cold War Canada* (Toronto, 2006), 2. See also Paula J. Draper, 'Canadian Holocaust Survivors: From Liberation to Rebirth,' *CJS/EJC* 4/5 (1996–7): 39–62; and Harry Henig, *Orphan of the Storm* (Toronto, 1974).
9 Ibid., 33.
10 David Rome, 'Canada,' *AJYB* 50 (1949): 290; Troper, 'Canada and the Survivors of the Holocaust,' 282–3; Louis Rosenberg, 'Canada,' *AJYB* 54 (1953): 221; Abella and Bialystok, 'Canada,' 759–60. See also Gerber, 'Immigration and Integration,' table 4.2, 'Total Immigration to Canada, General Displaced and Jewish Displaced, 1948–1953,' 39; Rabbi Abraham L. Feinberg, 'Recent Jewish Immigration Projects,' *Canadian Welfare* 25 (1950): 2–13, 4.
11 Gerber, 'Immigration and Integration,' 33, 36; *Vancouver News Herald*, 18 Dec. 1944, and *Jewish Western Bulletin*, 4 Jan. 1946, quoted in Gerber, 41.
12 Lappin, *Redeemed Children*, 158, 166.
13 See Iacovetta, *Gatekeepers*, ch. 2.
14 Gerber, 'Immigration and Integration,' 19.
15 Myra Giberovitch, 'The Contributions of Montreal Holocaust Survivor Organizations to Jewish Communal Life' (MSW thesis, McGill University, 1988), 52.

16 Percy Abrams, 'A Study of the Jewish Immigrants in Hamilton and Their Relationship with the Jewish Community Centre' (MSW thesis, University of Toronto, 1955), 29, 38, 79, 98.
17 Gerber, 'Immigration and Integration,' 93; 'Abstract,' 12, 63, 71, 76, 80, 83.
18 Feinberg, 'Immigration Projects,' 11–12.
19 Giberovitch, 'Montreal Holocaust Survivor Organizations,' 74, 77.
20 See Frank Bialystok, 'The Politicization of Holocaust Survivors in Toronto and Montreal, 1960–1973,' paper presented to the Canadian Historical Association, June 1996.
21 Paula J. Draper, 'Surviving Their Survival: Women, Memory, and the Holocaust,' in *Sisters or Strangers? Immigrant, Ethnic, and Radicalized Women in Canadian History*, ed. Marlene Epp, Franca Iacovetta, and Frances Swyripa (Toronto, 2004), 399–414, 411; Moses Znaimer, 'Our Remnant of a Family,' from *Passages to Canada* (Dominion Institute), with gratitude to Moses Znaimer; quoted in Norman J. Hillmer and J.L. Granatstein, *The Newly Found Land: Eyewitness Accounts of the Canadian Immigrant Experience* (Toronto, 2006), 233–9, 238.
22 Gerber, 'Immigration and Integration,' 31, 76, 93.
23 Abella and Bialystok, 'Canada,' 760; Rosenberg, 'Canada,' *AJYB* 57 (1956): 303; *AJYB* 58 (1957): 230; *AJYB* 66 (1965): 323. See Ibolya (Szalai) Grossman, *An Ordinary Woman in Extraordinary Times* (Toronto, 1990).
24 See Robertson Davies, *Discoveries: Early Letters, 1938–1975*, ed. Judith S. Grant (Toronto, 2002), 11, 35, 133, 145, 185, and 281, for examples of this snide antisemitism.
25 See Michael D. Behiels, *Prelude to Quebec's Quiet Revolution: Liberalism versus Neo-Nationalism, 1945–1960* (Montreal, 1985); René Lévesque, 'For an Independent Quebec,' in *Quebec since 1945: Selected Readings*, ed. Michael D. Behiels (Toronto, 1987), 265–73, as well as other articles in this useful collection; David Rome, 'Canada,' *AJYB* 44 (1942): 181; *AJYB* 45 (1943): 230; *AJYB* 46 (1944): 203; *AJYB* 47 (1945): 361, 363.
26 David Rome, 'Canada,' *AJYB* 48 (1946): 277; *AJYB* 50 (1949): 292–3.
27 Jack Jedwab, 'The Politics of Dialogue: Rapprochement Efforts between Jews and French Canadians: 1939–1960,' in *Renewing Our Days: Montreal Jews in the Twentieth Century*, ed. Ira Robinson and Mervin Butovsky (Montreal, 1995), 42–74, 54.
28 André Laurendeau, 'Bloc Notes,' *Le Devoir*, 28 Nov. 1952, quoted in ibid., 57n20.
29 Betty Sigler, 'Montreal: The Bonds of Community, the Town within the City,' *Commentary* 20, no. 4 (1950): 345–53, 352; Everett C. Hughes, *French Canada in Transition* (Chicago, 1963).

30 Michael D. Behiels, 'Georges Henri Levesque,' in *The Canadian Encyclopedia*, vol. 2, 2nd ed. (Edmonton, 1988), 1205; Pierre Elliott Trudeau, 'Separatist Counter Revolutionaries,' in *Federalism and the French Canadians* (Toronto, 1968), 206.
31 See also Max Nemni, *Young Trudeau: Son of Quebec, Father of Canada 1919–1944* (Toronto, 2006).
32 Jean Pierre Gaboury, *Le Nationalisme de Lionel Groulx: Aspects idéologiques* (Ottawa, 1970), 35–6. See Richard Jones, *L'Idéologie de l'Action Catholique* (Quebec, 1974); and Gérard Bouchard's *Les Deux Chanoines: Contradictions et ambivalences dans la pensée de Lionel Groulx* (Montreal, 2003), 149–58, for an interesting re-evaluation.
33 See Pierre Elliott Trudeau, in collaboration, *La Grève de l'amiante* (Montreal, 1956), app. 2, 'Le Rapport Custos,' 407–8; Yves Lavertu, *The Bernonville Affair: A French War Criminal in Quebec after World War II*, trans. George Tombs (Montreal, 1995), 58.
34 Quoted in Sol Littman, 'Barbie's Buddy in Canada,' *Canadian Dimension* 21, no. 6 (1987): 13–15, 14. See also *CJN*, 2 June 1994.
35 Xavier Gélinas to the author, 4 Dec. 1997. See also Xavier Gélinas, 'Le Droit intellectuel et la Révolution tranquille: Le Cas de la revue *Tradition et progrès*, 1957–1962,' *CHR* 77, no. 3 (1996): 353–87.
36 See Jedwab, 'The Politics of Dialogue,' 42–74.
37 See Jean-Phillipe Croteau, 'Les Relations entre les Juifs de la langue française et les Canadiens Français selon le *Bulletin du Cercle Juifs* (1954–1968)' (M.A. thesis, Université de Montréal, 2000).
38 Claude Ryan, 'How French Canadians See Jews,' in *A Stable Society*, ed. Robert Guy Scully and Marc Plourde, (Montreal, 1978), 322.
39 Yogev Tzuk, 'Challenge and Response: Jewish Communal Welfare in Montreal,' *Contemporary Jewry* 6, no. 2 (1983): 43–52, 49.
40 Janine Stingel, *Social Discredit: Anti-Semitism, Social Credit and the Jewish Response* (Montreal, 2000), 122–51; David Rome, 'Canada,' *AJYB* 52 (1951): 237.
41 See James W. St G. Walker, 'Canadian Anti-semitism and Jewish Community Response: The Case of Noble and Wolfe,' in *Multiculturalsim, Jews, and Identities in Canada*, ed. Howard Adelman and John H. Simpson (Jerusalem, 1996), 37–68; David Rome, 'Canada,' *AJYB* 51 (1950): 274; *AJYB* 53 (1952): 262.
42 See Martin Sable, 'George Drew and the Rabbis: Religious Education in Ontario's Public Schools,' *CJS* 6 (1998): 25–53.
43 Carmela Patrias and Ruth A. Frager, '"This Is Our Country, These Are Our Rights": Minorities and the Origin of Ontario's Human Rights Campaigns,'

CHR 82 (March 2001): 1–35; Carmela Patrias, 'Socialists, Jews, and the 1947 Saskatchewan Bill of Rights,' *CHR* 87, no. 2 (June 2006): 265–92, 267.
44 Ben Kayfetz to the author, 17 July 1977. See also Ben Kayfetz, 'On Community Relations in Ontario in the 1940s,' *Canadian Jewish Studies* 2 (1994): 57–66; Irwin Pollock, 'Civil Rights and the Anglo-Jewish Press in Canada: 1930–1970' (M.A. thesis, McGill University, 1979); John C. Bagnall, 'The Ontario Conservatives and the Development of Anti-discrimination Policy: 1944 to 1962' (Ph.D. diss., Queen's University, 1984), 20–2, 35, 71–2 (in an editorial in February 1944, the *Toronto Star* attacked anti-Semitism; quoted in ibid., 32); Roger Graham, *Old Man Ontario: Leslie M. Frost*, Ontario Historical Studies Series (Toronto, 1990), 263.
45 Joe T. Darden, 'Blacks, Jews, and Civil Rights in Canada and the United States,' paper presented at the 84th Annual Meeting of the Canadian Historical Association, London, 2005, p. 16.
46 Bruce Muirhead, *Against the Odds. The Public Life and Times of Louis Rasminsky* (Toronto, 1999), 3, 147–8; Lesley Marrus-Barsky, 'History of Mount Sinai Hospital' (unpublished manuscript), 105, 112.
47 Donald Creighton, *The Forked Road: Canada 1939–1957* (Toronto, 1976), 181–2; LAC, RG 33, Royal Commission on National Development in the Arts, Letters and Sciences, vol. 14, brief 132 (submission ... by the Canadian Jewish Congress, 14 Nov. 1949), microfilm C-2005.
48 Creighton, *The Forked Road*, 2.
49 Leo Driedger and Glenn Church, 'Residential Segregation and Institutional Completeness: A Comparison of Ethnic Minorities,' *CRSA/RCSA* 11, no. 1 (1974): 30–52, 39; Gerber, 'Immigration and Integration,' 43–4.
50 George Gamester, 'College and Spadina Gang Prove They're Pals for Life,' *Toronto Star*, 15 March 1998.
51 John R. Seeley, R. Alexander Sim, and Elizabeth W. Loosely, in collaboration with Norman W. Bell and D.F. Fleming, *Crestwood Heights* (Toronto, 1956), 212–15, 219, 286–7, 307, 308.
52 Louis Rosenberg, 'Canada,' *AJYB* 54 (1953): 228.
53 See *Baron de Hirsch Congregation, 1890 to 1990: 100th Anniversary Commemorative Book* (Halifax, 1990); *Agudas Israel Congregation Dedication Volume, 1905–1963* (Saskatoon, 1963).
54 Harvey Meirovitch, 'The Rise and Decline of a Toronto Synagogue: Congregation Beth Am,' *CJHSJ* 1, no. 2 (1977): 97–113, 99–100.
55 Ben Lappin, 'May Day in Toronto: Yesteryear and Now,' *Commentary* 19, no. 5 (1955): 476–9, 479.
56 See Gerald Tulchinsky, 'Family Quarrel: Joe Salsberg, the "Jewish" Question, and Canadian Communism,' *Labour/Le Travail* 56 (Fall 2005): 149–73.

See Kim Ellen Levis, 'Keeping the Flame Alive: The Story of the Toronto Jewish Folk Choir,' *CJO*, Dec. 1997, p. 20.
57 Bessie W. Batist, ed., *A Treasure for My Daughter: A Reference Book of Jewish Festivals with Menus and Recipes* (Montreal, 1950), 3.
58 Erna Paris, 'Growing Up a Jewish Princess in Forest Hill,' in *The Spice Box: An Anthology of Jewish Canadian Writing*, ed. Gerri Sinclair and Morris Wolfe (Toronto, 1981), 243–50, 246–7. The atmosphere in the Forest Hill Reform Holy Blossom Temple during the 1940s is effectively discussed by Michele Landsberg in Francine Zuckerman, ed., *Half the Kingdom: Seven Jewish Feminists* (Montreal, 1992), 57–69, 58, 60.
59 Yael Gordon-Brym, 'The Changing Role of Canadian Jewish Women,' in *Canadian Jewish Women of Today: Who's Who of Canadian Jewish Women*, ed. Edmond Y. Lipsitz (Downsview, 1983), 11–21, 14; Rachel Schlesinger, 'Changing Roles of Jewish Women,' in *Canadian Jewry Today: Who's Who in Canadian Jewry*, ed. Edmond Y. Lipsitz (Downsview, 1989), 60–70, 62, 63.
60 Louis Rosenberg, 'The Jewish Population of Canada: A Statistical Summary to 1943,' *AJYB* 48 (1947): 50; *AJYB* 56 (1955): 301; Louis Rosenberg, 'A Study of the Changes in the Population Characteristics: The Jewish Community in Canada 1931–1961,' *Canadian Jewish Population Studies*, Canadian Jewish Community Series 2, no. 2 (Montreal, 1965), 15, 40.
61 These figures are Jews by religion. See Daniel J. Elazar and Harold M. Waller, *Maintaining Consensus: The Canadian Jewish Polity in the Postwar World* (New York, 1990), 18.
62 Louis Rosenberg, 'Canada,' *AJYB* 65 (1964): 163; 56 (1955): 299; 52 (1951): 231; 58 (1957): 229; 68 (1967): 269.
63 See Morton Weinfeld, 'Intermarriage: Agony and Adaptation,' in *The Canadian Jewish Mosaic*, ed. M. Weinfeld, W. Shaffir, and I. Cotler (Toronto, 1981), 361, 365–82, 381.
64 Louis Rosenberg, 'Canada,' *AJYB* 53 (1952): 260–1.
65 Louis Rosenberg, 'Two Centuries of Jewish Life in Canada, 1760–1960,' *AJYB* 62 (1961): 42; Elazar and Waller, *Maintaining Consensus*, 18.
66 See Edward S. Shapiro, A *Time for Healing: American Jewry since World War II* (Baltimore, 1992), 125–6.
67 Louis Rosenberg, 'Canada,' *AJYB* 62 (1961): 41. See Abraham J. Karp, 'The Conservative Rabbi – "Dissatisfied but Not Unhappy,"' in *The American Rabbinate: A Century of Continuity and Change*, ed. Jacob R. Marcus and Abraham N. Peck (Hoboken, 1985), 98–172, 163.
68 All Conservative and Reform congregations had rabbis, though in 1951 only 96 of 146 Orthodox congregations had their own rabbis. See Rosenberg, 'Canada,' *AJYB* 52 (1951): 238; *AJYB* 62 (1961): 42.

69 Karp, 'The Conservative Rabbi,' 156.
70 See Etan Diamond, *And I Will Dwell in Their Midst: Orthodox Jews in Suburbia* (Chapel Hill, 2000), 15.
71 William Shaffir, *Life in a Religious Community: The Lubavitcher Chassidim in Montreal, Cultures and Communities: Community Studies* (Toronto, 1974), 12.
72 Rosenberg, 'Canada,' *AJYB* 58 (1957): 234–5.
73 Rosenberg, 'Two Centuries of Jewish Life,' 42.
74 Rome, 'Canada,' *AJYB* 44 (1942): 180; 45 (1943): 228; 47 (1945): 358.
75 Rosenberg, 'Canada,' *AJYB* 55 (1954): 169.
76 Mordecai Richler, 'This Year in Jerusalem,' in *Hunting Tigers under Glass: Essays and Reports* (London, 1971), 143–76, 163–4.
77 Elazar and Waller, *Maintaining Consensus*, 71, 161.
78 Rosenberg, 'Canada,' *AJYB* 53 (1952): 263–4.
79 See Morton Weinfeld, 'Introduction,' and 'Bibliography of Works by Louis Rosenberg,' in Louis Rosenberg, *Canada's Jews: A Social and Economic Study of Jews in Canada in the 1930s*, ed. Morton Weinfeld (Montreal, 1993).

13. Jewish Ethnicity in Multicultural Canada, 1960–1980

1 J.K. Johnson, ed., *The Canadian Directory of Parliament 1867–1967* (Ottawa, 1968), 243; *AJYB* (1970): 364.
2 *Census of Canada* (1961), vol. 3, part 1, 94–515; ibid. (1971), vol. 3, part 3, 94–731.
3 See Louis Greenspan and Graeme Nicholson, eds, *Fackenheim: German Philosophy and Jewish Thought* (Toronto, 1991).
4 See Richard Menkis, 'A Threefold Transformation: Jewish Studies, Canadian Universities and the Canadian Jewish Community,' in *A Guide to the Study of Jewish Civilization in Canadian Universities*, ed. Michael Brown (Toronto, 1998): 43–69.
5 See Leo Kolber with L. Ian MacDonald, *Leo a Life* (Montreal, 2003), 53.
6 Ann Gibbon and Peter Hadekel, *Steinberg: The Breakup of a Family Empire* (Toronto, 1990), 2, 11, 63.
7 Anthony Bianco, *The Reichmanns: Family, Faith, Fortune, and the Empire of Olympia & York* (Toronto, 1997), 257, 369.
8 Louis Rosenberg, 'Canada,' *AJYB* 65 (1964): 168.
9 Ibid., *AJYB* 66 (1965): 325; *AJYB* 68 (1967): 269.
10 Ibid., 270. See Mervin Butovsky and Ode Garfinkle, editors and translators, *The Journals of Yaacov Zipper, 1950–1982: The Struggle for Yiddishkeit* (Montreal, 2004), xiii–xv.
11 See Ben Kayfetz, 'Canada,' *AJYB* 69 (1968): 282–3.

12 Harold Troper, 'The Canadian Jewish Polity and the Limits of Political Action: The Campaign on Behalf of Soviet and Syrian Jews,' in *Ethnicity, Politics, and Public Policy in Canada: Case Studies in Canadian Diversity*, ed. Harold Troper and Morton Weinfeld (Toronto, 1999).
13 Mitchell Sharp, *Which Reminds Me ... A Memoir* (Toronto, 1994), 211.
14 See Wendy Eisen, *Count Us In: The Struggle to Free Soviet Jews: A Canadian Perspective* (Toronto, 1995), 45. See also Mindy B. Avrich-Skapinker, 'Canadian-Jewish Involvement with Soviet Jewry, 1970–1990: The Toronto Case Study' (PhD diss., University of Toronto, 1993).
15 Eisen, *Count Us In;* quoted in Troper, 'Canadian Jewish Polity,' 13.
16 See Harold Troper, *The Ransomed of God: The Story of One Woman's Role in the Rescue of Syrian Jews* (Toronto, 1999).
17 Roberta L. Markus and Donald V. Schwartz, 'Soviet Jewish Emigres in Toronto: Ethnic Self-Identity and Issues of Integration,' *CES/EEC* 16, no. 2 (1984): 71–88; Roberta L. Markus, *Adaptation: A Case Study of Soviet Jewish Immigrant Children in Toronto, 1970–1978* (Toronto, 1979), 15–16.
18 Markus, *Adaptation*, 17.
19 Kayfetz, 'Canada,' *AJYB* 69 (1968): 385.
20 Harold Waller, 'The Impact of the Six-Day War on the Organizational Life of Canadian Jewry,' in *The Six-Day War and World Jewry*, ed. Eli Lederhendler (Bethesda, 2000), 81–97, 82, 97.
21 Mordecai Richler, *This Year in Jerusalem* (Toronto, 1994), 115–16.
22 Melvin Fenson, 'Canada,' *AJYB* 75 (1974–5): 348, 350.
23 Haim Genizi, *The Holocaust, Israel, and the Canadian Protestant Churches* (Montreal, 2002), 24, 91–7.
24 Sharp, *Which Reminds Me*, 209.
25 Bernard Baskin, 'Canada,' *AJYB* 80 (1980): 179; J.L. Granatstein and Robert Bothwell, *Pirouette: Pierre Trudeau and Canadian Foreign Policy* (Toronto, 1990), 211; Bernard Baskin, 'Canada,' *AJYB* 76 (1976): 257.
26 Bernard Baskin, 'Canada', *AJYB* 77 (1977): 332.
27 Kayfetz, 'Canada,' *AJYB* 69 (1968): 363; W. Gunther Plaut, *Unfinished Business: An Autobiography* (Toronto, 1981), 281–2.
28 Plaut, *Unfinished Business*, 278–94; David Taras, 'A Church Divided: A.C. Forrest and the United Church's Middle East Policy,' in *The Domestic Battleground: Canada and the Arab-Israeli Conflict*, ed. David Taras and David H. Goldberg (Montreal, 1989), 86–101; Warren Bass, '"I Am Surprised You Still Speak to Me": The United Church *Observer* and the Jews, 1948–1987' (undergraduate essay, Queen's University, 1990), 8.
29 *CJN*, 7 June 1968.
30 Bass, '"I Am Surprised,"' 12–13.

31 *CJN*, 12 Dec. 1969, 13 March 1970.
32 Plaut, *Unfinished Business*, 286.
33 Taras, 'Church Divided,' 86; Reuben Slonim, *Family Quarrel: The United Church and the Jews* (Toronto, 1977), vii. See also Gary A. Gaudin, 'Protestant Church / Jewish State: The United Church of Canada, Israel and the Palestinian Refugees Revisited,' *Studies in Religion / Sciences Religieuses* 24, no. 2 (1995): 179–91.
34 See David J. Bercuson, *Canada and the Birth of Israel: A Study in Canadian Foreign Policy* (Toronto, 1985); Zachariah Kay, *The Diplomacy of Prudence: Canada and Israel, 1948–1958* (Montreal, 1997); David H. Goldberg, *Foreign Policy and Ethnic Interest Groups: American and Canadian Jews Lobby for Israel* (New York, 1990), 112–22; Bernard Baskin, 'Canada,' *AJYB* 79 (1979): 197.
35 Ibid., *AJYB* 80 (1980): 180; Granatstein and Bothwell, *Pirouette*, 213–14, 218, 217.
36 Goldberg, *Foreign Policy*, 140; Ronnie Miller, *From Lebanon to the Intifada: The Jewish Lobby and Canadian Middle Eastern Policy* (Lanham, 1991), 97.
37 Harold Waller, 'Canada,' *AJYB* 90 (1990): 311.
38 Baskin, 'Canada,' *AJYB* 79 (1979): 196, 198, 199.
39 Jack Wertheimer, 'The Disaffections of American Jews,' *Commentary* 105, no. 5 (1998): 44–9; Ruth R. Wisse, 'Between Passovers,' *Commentary* 88, no. 6 (1989): 42–7, 47.
40 Michael Brown, 'The Push and Pull Factors of Aliyah and the Anomalous Case of Canada: 1967–1982,' *JSS* 48, no. 2 (1986): 141–62, 143; Richler, *This Year in Jerusalem*, 237–8.
41 Michael M. Solomon, 'Canada,' *AJYB* 71 (1970): 362; Stuart E. Rosenberg, 'Canada,' *AJYB* 73 (1972): 398.
42 Kayfetz, 'Canada,' *AJYB* 69 (1968): 362.
43 See Zailig Pollock, *A.M. Klein: The Story of the Poet* (Toronto, 1994); Miriam Waddington, *A.M. Klein*, Studies in Canadian Literature (Toronto, 1970); and Adam G. Fuerstenberg, 'The Poet and the Tycoon: The Relationship between A.M. Klein and Samuel Bronfman,' *CJHSJ* 5, no. 2 (1981): 49–69. See also Ruth R. Wisse, 'Jewish Participation in Canadian Culture' (a study for the Royal Commission on Bilingualism and Biculturalism, n.d., manuscript); Ruth R. Wisse, *The Modern Jewish Canon: A Journey through Language and Literature* (New York, 2000), 259–66; Michael Greenstein, *Third Solitude: Tradition and Discontinuity in Jewish-Canadian Literature* (Montreal, 1989), 53.
44 Norman Ravvin, *A House of Words: Jewish Writing, Identity, and Memory* (Montreal, 1997), 33–47; Ruth R. Wisse, 'My Life without Leonard Cohen,' *Commentary* 100, no. 4 (1996): 27–33, 33; Mervin Butovsky, 'An Interview with Irving Layton,' in *Canadian Jewish Anthology / Anthologie Juive du Canada*,

ed. Chaim Spilberg and Yaacov Zipper (Montreal, 1982), 59–74; Ruth Panofsky, *The Force of Vocation: The Literary Career of Adele Wiseman* (Winnipeg, 2006).
45 Franklin Bialystok, *Delayed Impact: The Holocaust and the Canadian Jewish Community* (Montreal, 2000), 132–3; Rosenberg, 'Canada,' *AJYB* 73 (1972): 396–8.
46 Ibid., 397.
47 Stuart E. Rosenberg, 'French Separatism: Its Implications for Canadian Jewry,' *AJYB* 73 (1972): 407–27, 427.
48 Quoted in ibid., 409.
49 Fenson, 'Canada,' *AJYB* 75 (1974–5): 320.
50 *Montreal Gazette*, 17 Oct. 1979; Graham Fraser, *PQ: René Lévesque and the Parti Québécois in Power* (Toronto, 1984), 153–4.
51 Fenson, 'Canada,' *AJYB* 75 (1974–5): 321.
52 Bernard Baskin, 'Canada,' *AJYB* 78 (1978): 281; Fraser, *René Lévesque*, 67; Mordecai Richler, 'Language (and Other) Problems,' in *Home Sweet Home: My Canadian Album* (Toronto, 1986), 224–64, 241–2.
53 Ruth R. Wisse and Irwin Cotler, 'Quebec's Jews: Caught in the Middle,' *Commentary* 64, no. 3 (1977): 55–9.
54 Michel Laferrière, 'Quebec's Jews,' *Commentary* 65, no. 1 (1978): 4–5.
55 Ibid.
56 Irwin Cotler, 'Le Fait français et le fait juif: First Encounters,' *Report on Confederation* 1, no. 8 (1978): 26–8, 27.
57 Jean-François Lisée, 'Interview with Pierre Anctil,' in *Boundaries of Identity: A Quebec Reader*, ed. William Dodge (Toronto, 1992), 151–6, 153.
58 See Jean-Phillipe Croteau, 'Les Relations entre les Juifs de la langue française et les Canadiens français selon le *Bulletin du Cercle Juif* (1954–1968)' (M.A. thesis, Université de Montréal, 2000); Naim Kattan, 'Jewish Characters in the French-Canadian Novel,' *Viewpoints* 1, no. 3 (1966): 29–32, 29.
59 J.L. Granatstein, *Canada 1957–1967: The Years of Uncertainty and Innovation* (Toronto, 1986), 248; LAC, RG 33/80, Royal Commission on Bilingualism and Biculturalism, vol. 45, file 740252.
60 Harold Waller, 'Canada,' *AJYB* 86 (1986): 237.
61 Lisée, 'Pierre Anctil,' 154. But it was the law and it was enforced; see Harold Waller, 'Canada,' *AJYB* 97 (1997): 252.
62 Jean-Claude Lasry, 'A Francophone Diaspora in Quebec,' in *The Canadian Jewish Mosaic*, ed. M. Weinfeld, W. Shaffir, and I. Cotler (Toronto, 1981), 221–40. See also Jean-Claude Lasry, 'Sephardim and Ashkenazim in Montreal,' in *The Jews in Canada*, ed. Robert J. Brym, William Shaffir, and Morton Weinfeld (Toronto, 1993), 395–401; Marie Berdugo-Cohen,

Yolande Cohen, and Joseph Levy, *Juifs marocains à Montréal: Témoinages d'une immigration moderne* (Montreal, 1987).
63 Rosenberg, 'French Separatism: Its Implications,' 407–27, 420.
64 Fenson, 'Canada,' *AJYB* 75 (1974–5): 317–57, 321.
65 *CJN*, 27 Dec. 1963.
66 Ibid., 30 Aug. 1968.
67 Jean-Claude Lasry and Evelyn Bloomfield Schacter, 'Jewish Intermarriage in Montreal, 1962–1972,' *JSS* 37, nos. 3–4 (1975): 267–78, 272; Waller, 'Canada,' *AJYB* 86 (1986): 234; *AJYB* 89 (1989): 261.
68 Lasry, 'A Francophone Diaspora,' 227, 231.
69 *CJN*, 28 Jan. 1972, 22 June 1973; *CJO* (April 1975); *CJN*, 22 Nov. 1979.
70 This paragraph is based on Berdugo-Cohen et al., *Juifs marocains à Montréal*.
71 *CJN*, 25 June 1987.
72 See Janice Arnold, 'Plans Created for Ashkenazi-Sephardic Programmes' and 'Montreal Dialogue Boosts Sephardi-Ashkenazi Ties,' *CJN*, 9 Jan. and 11 Sept. 1986.
73 Margaret Spack, 'Integration of Jewish Immigrants from Morocco into the Toronto Community: The Use of Attitudes towards the Social Services' (M.S.W. thesis, University of Toronto, 1965), 2–3, 5.
74 Sylvia K. Baker, 'Integration of Jewish Immigrants from Morocco into the Toronto Community: A Comment on the Relationship between Integration and Disciplinary Problems with Their Children Experienced by Parents from Morocco' (M.S.W. thesis, University of Toronto, 1965), 2; Thomas H. Zador, 'Integration of Jewish Immigrants from Morocco into the Jewish Community: An Exploratory Study of Sephardic Jewish Immigrants Who Came to Canada after Morocco Gained Independence in 1956, with Special Reference to Psychological-Emotional as well as Socio-Economic Satisfactions and Dissatisfactions in Canada' (MSW thesis, University of Toronto, 1965), 7.
75 *CJN*, 27 Jan. 1967; 15 March 1968; 20 March and 24 Aug. 1973; 19 April 1974; 6 May 1977.
76 Quoted in Sarah Taieb-Carlen, 'Monocultural Education in a Pluralist Environment: Ashkenazi Curricula in Toronto Jewish Educational Institutions,' *CES/EEC* 24, no. 3 (1992): 75–86, 83.
77 *CJN*, 4 March 1977.
78 See Marion E. Meyer, *The Jews of Kingston: A Microcosm of Canadian Jewry?* (Kingston, 1983), 101–8.
79 Laura Wolfson to the author, 25 April 1997.
80 Meyer, *Jews of Kingston*, 107; Marion E. Meyer, 'Ten Years Later: Another Look at Our Community' (unpublished manuscript, 1997), 2.

81 *CJN*, 25 Feb. 1977.
82 *CJN*, 14 Jan.1972.
83 *CJN*, 10 May 1972.
84 *CJN*, 3 Nov. 1972.
85 Len Scher, *The Un-Canadians: True Stories of the Blacklist Era* (Toronto, 1992).
86 'Secular Jewish Schools: Proposed Statement of Principles,' *CJO* (March 1973); Marvin Klotz, quoted in Jack Cowan, 'Secular Jewish Life,' *CJO* (June 1973): 12.
87 Jerald Bain, 'Secular Jewish Viewpoint,' *CJO* (Aug.-Sept. 1973): 9. See M.J. Olgin, 'In Defense of Progressive Jewish Culture,' *CJO* (March 1973): 5, 6,13; Harold Benson, 'Some Aspects of Jewish Secular Identity,' *CJO* (July-Aug. 1974): 3–4; Maxine and Sol Hermolin, 'Searching for Meaning of Jewish Secularism,' *CJO* (July-Aug. 1976): 8–9; Michael Bodemann, 'Does the Jewish Left in Canada Have a Future?' *CJO* (March 1981): 3, 4, 15; and Bodemann, 'Jews in Canada: What Place for Progressives?' *CJO* (Oct. 1981): 10–12.
88 Jerald Bain, 'A Vision for the Future,' *CJO* (Dec. 1982): 13–16, 16; *CJN*, 29 March 1979.
89 See Ben Lappin, 'May Day in Toronto: Yesteryear and Now,' *Commentary* 19 (1955): 476–9, and Gerald Tulchinsky, 'Ben Lappin's Reflections on May Day Celebrations in Toronto's Jewish Quarter,' *L/Let* 49 (2002): 211–21, for a poignant look at the remnants of this old left; and Merrily Weisbord, *The Strangest Dream: Canadian Communists, the Spy Trials and the Cold War* (Montreal, 1994), 214–30.

14. Complexities and Uncertainties

1 See *26th Annual Holocaust Education Week, November 1–9*, 2006 (United Jewish Appeal Federation of Toronto, 2006); Ruth R. Wisse, 'Between Passovers" *Commentary* 88, no. 6 (1989): 42–7, 46.
2 See Morton Weinfeld and John J. Sigal, 'The Effect of the Holocaust on Selected Socio-Political Attitudes of Adult Children of Survivors' *CRSA/RCSA* 23, no. 3 (1986): 365–82; Jack Kuper, *Child of the Holocaust* (Toronto, 1967).
3 *National Post*, 7 Sept. 2006.
4 See Leslie Ann Hulse, 'The Emergence of the Holocaust Survivor in the Canadian Jewish Community' (MA thesis, Carleton University, 1979); Irving Abella and Frank Bialystok, 'Canada,' in *The World Reacts to the Holocaust*, ed. David Wyman (Baltimore, 1996), 749–81, 766; Frank Bialystok, *Delayed Impact: The Holocaust and the Canadian Jewish Community* (Montreal, 2000), 130–4.

5 See William Kaplan, 'Maxwell Cohen and the Report of the Special Committee on Hate Propaganda,' in *Law, Policy, and International Justice: Essays in Honour of Maxwell Cohen*, ed. William Kaplan (Montreal, 1993), 243–74.
6 See W. Gunther Plaut, *Page Two: Ten Years of 'News and Views'* (Toronto, 1971), 49.
7 Janine Stingel, 'From Father to Son: Canadian Jewry's Response to the Alberta Social Credit Party and the Reform Party of Canada,' *Canadian Jewish Studies* 9 (2001): 1–37.
8 However, one scholar argues – unconvincingly to some reviewers – that 'the overwhelming majority of Nazi war criminals and collaborators ... were admitted inadvertently, either as a result of the absence of information about their wartime activities or its inaccessibility' (Howard Margolian, *Unauthorized Entry: The Truth about Nazi War Criminals in Canada* [Toronto, 2000], 187).
9 *CJN*, 28 June 1963, 30 March 1973, 23 April 1971; *CJO* (Jan.-Feb. 1975): 21–2; *CJN*, 7 Feb. 1975; Harold Troper and Morton Weinfeld, *Old Wounds: Jews, Ukrainians and the Hunt for Nazi War Criminals in Canada* (Toronto, 1988), 383.
10 See Sol Littman, *War Criminals on Trial: The Rauca Case* (Markham, 1984).
11 Harold Waller, 'Canada,' *AJYB* 86 (1986): 235; Jules Deschênes, *Commission of Inquiry on War Criminals Report* (Ottawa, 1986), iii.
12 See Sol Littman, *Pure Soldiers or Sinister Legion: The Ukrainian 14th Waffen – SS Division* (Montreal, 2003).
13 Harold Waller, 'Canada,' *AJYB* 87(1987): 199; *CJN*, 16 Jan. 1986.
14 Ibid., 30 Jan. 1986.
15 Quoted in John Sopinka, Q.C., *Ukrainian Canadian Committee Submission to the Commission of Inquiry on War Criminals* (Toronto, 1986), 6.
16 *CJN*, 2 April 1987; 6 Feb. and 27 Nov. 1986;
17 Troper and Weinfeld, *Old Wounds*, 304; quoted in *CJN*, 13 Aug. 1987.
18 Ibid., 20 Aug. 1987. See also Harold Waller, 'Canada,' *AJYB* 89 (1989): 259–60.
19 Manoly R. Lupul, *The Politics of Multiculture: A Ukrainian-Canadian Memoir* (Edmonton, 2005), 197.
20 Waller, 'Canada,' *AJYB* 89 (1989): 260.
21 Ibid., *AJYB* 90 (1990): 306, 308. See David Matas, with Susan Charendoff, *Justice Delayed: Nazi War Criminals in Canada* (Toronto, 1987), 264.
22 Irving Abella, 'Eluding Justice: Nazi War Criminals in Canada,' paper presented to Conference on Canadian Jewish Studies, York University, June 1998; Harold Waller, 'Canada,' *AJYB* 91 (1991): 234.
23 *CJN*, 7 Nov. and 5 Dec. 1996. See Arnold Fradkin, 'Canada Ignored War Criminals for 27 Years' and 'War Crimes Cases Crawling Ahead at Snail's

Pace,' *CJN*, 2 and 9 Jan. 1997; R. Paltiel, 'Canada Portrayed as Sanctuary for War Criminals,' *Globe and Mail*, 31 Jan. 1997, 25 April 2005; B. Farber, 'The Nazi Enablers among Us,' *National Post*, 9 Feb. 2007; B'nai B'rith press release, 21 June 2007.
24 Waller, 'Canada,' *AJYB* 86 (1986): 236; quoted in Gabriel Weimann and Conrad Winn, *Hate on Trial: The Zundel Affair, the Media and Public Opinion in Canada* (Oakville, 1986), 29.
25 Waller, 'Canada,' *AJYB* 87 (1987): 198.
26 See Alan Davies, 'The Keegstra Affair,' and Manuel Prutschi, 'The Zundel Affair,' in *Antisemitism in Canada: History and Interpretation*, ed. Alan Davies (Waterloo, 1992), 227–47 and 249–77; David Bercuson and Douglas Wertheimer, *A Trust Betrayed: The Keegstra Affair* (Toronto, 1985), 56, 60, 62–3, 213–23; David R. Elliott, 'Anti-Semitism and the Social Credit Movement: The Intellectual Roots of the Keegstra Affair,' *CES/EEC* 17, no. 1 (1985): 78–89; Waller, 'Canada,' *AJYB* 87 (1987): 198.
27 Waller, 'Canada,' *AJYB* 87 (1987): 198; ibid., *AJYB* 88 (1988): 247.
28 Weimann and Winn, *Hate on Trial*, 125, 164–5; Waller, 'Canada,' *AJYB* 88 (1988): 248.
29 Ibid., *AJYB* 90 (1990): 313. See Randal F. Schnoor, 'Tradition and Innovation in an Ultraorthodox Community: The Hasidim of Outremont,' *CJS/EJC* (2002): 53–73.
30 See Dana Herman, 'In the Shadow of the Mountain: A Historical Re-evaluation of the 1988 Outremont Dispute' (MA thesis, McGill University, 2003).
31 *Globe and Mail*, 8 Nov. 2006, 18 June 2007.
32 See Michael Brown, 'Introduction: The Contemporary Campus Setting,' in *Approaches to Antisemitism: Context and Curriculum*, ed. Michael Brown (New York, 1994), 1–9, 7.
33 Mordecai Richler, *Oh Canada! Oh Quebec! Requiem for a Divided Country* (Toronto, 1992), 251–60.
34 Paul M. Sniderman, David A. Northrup, Joseph F. Fletcher, Peter H. Russell, and Philip E. Tetlock, 'Psychological and Cultural Foundations of Prejudice: The Case of Antisemitism in Quebec,' *CRSA/RCSA* 30, no. 2 (1993): 242–70.
35 Harold Waller, 'Canada,' *AJYB* 91 (1991): 233; ibid., *AJYB* 92 (1992): 289.
36 See Howard Adelman, 'Blacks and Jews: Racism, Anti-Semitism, and *Show Boat*,' in *Multiculturalism, Jews, and Identities in Canada*, ed. Howard Adelman and John H. Simpson (Jerusalem, 1996), 128–78; Eugene Kaellis, 'Jews and Blacks: An Uneasy Interface,' *CJO* (Jan.-Feb. 1998): 15, 28; Harold Waller, 'Canada,' *AJYB* 96 (1996): 199; *CJN*, 16 Jan. 1997.
37 Yaacov Glickman, 'Anti-Semitism and Jewish Social Cohesion in Canada,' in *Racism in Canada*, ed. Ormond McKague (Saskatoon, 1991), 45–63, 212–15;

Robert Brym and Rhonda L. Lenton, 'The Distribution of Anti-Semitism in Canada in 1984,' *CJS* 16, no. 4 (1991): 411–18, 411; *AJYB* 103 (2003), 299–334, 316.

38 Jean-François Lisée, 'Interview with Pierre Anctil,' in *Boundaries of Identity: A Quebec Reader*, ed. William Dodge (Toronto, 1992), 149–56, 153. See Pierre Anctil, *Le Devoir: Les Juifs et l'immigration de Bourassa à Laurendeau* (Quebec, 1988); *Le Rendez-vous manqué: Les Juifs de Montréal face au Québec de l'entre deux guerres* (Quebec, 1988); *Montreal foun Nekhtn Le Montreal juif d'autrefois*, de Israel Medresh (Sillery, 1997); *Yidishe Lider Poèmes yiddish, de Jacob Isaac Segal* (Montreal, 1992).

39 Brym and Lenton, 'Distribution of Anti-Semitism,' 415. See also Simon Langlois, 'The Distribution of Anti-Semitism in Canada: A Hasty and Erroneous Generalization by Brym and Lenton,' *CJS* 17, no. 2 (1992): 175–8; and Brym and Lenton, 'Anti-Semitism in Quebec: Reply to Langlois,' *CJS* 17, no. 2 (1992): 179–83.

40 Werner Cohn, 'English and French Canadian Public Opinion on Jews and Israel: Some Poll Data,' *CES/EEC* 2, no. 2 (1979): 31–48; *Antisemitism World Report 1995* (London, 1995), 14–23, 22.

41 Morton Weinfeld, 'Canada since 1960,' in *Encyclopedia Judaica*, 2nd ed., ed. Michael Berenbaum and Fred Skolnik, 22 Vols (Detroit, 2007), 4: 393–421, 415. See Harold Waller's *AJYB* entries on Canada, 1995 to 2004, for detailed surveys of these events; and *Jerusalem Report* 17, no. 26 (16 April 2007): 44.

42 Irving Abella, 'Antisemitism in Canada: New Perspectives on an Old Problem,' in Brown, ed., *Approaches to Antisemitism*, 46–56, 53.

43 *CJN*, 13 March 1997; Harold Troper, 'Ethnic Studies and the Classroom Discussion of Antisemitism,' in Brown, ed., *Approaches to Antisemitism*, 193–203, 203.

44 Waller, 'Canada,' *AJYB* 98 (1998): 191–210, 200; *AJYB* 99 (1999): 241.

45 Waller, 'Canada' *AJYB* 102 (2002): 277–303, 287.

46 Warren Kinsella, *Web of Hate: Inside Canada's Far Right Network* (Toronto, 1994), 349.

47 *CJO* (Sept. 1992); *CJN*, 3 Nov. 1994; Ron Rosenbaum, *Those Who Forget the Past: The Question of Anti-Semitism* (New York, 2004), 189–207, 207; Morton Weinfeld, 'The Changing Dimensions of Contemporary Canadian Antisemitism,' in *Contemporary Antisemitism: Canada and the World*, ed. Derek J. Penslar, Michael R. Marrus, and Janice G. Stein (Toronto, 2005) 35–51, 35; *Jerusalem Post*, 22 July 2005.

48 Waller, 'Canada,' *AJYB* 103 (2003): 299–334, 310–311; *AJYB* 104 (2004): 231–367, 241.

49 Bernard Baskin, 'Canada,' *AJYB* 77 (1977): 324.
50 Ibid., *AJYB* 76 (1976): 253.
51 Ibid., *AJYB* 77 (1977): 326; 78 (1978): 279; 84 (1984): 176; Leo Davids, 'Taking a Closer Look at Canada's Jewish Seniors,' in *A Maturing Community: Jewish Women and Seniors in Canada*, ed. Michael Brown and Leo Davids (Toronto, 2005), 34.
52 Bernard Baskin, 'Canada,' *AJYB* 79 (1979): 193; *AJYB* 80 (1980): 174, 176.
53 Leo Davids, 'Canada: Canadian Jewry: Some Recent Census Findings,' *AJYB* 85 (1985): 193; Waller, 'Canada,' *AJYB* 86 (1986): 232; Baskin, 'Canada,' *AJYB* 84 (1984): 176.
54 Waller, 'Canada,' *AJYB* 89 (1989): 261; *AJYB* 86 (1986): 232.
55 Ibid., *AJYB* 90 (1990): 309.
56 Baskin, 'Canada,' *AJYB* 83 (1983): 190; Waller, 'Canada,' *AJYB* 86 (1986): 232.
57 See Gerald L. Gold, 'A Tale of Two Communities: The Growth and Decline of Small Town Jewish Communities in Northern Ontario and Southwestern Louisiana,' in *The Jews of North America*, ed. Moses Rischin (Detroit, 1987), 224–34.
58 Melvin Fenson, 'Canada,' *AJYB* 75 (1974–5): 350–1; Baskin, 'Canada,' *AJYB* 76 (1976): 251; Waller, 'Canada,' *AJYB* 96 (1996): 201; *AJYB* 89 (1989): 262.
59 See Rachel Schlesinger, 'Changing Roles of Jewish Women,' in *Canadian Jewry Today: Who's Who in Canadian Jewry*, ed. Edmond Y. Lipsitz (Downsview, 1989), 60–70; Francine Zuckerman, ed., *Half the Kingdom: Seven Jewish Feminists* (Montreal, 1992), 9, 67, 102.
60 Michael Brown, 'Signs of the Times: Changing Notions of Citizenship, Governance and Authority as Reflected in Synagogue Constitutions,' paper presented to Conference on Canadian Jewish Studies, York University, 1998; Sheva Medjuck, 'If I Cannot Dance to It, It's Not My Revolution: Jewish Feminism in Canada Today,' in *The Jews in Canada*, ed. Robert J. Brym, William Shaffir, and Morton Weinfeld (Toronto, 1993), 328–43, 341.
61 Waller, 'Canada,' *AJYB* 91 (1991): 234.
62 Baskin, 'Canada,' *AJYB* 83 (1983): 189; *AJYB* 84 (1984): 177. Calgary had received some Soviet Jewish families since the early 1970s. See Arthur Levin, 'A Soviet Jewish Family Comes to Calgary,' *CES/EEC* 6, nos. 1–2 (1974): 53–66. See also Roberta L. Markus and Donald V. Schwartz, 'Soviet Jewish Emigres in Toronto: Ethnic Self-Identity and Issues of Integration,' in Brym, Shaffir, and Weinfeld, eds, *The Jews in Canada*, 402–20.
63 Robert J. Brym, 'Jewish Immigrants from the Former Soviet Union in Canada,' *East European Jewish Affairs* 31 (2001): 34–41, 40.
64 Marion Marks to the author, 24 March 1997; Dr Aubrey Groll to the author, 30 May 1997.

65 Baskin, 'Canada,' *AJYB* 78 (1978): 283; Waller, 'Canada,' *AJYB* 92 (1992): 293; Baskin, 'Canada,' *AJYB* 83 (1983): 189.
66 See Ruth Linn and Nurit Barkan Ascher, 'Imaginary Suitcases in the Lives of Israeli Expatriates in Canada: A Psychological Look at a Unique Historical Phenomenon,' *CJS/EJC* 2 (1994): 21–40, 21–3, 37.
67 Peter Kruitenbrower, 'Fleeing the Promised Land,' *Maclean's*, 13 Jan. 1997, p. 58–9; *Montreal Gazette*, 27 Jan. 2007.
68 *CJN*, 19 June 1964.
69 Ibid., 4 Feb. and 25 Aug. 1972; Baskin, 'Canada,' *AJYB* 78 (1978): 280; *AJYB* 79 (1979): 200; Waller, 'Canada,' *AJYB* 86 (1986): 233.
70 Ibid., *AJYB* 88 (1988): 253; Michael M. Rosenberg and Jack Jedwab, 'Institutional Completeness, Ethnic Organizational Style and the Role of the State: The Jewish, Italian and Greek Communities of Montreal,' *CRSA/RCSA* 29, no. 3 (1992): 266–87, 276.
71 *National Post*, 29 Sept. 2006.
72 Waller, 'Canada,' *AJYB* 86 (1986): 233.
73 Baskin, 'Canada,' *AJYB* 77 (1977): 325; Morton Weinfeld, 'Between Quality and Quantity: Demographic Trends and Jewish Continuity, in *Creating the Jewish Future*, ed. Michael Brown and Bernard Lightman (Walnut Creek, 1998), 234–47, 243.
74 Baskin, 'Canada,' *AJYB* 81 (1981): 188.
75 *CJC*, 19 Sept. 1952.
76 *CJN*, 12 Jan. 1962; 29 June 1973.
77 Ibid., 11 May 1973.
78 Ibid., 22 and 31 Aug. 1975; 18 Oct. 1974; 26 Nov. 1975, 9 May 1975; 1 Feb. 1975.
79 See Morton Weinfeld, 'Jewish Education: Some Modest Proposals,' *Viewpoints* 14, no. 1 (1986); *CJN*, 27 Aug. 1987; Morton Weinfeld and Susan Zelkowitz, 'Reflections on the Jewish Polity and Jewish Education,' in Brym, Shaffir, and Weinfeld, eds, *The Jews in Canada*, 142–52, 152.
80 *CJN*, 15 Dec. 1979; 28 April 1994; *Covenant*, 24 March 1994; *CJN*, 10 March 1972.

Epilogue: *Oyfn Veg* (On the Road)

1 Morton Weinfeld, 'Canada since 1960,' in *Encyclopedia Judaica*, 2nd ed., ed. Michael Berenbaum and Fred Skolnik, 22 vols (Detroit, 2007), 4: 410–21.
2 Jennifer Freed, 'Making Minyan,' *Salt* 11, no. 1 (Nov. 1991): 22–33.
3 Weinfeld, 'Canada since 1960,' 4: 410–21.
4 Ibid.

5 See Faydra L. Shapiro, 'Learning to Be a Diaspora Jew through the Israel Experience,' in *The Canadian Jewish Studies Reader*, ed. Richard Menkis and Norman Ravvin (Calgary, 2004), 224–40. The controversy in 1998 over a proposed Holocaust exhibit at the National War Museum is a case in point.
6 Jim L. Torczyner and Shari Brotman, 'Jewish Continuity in Canada,' *Viewpoints* 22, no. 2 (1994): 3-5, 5; Morton Weinfeld, 'Between Quality and Quantity: Demographic Trends and Jewish Survival,' paper presented at the conference, 'Creating the Jewish Future,' Centre for Jewish Studies, York University, Oct. 1996, p. 27.
7 Weinfeld, 'Canada since 1960,' 4: 410–21.
8 Moses Milstein, 'Memories of Montreal – and Richness,' *Globe and Mail*, 28 April 1998.
9 One of the most recent and widely distributed of these books is the richly illustrated anthology *Growing Up Jewish: Canadians Tell Their Own Stories*, ed. Rosalie Sharp, Irving Abella, and Edwin Goodman (Toronto, 1997).
10 The Association holds an annual conference where papers are presented by scholars on their research.
11 *Globe and Mail*, 5 Feb. 1998.
12 A term I have borrowed from Stephen J. Whitfield, 'The Enigmas of Modern Jewish Identity,' *JSS* 8, nos. 2–3 (2002): 162–7.
13 *National Post*, 12 sept. 2006; Peter Black, 'Quebec's Troubled Past – and Current – Relationship with Jews,' *Whig Standard*, 11 Aug. 2006; Mark Abley, 'Sympathy for Lebanon Widespreads,' *Toronto Star*, 19 Aug. 2006; Lysiane Gagnon, 'When Talk Becomes Anti-Semitic,' *Globe and Mail*, 3 July 2006.
14 Merrily Weisbord, 'Being at Home,' in *Boundaries of Identity: A Quebec Reader*, ed. William Dodge (Toronto, 1992), 157–9, 159.
15 Zvi Gittelman, 'The Decline of the Diaspora Jewish Nation: Boundaries, Content, and Jewish Identity,' *JSS* 4, no. 2 (1998): 112–32.

A Select Bibliography of Secondary Sources

Abella, Irving. *A Coat of Many Colours: Two Centuries of Jewish Life in Canada.* Toronto, 1990.
– ed. 'Portrait of a Jewish Professional Revolutionary: The Recollections of Joshua Gershman.' *Labour / Le Travail* 2 (1977): 185–213.
Abella, Irving, and Harold Troper. *None Is Too Many: Canada and the Jews of Europe, 1933–1948.* Toronto, 1982.
Anctil, Pierre, *Le Devoir, les juifs et l'immigration: de Bourassa à Laurendeau.* Quebec, 1988.
– *Le Rendez-vous manqué: les juifs de Montréal face au Québec de l'entre-deux-guerres.* Montreal, 1988.
– *Tur malka: flâneries sur les cimes de l'histoire juive montréalaise.* Sillery, 1997.
– ed. *Through the Eyes of the Eagle: The Early Montreal Yiddish Press, 1907–1916.* Translated from the Yiddish by David Rome. 2001. Montreal, 2001.
Anctil, Pierre, Ira Robinson, and Gérard Bouchard, eds. *Juifs et canadiens français dans la société québécoise.* Sillery, 1999.
Arnold, Abraham J. 'Jewish Immigration to Western Canada in the 1880s.' *CJHSJ*/SHJCJ 1, no. 2 (1977): 82–95.
Babcock, Robert H., 'A Jewish Immigrant in the Maritimes: The Memoirs of Max Vanger.' *Acadiensis* 16, no. 1 (Autumn 1986): 136–48.
Belkin, Simon. *Di Poale Zion Bavegung in Kanada: 1904–1920.* Montreal, 1956.
– *Through Narrow Gates: A Review of Jewish Immigration, Colonization and Immigrant Aid Work in Canada (1840–1940).* Montreal, 1966.
Bercuson, David J. *Canada and the Birth of Israel: A Study in Canadian Foreign Policy.* Toronto, 1985.
Berdugo-Cohen, Maria, Yolande Cohen, and Joseph Levy. *Juifs marocains à Montréal: Témoinages d'une immigration moderne.* Montreal, 1987.

Betcherman, Lita-Rose. 'Clara Brett Martin's Anti-Semitism.' *Canadian Journal of Women and the Law* 5 (1992): 280–97.
Bialystok, Frank. *Delayed Impact: The Holocaust and the Canadian Jewish Community.* Montreal, 2000.
Bianco, Anthony. *The Reichmanns: Family, Faith, Fortune, and the Empire of Olympia & York.* Toronto, 1997.
Biderman, Morris. *A Life on the Jewish Left: An Immigrant's Experience.* Toronto, 2000.
Brecher, M. 'Patterns of Accommodation in the Men's Garment Industry of Quebec, 1914–1954.' In *Patterns of Industrial Dispute Settlement in Five Canadian Industries.* Ed. W.D. Woods. Montreal, 1958.
Brown, Michael. 'The Americanization of Canadian Zionism, 1917–1982.' In *Contemporary Jewry: Studies in Honor of Moshe Davis.* Ed. Geoffrey Wigoder, 129–58. Jerusalem, 1984.
– 'The Beginnings of Reform Judaism in Canada.' *JSS* 34 (1972): 322–42.
– 'Divergent Paths: Early Zionism in Canada and the United States.' *JSS* 44 (Spring 1982): 149–68.
– *'Jew or Juif? Jews, French Canadians, and Anglo-Canadians, 1759–1914.* Philadelphia, 1987.
– 'The Push and Pull Factors of Aliyah and the Anomalous Case of Canada: 1967–1982.' *JSS* 48, no. 2 (1986): 141–62.
Brym, Robert. 'Jewish Immigrants from the Former Soviet Union in Canada.' *East European Jewish Affairs* 31 (2001): 34–41.
Brym, Robert, and Rhonda L. Lenton. 'The Distribution of Anti-Semitism in Canada in 1984.' *Canadian Journal of Sociology* 16, no. 4 (1994): 411–18.
Brym, Robert, William Shaffir, and Morton Weinfeld, eds. *The Jews in Canada.* Toronto, 1993.
Butovsky, Mervin, and Ode Garfinkle, eds. and trans. *The Journals of Yaacov Zipper, 1950–1982: The Struggle for Yiddishkeit.* Montreal, 2004.
Caplan, Usher. *Like One That Dreamed: A Portrait of A.M. Klein.* Toronto, 1982.
Chiel, Arthur A. *The Jews in Manitoba: A Social History.* Toronto, 1961.
Cohn, Werner. 'English and French Canadian Public Opinion on Jews and Israel: Some Poll Data.' *CES/EEC* 2, no. 2 (1979): 31–48.
Danson, Barney. *Not Bad for a Sergeant: The Memoirs of Barney Danson.* Toronto, 2002.
Davids, Leo. 'Taking a Closer Look at Canada's Jewish Seniors.' In *A Maturing Community: Jewish Women and Seniors in Canada.* Ed. Michael Brown and Leo Davids. Toronto, 2005.
Davies, Alan, ed. *Antisemitism in Canada: History and Interpretation.* Waterloo, 1992.

Davies, Alan, and Marilyn F. Nefsky. *How Silent Were the Churches? Canadian Protestantism and the Jewish Plight during the Nazi Era.* Waterloo, 1997.

Dekar, Paul R. 'From Jewish Mission to Inner City Mission: The Scott Mission and Its Antecedents in Toronto, 1908 to 1964.' In *Canadian Protestant and Catholic Missions, 1820–1860s: Historical Essays in Honour of John Webster Grant.* Ed. John S. Moir and C.T. McIntire. New York, 1988.

Delisle, Esther. *The Traitor and the Jew: Anti-Semitism and the Delirium of Extremist Right-Wing Nationalism in French Canada from 1929–1939.* Trans. Madelaine Hébert. Montreal, 1993.

Diamond, Etan. *And I Will Dwell in Their Midst: Orthodox Jews in Suburbia.* Chapel Hill, 2000.

Draper, Paula J. 'The Accidental Immigrants: Canada and the Interned Refugees: Part 1.' *CJHSJ/SHJCJ* 2, no. 1 (1978): 1–38; 'Part 2,' *CJHSJ/SHJCJ* 2, no. 2 (1978): 80–112.

– 'Canadian Holocaust Survivors: From Liberation to Rebirth.' *CJS/EJC* 4–5 (1996–7): 39–62.

– 'Surviving Their Survival: Women, Memory, and the Holocaust.' In *Sisters or Strangers: Immigrant, Ethnic, and Radicalized Women in Canadian History.* Ed. Marlene Epp, Franca Iacovetta, and Frances Swyripa, 399–414. Toronto, 2004.

Draper, Paula J., and Janice B. Karlinsky. 'Abraham's Daughters: Women, Charity and Power in the Canadian Jewish Community.' In *Looking into My Sister's Eyes: An Exploration in Women's History.* Ed. Jean Burnet. Toronto, 1986.

Eisen, Wendy. *Count Us In: The Struggle to Free Soviet Jews: A Canadian Perspective.* Toronto, 1995.

Elazar, Daniel J., and Harold Waller. *Maintaining Consensus: The Canadian Jewish Polity in the Postwar World.* New York, 1990.

Elliott, David R. 'Anti-Semitism and the Social Credit Movement: The Intellectual Roots of the Keegstra Affair.' *CES/EEC* 27, no. 1 (1985): 78–89.

Figler, Bernard, and David Rome. *Hananiah Meir Caiserman: A Biography with an Essay on Modern Jewish Times by David Rome.* Montreal, 1962.

Frager, Ruth. *Sweatshop Strife: Class, Ethnicity, and Gender in the Jewish Labour Movement of Toronto, 1900–1939.* Toronto, 1992.

Genizi, Haim. *The Holocaust, Israel, and the Canadian Protestant Churches.* Montreal, 2002.

Gidney, R.D., and W.P.J. Millar, '"We Wanted Our Children to Have It Better": Jewish Medical Students at the University of Toronto, 1910–1951.' *Canadian Historical Association Journal* 11 (2000): 109–24.

Glass, Joseph B. 'Isolation and Alienation: Factors in the Growth of Zionism in the Canadian Prairies, 1917–1939.' *CJS/EJC* 9 (2001): 85–123.

Godfrey, Sheldon, and Judith Godfrey. *'Burn This Gossip': The True Story of George Benjamin of Belleville, Canada's First Jewish Member of Parliament 1857–1863.* Toronto, 1991.
– *Search Out the Land: The Jews and the Growth of Equality in British Colonial America, 1740–1867.* Montreal, 1995.
Goldberg, David H. *Foreign Policy and Ethnic Interest Groups: American and Canadian Jews Lobby for Israel.* New York, 1990.
Gonick, Cy. *A Very Red Life: The Story of Bill Walsh.* St John's, 2001.
Gotheil, Allen. *Les juifs progressistes au Québec.* Montreal, 1988.
Greenstein, Michael. *Third Solitude: Tradition and Discontinuity in Jewish-Canadian Literature.* Montreal, 1989.
Gutkin, Harry. *Journey into Our Heritage.* Toronto, 1980.
Gutkin, Harry, with Mildred Gutkin. *The Worst of Times, the Best of Times: Growing Up in Winnipeg's North End.* Toronto, 1987.
Hart, Arthur D., ed. *The Jew in Canada: A Complete Record of Canadian Jewry from the Days of the French Regime to the Present Time.* Montreal, 1926.
Hiebert, Daniel. 'Discontinuity and the Emergence of Flexible Production: Garment Production in Toronto, 1901–1931.' *Economic Geography,* July 1990, 225–42.
Hoffer, Clara, and F.H. Kahan. *Land of Hope.* Illustrated by William Perehudoff. Saskatoon, 1960.
Jedwab, Jack. 'Uniting Uptowners and Downtowners: The Jewish Electorate and Quebec Provincial Politics, 1927–39.' *CES/EEC* 18, no. 2 (1986): 7–19.
Kahn, Alison. *Listen While I Tell You: A Story of the Jews of St. John's, Newfoundland.* St John's, 1987.
Katz, Y., and J. Lehr. 'Jewish and Mormon Agricultural Settlement in Western Canada: A Comparative Analysis.' *Canadian Geographer / Géographie Canadienne* 35, no. 2 (1991): 128–42.
Kay, Zachariah. *Canada and Palestine: The Politics of Non-commitment.* Jerusalem, 1978.
Klein, A.M. *Beyond Sambation: Selected Essays and Editorials, 1928–1955.* Ed. M.W. Steinberg and Usher Kaplan. Toronto, 1982.
Klein, Ruth, and Frank Dimant, eds. *From Immigration to Integration: The Canadian Jewish Experience.* Toronto, 2001.
Lappin, Ben. *The Redeemed Children: The Story of the Rescue of War Orphans by the Jewish Community of Canada.* Toronto, 1963.
Larrue, Jean-Marc. *Le théâtre yiddish à Montréal.* Montreal, 1996.
Layton, Irving. *Waiting for the Messiah.* Don Mills, 1985.
Levendel, Lewis. *A Century of the Canadian Jewish Press, 1880s-1980s.* Ottawa, 1989.
Levitt, Cyril H., and William Shaffir. *The Riot at Christie Pits.* Toronto, 1987.

Levitt, Sheldon, Lynne Milstone, and Sidney T. Tenenbaum. *Treasures of a People: The Synagogues of Canada*. Toronto, 1985.
Lewis, David. *The Good Fight: Political Memoirs, 1909–1958*. Toronto, 1981.
Linn, Ruth, and Nurit Barkan Ascher. 'Imaginary Suitcases in the Lives of Israeli Expatriates in Canada: A Psychological Look at a Unique Historical Phenomenon.' *CJS/EJC* 2 (1994): 21–40.
Lipinsky, Jack. 'The Apprenticeship of an Executive Director: M.A. Solkin, A.J. Paul and the Jewish Immigrant Aid Society of Canada.' *CJHSJ/SHJCJ* 9, no. 2 (1985): 67–81.
Littman, Sol. *War Criminals on Trial: The Rauca Case*. Markham, 1984.
Lo, Laurelle. 'The Path from Peddling: Jewish Economic Activity in Ottawa Prior to 1939.' In *Construire une capital / Ottawa / Making a Capital*. Ed. Jeff Keshen and Nicole St-Onge. Ottawa, 2001.
MacFadyen, Joshua D. '"Nip the Noxious Growth in the Bud": Ortenberg v. Plamendon and the Roots of Canadian Anti-hate Activism.' *CJS/EJC* 12 (2004): 73–96.
Marks, Lynne. 'Kale Meydelach or Shulamith Girls: Cultural Change and Continuity among Jewish Parents and Daughters – A Case Study of Toronto's Harbord Collegiate Institute in the 1920s.' *Canadian Women's Studies* 7, no. 3 (1986): 85–9.
Markus, Roberta L., and Donald V. Schwarts. 'Soviet Jewish Emigres in Toronto: Ethnic Self-Identity and Issues of Integration.' *CES/EEC* 16, no. 2 (1984): 71–88.
Marrus, Michael R. *Mr. Sam: The Life and Times of Samuel Bronfman*. Toronto, 1991.
Martz, Fraidie. *Open Your Hearts: The Story of the Jewish War Orphans in Canada*. Toronto, 1996.
Matas, David, with Susan Charendoff. *Justice Delayed: Nazi War Criminals in Canada*. Toronto, 1987.
Maynard, Fredelle Bruser. *Raisins and Almonds*. Toronto, 1985.
– *The Tree of Life*. Toronto, 1989.
McGrath, Robin. *Salt Fish and Shmattes: A History of the Jews in Newfoundland and Labrador from 1770*. St John's, 2006.
Medjuck, Sheva. *The Jews of Atlantic Canada*. St John's, 1986.
Medres, Israel. *Between the Wars: Canadian Jews in Transition*. Trans. from the Yiddish by Vivian Felsen. Montreal, 2003.
– *Montreal of Yesterday: Jewish Life in Montreal, 1900–1920*. Trans. from the Yiddish by Vivian Felsen. Montreal, 2000.
Meirovitch, Harvey. 'The Rise and Decline of a Toronto Synagogue: Congregation Beth Am.' *CJHSJ/SHJCJ* 1, no. 2 (1977): 97–113.

Menkis, Richard. 'Historiography, Myth and Group Relations: Jewish and Non-Jewish Québécois on Jews and New France.' *CES/EEC* 23, (1991): 24–38.
– '"In This Great, Happy and Enlightened Colony." Abraham De Sola on Jews, Judaism and Emancipation in Victorian Montreal.' In *L'antisemitisme éclairé: Inclusion and Exclusion: Perspectives and Jews from the Enlightenment to the Dreyfus Affair*. Ed. Ilana Zinquer et Sam W. Bloom, Leiden, 2003. 315–31.
Menkis, Richard, and Norman Ravvin, eds. *The Canadian Jewish Studies Reader*. Calgary, 2005.
Miller, Ronnie. *From Lebanon to the Intifada: The Jewish Lobby and Canadian Middle Eastern Policy*. Lanham, 1991.
Myers, Tamara. 'On Probation: The Rise and Fall of Jewish Women's Antidelinquency Work in Interwar Montreal.' In *Negotiating Identities in 19th- and 20th-Century Montreal*. Ed. Bettina Bradbury and Tamara Myers, 175–201. Vancouver, 2005.
Oliver, Peter. *Unlikely Tory: The Life and Politics of Allan Grossman*. Toronto, 1985.
Patrias, Carmela, and Ruth A. Frager. '"This Is Our Country, These Are Our Rights": Minorities and the Origin of Ontario's Human Rights Campaigns.' *Canadian Historical Review* 82 (March 2001): 1–35.
Penslar, Derek J., Michael R. Marrus, and Janice G. Stein, eds. *Contemporary Antisemitism: Canada and the World*. Toronto, 2005.
Pollock, Zailig. *A.M. Klein: The Story of the Poet*. Toronto, 1994.
Ravvin, Norman. *A House of Words: Jewish Writing, Identity, and Memory*. Montreal, 1997.
Reiter, Ester. 'Camp Naivelt and the Daughters of the Jewish Left.' In *Sister or Strangers? Immigrant, Ethnic, and Radicalized Women in Canadian History*. Ed. Marlene Epp, Franca Iacovetta, and Frances Swyripa, 365–80. Toronto, 2004.
Robinson, Ira. 'Kabbalist and Community Leader: Rabbi Yudel Rosenberg and the Canadian Jewish Community.' *CJS/EJC* 1 (1993): 41–58.
– *Rabbis and Their Community: Studies in the Eastern European Orthodox Rabbinate in Montreal, 1896–1930*. Calgary, 2008.
Robinson, Ira, and Mervin Butovsky, eds. *Renewing Our Days: Montreal Jews in the Twentieth Century*. Montreal, 1995.
Robinson, Ira, et al., eds. *An Everyday Miracle: Yiddish Culture in Montreal*. Montreal, 1990.
Rosenberg, Leah. *The Errand Runner: Reflections of a Rabbi's Daughter*. Toronto, 1981.
Rosenberg, Louis. *Canada's Jews: A Social and Economic Study of the Jews in Canada*. Montreal, 1939.
Rouillard, Jacques. 'Les travailleurs juifs de la confection à Montréal (1910–1980).' *Labour / Le Travail* 8/9 (1981/82): 253–9.

Sack, Benjamin G. *History of the Jews in Canada*. Montreal, 1965.
Saint-Pierre, Jocelyn. 'Les écoles juives et les débats parlementaires de l'Assemblée Législative du Québec. *CJS/EJC* 9 (2001): 210–50.
Samuel, Sigmund. *In Return: The Autobiography of Sigmund Samuel*. Toronto, 1963.
Scher, Len. *The Un-Canadians: True Stories of the Blacklist Era*. Toronto, 1992.
Shaffir, William. *Life in a Religious Community: The Lubavitcher Chassidim in Montreal*. Cultures and Communities: Community Studies. Toronto, 1974.
Sharp, Rosalie, Irving Abella, and Edwin Goodman, eds. *Growing Up Jewish: Canadians Tell Their Own Stories*. Toronto, 1997.
Sniderman, Paul M., et al. 'Psychological and Cultural Foundations of Prejudice: The Case of Antisemitism in Quebec.' *CRSA/RCSA* 30, no. 2 (1993): 242–70.
Speisman, Stephen A. *The Jews of Toronto: A History to 1937*. Toronto, 1979.
Steedman, Mercedes. *Angels of the Workplace: Women and the Construction of Gender Relations in the Canadian Clothing Industry, 1890–1940*. Toronto, 1997.
Stingel, Janine. *Social Discredit: Anti-Semitism, Social Credit and the Jewish Response*. Montreal, 2000.
Stone, Daniel, ed. *Jewish Radicalism in Winnipeg, 1905–1960*. Winnipeg, 2003.
Stortz, Paul. '"Rescue Our Family from a Living Death": Refugee Professors and the Canadian Society for the Protection of Science and Learning at the University of Toronto, 1935–1946.' *Canadian Historical Association Journal* (2003): 231–61.
Swerdlow, Max. *Brother Max: Labour Organizer and Educator*. Ed. Gregory S. Kealey. St John's, 1990.
Taras, David, and David H. Goldberg, eds. *The Domestic Battleground: Canada and the Arab-Israeli Conflict*. Montreal, 1989.
Taschereau, Sylvie. 'Les sociétés de prêt juives à Montréal, 1911–1945.' *Urban History Review / Revue Historique Urbain 33*, no. 2 (Spring 2005): 3–16.
Trachtenberg, H. 'The Winnipeg Jewish Community and Politics: The Interwar Years, 1919–1939.' *Historical and Scientific Society of Manitoba, Transactions*. ser. 3, nos. 34–5 (1977–8; 1978–9): 115–53, 119–20.
Troper, Harold. 'Canada and the Survivors of the Holocaust: The Crisis of the Displaced Person.' In *'She'erith Hapleta: 1944–1948: Rehabilitation and Political Struggle*. Ed. Y. Gutman and Avital Saf, 261–85. Jerusalem, 1990.
– 'The Canadian Jewish Polity and the Limits of Political Action: The Campaign on Behalf of Soviet and Syrian Jews.' In *Ethnicity, Politics and Public Policy in Canada: Case Studies in Canadian Diversity*. Ed. Harold Troper and Morton Weinfeld. Toronto, 1999.
– 'Jews and Canadian Immigration Policy, 1900–1950.' In *The Jews of North America*. Ed. Moses Rischin, 44–58. Detroit, 1987.

- *The Ransomed of God: The Story of One Woman's Role in the Rescue of Syrian Jews.* Toronto, 1999.
Troper, Harold, and Morton Weinfeld. *Old Wounds: Jews, Ukrainians and the Hunt for Nazi War Criminals in Canada.* Toronto, 1988.
Tulchinsky, Gerald. *Branching Out: The Transformation of the Canadian Jewish Community.* Toronto, 1998.
- 'Family Quarrel: Joe Salsberg, the "Jewish" Question, and Canadian Communism.' *Labour / Le Travail* 56 (Fall 2005): 149–73.
- 'Hidden among the Smokestacks.' In *Essays in Honour of J.M.S. Careless.* Ed. David Keane, 257–84. Toronto, 1990.
- 'Immigration and Charity in the Montreal Jewish Community to 1890.' *Histoire sociale / Social History* 16, no. 33 (November 2000): 370–91.
- *Taking Root: The Origins of the Canadian Jewish Community.* Toronto, 1992.
Usiskin, Michael. *Uncle Mike's Edenbridge: Memoirs of a Jewish Pioneer Farmer.* Trans. from Yiddish by Marcia Usiskin Basman, Winnipeg, 1983.
Usiskin, Roz. 'Continuity and Change: The Jewish Experience in Winnipeg's North End, 1900–1914.' *CJHSJ / SHJCJ* 4 (1980): 71–94, 84.
Walker, James W. St G. 'Canadian Anti-Semitism and Jewish Community Response: The Case of Noble and Wolfe.' In *Multiculturalism, Jews, and Identities in Canada.* Ed. Howard Adelman and John H. Simpson, 37–68. Jerusalem, 1996.
Waller, Harold. 'The Impact of the Six-Day War on the Organizational Life of Canadian Jewry.' In *The Six-Day War and World Jewry.* Ed. Eli Lederhendler, 81–97. Bethesda, 2000.
Weinfeld, M., W. Shaffir, and I. Cotler, eds. *The Canadian Jewish Mosaic.* Toronto, 1981.
Weinfeld, Morton. *Like Everyone Else ... but Different: The Paradoxical Success of Canadian Jews.* Toronto, 2001.
Wolofsky, Hirsh. *Journey of My Life.* Montreal, 1945.
Zuckerman, Francine, ed. *Half the Kingdom: Seven Jewish Feminists.* Montreal, 1992.

Index

1912 strike, 149–51, 153. *See also* Caiserman, Hananiah Meir
1912–13 boycotts, 323–4
1916–17 strike, 158–9; effects on Montreal's Jewish population, 160
1919 Winnipeg General Strike, 164, 188, 220

Aarons, Isaac, 33–4
Abella, (Professor) Irving, 326, 466–7
Aberhart, William 'Bible Bill,' 322
Abraham, Chapman, 18
Abraham Gradis of Bordeaux, 13
Abrahams, Israel, 14; potash manufacturer, 15
Abramowitz, (Rabbi) Dr Herman, 142, 143, 161, 174–5, 344
Abramson, Samuel, 278–81 passim
Achat Chez Nous, 255, 256
Action Catholique, L': antisemitic writings, 303–5
Action Française, L', 312–13
Action sociale, L', 141
Adams, Robert Chambliss, 66
Adilman, Max, 342
Adler, Dr N. (Chief Rabbi of the British Empire), 57
Adler, (Rabbi) Michael, 174
agriculture: Jewish pursuits in, 78, 88–9, 204–5; relief provided to Jews, 234; undercapitalization, 205
Agudath Israel Anshei Sepharade (Toronto), 201
Ahavath Achim (Saint John), 55
Albert, Louis: partnership with William Silverstone, 39–40
Aliyah, 9, 60, 341–3, 361
All for One Society. *See* Alle Far Einem
All-Canadian Congress of Labour, 243, 263
Alle Far Einem (Toronto), 254
Allenby, (General), 160, 178
Alliance Israélite Universelle (Paris), 84, 86, 99–100, 103
Almazoff, Moses, 188
Altman, Victor, 149
Amalgamated Clothing Workers of America (ACWA), 121, 161–2, 163, 188, 243, 261, 263, 551–2n67; board report recommendations, 162; formation of, 154; Joint Board, 162; Montreal Joint Board, 258; strike against John W. Peck, 154–60

American Jewish Agricultural Society, 251
American Jewish Congress: establishment of (1919), 179, 183–4; invitation for Canadian Jews to attend, 181, 184
American Jewish Joint Distribution Committee (the Joint), 225, 401
American Revolution, 15–16, 17, 22, 192
Anctil, (Professor) Pierre, 471
Anglo-Jewish Association, 73, 77
Ansell, David, 40, 84, 101, 519n21
Anthony, Lewis, 38
antisemitism, 8–9, 35–6, 109, 126–45 passim, 132, 236–7, 251, 254, 255, 258, 282, 299–327 passim, 402–3, 408, 409, 460, 469; attacks on Canadian Jews, 139; decline in, 473; desecration of Jewish cemetery at Trois-Rivières, 133, 137; in French Canada, 133, 412–13, 444–7, 471; German-Nazi influence on Canadians, 310; Heritage Front, 471; local Sunday closing legislation (1904), 133; within the military, 378, 382–4; in Montreal, 21; 'new antisemitism,' 473–4; Plamondon libel (*see* Plamondon libel [1910]); in post-war Canada, 415–16; and publications in Montreal, 104–6; in Quebec, 315–16, 471; re-emergence of school question (1901), 133; restrictive covenants as form of, 413–14; socio-economic factors, 302; in Toronto, 325, 471; within universities, 132–3, 319–20, 409–10, 415, 475
Arbeiter Ring (Workmen's Circle), 118, 124, 151, 210, 275–6; complaints of discrimination against Jewish workers, 254; influence of East European Bundist ideas, 275; lodge role, 119; school of (*see* Yiddisher Yugend Farein)
Arcand, Adrian, 299–300, 412; *Le Patriote*, 305, 307
Ascher, Gottschalk, 39
Ascher family, 45, 63
Ashinsky, (Rabbi), 107, 166
Association Canadienne de la Jeunesse Catholique, 140, 141
Association of Survivors of Nazi Oppression, 460
Association Sépharade Francophone. *See* Communauté Sépharade du Québec
Auschwitz: March of the Living, 459, 491

Balfour Declaration (1917), 176, 192, 329–30
Bank of Montreal, 29–30
Banting, Dr Frederick, 319
Baron Byng School (Montreal), 266
Baron de Hirsch Hebrew Benevolent Society (Halifax), 217
Baron de Hirsch Institute (Montreal), 11, 55, 87–8, 94, 103, 108, 117, 515–16n58, 517n79; formation (1891), 55; offshore funding, 104; plans to settle Jews in Northwest, 83–4; qualification that members be unmarried, 513n22; relief programs, 99; school, 99–102, 136. *See also* Young Men's Hebrew Benevolent Society (Montreal)
Barré, Laurent, 314, 409
Beaverbrook, Lord, 332–3
Beilis, Mendel. *See* Beilis 'blood libel'
Beilis 'blood libel,' 143–5 passim

Belkin, Simon, 189
Bellan, Ruth, 207
Bender, (Rabbi) Charles, 255
Ben-Gurion, David, 175, 353
Benjamin, George: as MP, 51; owner-editor of the *Belleville Intelligencer* and *Hastings General Advertiser*, 51
Benjamin, Henry, 43
Benjamin, I.J., 56
Benjamin, Samuel, 43, 72
Benjamin, William, 43
Benjamin family, 44, 95
Bennett, A.B. ('Archie'), 219, 380
Ben-Zvi, Yitchak, 175
Bercovitch, Peter, 150, 155, 161–2, 271, 286, 289, 290–1, 295, 314; election to Quebec Legislative Assembly, 155–6; preparation of the David Bill, 296
Betar, 339
Beth David (Montreal), 93–4
Beth Elohim congregation (Charleston), 67
Beth Yehuda (Montreal), 94
Bevis Marks (London), 62
Bindman, (Lieutenant) David, 384
Blair, Frederick C., 231–41 passim
Blumenberg, Sam, 164
BNA Act. *See* British North America Act
B'nai B'rith, 67, 311, 414, 449, 473–4
B'nai Jacob (Montreal), 93–4
Board of Delegates of Hebrew Congregations, 73–5
Bodeman, Michael, 456–7
Boer War (1899), 107
Bolshevik Revolution, 192, 263
Bond, (Bishop) William Bennett, 76–7
Borovoy, Alan, 467
Bourassa, Henri: condemnation of antisemitism, 308

Brahadi, Abraham, 42–3
Brainin, Reuben, 150, 158, 179, 183, 192; 1914 strike against Vineberg & Co., 529n71
Brandeau, Esther, 13
Brickner, (Rabbi) Barnett, 569n43
British North America Act (1867): education mandate, 100
British North American Jewry: English and German origin, 60–1
British policy: 1938 White Paper, 353–4, 356
Bronfman, Allan, 251, 258
Bronfman, Charles, 445
Bronfman, Samuel, 274, 286, 312, 371, 403, 426, 428
Brotman, Fanny (Pelenovsky), 82
Bruser, Fredelle, 207
Buck, Tim, 247
Buhay, Becky, 164, 265
Buhay, Michael, 164, 265
Buller, Annie, 265
Bumsel, Michael, 45; partnership with Michael Dinklespiel, 39
Businessmen's Strike Relief Committee, 158–9

Caiserman, Hananiah Meir, 154, 158, 180, 183–4, 185, 187, 189–90, 219–20, 220, 223–4, 254, 280, 290–1, 296–7, 308, 349–50, 401–2; establishment of Jewish Immigrant Aid Society, 190; role in 1912 strike, 149–51; support of separate school system, 288–9
Caisses Populaires movement, 94, 141
Calebro, Tony, 159
Canada: Arab/Israeli conflict, 435; as distinct from United States, 4, 73–5, 178, 191–2; immigration policy,

6, 76–8; influence of Jewish community, 4–5; Jewish colonization of, 88–9; Jewish detentions, 227–30, 239–41; multiculturalism, 5–6, 415–16, 439, 457. *See also* Canadian Jewish identity; immigrants; immigration
Canada-Israel Committee, 433–8 passim
Canadian Expeditionary Force (First World War): Jewish participation in, 533n35
Canadian Intelligence Service, 413
Canadian Jewish Alliance, 179–80, 182–3
Canadian Jewish Chronicle, 185–6, 218, 224–5, 239, 526n18; absence of rabbis, 161; fundraising campaign, 249; opposition to Communism, 268; perspectives on French-Canadian workers, 252–3; support of conscription, 375; on 'sweetheart contracts,' 253
Canadian Jewish Committee for Refugees: fundraising proposal for the United Palestine Appeal, 350
Canadian Jewish Conference. *See* Federation of Zionist Societies of Canada
Canadian Jewish Congress, 3, 6, 8, 183–7, 254, 426, 442–3; anti-defamation efforts, 308–10; collapse of, 219; creation of anti-Nazi committee, 460; denouncement of Soviet Union's denial of rights to Jews, 430–1; efforts to bring Holocaust survivors into Canada, 403–4; encouragement of Jewish enlistments, 380–1; entreaties, 466–7; establishment of, 179; financial situation of, 190; formation of (1917), 152; formation of National War Efforts Committee (WEC), 372; formation of Toronto Jewish Congress, 475; formation of Winnipeg Community Council, 475; goal to combat government anti-alien pressures, 187–8; impact on Canadian Jewry, 191–2; Joint Public Relations Committee of the, 311; leadership, 190–1; 1933 revival of, 306–7; principles of, 179–80; reaction to Canadian antisemitism, 309; request for investigation of condition of dependents of Canadian citizens in Ukraine, 189–90; resolution to promote a system of separate Jewish schools, 185, 190; and social fascism, 271; submission to 1949 Royal Commission on National Development in the Arts, Letters and Sciences, 415
Canadian Jewish identity, 7, 9, 23; characteristics of, 7–8; cultural dimensions of, 441–2; Israel as central feature of, 439–40
Canadian Jewish Review, 218
Canadian Jewish Times. *See Canadian Jewish Chronicle*
Canadian National Committee on Refugees and Victims of Political Persecution (CNCR), 235
Canadian Pacific Railway (CPR), 48–9, 59, 78, 82
Canadian Student Assembly (1940), 266
Canadian Zionist Federation, 438. *See also* Federation of Zionist Societies of Canada
Canadien, Le (Quebec), 26
Carr, Sam, 270, 271

Cass, (Rabbi Chaplain) Samuel, 383, 386, 388, 391–400 passim; assistance to Holocaust survivors, 398–9
Cassidy, (Professor) Harry, 261–2
cemeteries, 211
censorship: of Jews, 163–4
Central Canada: colonization, 115–17, 205–7, 234; Jewish population growth, 110–11, 115–16
Central Committee for Interned Refugees (CCIR), 240
Chagelle, Marc, 279
Chalifoux, J.A.: leader of fascist group, 306
chalutz ideal, 360
Charbonneau, (Archbishop), 409
Charbonneau, Yvan, 445
Chevra Bikkur Cholim V'Kedusha (benevolent society in Victoria), 57
Chevra Kadisha (Montreal), 94
Chevra Thilim (Montreal), 94
child labour, 122–3
Chisolm, (Reverend) John, 132
Chovevei Zion (Lovers of Zion), 165
Chown, (Reverend) S.D., 131
Christian Council for Palestine, 355–7
Chronicle, The. See Canadian Jewish Chronicle
Citizen's Committee Jewish Relief Fund (Montreal), 76
Citron, Sabina: founder of Canadian Holocaust Remembrance Association, 466
Clark, (Prime Minister) Joe, 437
Clarke, Dr C.K., 131–2
cloak-makers. *See* International Ladies' Garment Workers' Union
clothing industry, 42–3, 94–5, 162–3, 184, 242–82 passim, 254, 546n154; class conflict within, 258, 263; French-Canadian labourers, 246–8, 252–3, 256; Jewish leadership of joint-boards, 247; Jewish participation in, 145–64 passim, 548n17; 1925 general strike, 247, 248; 1937 strike, 257–8; relocation of production, 261; unions, 145–60 passim, 243, 246–65 passim, 492; use of non-unionized labour, 260; working conditions, 96–9, 146–7, 244, 255–6
CNCR. *See* Canadian National Committee on Refugees and Victims of Political Persecution
Cohen, Isaac, 163, 167
Cohen, Jacob, 95
Cohen, Jacob Raphael, 21
Cohen, Joseph, 289, 291, 292–3
Cohen, Lazarus, 79, 87
Cohen, Leonard, 441–2
Cohen, Lyon, 95, 106, 107, 140, 147, 148–9, 157, 158, 219, 222, 271; controversial role in 1916–17 strike, 184–5; establishment of brass foundry, 148; founding of *Jewish Times*, 148; head of Congress deliberations, 184–5; president of Manufacturers' Association, 155–6. *See also* Freedman Company
Cohen, (Professor) Maxwell, 460
Cohen, M.R., 58
Cohen, (Lieutenant) Myer Tutzer, M.C.; at Battle of Passchendaele (1917), 174
Cohen, Nathan, 374
Cohen, (Reverend), 58
Coleman, Thomas, 50
Colonization Committee, 84, 85
Colville, (Colonel) F.H.M., 413
Commission on the Sweating System in Canada (1896), 96, 97

Committee for the Relief of Ukrainian Orphans, 224
Committee of Nine. *See* Taschereau, Louis-Alexandre
Committee of Trade (Montreal): formation (1822), 29
Committee on Jewish-Gentile Relations: counter-propaganda campaigns, 310
Communauté Sépharade du Québec, 449, 450
Communism, 263–72; attacks against Zionism, 340–1; Jewish Communists, 271–5, 281, 341, 376
Communist IUNTW: 1934 strike, 252, 254
Communist Party of Canada, 243, 247, 264, 279–82; Central Control Commission, 269; *Clarion*, 270; emergence in 1921, 189; establishment of the Jewish National Bureau, 265–6; renaming due to 1940 outlawing of, 269; role of women, 265, 266
Connor, Ralph: *The Foreigner*, 132
Co-operative Commonwealth Federation (CCF), 277–8, 374
Corcos, (Rabbi) Joseph, 292
Cotler, (Professor) Irwin, 445–7, 463, 474, 494
Coughlin, (Father) Charles, 307, 310
Creelman, (Colonel) J.J., 291
Crerar, Thomas A., 235–6
Crestohl, Leon, 364
Croix de Montréal, La, 102, 104; call for boycott of Jewish businesses, 302
Crowley, John, 246
Cuthbert Company: 1937 strike, 271

DaCosta, Isaac, 15
Danson, Barney, 326, 384

Daughters of Zion, 171
David, Athanase, 296
David, David, 19: admission into the Beaver Club, 29; board member of the Lachine Canal Company, 30; as founding director of the Bank of Montreal, 29–30; St James Street synagogue property, 32
David, Dr Aaron Hart, 72
David, Eleazar (s. of Samuel David), 31
David, Phoebe, 23
David bill, 296; repeal of, 299
David family, 63
Davidson, Justice, 137
Davis, Sir Mortimer (s. of Samuel Davis), 41, 229
Dawson, William, 64, 66
de Bernonville, Comte Jacques Duge, 411
de Haas, Jacob, 168
de Hirsch, (Baron) Maurice, 84
de Hirsch, Baroness, 103
de la Penha, Joseph, 13
de Lara, Hazan, 21
de Maurera, Jacob, 13–14
de Sola, (Reverend) Abraham, 62–72, 192; committment to Orthodox Judaism, 66–8; disrespect for 'German school,' 72; as McGill College teacher, 63, 66; opening prayer at the U.S. House of Representatives, 64; opposition to Reform movement, 67; participation in English-language cultural activities, 63–4; philanthropic activities, 65, 69–70; philosophy of Zionism, 169; prejudice against Ashkenazi ritual, 68, 71; recipient of honorary degree, 64; reputation as scholar, 512n8;

research and writing activities, 64–5; spiritual leader of Shearith Israel, 62–4. *See also* Hebrew Philathropic Society
de Sola, Clarence, 72, 135, 166–70 passim, 178, 181, 191; disillusionment with, 173; involvement in Jewish communal welfare, 73–4; letter to the Central Zionist Bureau, 167; as nationalist, 192; view that Zionism was solution to 'Jewish problem,' 182
de Sola, (Rabbi Reverend) Meldola (s. of Abraham de Sola), 100, 101, 161, 192
Delapratz (cigar-maker), 42
Denault, Amédée, 104
Denberg, (Rabbi) Chaim: appointment at Université de Montréal, 409–10
Der Kamf, 266
Dershowitz, Alan, 490
Desbecker, I., 49
Deschênes, Justice Jules: inquiry into war criminals in Canada, 462–6 passim
Deutscher Bund Canada, 310
Devoir, Le (Montreal), 135–6
Dinklespiel, Michael: partnership with Michael Bumsel, 39
discrimination: within universities, 318–21
Disraeli, Benjamin, 127
Dominion Cloak Company, 153
Dominion Lands Act (1872), 77, 80
Dorion, Jules, 298, 299
Dos Yiddishe Vort (Winnipeg), 113, 166
Douglas, (Major) Clifford H., 322
Drapeau, Jean, 269
Dray family, 49
Dreyfus affair, 105–6, 137; effect on Montreal Jewry, 106–7

Droege, Wolfgang: leader of the Heritage Front, 471
Drumont, Édouard, 104, 142; *La France juive*, 134–5
Duhamel, Roger, 412
Dun and Company: antisemitism, 37–8; commercial beginnings, 51; credit reports, 37–61 passim
Dunkelman, Ben, 342, 373, 383
Dunkelman, David, 260, 342–3, 363
Dunkelman, Rose, 172, 342–3; as Ontario Hadassah leader, 340
Duplessis, Maurice, 314, 408; opposition to Communism, 268

Eastern Canada: decline in population, 216–18; Jewish population growth, 110–11, 200
Eastern Europe: Jewish minority rights, 185, 187. *See also* Canada, immigration policy; immigration, from Eastern Europe; Russia
Eaton's. *See* T. Eaton Company
Edelstein, Hyman, 182
Edmonton, 115
education, 190, 283–301 passim, 420–1, 456, 482–3; equality, 138–9, 283–7, 484–5; francophone, 450; funding of Jewish, 483–6; integration, 208. *See also* Quebec, school question
Eisendrath, (Rabbi) Maurice N., 310, 340
Englehart, Jacob, 46
Erlick, Muni, 279–80
European Zionist Federation, 178
Ezekiel, J.W., 50

Factor, Sam, 546n154
Falconer, Sir Robert, 238
family connections, 40–1

farming. *See* agriculture
Farrar, William, 225, 226
Farthing, (Reverend) John, 291–2
fascism, 280–1; threat to French Canadians, 281
Federated Zionist Organization of Canada, 440
Federation of American Zionists, 168
Federation of Jewish Philanthropies (Montreal), 249, 255; establishment of (1916), 214–15; in Toronto, 251
Federation of Zionist Societies of Canada, 165–77, 182–3, 328; Canadian Jewish Conference, 180–3; effects of First World War on program of, 174, 177; establishment (1899), 165–6; fundraising, 170–1, 177–8; membership, 167; opposition to push for a congress, 180; role in communal affairs post–First World War, 173
Feintuch, M., 45
Finkelstein, Sam, 384, 389
Finklestein, M.J., 166
Finta, Imre: prosecution of, 466
First World War, 173–7; Canadian Expeditionary Force, 174; Military Service Act, 174
Fitch, Louis, 142–3, 181, 185, 190, 288, 290, 294, 315
Florentine, Abram, 15
Foreign Enlistment Act: violation of, 278
Forman, Chaya Rivka Wolodarsky, 219
Forrest, (Reverend) Alfred C., 435–7
Fort Henry (Kingston), 163
Frager, (Professor) Ruth, 243
France Juive, La, 104

Francq, Gustave, 248–9
Franklin, Lumley, 56
Franklin, Selim, 56; election to Vancouver Island legislative assembly (1860), 58
Franks, David Salisbury, 22
Franks, Jacob, 14
Franks, Zebulon, 59; later career of, 504n30
Freedman, (Captain) Isidore, 173–4
Freedman Company, 147, 148. *See also* Cohen, Lyon
Freiman, Archie J. (h. of Lillian Freiman), 177, 178, 222, 229, 343, 346–7, 349, 350–1; head of the Federation, 184; as president of the Zionist Organization of Canada, 254, 328–9, 332
Freiman, Lillian (w. of Archie Freiman), 120, 172, 177–8, 222, 227, 334; negotiation of agreement for admission of orphans, 224–7
French-Canadian nationalism, 108, 281, 412–13; antisemitic aspect of, 313–14, 410, 469–70
French Canadians: business ventures of, 302–3
Frères Chasseurs. *See* Hunters' Lodges
Friedman, David (s. of Noah Friedman), 95
Friedman, Noah, 51, 95

Galt, Alexander T., 77–8, 79–81, 83
Garber, Michael, 290
Gauthier, (Monseigneur) Georges, 298
Gelber, Lionel, 320, 337, 564n115
General Federation of Labour, 276
Genkind, Ethel Ostry, 403

Gerber, Jean, 403–4, 405, 407
Gershman, Joshua, 263–4; migration from Poland to Canada, 121; organizer of the Labor Progressive Party, 272–3
Glazer, (Rabbi) Simon, 138, 142
Godbout, Adélard (premier of Quebec), 317
Goel Tzedec (Toronto), 118
Goglu, Le, 315
Goldbloom, Dr Victor, 413
Goldman, Emma, 268
Goldman, Leon, 168–9, 181–2, 331
Goldstein, Maxwell, 137–9, 287, 291
Goodman, Edwin, 383
Gordon, (Rabbi) Nathan, 120, 161
Gouin, Sir Lomer, 290
Gouzenko, Igor, 270, 281–2
Grant, George Munro, 130
Green, Nathan, 54
Grégoire, J.E., 314
Grossman, Allan, 121
Grossman, Vladimir, 205, 234
Groulx, (Abbé) Lionel, 281, 307, 411; attacks on Quebec's Jews, 312; influence on by French racist nationalism, 312–13
Guilbeault, J.A., 252
Guillemette, Aldea, 257
Gunther, E., 44–5
Guralnick, Harry, 267
Gutkin, Mildred, 204
Gutman, Moses, 44
Guttstam, I., 45

Hadassah-WIZO Organization of Canada ('Hadassah'), 171–2, 328, 333–5; class culture of, 124; formation of (1917), 124; women's role in, 333–4; Youth Aliyah, 334–5. *See also* immigrants, women's experiences
Haid, Morris, 245–6
Halifax, 55, 108; establishment of the Hebrew Community Council, 387; Halifax explosion, 217; Jewish community within, 386–7; Starr Street synagogue, 55
Halifax Gazette, 14
Ha-Melitz (Odessa), 79
Hamilton, 49; Jewish population growth, 108–9
Harkavy, Alexander, 165
Harris, Dr J. Alton, 107
Harris, Eliza, 31
Harris, Sidney, 483–4
Hart, Aaron, 18–19, 22–3
Hart, Aaron Philip (n. of Ezekiel Hart), 25, 29
Hart, Abraham, 32, 33
Hart, A.J., 147
Hart, Alexander, 41
Hart, Arthur D., 218
Hart, Benjamin, 25, 30, 32–3
Hart, Dorothea (w. of Aaron Hart), 22–3
Hart, Ezekiel (s. of Aaron Hart), 27–8, 34, 36, 58; election to Quebec Legislative Assembly, 505n44; election to the House of Assembly, 25–7
Hart, Moses (s. of Aaron Hart), 18–19, 25, 29, 507n68; *Modern Religion*, 34–5
Hart, Naphthali, Jr, 15
Hart, Philip (s. of Simon Hart), 39–40
Hart, Samuel: move to Halifax, 15–16; pewholder in St George's Church, 16

Hart, Sarah (d. of Aaron Hart), 23, 31
Hart, Solomon, 54
Hart family, 22–3, 28–30 passim, 63; real estate acquisitions of, 29
Hashomayim, Shaar (Montreal), 107
Hashomer Hatzair, 338–9, 361; establishment of *hachshara* training farm, 360–1
Haskalah, 109–10
Hayes, Moses Judah, 30; role in Montreal's economic development, 30
Hayes, Saul, 237, 274, 412, 415–16, 430
Hays, Andrew: member of first junto, 20
Hayward, Constance, 235
Hazan, Haim, 452
Hebrew Benevolent Society: formation of, 63; reorganization into United Hebrew Charities, 119
Hebrew Immigrant Aid Society (New York), 228, 232
Hebrew Philanthropic Society (Montreal), 63, 69
Helbronner, Jules, 135
Helping Hand Fund, 330
Hershman, Harry, 225; support for Jewish orphans, 226–7
Herzl, Theodor, 108, 165, 167, 169. *See also* Zionism, territorial
Herzl Health Clinic (Montreal), 117
Hester How Public School (Toronto), 118
Hillman, Sidney, 155
Hirsch. *See* Northwest Territories
Hirsch, Baron. *See* de Hirsch, (Baron) Maurice
Hirsch, Michael, 161–2, 291, 292–3
Hirsch cadets. *See* Baron de Hirsch Institute, school

Hirschfield, J., 50
Hoffer, Israel (h. of Clara Hoffer), 116; *Land of Hope*, 206
Hoffman, Abraham, 57
Hoffnung, Abraham, 38–9, 41
Hoffnung family, 47
Holocaust, 3, 9, 365–6, 396–8, 431, 459, 487; denial of, 460; exhibit at the National War Museum (1998), controversy of, 597n5; survivors of the, 401, 403–6, 425, 460
Holy Blossom synagogue (Toronto), 109, 201
Houde, Camillien, 299
Howe, Irving, 457
Howse, (Reverend) Ernest M., 239, 435–6
Hunters' Lodges, 36
Huot, (Abbé) Antonio, 144, 298

ICOR, 266–8
immigrants: 'accidental immigrants,' 240–1; deportation of, 227; discomfort with Canadian Jewish community, 404–7; juvenile delinquency of, 120–1; ties with kinfolk in Europe, 215–16; women's experiences, 123–4
immigration, 74, 108–25 passim, 138, 235, 237, 422; anti-immigrant sentiment, 187, 189, 234–6; from Eastern Europe, 70, 73, 75–6, 93–4, 108–10, 184, 185, 191, 218–19, 221, 232–3, 404, 431–2, 480–2 (*see also* Russia); in the 1870s, 69–70; from Israel, 407, 431–2, 481–2; law of 1910, 220; myths, 5–6; 'permit system,' 236; policy, 189, 220–2, 230–41 passim, 403, 460, 482; resistance to admission of Jewish refugees,

233–41 passim; from South Africa, 481; to urban centres, 117–25, 201–2, 208–9
Immigration Act of 1919, 220–1
Independent Arbeiter Ring, 276
Independent Cloakmakers' Union of Toronto: 1910 strike, 153
Independent Hebrew Association (Kingston): 1902 constitution, 111–12
Industrial Removal Office (IRO), 122
Industrial Union of Needle Trade Workers (IUNTW), 243, 248; attempts to organize Toronto dressmakers, 259; Delight Dress strike (1932), 259
International Colonization Association, 79
International Ladies' Garment Workers' Union (ILGWU), 146, 151, 153, 163, 187, 243, 248, 251–2; battle with Catholic syndicates, 256; call for general strike at all Toronto cloak factories, 259–60; French-Canadian workers, 243; internal tensions, 243; organization of Toronto's dressmakers and cloakmakers, 259; struggles, 246–7
Isaacs, Abraham, 54–5
Israel: migration to, 9 (*see also* Aliyah); militancy of, 435–6; policies of, 431–9, 440. *See also* Zionism
Israel Defense Force (IDF): Canadian Jews' participation in, 364
Iyr Hamelech (Kingston), 454

Jabotinsky, Vladimir: head of Zionist Revisionists, 332
Jacobs, Abraham, 51, 95
Jacobs, Henry, 42

Jacobs, Samuel, 106, 107, 126, 142–3, 186, 219, 222, 230, 233, 286, 308; as MP (1917), 186–7; *shtadlanutl*, 221–2
Jacobs, Samuel (18th-century merchant), 15, 18, 19, 31; partner in brewery at Louisbourg, 15
JCA. *See* Jewish Colonization Association (Paris)
'Jew bill.' *See* Legislative Assembly of Lower Canada, 1831 bill
Jewish Agricultural and Industrial Aid Society, 115. *See also* Jewish Colonization Association (JCA)
Jewish Aid Society of Montreal, 272
Jewish Brigade, 359
Jewish Bund, 110
Jewish Chronicle (London, UK), 71
Jewish Cloakmakers' Union, 147–8
Jewish Colonial Trust, 165–6
Jewish Colonization Association (JCA), 84, 86, 88, 93, 100, 103, 104, 205, 206–8 passim, 232; attempts to alleviate immigrants' distress, 228; establishment of Canadian organization, 115–16; policies of, 206
Jewish community: assimilation, 31; factory workers, 95; ghetto in Montreal, 108–9; isolation of, 60; and the labour movement, 98–9; need for credit, 94; petty commerce, 94; in Quebec's education system, 100–1; reflective of economic opportunities, 110–11; religious education, 32–3
Jewish Community Council (JCC) (Montreal), 286, 288
Jewish Educational Committee (Montreal), 286–7, 291
Jewish educational system. *See* education

Jewish Emigration Aid Society
  (JEAS), 77, 79
Jewish Emigration Society (London,
  UK), 71
Jewish Fraternal Order (Winnipeg),
  272
Jewish Immigrant Aid Society (JIAS),
  190, 222–33 passim, 236–7,
  565n117; criticisms of, 223; financial situation of, 228–9
Jewish Labour Committee, 448
Jewish Labour League, 188
Jewish labour movement, 5–6, 276–7;
  social consciousness, 6
Jewish Legion, 174; recruiting campaign, 175
Jewish liberalism, 455–6
Jewish National Fund, 170, 341,
  345–7
Jewish National Workers' Alliance,
  210; Peretz branch, 210
Jewish nationalism. See Zionism
Jewish People's Restaurant for the
  Unemployed (Montreal), 249
Jewish population: appeal of Communism, 263–4; in Canada, 10,
  75–6, 109–10. (see also immigration); civil rights, 25, 181, 414–15;
  commercial beginnings, 37; criminality, 209–10; decline in formal
  religiosity, 22, 62; demographics
  of, 421, 478–9; education of (see
  education; Quebec, school question); equal rights, 184, 283; family size, 204; French, 13–16; future
  of, 480–1; German and Polish
  split, 34; governance, 214; intermarriage, 22–3, 421–2, 490–1;
  Liberal support, 315; in Montreal,
  70–1; myths and superstitions
  about, 140–3, 411; occupational
  diversity, 208–9; philanthropy, 214–
  15, 344, 424–6; Portuguese, 13–16;
  post-war distribution of, 415–19
  passim; post-war family values, 419;
  post-war migration, 9–10; proclivity for self-employment, 421; religious devotion, 32–3; as second-
  class citizens, 28, 209, 300; separate
  school system, 283–301, 288–9;
  split within, 438–43; suburbanization of, 416, 490; support for Israel,
  432–4; threat of modernity, 193–5,
  489; use of Yiddish within, 491–2;
  violence against, 314–15
Jewish refugees. See immigration,
  resistance to admission of Jewish
  refugees
Jewish Reinforcement Company
  (1917), 174
Jewish school board, 296–7; contract
  with Protestant boards, 297;
  requests from Protestants, 297
Jewish Socialist Democratic Party of
  Canada, 188
Jewish Socialist Party: of Toronto, 188
Jewish Standard (Toronto), 218
Jewish Times (Montreal), 96, 105, 106–
  8, 150–1; racist direction, 107; on
  sectarian education, 139; support
  of Zionism, 108, 169
Jewish trade: in the colonial era, 13–19;
  observers of ancient tradition, 16
Jewish Western Bulletin, 113, 218
Jewish women. See women
Jewish Women's Labour League. See
  Yiddisher Arbeiter Froyen Farein
Jewish Workers' Conference, 288
Jewish Youth Organization. See
  Yiddisher Yugend Farein

Jews: business partnerships, 38–40; commercial pursuits, 112–13; communal experience, 110–12; family connections, 38–40; fundraising activities, 160, 249
JIAS. *See* Jewish Immigrant Aid Society
Jodoin, Claude, 252
Joint Board. *See* Amalgamated Clothing Workers of America (ACWA)
Joseph, Abraham, 31
Joseph, Bernard, 175–6; formation of Young Judaea, 175
Joseph, Jacob Henry, 40–1
Joseph, Jesse, 70; president of Montreal Gas Company, 38
Joseph, Judah George, 45–6
Joseph, (Professor) Norma, 479–80
Joseph family, 53, 63
Journeymen Tailors' Union, 152
Judaean Benevolent and Friendly Society, 119
Judah, Bernard, 23
Judah, Uriah: as gabay, 20
Judaism: Orthodox congregation, 422–4, 454; Reform congregation (*see* Reform movement); 'traditional', 423, 454

Kadima. *See* Reform movement
Kanigsberg, R., 565n117
Kattan, Naim, 412
Kaufman, Yehuda, 180, 185
Kayfetz, Ben, 414
Keegstra, James, 467, 468
Kellert, Harris, 51, 95. *See also* Freedman Company
Keneder Adler, 160–1, 218, 230; fundraising campaign, 249
Keren Hatarbut, 440–1

Keren Hayesod, 339–40, 345; fundraising campaigns, 343, 344
Keren Kayemeth. *See* Jewish National Fund
Kesher Shel Barzel, 67–8
King, (Prime Minister) William Lyon Mackenzie, 4, 131, 231, 234–5, 237, 330, 507n69, 545n142; exploitation of labour investigations, 96–7; policy on immigration, 235–8 passim
Kirkconnell, Watson, 238
Kirschbaum, Dr Josef, 462
Kishinev: pogroms (1902), 108
Klein, Abraham Moses, 239, 261, 317, 336–7, 381–2, 409, 441, 493
Knesset Israel, 201
Kogan, Schmil. *See* Carr, Sam
Kohn, Samuel, 50
Koldofski, M., 153
Kon, Louis, 187–8
Koopman, Levi. *See* Marchand, Louis
Kraisman, Sam, 259
Ku Klux Klan, 321
Kuntz, Prof. Charles, 267

L. Loeb and Co., 49–50
Labour League of Toronto, 272
labour legislation: Collective Labour Agreements Extension Act (Quebec), 262; Industrial Standards Act (Ontario), 262
labour movement. *See* clothing industry, unions
Labor Progressive Party, 274
Labour Zionism, 328
Labour Zionist Movement of Canada: establishment of (1938), 276
Labour Zionists. *See* Poale Zion
Lachine Canal Company, 30

Ladies Garment Manufacturers' Association of Canada, 245
Ladies' Hebrew Benevolent Society (Montreal), 72, 73, 77, 108
Laferrière, Michel, 446
Laister, Joseph, 128
Lancaster (Ontario), 51
Lander, Julius, 39
landsmanshaften (hometown association), 94, 117, 118–19; Anshei New York, 210; Hebrew Men of England, 210; origins of, 210–11
Lapointe, Ernest, 237, 314, 546n154
Laporte, Pierre, 444–5
Laskin, (Professor) Bora, 320
Laurendeau, André, 409, 412; student activist leader, 305
Laurier, (Prime Minister) Sir Wilfrid, 4; position on refugees in Canada, 144–5
Lavergne, (Abbé) Édouard, 304, 306
Lavergne, Armand, 135
Layton, Irving, 441–2
League of Nations, 185, 187; impact on Zionism in Canada, 176
Leavitt, Dr Joseph, 225, 226
Leeser, Isaac, 64–8 passim, 72; attempts to form a Board of Delegates of Hebrew Congregations, 73–4
Legislative Assembly of Lower Canada, 23–4, 25; 1831 bill, 35
Leroux, Henri, 302
Lesser, A., 160
Lesser, Mona, 44
Lévesque, (Father) Georges-Henri, 410
Lévesque, René (premier of Quebec), 412

Levey, Abraham, 42, 514n25
Levi, (Rabbi Chaplain) Gershon, 384–8 passim, 394
Levi, L., 50
Levin, Bernard, 43
Levinson, Solomon, 95
Levy (jeweller), 49
Levy, Bert 'Yank,' 280
Levy, Daniel, 55
Levy, John, 39, 41–2
Levy, Morden, 54
Levy, Nathan, 14–15
Lewis, David, 277–8, 374
Libre Parole (Illustrée), La, 106, 140–1
Lightstone, (Captain) Hyman, 107
Ligue du dimanche, 251
Lipschitz, Sam, 401
Littman, Sol, 464
London (England), 16; religious leadership, 61
London (Ontario), 108
London Ladies Emigration Society, 71
Lopez, Aaron, 15
Lord's Day Act, 251
Lord's Day Alliance: 1904 attack on Orthodox Jews, 131
Louis, B., 53
Louisbourg, 14
Louzada, Jacob, 15
Lower, (Professor) Arthur, 235
Lower Canada: conflicting visions of, 25; in the 1840s, 63; political discrimination, 35–6
Loyalists: Jewish, 505n31
Ludwig, Jack, 441
Lunan, Gordon, 281–2
Lunenburg, Nova Scotia, 14–15
Lyons, Jacques J., 64

Macdonald, (Prime Minister) John A., 78
Machon (Institute), 364–5
Machzikei Ha Das, 118
Mallach, L., 206
Mandel, Eli, 441
Mansion House Committee (London), 77, 80–1, 84, 93
Manufacturers' Protective Association: complaints of discrimination by, 254
Marchand, Louis, 31
Marcus, (Professor) Jacob, 18, 22
Marcus, John, 388–9
Margulies, Mrs, 232–3
marriage: among early settlers, 22–3. *See also* women
Martin, Clara Brett: antisemitic beliefs, 131
Martin, Médéric, 158
Massey, Vincent, 237
Matas, David, 466
McDiarmid, Mr C., 84–5
McEvoy, (Reverend) A.N., 145
McGill University, 132–3, 318
Mechanics Institute, 64
Meighen, Mrs Arthur, 222, 224
Meighen, (Prime Minister) Arthur, 229–30
Mennonites, 310, 323
Merritt, (Rabbi) Max J., 287–8
Michaels, Humphry, 42
Michaels, Michael, 42
Mikveh Israel (congregation at Philadelphia), 63, 64
military: Jewish chaplains in the, 384–400 passim; Jewish conscripts, 377–8; Jewish participation in, 173–6, 371–400 passim, 533n35, 533n37

Military Service Act of 1917, 533n35
Minerve, La (Montreal), 106
minhag, 34; Ashkenazic (Dutch-German) tradition, 32–3, 34, 68–9, 450; Sephardic (Portuguese) tradition, 32–3, 34, 68–9, 449–50, 451–3
Minimum Wage Commission, 255
Mizrachi (Religious Zionism), 171, 177, 329, 350–1, 534n50; impact on ZOC fundraising campaigns, 347–8
Mondelet, Jean-Marie, 27
Monk, Henry Wentworth, 165
Monson, (Rabbi Chaplain) David, 375–6, 384
Montefiore, (Sir) Moses, 32, 57, 63
Montreal, 8, 146–7; class structure, 108–9; clothing industry, 8, 95, 147–8, 151, 162–3; commercial beginnings, 17–36; diversification of Jewish community within, 449–50; 1871 census, 70; establishment of congregation, 19–21; French-speaking immigrants to, 449–50; Jewish association membership, 213; Jewish population, 93, 199–200, 449, 477; 'Jewish quarter,' 212; poverty in, 249; Roman Catholic cathedral at, 74–5; St James Street synagogue, 32; suburbanization of, 213; synagogue attendance, 213–14; traditional Jewish community, 213–14
Montreal Clothing Manufacturers' Association, 148, 155–7, 161–2
Montreal Committee for the Relief of the Persecuted Persian Jews, 65–6
Montreal Dress Manufacturers' Guild, 252
Montreal Federation of Jewish Charities, 251

Montreal Gas Company. *See* Joseph, Jesse
Montreal Gazette, 76
Montreal Hebrew Free Loan Association, 94, 117
Mordecai, Adolphus, 28
Mormons: colonization by, 206–7
Morris, Edward, 44
Morris, William. *See* Buhay, Michael
Morritz, B., 50
Mosley, Oswald, 326
Moss family, 43–4, 53, 63, 95
Mowat, Herbert, 356–9 passim
Moyse, Dean, 132–3
Mulock, (Sir) William, 238
Murphy, Harvey, 264
Muter Farein (Toronto), 124. *See also* immigrants, women's experiences
Myer, Bereskin, 534n46
Myerson, H.M., 375

Namier, (Professor) Lewis, 133
Nathan, Henry: election to legislature of British Columbia (1870), 58–9
Nathans family, 14
National Associated Women's Wear Bureau, 250
National Clothing Workers of Canada, 243
National Conference for Israel and Jewish Rehabilitation, 426
National Council for Refugees (NCR), 240
National Council of Jewish Women, 104, 120
National Council of Women of Canada, 104
National Desertion Bureau: establishment (1911), 122

National Socialist Party, 310
National War Efforts Committee (WEC), 372, 375–6, 399
Nationale Radicale Schule (Winnipeg), 275
nationalism: French-Canadian, 25; Jewish, 296
Nazism, 323, 353, 358, 362, 371–5; antisemitic propaganda in Canada, 310; denunciation from Canadian churches, 238; influence on Mennonite community, 310; war criminals, 461–7, 473–4
needle industry. *See* clothing industry
Neumann family: immigration to Canada, 237
New Clothing Workers of Canada, 261
New York: connections with Canadian Jewish community, 16
Newfoundland, 54
Nissim ben Solomon, (Rabbi), 65
Noah, Mordecai: attempted establishment of asylum for Jews, 35
Nordheimer, Abraham, 51
Nordheimer family, 109
North West Company, 29
Northern Canada: Jewish population growth, 110–11
Northway, John, 244
Northwest Territories: Hirsch settlement, 85–8, 115–16, 205; Jewish settlement efforts in, 83–8
Novak, Hershl, 151. *See also* Poale Zion
Nurenberger, M.J., 436, 485

Oberndorfer, Simon, 51
O'Brien, James, 95–6
Occident, The, 34, 65, 66, 69

Index 623

October Revolution (1917): as 'Jewish plot,' 282
Ollendorf, Moses, 38
Olympic Games (Berlin), 308
One Big Union, 188, 265, 535n74
Ontario: Fair Employment Practices Act (1951), 414; Insurance Act, 311; Racial Discrimination Act (1944), 414
Ontario Committee for Government Aid to Jewish Day Schools, 442
Oppenheimer, David: involvement in Vancouver (BC) politics, 59
Oppenheimer brothers, 56–7, 58
Oschenski brothers, 188
Ottawa, 519n19; growth of Jewish population, 521n58
Outremont (Quebec): construction of synagogue at, 469–70; 'Jewish problem' at, 469

Palestine: Canadian immigrants to, 341–2; as Jewish 'national home,' 9, 184, 185
Papineau, Louis-Joseph, 35; leader of the Parti Patriote, 28
Paré, (Father) Joseph, S.J., 311
Paris, Erna, 420
Parti Canadien, 27–8. *See also* Parti Patriote
Parti Patriote, 28
Parti Québécois, 443–6; nationalist program of, 446–8; 1976 victory of, 445
Patrie, La (Montreal), 105
Patterson, (Colonel) A.H., 343. *See also* Zionism, Patterson tour of 1923
Pelletier, Georges: editor of *Le Devoir*, 307
Pelletier, Louis, 101

Peoples' Kitchen (Montreal), 249
Peretz Shule, 124
Perlin, Israel, 217–18
Perri, Rocco (h. of Bessie Starkman), 210
Pesotta, Rose, 252, 257
Petach Tikvah Anshei Castilia (Toronto), 453
philanthropic organizations. *See* Federation of Zionist Societies of Canada; Hadassah; Ladies' Hebrew Benevolent Society; Young Men's Hebrew Benevolent Society; Young Judaea
Philip, Aaron, 28
Philo, Solomon, 59
Pierce, Ascher, 82, 84; investments in Palestine, 342
Pinsler, Jacob, 136–7
Piza, David, 32
Plamondon, Joseph Édouard, 141–2
Plamondon libel (1910), 133, 141–4; appeal, 143–4
Plaut, (Rabbi) Gunther, 430–1, 435, 455
Poale Zion, 150, 151, 171, 177, 275, 276, 288, 329, 350–1; clubs, 183; influence on clothing workers, 158
Poland. *See* immigration
Polish Canadians, 324–5
Pope Pius XII, 465
Popular Cloak: strike (1934), 259
Posluns, Abraham, 245
Posluns, Samuel, 259–60
Presbyterian Church: missionary efforts, 134
Presse, La (Montreal), 105
Price, (Rabbi) Dr, 181
Price Spreads Commission. *See* Royal Commission on Price Spreads and Mass Buying

Pride of Israel (Toronto), 119
Prince (jeweller), 49
Prince Edward Island, 54
Protestant Board of School Commissioners, 102, 283–4; equality of Jewish students within the, 408, 429–30; Montreal, 136–7
Prutschi, Manuel, 464–5
Pullan, Elias, 245

Quebec: antisemitism, 408, 411, 444–7; Council of Public Instruction, 296, 299; efforts to change traditional views, 410; fascism within, 411; Jews, 412, 443–4, 447–8; passing of Bill 178, 448–9; relationship of church and state in, 410; school question, 136–9, 185, 283, 283–301, 413, 519n19 (*see also* education); separatist movement in, 443–5. *See also* Montreal
Quebec Act (1774), 23–4
Quebec City: British capture of, 17, 22; Jewish population growth, 109; opposition to synagogue, 316–18
Quebec Mercury, 25, 27
Quebec Royal Commission of Inquiry on Education (1960), 429
Quebec Women's Minimum Wage Board, 248–9
Queen's University, 132–3, 318–19, 320–1

Rabinovitch, Dr I.M.: lecture to Canadian Club of Montreal (1946), 571n87
Rabinovitch, Dr Samuel, 313
Rabkin, Elias, 154
Racial Discrimination Bill, 311
rag trade. *See* clothing industry

Raginsky, Anna, 172
railways. *See* Canadian Pacific Railway
Rambam, Steve, 467
Rasminsky, Louis, 337–8, 415
Rauca, Albert Helmut, 462
RCMP. *See* Royal Canadian Mounted Police
Reading, Lord, 181
Rebellions of 1837, 31, 36
Rebelsky, David, 345
'Red Scare,' 164, 220
Reform congregation. *See* Temple Emanuel
Reform movement, 61, 422, 429–30, 454; establishment of Kadima (Forward), 438–9; in Kingston (Ontario), 454; in Toronto, 109
Reichmann family, 428–9
Restoration Funds, 330
Revisionists, 348–9, 357
Rexford, (Reverend Canon) Elson I., 284–5
R.G. Dun and Company. *See* Dun and Company, credit reports
Rhinewine, Abraham, 218
Richler, Mordecai, 425, 433, 440, 441–2
Roback, Leah, 250–1, 252, 256–7
Rodal, Alti, 465
Rodfei Sholem (Toronto), 201
Rodrigues family, 14
Roher, Martin, 373
Rohold, Shabbatai Benjamin, 134
Roman Catholic board of school commissioners, 100
Roman Catholic Church, 251–2; antisemitic propoganda, 140–1; antisemitism within, 134–5; attitude towards international unions, 245; consultation with Catholic committee of the Quebec Council

of Public Instruction, 297–8; liberalization of in Quebec, 410–11; opposition to Jews sitting on Council of Public Instruction, 299; school deal with Spanish and Portuguese Jews, 100–1; and unions, 253, 255, 256, 257

Romania: Jewish emigrants from, 103–4

Rome, David, 408, 409–10, 412

Rose (Rosenberg), Fred, 268–70, 281; arrest and sentencing of, 269–70; as campaigner, 269

Rosenband, Leopold, 49

Rosenberg, Louis, 193–4, 199, 200–1, 205, 255, 426; on the future of Quebec Jewry, 443–4

Rosenbloom, H.D., 230

Rosh Pina (Head of the Corner) congregation. *See* Winnipeg

Ross, Ellen, 66

Ross, Malcolm, 468–9

Rossin, Marcus, 46, 47

Rothschild, Baron, 57, 78

Rothschild, (General) Robert, 382–3

Rouleau, Raymond-Marie (Cardinal), 298

Royal Canadian Mounted Police, 164, 187, 188; scrutiny of United Jewish People's Order (UJPO), 273–4; surveillance of Jewish Communist participation, 266, 271–3

Royal Commission on Bilingualism and Biculturalism, 443, 448

Royal Commission on Education (1924) (Quebec), 292–3. *See also* Gouin, Sir Lomer

Royal Commission on Price Spreads and Mass Buying (1934), 245, 249–51, 255, 261–2

Royal Commission on the Relations of Labour and Capital, 95–7; report (1889), 518n13

Royal Montreal Cavalry, 31

Royal North-West Mounted Police. *See* Royal Canadian Mounted Police

Rubin, Sam, 260

Ruppin, Arthur, 515n42, 569n43

Russia, 189, 515n42; Jewish emigrants from, 75, 77–8, 103, 109–10, 515–16n58; pogroms in, 144–5

Ryan, Claude, 412–13

Sack, Benjamin Gutl, 218

Saint John, New Brunswick, 53–5, 108; congregation at (*see* Ahavath Achim); Jewish population growth, 109

Salsberg, Joseph B., 272, 280, 281

Samuel, Joseph, 54

Samuel, Mark, 37, 42–3, 47–9

Samuel, Sigmund (s. of Lewis Samuel), 47–9; education, 109

Samuel family, 46, 48–9

Sanhedrin: re-establishment of, 178

Sansregret, J.E.: vice-president of Retail Merchants Association of Canada, 303

Saunders, Alexander, 44

Saunders, Leslie, 379–80

Sauvé, Hon. Arthur, 314

Scher, Morris, 270

Schlossberg, Joseph, 155, 158, 254

schochet (killer, or ritual slaughterer), 32, 34

Schomberg, (Lieutenant, Royal Navy) Alexander: commander of the *Diana*, 17

school system. *See* education; Quebec, school question

Schubert, Joseph, 247

Schwartz, Frederick, 49

Schwartz, (Rabbi) Jesse, 342
Scott, (Canon), 142, 143
Scott, (Professor) Frank, 237, 261
secularists, 456–7
Segal, (Yacov Yitzchak) Jacob I., 192–3, 218
Selick, Anna, 171
Semi-Ready, 155–7
Senese, (Professor) Phyllis: study of the reaction to the Dreyfus case, 131
Shaar Hashomayim (Montreal), 84–5, 201, 288; relocation of, 93
Sha'ar Hashomayim (Windsor), 201
Shaarey Zedek congregation (Winnipeg), 114–15
Sharp, Mitchell, 431, 434
Shavei Zion, 165
Shearith Hapleta, 406
Shearith Israel (Montreal), 16; affiliation with Shearith Israel (New York), 16–17; Ashkenazim foundations, 16, 72; benevolent activities, 63; day school, 100; educational activities, 63; emphasis on Sephardic worship, 36; first Canadian congregation, 13; leadership of, 62–3; Sephardim foundations, 16, 72; tensions, 72
Shearith Israel (New York), 64
Shemen, Nachman, 218
Shields, (Reverend) Tommy, 238
shmata business. *See* clothing industry
Shomrei Shabbos synagogue (Toronto), 118, 453
Shulemson, (Flying Officer, RCAF) Sydney, 389
Sidor, Karol, 465
Siegler, Alderman Max, 309

Silcox, (Reverend) Claris E., 238, 310; of the Canadian Council of Christians and Jews, 317
Silverman, Lyon, 41
Silverman, Samuel, 39
Silverman family, 63
Silverstone, William, 39–40
Simon Wiesenthal Centre, 466
Singer, E. Frederick, 311
Sirluck, (Professor) Ernest, 373, 377
Slonim, (Rabbi) Reuben, 394–5
Smith, Goldwin: as antisemite, 127–31
Social Credit Party: of Alberta, 322–3; antisemitic views of, 413
Social Democratic Party, 110, 275; East European influence on, 8–9; emergence of, 189; Jewish membership, 163–4, 187
Socialist Party of Canada: Jewish membership, 163–4, 187
Soleil, Le (Quebec), 298–9
Solomon, Henry, 30
Solomons, Ezekiel, 18, 20
Solomons, Lucius Levy, 18, 20, 22, 30
Solomons, Solomon: Newfoundland's first postmaster, 54
Sommer, Abraham, 146, 245; construction of Sommer Building, 245; establishment of Queen Dress and Waist Company, 245
Sommer, Charles, 245, 252, 255, 256
Sommer and Abraham Gittelson. *See* Ladies Garment Manufacturers' Association of Canada
Sonneborn Dryfoos and Company, 46
Sonnenfeldt, Dr: director of the Jewish Colonization Association, 84; JCA agricultural expert, 89
Sopinka, Justice John, 464

Soviet Union: support for Jews in, 430–2
Spanish Civil War, 278–81; International Brigades disbandment, 281; Mackenzie-Papineau Battalion, 278
Special Committee on Hate Propaganda: federal anti-hate legislation, 460
Spector, Maurice, 264–5
Sperber, Marcus, 150
sport: as vehicle for Jewish identity, 215
S.S. *Grampian*, 227
St Laurent, (Prime Minister) Louis, 411, 465
Stanley, (Professor) Carleton W., 321
Star Mantle Manufacturing Company, 146
Starkman, Bessie (w. of Rocco Perri), 210
Steinberg, Harry, 246
Steinberg, Sam, 428
Sterlin, (Lieutenant) Mitchell, 384
Stern, (Rabbi) Harry, 253, 255, 258, 278–9, 311, 355–6, 572n101; as head of grievance board, 248
Stern, Shalom, 360
Stine, Isaac, 50
St-Jean-Baptiste Society, 237, 238
Stuchen, Phillip, 401
Sunday Observance Act (Quebec): removal of Jewish exemption (1936), 300
Superior Cloak, 245; strike (1934), 259. *See also* Posluns, Abraham
Sutro brothers, 56
swastika clubs, 325–6; in Ontario, 307
'sweating system.' *See* clothing industry, working conditions
Sylvester, Frank, 56

synagogues: as centre of Jewish life, 111–12; as community, 24–5, 32–3; construction of, 201; financial situation of, 454–5; post-war characteristics of, 422–3; in Montreal, 32–4 (*see also* Montreal)

T. Eaton Company, 148, 152–3
Taillon, (Premier), 101
Tardivel, Jules-Paul, 104
Taschereau, (Premier) Louis-Alexandre, 254, 289–99 passim, 315; attacks on ILGWU, 252; Committee of Nine, 290
Taylor, Dr R. Bruce, 132–3
Temple Emanuel (Montreal), 93, 201
Territorialist Organization, 108
"The Amalgamated." *See* Amalgamated Clothing Workers of America (ACWA)
Tifereth Israel (Windsor), 111
Toronto: adoption of Reform elements by congregation, 109; city 'Ward,' 118–19; construction of first synagogue, 38; Holy Blossom synagogue, 109; Jewish community, 208–9; Jewish population, 477; Jewish population growth, 108–9, 199–201; *landsmanshaften*, 210; mutual benefit societies, 118–19, 210–11
Toronto Jewish Congress, 475, 478
Toronto Jewish Folk Choir, 272
Toronto Social Survey Commission (1915), 120
Treasure for My Daughter, A, 419
Trudeau, (Prime Minister) Pierre Elliott, 238, 410, 427, 430, 439, 462, 465; Middle Eastern policy of, 437; role in 1949 Asbestos strike, 410

True Witness and Daily Chronicle (Montreal), 105, 106
tuberculosis: Royal Commission on Tuberculosis (1910) findings, 528n63

Ukraine, 3–4; pogroms, 3, 189
Ukrainian Civil Liberties Association, 467
Ukrainian Farband. *See* Belkin, Simon
Ukrainians: antisemitic beliefs, 323–4; disagreements with Jews over wartime events, 464; Ukrainian Canadian Committee, 464
Underhill, (Professor) Frank, 237, 320, 564n115
Union Nationale, 315; 1936 election victory, 314
United Clothing Workers, 263
United Garment Workers of America (UGWA), 98, 146–51 passim, 163; participation in Socialist Labour Party meetings, 528n64
United Hat, Cap and Millinery Workers' International Union, 243
United Hebrew Charities (New York), 72
United Israel Appeal (UIA), 367, 475
United Jewish People's Order (UJPO), 272–6; agenda, 273; fund-raising campaign, 274; recruitment, 275; sponsorship of children's summer camps, 274, 275; support for, 273–4
United Jewish Refugee and War Relief Agency (UJRA), 240, 424
United Jewish Welfare Fund (UJWF) (Toronto), 475
United Palestine Appeal, 350, 352
Université de Montréal, 133, 281, 312, 314–15, 410
Université Laval à Montréal, 133
universities, 318–21; appointment of Jewish faculty at, 427–8. *See also* antisemitism, within universities
University of Toronto, 133, 318, 320, 415
Usher, Moe (pilot officer, RCAF), 389
Usiskin, ('Uncle Mike') Michael, 116–17, 207; Edenbridge, 205–6
Ussishkin, Menachem, 341, 346–7

Valentine, Isaac, 33
Valiquette, (Father) Stéphane, S.J., 311, 408; establishment of the Council of Christians and Jews in Quebec, 408
Vancouver: construction of synagogue (1910), 59; formation of Reform congregation, 59; Jewish community, 59
Vérité, La (Montreal), 104, 106
Versailles Peace Conference, 185, 187
Victoria, 55–8, 108; benevolent societies, 58; construction of synagogue, 55, 57
Vineberg, Harris, 95

Waddington, Miriam, 441
Wade, Mason, 36
Wallenberg, Raoul, 459
Wallot, Jean-Pierre, 27
Walsh, Bill (s. of Hirsch Wolofsky), 264, 272
war criminals. *See* Nazism, war criminals
War Relief Conference, 179
Warner, Rebecca, 42
Wasserstein, Bernard, 490
Weinfeld, Henry, 258
Weinfeld, (Professor) Morton, 421–2, 474, 491

Weisgal, Meyer, 340, 360–1
Weizmann, Chaim, 329, 330, 332–3, 343–5 passim, 350, 352, 353–4
Western Canada: Jewish colonization of, 89–90; Jewish population growth, 110–11, 200
Western Shirt and Overall Company, 245–6. *See also* Haid, Morris; Steinberg, Harry
Wilder, Harry, 232, 328–9
Willinsky, Abraham I., 133, 526n26
Wilson, (Senator) Cairine, 235, 240
Winchevsky, Morris, 150, 274, 275
Windsor, 109
Winnipeg, 109, 113–15; arrival of Russian Jewish immigrants in (1882), 78–83; B'nai Zion synagogue, 114; establishment of parochial school system, 113; growth of Jewish population, 114–15, 202–4; Hebrew Benevolent Society, 119; Jewish Old Folks Home of Western Canada, 119; Jewish population, 416, 478; Jewish population growth, 199–200; orphanages, 119–20; political rivalry between Jews and Ukrainians, 114; rise of antisemitism, 109; Rosh Pina congregation (1890), 109; Shaarey Zedek congregation (1880), 109
Winnipeg General Strike of 1919, 187; anti-foreign sentiment, 126
Wiseman, Adele, 441
Wisse, (Professor) Ruth, 445–7, 474
Wolfe, Bernard, 413–14
Wolfe, George, 39
Wolff, Martin, 218
Wolofsky, Hirsch, 272, 288, 292, 293, 295

women, 479–80; education of, 203; feminism, 420, 493–4; involvement in war effort, 376; in post-war Canada, 419–20; role in business affairs, 23; roles of immigrant, 123–4; traditional roles of, 203–4; in the workforce, 420. *See also* Hadassah-WIZO; Zionism, women's involvement in
Women's Consumers League, 254
Woodsworth, James S.: CCF leader, 278; *Strangers within Our Gates*, 126
Worker, 265
Workers' Unity League, 243, 263
Workman, Mark, 95, 146, 157, 191, 219
World Conference against Racism (Durban), 494
World Zionist Organization, 328, 348
Wrong, George M., 238

Yiddish publications, 218, 221–2
Yiddishe Vort, 218
Yiddisher Arbeiter Froyen Farein (Toronto): Camp Naivelt, 266; establishment of (1923), 266
Yiddisher Yugend Farein: Arbeiter Ring (Workmen's Circle) School, 114; National Radical School (1914), 114
Yiddisher Zhurnal (Toronto), 218
Young, Dr Ainslie, 142, 143
Young Communist League (YCL), 264, 268; Jewish participation in, 266
Young Jewish Socialist Club, 264
Young Judaea, 172–3, 207, 338–9; Zionist enthusiasm in, 335–7
Young Ladies' Sewing Circle, 108
Young Men's Hebrew Benevolent Society (Montreal), 69–70, 72–3,

77, 79, 213, 215; renamed Baron de Hirsch Institute, 83
Young Socialist League, 264
Young Women's Hebrew Association (YWHA), 213, 215

Zacharias (cigar-maker), 42
Zacks, Samuel, 360–1, 363–4; leadership role in ZOC, 351–3, 354, 357, 358
Zionism, 6–10, 108, 110, 271, 282, 432–3; in Canada, 9, 165–85 passim, 532n19; Christian sympathies for, 355, 356; critiques of, 339–41; establishment of Winnipeg Hebrew School (Talmud Torah), 114; fundraising, 330–2, 337, 339, 351–2, 359, 365; and the Jewish identity, 440; leadership, 6; organizations, 3; Patterson tour of 1923, 343–4; post-war appeal of, 408; public relations activities, 353–4, 365; summer camps, 361–2; support for education, 359–60; support from Montreal Jewish elite, 108; territorial, 108; in United States, 9; women's involvement in, 171–2, 420; youth involvement in, 172–3; youth movements in, 360–2, 363
Zionist Order of Habonim. *See* Zionist Organization of Canada, men's associations
Zionist Organization of America: objection to mandate of Keren Hayesod, 339–40
Zionist Organization of Canada (ZOC), 254, 312, 346–7, 328–67 passim; fundraising, 344, 349–53 passim; leadership, 351; loss of significance of, 367; men's associations, 362–3; resolution to create a Jewish Commonwealth, 353; United Palestine Appeal, 362
Zlotnick, (Rabbi) Judah, 345–8 passim; as executive director of the Zionist Organization of Canada, 341, 342
Zuken, Joe, 272
Zuken, Louis: migration from Ukraine to Canada, 121
Zundel, Ernst: trial of, 467–8